PHIL EDMONSTON'S

LEMON-AID

SUVS, VANS, AND TRUCKS

2005

PHIL EDMONSTON

PENGUIN
CANADA

PENGUIN CANADA

Published by the Penguin Group

Penguin Group (Canada), 10 Alcorn Avenue, Toronto, Ontario, Canada M4V 3B2
(a division of Pearson Penguin Canada Inc.)

Penguin Group (USA) Inc., 375 Hudson Street, New York, New York 10014, U.S.A.
Penguin Books Ltd, 80 Strand, London WC2R 0RL, England
Penguin Ireland, 25 St Stephen's Green, Dublin 2, Ireland (a division of Penguin Books Ltd)
Penguin Group (Australia), 250 Camberwell Road, Camberwell, Victoria 3124, Australia
      (a division of Pearson Australia Group Pty Ltd)
Penguin Books India Pvt Ltd, 11 Community Centre, Panchsheel Park, New Delhi – 110 017, India
Penguin Group (NZ), Cnr Airborne and Rosedale Roads, Albany, Auckland, New Zealand
      (a division of Pearson New Zealand Ltd)
Penguin Books (South Africa) (Pty) Ltd, 24 Sturdee Avenue, Rosebank, Johannesburg 2196, South Africa

Penguin Books Ltd, Registered Offices: 80 Strand, London WC2R 0RL, England

First published 2004

(FR) 10 9 8 7 6 5 4 3 2 1

Copyright © Les Editions Edmonston, 2004

Manufactured in Canada.

Library and Archives Canada Cataloguing in Publication data available upon request.

Visit the Penguin Group (Canada) website at **www.penguin.ca**

CONTENTS

PART FOUR VEHICLE RATINGS   145

Sport-Utility Vehicles   152

KEY DOCUMENTS

The following photos, charts, documents, memos, court filings and decisions, and service bulletins are included in this index so that you can easily find and photocopy whichever document will prove helpful in your dealings with automakers, government agencies, dealers, or service managers. Most of the service bulletins outline repairs or replacements that should be done for free.

Minivans and Vans

Pickup Trucks

PART TWO   USED, BUT NOT ABUSED

PART THREE   GET YOUR MONEY BACK

PART FOUR   VEHICLE RATINGS

DEADLY SECRETS

Paralysed from the chest down last October after a rollaway Chrysler minivan crushed her in front of her own home, Darlene Hellerman can no longer tuck her two young sons into bed....

And now she knows she can't sue Chrysler, the company she blames for her tragically altered life.

Because the full-time mom, a native of Ontario, lives in Manitoba and this province has no-fault insurance, she cannot go after the car manufacturer. The Manitoba Public Insurance Corporation Act flatly denies Manitoba drivers the right to sue not just other drivers, but even the makers of possibly defective cars.

Lindor Reynolds, *Winnipeg Free Press*
July 7, 2004

2004 Chrysler Caravan: Chrysler rejected the interlock safety feature found on most other vehicles and then misled buyers that the safety device was installed, even though it wasn't. The automaker sent owners a sticker correction to paste in their owners manual.

Buckle your seat belt and take a ride on the "dark side" of auto ownership. In the following pages you will be astounded and disgusted by the lies, arrogance, and murderous behaviour exhibited by the automobile industry. Additionally, you will be given copies of secret warranties, confidential service bulletins, and pricing info that can save you thousands of dollars in buying or repairing your vehicle. And, finally, don't forget the many court decisions and ratings that will steer you clear of an overpriced lemon and give you the tools to get your money back.

The Death of Detroit

General Motors (GM) and Ford are banks on wheels, getting their profits from lending money, not from selling cars. As far as auto production is concerned, Detroit's Big Three automakers are "dead men, walking," run by incompetent, scared executives, hoping for a fat pension before the Japanese change the locks.

Take Ford's recently fired president Jac Nasser, the poster boy for Detroit deceit and arrogance. Blustering and dishonest, Nasser spent millions on TV ads blaming Firestone for Explorer rollovers, all the while knowing that several years earlier he screwed owners during his watch in Venezuela by using secret warranties and settlement gag orders to cover up catastrophic tire failures and vehicle rollovers in that country. Then Nasser pushed stupidity into unbelievability by proposing that Ford recall Explorers in only five American States where seasonal temperatures were the highest. Shortly thereafter, an angry public forced him to recall Explorers everywhere.

Now that Ford and Bridgestone/Firestone have paid off plaintiffs, they want to sell tires together, again.

The Nasser legacy lives on at Ford Canada where the company is actively engaged in stonewalling owner complaints over sudden tie-rod failures on its 1996–2004 F-series pickups.

WHY CAN'T FORD TELL THE TRUTH? A Toronto 2004 Ford F-150 owner writes: "I have now received a notice from Ford to have the tie-rods inspected every 20,000 km, at my expense, to check for wear. Ford will fix it for free if the vehicle is still under warranty. Should this not be Ford's problem? Where is the recall? Apparently these can come completely apart. Is a Firestone tire problem in the waiting? Quality is not 'Job One'..."

The Automobile Protection Association (*APA.ca*), a Montreal-based national auto consumer group, has received reports that steering tie-rod ends on 1997–2003 Ford F-150 and F-250 light duty pickups and 1997–2002 Ford Expeditions are wearing prematurely. It also appears that the tie-rod ends can suddenly separate, causing a total loss of steering. Goodbye Explorer rollover, hello out-of-control F-series trucks.

Enough on Ford, what about GM?

General Motors is in the midst of a decades-long slide that saw its U.S. market share crash from 60 percent to 28 percent. Now it's hyping a former Chrysler president, 72-year-old Bob Lutz, as its new North American vice chairman and product czar, responsible for generating change and making the company profitable.

Lutz, the car journalists' flavour of the month, doesn't pass muster

He is the same "bright light" that brought out the failure-prone Chrysler LH cars (Concorde, Intrepid, New Yorker, and Vision), jumped ship for $24.2 million as Chrysler was date-raped by Mercedes who regarded the company and Lutz with thinly veiled contempt, ran Exide into bankruptcy, and then set up and bankrupted Cunningham Motors, manufacturer of a $250,000 V-12-equipped sports coupe prototype that never saw the light of day. Lutz convinced GM to invest in Cunningham. GM lost its investment and continues to lose money under Lutz.

Chrysler continues to lurch from good news to bad

Although Chrysler helped DaimlerChrysler AG's bottom line with a big 2004 second-quarter turnaround, the parent company is in organizational chaos, losing many top people and contending with a dramatic decline in Mercedes-Benz sales. Unlike Chrysler's rosy results, Mercedes' second-quarter operating profits slipped 18 percent on sluggish car sales, expensive new product launches, and efforts to improve quality, following scathing criticism from owners, dealers, and private and public consumer advocacy agencies.

DaimlerChrysler is also back-pedalling away from its joint ventures with Mitsubishi after that company's executives were hauled off to jail in Japan earlier this year and charged with hiding safety defects.

Hmmmm, hiding safety defects, now that's something Chrysler is good at after years of rejecting 1998–2003 Dodge Durango/Dakota complaints of sudden steering loss caused by collapsing ball joints.

Wary shoppers

Canadian buyers are fed up with Detroit's deception. Described by Toronto-based auto consultant Dennis DesRosiers as the most loyal owners in North America, Canadians are resisting Detroit's rebate-laden bargains because they don't want overpriced, unreliable vehicles, or service managers trained by the Marquis de Sade.

Here's what makes shoppers especially wary: For almost a decade GM, Ford and Chrysler have used plastic engine intake manifolds that crack, and automatic transmissions that suddenly go into "limp mode" after a few years or when passing by a radar installation (yikes!).

GM's "secret" engine warranty

Defective Intake Manifold Gasket

Engine Oil or Coolant Leak (Install New Intake Manifold Gasket)

Bulletin No.: 03-06-01-010B   Date: 10/24/2003

2000–03 Buick Century
2002–03 Buick Rendezvous;
1996 Chevrolet Lumina APV
1997–2003 Chevrolet Venture
1999–2001 Chevrolet Lumina
1999–2003 Chevrolet Malibu, Monte Carlo
2000–03 Chevrolet Impala
1996–2003 Oldsmobile Silhouette
1999 Oldsmobile Cutlass
1999–2003 Oldsmobile Alero
1996–99 Pontiac Trans Sport
1999–2003 Pontiac Grand Am, Montana
2000–03 Pontiac Grand Prix
2001–03 Pontiac Aztek with 3.1L or 3.4L V-6 engine.

Condition: Some owners may comment on an apparent oil or coolant leak. Additionally, the comments may range from spots on the driveway to having to add fluids. Cause: Intake manifold may be leaking allowing coolant, oil or both to leak from the engine. Correction: Install a new design intake manifold gasket. The material used in the gasket has been changed in order to improve the sealing qualities of the gasket.

Every year, millions of dollars are stolen from owners who replace cracked engine intake manifolds covered by automaker "secret" warranties. Owners never see service bulletin "smoking gun" proof like GM's service bulletin, above. Although these engines should last at least 7 years/160,000 km, they barely survive half as long.

General Motors says it has learned from past mistakes and now builds high-quality vehicles.

Yeah, like 1999–2004 trucks with defective in-tank fuel gauge sensors?

GM's faulty fuel gauges

Bulletin No.: 04-08-49-018A   Date: June 2004
Technical
Subject: Cranks but no start, stall, inaccurate/incorrect fuel gauge reading, no fuel, vehicle is out of fuel and fuel gauge reads above empty (replace fuel level sensor)
Models: 2001–04 Cadillac Trucks
1999–2004 Chevrolet and GMC Trucks
with gasoline engine (VINs X, V, T, U, N, G — RPOs LU3, LR4, LM7, LQ4, LQ9 or L18)

GM Trucks and cars run out of fuel, even though the fuel gauge says there's plenty of gas left. This $500 repair is GM's responsibility, says the above confidential service bulletin.

How about 2002–04 GM SUVs with $300 melting tail lights? Just last month, a GM whistle-blower sent me the automaker's latest secret warranty, used to cover melted tail light circuit boards on almost a million SUVs. GM's executives are the real "dim bulbs."

Limited alternative choices

The Detroit Big Three are lying when they say safety, fuel economy, and quality are their top concerns. They are still manufacturing unsafe, gas guzzling junk cars, trucks, and vans; hiding their service bulletins (not from *Lemon-Aid*, though); selling vehicles at inflated prices; getting less fuel economy than decades ago; and using secret warranties as a substitute for quality. Exactly what they were doing 33 years ago, when I wrote the first *Lemon-Aid* guides.

Unfortunately, Asian automakers have also become less than forthright in dealing with customers as their product quality declines. While Mitsubishi executives were hauled off to jail earlier this year, Toyota, Hyundai, and Kia bought themselves out of trouble. ("Honest, officer, we weren't speeding. But we will give your Brotherhood a few hundred dollars and drive more slowly, if you don't write us up. OK? OK?")

While carefully explaining that its recent "gift" of over $2 million to Canadian charities was not an admission of guilt, Toyota's settlement ended a price-fixing probe by Ottawa's Competition Bureau based on *Lemon-Aid*'s formal complaint against its Access program. A similar settlement for 12 million Rand ($2.3 million in Canadian dollars) is in the offing in South Africa. Interestingly, Toyota's usually loquacious PR honchos are closed-mouthed over the bad rap Access gave the company, three years after I warned Toyota via *Lemon-Aid* that the company was morally adrift with its "no-haggle" Access scheme. Hyundai and Kia couldn't count horsepower for almost a decade and have just refunded millions of dollars to buyers following another *Lemon-Aid* complaint lodged with Ottawa's Competition Bureau. Both automakers say this was just a recurring math problem—one that apparently erred mostly in the companies' favour.

In Part Four, you will learn that certain Honda, Toyota, and Nissan vehicles have had a resurgence of engine and transmission problems in addition to an apparent overall decline in reliability. For example, Nissan engineers are presently falling over themselves trying to correct Altima and Quest glitches. As they capture the market share, it seems the Asian automakers are skating on their earlier reputations and cutting quality, thereby committing the same mistake as Detroit did years ago.

Nevertheless, there is a marked difference with Asian complaint handling. "Secret warranties" are shunned and coverage is usually publicly extended to everybody up to eight years.

Don't get spooked by high fuel prices and jump into a hybrid

Automotive News reports that few people get the fuel economy claimed and that rescue workers have been warned that a 500-volt fatal shock could await them when cutting through a wrecked hybrid.

Don't look for GM, Ford, or Chrysler hybrid pickups or SUVs to be available in any large quantity in the near future. These companies don't really believe in hybrids and have given a discreet word to production to go slow.

Remember, for the price of a Toyota Prius (recommended by *Lemon-Aid*) or a Honda Insight/Hybrid you can buy two used Toyota Echos or Honda Civics that are almost as fuel frugal and can be repaired and serviced anywhere. Want an SUV fuel-miser? Get a used Hyundai Santa Fe.

Dealer Deceit

What about the honesty of Canadian auto dealers as a check on automaker abuses? To quote tennis champ John McEnroe: "You can't be serious?"

Canadian car dealers are a pitiful breed, kept on a short leash by automobile manufacturers that can close them down in a minute, due to the absence of the franchise protection that has existed for decades in the States. Sure, Ford was successfully sued for shutting down Mercury dealers in Canada, but what did the former dealers get? Very little. And the Mercury franchise is still long gone.

Dealers huff and puff about being independent businesspeople and contribute to many community causes, but in the end, with automaker complicity, they run systematic scams that would embarrass Enron and BRE-X flim-flammers. Newspaper ads carry fine print that defies comprehension, warranty service charges may be almost double what's acceptable (CBC TV *Marketplace* Mazda survey at *www.cbc.ca/consumers/market/files/cars/mazda_warranty*), and sales contracts routinely list spurious $300–$500 extra charges for "administrative costs" and "acquisition fees."

I own a used 1995 GMC Vandura full-sized, fully converted van, bought four years ago for $9,000, and a 2001 Hyundai Elantra with seven years left on its warranty.

Lemon-Aid regional reporters

Auto industry executives hate to see their secrets exposed in each year's *Lemon-Aid.* They take special measures to keep things hidden, but industry whistleblowers and reader feedback ensure that we get regular reports on auto defects, scams, and just plain abusive behaviour. If you would like to be a volunteer *Lemon-Aid* regional reporter write us at: *lemonaid@earthlink.net.*

Volunteers will report on their own vehicle's performance and defects, expose scams, and highlight both unacceptable and exemplary behaviour by dealers and automakers. Information received from regional reporters will help us to compile future car guides and investigate auto-industry practices, enabling other car owners and buyers to make informed decisions and avoid auto-industry shenanigans.

Our goal: Empower auto owners, find the secrets, and clean up the industry through surveillance and enforcement.

No ads, no favourites, and no bull.

Phil Edmonston
November, 2004

PART ONE

GET THE BEST FOR LESS

1

Media Madness

All publications want access to the hot new cars. They want a test drive or spy shot, computer mock-up, something, anything before their rivals. Commercial necessity gives manufacturers power over both the car mags and their jobbing journos. Again, I've never heard of a manufacturer saying: "I'll give you our latest car as long as you play nice." The relationship between carmakers and the press is as complicated as that of an alcoholic and his wife. But co-dependency doesn't change the basic implication: screw us this time, and we'll screw you next....

thetruthaboutcars.com
Robert Farago

Don't be guilt-ridden because you want a pickup or sport-utility; you're actually no different than most Canadians. In fact, more than half of all new vehicles sold in Canada today, such as this 2005 Hyundai Sonata, are classed as trucks. The major differences between us and Americans is that we opt for smaller models, we keep our vehicles longer, and we are more loyal to minivans.

A Buyer's Market

Passenger car sales by Detroit's Big Three are in deep trouble. Not only have the Japanese and South Koreans completely dominated every niche but trucks, but GM complains high production costs mean it loses $1,000 every time a Cavalier or Sunfire is sold. So, this year more than ever, American automakers are counting on profitable $30,000 SUVs, trucks, and vans (which earn them about $10,000 profit per vehicle) to stay afloat. General Motors has the most balanced mixture of trucks and cars, while Ford and Chrysler are kept on life-support by their SUV and truck sales, augmented by a few car purchases.

Nevertheless, 2005 is going to be a brutal year for automakers, say analysts at Goldman Sachs. They see aggressive rebating by GM in an effort to reduce its over-supply of SUVs and trucks, and a decline in sales and profits caused by high fuel prices, Asian competition, and the higher cost of borrowing. Already, prices of new and used large trucks and SUVs, like the Ford Expedition and Excursion and the GM Yukon and Tahoe, are down over twenty percent.

2004 and 2005 price-cutting this year promises to be brutal.

New or used?

Used, of course. Even though high fuel costs have driven down prices of new, large SUVs and trucks by up to $8,000, used vehicles are still the better buy because they cost about half the price of discounted new models, putting less money at risk. In fact, the ideal situation would be to buy a relative's vehicle and add an insurance rider to the family policy, if everyone lives under the same roof. Another viable alternative is to register the vehicle in your company's name to get additional tax benefits. We'll look at all the used options in Part Two.

2005 "backdoor" price increases

The first half of 2004 has been a lousy year for auto profits with sales expected to fall 7 or 8 percent by year's end. Consequently, auto manufacturers will likely raise 2005 model prices only a moderate 2 percent as they concentrate upon "backdoor" profits from high delivery and administrative fees, and "option-packing" vehicles with extra-cost side airbags, anti-lock brakes, and sophisticated audio and entertainment systems. In the following June sales chart, the companies with the most year-to-date losses are the ones where price haggling will have the most success—if the vehicles are worth it!

June 2004 Truck Sales Slump

Company	Sold per Month	Change '04/'03	Year-to-date	Change '04/'03
GM	19,265	+9.0%	111,921	+1.7%
Ford	18,050	-3.7	84,940	-7.6
DaimlerChrysler	18,018	+11.9	89,796	+6.2
Toyota	3,887	-7.2	22,238	-0.1
Honda	3,452	+5.7	17,408	-12.1
Nissan	2,401	+54.8	11,571	-18.0
Hyundai	1,129	-6.8	6,295	-0.3
Mazda	1,096	-13.8	6,003	-25.1
Kia	808	-32.8	4,345	-26.8
BMW	592	+122.6	2,078	+36.7
Subaru	324	-10.5	2,018	+2.7
Mitsubishi	245	-11.9	1,913	+49.9
Suzuki	243	-46.4	1,618	-20.5
Mercedes	214	+1.9	1,110	+3.1
Land Rover	105	-8.7	639	-7.7
Porsche	92	-7.1	505	+51.7
Volkswagen	88	+1,000.0	611	+1,146.9
Total	**70,019**	**+4.5%**	**365,009**	**-0.7%**

Poor sales have forced many automakers to come up with unique incentives to close deals. These include Nissan's offer of 500 litres of free gas and Chrysler's 5-year, interest-free loans on Chrysler Grand Caravans.

Mitsubishi sales are plummeting in the United States leading to more flexible prices in Canada, and Mazda's cars are red hot, despite a lull in truck and van sales.

Fortunately, as in previous years, these price increases aren't likely to hold up for long—not with DaimlerChrysler, Ford, and GM struggling to gain market share. Expect to see all sorts of sales incentives beginning in late fall that will cut prices by about $3,000, led by GM's inevitably aggressive rebate and low-cost financing programs.

Canadian versus American prices

The average new vehicle transaction price in Canada is a bit over $30,000, says Dennis DesRosiers, a Richmond Hill, Ontario-based automobile industry consultant. As in previous years, he has found that Canadian auto prices are lower than what Americans pay, particularly on some compact and intermediate car models. However, this year's truck and van prices have risen appreciably, due to a strengthened Canadian dollar. For example, a 2004 intermediate SUV costs $39,588, or 7.2 percent more in Canada than in the United States. Last year, the average sport-utility price was about $6,000 less in Canada.

All things considered, the average manufacturer's suggested retail price of a 2004 car or truck sold in Canada is $773 more expensive than in the United States. Last year it was about $5,000 cheaper, although higher Canadian taxes ate up much of the advantage.

The most obvious effect of this narrowing of the price gap with American-sold vehicles has been the drying up of cross-border marketing into the United States. Canadian shoppers in cities close to the American border are now finding new and used prices more competitive as more vehicles remain in their country.

If you *must* buy a new sport-utility, truck, or van this year, seriously consider buying a cheaper 2004 model off the dealer's lot, particularly if that model hasn't been substantially upgraded this year (check Part Four). It will likely offer more standard features than the 2005 version and be eligible for generous factory rebates as well. Of course, if you can afford to wait six months, most of the 2005 price increases will be wiped out by a new round of factory rebates and low-cost financing programs, and cars and trucks will be cheaper on both sides of the border.

Why a New SUV, Truck, or Van?

Even if you do spend more than you should for a new truck, sport-utility, or van, you won't lose much money through depreciation, unless you go for the largest models—and even they are carrying price tags cut by as much as 25 percent.

The phenomenal popularity of these vehicles is due to a number of factors: They are practical, most are safer and more reliable than they were a decade ago, and zero percent financing incentives will eventually trim $2,000–$4,000 from base prices. In fact, sport-utilities and pickups, especially, depreciate so slowly that they've dethroned minivans and vans as the classes of vehicles that retain their value the longest.

Trucks and vans can easily be converted to suit anyone's needs or tastes. If you fish, you can get a 4X4 sport-utility or pickup that'll go practically anywhere and haul your boat as well. Born to party? Pickups will bring joy to your achy-breaky heart with their aerodynamic exterior styling, roomier luxury interiors, extended cabs with a bench seat in the rear, and four doors. Retired? No problem. A van can be transformed into a home on wheels (without the lawn maintenance or municipal taxes). And if you need to haul kids, lots of odds and ends, small appliances, or lumber, a minivan or small SUV may be just the ticket, a vital accessory for the do-it-yourself home improvement craze.

Most owners also feel safer driving trucks and vans, which now offer many standard safety features like airbags and adjustable pedals. Driver confidence is further increased by these vehicles' improved crashworthiness, larger size, extra weight, all-wheel-drive (AWD) capability, and high driver vantage point.

One compromise you'll have to make is fuel economy. The cheaper, hard riding, truck-based SUVs and vans will generally use more fuel than vehicles set upon an extended car platform. And, any choice equipped with AWD capability will be more fuel thirsty. So, if you want to protect the environment, save fuel, and have a comfortable ride, you should consider a small model built on a car platform, without the AWD option.

Ask the right questions (and don't go alone)

There are about 4,000 vehicle dealerships in Canada and they all want your money—over $30,000 for the average vehicle, and lots more for fully equipped sport-utilities, trucks, and vans.

According to the Canadian Automobile Association (CAA), the average household owns two vehicles, which are each driven about 20,000 km annually and cost $806 for maintenance and $962 for insurance (an average of $1,774 for a Chrysler Caravan). The CAA also estimates in its 2004 "Driving Costs" study (*www.caa.ca/e/automotive/pdf/driving-costs-04.pdf*) that the per-kilometre cost of driving a 2004 Caravan minivan 24,000 kilometres would be 46.9 cents, or $11,264.85 a year. Amazingly, a 2004 Chevrolet Cavalier compact wouldn't offer that much savings, costing 44 cents/km, or $10,567.05 for the year.

Keep in mind that it's practically impossible to buy a bare-bones SUV, truck, or van because automakers cram them with costly, non-essential performance and convenience features so they can maximize profits. Nevertheless, money-wasting gadgets like electronic navigation and sophisticated entertainment systems can be easily passed up with little impact upon safety or convenience.

Before paying big bucks, you should know what your real needs are and how much you can afford to spend. Don't confuse *needs* with *style,* or *trendy* with *essential.* Visiting the showroom with your spouse or a level-headed relative or friend will help you steer a truer course through all the non-essential options you'll be offered.

Most sales agents admit that female shoppers are far more knowledgeable about what they want and more patient in negotiating the contract's details than men, who tend to be mesmerized by many of the techno-toys available and often skip over the fine print and bluff their way through the experience. In increasing numbers, women have discovered that minivans and 4X4 sport-utilities are more versatile than passenger cars and station wagons. In the United States, for example, GM dealers have found that although most 4X4 owners are men, the majority of 4X4s are driven by women who are attracted to the high seating position, the easy loading and unloading of children, and the styling, which is sportier than most minivans'.

Automakers market sport-utilities and pickups to appeal to the macho crowd (look at the ads) by emphasizing luxury, power, adventure, and ruggedness. This is quite a marketing coup when you consider that *Popular Mechanics* estimates that 95 percent of all sport-utilities are driven on paved roads 95 percent of the time—that is, they aren't purchased for off-road use—and that *Consumer Reports* doesn't consider sport-utilities all that rugged or dependable anyway.

Am I spending too much?

Determine how much money you can spend, and then decide on what vehicles in that price range interest you. Have several models in mind so that the overpriced one won't tempt you. As your benchmarks, use the ratings, alternative models, estimated purchase cost, and residual value figures shown in Part Four of this guide. Remember, logic and prudence are the first casualties of showroom hype, so carefully consider your actual requirements and how much you can budget to meet them before comparing models and prices at a dealership. Write down your first, second, and third choices relative to each model and the equipment offered. Browse the automaker websites and *www.carcostcanada.com* for the manufacturer's suggested retail price (MSRP), promotions, and package discounts. Look for special low prices that may only apply to Internet-generated referrals. Once you get a good idea of the price variations, get out the fax machine or PC at home or work and make the dealers bid against each other (see pages 60–61). Then call the lowest-bidding dealership and ask for an appointment to be assured of getting a sales agent's complete attention, and take along the downloaded info from the automaker's website to avoid arguments.

Can I get more for less?

Sure. Sometimes a cheaper twin will fill the bill. Twins are those nameplates made by different auto manufacturers or different divisions of the same company that are virtually identical in body design and mechanical components, like the Toyota Matrix and Pontiac Vibe, Mercury Villager and Nissan Quest (until 2004), or the Chrysler Caravan and Voyager.

American manufacturers are a wily bunch. While beating their chests over the need to buy "American," they have joined Asian automakers in co-ventures where they know they can't compete on their own. This has resulted in models whose parentage is impossible to nail down but that incorporate a high degree of quality control. Suzuki builds the Chevrolet Tracker (formerly known as Geo) 4X4 in Ontario, and Ford and Mazda churn out identical Rangers and B Series pickups in the United States.

Sometimes choosing a higher trim line will cost you less when you take all the standard features into account. It's hard to compare value prices with the manufacturer's base price, though, because the base prices are inflated and can be negotiated downward, while value-priced cars are usually offered as "take it or leave it" with bundled options.

Twins and hybrids are only two of the alternatives; there are plenty of others. Minivans, for example, often come in two versions; a base commercial, or cargo, version and a more luxurious model for private use. The commercial version doesn't have as many bells and whistles, but it's more likely to be in stock and will probably cost much less. And if you're planning to convert it, there's a wide choice of independent customizers that will likely do a better job than the dealer, and for less. Of course, you will want a written guarantee from the dealer, the customizer, or sometimes both that no changes will invalidate the manufacturer's warranty.

Representing about one-fourth of the new-vehicle market, leasing is an alternative used to make vehicles seem more affordable, but it's really more expensive than buying, and for most people the pitfalls will far outweigh any advantages. If you have to lease, keep your losses to a minimum by leasing for the shortest time possible and by making sure that the lease is close-ended (meaning that you walk away from the vehicle when the lease period ends). The CAA estimates that 75 percent of lessees return their vehicles when the lease expires.

Instead of leasing, consider purchasing used. Look for a 3- to 5-year-old vehicle with 60,000–100,000 km on the clock and some of the original warranty left. Such a vehicle will be just as reliable, for less than half the cost of one bought new or leased. Parts will be easier to find, independent servicing should be a breeze, insurance premiums will come down from the stratosphere, and your financial risk is lessened considerably if you get a lemon.

On both new and used purchases, be wary of unjustified hidden costs like a $495 "administrative" or "disposal" fee, an "acquisition" charge, and boosted transport and freight costs that can collectively add several thousand dollars to the retail price.

What are my driving needs?

Our driving needs are influenced by where we live, our lifestyle, and our age. In the city, a small wagon or hatchback is more practical and less expensive than a minivan. However, if you're going to be doing a lot of highway driving, transporting small groups of people (especially kids), or loading up on accessories, a small SUV like a Honda CR-V or Toyota RAV4 could be the more logical choice for price, comfort, and reliability.

Most families who travel less than 20,000 km per year should avoid the smallest and largest engines available with a given model. The smallest engines usually come with bare-bones models where fuel economy trumps high-speed merging into traffic and driving comfort isn't important. Try a small engine (not necessarily the smallest one) that offers economy, performance, and a comfortable ride and interior; conversely, driving more than 20,000 km a year means spending a lot more time in a larger vehicle, requiring more reserve power for better performance/handling and accomodating the energy drain from additional safety, comfort, and convenience accessories. If you spend lots of time on the road or plan on buying a minivan or van, you'll definitely need a large 6- or 8-cylinder power plant to handle the air conditioning (AC) and other power-hungry accessories essential to your driving comfort and convenience. Fuel savings will be the last thing on your mind if you buy an underpowered truck or van, like Honda's early Odyssey minivans or GM's 2005 Canyon and Colorado small pickups.

Pushrod or overhead cam?

Most North American automakers prefer overhead valve engines because they cost about $800 less, provide better low-end power, use fewer parts, and weigh less than the overhead cam (multi-valve) engines favoured by automakers globally. Still, the more popular overhead cam configuration is used extensively by Japanese manufacturers because it offers more power at higher rpm, and uses variable valve timing for a better torque range, smoother idling, increased fuel economy, and cleaner emissions.

GM's popular Silverado/Sierra full-sized trucks use pushrod V8s, while Ford's F-150 pickups sport overhead cam V8s. Dodge has it both ways: Its Ram pickup comes with an overhead cam V8, as well as an optional 5.7L Hemi pushrod V8.

From a quality/performance perspective, cheaper pushrods are low-tech and outdated. Recent versions have not been particularly reliable and maintenance costs are about the same as with multi-valve engines.

Be especially wary of towing capabilities bandied about by automakers. They routinely exaggerate towing capability and seldom mention the need for expensive optional equipment or that the maximum safe towing speed may be only 72.4 km/h (45 mph), as is the case with some Japanese minivans and trucks. Chrysler, for example, bought back many 1997–99 Ram pickups because they would only tow 900 kg (2,000 lb.), not the 2,700 kg (6,000 lb.) advertised. GM pickups and vans have been the object of similar complaints.

Finally, remember that crew cab pickups sacrifice some utility with a shorter bed, but provide a much roomier interior—essential for carrying rear passengers in greater comfort or for keeping some cargo out of the weather.

Do I feel comfortable in this vehicle?

The advantages of many sport-utilities, pickups, and vans quickly pale in direct proportion to your tolerance for a harsh ride, noise, a high step-up, a cold interior, lots of buffeting from wind and passing trucks, and rear visibility blocked by the spare tire hanging on the rear tailgate.

Check to see if the vehicle's interior is user-friendly. Can you reach the sound system and AC controls without straining or taking your eyes off the road? Are the controls just as easy to operate by feel as by sight? What about dash glare onto the front windshield? Do rear-seat passengers have to be contortionists to enter or exit?

To answer these questions you need to drive the vehicle over a period of time to test how well it responds to the diversity of your driving needs, without having some impatient sales agent yapping in your ear. If this isn't possible, you may find out too late that the handling is more trucklike than you'd wanted. But you can conduct the following showroom test. Adjust the seat to a comfortable setting, buckle up, and settle in. Can you sit a foot away from the steering wheel and still reach the accelerator and brake pedals? When you look out the windshield and use the rear- and side-view mirrors, do you detect any serious blind spots? Will optional mirrors give you an unobstructed view? Does the seat feel comfortable enough for long trips? Can you reach important controls without moving off the seatback? If not, shop for something that better suits your requirements.

Do I have the required driving skills?

Probably not. You will have to drive more conservatively when you're behind the wheel of an SUV, truck, or van to avoid rolling over or losing control. Front-drive braking (especially with anti-lock brakes) is quite different from braking with a rear-drive. Rear-drive minivans handle like trucks, and full-sized vans tend to scrub the right rear tire during sharp right-hand turns until you get the hang of making wider turns. Limited rear visibility is another problem with larger sport-utilities and vans, forcing drivers to carefully survey side and rear traffic before changing lanes or merging with traffic.

What safety features are unsafe?

Automakers are loading 2004–05 models with features that wouldn't have been imagined several decades ago because safety devices appeal to families and can boost profits almost 500 percent. Yet some safety innovations, like anti-lock brakes and full-powered airbags, don't deliver the safety payoffs promised by automakers and may create additional dangers. Some of the more effective safety features are superior front, side, and offset crash protection, a high resistance to rollovers, head-protecting side and de-powered airbags, adjustable brake and accelerator pedals, standard integrated child safety seats, seat belt pretensioners, innovative head restraints, and sophisticated communication systems.

Seat belts provide the best means of reducing the severity of injury arising from both low- and high-speed frontal collisions. In order to be effective, though, seat belts must be adjusted properly and feel comfortably tight without undue slack. But owners often complain that seat belts don't retract enough for a snug fit, are too tight, chafe the neck, and don't properly fit children. Some automakers have corrected these problems with adjustable shoulder-belt anchors that allow both tall and short drivers to raise or lower the belt for a snug, more comfortable fit. Another important seat belt innovation is the front seat belt pretensioner (not found on all vehicles), a device that automatically tightens the safety belt in the event of a crash.

Safety Considerations

There are no easy safety solutions. According to the National Highway Traffic Safety Administration (NHTSA), 59 percent of the vehicle occupants who died in 2002 were not wearing seat belts, and 42 percent of the highway deaths were in alcohol-related crashes. Although figures show a dramatic reduction in fatalities and injuries over the past three decades, safety experts feel more built-in safety features will henceforth pay small dividends.

It's time to target the driver. NHTSA says 76 percent of almost 7 million annual crashes on North American highways are caused by driver error. This means safety programs that concentrate primarily upon motor vehicle standards won't be as effective as measures that target the driver, like stricter license requirements and law enforcement.

Incidentally, police studies have shown an important side benefit to arresting traffic law scofflaws: They often net dangerous career criminals and seriously impaired drivers before they harm others. Apparently, sociopaths and substance abusers don't care which laws they break.

Active safety

Advocates of active safety stress that accidents are caused by the proverbial "nut behind the wheel" and believe that safe driving can best be taught through schools or by private driving courses. Active safety components are generally those mechanical systems, such as anti-lock brake systems (ABS), high-performance tires, and traction control, that may help avoid accidents if the driver is skillful and mature.

The theory of active safety has several drawbacks. First, about forty percent of all fatal accidents are caused by drivers who are under the influence of alcohol or drugs. Surely all the high-performance options and specialized driving courses in the world will not provide much protection from impaired drivers who draw a bead on your vehicle. Second, because active safety components get a lot of use—you're likely to need anti-lock brakes 99 times more often than an airbag—they have to be well designed and well maintained to remain effective. Finally, consider that independent studies show that safe driving taught to young drivers actually contributes to their deaths and injuries by putting immature drivers on the road (*Lancet*, July 2001; 1978 DeKalb County, Georgia study).

Passive safety

Passive safety assumes that you will be involved in life-threatening situations and should be warned in time to avoid a collision or automatically protected from collision forces when they occur. Daytime running lights, a third, centre-mounted brake light, and head-protecting airbags are three passive safety features that have paid off handsomely in reduced injuries and lives saved.

Passive safety features also assume some accidents aren't avoidable and that, when an accident occurs, the vehicle should provide as much protection as possible to the driver, the vehicle's other occupants, and others who may be struck—without depending on the driver's reactions. Passive safety components that have consistently proven to reduce vehicular deaths and injuries are seat belts, vehicle structures that enhance crashworthiness by absorbing or deflecting crash forces away from the vehicle's occupants, and designs that reduce rollovers.

Rollovers

When you buy a pickup, van, or SUV, you should be concerned the vehicle may roll over. Although rollovers represent only 3 percent of crashes (10,000 annual U.S. road accidents), they cause a third of all traffic deaths. And these crashes aren't with other vehicles. Most rollover deaths occur in single-vehicle accidents, representing nearly 40 percent of fatal accidents that involved SUVs—an increase of 10 percent in 2003.

Incidentally, while additional passengers make low-riding sedans more stable, additional passengers make high-riding SUVs more unstable, says Consumers Union, publisher of *Consumer Reports* magazine.

Ford's Explorer Sport Trac 4X2 drive posted the single worst rating for rollover propensity among all 2004 vehicles analyzed—including cars, vans and SUVs. Its two-star rating indicated a nearly 35 percent chance of tipping over.

In the NHTSA's August 2004 rankings of one to five stars The Explorer Sport Trac 4X4 drive, the Explorer four-door 2X2 drive, and the Mountaineer four-door 2X2 drive were in the bottom six of the SUV class, which as a group posted the lowest three-star scores.

For the first time, 2004 results include dynamic tests, which simulate real-world performance, instead of the previously used mathematical formula. This has led to striking differences in results. For example, Saturn's Vue SUV received three stars out of a possible five in the earlier test. However, when two models were tested dynamically, the rear wheels collapsed. GM voluntarily recalled all 2002–2004 models. This raises some questions about other vehicles that are based on the Vue platform, like the 2005 Chevrolet Equinox.

All of the results for 2004 and prior years and models can be found in Part Four or at *www.nhtsa.dot.gov/ncap.*

2004 NHTSA Rollover Results (% Chance of Tipping Over)

Passenger cars
Best: Mazda RX-8—8%
Worst: Subaru Outback wagon—15.5%

Pickup trucks
Best: Chevrolet Silverado 4X2—15.9%
Worst: Toyota Tacoma 4X4—28.3%

Sport-utility vehicles
Best: Chrysler Pacifica 4X4—13%
Worst: Ford Explorer Sport Trac 4X2—34.8%

Vans
Best: Nissan Quest—12.1%
Worst: Toyota Sienna—15%

2004 SUV Rollover Crash Ratings

Make	Model	Class	Rollover Star Rating	% Chance of Rollover in Single Vehicle Crash	Tip/No Tip
Chrysler	Pacifica 4X4	SUV	4	13.0	No Tip
Chrysler	Pacifica 4X2	SUV	4	14.0	No Tip
Nissan	Murano 4X4	SUV	4	15.1	No Tip
Honda	Pilot 4X4	SUV	4	15.9	No Tip
Nissan	Murano 4X2	SUV	4	15.9	No Tip
Volvo	XC90 4X4	SUV	4	17.9	No Tip
Buick	Rainier 4X4 (3)	SUV	4	19.1	No Tip
Chevrolet	Trailblazer 4X4	SUV	4	19.1	No Tip
Dodge	Durango 4X4	SUV	4	19.1	No Tip
GMC	Envoy 4x4 (3)	SUV	4	19.1	No Tip
Olds	Bravada 4X4 (3)	SUV	4	19.1	No Tip
Buick	Rainier 4X2 (4)	SUV	3	20.4	No Tip
Chevrolet	Trailblazer 4X2	SUV	3	20.4	No Tip
GMC	Envoy 4X2 (4)	SUV	3	20.4	No Tip
Olds	Bravada 4X2 (4)	SUV	3	20.4	No Tip
Toyota	4Runner 4X4	SUV	3	20.4	No Tip
Ford	Escape 4X4	SUV	3	20.9	Tip
Mazda	Tribute 4X4 (5)	SUV	3	20.9	Tip
Mercury	Mariner 4X4 (5)	SUV	3	20.9	Tip
Dodge	Durango 4X2	SUV	3	21.2	No Tip
Jeep	Liberty 4X4	SUV	3	21.9	No Tip
Toyota	4Runner 4X2	SUV	3	21.9	No Tip
Ford	Explorer 4-DR 4X4	SUV	3	22.8	No Tip
Mercury	Mountaineer 4-DR 4X4 (6)	SUV	3	22.8	No Tip
Ford	Escape 4X2	SUV	3	23.7	Tip

Mazda	Tribute 4X2 (7)	SUV	3	23.7	Tip
Mercury	Mariner 4X2 (7)	SUV	3	23.7	Tip
Jeep	Liberty 4X2	SUV	3	24.6	No Tip
Chevrolet	Tahoe 4X4	SUV	3	26.3	Tip
GMC	Yukon 4X4 (8)	SUV	3	26.3	Tip
Ford	Explorer Sport Trac 4X4	SUV	3	27.9	No Tip
Chevrolet	Tahoe 4X2	SUV	3	28.3	Tip
Ford	Explorer 4-DR 4X2	SUV	3	28.3	Tip
GMC	Yukon 4X2 (9)	SUV	3	28.3	Tip
Mercury	Mountaineer 4-DR 4X2 (10)	SUV	3	28.3	Tip
Ford	Explorer Sport Trac 4X2	SUV	2	34.8	Tip

The best rollover ratings for 2004 models tested were: Mazda RX-8 four-door (passenger car); Chevrolet Silverado 4X2 extended cab (pickup truck); Chrysler Pacifica 4X4 (sport utility vehicle); and the Nissan Quest (van).

These results give a black eye to Ford and add credibility to Firestone's claims that previous Explorer rollover accident deaths and injuries were due to the Explorer's design, rather than to faulty tires. Bridgestone/Firestone raised the design argument at hearings in 2001 where the tiremaker disclosed that independent tests showed conclusively that the Explorer would roll over when equipped with competitors' tires. Ford claimed the tests were rigged.

When asked to comment upon the latest NHTSA tests, Ford spokeswoman Kristen Kinley dropped the "rigged" excuse and simply said:

> While we believe the NHTSA rating system has some value, we don't believe it's a good indicator of how a vehicle performs in the real world....

Crashworthiness

A vehicle with a high crash protection rating is a lifesaver. In fact, crashworthiness is the one safety improvement over the past 30 years that everyone agrees has paid off handsomely without presenting any additional risks to drivers or passengers. By surrounding occupants in a protective cocoon and deflecting crash forces away from the interior, auto engineers have successfully created safer vehicles without increasing size or cost. And purchasing a vehicle with the idea that you'll be involved in an accident some day is not unreasonable. According to the Insurance Institute for Highway Safety (IIHS), the average car will likely have two accidents before ending up as scrap and is twice as likely to be in a severe front-impact crash as a side-impact crash.

Since some vehicles are more crashworthy than others, and since size doesn't always guarantee crash safety, it's important to buy one that gives you the best protection from a frontal, a frontal offset, and a side collision, while keeping rollover potential to a minimum.

For example, the Chrysler Caravan and Ford Windstar minivans are similarly designed, but your chance of surviving a high-speed collision with the Windstar is far greater than it is with a Caravan or any other Chrysler minivan.

2004 Silverado crash (courtesy: NHTSA)

Chevrolet's redesigned 2004 Silverado/Sierra Extended Cab 4X2 earned only three stars for passenger frontal crash protection, while the low-tech 2004 Dodge Ram 1500 Quad Cab 4X2 garnered five stars for driver and passenger frontal protection.

Don't get taken in by the five-star crash rating hoopla touted by carmakers. There isn't any one vehicle that can claim a prize for being safest. Vehicles that do well in NHTSA side- and front-crash tests may not do very well in IIHS offset crash tests, or may have poorly designed head restraints that would increase the severity of neck injuries. Or a vehicle may have a high number of airbag failures, such as the bags deploying when they shouldn't or not deploying when they should.

Before making a final decision on the vehicle you want, look up its crashworthiness and overall safety profile in Part Four.

Two Washington-based agencies monitor how vehicle design affects crash safety: NHTSA and IIHS. Crash information from these two groups doesn't always correspond because, while IIHS's results incorporate all kinds of accidents, including offset crashes and bumper damage sustained from low-speed collisions, NHTSA's figures relate only to 56 km/h (35 mph) frontal and some side collisions. The frontal tests are equivalent to two vehicles of equal weight hitting each other head-on while travelling at 56 km/h (35 mph) or to a car slamming into a parked car at 114 km/h (70 mph). Bear in mind that a vehicle providing good injury protection may also cost more to repair because its structure, not the occupants, absorbs most of the collision forces. That's why safer vehicles don't always have lower insurance rates.

Cars versus trucks (size usually does matter)

Occupants of large vehicles have fewer severe injury claims than do occupants of small vehicles. This was proven conclusively in a 1996 NHTSA study that showed collisions between light trucks or vans and small cars resulted in an 81 percent higher fatality rate for the occupants of the small cars than occupants of the light trucks or vans.

Vehicle weight offers the most protection in two-vehicle crashes. In a head-on crash, for example, the heavier vehicle drives the lighter one backward, which decreases forces inside the heavy vehicle and increases forces in the lighter one. All heavy vehicles, even poorly designed ones, offer this advantage in two-vehicle collisions. However, they may not offer good protection in single-vehicle crashes.

Crash test figures show that SUVs, vans, and trucks also offer more protection to adult occupants than passenger cars in most crashes, because their higher set-up allows them to ride over other vehicles (Ford's 2002 4X4 Explorer lowered its bumper height to prevent this hazard). Conversely, due to their high centre of gravity, easily overloaded tires, and unforgiving suspensions, these vehicles have a disproportionate number of single-vehicle rollovers, which are far deadlier than frontal or side collisions. In the case of the early Ford Explorer, Bridgestone/Firestone CEO John Lampe testified in August 2001 that 42 of 43 rollovers involving Ford Explorers in Venezuela were on competitor's tires—shifting the rollover blame to the Explorer's design and crashworthiness.

IIHS figures show that for every 450 kg (1,000 lb.) added to a vehicle's mass, the risk of injury to an unrestrained driver is lowered by 34 percent, and the risk of injury to a restrained driver is lowered by 25 percent. GM's series of two-car crash tests carried out a decade ago dramatically confirm this fact. Its engineers concluded that if two cars collide, and one weighs half as much as the other, the driver in the lighter car is 10 times more likely to be killed than the driver in the heavier one. This held true no matter how many stars the smaller car was awarded in government crash tests.

Interestingly, a vehicle's size or past crashworthiness rating doesn't always guarantee that you won't be injured. For example, a 2004 Honda Civic earned five stars for front collision protection and four stars in side-impact tests. However, four years earlier, the 2000 Civic garnered only four stars in frontal and two stars in side-impact crashes. GM's 2004 Extended Cab Silverado pickup earned four stars for the driver and three for the passenger in similar frontal crash tests.

Unsafe designs

Although it sounds hard to believe, automakers *will* deliberately manufacture a vehicle that will kill or maim simply because, in the long run, it costs less to stonewall complaints and pay off victims than to make a safer vehicle. I learned this lesson after reading the court transcripts of *Grimshaw v. Ford* (fire-prone Pintos) and listening to court testimony of GM engineers who deliberately placed fire-prone "sidesaddle" gas tanks in millions of pickups to save $3 per vehicle.

More recent examples of corporate greed triumphing over public safety: Pre-1997 airbag designs that maim or kill women, children, and seniors; anti-lock brake systems that don't brake (a major problem with some GM minivans, trucks, and sport-utilities, and Chrysler sport-utilities and mini-vans); flimsy front seats and seatbacks; the absence of rear head restraints; and fire-prone GM pickup and Ford Crown Victoria fuel tanks. Two other examples of hazardous engineering designs that put profit ahead of safety are failure-prone Chrysler, Ford, and GM minivan sliding doors; automatic transmissions that suddenly shift into Neutral, or allow the vehicle to roll away when parked on an incline, or break down in traffic; and rear pickup seats that injure children.

Children in the rear jump seats of compact extended-cab pickup trucks run a higher risk of injury in an accident because they are more likely to hit something in the confined space, according to a University of Pennsylvania School of Medicine study, published in the April 2002 *Journal of the American Medical Association.*

"Children in rear side-facing, fold-down or jump seats of compact pickup trucks are at substantially increased risk of injury compared with children in the rear seats of other vehicles," it said. "This increase in risk appears to be caused at least in part by contact with the interior of the vehicle at impact."

Flying seats and seatbacks

Seat anchorages have to conform to government load regulations, but the regulations are so minimal that seats can easily collapse or tear loose from their anchorages, leaving drivers and passengers vulnerable in accidents. NHTSA's complaint database is replete with instances where occupants report severe injuries caused by collapsing seatbacks that have injured front-seat occupants or crushed children in safety seats placed in the rear seat.

Driver and passenger seatbacks frequently collapse in rear-end collisions. In one Illinois Appeal Court decision (*Carillo v. Ford*, Cook County Circuit Court), a $14.5 million jury verdict was sustained against Ford after a driver's 1991 Explorer seatback failed, leaving the driver paralyzed from the chest down.

Experts testified that the seatback design was unreasonably dangerous in high-speed, rear-impact collisions. Ford's experts countered that the "yielding seats" were reasonably safe and met the NHTSA safety standard for seatback strength established in 1971, based on a 1963 recommendation by the Society of Automotive Engineers. This standard requires a seat to withstand 200–300 lb. of force. However, in a typical rear-impact crash, seats are subjected to forces four or five times that, according to Kenneth Saczalski, an engineering consultant who specializes in seat design.

The Appeal Court rejected Ford's plea.

Safety features that kill

In the late '60s, Washington forced automakers to include essential safety features like collapsing steering columns and safety windshields in their cars but exempted trucks and vans, and later, SUVs and minivans. As the years passed, the number of mandatory safety features increased to include seat belts, airbags, and crashworthy construction and fewer vehicles were exempted. These improvements met with public approval until quite recently, when reports of deaths and injuries caused by anti-lock brake systems (ABS) and airbag failures showed that defective components and poor engineering negated the potential life-saving benefits associated with these devices.

For example, one out of every five ongoing NHTSA defect investigations concerns inadvertent airbag deployment, failure of the airbag to deploy, or injuries suffered when the bag did go off. In fact, airbags are the agency's single largest cause of current investigations, exceeding even the full range of brake problems, which runs second.

Transport Canada allows car owners to have a mechanic disengage airbags for several reasons: Having to sit fewer than 25 cm from the steering wheel, having to put children in the front seat, or having adult passengers with medical conditions that may induce airbag injuries. Motorists are required by regulation to submit the forms, but Transport Canada does not verify the accuracy of the information. People can have the work done without waiting for a response from the government. The department does not track people who disconnect their bags without going through the official route.

Anti-lock brake systems (ABS)

I am not a fan of ABS brakes. They are often ineffective, failure-prone, and expensive to service.

Essentially, ABS prevents a vehicle's wheels from locking when the brakes are applied in an emergency situation, thus reducing skidding and the loss of directional control. When braking on wet and dry roads, your stopping distance will be about the same as with conventional braking systems. But in gravel, slush, or snow, your stopping distance will be greater.

The most important feature of ABS is that it preserves steering control. As you brake in an emergency, ABS will release the brakes if it senses wheel lock-up. Braking distances will lengthen accordingly, but at least you'll have some steering control. On the other hand, if you start sliding on glare ice, don't expect ABS to help you out very much. The laws of physics (no friction, no stopping!) still apply on ABS-equipped vehicles. You can decrease the stopping distance, however, by removing your all-season tires and installing four snow tires that are the same make and size.

Transport Canada studies show ABS effectiveness is highly overrated. The Insurance Institute for Highway Safety (IIHS)—an American insurance research group that collects and analyzes insurance claims data—says that cars with ABS brakes are actually more likely to be in crashes where no other car is involved but a passenger is killed. Other insurance claim statistics show that ABS brakes aren't producing the overall safety benefits that were predicted by the government and automakers. One IIHS study found that a passenger has a 45 percent greater chance of dying in a single-vehicle crash in a car with anti-lock brakes than in the same car with old-style brakes. On wet pavement, where ABS supposedly excels, that figure rises to a 65 percent greater chance of being killed. In multi-vehicle crashes, ABS-equipped vehicles have a passenger death rate 6 percent higher than vehicles not equipped with ABS.

The high cost of ABS maintenance is one disadvantage that few safety advocates mention, but consider the following: Original parts can cost five times more than regular braking components, and many dealers prefer to replace the entire ABS unit rather than troubleshoot a very complex system.

Keep in mind that anti-lock brakes are notoriously unreliable on all makes and models. They often fail completely, resulting in no braking whatsoever, or they may extend stopping distance by 30 percent. This phenomenon is amply documented throughout NHTSA's complaint database.

Airbag dangers (unsafe at any speed?)

First the good news. It is estimated that airbags have reduced head-on crash fatalities by up to 30 percent and moderate-to-severe injuries by 25 to 29 percent. Injury claims at hospitals resulting from traffic crashes have dropped 24 percent as a result of airbags.

Now for the bad news. To begin with, no airbag is safe, although some model years are safer than others. Pre-'97 airbags explode too forcefully and can seriously injure or kill occupants vulnerable to injury. Later, de-powered "smart" devices are less hazardous, but they're not that smart. Many systems will disable the airbag even though the passenger seat is occupied by a normal-sized adult, as may be the case with Nissan's Quest minivan and Titan pickup, Hyundai's Elantra, and Jaguar, Jeep, Lexus, and Toyota models.

Inadvertent airbag deployment

Airbags frequently go off for no apparent reason, usually due to faulty sensors. Causes of sudden deployment include passing over a bump in the road; slamming the car door; having wet carpets; or, in some Chrysler minivans, simply putting the key in the ignition.

This happens more often than you might imagine, judging by the frequent recalls and thousands of complaints recorded on NHTSA's website at *www.nhtsa.dot.gov/cars/problems/complain/Index.cfm.* Incidentally, dealers and manufacturers are routinely denying claims by alleging that airbags don't go off without a collision. They usually back down if the insured presses the issue.

> On June 17, 2004, after dropping my son off for baseball practice in Toronto, I decided to run a couple of errands. Upon returning to the ball field, I put my 1998 Dodge Grand Caravan in park and turned off the ignition. Immediately thereafter, my air bag deployed. I was struck on the left side of my face and neck and my left ear received some trauma. The BANG from the air bag deploying was so loud that people from 3 surrounding ball fields heard the blast....

•

> Our airbags on our 2003 Volkswagen Jetta TDI deployed for no reason on a smooth surface July 3, 2004. We were denied warrantee because the Calgary Volkswagen field technician found two small dents on the bottom of the car. We met another Volkswagen Jetta TDI driver who experienced basically the same as us on July 1, 2004 and was also denied warranty. An employee at the dealership stated that another customer had an airbag deploy on a Jetta one month earlier causing $5600 in damage.... The deployment of our airbag tore open the ceiling along the passenger side of the car, ruptured the seat, damaged the panel beside the passenger seat, and immobilized the front passenger seatbelt.... These airbags instead of bringing safety are more of a danger. If we had been aware of this or the way Volkswagen would respond to this problem, we never would have bought from them....

Airbag benefits generally outweigh their shortcomings and they shouldn't be disabled. If you feel vulnerable, you'll want to choose a vehicle with adjustable brake and accelerator pedals or an adjustable seat that can travel backward far enough to keep you at a safe distance (over 25 cm or one foot) from the front airbag's explosive force. Children's safety can be assured by getting a vehicle with an airbag shut-off switch, or by having the children sit in the rear middle-seat position, away from front seatbacks that frequently collapse in rear-enders.

Nevertheless, airbags are still dangerous, even when they work properly. In fender-benders, for example, where no one would have been hurt if the airbag hadn't deployed, full-power, early airbag systems can kill women, seniors, and children—or leave them horribly scarred or deaf.

If you are hit from the rear and thrown within 25 cm of the steering wheel as the airbag deploys, you risk severe head, neck, or chest trauma, or even death. If you are making a turn with your arms crossing in front of the steering wheel, you are out of position and risk fractures to both arms. If you drive with your thumbs extended a bit into the steering hub area as I often do, you risk losing both thumbs when the housing cover explodes.

Sometimes, just being female is enough to get you killed.

Two startling Transport Canada studies were uncovered in October 1999 as part of a CBC *Marketplace* investigation into airbag safety. The consumer TV show unearthed government-financed research that showed airbags reduce the risk of injury by *only 2 percent* for adults who wear seat belts. Even more incredible, the studies confirm that airbags actually *increase* the risk of injury to women by 9 percent and the risk of death for children by 21 percent.

The research was conducted in 1996 and 1998 on early, full-powered airbags. Fearing the public disclosure of the findings, it took Transport Canada four months to release the studies to *Marketplace*. American government officials have refused to comment on the Canadian research, despite the fact that it contradicts the basic premise of airbag use—they are safe at any speed, regardless of gender.

In fact, the danger to women is so great that an earlier 1996 Transport Canada and George Washington University study of 445 drivers and passengers drew these frightening conclusions:

> While the initial findings of this study confirm that belted drivers are afforded added protection against head and facial injury in moderate to severe frontal collisions, the findings also suggest that these benefits are being negated by a high incidence of bag-induced injury. The incidence of bag-induced injury was greatest among female drivers. Furthermore, the intervention of the airbag can be expected to introduce a variety of new injury mechanisms such as facial injuries from "bag slap," upper extremity fractures, either directly from the deploying airbag module or from arm flailing, and thermal burns to the face and arms.

A frightening admission. Don't look for the above study on Transport Canada's website. It's not there.

Side airbags—good and bad

In crashes with another passenger vehicle, 51 percent of driver deaths in recent model cars during 2000–01 occurred in side impacts, up from 31 percent in 1980–81.

Side airbags and side curtains are designed to protect drivers and passengers in rollovers and side-impact crashes, which are estimated to account for almost a third of vehicular deaths. They also have been shown to help keep unbelted occupants from being ejected in rollovers. Head-protecting side airbags can reduce serious crash injuries by 45 percent. Side airbags without head protection reduce injuries by only 10 percent. Ideally, you want a side airbag system that protects both the torso and head.

Because side airbags aren't required by federal regulation in the States or in Canada, neither government has developed any tests to measure their safety for children and small adults. IIHS hopes its test results will goad government regulators and automakers into standardizing side airbag design and increasing their effectiveness and safety.

In the meantime, keep in mind that preliminary safety studies show side airbags may be deadly to children or any occupant not sitting in the correct position. Research carried out in 1998 by safety researchers (Anil Khadikar, Biodynamics Engineering Inc., and Lonney Pauls, Springwater Micro Data Systems, "Assessment of Injury Protection Performance of Side Impact Airbags") shows there are four hazards that have not been fully addressed by automakers:

1. Inadvertent airbag firing (short circuit, faulty hardware or software)
2. Unnecessary firing (sometimes opposite side airbag will fire; airbag may deploy when a low-speed side-swipe wouldn't have endangered occupant safety)
3. A three-year-old restrained in a booster seat could be seriously injured
4. Out-of-position restrained occupants could be seriously injured

The researchers conclude with the following observation: "Even properly restrained vehicle occupants can have their upper or lower extremities in harm's way in the path of an exploding [side] airbag."

The above study and dozens of other scientific papers confirm that small and tall restrained drivers face death or severe injury from frontal and side airbag deployments for the simple reason that they are outside of the norm of the 5'8", 180 lb. male test dummy.

These studies also debunk the safety merits of ABS brakes, so it's no surprise they go unheralded by Transport Canada and other government and private safety groups. With a bit of patience, though, you can find this research at *www.nhtsa.dot.gov/esv.*

In the meantime, don't forget the NHTSA's side airbag warning issued on October 14, 1999:

Side impact airbags can provide significant supplemental safety benefits to adults in side impact crashes. However, children who are seated
in close proximity to a side airbag may be at risk of serious or fatal
injury, especially if the child's head, neck, or chest is in close proximity
to the airbag at the time of deployment.

Protect yourself

Additionally, you should take the following steps to reduce the danger from
airbag deployment:

- Don't buy a vehicle with side airbags unless it offers head protection and
  you are confident that all occupants will remain properly positioned out of
  harm's way.
- Make sure that seat belts are buckled and all head restraints are properly
  adjusted (about ear level).
- Make sure the head restraints are rated "good" by IIHS in Part Four.
- Insist that passengers who are frail, short, or have recently had surgery sit in
  the back.
- Make sure that the driver's seat can be adjusted for height and has tracks
  with sufficient rearward travel to allow short drivers to remain a safe distance (25 centimetres) away from the bag's deployment.
- If you are short-statured, consider buying aftermarket pedal extensions from
  auto parts retailers or buying optional adjustable accelerator and brake
  pedals to keep you a safe distance away from a deploying airbag.
- Buy a vehicle that comes with manual passenger-side airbag disablers.
- Buy a vehicle that uses sensors to detect the presence of an electronically
  tagged child safety seat in the passenger seat and disables the airbag for
  that seat.

Top 20 safety defects

The U.S. federal government's online safety complaints database contains well
over 100,000 entries, going back to vehicles made in the late '70s. Although
the database originally intended to record incidents of component failures that
only relate to safety, you will find every problem imaginable dutifully recorded
by clerks working for NHTSA.

A perusal of the listed complaints shows that some safety-related failures
occur more frequently than others and often affect one manufacturer more
than another. Here is a summary of some of the more commonly reported failures, in order of frequency:

1. Airbags not deploying when they should, or deploying when they
   shouldn't
2. ABS total brake failure; wheel lock-up
3. Tire tread separation
4. Electrical or fuel system fires
5. Sudden acceleration

6. Sudden stalling
7. Sudden electrical failure
8. Transmission failing to engage or suddenly disengaging
9. Transmission jumping from Park to Reverse or Neutral; vehicle rolling away when parked
10. Steering or suspension failure
11. Seat belt failures
12. Collapsing seatbacks
13. Defective sliding door, door locks, and latches
14. Poor headlight illumination
15. Dash reflecting onto windshield
16. Hood flying up
17. Wheel falling away
18. Steering wheel lifting off
19. Transmission lever pulling out
20. Exploding windshields

Senior safety

According to the Canada Safety Council, almost 30 percent of Canada's population was over age 50 in 2002 and half of Canadians 65 and older living in a private household drive a motor vehicle, though most drive only a few times a week. Furthermore, drivers over 80 are the fastest-growing segment of the driving population. Husbands do the bulk of family driving, which usually involves short trips (11–17 km per day, on average) for medical appointments and visits to family, friends, and shopping malls. This puts older women, who tend to outlive their husbands, in a serious bind due to their lack of driving experience—particularly in rural areas, where driving is a necessity rather than a choice.

Safe, reliable choices

Older drivers, like most of us, want cars that are reliable, relatively inexpensive, and fuel-efficient. Additionally, they require vehicles that compensate for some of the physical challenges associated with aging and that provide protection for accidents more common to mature drivers (side-impacts, for example). Furthermore, as drivers get older, they find that the very act of getting in a car (sitting down while moving sideways, without bumping their heads or twisting their necks) demands considerable acrobatic skill.

No wonder vans, small SUVs set upon car platforms, and Cadillac SUVs, such as the Escalade, are so popular with senior drivers with limited mobility.

Access and comfort

Sometimes drivers with arthritic hands may have to insert a pencil into their key ring to twist the key in the ignition. Make sure your ignition lock doesn't require that much effort. Power locks and windows are a must, especially if the vehicle will be operated with hand controls. A remote keyless entry will allow entry without having to twist a key in the doorlock. A vehicle equipped with a buttonless shifter will be less difficult to activate for arthritis sufferers and drivers with limited upper-body mobility. Cruise control can be helpful for those with lower-body mobility challenges.

Get a vehicle that's easy to enter and exit. Check for door openings that are wide enough to get in and out of easily, both for you and for any wheelchairs or scooters that may need to be loaded. Of course, your trunk or rear cargo area needs a low liftover and room to stow your wheelchair or scooter. Bench seats are preferable because they're roomier and easier to access; a power-adjustable driver seat is also a good idea. Make sure the seat is comfortable—take a trip of several hours—and has plenty of side bolstering.

Forget minivans and large trucks, unless you invest in a step-up, have an easily reached inside grip handle, and don't mind bumping the left-side steering column stalk with your knee each time you slide into the driver's seat.

Drivers with limited mobility or those who are recovering from hip surgery give kudos to the Buick LeSabre, Cadillac Escalade, and GM Venture/ Montana minivans; Toyota's Echo, Matrix, and Avalon; and small SUVs like the Honda CR-V, Hyundai Santa Fe, or Toyota RAV4.

Incidentally, General Motors' minivans offer a Sit-N-Lift option which is a motorized, rotating, lift-and-lower rear passenger seat that's accessed through the middle door and can be taken out when not needed. An $8,600 option, this seat was introduced in October 2003 and will be offered with GM's 2005 Crossover Sport Vans. 2001 model year and later GM minivans can also be retrofitted. The seat can support 136 kg (300 lbs.), includes a slide-out footrest, and can be lowered to approximately 42.5 cm (17 inches) from seat bottom to ground.

Safety

The driver's seat should be mounted high enough to give a commanding view of the road (with a bit slower reaction time, we need earlier warnings). Driver seats must offer enough rearward travel to attenuate the force of an exploding airbag, which can be particularly hazardous to older, small-statured occupants, children, and anyone recovering from surgery. Adjustable gas and brake pedals are a must for short-legged drivers.

And, while we're discussing airbags, remember that prior to 1997 most airbags were full-force, making it especially important that you put at least 25 cm between your upper torso and the front airbag. As full-powered air bags deploy, they expand with an explosive force which is greatest in the first 8 cm of travel. Sit within this zone and you are likely to be killed or seriously injured from the explosion. Tests have shown that short drivers tend to sit about 24 cm (measured from the chest) from the steering wheel in comparison to an average male who sits at a distance of about 39 cm. Moreover, pre-impact braking may throw you even closer to the air bag prior to its deployment, which certainly isn't a confidence-builder, is it?

Transport Canada recommends that adults sit more than 25 cm away from the air bag housing and that children (ages 12 and under) sit in the rear of the vehicle. Also, since most intersection collisions involving mature drivers occur when drivers are making a turn into oncoming traffic, head-protecting side airbags are a must.

Look for handles near the door frame that can be gripped for support when entering or leaving the vehicle, bright dashboard gauges that can be seen in sunlight, and instruments with large-sized controls.

Remote-controlled mirrors are a must, along with adjustable, unobtrusive head restraints, and a non-reflective front windshield (many drivers put a cloth on the dash top to cut the distraction). Make sure brake and accelerator pedals aren't mounted too close together.

Safety features

As far as safety features are concerned, a superior crashworthiness rating is essential, as well as torso and head-protecting side airbags. The extra head protection can make a critical difference in side impacts. For example, Toyota's 2004 RAV4, with $680 head-protecting side airbags earned a "best pick" designation from the Insurance Institute for Highway Safety (IIHS). When tested without the head protection, it received a "poor" rating in the side test.

Don't be overly impressed by anti-lock brakes, since their proper operation (no tapping on the brakes) runs counter to everything you have been taught, and they aren't that reliable. Look for headlights that give you a comfortable view at night, as well as easily seen and heard dash-mounted turn signal indicators. Ensure that the vehicle's knobs and switches are large and easy to identify. An easily accessed, full-sized spare tire and user-friendly lug wrench and jack stand are also important.

Trip tips

Before you begin a driving vacation (an oxymoron?), make sure that the vehicle is properly serviced, baggage and occupants don't exceed a safe limit, and visibility is unobstructed. Above all, don't treat the trip as an endurance marathon. Plan your route with rest stops scheduled every two hours or 200 km, don't drive at night (even with glasses, vision can be poor) or during weekends (lots of impaired, crazy drivers are partying), and if you fall behind schedule, call ahead to say you'll be a bit late.

Sooner or later you will find out that everyone on the highway is going much faster than you. Although the speed limit says 100 km/h, most drivers will speed by at 120 km/h. Plus, it will seem like every vehicle in your rearview mirror is a huge commercial truck, hugging your rear bumper. All the more reason to stay in the middle lane and let the speeders pass you by. Why not simply stay all the way to the right? Too many exits that cut off the right lane, or merging cars entering the highway. Your slow speed will likely cause them to speed up and cut you off as they dart from the far-right lane to the middle lane, where you should be anyhow.

When to stop driving

Most older drivers know when it's time to stop driving, but many continue driving because they have to. The Ontario Ministry of Transportation lists the following five warning signs that tell you to stop driving:

1. Frequent near collisions
2. Direct involvement in minor collisions
3. Difficulty seeing pedestrians, objects, and other vehicles
4. Difficulty coordinating hand and foot movements
5. Increased nervousness behind the wheel

Other Buying Considerations

When "new" isn't new

There's no guarantee that what you buy is really new. The odometer may have been disconnected, or the vehicle could have been involved in an accident, both common occurrences.

Even if the vehicle hasn't been used, it may have been left outdoors for a considerable length of time, causing the deterioration of rubber components, premature body and chassis rusting, or severe rusting of internal mechanical parts (leading to brake malfunction, fuel line contamination, hard starting, and stalling).

You can check a vehicle's age by looking at the date-of-manufacture plate found on the driver-side door pillar. If the date of manufacture is 7/02, your vehicle was probably one of the last 2002 models made before the September changeover to the 2003s. Redesigned vehicles or those new to the market are exceptions to this rule. They may arrive at dealerships in early spring or mid-summer, and are considered to be next year's models. They also depreciate more quickly, owing to their earlier launching, but this difference narrows over time.

Carryover models generally have fewer problems than vehicles that have been significantly reworked or just introduced to the market. Newly redesigned vehicles get quality scores that are, on average, 2 percent worse than vehicles that have been around for a while, says J.D. Power.

Because they were the first off the assembly line for that model year, most vehicles assembled between September and February are called "first series" cars. "Second series" vehicles, made between March and August, incorporate more assembly-line fixes and are better built than the earlier models, which may depend on ineffective "field fixes" to mask problems until the warranty expires. Both vehicles will initially sell for the same price, but the post-February ones will be a far better buy, since they benefit from more assembly-line upgrades and rebates.

There's also the very real possibility that the new vehicle you've just pur-chased was damaged while being shipped to the dealer and was fixed by the dealer during the pre-delivery inspection. It's estimated that this happens to about 10 percent of all new vehicles. There's no specific Canadian legislation allowing buyers of vehicles damaged in transit to cancel their contracts. However, in B.C., legislation says that dealers must disclose damages of $2,000, or more. In a more general sense, Canadian common-law jurispru-dence *does* allow for cancellation or compensation whenever the delivered product differs markedly from what the buyer expected to receive.

Fuel economy fantasies

Oh, we wanted so badly to believe in the 200-mpg Pogue carburetor invented in 1953 by Charles Nelson Pogue, a Montreal automotive engineer. As his 15 minutes of fame approached the 14-minute mark, Pogue recanted, saying that he had never claimed his carburetor would get 200 miles per gallon, "or even half of that," declaring all such numbers were "violently distorted by newspapermen and magazine writers."

And who can forget '70s icon, Liz Carmichael, a six-foot, 200-pound transsexual born Jerry Dean Michael, who built a three-wheeled prototype car called the Dale that was to be powered by a two-cylinder engine, get 70 mpg, and sell for under $2,000. Dealers bought franchises, no cars were delivered, and "she" confessed to being a "he," and was hauled off to jail.

Now, after we've had our hopes dashed by Pogue and Carmichael, Transport Canada hoodwinks us with gas mileage figures that are impossible to achieve.

Gas mileage claims on individual models trumpeted by the manufacturers or Transport Canada aren't that reliable; they can be lower by 40–45 percent in city driving and about 20–23 percent overall, says *Consumer Reports*. Automakers submit their own test results to the government after running the vehicles under optimum conditions, and Transport Canada then publishes these self-serving "cooked" figures. In fact, one Ford bulletin warns dealers:

> Very few people will drive in a way that is identical to the EPA [sanctioned] tests.... These [fuel economy] numbers are the result of test procedures that were originally developed to test emissions, not fuel economy.

Stephen Akehurst, a senior manager at Natural Resources Canada, which tests vehicles and publishes the annual *Fuel Consumption Guide*, admits that his lab tests vehicles under ideal conditions. He says that actual driving may burn about 25 percent more fuel than what the government tests show.

Some examples: One of the biggest gas-guzzlers tested, the Lincoln Aviator, burned 44 percent more than the *Fuel Consumption Guide*'s estimate. A Nissan Quest burned twice as much fuel as was advertised in the *Fuel Consumption Guide*. Only the Hyundai Elantra did well. It burned a full litre less than predicted by the guys in the white coats.

It's not surprising, therefore, that J.D. Power and Associates' 2003 quality survey showed that poor gas mileage was one of the top complaints among owners of 2003 model cars and trucks. Environment Canada also confirms that 2003–04 models are much less fuel efficient than vehicles built 15 years ago. At that time, the fleet averaged 10.5L/100 km; now it's estimated to be 11.2L/100 km.

In theory this fuel-economy misrepresentation is actionable, but only one successful, $300, small claims court lawsuit has been reported in Canada. Most people simply keep the car they bought and live with the fact that they were fooled.

Although good fuel economy is important, it's hardly worth a harsh ride, excessive highway noise, side-wind buffeting, anemic acceleration, and a cramped interior. You may end up with much worse gas mileage than advertised and a vehicle that's underpowered for your needs.

If you never quite got the hang of metric fuel economy measurements, use the fuel conversion table that follows to establish how many miles to a gallon of gas your vehicle provides.

Fuel Economy Conversion Table

L/100 km	mpg	L/100 km	mpg	L/100 km	mpg
5.0	56	7.4	38	12.5	23
5.2	54	7.6	37	13.0	22
5.4	52	7.8	36	13.5	21
5.6	50	8.0	35	14.0	20
5.8	48	8.5	33	15.0	19
6.0	47	9.0	31	15.0	18
6.2	46	9.5	30	17.0	17
6.4	44	10.0	28	18.0	16
6.7	43	10.5	27	19.0	15
6.8	42	11.0	26	20.0	14
7.0	40	11.5	25	21.0	13
7.2	39	12.0	24	23.0	12

Fuel economy figures are published by Natural Resources Canada (a free copy of its Fuel Consumption Guide [an engrossing work of fiction!] can be obtained on the Internet at *oee.nrcan.gc.ca/autosmart/fcg/index.cfm* or by calling 1-800-387-2000).

Excessive maintenance fees

Maintenance inspections and parts costs represent hidden costs that are usually exaggerated by dealers and automakers to increase their profits on vehicles that rarely require fixing or that are sold in insufficient numbers to support a service bay. Both Mazda and Honda owners suspect this to be the case, as the following Honda owner reports and a CBC *Marketplace* Mazda dealer survey confirms.

In an investigative report shown on February 18, 2003, CBC TV's *Marketplace* surveyed 12 Mazda dealers across the country to determine how much they charged for a "regularly scheduled maintenance inspection" as listed in the owner's manual of a 2001 Mazda MPV with 48,000 km (*www.cbc.ca/consumers/market/files/cars/mazda_warranty*). Even with different labour rates, Mazda says the check-up should not cost more than about $280 anywhere in Canada. Here are the prices they were quoted:

- $400 (Montreal)
- $546 (Burlington)
- $225 (Toronto)
- $253 (Calgary)
- $340 (Calgary)
- $450 (Calgary)

- $300 (Toronto)
- $271 (Winnipeg)
- $700 (Winnipeg)

- $350 (Vancouver)
- $500 (Vancouver)
- $525(Vancouver)

The first quote for service in Winnipeg was $700. A service technician told *Marketplace*'s producer that the price varied between $400 and $500 and warned that the work was needed to maintain the warranty. However, a check of the owner's manual didn't not show any connection between the service and keeping the warranty in place. Gregory Young, director of Corporate Public Relations for Mazda Canada said, "There's nothing in the owner's manual that says if you don't have this work done in its entirety at a prescribed time that automatically your warranty is void."

Who Can You Trust?

Most investigative stories done on the auto industry in Canada (such as secret car warranties, dangerous airbags, and Chrysler minivan defects) have been written by business columnists, freelancers, or "action line" troubleshooters rather than by reporters on the auto beat. Jeremy Cato and Michael Vaughn, who host *The Globe and Mail* newspaper-affiliated *Report on Business* daily TV show out of Toronto, epitomize the best combination of auto journalism and business reporting. This duo asks the tough questions automakers hate to answer. On Saturday nights, Toronto's CityPulse24 goes after dishonest or incompetent dealers and automakers as Mohamed Bouchama, president of Car Help Canada, shakes up car dealers and manufacturers by rating new and used cars, providing legal advice, and teaching consumers the art of complaining. Another good source of auto information is CFRB radio in Toronto. Every Saturday afternoon, expert mechanic Alan Gelman gives out hard-hitting auto repair tips. The *Vancouver Sun*'s Linda Bates also does an outstanding job without compromising her integrity. There's also the *Toronto Star*'s Ellen Roseman, one of Canada's foremost consumer advocates and business columnists, and Maryanna Lewyckyj, a *Toronto Sun* business and consumer columnist who is more car-savvy than most automaker PR stuffed shirts. Finally, the *Canadian Driver* website offers a cornucopia of Canadian car critics that are relatively independent of industry influence.

These reporter/advocates are the exception, not the rule. Even the most ardent reporters frequently have to jump through hoops to get their stories out, simply because their editors or station managers have bought into many of the fraudulent practices so common to the auto industry. Haranguing staff for more "balance" is the pretext *du jour* for squelching hard-hitting stories implicating dealers and automakers. News editors don't want truth, they want copy and comfort. They'll spend weeks sifting through Paul Martin's or Stephen Harper's trash cans looking for conflicts of interest, while ignoring the auto industry scams threaded throughout their own classified ads.

Want proof? Go ahead and try to decipher the fine print in *The Globe and Mail* or *Toronto Star* leasing ads or, better yet, tell me what the fine print scrolled at breakneck speed on television new-vehicle commercials really says.

Probably something to the effect that "everything said or shown before in this ad may or may not be true." Where is the investigative reporter who will submit these ads to an optometrists' group that will confirm that the message is unreadable?

Think about this: Dealers selling used cars from residences, posing as private parties ("curbsiders"), are periodically exposed by dealer associations and "crusading" auto journalists. Yet these scam artists place dozens or more ads weekly in the classified section of local newspapers, where the same phone numbers and billing addresses constantly reappear. The ad order takers know who these crooks are. Why isn't there an exposé by reporters working for these papers? Why don't they publish the fact that it's mostly new-vehicle dealers who supply curbsiders with their cars? That's what I'd call balanced reporting, but it never seems to be done. Classified ad sellers care only about selling ads, not whether the seller is a dishonest used-car salesman or an escort agency that's a front for prostitution. Speaking of prostitution, although car columnists claim that their integrity is not for sale, there's no doubt that it can be rented. Travel junkets and public relations and advertising contracts all sweeten the pot for these pseudo-journalists.

Steer clear of the "Car of the Year"

Once you've established a budget and selected some vehicles that interest you, the next step is to ascertain which ones have high safety and reliability ratings. Be wary of the ratings found in some enthusiast magazines and car enthusiast websites; their supposedly independent tests are a lot of baloney (see "Rating the ratings" in Part Four).

You want proof of how misleading these ratings can be? Take *Car and Driver* as an example. It rated the Ford Focus as a "Best Buy" during its first three model years, while government and consumer groups decried the car's dozen or so recall campaigns and the huge number of owner safety and reliability complaints.

There are dozens of organizations and magazines that rate cars for everything from their overall reliability and frequency of repairs (J.D. Power and *Consumer Reports*) to their crashworthiness and appeal to owners (NHTSA, IIHS, and Strategic Visions Total Quality Survey (TQS)). These ratings don't always match. For instance, BMW's Mini ranked 25th of 28 brands in J.D. Power's Initial Quality Survey (IQS). But the popular British import ranks second of 30 brands included in Strategic Vision's Total Quality Survey (TQS).

Getting reliable info

Funny, as soon as they hear that you're shopping for a new vehicle, everybody wants to tell you what to buy—relatives, co-workers, friends, and everyone else who thinks they know what's best for you. After a while, you'll get so many conflicting opinions that it'll seem as if any choice you make will be the wrong one. Before making your decision, remember that you should invest a couple of months in researching costs and models. The following sources provide a variety of useful information that will help you ferret out what vehicle best suits your needs and budget.

Auto shows

Auto shows are held from January through March throughout Canada, starting in Montreal and ending in Vancouver. Although you can't buy or drive a car at the show, you can easily compare prices and the interior/exterior styling of different vehicles. In fact, show officials estimate that about 20 percent of auto show visitors are actively seeking info for an upcoming new-car purchase. Interestingly, while the shows are open, dealer traffic nosedives, making for much more generous deals in showrooms. Business usually picks up following the show.

Internet and online services

Anyone with access to a computer and a modem can now obtain useful information relating to the auto industry in a matter of minutes, and at little or no cost. This is accomplished in two ways: Subscribing to an online service, like America Online (AOL), that offers consumer forums and easy Internet access, or going directly to the Internet through a low-cost Canadian Internet service provider (ISP) and a browser like Google that helps you cruise thousands of helpful sites.

Shopping on the Internet

The key word here is "shopping," because *Consumer Reports* magazine has found that barely 2 percent of Internet surfers actually buy a new or used car online. Yet, over 50 percent of buyers admit to using the Internet to get prices and specifications before visiting the dealership. Apparently, few buyers want to purchase a new or used vehicle without seeing what's offered and knowing all money paid will be accounted for.

New-vehicle shopping through automaker and independent websites is a quick and easy way to compare prices and model specifications, but you will have to be careful. Many so-called independent sites are merely fronts for dealers and automakers and tailor their information to steer you into their showroom, or convince you to buy a certain brand of car.

Nevertheless, shoppers now have access to information they once were routinely denied or had trouble finding, such as dealer price markups and incentive programs, the book value for trade-ins, and considerable safety data. Canadian shoppers can get Canadian invoice prices and specs by contacting the Automobile Protection Association (APA) by phone or fax, or by accessing *www.carcostcanada.com*.

Other advantages to online shopping: Some dealers offer a lower price to online shoppers, and the entire transaction, including financing, can be done on the Internet. Buyers don't have to haggle; they merely post their best offer electronically to a number of dealers in their area code (for more convenient servicing of the vehicle) and await counter offers. Three caveats: 1) You will have to go to a dealer to finalize the contract and be preyed upon by the financing and insurance (F&I) sales agents; 2) as far as bargains are concerned, *Consumer Reports* says its test shoppers found that lower prices are more frequently obtained by visiting the dealer showroom and concluding the sale there; and 3) only a third of online dealers respond to customer queries.

Auto Quality Rankings

There are two major surveyors of automobile quality: J.D. Power and Associates, a private American automobile consulting organization, and Consumers Union, an American non-profit consumer organization that publishes *Consumer Reports*.

J. D. Power

Each year, J. D. Power and Associates publishes the results of two important surveys measuring vehicle quality and owners' customer service satisfaction (CSI). Interestingly, these two polls often contradict each other. For example, its Dependability Index places Saturn near the bottom of the list; however, Saturn's placed sixth from the top in the Power Service Index. This leads one to conclude that the car isn't very reliable, but service is given with a smile!

Power's criticism of Nissan's 2004 Quest minivan has company engineers working overtime. They have already authorized a number of recalls to fix sliding doors, replace the driver's power window switch, repair faulty interior reading lights, replace second-row seat levers, and correct airbag sensors that don't work. Engineers were tipped off to the Quests' glitches in the 2004 J.D. Power and Associates Initial Quality Study, which rated the Quest last among minivans in consumer perceptions of quality during the first 100 days of ownership. Nissan's Titan full-sized pickup and Armada full-sized SUV also placed last in their segments for other problems.

Consumer Reports and CAA's *Autopinion* (Carguide)

Consumer groups and non-profit auto associations are your best bets for the most unbiased auto ratings. They're not perfect, though, so it's a good idea to consult several and look for ratings that match from publication to publication. My favourites are *Consumer Reports* and the Canadian Automobile Association's (CAA) *Autopinion*. Both publications list only the manufacturer's suggested retail price (MSRP), not the invoice price.

Consumer Reports (*CR*) is an American publication that once had a tenuous affiliation with the Consumers Association of Canada. Its ratings, extrapolated from Consumers Union's annual U.S. member survey, accurately mirror the Canadian experience. There are two exceptions, however. Components that are particularly vulnerable to our harsh climate usually don't perform as well as the *CR* reliability ratings indicate, and poor servicing caused by a weak dealer body in Canada can make some service-dependent vehicles a nightmare to own in Canada, whereas the American experience may be benign.

Based on 600,000-plus American and Canadian member responses, *CR* lists used vehicles that, according to owner reports, are significantly better or worse than the industry average. Statisticians agree that *CR*'s sampling method leaves some room for error, but, with a few notable exceptions, the ratings are fair, conservative, and consistent guidelines for buying a reliable new vehicle. My only criticisms of the ratings are that many models, like Toyota and Honda, can do no wrong, yet service bulletins and extended warranties show they have serious engine, transmission, and electrical problems. Plus, older vehicles are excluded from *CR*'s ratings and many of the ratings about the frequency of repair of certain components aren't specific enough. For example, don't just tell me there are problems with the fuel or electrical system. Rather, let me know about specific components—is it the fuel pumps that are failure-prone, or the injectors that clog up, or the battery that suddenly dies?

There's also the CAA's annual "Vehicle Ownership Survey," found in the February issue of *Carguide* magazine. It's available from CAA and news-stands for $5.95 and is kept on display through June. A one-year subscription costs $17.99 in Canada (GST included) and $25.99 elsewhere (*www.carguidemagazine.com*; 905-842-6591).

Carguide is published six times a year. It contains reams of automaker advertising and publishes mostly general-interest articles as well as summaries of new cars and trucks. Its most useful feature is its used-vehicle ratings, based on CAA's annual sampling of 20,000 owners—that's less than 5 percent of *Consumer Reports*' survey, but at least you know they're all Canadian drivers. The *Autopinion* supplement gives you a good general idea of those vehicles that have generated the most problems for CAA members (Chrysler Neon, Ford Windstar, and Ford F-Series trucks), but its conclusions should be compared with *Consumer Reports*' or *Lemon-Aid*'s recommendations before a definite decision is made.

Lemon-Aid *versus* Consumer Reports

CR and *Lemon-Aid* ratings are often in agreement. Where they differ is in *Lemon-Aid*'s greater reliance upon NHTSA safety complaints, service bulletin admissions of defects, and owner complaints received through the Internet (rather than from a subscriber base, which may simply attract owners singing from the same hymnal).

In looking over *CR*'s best new- and used-vehicle picks for 2003, as published in its December 2002 edition, there are a number of recommended vehicles that defy all logic.

Foremost is the Ford Windstar, followed by the Saturn Vue and the Jeep Liberty. It is inconceivable that *CR* isn't aware of the multiplicity of power-train, body, and suspension failures affecting these vehicles. Then there's the assorted Chrysler lineup. Now, you'd have to live on another planet not to know that Chryslers are afflicted by chronic automatic transmission, ball joint, body, brake, and AC defects. In fact, *Consumer Reports*' "Frequency of Repair" tables in the same edition give out plenty of black marks to the aforementioned models and components. Yet sloppy research and editing failed to pick up on these contradictions.

Look Before You Lease

Why leasing costs more

Leasing means paying more than you have to. Lessees usually pay the full manufacturer's suggested retail price (MSRP) on a vehicle loaded with costly options, plus hidden fees and interest charges that wouldn't be included if the vehicle were purchased instead. DesRosiers Automotive Research Inc. found that some fully loaded entry-level cars *leased* with high interest rates and deceptive "special fees" could cost more than what some luxury models would cost to *buy*. A useful website that takes the mystery out of leasing is at *www.federalreserve.gov/pubs/leasing*, run by the United States Federal Reserve Board. It goes into incredible detail, comparing leasing versus buying, and has a handy dictionary of terms you're most likely to encounter.

Decoding leasing ads

Take a close look at the small print found in most leasing ads. Pay particular attention to the "weasel" words relating to the model year, kind of vehicle (demonstration or used), equipment, warranty, interest rate, buy-back amount, down payment, security payment, monthly payment, transportation and preparation charges, administration fee ("acquisition" and "disposal" fees), insurance premium, number of free kilometres, and excess kilometre charge.

When and Where to Buy

When to buy

A good time to buy a new sport-utility, van, or truck that hasn't been redesigned is in the winter, between January and March, when you get the first series of rebates and dealer incentives, and production quality begins to improve. Try not to buy when there's strike action—it will be especially tough to get a bargain because there's less product to sell and dealers have to make as much profit as possible on each vehicle remaining in their diminishing stock. Furthermore, work stoppages increase the chances that online defects will go uncorrected and the vehicle will be delivered, as is, to product-starved dealers.

Instead, lie low for a while and then return in force in the summer and early fall, when you can double-dip from additional automakers' dealer incentive and buyer rebate programs, which can mean thousands of dollars in additional savings. Remember, too, that vehicles made between March and August offer the most factory upgrades, based on field complaints from those unfortunate fleet managers and rental car agencies who bought the vehicles when they first came out.

Allow yourself at least two weeks to finalize a deal if you're not trading in your vehicle, and longer if you sell your vehicle privately. Visit the showroom at the end of the month, just before closing, when the salesperson will want to make that one last sale to meet the month's quota. If sales have been terrible, the sales manager may be willing to do some extra negotiating in order to boost sales-staff morale.

Where to buy

Good dealers aren't always the ones with the lowest prices. Dealing with someone who gives honest and reliable service is just as important as getting a good price. Check a dealer's honesty and reliability by talking with motorists who drive vehicles purchased from that dealer (identified by the nameplate on the trunk). If these customers have been treated fairly, they'll be glad to recommend their dealer. You can also ascertain the quality of new-vehicle preparation and servicing by renting one of the dealer's minivans or pickups for a weekend or by getting your trade-in serviced.

How can you tell which dealers are the most honest and competent? Well, judging from the thousands of reports I receive each year, dealerships in small suburban and rural communities are more fair than big-city dealers, because they're more vulnerable to negative word-of-mouth advertising and to poor sales—when their vehicles aren't selling, good service takes up the slack. Their prices may also be more competitive, but don't count on it.

Dealers selling more than one manufacturer's product line present special problems. Overhead can be quite high, and cancellation of a dual dealership by an automaker in favour of an exclusive franchise elsewhere is an ever-present threat. Parts availability may also be a problem, because a dealer with two separate vehicle lines must split the inventory and may therefore have an inadequate supply on hand.

The quality of new-vehicle service is directly linked to the number and competence of dealerships within the network. If the network is weak, parts are likely to be unavailable, repair costs can go through the roof, and the skill level of the mechanics may be questionable. Among foreign manufacturers, Asian automakers have the best overall dealer representation across Canada, except for Mitsubishi and Kia.

Kia's dealer network is very weak, having been left by its owner, Hyundai, to fend for itself for many years, but is strengthening. Mitsubishi dealers piggy-backed onto existing Chrysler franchises, however, have been seriously weakened by Chrysler's decision to dump parts of Mitsubishi.

European imports are highly dealer-dependent for parts and service. Furthermore, since parts aren't easily found outside of the dealer network, they tend to be pricier than Japanese and American components. Servicing in Canada has been woefully inadequate, with VW's lack of a Canadian customer assistance office making a bad situation worse.

And, talking about bad situations, Mercedes-Benz has gained a reputation for poor quality vehicles encompassing its SUVs, C-series, and E-series cars (complaints include engine "sludge" and electrical system problems).

No matter where your car comes from, it's always a good idea to patronize dealerships that are accredited by auto clubs such as CAA affiliates or consumer groups like the APA. Auto club accreditation is no iron-clad guarantee of honest or competent business practices, but if you're cheated or fall victim to poor servicing from one of their recommended garages (look for the accreditation symbol in their phone book ads or on their shop windows), the accreditor is one more place to take your complaint and apply additional mediation pressure. And as you'll see under "Repairs" in Part Three, plaintiffs have won in court by pleading that the auto club is legally responsible for the consequences of the recommendations it makes.

Automobile brokers/vehicle buying services

Brokers are independent agents who try to find the new or used vehicle you want at a price below what you'd pay at a dealership (including the extra cost of the broker's services). Broker services appeal to buyers who want to save time and money while simultaneously avoiding most of the stress and hassle associated with the dealership experience, which for many people is like a swim in shark-infested waters.

Brokers get new vehicles through dealers, while used vehicles may come from dealers, auctions, private sellers, and leasing companies. The broker's job is to find a vehicle to meet the client's expressed needs, and then negotiate its purchase (or lease) on behalf of the client. The majority of brokers tend to deal exclusively in new vehicles, with a small percentage dealing in both new and used vehicles. Ancillary services vary among brokers, and may include such things as comparative vehicle analysis and price research.

The cost of hiring a broker ranges anywhere from a flat fee of a few hundred dollars to a percentage of the value of the vehicle (usually 1–2 percent). A flat fee is usually best because it encourages the broker to keep the selling price low. Reputable brokers are not beholden to any particular dealership or make, and will disclose their flat fee up front or tell the buyer the percentage amount they will charge on a specific vehicle.

Finding the right broker

This is a tall order, because good brokers are hard to find, particularly in Western Canada and British Columbia. Buyers who are looking for a broker should first ask friends and acquaintances if they can recommend one. Word-of-mouth referrals are often the best, because people won't refer others to a service with which they were dissatisfied. Your local credit union or the regional CAA office is a good place to get a broker referral from people who see their work every day.

Toronto's Metro Credit Union (contact David Lawrence or Rob LoPresti at 1-800-777-8507 or 416-252-5621) has a vehicle counselling and purchasing service (Auto Advisory Services Group, comprising CarFacts and AutoBuy) where members can hire an expert "car shopper" who will do the legwork—including the tedious and frustrating dickering with sales staff—and save members time and hassle. This program can also get that new or used vehicle at a reduced (fleet) rate, arrange top-dollar prices for trade-ins, provide independent advice on options like rustproofing and extended warranties, carry out lien searches, and even negotiate the best settlement with insurance agents. The credit union also holds regular car-buying seminars throughout the year in the Greater Toronto Area and maintains a website.

Choosing an Inexpensive Vehicle

Watch the warranty

There's a big difference between warranty promise and warranty performance. Most automakers offer bumper-to-bumper warranties good for at least the first

3 years/60,000 km, and some problem-prone models and luxury makes get additional base coverage up to 5 years/100,000 km. DaimlerChrysler and South Korean automakers are also using more comprehensive five- to seven-year warranties as important marketing tools to give their cars luxury cachet, or to allay buyers' fears of poor quality/reliability. It's also becoming an industry standard for car companies to pay for roadside assistance, a loaner car, or hotel accommodations if your vehicle breaks down while you're away from home and it's still under warranty. *Lemon-Aid* readers report few problems with these ancillary warranty benefits.

However, just like the weight-loss ads you see on TV, what you see isn't always what you get. For example, bumper-to-bumper coverage usually excludes stereo components, brake pads, clutch plates, and many other expensive components.

Insurance deals

Insurance costs can average between $900 and $2,000 per year, depending on the type of vehicle you own, your personal statistics and driving habits, and whether you can obtain coverage under your family policy. Even though it seems unfair, small SUVs and pickups are usually classed in the high-risk category (accident and theft) and therefore usually cost more than passenger cars to insure.

There are some general rules to follow when looking for insurance savings. For example, vehicles older than five years do not necessarily need collision coverage and you may not need loss-of-use coverage or a rental car. Other factors that should be considered:

- A low damageability rating and an average theft history also can reduce rates by 10–15 percent. These rankings can be checked at *www.ibc.ca/vehinfo_pub_howcarsmeasureup.asp*. Don't be surprised, though, if there appears to be no rhyme or reason for the disparity in the ratings of similar vehicles. Insurance statistics aren't as scientific as insurers, who often charge what the market will bear, pretend.
- When you phone for quotes, make sure you have your serial number in hand. Many factors, such as the make of the car, the number of doors, if there's a sports package, and the insurer's experience with the car, affect the quote. And be honest, or you'll find your claim denied, the policy cancelled, or your premium cost boosted.
- Where you live and work also determine how much you pay. Auto insurance rates are 25–40 percent lower in London, Ontario, than in downtown Toronto because there are fewer cars in the city and fewer kilometres to drive to work. Similar disparities are found in B.C. and Alberta.
- A driver-training course can save you thousands of premium dollars. For example, a policy on a '98 Honda Civic for a schooled driver under 25 may be $3,000 less than the regular premium price.
- You may be able to include your home or apartment insurance as part of a premium package eligible for additional discounts.

The Consumer's Guide to Insurance website (*www.insurancehotline.com*), based in Ontario, but with quotes for other provinces, says it pays to shop around for cheap auto insurance rates. In February 2003, the group discovered that the same insurance policy could vary in cost by a whopping 400 percent.

For example, a 41-year-old married female driving a 2002 Honda Accord and a 41-year-old married male driving a 1998 Dodge Caravan, both with unblemished driving records, should pay no more than $1,880, but some companies surveyed asked as much as $7,515. And that's what they would have paid, if they hadn't shopped around.

The Consumer's Guide to Insurance (*www.insurancehotline.com*) tells consumers which companies have the lowest car insurance rates. The service can be accessed by telephone at 416-686-0531.

Use "secret" warranties

Automobile manufacturers are reluctant to publicize their secret warranty programs because they feel that such publicity would weaken consumer confidence in their products and increase their legal liability. The closest they come to an admission is to send out a "goodwill policy," "special policy," or "product update" service bulletin for dealers' eyes only. These bulletins admit liability and propose free repairs for defects that include faulty paint, engine, and transmission failures on Chrysler, Ford, and GM vehicles (see Part Three).

If you're refused compensation, keep in mind that secret warranty extensions are, first and foremost, an admission of manufacturing negligence. You can usually find them in technical service bulletins (TSBs) that are sent daily to dealers by automakers. Your bottom-line position should be to accept a pro rata adjustment from the manufacturer, whereby you share a third of the repair costs with the dealer and automaker. If polite negotiations fail, challenge the refusal in court on the grounds that you should not be penalized for failing to make a reimbursement claim under a secret warranty that you never knew existed!

Service bulletins are great guides for warranty inspections (especially the final one), and they're useful in helping you decide when it's best to trade in your car. They're written by automakers in "mechanic-speak" because service managers relate better to them that way, and manufacturers can't weasel out of their obligations by claiming that they never wrote such a bulletin.

If your vehicle is out of warranty, show these bulletins to less expensive independent garage mechanics, so they can quickly find the trouble and order the most recent *upgraded* part, ensuring that you don't replace one defective component with another.

Because these bulletins are sent out by U.S. automakers, Canadian service managers and automakers may deny, at first, that they even exist (are you listening, Chrysler and Ford?). However, when they're shown a copy they usually find the appropriate Canadian part number or bulletin in their files. The problem and its solution don't change from one side of the border to another. Imagine American and Canadian tourists being towed across the border because each country's technical service bulletins were different. Mechanical fixes do differ in cases where a bulletin is for California only, or relates to a safety or emissions component used only in the States. But these instances are rare indeed.

The best way to get bulletin-related repairs carried out is to visit the dealer's service bay and attach the specific ALLDATA-supplied service bulletin covering your vehicle's problems to a work order.

Getting your vehicle's service bulletins

Free summaries of automotive recalls and technical service bulletins listed by year, make, model, and engine can be found at the ALLDATA (*www.alldata.com/TSB*) and NHTSA websites. Like the NHTSA summaries, ALLDATA's summaries are so short and cryptic that they're of limited use. So pay the $24.95 (U.S.) subscription fee and download the complete contents of all the bulletins applicable to your vehicle from ALLDATA at *www.alldatadiy.com*.

Asian automakers

Many well-meaning Canadian buyers want to encourage domestic auto production by purchasing a product made by the Detroit Big Three, even though they know Asian vehicles have a better reputation for quality. Now that Chrysler is owned by German automaker Daimler and so many vehicles and components are manufactured in the United States, Brazil, China, and Mexico, this should be less of a dilemma. Although Chrysler's Daimler connection hasn't resulted in better quality scores (Daimler has its own quality problems), automakers have found that offshore factories can actually raise quality to higher levels than what factories in their own countries can manage. For example, American auto manufacturers have known for decades that Canadian plants build higher-quality vehicles than factories in the United States. That's one of the reasons I recommend the Cambridge, Ontario-built Matrix over GM's identical American-built Pontiac Vibe. Surprisingly, BMW's highest-quality factory is found in Rosslyn, South Africa.

Nevertheless, most studies show that, in spite of improvements attempted over the past two decades, vehicles made by DaimlerChrysler, Ford, and, to a lesser extent, GM still don't measure up to Japanese and some South Korean products (Hyundai) in terms of quality and technology. This is particularly evident in SUVs and minivans, where Honda, Nissan, and Toyota have long retained the highest reliability and dependability ratings, despite a handful of recent missteps.

Whether you buy domestic or imported, overall vehicle quality for all brands has improved a great deal during the past three decades. Premature rusting is less of a problem and reliability is improving. On the other hand, repairs are outrageously expensive and complicated. Owners of cars and minivans made by GM, Ford, and Chrysler still report serious powertrain deficiencies, often during the first year in service. These defects include electrical system failures caused by faulty computer modules; malfunctioning ABS systems, brake rotor warpage, and early pad wearout; failure-prone air conditioning and automatic transmissions; and defective engine head gaskets, intake manifolds, fuel systems, suspensions, steering, and paint.

Don't buy the myth that parts for imports are overpriced or hard to find. It's actually easier to find parts for Japanese vehicles than for domestic vehicles due to the large number of units produced, the presence of hundreds of independent suppliers, the ease with which relatively simple parts can be interchanged among different models, and the large reservoir of used parts stocked by junkyards. Incidentally, when a part is hard to find, the *Mitchell Manual* is a useful guide to substitute parts that can be used for many different models. It's available in some libraries, most auto parts stores, and practically all junkyards.

Sadly, customer relations is the Japanese automakers' Achilles heel. Dealers are spoiled rotten by decades of easy sales and have developed a "take it or leave it" showroom attitude, which is often accompanied by a woeful ignorance of their own model lineup. This was once a frequent complaint of Honda and Toyota shoppers, though recent APA undercover surveys show a big improvement among Toyota dealers.

Where it has gotten worse is in the service bay, where periodic maintenance visits and warranty claims are like sessions with Tony Soprano. Well-known factory-related defects (Honda engine oil leaks, Nissan exhaust manifolds, and Toyota engine and tranny problems) are corrected under extended warranties, but you always have the feeling *you owe the family*.

There's no problem with discourteous or ill-informed South Korean automakers. Instead, poor quality has been their bugaboo. Yet, like Honda and Toyota's recovery following their own first first-series quality glitches, Hyundai, South Korea's biggest carmaker, has made considerable progress in bringing up quality quite dramatically.

Kia is a small South Korean automaker bought by Hyundai in October 1998. It has kept its own identity and dealer network, but sales and product improvements have stagnated since the sale. Kia models can usually be found next to Daewoo (also South Korean) in the basement of most quality rankings. Nevertheless, Hyundai says it will work hard to improve Kia quality this year and promises to show its commitment with the return of the Kia Sportage SUV (absent since 2002) in 2005.

Up to the mid-'90s, South Korean vehicles were merely cheap, poor-quality knock-offs of their Japanese counterparts. They would start to fall apart after their third year due to subpar body construction, unreliable automatic transmission and electrical components, and parts suppliers who put low prices ahead of reliability and durability. This was particularly evident with Hyundai's Pony, Stellar, Excel models, and early Sonata models. During the past several years, though, Hyundai's product lineup has been extended and refined and quality is no longer a worry. Plus, Hyundai's comprehensive base warranty protects owners from most of the more expensive breakdowns that may occur.

Hyundais are easily repaired by independent garages, and their rapid depreciation doesn't mean much because they cost so little initially and entry-level buyers are known to keep their cars longer than most, thereby easily amortizing the higher depreciation rate.

European models

Lemon-Aid doesn't recommend any new or used European SUV or minivan. We all know the European automakers have fallen all over themselves trying to get a larger piece of the lucrative SUV and minivan markets—such is the pull of sky-high profits (a Lincoln Navigator may garner $15,000) and soaring sales. But they haven't given us the same high-quality vehicles offered by many Asian automakers. Heck, even the Germans have abandoned their own products. For example, a 2002 J.D. Power survey of 15,000 German car owners found that German drivers are happiest at the wheel of a Japanese car. This conclusion included compact and luxury cars as well as off-roaders. Toyota won first place on quality, reliability, and owner satisfaction, while Nissan's Maxima headed the luxury class standings. BMW was the first choice among European offerings.

Money-losing Land Rover, now owned by Ford, is still struggling since it moved into the North American market with its overpriced, quality-challenged, and under-serviced SUVs. But Land Rover of North America shrugs off its quality problems, and Ford isn't likely to improve things much while it struggles with its own mismanagement and poor-quality woes. For many years, Land Rovers got a free ride from fawning car columnists on this side of the Atlantic (British press criticism had been merciless due to the vehicle's terrible quality control and marginal sales figures). Nevertheless, when Matt Joseph, a Madison, Wisconsin, newspaper and radio car reviewer, published a mildly critical review of the 2000 Discovery, he paid for his audacity—with his job.

Still, Matt got the last laugh after all: A 2003 study of 34,000 car owners with vehicles up to eight years old published by Britain's Consumers' Association found that less than half of British owners would recommend a British-made Rover or Vauxhall to a friend. The most highly rated cars in the study were the Japanese Subaru, Isuzu, and Lexus. Over 85 percent of drivers would recommend them.

Here's another surprise: Although it builds some fine vehicles, Mercedes-Benz's SUV quality control isn't equal to that company's pretensions. After stumbling badly when it first launched its rushed-to-production, American-made ML320 for the 1998 model year, the automaker has sent out many urgent service bulletins that seek to correct a surprisingly large number of production deficiencies. Judged by its own confidential service bulletins, Mercedes' quality control is an embarrassment.

Volkswagen isn't a whole lot better than Mercedes. True, it has always been early on the scene with great concepts, but they have always been accompanied by poor execution and a weak servicing network. With its failure-prone and under-serviced EuroVan and Camper, the company hasn't been a serious minivan player since the late '60s, and VW's few sport-utility and pickup variants have been resounding duds.

With European models, your service options are limited and customer relations staffers can be particularly insensitive and arrogant. Plus, you can count on lots of aggravation and expense due to the unacceptably slow distribution of parts and their high markup. Because these companies have a quasi-monopoly on replacement parts, there are few independent suppliers you can turn to for help. And auto wreckers, the last-chance repository for inexpensive car parts, are unlikely to carry European parts for vehicles that are more than three years old or were manufactured in small numbers.

These vehicles also age badly. The weakest areas remain the drivetrains, electronic control modules, electrical and fuel systems, brakes, accessories (sound system, AC, etc.), and body components.

Just When You Thought Your Brain Was Full

Depreciation

Depreciation is the biggest—and most often ignored—expense you encounter when you trade in your vehicle or when an accident forces you to buy another vehicle before the depreciated loss can be amortized. Most new cars depreciate a whopping 30–40 percent during the first two years of ownership. Fortunately, average-sized minivans, vans, trucks, and sport-utilities don't lose that much of their value before their fifth year in use. The best way to use depreciation rates to your advantage is to choose a vehicle listed as being both reliable and economical to own and keep it for five to 10 years. Alternatively, you may buy insurance to protect you from depreciation's bite.

Performance promises (ya gotta be kidding!)

Take the phrase "carlike handling" with a large grain of salt. Since many rear-drive models are built on a modified truck chassis and use steering and suspension components from their truck divisions, they tend to handle more like trucks than cars, in spite of automakers' claims to the contrary. Also, what you see is not necessarily what you get when you buy or lease a new sport-utility, van, or pickup, because these vehicles seldom come with enough standard features to fully exploit their versatility. Additional options are usually a prerequisite to make them safe and comfortable to drive. Consequently, the term "multipurpose" is a misnomer unless you are prepared to spend multi-bucks to outfit your sport-utility, van, or pickup. Even fully equipped, these vehicles don't always provide the performance touted by automakers. And bear in mind that off-roading requires suspension, engine, and drivetrain packages, as well as other components, such as off-road tires and a skid plate, that may not come as standard equipment. Also be wary of ABS brakes when going off-road; they can degrade handling considerably.

Front-drives handle better than rear-drives, but the size and weight of multi-purpose vehicles still require a whole new set of driving skills when cornering at moderate speeds, parking, or turning. Sport-utilities and pickups are more likely to roll over than passenger cars. A moment's inattention can easily lead to a deadly rollover.

Four-wheel drive

Four-wheel drive (4X4) directs engine power through a transfer case to all four wheels, which *pull and push* the vehicle forward, giving you twice as much traction. On most models, when four-wheel drive isn't engaged, the vehicle reverts to rear-drive. The large transfer case housing makes the vehicle sit higher, giving you additional ground clearance.

Keep in mind that extended driving over dry pavement with 4X4 engaged will cause the driveline to bind and result in serious damage. Some buyers are turning instead to rear-drive pickups equipped with winches and large, deep-lugged rear tires.

Many 4X4 customers have been turned off by the typically rough and noisy driveline; a tendency for the vehicle to tip over when cornering at moderate speeds (a Ford Bronco and Isuzu Rodeo specialty); vague, trucklike handling; high repair costs; and poor fuel economy. No wonder car-based SUVs like the Toyota RAV4 and the Honda CR-V are so popular: Buyers want versatility without sacrificing fuel economy, comfort, or handling.

All-wheel drive

Essentially, this is four-wheel drive *all* the time, a feature epitomized by Subaru's engineering, and used mostly in sedans and minivans, all-wheel drive (AWD) never needs to be de-activated when running over dry pavement and doesn't require the heavy transfer case (although some sport-utilities and pickups do use a special transfer case) that raises ground clearance and cuts fuel economy. AWD-equipped vehicles aren't recommended for off-roading because of their lower ground clearance and fragile driveline parts, which aren't as rugged as 4X4 components.

Diesels

Diesel engines are up to 30 percent more efficient than gasoline engines. They become more efficient as the engine load increases, whereas gasoline engines become less so. This is the main reason diesels are best used where the driving cycle includes a lot of city driving, with slow speeds, heavy loads, frequent stops, and long idling times. At full throttle, both engines are essentially equal from a fuel-efficiency standpoint. The gasoline engine, however, leaves the diesel in the dust when it comes to high-speed performance. Many owners of diesel-equipped vehicles are frustrated by excessive repair costs and poor road performance on vehicles that lack turbo. Bear in mind that before the fuel savings can outweigh the high cost of a diesel purchase, the average owner would have to drive 40,000–50,000 km per year. Other diesel disadvantages: engine clatter, smelly exhaust, high nitrous oxide emissions (a cause of acid rain), and excessive particulates (soot) that aggravate respiratory maladies.

Diesel engines aren't all equally reliable, either. Chrysler trucks equipped with Cummins diesels are also good all-around performers. Its new Jeep Liberty and Dodge Sprinter diesels, however, are unproven. But when it comes to Ford and GM diesels, owners report subpar performance, frequent break-downs, and poor dealer servicing.

Rust protection

First off, remember that the best rustproofing protection is to keep your vehicle in a dry, unheated garage or outside. Never bring it in and out of a heated garage during the winter months. Your vehicle is most prone to rust when temperatures are just a bit above freezing; keep it especially clean and dry during that time.

If you live in an area where roads are heavily salted in winter, or in a coastal region, have undercoating sprayed annually, and make sure to include the rocker panels (inside the door bottoms), the rear hatch's bottom edge, the tailgate, and the wheelwells. This treatment, costing less than $100, will protect vital suspension and chassis components, make the vehicle ride more quietly, and allow you to ask a higher price at trade-in time. The only downside, which can be checked by asking for references, is that the undercoating may give off an unpleasant odour for months, and it may drip, soiling your driveway.

Surviving the Options Jungle

The best options for your buck are an automatic transmission, an anti-theft immobilizer, air conditioning, a premium sound system, and higher quality tires, features that may bring back a third to half their value. Rustproofing makes cars easier to sell in some provinces with salt on the roads, but paint protection and seat sealants are a waste of money.

Most option prices can be cut by 20 percent. Extended warranties are overpriced by about 75 percent. Plus, why are you buying a vehicle that is so doubtful as far as reliability is concerned that you have to pay over a thousand dollars to protect yourself from factory mistakes? And when the warranty runs out...?

Dealers make more than three times as much profit selling options as they do selling most cars (50 percent profit versus 15 percent profit). No wonder their eyes light up when you start perusing their options list. If you must have some options, compare prices with independent retailers and buy where the price is lowest and the warranty is the most comprehensive. Buy as few options as possible from the dealer, since you'll get faster service, more comprehensive guarantees, and lower prices from independent suppliers. Remember, extravagantly equipped vehicles hurt your pocketbook in three ways: They cost more to begin with, they cost more to maintain, and they often consume extra fuel.

A heavy-duty battery and suspension and perhaps an upgraded sound system will generally suffice for American-made vehicles; most imports already come well equipped. An engine block heater with a timer—favoured by 39 percent of new car shoppers—isn't a bad idea, either. It's an inexpensive investment that ensures winter starting and reduces fuel consumption by allowing you to start out with a semi-warm engine.

When ordering parts, remember that purchases from American outlets can be slapped with a small customs duty, if the part isn't made in the United States. Then you'll pay the inevitable GST levied on the part's cost and customs duty. Finally, your freight carrier may charge a $15–$20 brokerage fee for representing you at the border.

Smart Options

Adjustable pedals and extensions

This device moves the brake and accelerator pedals forward or backward about 10 cm (4 inches) to accommodate short-statured drivers and protect them from airbag-induced injuries.

If the manufacturer of your vehicle doesn't offer optional power-adjustable pedals, several companies sell inexpensive pedal extensions through the Internet; go to *stores.yahoo.com/hdsmn/pedex.html.* If you live in Toronto or London, Ontario, check out *www.kinomobility.com.*

Adjustable steering wheel

This option facilitates access to the driver's seat and permits a more comfortable driving position. It's particularly useful if a vehicle will be driven by more than one person.

Air conditioning

Why not? AC systems are far more reliable than they were a decade ago and they have a lifespan of 5–7 years. Sure, replacement/repair costs can hit $1,000, but that's very little when amortized over an eight- to ten-year period. In the same way that buying an underpowered van to save on fuel costs can leave you regretting its poor performance, your savings will be the last thing on your mind when you're sweltering in your vehicle some summer day.

Air conditioning increases fuel consumption by 3–4 percent at highway speeds. It provides extra comfort, reduces wind noise (from not having to roll down the windows), and improves window defogging. Buy a factory-installed unit. You'll get a longer warranty and reduce the chance that other mechanical components will be damaged during installation.

Anti-theft systems

You'd be a fool not to buy an anti-theft system for your much-coveted-by-thieves sport-utility, van, or pickup. Auto break-ins and thefts cost Canadians more than $400 million annually, meaning that there's a one in 130 chance that your vehicle will be stolen and only a 60 percent chance that you'll ever get it back. In fact, older pickups are particularly easy pickings for thieves. Chevrolet and GMC trucks are at the top of the list, say Calgary police, mainly because most Chrysler keys will open GM truck doors and the steering column locks are easily bypassed. Chrysler minivans are also theft-prone due to their rudimentary door lock assemblies. Car security specialist Dan Friesen told the Canadian Press in July 2001 that he's not surprised pickups are so popular: "Most of these trucks are so easy to break into, it's a joke. I tell some people they shouldn't even lock their doors because it will save them money in the end."

Since most vehicles are stolen by amateurs, the best theft deterrent is a visible device that complicates the job while immobilizing the vehicle and sounding an alarm. For less than $150, you can install both a steering-wheel lock and a hidden remote-controlled ignition disabler. Satellite tracking systems like GM's OnStar feature are also very effective.

Auxiliary lighting

Essential only for serious off-roaders, extra lighting improves safety and makes night driving less fatiguing. In the city, it's a pain in the butt to other drivers, who are constantly blinded by the lights' intensity and high placement.

Battery (heavy-duty)

The best battery for northern climates is the optional heavy-duty type offered by many manufacturers for about $80. It's a worthwhile purchase, especially for vehicles equipped with lots of electric options. Most standard batteries last only two winters; heavy-duty batteries give you an extra year or two for about 20 percent more than the price of a standard battery.

Bed protectors (pickups)

Selling for $100–$200, these protectors range from simple mats to deluxe moulded polyethylene liners. They guard against rusting in the panel joints and bolt areas by preventing water accumulation, and protect the cargo bed walls and tailgate from scratches and dents. These benefits help to keep resale value high.

Central locking control

Costing around $200, this option is most useful for families with small children, car-poolers, or drivers of pickups, minivans, and vans who can't easily slide across the seat to lock the other doors.

Child safety seat (integrated)

Integrated safety seats are designed to accommodate any child more than one year old or weighing over 9 kg (20 lb.). Since the seat is permanently integrated into the seatback, it takes the fuss out of installing and removing the safety seat and finding some place to store it. When not in use, it quickly folds away out of sight, becoming part of the seatback. Two other safety benefits: You know the seat has been properly installed, and your child gets used to having his or her "special" seat in back, where it's usually safest to sit.

Electric winch

Ideal for hauling logs, boats, rocks, and stumps and getting you out of rough terrain. Serious off-roaders will find that an electric winch that can pull 675–1,350 kg (1,500–3,000 lb.) is a worthwhile $200–$350 investment.

Engines

Choose the most powerful 6- or 8-cylinder engine available if you are going to be doing a lot of highway driving, plan to carry a full passenger load and luggage on a regular basis, or intend to load up the vehicle with convenience features like air conditioning. Keep in mind that multipurpose vehicles with larger engines are easier to resell and retain their value the longest. For example, Honda's '96 Odyssey minivan was a sales dud in spite of its bullet proof reliability, mainly because buyers didn't want a minivan with a wimpy 4-cylinder power plant. Some people buy underpowered vehicles in the mistaken belief that increased fuel economy is a good trade-off for decreased engine performance. It isn't.

Engine and transmission cooling system (heavy-duty)

This relatively inexpensive option provides extra cooling for the transmission and engine. It can extend the life of these components by preventing over-heating when heavy towing is required.

Extended warranties

A waste of $1,000–$1,500 for vehicles recommended in *Lemon-Aid* or vehicles sold by automakers that have written goodwill warranties covering engine and transmission failures (Ford and GM). If you can get a great price for a vehicle rated just Average or Above Average, but want to protect yourself from costly repair bills, frequent garages that offer lifetime warranties on parts listed here as failure-prone such as powertrains, exhaust systems, and brakes. Only buy an extended warranty as a last resort and make sure you know what it covers and for how long.

Gas tank (extra capacity)

If full-sized vans weren't such gas hogs, a larger gas tank wouldn't be necessary. Nevertheless, owners will appreciate the extra cruising range a larger tank provides. Expect to spend about $250.

Keyless entry (remote)

A safety and convenience option. You don't need to fiddle with the key in a dark parking lot or take off a glove in cold weather to unlock or lock the vehicle. Try to get a keyless entry system combined with anti-theft measures, such as an ignition kill switch or some other disabler. Incidentally, many car-makers no longer make vehicles with an outside keylock on the passenger side.

Mirror options

Power mirrors are particularly convenient on vehicles that have a number of drivers, or on minivans, vans, or trucks.

Paint colour

Choosing a popular colour can make your vehicle easier to sell at a good price. DesRosiers automotive consultants say blue is the preferred colour overall, but green and silver are also popular with Canadians. Remember that certain colours require particular care. For example:

Black (and other dark colours): These are most susceptible to sun damage because of their heavy absorption of ultraviolet rays.

Pearl-toned colours: These are the most difficult to work with. If the paint needs to be retouched, it must be matched to look right from both the front- and side-angle views.

Red: This also shows sun damage, so keep your car in a garage or shady spot whenever possible.

White: Although grime looks terrible on a white car, it's the easiest colour to care for.

Power-assisted doors, windows, and seats

Merely a convenience feature with cars, power-assisted windows, doors, and seats are a necessity with minivans—crawling across the front seat a few times to roll up the passenger-side window or lock the doors will quickly convince you of their value. Power seats with memory are particularly useful if a vehicle is driven by more than one person. Automatic window and seat controls currently have few reliability problems, and they're fairly inexpensive to install, troubleshoot, and repair. Power sliding doors are especially failure-prone on all makes and shouldn't be purchased by families with children.

Roll bars

Roll bars protect sport-utility occupants from rollovers. This is an essential safety item because these vehicles have a nasty habit of suddenly overturning without warning. A good roll bar and cage kit sells for about $350.

Running boards

Throughout this guide you'll see my recommendation that you buy optional running boards. Far from returning you to '50s styling, running boards are practically essential for climbing into most full-sized vans, sport-utilities, and pickups. They can be purchased from independent suppliers for $65–$200, which is much less than the $250–$700 charged by the automakers.

Side airbags

A worthwhile feature if you are the right size and properly seated, side airbags are presently way overpriced and aren't very effective unless both the head and upper torso are protected. Side airbags are often featured as a $700 add-on to the sticker price, but you would be wise to bargain aggressively, since a supplier source told *Automotive News* that automakers pay about $100 for a pair of side curtain airbags.

Skid plates

A steel skid plate protects a sport-utility or pickup from rocks and other obstacles when off-roading. It should be at least a quarter inch thick and cover the rear differential and oil pan. Some sport-utilities and pickups have a low-slung front gear housing that is easily damaged and pushes large amounts of mud and debris up into the front end, raising it to the point that front-end traction is lost.

Suspension (heavy-duty)

Always a good idea, this inexpensive option pays for itself by providing better handling, allowing additional ride comfort (though a bit on the firm side), and extending shock life an extra year or two.

Tires

There are two types of tires: All-season and performance. Touring is just a fancier name for all-season tires. All-season radial tires cost between $90 and $150 per tire. They're a compromise, since according to Transport Canada they won't get you through winter with the same margin of safety as snow tires will, and they don't provide the same durability on dry surfaces as do regular summer tires. In areas with low to moderate snowfall, however, these tires are adequate as long as they're not pushed beyond their limits.

Mud or snow tires provide the best traction on snowy surfaces, but traction on wet roads is actually decreased. Treadwear is also accelerated by the use of softer rubber compounds. Beware of using wide tires for winter driving; 70-series or wider give poor traction and tend to "float" over snow.

Spare tires

Be wary of space-saver spare tires. They often can't match the promised mileage and seriously degrade steering control. Furthermore, they are usually stored in spaces inside the trunk that won't hold a normal-sized tire. Where the spare is stored can also have safety implications. Watch out for spares stowed under the chassis or mounted on the rear hatch on some sport-utilities. Frequently, the attaching cables and bolts rust out or freeze, permitting the spare to fall off or making it next to impossible to access when needed.

Self-sealing and run-flat tires

Today there are two technologies available to help maintain vehicle mobility when a tire is punctured: Self-sealing and self-supporting/run-flat tires.

Self-sealing: Ideal if you drive long distances. Punctures are fixed instantly and permanently with a sealant which seals most punctures from nails, bolts, or screws up to 5 mm (3/16 of an inch) in diameter. A low air pressure warning system isn't required. Expert testers say a punctured self-sealing tire can maintain air pressure for up to 200 km—even in freezing conditions. The Uniroyal Tiger Paw NailGard ($85–$140, depending on size) is the overall winner in a side-by-side test conducted by The Tire Rack.

Self-supporting/run-flat: Priced from $175 to $350 per tire, 25–50 percent more than the price of comparable premium tires, Goodyear's EMT run-flat tires were first offered as an option on the 1994 Chevrolet Corvette, and then became standard on the 1997 model. These tires reinforce the sidewall, so it can carry the weight of the car for 90 km, or about an hour's driving time, even after all air pressure has been lost. You won't feel the tire go flat and must depend upon a $250–$300 optional tire pressure monitor to warn you before the sidewall collapses and you begin riding on your rim. Plus, not all vehicles can adapt to run flat tires; you may need to upgrade your rims. Experts say run-flats will give your car a harder ride and you'll likely notice more interior tire and road noise. The car might also track differently. The 2004 Sienna Dunlop Run Flat Tech tires have a terrible reputation for premature wear. At 25,000 km, one owner complained her Sienna needed a new set at $200 each. You can expect a backlog of a month or more to get a replacement, and Toyota doesn't include any type of spare. Goodyear has had their EMT (Extended Mobility Tire) and Pirelli their P-Zero tires for some time now and they seem to perform adequately. Don't make a final choice before talking with an auto manufacturer rep as to what's recommended and how your warranty will be affected.

Like its Toyota Sienna rival, Honda's 2005 Odyssey minivan will also offer a run-flat Michelin Pax tire that can run flat for more than 120 miles at 50 mph. First introduced in 1998, the system includes a tire, a wheel, an inner support ring, and a tire pressure monitor.

Which tires are best?

There is no independent Canadian agency that evaluates tire performance and durability. However, U.S.-based NHTSA rates treadwear, traction, and resistance to sustained high temperatures and etches the ratings onto all tires sold in the States and Canada and regularly posts its findings on the Internet (*www.nhtsa.dot.gov*). The treadwear grade is fixed at a base 100 points and the tire's wear rate is measured after the tire is driven through a course that approximates most driving conditions. A tire rated 300 will last three times as long as one rated 100.

I've come up with the following tire ratings after researching government tests, consumer comments, and industry insiders. Remember, some of the brand names may be changed.

Dunlop D65 Touring and SP20 AS: Treadwear rated 520, these tires are the bargain of the group. They provide excellent wet and dry cornering and good steering response. Cost: $146 list; sells for $100.

Goodrich Control TA M65: Treadwear rated 360, this tire excels at snowbelt performance and is bargain priced at $120.

Goodyear Aquatred #3: Treadwear rated 340, this tire is a bit noisy and its higher-rolling resistance cuts fuel economy. Still, it's an exceptional performer on wet roads and works especially well on front-drive cars where the weight is over the front tires. Average performance on dry pavement. Costs about $130; no discounts.

Goodyear Regatta #2: Treadwear rated 460, this $100 tire does everything well, including keeping tire noise to a minimum.

Michelin MX4: Treadwear rated 320, this tire gives a smoother ride and a sharper steering response than the Goodyear Aquatred. Cost: $144 list; often discounted to $100. MX1 is also an excellent winter performer.

Pirelli P300 and P400: Treadwear rated 460 and 420, these are two of the best all-around all-season tires. Cost: $173 list; sell for about $120.

Yokohama TC320: Treadwear rated 300, these are two other Aquatred knock-offs that perform almost as well for half the price.

Other good tire choices: Dayton Timberline A/T, General XP, Goodrich Touring T/A HR4, Goodyear Eagle LS, Kelly Navigator Platinum TE, Pirelli P3000, and Scorpion A/T. Winter tires: Futura Euro-Metric, Goodyear Ultra Grip Ice, Michelin Arctic Alpin, and Pirelli Winter Ice Assimmetrico.

The following tires aren't recommended: Bridgestone Potenza RE 92; Continental truck tires; Cooper Lifeline Classic II; all Firestone makes; Goodrich Advantage; Hydro 2000 and Ameri G4S; Goodyear Eagle GA, Wrangler, and WeatherHandler; Michelin XGT H4, XW4, and MXV4 Green X; Pirelli P4000 Super Touring (not to be confused with the recommended P400); and Toyo 800 Plus.

Trailer-towing equipment

Just because you need a vehicle with towing capability doesn't mean that you have to spend big bucks. The first things you should determine before choosing a towing option are whether a pickup or small van will do the job and whether your tires will handle the extra burden. For most towing needs (up to 900 kg/2,000 lb.), a passenger car, small pickup, or minivan will work just as well as a full-sized pickup or van (and cost much less). If you're pulling a trailer that weighs more than 900 kg, most passenger cars won't handle the load unless they've been specially outfitted according to the automaker's specifications. Pulling a heavier trailer (up to 1,800 kg/4,000 lb.) will likely require a compact passenger van. You may, however, have to keep your speed at 70 km/h (45 mph) or less as Toyota suggests with the 2004 Sienna.

A full-sized van can handle up to 4,500 kg (10,000 lb.) and may be cheaper and more versatile than a multipurpose vehicle, which would have to be equipped with a V8 engine and heavy-duty chassis components to be effective. Don't trust the towing limit found in the owner's manual. Automakers publish tow ratings that are on the optimistic side and sometimes outright wrong, as has been alleged by some 2002–04 Toyota Tacoma owners.

Automakers reserve the right to change limits whenever they feel like it, so make any sales promise an integral part of your contract (see "False Advertising" in Part Three). A good rule is to reduce the promised tow rating by 20 percent. In assessing towing weight, factor in the cargo, passengers, and equipment of both the trailer and the tow vehicle. Keep in mind that five people and luggage add 450 kg (1,000 lb.) to the load, and that a full 227-litre (50-gallon) water tank adds another 225 kg (500 lb.). The manufacturer's gross vehicle weight rating (GVWR) takes into account the anticipated average cargo and supplies that your vehicle is likely to carry.

Automatic transmissions are fine for trailering, although there's a slight fuel penalty to pay. Manual transmissions tend to have greater clutch wear due to towing than do automatic transmissions. Both transmission choices are equally acceptable. Remember, the best compromise is to shift the automatic manually for maximum performance going uphill and to maintain control while not overheating the brakes when descending mountains.

Unibody vehicles (those without a separate frame) can handle most trailering jobs as long as their limits aren't exceeded. Front-drives aren't the best choice for pulling heavy loads in excess of 900 kg (2,000 lb.), since they lose some steering control and traction with all the weight concentrated in the rear.

Whatever vehicle you choose, keep in mind that the trailer hitch is crucial. It must have a tongue capacity of at least 10 percent of the trailer's weight; otherwise it may be unsafe to use. Hitches are chosen according to the type of tow vehicle and, to a lesser extent, the weight of the load.

Most hitches are factory installed, even though independents can install them more cheaply. Expect to pay about $200 for a simple boat hitch and a minimum of $600 for a fifth-wheel version.

Equalizer bars and extra cooling systems for the radiator, transmission, engine oil, and steering are a prerequisite for towing anything 900 kg (2,000 lb.) or heavier. Heavy-duty springs and brakes are a big help, too. Separate brakes for the trailer may be necessary to increase your vehicle's maximum towing capacity.

Transmission: Automatic, manual, and CVT

Despite its many advantages, the manual transmission is an endangered species in North America, where manuals equip only 12 percent of all new vehicles (mostly econocars, sports cars, and budget trucks), whereas European buyers opt for a manual transmission almost 90 percent of the time.

A transmission with four or more forward speeds is usually more fuel efficient than one with three forward speeds, and manual transmissions are usually more efficient than automatics, although this isn't always the case.

Shoppers who want a Dodge truck with the highly recommended Cummins diesel engine, but don't want to be stuck with Chrysler's infamous automatic transmission breakdowns, should opt for the six-speed transmission.

Don't invest in a continuously variable transmission (CVT) used by Ford, GM or Chrysler. GM is ditching theirs and Ford is just going into its first-year production. Sure, CVTs improve fuel economy by about 10 percent through the use of pulleys connected by a steel belt or chain to drive the wheels. But the system is relatively new in North America, where automakers like GM haven't quite worked the bugs out. However, CVTs have been used for decades in the rest of the world with few problems by companies like Audi, Honda, and Nissan.

GM has put an optional Fiat-built CVT in its Saturn Ion and Vue ($900 and $1,990, respectively) since 2002 and has had to extend the warranty to deal with chronic drivetrain failures.

Special Policy Adjustment — Extended Transmission Warranty Coverage for Variable Transmission with Intelligence (VTi) Transmission

Bulletin No.:04020   Date:(04/21/02004)

Table 1: Chart A   Table 2: Chart B

04020 - Special Policy Adjustment - Extended Transmission Warranty Coverage for Variable Transmission with Intelligence (VTi) Transmission
2002–04 VUE Vehicles
Equipped with VTi (M75 and M16)
2004 ION Quad Coupe Vehicles
Equippped with VTi (M75)
All Saturn Retailers and Authorized Service Providers

Condition: Saturn has determined that 2002–04 VUE and 2003–04 ION Quad Coupe vehicles equipped with the VTi transmission may experience certain transmission concerns that might affect customer satisfaction, and may require repair or replacement.

Special policy adjustment: This special policy bulletin has been issued to extend the warranty on the VTi transmission assembly for a period of 5 yars or 75,000 miles (120,000 km), whichever occurs first, from the date the vehicle was originally placed in service, regadless of ownership. The repairs will be made at no charge to the customer.

Rumour has it 2005 will be the Saturn CVT's last year, although Ford plans to offer it in the 2005 Five Hundred, Freestyle, and Montego (Lord help us!).

Unnecessary Options

Cruise control

Mainly a convenience feature, automakers provide this $250–$300 option to motorists who use their vehicles for long periods of high-speed driving. Some fuel is saved owing to the constant rate of speed, and driver fatigue is lessened during long trips. Still, the system is particularly failure-prone and expensive to repair, can lead to driver inattention, and can make the vehicle hard to control on icy roadways. Malfunctioning cruise control units are also one of the major causes of sudden acceleration incidents. At other times, cruise control can be very distracting, especially to inexperienced drivers unaccustomed to sudden speed fluctuations.

Electronic instrument readout

If you've ever had trouble reading a digital watch face or resetting your VCR, you'll feel right at home with this electronic gizmo. Gauges are presented in a series of moving digital patterns that are confusing, distracting, and unreadable in direct sunlight. This system is often accompanied by a trip computer and a vehicle monitor that computes fuel use and kilometres to empty, indicates average speed, and signals component failures. Figures are frequently in error or slow to catch up.

Foglights

A pain in the eyes for other drivers, foglights aren't necessary for most drivers with well-aimed original-equipment headlights.

Gas-saving gadgets/fuel additives

Because full-sized sport-utilities, vans, and trucks are notorious fuel burners, the accessory market has been flooded with hundreds of gas-saving gadgets and fuel additives that purport to make these vehicles less fuel-thirsty. There isn't one on the Canadian market that works, according to Transport Canada, and the use of any of these products is a quick way to render your warranty invalid.

GPS navigation systems

Optional $1,500–$2,000 navigation systems are red-hot moneymakers for auto manufacturers. First offered only on luxury nameplates, the electronic maps are now available on 107 out of 247 popular models.

Many of the systems are obtrusive, distracting, washed out in sunlight, and hard to calibrate. A portable Garmin GPS unit is one of the more user-friendly models that's also reasonably priced.

ID etching

This $150–$200 option is a scam. The government doesn't require it, and thieves and joyriders aren't deterred by the etchings. If you want to etch your windows for your own peace of mind, several private companies will sell you a $15–$30 kit that does an excellent job (*www.autoetch.net*), or you can wait for your municipality or local police agency to conduct one of their periodic free VIN ID etching sessions in your locality.

Paint and fabric protectors

Selling for $200–$300, these "sealants" add nothing to a vehicle's resale value. Although paint lustre may be temporarily heightened, this treatment is less effective and more costly than regular waxing, and it may also invalidate the manufacturer's guarantee at a time when the automaker will look for any pre-text to deny your paint claim.

Auto fabric protection products are nothing more than Scotchguard variations, which can be bought in aerosol cans for a few dollars, instead of the $50–$75 charged by dealers.

Rooftop carrier

Although this inexpensive option provides additional baggage space and may allow you to meet all your driving needs with a smaller vehicle, a loaded roof rack can increase fuel consumption by as much as 5 percent. An empty rack cuts fuel economy by about 1 percent.

Rustproofing

Rustproofing is no longer necessary now that the automakers have extended their own rust warranties. In fact, you have a greater chance of seeing your rustproofer go belly up than having your untreated vehicle ravaged by premature rusting. Even if the rustproofer stays in business, you're likely to get a song and dance about why the warranty won't cover so-called "internal" rusting, or why repairs will be delayed until the sheet metal is actually rusted through.

Stability control

Save your money. Buy a stable vehicle and drive safely.

This option is designed to prevent a vehicle from sliding or skidding in a turn or when passing over uneven terrain. Problem is, it doesn't always work that way. In tests carried out by *Consumer Reports* magazine, the stability-control system used in the Mitsubishi Montero was rated "unacceptable," BMW's X5 3.0i system provided poor emergency handling, and Acura's MDX and Subaru's Outback VDC stability systems left much to be desired.

Sunroof

Unless you live in a temperate region, the advantages of a sunroof are far outweighed by its disadvantages. You're not going to get better ventilation than a good air-conditioning (AC) system would provide, and a sunroof may grace your environment with painful "booming" wind noises, rattles, water leaks, and road dust accumulation. Gas consumption is increased, night vision is reduced by overhead highway lights shining through the roof opening, and several inches of headroom can be lost.

Tinted glass

Tinting jeopardizes your safety by reducing night vision. On the other hand, it does keep the interior cool in hot weather, reduces glare, and hides the car's contents from prying eyes. Factory applications are worth the extra cost, since cheaper aftermarket products (costing about $100) distort visibility and peel away after a few years. Some tinting done in the U.S. can run afoul of provincial highway codes that require more transparency.

Cutting the Price

Bidding by fax/email

What, shop by fax? Get bids by email?

Sure, simply fax or email an invitation for bids (sending a cover letter with your company logo will help impress) to area dealerships, asking them to give their bottom-line price for a specific make and model and clearly stating that all final bids must be sent within a week. Because no salesperson is acting as a commission-paid intermediary, the dealers' first bids are likely to start off a few hundred dollars less than advertised. When all the bids are received, the lowest bid is sent to the other dealers to give them a chance to beat that price. After a week of bidding, the lowest price gets your business.

Dozens of *Lemon-Aid* readers have told me how this approach has kept the price down and prevented the showroom song-and-dance routine between the sales agent and the sales manager ("he said, she said, they said").

A *Lemon-Aid* reader sent in the following suggestions for buying by fax:

> First, I'd like to thank you for writing the *Lemon-Aid* series of books, which I have used extensively in the fax-tendering purchase of my '99 Accord and '02 Elantra. I have written evidence from dealers that I saved a bare minimum of $700 on the Accord (but probably more) and a whopping $900 on the Elantra through the use of fax-tendering, over and above any deals possible through Internet-tendering and/or showroom bargaining.
>
> Based on my experience, I would suggest that in reference to the fax-tendering process, future *Lemon-Aid* editions emphasize:
>
> • Casting a wide geographical net, as long as you're willing to pick the car up there. I faxed up to 50 dealerships, which helped tremendously in increasing the number of serious bidders. One car was bought locally in Ottawa, the other in Mississauga.
> • Unless you don't care much about what car you end up with (e.g. the author of the fax letter in the *Lemon-Aid* guide) be very specific about what you want. If you are looking at just one or two cars, which I recommend, specify trim level and all extended warranties and dealer-installed options in the fax letter. Otherwise, you'll end up with quotes comparing apples and oranges, and you won't get the best deal on options negotiated later. Also, specify that quotes should be signed—this helps out with errors in quoting.
> • Dealerships are sloppy—there is a 25–30% error rate in quotes. Search for errors and get corrections, and confirm any of the quotes in serious contention over the phone.
> • Phone to personally thank anyone who submits a quote for their time. Salespeople can't help themselves, they'll ask how they ranked, and often want to then beat the best quote you've got. This is much more productive than faxing back the most competitive quote (I know, I've tried that too).

Fax Bid Request

Date

Attention: New Car Sales Manager:

I am planning on buying a new_____and am requesting a price
quote for the above vehicle with the following equipment:

* _____

* _____

* _____

* _____

* _____

I am interested in the following colours, in order of preference:

* _____

* _____

Please include the price of all items, and the extras, such as tire tax, air
conditioning tax, delivery, and inspection, etc.

I am sending this fax to several dealers, and the best quote will get my
business. I am willing to drive out of town if the savings warrant.

If you are interested in selling me a car, please send me a quote by fax or
email by _____. I shall give you a second opportunity to beat the
lowest bid within the week and will contact the winning dealer to confirm
the order.

I am flexible to purchase the car off your lot, or on order, whatever works
best for you.

Thank you in advance for your assistance.

Jane Consumer
Fax: 555-555-5555

Getting a Fair Price

What's the dealer's cut?

Most new car salespeople are reluctant to give out information on the amount
of profit figured into the cost of each new car, but a few years back *Automotive
News* gave American dealer markups based on MSRP. I've reduced the

percentages a bit to reflect what Canadian dealers now receive and I've included negotiable freight, PDI, and administrative fees, all of which you should bargain down.

Dealer markup (American vehicles)

minivans: 16+%
high-end minivans: 17+%
base pickups: 14+%
high-end pickups: 16+%
vans and sport-utility vehicles: 16+%
fully equipped, top-of-the-line vans and SUVs: 20+%

Dealer markup (Japanese vehicles)

minivans: 11+%
high-end minivans: 13+%
base pickups: 12+%
high-end pickups: 14+%
sport-utility vehicles: 13+%
fully equipped, top-of-the-line vans and SUVs: 15+%

South Korean prices are the most negotiable, while Japanese and European vehicle prices are much firmer. In addition to the dealer's markup, some vehicles may also have a 3 percent carryover allowance paid out in a dealer incentive program. Finance contracts may also tack on a 3 percent dealer commission.

What's a fair price?

New-car negotiations aren't wrestling matches where you have to pin the sales agent's shoulders to the mat to win. If you feel that the overall price is fair, don't jeopardize the deal by giving no quarter. For example, if you've brought the contract price 10 percent or more below the MSRP and the dealer sticks you with a $200 "administrative fee" at the last moment, let it pass. You've saved money and the sales agent has saved face.

To come up with a fair price, subtract one-half the dealer markup from the MSRP and trade the carryover and holdback allowance for a reduced delivery and transportation fee. Compute the options separately. Buyers can more easily knock $1,000–$2,000 off a $20,000 base price if they wait until January or February (when sales are stagnant), choose a vehicle in stock, and resist unnecessary options.

Once you and the dealer have settled on the vehicle's price, you aren't out of the woods yet. You'll likely be handed over to an F&I (financing and insurance) specialist, whose main goal is to convince you to buy additional financing, loan insurance, paint and seatcover protectors, rustproofing, and extended warranties. These items will be presented on a computer screen as costing only "a little bit more each month." Compare the dealer's insurance and financing charges with an independent agency that may offer better rates and better service. Often the dealer gets a kickback for selling insurance and financing, and guess who pays for it? Additionally, remember that if the financing rate looks too good to be true, you're probably paying too much for the vehicle. The F&I closer's hard-sell approach will take all your willpower and patience to resist, but when he gives up, your trials are over.

Add-on charges are the dealer's last chance to stick it to you before the contract is signed. Dealer pre-delivery inspection (PDI) and transportation charges, "documentation" fees, and extra handling costs are ways that the dealer gets extra profits for nothing. Dealer preparation is often a once-over-lightly affair, with a vehicle seldom getting more than a wash job and a couple of dollars of gas in the tank. It's paid for by the factory in most cases and, when it's not, should cost no more than 2 percent of the selling price. Reasonable transportation charges are acceptable, although dealers who claim that the manufacturer requires the payment often inflate them.

The myth of "no haggle" pricing

It's all smoke and mirrors. In effect, all dealers bargain. They hang out the "No dickering, one price only" sign simply as a means to discourage customers from asking for a better deal. Like parking lots and restaurants that claim they won't be responsible for lost or stolen property, they're bluffing. Still, you'd be surprised by how many people believe that if it's posted, it's non-negotiable.

Toyota Canada abandoned its Access no-haggle price strategy sales system in June 2004, after settling out of court a price-fixing probe undertaken by Ottawa. Toyota is still the target of class-action lawsuits in Quebec and British Columbia, however.

If you bought your Toyota in B.C. and feel you paid too much under Access, contact Leslie Mackoff at *lmackoff@mackoff.ca*. Mackoff's class-action lawsuit alleges dealers set prices unlawfully, refused to offer discounts from the Access price and would not offer free options or extra features. Quebec buyers may file a similar claim with Daniel Belleau (*APA.ca*), a Montreal lawyer who has also filed a class-action claim in that province

Price guidelines

When negotiating the price of a new vehicle, remember there are several price guidelines, and dealers use the one that will make the most profit on each transaction. Two of the more common prices quoted are the MSRP (what the automaker advertises as a fair price) and the dealer's invoice cost, which is supposed to indicate how much the dealer paid for the vehicle. Both price indicators leave considerable room for the dealer's profit margin, along with some extra padding in the form of inflated transportation and preparation charges. If presented with both figures, go with the MSRP, since it can be verified by calling the manufacturer. Any dealer can print up an invoice and swear to its veracity. If you want an invoice price from an independent source, contact *Carcostcanada.com* (or phone 1-800-805-2270).

Buyers who live in rural areas and Western Canada are often faced with grossly inflated auto prices compared to those charged in major metropolitan areas. A good way to get a more competitive price without buying out of province is to buy a couple of out-of-town newspapers (the Saturday *Toronto Star* "Wheels" section is especially helpful) and demand that your dealer bring his selling price, preparation, and transportation fees into line with the prices advertised.

Another tactic is to take a copy of a local competitor's car ad to a competing dealer selling the same brand and ask for a better price. Chances are, they've already lost a few sales due to the ad, and will work a little harder to match the deal; if not, they're almost certain to reveal the tricks in the competitor's pro-motion to make the sale.

Dealer incentives and customer rebates

When vehicles are first introduced in the fall, they're generally overpriced. Later on, near the end of summer, automakers offer customer cash rebates of $750–$3,000, plus increased dealer cash incentives for almost as much. Incentives are first offered during the winter months and boosted in late summer or early fall when dealer showroom traffic has fallen off. Smart shop-pers who buy during these months can shave 10 percent off a vehicle's list price (about $3,000 on a $30,000 MSRP) by double-dipping from both of these automaker rebate programs or by using zero percent financing.

In most cases, the manufacturer's rebate is straightforward and mailed directly to the buyer from the automaker. There are other rebate programs that require a financial investment on the dealer's part, however, and these shared programs tempt dealers to offset losses by inflating the selling price or pock-eting the manufacturer's rebate. Therefore, when the dealer participates in the rebate program, demand that the rebate be deducted from the MSRP, and not from some inflated invoice price concocted by the dealer.

Some rebate ads will include the phrase "from dealer inventory only." If your dealer doesn't have the vehicle in stock, you won't get the rebate.

Sometimes automakers will suddenly decide that a rebate no longer applies to a specific model, even though their ads continue to include it. When this happens, take all brochures and advertisements showing your eligibility for the rebate plan to provincial consumer protection officials. They can use false advertising statutes to force automakers to give rebates to every purchaser who was unjustly denied one. If you want more immediate relief, simply file a claim in small claims court.

Finally, when buying a heavily discounted vehicle, be wary of "option pack-aging" by dealers who push unwanted protection packages (rustproofing, paint sealants, upholstery finishes, etc.), or who levy excessive charges for prepara-tion, filing fees, loan guarantee insurance, and credit life insurance.

Rebates and quality

Forget the old adage, "You get what you pay for." Many reliable, top-performing vehicles come with rebates—they just aren't as generous as what you'll find with more mediocre choices. For example, rarely will Toyota and Honda offer more than $1,000 rebates, whereas Chrysler, Ford, and GM routinely hand out $3,000 discounts and other sales incentives. To come out ahead, you have to know how to play this rebate game by choosing quality first.

Customer and dealer incentives are frequently given out to stimulate sales of year-old models that are unpopular, scheduled to be redesigned, or headed for the axe. By choosing carefully which rebated models you buy, it's easy to realize important savings with little risk. For example, GM's $2,000 incentives are good deals when applied to its reasonably reliable SUVs and full-sized vans, but not worth it when applied to the company's glitch-prone 2004 Silverado and Sierra pickups. Ford's F-150 pickup and Windstar minivan rebates ($3,000+) also aren't sufficient to offset the greater risk of factory-related defects afflicting these failure-prone models. DaimlerChrysler rebates can be a good deal when applied to minivans, but not advisable as a reason to buy the company's less-reliable SUVs and trucks.

Inflated and deflated prices

Generally, vehicles are priced according to what the market will bear and then are discounted as the competition heats up, or as the economy sours. A vehicle's stylishness, upgrades, scarcity, or general popularity can inflate its value considerably. For example, despite a worrisome increase in factory glitches, Toyota's revamped 2004 Sienna has such a high prevailing market value that most buyers pay the full MSRP. Usually, though, prices moderate in the following years (think of all the unsold PT Cruisers and VW New Beetles that are heavily discounted). On the other hand, if your choice has a deflated market value (like Kia and Daewoo), find out why it's so unpopular and then decide if the savings are worth it. Vehicles that don't sell because of their weird styling are no problem, but poor quality control, as with the Ford Windstar/Freestar and Land Rover, can cost big bucks.

Leftovers

In the fall, at the beginning of each new model year, most dealers still have a few of last year's vehicles left. Some are new, some are demonstrators with less than a few thousand miles on them. The factory gives the dealer a 3–5 percent rebate on late-season vehicles, and dealers will often pass on some of these savings to clients. But are these leftovers really bargains?

They might be, if you can amortize the first year's depreciation by keeping the vehicle for eight years. But if you're the kind of driver who trades every two or three years, you're likely to come out a loser by buying an end-of-the-season van or sport-utility vehicle. The simple reason is that as far as trade-ins are concerned, a leftover is a used vehicle that has depreciated at least 20 percent. The savings the dealer gives you may not equal that first year's depreciation (a cost you'll incur without getting any of the first year's driving benefits). If the dealer's discounted price matches or exceeds the 20 percent depreciation, then you're getting a pretty good deal. But if the next year's model is only a bit more expensive, has been substantially improved, or is covered by a more extensive, comprehensive warranty, it could represent a better buy than a cheaper leftover.

Ask the dealer for all work orders relating to the vehicle, including the PDI checklist, and make sure that the odometer readings follow in sequential order. Remember as well that most demonstrators should have less than 5,000 km on the ticker, and that the original warranty has been reduced from the day the vehicle was first put on the road. Have the dealer extend the warranty or lower the price accordingly—about $100 for each month of warranty that has expired. If the vehicle's file shows that it was registered to a leasing agency or any other third party, you're definitely buying a used vehicle disguised as a demo. You should walk away from the sale because you're dealing with a crook.

Cash versus Financing

Let's clear up one myth right away: Dealers won't treat you better if you pay cash. They want you to buy a fully loaded vehicle and finance the whole deal. Paying cash is not advantageous to the dealer, since kickbacks on finance contracts represent an important part of the F&I division's profits. Actually, barely 8 percent of new-car buyers pay cash. They may be making a big mistake. Financial planners say it may be smarter to borrow the money to purchase a new vehicle even if you can afford to pay cash, because if you use the vehicle for business a portion of the interest may be tax deductible. The cash that you free up can then be used to repay debts that aren't tax deductible (mortgages or credit card debt, for example).

Rebates versus low or zero percent financing

If you are buying an expensive vehicle and going for longer financing, the low-rate financing will be a better deal than the rebate. A zero percent loan will save you $80 per $1,000 financed over 24 months, or $120 per $1,000 financed over 36 months. If you were financing a $30,000 car for two years, you'd multiply $80 x 30 and save about $2,400.

Low-rate financing programs have the following disadvantages:

• Buyer must have exceptionally good credit.
• Shorter financing period means higher payments.
• Cash rebates are excluded.
• Only fully equipped or slow-selling models are eligible.
• Buyer pays full retail price.

Remember, to get the best price, whether you're paying cash or financing the purchase, first negotiate the price of the vehicle without disclosing whether you are paying cash or financing the purchase (simply say you haven't yet decided). Once you have a fair price, then take advantage of the financing.

Getting a loan

Borrowers must be at least 18 years old (age of majority), have a steady income, prove that they have discretionary income sufficient to make the loan payments, and be willing to guarantee the loan with additional collateral, or their parent or spouse as a co-signer.

Before applying for a loan, you should have established a good credit rating via a paid-off credit card and have a small savings account with your local bank, credit union, or trust company. Then, prepare a budget listing your assets and obligations. This will quickly show whether or not you can afford a car. Next, pre-arrange your loan with a simple phone call. This will protect you from much of the smoke and mirrors showroom shenanigans.

Incidentally, if you do get in over your head and require credit counselling, contact Credit Counselling Service (CCS). This is a non-profit organization located in many of Canada's major cities (*www.creditcanada.com*).

Hidden loan costs

Don't trust anyone. The Montreal-based Automobile Protection Association's undercover shoppers have found the most deceptive deals often involve major banking institutions, rather than automaker-owned companies.

In your quest for an auto loan, remember that the Internet offers help for people who need a loan and want quick approval, but don't like to face a banker. The Bank of Montreal (*www.bmo.com*) was the first Canadian bank to allow vehicle buyers to post a loan application on its website, and it promises to send a loan response within 20 seconds. Other banks, such as the Royal Bank, are offering a similar service. Loans are available to any web surfer, including those who aren't current Bank of Montreal or Royal Bank customers.

Be sure to call various financial institutions to find out the following:

- The annual percentage rate on the amount you want to borrow and for the duration of your repayment period
- The minimum down payment that the institution requires
- Whether taxes and licence fees are considered part of the overall cost and, thus, are covered by part of the loan
- Whether lower rates are available for different loan periods or for a larger down payment
- Whether discounts are available to depositors and, if so, how long you must be a depositor before qualifying

When comparing loans, consider the annual rate and calculate the total cost of the loan offer; that is, how much you'll pay above and beyond the total price of the vehicle.

Dealers can finance your purchase at interest rates that are competitive with the banks' because of the rebates they get from the manufacturers and some lending institutions. Some dealers, though, mislead their customers into thinking they can borrow money at as much as five percentage points below the prime rate. Actually, they're jacking up the retail price to more than make up for the lower interest charges. Sometimes, instead of boosting the price, dealers reduce the amount they pay for the trade-in. In either case, the savings are illusory.

When dealing with banks, keep in mind that the traditional 36-month loan has now been stretched to 48 or 60 months. Longer payment terms make each month's payment more affordable, but over the long run they increase the cost of the loan considerably. Therefore, take as short a term as possible.

Be wary of lending institutions that charge a "processing" or "document" fee ranging from $25 to $100. Sometimes consumers will be charged an extra 1–2 percent of the loan up front in order to cover servicing. This is similar to lending institutions adding "points" to mortgages, except that with auto loans it's totally unjustified. In fact, dealers in the States are the object of several state lawsuits and class actions for inflating loan charges.

Some banks will cut the interest rate if you're a member of an automobile owners association or if loan payments are automatically deducted from your chequing account. This latter proposal may be costly, though, if the chequing-account charges exceed the interest-rate savings.

Finance companies affiliated with GM, Ford, and Chrysler have been offering low-interest loans many points below the prime rate. In many cases, this low rate is applicable only to hard-to-sell models or vehicles equipped with expensive options. The low rate frequently doesn't cover the entire loan period. If vehicles recommended in this book are covered by low-interest loans, however, then the automaker-affiliated finance companies may be a useful alternative to regular banking institutions.

Loan protection

Credit insurance guarantees that the vehicle loan will be paid if the borrower becomes disabled or dies. There are three basic types of insurance that can be written into an installment contract: Credit life, accident and health, and comprehensive. Most bank and credit union loans are already covered by some kind of loan insurance, but dealers sell the protection separately at an extra cost to the borrower. For this service, the dealer gets a hefty 20 percent commission. The additional cost to the purchaser can be significant. The federal 7 percent GST is applied to loan insurance, but PST may be exempted in some provinces.

Collecting on these types of policies isn't easy. There's no payment if your illness is due to some condition that existed prior to your taking out the insurance. Nor will the policy cover strikes, layoffs, being fired, etc. Generally, credit insurance is unnecessary if you're in good health, you have no dependents, and your job is secure.

Personal loans from financial institutions now offer lots of flexibility. Most offer financing (with a small down payment), fixed or variable interest rates, a choice of loan terms, and no penalties for prepayment. Precise conditions depend on your personal credit rating. Finally, credit unions can also underwrite new vehicle loans that combine a flexible payment schedule with low rates.

Leasing contracts are less flexible. There's a penalty for any prepayment, and rates aren't necessarily competitive.

Negotiating the Contract

How likely are you to be cheated when buying a new car? Automobile Protection Association (APA) staffers posing as buyers visited 42 dealerships in four Canadian cities in early 2002. The APA says that almost half the dealers they visited (45 percent) flunked their test, and auto buyers in Western Canada are especially vulnerable to dishonest dealers.

In Vancouver and Edmonton, dealer ads left out important information, vehicles in the ads weren't available, or they were selling at higher prices. Fees for paperwork and vehicle preparation were frequently excessive, with Chrysler dealerships in Vancouver and Toronto charging the most ($299–$632). In some cases, the dealers may have double-billed the buyer. In Toronto, pre-delivery charges of $343 and $89 were levied on top of Chrysler's $955 PDI/transport fee.

Chrysler and Ford dealerships performed the worst overall, Toyota and General Motors performed best, and Mazda and Hyundai dealers were mediocre (they charged extra for items other automakers include in the base price). The APA found Toyota dealers demonstrated a superior level of product knowledge, covered all the bases more consistently, and applied the least pressure to make a sale. But Toyota dealers in the regions with Access-fixed selling prices appeared to charge substantially more.

You sign, you buy

Watch what you sign, since any document that requires your signature is a contract. Don't sign anything unless all the details are clear to you and all the blanks have been filled in. Don't accept any verbal promises that you're merely putting the vehicle on hold. And when you are presented with a contract, remember, it doesn't have to include all the clauses found in the dealer's pre-printed form. You and the sales representative can agree to strike some clauses and add others.

When the sales agent asks for a deposit, make sure that it's listed on the contract as a deposit and try to keep it as small as possible (a couple hundred dollars at the most). If you decide to back out of the deal on a vehicle taken from stock, let the seller have the deposit as an incentive to cancel the contract (believe me, it's cheaper than a lawyer and probably equal to the dealer's commission).

Scrutinize all references to the exact model (there is a heck of an upgrade from base to LX or Limited), prices, and delivery dates. Delivery can sometimes be delayed three to five months, and you'll have to pay all price increases announced during the interim (1–2 percent) unless you specify a delivery date in the contract, which protects the price.

Make sure that the contract indicates that your new vehicle will be delivered to you with a full tank of gas. Once this was the buyer's responsibility, but now, with drivers spending over $30,000 for the average new vehicle, dealers usually throw in the tank of gas.

Essential clauses

You can put things on a more equal footing by negotiating the inclusion of as many clauses as possible from the sample additional contract clauses found below. To do this, write in a "Remarks" section on your contract, and add "See attached clauses, which form part of this agreement." Then attach a photocopy of the "Additional Contract Clauses" page and persuade the sales agent to initial as many of the clauses as possible. Although some clauses may be rejected, the inclusion of just a couple of them can have important legal ramifications later on if you want a full or partial refund.

Additional Contract Clauses

1. **Original contract:** This is the ONLY contract; i.e., it cannot be changed, retyped, or rewritten, without the specific agreement of both parties.

2. **Financing:** This agreement is subject to the purchaser obtaining financing at _____% or less within _____ days of the date below.

3. **"In-service" date and mileage:** To be based on the closing day, not the day the contract was executed and will be submitted to GM for warranty and all other purposes. The General dealership will have this date corrected by GM if it should become necessary.

4. **Delivery:** The vehicle is to be delivered by _____, failing which the contract is cancelled and the deposit will be refunded.

5. **Cancellation:**
   (a) The purchaser retains the right to cancel this agreement without penalty at any time before delivery of the vehicle by sending a notice in writing to the vendor.
   (b) Following delivery of the vehicle, the purchaser shall have two days to return the vehicle and cancel the agreement in writing, without penalty. After two days and before thirty-one days, the purchaser shall pay the dealer $25 a day as compensation for depreciation on the returned vehicle.
   (c) Cancellation of contract can be refused where the vehicle has been subjected to abuse, negligence or unauthorized modifications after delivery.
   (d) The purchaser is responsible for accident damage and traffic violations while in possession of the said vehicle.

6. **Protected Price:** The vendor agrees not to alter the price of the new vehicle, the cost of preparation or the cost of shipping.

7. **Trade-in:** The vendor agrees that the value attributed to the vehicle offered in trade shall not be reduced, unless it has been significantly modified or has suffered from unreasonable and accelerated deterioration since the signing of the agreement.

8. **Courtesy Car:**
   (a) In the event the new vehicle is not delivered on the agreed-upon date, the vendor agrees to supply the purchaser with a courtesy car at no cost. If no courtesy vehicle is available, the vendor agrees to reimburse the purchaser the cost of renting a vehicle.
   (b) If the vehicle is off the road for more than five days for warranty repairs, the purchaser is entitled to a free courtesy vehicle for the duration of the repair period. If no courtesy vehicle is available, the vendor agrees to reimburse the purchaser the cost of renting a vehicle of equivalent or lesser value.

9. **Work Orders:** The purchaser will receive duly completed copies of all work orders pertaining to the vehicle, including warranty repairs and the pre-delivery inspection (PDI).   ➤

10. **Dealer Stickers:** The vendor will not affix any dealer advertising, in any form, on the vehicle.
11. **Fuel:** Vehicle will be delivered with a free full tank of gas.
12. **Excess Mileage:** New vehicle will not be acceptable and the contract will be void if the odometer has more than 50 km at delivery/closing.
13. **Tires:** Original equipment Firestone, Bridgestone, or Goodyear tires are not acceptable.

_____   _____   _____
        Date   Vendor's Signature   Buyer's Signature

And don't take the dealer's word that "we're not allowed to do that"—heard most often in reference to your reducing the pre-delivery inspection (PDI) or transportation fee. Some dealers have been telling *Lemon-Aid* readers that they are "obligated" by the automaker to charge a set fee and could lose their franchise if they charge less. This is pure hogwash. No dealer has ever had their franchise licence revoked for cutting prices. Furthermore, the automakers clearly state that they don't set a bottom price, since doing so would violate Canada's Competition Act—that's why you always see them putting disclaimers in their ads saying the dealer can charge less.

The pre-delivery inspection

The best way to ensure that the PDI (written as PDE in some regions) will be done is to write in the sales contract that you'll be given a copy of the completed PDI sheet when the vehicle is delivered to you. Then, with the PDI sheet in hand, verify some of the items that were to be checked. If any items appear to have been missed, refuse delivery of the vehicle. Once you get home, check out the vehicle more thoroughly and send a registered letter to the dealer if you discover any incomplete items from the PDI.

Selling Your Trade-In

Buy, sell, or hold?

It doesn't take a genius to figure out that the longer one keeps a vehicle, the less it costs to own—up to a point. The Hertz Corporation has estimated that a small car equipped with standard options, driven 16,000 km (10,000 miles), and traded each year, costs approximately 6 cents/km more to run than a comparable compact traded after five years. A small car kept for 10 years and driven 16,000 km a year would cost 6.75 cents/km less than a similar vehicle kept for five years, and a whopping 12.75 cents/km less (20.38 cents/mile less) than a comparable vehicle traded in each year. That would amount to savings of $20,380 over a 10-year period. Obviously, savings are more substantial with trucks and vans due to their slow rates of depreciation.

If you're happy with your vehicle's styling and convenience features, and it's safe and dependable, there is no reason to get rid of it. But when the cost of repairs becomes equal to or greater than the cost of payments for a new car, then you need to consider trading it in. Shortly after your vehicle's fifth birthday (or whenever you start to think about trading it in), ask a mechanic to look at it to give you some idea of what repairs, replacement parts, and maintenance work it will need in the coming year. Find out if dealer service bulletins show that it will need extensive repairs in the near future. (See Appendix I for how to order bulletins from ALLDATA.) If it's going to require expensive repairs, you should trade the vehicle right away; if expensive work isn't necessary, you may want to keep it. Auto owner associations provide a good yardstick. They estimate that the annual cost of repairs and preventive maintenance for the average vehicle is between $700 and $800. If your vehicle is five years old and you haven't spent anywhere near $3,500 in maintenance, it would pay to invest in your old vehicle and continue using it for another few years.

Consider whether your vehicle can still be serviced easily. If it's no longer on the market, the parts supply is likely to dry up and independent mechanics will be reluctant to repair it.

Don't trade for fuel economy alone. Most fuel-efficient vehicles, such as front-drives, offset the savings through higher repair costs. Also, the more fuel-efficient vehicles may not be as comfortable to drive, due to excessive engine noise, lightweight construction, stiff suspension, and torque steer.

Reassess your needs. Does your family growth require a different vehicle? Are you driving less? Are you taking fewer long trips? Let your truck or van rust in peace and pocket the savings if its deteriorating condition doesn't pose a safety hazard and isn't too embarrassing. On the other hand, if you're in sales and are constantly on the road, it makes sense to trade every few years—in that case, the vehicle's appearance and reliability become a prime consideration, particularly since the increased depreciation costs are mostly tax deductible.

Drawing up your bill of sale

The province of Alberta has prepared a useful bill of sale applicable throughout Canada that can be accessed at *www3.gov.ab.ca/gs/pdf/registries/reg3126.pdf*.

Your bill of sale should identify the vehicle (including the serial number) and include its price, whether a warranty applies, and the nature of the examination made by the buyer. The buyer may ask you to put in a lower price than what was actually paid in order to reduce the sales tax. If you agree to this, don't be surprised when a Revenue Canada agent comes to your door. Although the purchaser is ultimately the responsible party, you're an accomplice in defrauding the government. Furthermore, if you turn to the courts for redress, your own conduct may be put on trial

Summary

Purchasing a used vehicle and keeping it at least five years saves you the most money. It takes about eight years to realize similar depreciation savings when buying new. Paying cash (or with the biggest down payment you can afford), using zero percent financing programs, and piling up as many kilometres and years as possible on your trade-in are the best ways to save money with new vehicles. Remember that safety is another consideration that depends largely on the type of vehicle you choose. Focus on the following objectives.

Buy safe

Safety features to look for:

1. A high NHTSA and IIHS crashworthiness rating and low rollover potential
2. Good-quality tires; be wary of "all-season" tires and Firestone makes
3. Three-point belts with belt pretensioners and adjustable shoulder belt anchorages
4. Integrated child safety seats and seat anchors, safety door locks, and over-ride window controls
5. De-powered dual airbags with a cut-off switch, side airbags with head protection, unobtrusive, effective head restraints, and pedal extenders
6. Front driver's seat with plenty of rearward travel and a height adjustment
7. Good all-around visibility; dash that doesn't reflect onto the windshield
8. An ergonomic interior with an efficient heating and ventilation system
9. Headlights that are adequate for night driving
10. Dash gauges that don't wash out in sunlight or produce windshield glare
11. Head restraints for all seating positions
12. Delaminated side window glass
13. Easily accessed sound system and climate controls
14. Navigation systems that don't require an MIT degree to calibrate
15. Manual sliding doors in vans (if children are transported)

Buy smart

1. Buy the vehicle you need and can afford, not the one someone else wants you to buy, or one loaded with options that you'll probably never use. Take your time. Price comparisons and test-drives may take a month, but you'll get a better vehicle and price in the long run.
2. Buy in winter or later in the new year to double-dip from dealer incentives and customer rebate or low-cost financing programs.
3. Sell your trade-in privately.
4. Arrange financing before buying your vehicle.
5. Test-drive your choice by renting it overnight or for several days.
6. Buy through the Internet or by fax, or use an auto broker if you're not confident in your own bargaining skills, lack the time to haggle, or want to avoid the "showroom shakedown."
7. Ask for at least a 5 percent discount off the MSRP, and cut PDI and freight charges by at least 50 percent. Insist on a specific delivery date written in the contract, as well as a protected price in case there's a price increase between the time the contract is signed and when the vehicle is delivered. Also ask for a free tank of gas.

8. Order a minimum of options and seek a 30 percent discount on the entire option list. Try not to let the total option cost exceed 15 percent of the vehicle's MSRP.

9. Avoid leasing. If you must lease, choose the shortest time possible, drive down the MSRP, and refuse to pay an "acquisition" or "disposal" fee.

10. Japanese vehicles made in North America, co-ventures with American automakers, and re-badged imports often cost less than imports and are just as reliable. However, some Asian and European imports may not be as reliable as you might imagine—Kia's Sportage and Mercedes' M-Class sport-utilities, for example. Get extra warranty protection from the automaker if you're buying a model that has a poorer-than-average repair history. Use auto club references to get honest, competent repairs at a reasonable price.

If you find a new vehicle too expensive to own, take a look at Part Two, where we show you how to save money buying a used sport-utility, truck, or van.

USED, BUT NOT ABUSED

2

A Buyer's Market

Prices are falling—two to three percent—and that's significant in the used-car market. Why? Because the profit derived from the average new-car sale is typically less than $1,000 to the dealer while a used-car sale can generate $1,500 to $2,500 or more.

Dennis DesRosiers
DesRosiers Automotive Consultants

Full-Sized SUVs and Vans: An Endangered Species!

This year's high fuel prices and insurance premiums have driven down trade-in prices of large vans and SUVs like the Ford Expedition, Lincoln Navigator, and GM Tahoe (shown above) and Yukon, by at least 15 percent.

High-mileage, older bargains

Although the GST favours private sales, new-car dealers have become a major force in used-car sales in Canada: 10 years ago, dealers sold about a third of all used cars; now it's 44 percent. Conversely, in 1993, half of used cars were sold by their owners privately; that's been reduced to 38 percent today.

The used fleet mileage has almost doubled in the past thirty years. Back in the 1970s, the average car racked up 160,000 km before it got dropped off at the junkyard. In the 1990s, the average car reached 240,000 before it got "recycled." Now, 2005 models are expected to see 300,000 km before they're discarded.

One CAA ownership survey revealed that less than 10 percent of owners of cars five years or younger got rid of them because of reliability problems or high maintenance costs.

Far more common reasons for selling a car five years old or younger: 43 percent were sold because the lease expired, 30 percent of owners said they just wanted a change, and 21 percent said the vehicle no longer met their requirements.

Only 22 percent of owners of vehicles six to 10 years old got rid of them due to reliability problems.

There are lots of reasons why 2005 is a great time to buy a used SUV, truck, or van—as long as you stay away from many of the rotten products. Fortunately, there's not as much late '70s and early '80s junk out there as there once was, and vehicles are safer, more fuel efficient, and loaded with extra convenience and performance features. Additionally, there's a lot of cheap product to choose from and dealers are cutting prices due to pressure from zero percent interest programs and unrealistically high residual values used to keep monthly payments small.

And, you don't have to feel like a cheapskate when you pass up the chance to buy a new SUV, truck, or van. In fact, an ever-increasing number of first-time car buyers are choosing used models, while only the upper third in income earners are buying new.

But dealers aren't giving anything away. Popular, car-based, 2-year-old SUVs and minivans are selling at about two-thirds of their original price, and aren't likely to depreciate much over the next few years. This has forced shoppers to downsize their choices or go to the South Koreans to keep costs manageable. Rather than getting a used Jeep Grand Cherokee, Ford Expedition, or GM Suburban, buyers are opting for Hyundais and Kias and cheaper off-lease vehicles like the Ford Escape, Hyundai Santa Fe, Jeep Wrangler, Honda CR-V, Kia Sportage, Subaru Forester, or Toyota RAV4. In trucks, customers are attracted to smaller pickups like the Ford Ranger, Mazda B2000 and Tribute, Nissan Frontier, or Toyota Tacoma.

The American quality gap

Chrysler continues to make a lot of low-quality vehicles, and the company's transferable 7-year/100,000 km warranty gives only buyers of 2001 or later models the protection they need when faced with Chrysler's traditional engine and transmission defects, and excludes common ball joint failure.

Nevertheless, used Fords are an even greater risk to your pocketbook. Whatever quality improvements there have been haven't yet worked their way through the lineup. Meanwhile, the automaker's base warranty continues to lag behind the competition. The redesigned 2004 F-150 pickups will be the first test of Ford's commitment to quality.

GM also has its share of lemons, as any early Suburban and AWD Astro/Safari owner will confirm. However, beginning with the '99 models, General Motors made substantial improvements in its truck and minivan quality and performance, though major engine, transmission, suspension, and brake problems have returned with a vengeance since 2001.

Defects run the gamut, from collapsing tie-rod ends on 1997–2004 pickups to coil spring breakage that sends 1995–98 Windstars careening out of control. And if your Explorer doesn't roll over after losing its tire tread, it's just as likely to suddenly accelerate.

You can reduce your risk of buying a lemon by getting a used vehicle rated as "Recommended" in this guide—one that has some of the original warranty still in effect. This protects you from some of the costly defects that are bound to crop up shortly after your purchase. The warranty allows you to make one final inspection before it expires and requires both the dealer and the automaker to compensate you for all warrantable defects found at that time, even though they are fixed after the warranty expires.

Why Canadians Buy Used

We *are* different. We are frugal, unpretentious, and faithful. We don't have short love affairs—with cars or trucks. We are very reluctant to trade in a vehicle or abandon a model that suits our needs. In fact, over half of the vehicles on Canada's roads are nine years old or older, says Toronto-based industry analyst Dennis DesRosiers. We are also more conservative than Americans in our vehicle choice. We still love minivans, while Americans embrace SUVs; we buy downsized sport-utilities, while Americans go for humongous Hummers; and we still support economy cars, because of our higher fuel costs.

Cheaper prices, no transport or "administration" fees, slower depreciation, "secret" warranty repair refunds, and better and cheaper parts availability

New-vehicle prices have moderated somewhat over the past few years, but they're still quite high. Insurance is another wallet buster, costing about $2,000 a year for young drivers not fortunate enough to fall under their parents' policy. And once you add financing costs, main-tenance, taxes, and a host of other expenses, CAA calculates the yearly outlay for a medium-sized car at over $8,252, or 36.7 cents/km; trucks or SUVs may run you about 10 cents/km more. For a comprehensive, though depressing, comparative analysis (cars versus trucks, minivans, SUVs, etc.) of all the costs involved over a 1- to 10-year period, access Alberta's consumer information website at *www1.agric.gov.ab.ca/ app24/costcalculators/vehicle/getvechimpls.jsp.*

Another advantage is that used vehicles aren't usually sold with $700–$1,400 transport fees or $495 "administration" charges. And you can legally avoid paying sales tax when you buy privately. That's right, you'll pay at least 10 percent less than the dealer's price and you may avoid the 7 percent federal Goods and Services Tax (GST) that applies in some provinces to dealer sales only.

Depreciation savings

If someone were to ask you to invest in stocks or bonds guaranteed to be worth about half their initial purchase value after four to five years, you'd probably head for the door. But this is exactly the trap you're falling into when you buy a new SUV, truck, or van that will likely depreciate 20 percent in the first year and 15 percent each year thereafter.

Now, the motorist buying a new vehicle is certain that the warranty and status far outweigh any inconvenience. He or she forks over $32,200 and drives away in a brand new sport-utility or truck. If he or she had a trade-in, its value would be subtracted from the negotiated price of the new vehicle, and GST/PST sales tax would be paid on the reduced amount.

When you buy used, the situation is altogether different. That same truck can be purchased four years later, in good condition, and with much of the manufacturer's warranty remaining, for one-half to two-thirds of its original cost, without paying the 7 percent GST sales tax. Furthermore, the depreciation "hit" will be much less in the ensuing years.

Secret warranty slush funds

Believe it or not, some free repairs—like those related to Chrysler brakes, Nissan exhaust systems, and Toyota engines—are authorized up to 10 years under automaker "goodwill" programs. Still, most secret warranty extensions hover around the 5- to 10-year mark and seldom cover vehicles exceeding 160,000 km (100,000 miles).

Knowing which after-warranty repairs will be reimbursed can cut your maintenance costs dramatically. Incidentally, automakers and dealers claim that there are no secret warranties—that they are all expressed in service bulletins. Although this is technically correct, the sources that supply these bulletins are somewhat obscure to most vehicle owners, and the bulletins seldom state flat-out that the factory goofed.

Parts

Used parts can have an unusually long lifespan. Generally, a new gasoline-powered car or minivan can be expected to run, relatively trouble-free, at least 200,000–240,000 km (125,000–150,000 miles) in its lifetime, and a diesel-powered vehicle can easily triple those figures. Some repairs will crop up at regular intervals, and along with preventive maintenance, your yearly running costs should average about $700–$800. Buttressing the argument that vehicles get cheaper to operate the longer you keep them, the U.S. Department of Transportation points out that the average vehicle requires one or more major repairs after every five years of use. However, once these repairs are done, it can then be run relatively trouble-free for another five years or more. In fact, the farther west you go in Canada, the longer owners keep their vehicles—an average of 10 years or more in some provinces.

Time is on your side in other ways, too. Three years after a model's launching, the replacement-parts market usually catches up to consumer demand. Dealers stock larger inventories, and parts wholesalers and independent parts manufacturers expand their output. Used replacement parts are unquestionably easier to come by, through bargaining with local garages or through a careful search of auto wreckers' yards or the Internet. A reconditioned or used part usually costs one-third to one-half the price of a new part. There's generally no difference in the quality of reconditioned mechanical components, and they're often guaranteed for as long as, or longer than, new ones. In fact, some savvy shoppers use the ratings in Part Four of this guide to see which parts have a short life and then buy those parts from retailers that give lifetime warranties on their brakes, exhaust systems, tires, batteries, etc.

Also, buying from discount outlets or independent garages, or ordering through mail order houses, can save you big bucks (30–35 percent) on the cost of new parts and another 15 percent on labour when compared with dealer charges. Costco is another good source of savings realized through independent retailers. The retailer sells competitively priced replacement tires and offers free rotation, balancing, and other inspections during the life of the tire.

Body parts are a different story, however. Although car company repair parts cost 60 percent more than certified generic aftermarket parts, buyers would be wise to buy only original equipment manufacturer (OEM) parts supplied by automakers in order to get body panels that fit well, protect better in collisions, and have maximum rust resistance, says *Consumer Reports* in its February 1999 study. Although insurance appraisers often substitute cheaper, lower-quality aftermarket body parts in collision repairs, *Consumer Reports* found that 71 percent of those policyholders who requested OEM parts got them with little or no hassle. It suggests that consumers complain to their provincial Superintendent of Insurance if OEM parts aren't provided. Ontario car owners have filed a class action against that province's major insurers alleging that making repairs with non-OEM parts is an unsafe practice and it violates insureds' rights.

With some European models, you can count on a lot of aggravation and expense caused by the unacceptably slow distribution of parts and the high markup. Because these companies have a quasi-monopoly on replacement parts, there are few independent suppliers you can turn to for help. And junkyards, the last-chance repository for inexpensive car parts, are unlikely to carry foreign parts for vehicles more than three years old or manufactured in small numbers.

Finding parts for Japanese and domestic cars and vans is hardly a problem, though, due to the large number of vehicles produced, the presence of hundreds of independent suppliers, the ease with which relatively simple parts can be interchanged from one model to another, and the large reservoir of used parts stocked by junkyards.

Lower insurance rates

Insurance for a used vehicle is a lot cheaper, and by carefully negotiating the deductible, smart shoppers can further reduce insurance premiums. As a vehicle gets older, the amount of the deductible should increase. It may reach a maximum of $500 per collision. As the deductible increases, the annual premium for collision coverage decreases.

The Insurance Bureau of Canada's Vehicle Insurance Information Centre (1-800-761-6703 or 416-445-5912; *www.ibc.ca/vehinfo.asp*) provides a comprehensive look at the insurance claims experience of the most popular Canadian models of private passenger vehicles. It includes collision, comprehensive, personal injury, and theft results for vehicles three or more years old. One would expect the best-rated vehicles would cost less to insure; however, this isn't necessarily the case. Instead, use the figures as a guide to parts costs and the crashworthiness of different models.

Fewer "hidden" defects

You can easily avoid nasty surprises by having your choice checked out by an independent mechanic (for $75–$100) before paying for a used vehicle. This examination before purchase protects you against any hidden defects the vehicle may have. It's also a tremendous negotiating tool, since you can use the cost of any needed repairs to bargain down the purchase price.

It's easier to get permission to have the vehicle inspected if you promise to give the seller a copy of the inspection report should you decide not to buy it. If you still can't get permission to have the vehicle inspected elsewhere, walk away from the deal, no matter how tempting the selling price. The seller is obviously trying to put something over on you. Ignore the standard excuses that the vehicle isn't insured, the licence plates have expired, or the vehicle has a dead battery.

You know the vehicle's history

Smart customers will want answers to the following questions before signing the contract: What did it first sell for and what is its present value? How much of the original warranty is left? How many times has the vehicle been recalled for safety-related defects? Are parts easily available? Does the vehicle have a history of costly performance-related defects that can be corrected under a secret warranty, through a safety recall campaign, or with an upgraded part? (See "Secret Warranties/Service Tips" in Part 4.)

Litigation is quick, easy, and relatively inexpensive

A multitude of federal and provincial consumer protection laws that you can personally call upon go far beyond whatever protection may be offered by the standard new-vehicle warranty. Furthermore, buyers of used vehicles don't usually have to conform to any arbitrary rules or service guidelines to get this protection.

Let's say you do get stuck with a vehicle that's unreliable, has undisclosed accident damage, or doesn't perform as promised. Most small claims courts have a jurisdiction limit of $3,000–$10,000 (Alberta sets it at $25,000), which should cover the cost of repairs or compensate you if the vehicle is taken back. That way, any dispute between buyer and seller can be settled within a few months, without lawyers or excessive court costs. Furthermore, you're not likely to face a battery of lawyers standing in for the automaker and dealer in front of a stern-faced judge. Actually, you may not have to face a judge at all, since many cases are settled through court-imposed mediators at a pre-trial meeting usually scheduled a month or two after filing.

Choosing the Right Seller

When to buy

In the fall, dealer stocks of good-quality trade-ins and off-lease returns are at their highest level, and private sellers are moderately active. Prices will be higher, but there will be a greater choice of vehicles available. In winter, prices decline substantially. Dealers and private sellers are generally easier to bargain with because buyers are scarce and weather conditions don't present their wares in the best light. In spring and summer, prices go up a bit as private sellers become more active and dealers try to get full price for their diminishing stock.

Private sellers

Private sellers are your best source for a cheap and reliable used vehicle, because you're on an equal bargaining level with a vendor who isn't trying to profit from your inexperience. Remember, no seller, be it a dealer or private party, expects to get his or her asking price. As with price reductions on home listings, a 10–20 percent reduction on the advertised price is common with private sellers. Dealers usually won't cut more than 10 percent off their advertised price.

Don't be surprised to find that many national price guides have an eastern Ontario/Quebec price bias. They often list unrealistically low prices compared with what you'll actually see in the eastern and western provinces and in rural areas, where good used cars are often sold for outrageously high prices or simply passed down through the family.

Promises and precautions

As a buyer, you should get a printed sales agreement, even if it's just hand-written, that includes a clause stating there are no outstanding traffic violations or liens against the vehicle. It doesn't make a great deal of difference whether the car will be purchased "as is" or as certified under provincial regulation. As a buyer, you should get a printed sales agreement, even if it's just handwritten, that includes a clause stating there are no outstanding traffic violations or liens against the vehicle. It doesn't make a great deal of difference whether the car will be purchased "as is" or as certified under provincial regulation. In either case, you can get your money back if you are deceived or sold a substandard vehicle.

If you suspect your vehicle is a rebuilt wreck from the States or was once a taxi, use Carfax (*www.carfax.com*; Tel.: 1-888-422-7329) to carry out a background check to see if the vehicle has been part of a fleet, has been wrecked, has flood damage, is stolen, or shows incorrect mileage on the odometer. The $20 fee by telephone is cut to $14.95 (U.S.) if the order is placed via the Internet. A typical search takes only a few minutes and most Canadian provinces are included in the database. The search will also turn up vehicles that were trucked across the border as "parts" and then sold to resellers. An initial, free search on the Internet will confirm whether or not your vehicle is listed in the database.

In most provinces, you can do a lien and registration search yourself. If a lien does exist, you should contact the creditor(s) listed to find out whether any debts have been paid. If a debt is outstanding, you should arrange with the vendor to pay the creditor the outstanding balance. If the debt is larger than the purchase price of the car, it's up to you to decide whether or not you wish to complete the deal. If the seller agrees to clear the title personally, make sure that you receive a written relinquishment of title from the creditor before paying any money to the vendor. Make sure the title doesn't show an "R" for "restored," since this indicates the vehicle was written off as a total loss and may not have been properly repaired.

Even if all documents are in order, ask the seller to show you the vehicle's original sales contract and a few repair bills in order to ascertain how well it was maintained. The bills will show you if the odometer was turned back, and will also indicate which repairs are still guaranteed. If none of these can be found, run (don't walk!) away. If the contract shows that the car was financed, verify that the loan was paid. If you're still not sure that the vehicle is free of liens, ask your bank or credit union manager to check for you. If no clear answer is forthcoming, look for something else.

Repossessed vehicles

Repossessed pickups and SUVs are quite common among contractors and other small businesses that have gone bankrupt. They are usually found at auctions, but they're sometimes sold by finance companies or banks as well. Canadian courts have held that financial institutions are legally responsible for defects found in what they sell, so don't be surprised at all by the disclosure paperwork shoved under your nose. Also, as with rental car company transactions, these companies' deep pockets and abhorrence of bad publicity means you'll likely get your money back if you make a bad buy. The biggest problem with repossessed vans, sport-utilities, and pickups, in particular, is that they were likely abused or neglected by their financially troubled owners. Although you rarely get to test-drive or closely examine these vehicles, a local dealer may be able to produce a vehicle maintenance history by running the VIN through its manufacturer's database.

Rental and leased vehicles

The second-best choice for getting a good used vehicle is a rental company or leasing agency. Due to a slumping economy, Budget, Hertz, Avis, and National are selling, at cut-rate prices, vehicles that have one to two years of service and approximately 80,000–100,000 km. These rental companies will gladly provide a vehicle's complete history and allow an independent inspection by a qualified mechanic of the buyer's choice, as well as arranging competitive financing.

Rental vehicles are generally well maintained, sell for a few thousand dollars more than privately sold vehicles, and come with strong guarantees, like Budget's 30-day money-back guarantee. Rental car companies also usually settle customer complaints without much hassle so as not to tarnish their image with rental customers.

Rental agencies keep their stock of cars on the outskirts of town near the airport, and advertise in the local papers. Sales are held year-round as inventory is replenished. Late summer and early fall are usually the best times to get the best choice, as the new rentals arrive during that time period.

Vehicles that have just come off a 3- or 5-year lease are much more competitively priced, generally have less mileage, and are usually as well maintained as rental vehicles. You're also likely to get a better price if you buy directly from the lessee rather than going through the dealership or an independent agency, but remember, you won't have the dealer's leverage to extract post-warranty "goodwill" repairs from the automaker.

New-car dealers

New-car dealers aren't a bad place to pick up a good used car or minivan. Prices are 15–20 percent higher than those for vehicles sold privately, but rebates and zero percent financing plans can trim used values dramatically. Plus, dealers are insured against selling stolen vehicles or vehicles with finance or other liens owing. They also usually allow prospective buyers to have the vehicle inspected by an independent garage, offer a much wider choice of models, and have their own repair facilities to do warranty work. Additionally, if there's a possibility of getting post-warranty "goodwill" compensation from the manufacturer, your dealer can provide additional leverage, particularly if the dealership is a franchisee for the model you have purchased. Finally, if things do go terribly wrong, dealers have deeper pockets than private sellers, so there's a better chance of getting a court judgment.

"Certified" vehicles

Almost all automakers provide "certified" used vehicles that have been refurbished by the dealer according to the manufacturer's guidelines. Sometimes, an auto association will certify a vehicle that has been inspected and had the designated defects corrected. In Alberta, the Alberta Motor Association (AMA) will perform a vehicle inspection at a dealer's request. On each occasion, the AMA gives a written report to the dealer that identifies potential and actual problems, required repairs, and serious defects.

Automaker-certified vehicles guarantee the vehicle's mechanical fitness and provide a warranty according to the age of the vehicle. But these vehicles don't come cheap, mainly because manufacturers force their dealers to bring them up to better-than-average condition before certifying them. The higher price can be reduced by choosing an older certified model, or amortized by keeping the vehicle longer.

Used-car leasing

A lousy idea for new or used vehicles. Leasing has been touted as a method of making the high cost of vehicle ownership more affordable. Don't you believe it: Leasing is generally costlier than an outright purchase, and for most people the pitfalls far outweigh any advantages. If you must lease, do so for the shortest time possible and make sure the lease is close-ended (meaning that you walk away from the vehicle when the lease period ends). Also, make sure there's a maximum allowance of at least 25,000 km a year and that the charge per excess kilometre is no higher than 8–10 cents.

Used-car dealers

Used-car dealers usually sell their vehicles for a bit less than what new-car dealers charge. However, their vehicles may be worth a lot less, because they don't get the first pick of top-quality trade-ins. Many independent urban dealerships are marginal operations that can't invest much money in reconditioning their vehicles, which are often collected from auctions and new-car dealers reluctant to sell the vehicles to their own customers. And used-car dealers don't always have repair facilities to honour what warranties they do provide. Often, their credit terms are easier (but more expensive) than those offered by franchised new-car dealers.

That said, used-car dealers operating in small towns are an entirely different breed. These small, often family-run businesses recondition and resell cars and trucks that usually come from within their community. Routine servicing is often done in-house and more complicated repairs are subcontracted out to specialized garages nearby. These small outlets survive by word-of-mouth advertising and would never last long if they didn't deal fairly with local buyers. On the other hand, their prices will likely be higher than elsewhere, due to the better quality of used vehicles they offer and the cost of reconditioning and repairing what they sell under warranty.

Auctions

First of all, make sure it's a legitimate auction. Many auctions are fronts for used-car lots where sleazy dealers put fake ads in complicit newspapers, pretending to hold auctions that are really no more than weekend selling sprees.

Furthermore, you'll need lots of patience, smarts, and luck to pick up anything worthwhile. Government auctions—places where the mythical $50 Jeep is sold—are fun to attend but highly overrated as places to find bargains. Look at the odds against you: It's impossible to determine the condition of the vehicles put up for bid; prices can be bid way out of control; and auction employees, their relatives, and friends usually pick over the good stuff long before you ever see it.

Paying the Right Price

If you don't want to pay too much when buying used, you've got the following four alternatives.

- Buy an older vehicle. Choose one that's five years old or more and has a good reliability and durability record. Buy extra protection with an extended warranty. The money you save from the extra years' depreciation and lower insurance premiums will more than make up for the extra warranty cost.
- Look for off-lease vehicles sold privately by owners who want more than what their dealer is offering. If you can't find what you're looking for in the local classified ads, put in your own ad asking for lessees to contact you if they're not satisfied with their dealer's offer.
- Buy a vehicle that's depreciated more than average simply because of its bland styling, lack of high-performance features, or discontinuation. For example, many of the Japanese pickups cost less to own than their flashier American-made counterparts, yet are more reliable and equally functional for most driving chores.
- Buy a twin or re-badged model. They usually share the same basic design, appearance, dimensions, and mechanical components, but their resale values may differ considerably.

Prices and price scams

Several price books, like the *Red Book* and *Black Book*, are available for perusal at your local library, credit union, or bank. *Lemon-Aid*'s prices are a synthesis of both guides, with auction figures thrown in. Remember, both buyers and sellers use the guide that will make them the most profit on each transaction: Sellers quote the retail price, while buyers try to get as close to wholesale as they can. The most common price guide quoted is the *Red Book* (*www.canadianredbook.com*), which shows a used vehicle's retail and wholesale worth across the country, while the *Black Book* is more regionally oriented. To find Canadian *Black Book* trade-in values online, go to either *www.daimlerchrysler.ca* or *www.toyota.ca*, or use the CAA's members-only link at *www.caasco.on.ca/automotive/blackbook.jsp*.

In spite of what you'll be told, wholesale and retail prices leave considerable room for the dealer's profit margin and some extra padding, like inflated preparation charges and administration fees that should be turned down flat.

> Your *Lemon-Aid* guide has levelled the playing field for the consumer when it comes to shopping for new or used vehicles. *Lemon-Aid* has also helped us consumers get the inside edge on how to protect ourselves from car manufacturers, secret warranties, goodwill service, etc.
>
> I recently used your publication to help me in my decision to purchase a 1999 Toyota Tercel. Your *Lemon-Aid* guide also helped me

avoid paying an "administration fee." I just walked out of the dealer's showroom. They must have thought I was crazy.

I didn't even have time to take my shoes off when my wife called me and said the Toyota dealership was on the telephone. She had no idea what had happened.

Suffice it to say, this wise consumer didn't pay an "administration fee" so someone could have dinner on me. If there is value in something I will pay it. If not, this customer walks. Here's to many years of carefree driving with my Toyota.

Just an off note. After 17 years of working for General Motors I thought I knew it all about vehicles, making deals, problems, defects, warranties, etc.

Was I wrong. You can never know it all. Keep publishing *Lemon-Aid* and I will keep reading it.

I'm a long-time GM employee who bought his first foreign-made vehicle with the help of Phil Edmonston. Patriotism is one thing, but blowing your hard-earned money for junk is another, just so you can wave the flag.

Sincerely, L. C.

Financing Choices

No one should spend more than 30 percent of his or her annual gross income on the purchase of a new or used vehicle. By keeping the initial cost low, there is less risk, and the purchaser may be able to pay mostly in cash. This can be an effective bargaining tool to use with private sellers, but dealers are less impressed by cash sales because they lose their kickback from the finance companies.

Credit unions

A credit union is the preferred place to borrow money at low interest rates and with easy repayment terms. You'll have to join the credit union or have an account with it before the loan is approved. You'll also probably have to come up with a larger down payment relative to what other lending institutions require.

In addition to giving you reasonable loan rates, credit unions help car buyers in a number of other ways. Toronto's Metro Credit Union (*www.metrocu.com*), for example, has a CarFacts Centre, which provides free, objective advice on car shopping, purchasing, financing, and leasing. CarFacts advisors provide free consultations in person or by phone.

Banks

Banks are a bit leery of financing used cars, because they fear you'll stop your payments if the vehicle turns out to be a dud. Nevertheless, with interest rates as high as 10 percent, they're not likely to turn you away.

In your quest for a bank loan, keep in mind that the loan officer will be impressed by a prepared budget and sound references. It also wouldn't hurt to have a vehicle already picked out at the local dealer, since banks like to encourage businesses in their area.

The Internet also offers help for people who need an auto loan and want quick approval, but don't like to face a banker. Used car buyers can post a loan application on a bank's website, even if they don't have an account with that bank.

Dealers

Dealer financing isn't the rip-off it once was, but still be watchful for all the expensive little "extras" the dealer may try to pencil into the contract. Dealers can finance the cost of a used vehicle at rates that compete with those of banks and finance companies. This is because they agree to take back the vehicle if the creditor defaults on the loan. Some dealers mislead their customers into thinking they can get financing at rates far below the prime rate. Actually, the dealer jacks up the base price of the vehicle to compensate for the lower interest charges.

Dealer Scams

First, avoid the usual scams by following three important rules:

- *Never* buy a vehicle imported from another province.
- *Walk away* if you aren't given the previous owners name and service records.
- *Check out* the vehicle with an independent garage or agency (Carfax, *icbc.com*, etc.).

Used vehicles are subject to the same deceptive sales practices employed by dealers who sell new vehicles. One of the more common tricks is to not identify the previous owner because the vehicle either was used commercially or had been written off as a total loss from an accident. It's also not uncommon to discover that the mileage has been turned back, particularly if the vehicle was part of a company's fleet. These scams can be thwarted if you demand the name of the vehicle's previous owner and run a VIN check through Carfax as a prerequisite to purchasing the vehicle.

It would be impossible to list all the dishonest tricks employed in used-vehicle sales. As soon as the public is alerted to one scheme, crooked sellers use other, more elaborate frauds. Nevertheless, under industry-financed provincial compensation funds, buyers can get substantial refunds if defrauded by a dealer.

Here are some of the more common fraudulent practices you're likely to encounter.

Failing to declare full purchase price

Here's where your own greed will do you in. A tactic used almost exclusively by small, independent dealers and some private sellers, the buyer is told that he or she can pay less sales tax by listing a lower selling price on the contract. But what if the vehicle turns out to be a lemon or the sales agent has falsified the model year or mileage? The hapless buyer is offered a refund on the fictitious purchase price indicated on the contract. If the buyer wanted to take the dealer to court, it's quite unlikely that he or she would get any more than the contract price. Moreover, both the buyer and dealer could be prosecuted for making a false declaration to avoid paying sales tax.

Phony private sales ("curbsiders")

Individuals sell about three times as many used vehicles as dealers, and crooked dealers get in on the action by posing as private sellers. They lure unsuspecting buyers through lower prices, cheat the federal government out of the GST, and routinely violate provincial registration and consumer protection regulations.

This scam is easy to detect if the seller can't produce the original sales contract or show some repair bills made out in his or her own name. You can usually identify a car dealer in the want ads section of the newspaper—just check to see if the same telephone number is repeated in many different ads. Sometimes you can trip up a curbsider by requesting information on the phone, without identifying the specific vehicle. If the seller asks you which car you are considering, you know you're dealing with a dealer.

Legitimate car dealers deplore the dishonesty of curbsider crooks, yet they are their chief suppliers. Dealership sales managers, auto auction employees, and newspaper classified ad sellers all know the names, addresses, and phone numbers of these thieves, but they don't act. Newspapers want the ad dollars, auctions want the action, and dealers want someplace to unload their wrecked, rust-cankered, and odometer-tricked junkers with impunity. Talk about hypocrisy, eh?

Curbsiders are particularly active in the west, importing vehicles from other provinces where they were sold by dealers, wreckers, insurance companies, and junkyards (after having been written off as total losses). They then place private classified ads in B.C. and Alberta papers, sell their stock, and import more.

If you get taken by one of these scams, don't hesitate to sue the publication carrying the ad through small claims court for allowing this rip-off artist to operate.

"Free-exchange" privilege

Dealers get a lot of sales mileage out of this deceptive offer. The dealer offers to exchange any defective vehicle for any other vehicle in stock. What really happens, though, is that the dealer won't have *anything else* selling for the same price and so will demand a cash bonus for the exchange…or you may get that dubious privilege of exchanging one lemon for another.

"Money-back" guarantee

Once again, the purchaser feels safe in buying a used car with this kind of guarantee, because what could be more honest than a money-back guarantee? Dealers using this technique often charge exorbitant handling charges, rental fees, or mechanical repair costs to the customer who's bought one of these vehicles and then returned it.

"50/50" guarantee

This means that the dealer will pay half the repair costs over a limited period of time. It's a fair offer if an independent garage does the repairs. If not, the dealer can always inflate the repair costs to double their actual worth and write up a bill for that amount (a scam sometimes used in "goodwill" settlements). The buyer winds up paying the full price of repairs that would probably have been much cheaper at an independent garage. The best kind of used-vehicle warranty is 100 percent with full coverage for a fixed term, even if that term is relatively short.

"As is" warranties

Buying a vehicle "as is" usually means that you're aware of mechanical defects, you're prepared to accept the responsibility for any damage or injuries caused by the vehicle, and all costs to fix it shall be paid by you. However, the courts have held that the "as is" clause is not a blank cheque to cheat buyers and therefore must be interpreted in light of the seller's true intent. That is, was there an attempt to deceive the buyer by including this clause? Did the buyer really know what the "as is" clause could do to his or her future legal rights? It's also been held that the courts may consider oral representations ("parole evidence") that were never written into the formal contract. So, if a seller makes claims as to the fine quality of the used vehicle, these claims can be used as evidence. Courts generally ignore "as is" clauses when the vehicle has been intentionally misrepresented, when the dealer is the seller, or when the defects are so serious that the seller is presumed to have known of their existence. Private sellers are usually given more credibility than dealers or their agents.

Odometer tampering

Most commonly found on vehicles brought in from other provinces, odometer fraud is quite common throughout Canada. In theory, sellers face hefty fines and even imprisonment if they're caught altering the mileage of any vehicle they sell, but in practice, few odometer tampering cases make it to court because intent to defraud is so difficult to prove. Also, RCMP officers responsible for enforcing the federal statutes are discouraged by the small fines leavied on odometer tricksters who ostensibly visit dealers to "fix" odometers, thereby skirting Canadian federal and provincial laws.

Misrepresentation

Used vehicles can be misrepresented in a variety of ways. A used airport commuter minivan may be represented as having been used by a Sunday school class. A mechanically defective pickup that's been rebuilt after several major accidents may have plastic filler in the body panels to muffle the rattles or hide rust damage, heavy oil in the motor to stifle the "clanks," and cheap retread tires to eliminate the "thumps." Your best protection against these dirty tricks is to have the vehicle's quality completely verified by an independent mechanic before completing the sale. Of course, you can still cancel the sale if you only learn of the misrepresentation after taking the vehicle home, but your chances dwindle as time passes.

> On another note, I'm finding it difficult finding a reasonably priced used car in the Toronto area. Many of the ads for private sales here turn out to be dealers or mechanics pretending to be private persons selling cars. Also, the prices are ridiculously inflated. Your books are a great read and have made me at least slow down and ask questions. For example, I almost got caught in a lease the other day and pulled out at the last minute. All this advertising had me believe there would be zero down, zero delivery, etc. until I found out there would be a $350 lease acquisition fee and a $250 admin. fee and all kinds of other charges—some legitimate, such as licensing. However, my zero down turned into a whopping $1,200! I'm just now getting into your leasing section.

Private Scams

A lot of space in this guide has been used to describe how used-car dealers and scam artists cheat uninformed buyers. Of course, private individuals can be dishonest too. In either case, protect yourself at the outset by keeping your deposit small and getting as much information as possible about the seller and the vehicle you're considering. Then, after a test drive, you may sign a written agreement to purchase the vehicle and give a deposit of sufficient value to cover the seller's advertising costs, subject to cancellation if the automobile fails its inspection. After you've taken these precautions, watch out for the following private sellers' tricks.

Used vehicles that are stolen or have finance owing

Many used vehicles are sold privately without free title because the original auto loan was never repaid. You can avoid being cheated by asking for proof of purchase and payment from a private seller. Be especially wary of any individual who offers to sell a used vehicle for an incredibly low price. Check the sales contract to determine who granted the original loan and call the lender to see if it's been repaid. Place a call to the provincial Ministry of Transportation to ascertain whether the car is registered in the seller's name.

Find out if a finance company is named as beneficiary on the auto insurance policy. Finally, call up the original dealer to determine whether there are any outstanding claims.

In Ontario, the Used Vehicle Information Package (mandatory for private sellers) will alert buyers to any problems with the title, but in other provinces buyers don't have access to this information. Generally, you have to contact the provincial office that registers property and pay a small fee for a computer printout that may or may not be accurate. You'll be asked for the current owner's name and the car's VIN, which is usually found on the driver's side of the dashboard.

There are two high-tech ways to get the goods on a dishonest seller. First, have a dealer of that particular model run a "vehicle history" check through the automaker's online network. This will tell you who the previous owners and dealers were, what warranty and recall repairs were carried out, and what other free repair programs may still apply. Second, you could use Carfax (*www.carfax.com*; Tel.: 1-888-422-7329) to carry out a background check.

Wrong registration

Make sure the seller's vehicle has been properly registered with provincial transport authorities. If it isn't, it may be stolen or you could be dealing with a curbsider. Be careful that you're not dealing with a simple typographical error caused by someone punching in the wrong vehicle identification number. This is very common and can be cross-checked by comparing the VIN with the insurance policy vehicle number.

Summary: Saving Money and Keeping Safe

You can get a good used vehicle at a reasonable price—it just takes lots of patience and homework. You can further protect yourself by becoming thoroughly familiar with your legal rights, as outlined in Part Three, and buying a vehicle recommended in Part Four. Following is a summary of the steps to take to keep your risk to a minimum:

1. Buy a full-sized, rear-drive delivery van and convert it yourself instead of opting for a more expensive, smaller, less powerful minivan.
2. Trade in your vehicle if the GST and PST sales tax reduction is more than the potential profit of selling privately.
3. Sell to a private party.
4. Buy from a private party, rental car outlet, or dealer (in that order).
5. Use an auto broker to save time and money.
6. Buy a *Lemon-Aid*-recommended vehicle for depreciation, parts, and service savings.
7. Buy a 3- or 4-year-old vehicle with lots of original warranty that can be transferred (35–50 percent savings over a new vehicle).
8. Choose a vehicle that's crashworthy and cheap to insure.

9. Carefully inspect Japanese-built vehicles that have reached their fifth year (engine head gasket, CV joints, steering box, and front brakes).
10. Don't buy an extended warranty unless it's recommended in this guide.
11. Have non-warranty repairs done by independent garages offering lifetime warranties.
12. Install used or reconditioned parts.
13. Keep all the previous owner's repair bills to facilitate warranty claims and to help mechanics know what's already been replaced or repaired.
14. Upon delivery, adjust mirrors to eliminate blind spots and adjust head restraints to prevent your head from snapping back in the event of a collision. On airbag-equipped vehicles, move the seat backward more than half its travel distance and sit at least a foot away from the airbag housing. Ensure that the airbag, spare tire, and tire jack haven't been removed.
15. Make sure the dealer and automaker have your name in their computers as the new owner of record. Ask for a copy of your vehicle's history, which is also stored in the same computer.

PART THREE

GET YOUR MONEY BACK

3

Windstar "mental distress" worth $7,500!

The plaintiff and his family have had three years of aggravation, inconvenience, worry, and concern about their safety and that of their children. Generally speaking, our contract law did not allow for compensation for what may be mental distress, but that may be changing.... In my view, a defect in manufacture (a faulty 2000 Windstar sliding door) which goes to the safety of the vehicle deserves a modest increase. I would assess the plaintiff's damage for mental distress resulting from the breach of the implied warranty of fitness at $7,500.

> Justice Shepard, Ontario Superior Court of Justice
> *Sharman v. Ford*
> October 7, 2003

Dodge Ram wandering, leaking

The defects in question were serious, expensive, and repetitive. Dawe describes that he was afraid to drive his 2001 pickup because it was wandering all over the road. He brought the truck in for treatment on numerous occasions prior to ultimately selling the vehicle in August 2002. On many occasions that the vehicle was repaired, similar problems would resurface later.

> Justice Patrick L. Casey, Nova Scotia Small Claims Court
> *Dave v. Courtesy Chrysler*
> July 30, 2004

Welcome to the "lemon" grove

Minivans with sliding doors that open on their own, Toyotas that suddenly accelerate, Chryslers that stall near radar installations, Pacificas that stink— today's cars don't need mechanics, they need exorcists.

"Stay away from radar"

Minivan Stalling, Jerking, Bucking Near Radar

Bulletin No: 18-16-96   Date: May 3, 1996
Intermittent Driveability Problems When Driving Near Radar
1996 (NS) Town & Country/Caravan/Voyager
NOTE: THE INSTALLATION OF THE "HARDENED" CRANK SENSOR APPLIES TO ALL VEHICLES
BUILT PRIOR TO NOVEMBER 1, 1995 (MDH 11-01-XX).
CONDITION: Some vehicles may experience intermittent driveability concerns or problems when
driven in close proximity to military or air traffic control radar installations.

"Officer, would you please not point that radar gun at my Caravan?"

As unbelievable as it seems, these defects aren't that rare. Even the staid
Runzheimer Consultants organization says that one out of every 10 American
vehicles produced by the Detroit Big Three is a "lemon." Owners of engine-
and transmission-challenged Chrysler Caravans and Ford Windstars, GM vans
with peeling paint and rust holes in the roof, and failure-prone Silverados and
Sierras would probably put that number much higher.

"Raindrops keep falling on my head"

Front/Rear Roof Rust Perforation

Bulletin No.: 02-08-67-006B   Date: March, 2003
Roof Perforation (Replace Roof) : 1997–2003 Chevrolet Venture
                                    1997–2003 Oldsmobile Silhouette
                                    1997–2003 Pontiac TranSport/Montana
Important: Implementation of this service bulletin by "GM of Canada" dealers requires prior
District Service Manager approval.
Condition: Some customers may comment that there is rust forming around the front or rear
portion of the roof.
Cause: During production, the E-coating (ELPO primer) may have been missed in concealed areas
of the front or rear portions of the outer roof panel.
Correction: Partial repairs to the roof panel are not permitted.
1. Remove the headliner.
2. Replace the roof. Important: Adhesive Bonding is the preferred installation method.
3. Reinstall the headliner.

Don't cause a stink!

Front seat belt foul odor

Bulletin No: 23-026-04   Date: July 16, 2004

Overview: This bulletin involves replacing the seat belt assembly and removing the foam material behind the seat belt retractor.

Models: 2004 (CS) Pacifica

Symptom/Condition: The vehicle operator may describe a foul odor from the front seat belt(s).

The odor does not originate from the seat belt but from the foam material that is located in the B-pillar. Under warm ambient temperatures, the odor is given off and permeates the plastic cup behind the seat belt retractor, into the seat belt itself. Replacing only the seat belt assembly will not correct the condition.

I don't want to cause a stink, but Chrysler/Jeep engineers have apparently lost their sense of smell for over a decade. Look below at the 1993–94 Jeep Grand Cherokee bulletin disclosed in the *1999 Lemon-Aid SUV, Van, and Truck Guide*.

Headliner – Offensive Odour

Bulletin No: 23-58-94   Date: Aug. 5, 1994

1993–94 (ZJ) Grand Cherokee/Grand Wagoneer

SYMPTOM/CONDITION: Headliner may exhibit an offensive smell often described as a "fish odour."

DIAGNOSIS: Smell the headliner (rubbing or tapping the headliner may make the odour more pronounced). If the headliner exhibits the odor, perform the repair procedure.

Stinky Chryslers aside, if you've bought an unsafe or unreliable vehicle, whether new or used, this section's for you. Its intention is to help you make a successful claim—without "fear and loathing," going to court, or getting frazzled. But if going to court is your only recourse, here is 35 years' worth of information on strategy, tactics, negotiation tools, and jurisprudence you may cite to "hang tough" and get an out-of-court settlement, or to win your case without spending a fortune on lawyers and research.

Four Ways to Get a Refund

Remember the "money-back" guarantee? Well, automakers are reluctant to offer any warranty that requires them to take back a defective truck or van. Fortunately, our provincial consumer protection laws have filled the gap so that now, any sales contract for a new or used vehicle can be cancelled—or free repairs can be ordered—if the vehicle:

• is unfit for the purpose for which it was purchased
• is misrepresented

- is covered by a secret warranty, or a "goodwill" warranty extension
- hasn't been reasonably durable, considering how well it was maintained, the mileage driven, and the type of driving done (particularly applicable to engine, transmission, and paint defects)

These four legal concepts enumerated above can lead to the contract being cancelled, the purchase price partially refunded, and damages awarded.

For example, if the seller says that an SUV or truck can pull a 900 kg (2,000 lb.) trailer and you discover that it can barely tow half that weight or won't reach a reasonable speed, you can cancel the contract for misrepresentation. The same principle applies to a seller's exaggerated claims concerning a vehicle's fuel economy or reliability, as well as to "demonstrators" that are in fact used cars with false (rolled back) odometer readings. GM's secret paint warranties and Ford's Windstar engine head gasket "goodwill" programs have all been successfully challenged in small claims court, as the jurisprudence in this section attests. And reasonable durability is an especially powerful legal argument that allows a judge to determine what the dealer and auto manufacturer will pay to correct a premature failure long after the original warranty has expired.

Unfair contracts

New and used sales contracts aren't meant to be fair. Dealers' and automakers' lawyers spend countless hours making sure their clients are well protected with iron-clad standard-form contracts.

Called "contracts of adhesion," judges look upon these agreements with a great deal of skepticism. They know these are contracts in which you have little or no bargaining power, such as loan documents, insurance contracts, and automobile leases. So when a dispute arises over terms or language, provincial consumer protection statutes require that judges interpret these contracts in the way most favourable to the consumer.

"Hearsay" not allowed

It's essential that printed evidence and/or witnesses (relatives are not excluded) are available to confirm that a false representation actually occurred, that a part is failure-prone, or that its replacement is covered by a secret warranty. Stung by an increasing number of small claims court defeats, automakers are now asking small claims court judges to disallow evidence from *Lemon-Aid*, service bulletins, or memos, on the pretext that such evidence is hearsay (not proven), unless confirmed by an independent mechanic or unless the document is recognized by the automaker or dealer's representative at trial. This is why you should bring in an independent garage mechanic or body expert to buttress your allegations. Sometimes, though, the service manager or company representative will make key admissions if questioned closely by you, a court mediator, or the trial judge. Some questions to ask: Is this a common problem? Do you recognize this service bulletin? Is there a case-by-case "goodwill" plan covering this repair? That questioning can be particularly effective if you call for the exclusion of witnesses until they're called (let them mill around outside the courtroom wondering what their colleagues have said).

Automakers often blame owners for having pushed their vehicle beyond its limits. Therefore, when you seek to set aside the contract or get a repair reimbursed, it's essential that you get the testimonies of an independent mechanic and co-workers in order to prove that the vehicle's poor performance isn't caused by negligent maintenance or abusive driving.

The reasonable durability claim is your ace in the hole, especially if you have an independent mechanic or body expert available to describe how long parts or paint should last. It's probably the easiest allegation to prove, since all automakers have benchmarks as to how long body components, trim and finish, and mechanical and electronic parts should last (see the durability chart on pages 108–109). Vehicles are expected to be reasonably durable and merchantable. What is reasonably durable depends on the price paid, kilometres driven, the purchaser's driving habits, and how well the vehicle was maintained by the owner. Judges carefully weigh all these factors in awarding compensation or cancelling a sale.

Whatever the reason you use to get your money back, don't forget to conform to the "reasonable diligence" rule that requires you to file suit within a reasonable time after purchase or after you've discovered the defect. If there have been no negotiations with the dealer or automaker, this period cannot exceed a few months. If either the dealer or the automaker has been promising to correct the defects for some time or has carried out repeated unsuccessful repairs, the delay for filing the lawsuit can be extended.

Refunds for other expenses

It's a lot easier to get the automaker to pay to replace a defective part than it is to obtain compensation for a missed day of work. Manufacturers seldom pay for consequential expenses like a ruined vacation, the vehicle not living up to its advertised hype, or the owner's mental distress because they can't control the amount of the refund. Courts, however, are more generous, having ruled that all expenses (damages) flowing from a problem covered by a warranty or service bulletin are the manufacturer's/dealer's responsibility under both common law (all provinces except Quebec) and Quebec civil law. Fortunately, when legal action is threatened—usually through small claims court—automakers quickly up their ante to include most of the owner's expenses because they know the courts will be more generous.

One precedent-setting judgment (cited in *Sharman v. Ford*, found in the Windstar section) giving generous damages to a motorist fed up with his "lemon" Cadillac was rendered in 1999 by the British Columbia Supreme Court in *Wharton v. Tom Harris Chevrolet Oldsmobile Cadillac Ltd.*, [2002] B.C.J. No. 233, 2002 BCCA 78*d*. In that case, Justice Leggatt threw the book at GM and the dealer in awarding the following amounts:

(a) Hotel accommodations: $217.17

(b) Travel to effect repairs at 30 cents per kilometre: The plaintiff claims some 26 visits from his home in Ucluelet to Nanaimo.

Some credit should be granted to the defendants since routine trips would have been required in any event. Therefore, the plaintiff is entitled to be compensated for mileage for 17 trips (approximately 400 km from Ucluelet to Nanaimo return) at 30 cents per kilometre.

$2,040.00

TOTAL: $2,257.17

[20] The plaintiff is entitled to non-pecuniary damages for loss of enjoyment of their luxury vehicle and for inconvenience in the sum of $5,000.

Warranties

The manufacturer's or dealer's warranty is a written legal promise that a vehicle will be reasonably reliable, subject to certain conditions. Regardless of the number of subsequent owners, this promise remains in force as long as the warranty's original time/kilometre limits haven't expired. Unfortunately, these warranties are full of so many loopholes ("you abused the car; it was poorly maintained; it's normal wear and tear") that they may be useless when a vehicle breaks down.

Thankfully, car owners get another kick at the can. As clearly stated in *Frank v. GM*, every vehicle sold new or used in Canada is also covered by an *implied* warranty—a collection of federal and provincial laws and regulations that protect you from hidden defects, misrepresentation, and a host of other scams. Furthermore, Canadian law presumes that car dealers, unlike private sellers, are aware of the defects present in the vehicles they sell. That way, they can't just pass the ball to the automakers and walk away from the dispute. For instance, in British Columbia a new car dealer is required to disclose damage requiring repairs costing more than 20 percent of the price or, in the case of a used motor vehicle, damage amounting to more than $2,000 (the Motor Dealer Act regulations).

Warranty denials

Safety restraints such as airbags and safety belts have warranty coverage extended for the lifetime of the vehicle, following an agreement made between U.S. automakers and importers. In Canada, though, some automakers try to dodge this responsibility because they are incorporated as separate Canadian companies. That distinction didn't fly with B. C.'s Court of Appeals in the 2002 *Robson* decision (*www.courts.gov.bc.ca/jdb-txt/ca/02/03/2002bcca0354.htm*). In that class action petition the court declared that both Canadian companies *and* their American counterparts can be held liable in Canada for deceptive acts that violate the provincial Trade Practices Act (in this case, Chrysler and GM paint delamination):

At this stage, the plaintiffs are only required to demonstrate that they have a "good arguable case" against the American defendants. The threshold is low. A good arguable case requires only a serious question to be tried, one with some prospect of success: see *AG Armeno Mines*, *supra*, at para. 25 [*AG Armeno Mines and Minerals Inc. v. PT Pukuafu Indah* (2000), 77 B.C.L.R. (3d) 1 (C.A.)]....

Aftermarket products and services—such as gas-saving gadgets, rustproofing, and paint protectors—can render the manufacturer's warranty invalid, so make sure you're in the clear before purchasing any optional equipment or services from an independent supplier.

How fairly a warranty is applied is more important than how long it remains in effect. Once you know the normal wear rate for a mechanical component or body part, you can demand proportional compensation when you get less than normal durability—no matter what the original warranty said.

Some dealers tell customers that they need to have original-equipment parts installed in order to maintain their warranty. A variation on this theme requires that routine servicing—including tune-ups and oil changes (with a certain brand of oil)—be done by the selling dealer, or the warranty is invalidated.

Nothing could be further from the truth.

Canadian law stipulates that whoever issues a warranty cannot make that warranty conditional on the use of any specific brand of motor oil, oil filter, or any other component, unless it's provided to the customer free of charge (listen up, Mercedes, Audi, and VW).

Sometimes dealers will do all sorts of minor repairs that don't correct the problem, and then after the warranty runs out they'll tell you that major repairs are needed. You can avoid this nasty surprise by repeatedly bringing your vehicle in to the dealership before the warranty ends. During each visit, insist that a written work order include the specific nature of the problem as *you* see it and that the work order carry the notation that this is the second, third, or fourth time the same problem has been brought to the dealer's attention. Write it down yourself, if need be. This allows you to show a pattern of non-performance by the dealer during the warranty period and establishes that it's a serious and chronic problem. When the warranty expires, you have the legal right to demand that it be extended on those items consistently reappearing on your handful of work orders. *Lowe v. Fairview Chrysler* (see page 140) is an excellent judgment that reinforces this important principle. In another lawsuit, *François Chong v. Marine Drive Imported Cars Ltd. and Honda Canada Inc.* (see page 139), a Honda owner forced Honda to fix his engine seven times—until they got it right.

A retired GM service manager gave me another effective tactic to use when you're not sure a dealer's warranty "repairs" will actually correct the problem for a reasonable period of time after the warranty expires. Here's what he says you should do:

When you pick up the vehicle after the warranty repair has been done, hand the service manager a note to be put in your file that says you appreciate the warranty repair, however, you intend to return and ask for further warranty coverage if the problem reappears before a reasonable amount of time has elapsed—even if the original warranty has expired. A copy of the same note should be sent to the automaker.... Keep your copy of the note in the glove compartment as cheap insurance against paying for a repair that wasn't fixed correctly the first time.

Extended (supplementary) warranties

Supplementary warranties providing extended coverage may be sold by the manufacturer, dealer, or an independent third party, and are automatically transferred when the vehicle is sold. They cost between $1,000 and $1,500, and should be purchased only if the vehicle you're buying is off its original warranty, if it has a reputation for being unreliable or expensive to service (see Part Four), or if you're reluctant to use the small claims courts when factory-related trouble arises. Don't let the dealer pressure you into deciding right away.

Generally, you can purchase an extended warranty any time during the period in which the manufacturer's warranty is in effect, or, in some cases, shortly after buying the vehicle from a used-car dealer. An automaker's supplementary warranty is the best choice but will likely cost about a third more than warranties sold by independents. And in some parts of the country, notably British Columbia, dealers have a quasi-monopoly on selling warranties, with little competition from the independents.

Dealers love to sell extended warranties, whether you need them or not, because up to 60 percent of the warranty's cost represents dealer markup. Out of the remaining 40 percent comes the sponsor's administration costs and profit margin, calculated at another 15 percent. What's left to pay for repairs is a minuscule 25 percent of the original amount. The only reason that automakers and independent warranty companies haven't been busted for operating this warranty Ponzi scheme is that only half of the car buyers who purchase extended service contracts actually use them.

It's often difficult to collect on supplementary warranties because independent companies frequently go out of business or limit the warranty's coverage through subsequent mailings. Both situations are covered by provincial laws. If the bankrupt warranty company's insurance policy won't cover your claim, take the dealer to small claims court and ask for the repair cost and the refund of the original warranty payment. Your argument for holding the dealer responsible is a simple one: By accepting a commission to act as an agent of the defunct company, the dealer took on the obligations of the company as well. As for limiting the coverage after you have bought the warranty policy, this is illegal, and it allows you to sue both the dealer and the warranty company for a refund of both the warranty and repair costs.

Emissions control warranties

These little-publicized warranties can save you big bucks if major engine or exhaust components fail prematurely. They come with all new vehicles and cover major components of the emissions control system for up to 8 years/ 130,000 km. Unfortunately, although owners' manuals vaguely mention the emissions warranty, most don't specify which parts are covered. Fortunately, the U.S. Environmental Protection Agency has intervened on several occasions with hefty fines against Chrysler and Ford for stonewalling emission-system claims and ruled that all major motor and fuel-system components are covered. These include fuel metering, ignition spark advance, restart, evaporative emissions, positive crankcase ventilation, engine electronics (computer modules), and catalytic converters, as well as hoses, clamps, brackets, pipes, gaskets, belts, seals, and connectors. Canada, however, has no government definition, and it's up to each manufacturer and the small claims courts to decide which components are covered.

Many of the confidential technical service bulletins listed in Part Four show parts failures that are covered under the emissions warranty, even though motorists are routinely charged for their replacement. The following example, applicable to Ford's 2002–2005 Taurus and Sable, shows the automaker will pay for fuel gauge repairs under the emissions warranty. Applying the same principles to other automakers' vehicles should be a breeze.

Fuel Gauge does not read Full after Filling Tank

Bulletin No.: 04-14-14

2002–05   Ford Taurus, Sable

Issue: Some 2002–05 Taurus/Sable vehicles may exhibit a fuel gauge which indicates the tank is only 7/8 full after filling the fuel tank. This may be due to the the caolbration of the fuel level indication unit.

Action: To service, remove the fuel delivery module and replace the fuel level indication unit. DO NOT REPLACE THE ENTIRE FUEL DELIVERY MODULE FOR THIS CONDITION.

Warranty Status: Eligible under provisions of new vehicle limited warranty coverage and emissions warranty coverage.

Operation	Description	Time
041414A	Replace Fuel Gauge tank unit (includes time to remove tank, drain and refill)	1.3hrs

---

Arm yourself with this internal bulletin when asking for a "goodwill" refund from any automaker who tries to hide behind the base warranty.

Unfortunately, few owners will ever see these bulletins, and most will end up paying for repairs that are really Ford's responsibility.

Make sure you get your emissions system checked out thoroughly by a dealer or independent garage before the emissions warranty expires and before having the vehicle inspected by provincial emissions inspectors. In addition to ensuring you pass provincial tests, this precaution could save you up to $1,000 if both your catalytic converter and other emissions components are faulty.

The secret warranty jungle

Few vehicle owners know that secret warranties exist. Automakers are reluctant to make these free repair programs public because they feel that doing so would weaken confidence in their product and increase their legal liability. The closest they come to an admission is sending a "goodwill policy," "product improvement program," or "special policy" technical service bulletin (TSB) to dealers or first owners of record. Consequently, the only motorists who find out about these policies are the original owners who haven't moved or leased their vehicles. The other motorists who get compensated for repairs are the ones who read *Lemon-Aid* each year, staple TSBs to their work orders, and yell the loudest.

Remember, second owners and repairs done by independent garages are included in these secret warranty programs. Large, costly repairs, such as blown engines, burned transmissions, and peeling paint, are often covered. Even mundane little repairs, which can still cost you a hundred bucks or more, are frequently included in these programs.

If you have a TSB, but you're still refused compensation, keep in mind that secret warranties are an admission of manufacturing negligence. Try to compromise with a pro rata adjustment from the manufacturer. If polite negotiations fail, challenge the refusal in court on the grounds that you should not be penalized for failing to make a reimbursement claim under a secret warranty you never knew existed!

Here are a few examples of the latest, most comprehensive secret warranties that have come across my desk in the last several years.

Chrysler

1998–2003 Dodge Durango and Dakota

Problem: Worn, rusted, and broken upper ball joint failure may cause the wheel to fall off; steering loss. Over 1,000 complaints have been recorded by NHTSA. **Warranty coverage:** Chrysler will replace the ball joints at half-cost, on a case-by-case basis up to 5 years/80,000 km. Check out prices: Some owners say their bills were inflated, making the discount illusory.

> I paid $540.70 to have the upper and lower ball joints replaced on the front passenger side of my 2001 Durango. All was fine until I got home and noticed that it was still squeaking. I brought it back to the Dodge dealership and, upon further inspection, was told the new problem was my lower control arm bushings on the same side as my recently replaced ball joints. This time it was going to cost me nearly $1,000 because I was told the bushings were not available separately from the control arm. It finally cost me $180 at an independent tire and alignment shop.

Control arm bushings $7.33

Chrysler, Ford, General Motors, and Asian automakers

All years, all models

Problem: Faulty automatic transmissions that self-destruct, shift erratically, gear down to "limp mode," are slow to shift in or out of Reverse, or are noisy. **Warranty coverage:** If you have the assistance of your dealer's service manager, expect an offer of 50–75 percent (about $1,500). File the case in small claims court and a full refund will be offered up to 7 years/160,000 km. Acura, Honda, Hyundai, Lexus, and Toyota coverage varies between 7 and 8 years.

All years, all models

Problem: Premature wearout of brake pads, calipers, and rotors, especially on SUVs, trucks, and vans. **Warranty coverage:** *Calipers and pads:* Goodwill settlements confirm that brake calipers and pads that fail to last 2 years/40,000 km will be replaced for 50 percent of the repair cost; components not lasting 1 year/20,000 km will be replaced for free. *Rotors:* If they last less than 3 years/60,000 km, they will be replaced at half price; replacement is free up to 2 years/40,000 km. Interestingly, early brake wearout, once mainly a Detroit failing, is now quite common with Asian makes as well.

Apparently, brake suppliers are using cheaper calipers, pads, and rotors that can't handle the heat generated by normal braking on heavier passenger cars, trucks, and vans. Consequently, drivers find routine braking causes rotor warpage that produces excessive vibrations, shuddering, noise, and pulling to one side when braking.

All years, all models

Problem: A nauseating "rotten-egg" smell permeates the interior. **Warranty coverage:** At first owners are told they need a tune-up. Then they are told to change fuel and to wait a few months for the problem to correct itself. When this fails, the catalytic converter will likely be replaced and the power control module recalibrated. Toyota has been particularly hard hit by this stink (see below).

Excessive Sulfur Dioxide Odor

Bulletin No: EG021-04   Date: June 14, 2004

2001–04 Sequoia

Introduction: Some customers may complain of excessive sulfur dioxide odor on 2001–04 model year Sequoia vehicles under the following conditions:

^ Stop and go driving

^ Heavy acceleration

In order to reduce the sulfur dioxide odor, the Electronic Control Module (ECM) (SAE term: Powertrain Control Module/PCM) fuel cut control logic has been modifed and a new catalyst is provided. Follow the repair procedure to reflash the ECM and replace the catalytic converter assembly.

Stinking interiors have affected Toyota's entire model lineup for at least the past five years.

Chrysler, Ford, General Motors, and Honda

All years, all models

Problem: Faulty paint jobs that cause paint to turn white and peel off horizontal panels. **Warranty coverage:** Automakers will offer a free paint job or partial compensation up to 6 years/ no mileage limitation. Thereafter, most manufacturers offer 50–75 percent refunds on the small claims courthouse steps.

In *Frank v. GM*, the Saskatchewan small claims court set a 15-year benchmark for paint finishes, and three other Canadian small claims judgments have extended the benchmark to seven years, second owners, and pickups.

In *Del Guidice v. Honda Canada Inc*, Quebec Superior Court, August, 2004, a class action petition is pending against Honda Canada for paint peeling on 1998–99 Hondas.

Paint peeling on blue/mauve Civic hatchbacks is quite common (*www.adamsgareau.com*).

I wanted to let you and your readers know that the information you publish about Ford's paint failure problem is invaluable. Having read through your "how-to guide" on addressing this issue, I filed suit against Ford for the "latent" paint defect. The day prior to our court date, I received a settlement offer by phone for 75 percent of what I was initially asking for.

This settlement was for a 9-year-old car. I truly believe that Ford hedges a bet that most people won't go to the extent of filing a lawsuit because they are intimidated or simply stop progress after they receive a firm no from Ford.

M. D.

Chrysler, Ford, General Motors, and Hyundai

1994–2003 engine head gasket and intake manifold failures; 1998–99 Hyundai Accent

Problem: Around 60,000–100,000 km the engine may overheat, lose power, burn extra fuel, and, possibly, self-destruct. Under the best of circumstances, the repair will take a day and cost about $800–$1,000. **Warranty coverage:** If you have the assistance of your dealer's service manager, expect a 50 percent offer up to 5 years/100,000 km (about $1,500, if other parts are damaged). 1996 and later Windstars will be covered up to 7 years/160,000 km if you threaten small claims court and cite the *Dufour* or *Reid* Windstar judgments (see page 132).

Engine claims are entering a second phase where the original free repair has to be repaired again. Car owners are told they had one kick at the can and that's it, but, once again, small claims court judges don't always see it that way. Courts have held that the company's first repair was an admission that the product was faulty; its correction must last a reasonable period of time, or be redone.

> I just wanted to let you know that after contacting you back in January regarding our 2001 Chevy Venture head gasket problem, I have just received my judgment through the Canadian Arbitration Program.
>
> I used the sample complaint letter as well as the judgment you have posted in the *Ford Canada v. Dufour* court case. This combined with an avalanche of similar Chevy Venture complaints that are posted on the Internet helped us to win a $1,700 reimbursement of the $2,200 we were looking for.

Ford

1992–2004 coil spring failures

Problem: Defective front coil springs may suddenly break, puncturing the front tire and leading to loss of steering control; particularly troublesome with Focus (2000 model), Taurus, Sable, Aerostar, and Windstar. **Warranty coverage:** Under a "Safety Improvement Campaign," negotiated with NHTSA, Ford will replace *broken* coil springs at no charge up to 10 years/unlimited mileage. The company says it won't replace the springs until they have broken—if you're alive to submit a claim—but has relented when threatened with a lawsuit. 1997–98 models that are registered in rust-belt states and Canada have been recalled for the installation of a protective shield (called a spring catcher bracket in the Canadian recall) to prevent a broken spring from shredding the front tire.

1996–2004 F-series trucks, SUVs, and Windstar vans

Problem: Sudden steering loss due to the premature wear and separation of the steering tie rod ends. **Warranty coverage:** Presently Ford is advising owners to have their vehicles inspected regularly. If pressed, the dealer will replace the component for free up to 5 years/ 100,000 km.

1999–2001 F-150 and Super Duty F-Series pickups, Econoline, Expedition, and Lincoln Navigator

Problem: Faulty engine head gaskets cause oil or coolant leakage, resulting in loss of power, excessive fuel consumption, engine overheating, or complete engine destruction. **Warranty coverage:** Ford will repair or replace affected engines. Insiders say the automaker is spending up to $4,500 (U.S.) to replace the engine and $800 to replace the cylinder heads and head gasket. Ford says that the faulty engines usually fail within the warranty period (according to the April 1, 2002, issue of *Automotive News*), but independent warranty data suggests they may leak at any time.

1997–2001 F-150, 250LD F-Series pickups, Econoline, Expedition, and Lincoln Navigator

Problem: Extensive door bottom and tailgate rusting; cracked outer door panel. **Warranty coverage:** Ford will repair or replace the door or body panels for free up to six years.

CORROSION AT BOTTOM OF DOOR OR TAILGATE
AT HEM FLANGE – REPAIR PROCEDURES

Article No.: 01-9-8   Date: 05/14/0
MODELS: 1997–2001 F-150, F-250LD
ISSUE: Some vehicles may exhibit corrosion at the hem flange at the bottom of any door/tailgate where the outer panel is folded over the inner panel. This may be caused by the adhesive absorbing water during the production process.
ACTION: Repair corrosion at hem flange using new design special hem flange tools and procedures. Refer to the following Service Procedure for details.

CRACK IN OUTER DOOR PANEL – LOWER
REAR CORNER OF WINDOW OPENING

Article No.: 01-18-2   Date: 09/17/01
MODELS: 1997–2000 F-150
          1997–98 F-250LD
ISSUE: Some vehicles may exhibit a cosmetic crack in the outer door panel at the lower rear corner of the window opening. This may be caused by excessive stress on the outer door panel.
ACTION: Inspect, repair, or replace outer door panel.

General Motors

1999–2004 trucks equipped with 3.1, 3.4, 4.3, 4.6 (Northstar), 4.8, 5.3, 5.7(LS1), 6.0 or 8.1L engines

Problem: Engine-damaging piston slap; engine knock; excessive oil consumption; engine failure (*www.pistonslap.com*). **Warranty coverage:** 5 years/ 100,000 km on a case-by-case basis and considerable service manager jawboning.

1994–2000 trucks equipped with a 6.5L diesel engines

Problem: Fuel injection pump failure. **Warranty coverage:** 11 years (Bulletin No.: 00064C; September, 2002).

1996–97 Blazer, Jimmy, and Bravada

Problem: Complete or partial ball joint separation or corrosion. In July 2001, GM recalled 1996 Blazer/Jimmy/Bravada models to replace corroded upper ball joints, but limited its recall to the snowbelt states. However, in November 2001, GM sent dealers a confidential service bulletin (No. 01049) that dropped the snowbelt state limitation and added an additional model year. **Warranty coverage:** All 1996–97 models are covered by a special policy to pay for upper ball joints that have separated up to 8 years or 100,000 miles (161,000 km).

1997–2003 Venture, TranSport/Montana, and Silhouette

Problem: Roof paint delamination and peeling; rust perforation. **Warranty coverage:** GM will replace, repair, or repaint the roof for free up to 6 years/ 100,000 km.

Honda

1998–2003 6-cylinder-engine-equipped Accord, Odyssey, and Pilot models

Problem: Defective aluminum engine block. **Warranty coverage:** Repair or replace engine under a "goodwill" program.

1997–99 CR-V

Problem: Harsh-shifting automatic transmission and torque converter. **Warranty coverage:** Honda will fix or replace the transmission free of charge up to 7 years/160,000 km under a "goodwill" program, whether owners bought their vehicle new or used (bulletin #00-012, published June 26, 2001).

Toyota

1997–2002 Toyota and Lexus vehicles with 2.2L 4-cylinder or 3.0L V6 engines

Problem: Sludge buildup may require a rebuilt engine. **Warranty coverage:** Toyota will repair or replace the engine at no charge up to 8 years/160,000 km (100,000 miles), whether you bought the vehicle new or used. Toyota has said owners will not be forced to show oil change receipts. Some dealers, apparently, haven't gotten the word.

> The service manager quietly told me that there was a "flaw" in the engine but would not elaborate. When I asked if there was a flaw why wouldn't Toyota warranty it, I was told "because you can't prove you did the oil change there is no use taking it to Toyota."
>
> In May 2002 we received the letter mentioned in your article, and we took our 1998 Sienna into the dealer (after spending three weeks talking to them and producing all the oil change records except the

missing one). The engine could not be rebuilt—it had to be replaced. The cost was $5,017.22, finally covered by this goodwill warranty.

T. C., Toronto
Automotive News, February 10, 1997

How Long Should a Part or Repair Last?

How do you know when a part or service doesn't last as long as it should and whether you should seek a full or partial refund? Sure, you have a gut feeling based on the use of the vehicle, how you maintained it, and the extent of work that was carried out. But, you'll need more than emotion to win compensation from garages and automakers.

You can definitely get a refund if a repair or part lasts longer than its guarantee, but not as long as is generally expected. But you'll have to show what the auto industry considers to be reasonable durability.

Automakers, mechanics, and the courts have their own benchmarks as to what's a reasonable period of time or amount of mileage one should expect a part or adjustment to last. Consequently, I've prepared the following table to show what most automakers consider is reasonable durability, as expressed by their original and "goodwill" warranties.

ACCESSORIES

Air conditioner	7 years
Cruise control	5 years/ 100,000 km
Power antenna	5 years
Power doors, windows	5 years
Radio	5 years

BODY

Paint (peeling)	7 years
Rust (perforations)	7 years
Rust (surface)	5 years
Water/wind/air leaks	5 years

BRAKE SYSTEM

Brake drum	120,000 km
Brake drum linings	35,000 km
Brake rotor	60,000 km
Disc brake calipers	30,000 km
Disc brake pads	30,000 km
Master cylinder, rebuild	100,000 km
Wheel cylinder, rebuild	80,000 km

ENGINE AND DRIVETRAIN

Constant velocity joint	6 years/ 160,000 km
Differential	7 years/ 160,000 km
Engine (gas)	7 years/ 160,000 km
Head gasket/Intake manifold	7 years/ 160,000 km
Transfer case	7 years/ 150,000 km
Transmission (auto.)	7 years/ 150,000 km
Transmission (man.)	10 years/ 250,000 km
Transmission oil cooler	5 years/ 100,000 km

EXHAUST SYSTEM

Catalytic converter	5–7 years/ 100,000 km or more
Muffler	2 years/ 40,000 km
Tailpipe	3 years/ 60,000 km

IGNITION SYSTEM

Cable set	60,000 km
Electronic module	5–7 years/ 160,000 km
Retiming	20,000 km
Spark plugs	40,000 km
Tune-up	20,000 km

SAFETY COMPONENTS

Airbags	life of vehicle
ABS brakes	7 years/ 160,000 km
ABS computer	10 years/ 160,000 km
Seatbelts	life of vehicle

STEERING AND SUSPENSION

Alignment	1 year/ 20,000 km
Ball joints	80,000 km
Power steering	5 years/ 80,000 km
Shock absorber	2 years/ 40,000 km
Struts	5 years/ 80,000 km
Tires (radial)	5 years/ 80,000 km
Wheel bearing	3 years/ 60,000 km

VISIBILITY

Halogen/foglights	3 years/ 60,000 km
Sealed beam	2 years/ 40,000 km
Windshield wiper motor	5 years/ 80,000 km

Much of the preceding guidelines were extrapolated from Chrysler and Ford payouts to thousands of dissatisfied customers over the past decade, in addition to Chrysler's original 7-year powertrain warranty applicable from 1991–95 and re-applied since 2001. Other sources for this chart were the Ford and GM transmission warranties outlined in their secret warranties; Ford, GM, and Toyota engine "goodwill" programs laid out in their internal service bulletins; and court judgments where judges have given their own guidelines as to what is reasonable durability.

Safety features—with the exception of ABS—generally have a lifetime warranty. Chrysler's 10-year "free-service" program portion of its 1993–99 ABS recall can serve as a handy benchmark as to how long one can expect these components to last on more recent models.

Airbags are a different matter. Those that are deployed in an accident—and the personal injury and interior damage their deployment will likely have caused—are covered by your accident insurance policy. However, if there is a sudden deployment for no apparent reason, the automaker and dealer should be held jointly responsible for all injuries and damages caused by the airbag.

You can prove their liability by downloading your vehicle's data recorder data. This will likely lead to a more generous settlement from the two parties and prevent your insurance premiums from being jacked up. Inadvertent deployment may occur after passing over a bump in the road, slamming the car door, or, in some Chrysler minivans, simply putting the key in the ignition. This happens more often than you might imagine, judging by the hundreds of recalls and thousands of complaints recorded on NHTSA's website.

Use the manufacturer's emissions warranty as your primary guideline for the expected durability of high-tech electronic and mechanical pollution control components, such as powertrain control modules (PCM) and catalytic converters. Look first at your owner's manual for an indication of which parts on your vehicle are covered. If you come up with few specifics, ask the auto manufacturer for a list of specific components covered by the emissions warranty. If you're stonewalled, ask your local MP to get the info from Transport Canada or Environment Canada, and invest $25 (U.S.) in an ALLDATA service bulletin subscription.

Recall repairs

Vehicles are recalled for one of two reasons: They may be unsafe or they don't conform to federal pollution control regulations. Whatever the reason, recalls are a great way to get free repairs—if you know which ones apply to you and you have the patience of Job.

Almost a half billion unsafe vehicles have been recalled by automakers for the free correction of safety-related defects since American recall legislation was passed in 1966 (a weaker Canadian law was enacted in 1971). During that time, about one-third of the recalled vehicles never made it back to the dealership for repairs because owners were never informed, they just didn't consider the defect that hazardous, or they gave up waiting for corrective parts.

Subsequent American legislation targets automakers who drag their feet in making recall repairs. Owners on both sides of the border may wish to cite the following NHTSA guidelines for support:

Dealer Recall Responsibility—For U.S. and IPC (U.S. States, Territories, and Possessions)

The U.S. National Traffic and Motor Vehicle Safety Act provides that each vehicle that is subject to a recall must be adequately repaired within a reasonable time after the customer has tendered it for repair. A failure to repair within 60 days after tender of a vehicle is *prima facie* evidence of failure to repair within a reasonable time. If the condition is not adequately repaired within a reasonable time, the customer may be entitled to an identical or reasonably equivalent vehicle at no charge or to a refund of the purchase price less a reasonable allowance for depreciation. To avoid having to provide these burdensome remedies, every effort must be made to promptly schedule an appointment with each customer and to repair their vehicle as soon as possible.

(GM Bulletin No.: 00064C, issued September, 2002)

If you've moved or bought a used vehicle, it's smart to pay a visit to your local dealer, give him your address, and get a "report card" on which recalls, free-service campaigns, and warranties apply to your vehicle. Simply give the service advisor the identification number (VIN)—found on the dash just below the windshield on the driver's side, or on your insurance card—and have the number run through the automaker's computer system. Ask for a computer printout of the vehicle's history (have it faxed to you, if you're so equipped) and make sure you're listed in the automaker's computer as the new owner. This ensures that you'll receive notices of warranty extensions and emissions and safety recalls.

Regional recalls

Don't let any dealer refuse you recall repairs because of where you live.

In order to cut recall costs, many automakers try to limit a recall to vehicles in a certain designated region. This practice doesn't make sense, since cars are mobile and an unsafe, rust-cankered steering unit can be found anywhere— not just in certain Rust Belt provinces or American states.

In 2001, Ford attempted to limit to five American states its recall of faulty Firestone tires. Public ridicule of the company's proposal led to an extension of the recall throughout North America.

In July 2004, Ford announced a regional recall to install protective spring shields on almost one million 1999, 2000, and 2001 model-year Taurus and Sable sedans to correct defective front springs that can break and puncture a tire. As it did for Windstars and Aerostars recalled earlier for the same problem, Ford says it will send recall letters only to owners whose vehicles are registered in high-corrosion areas, or where salt is used on roads.

Wherever you live or drive, don't expect to be welcomed with open arms when your vehicle develops a safety- or emissions-related problem that's not yet part of a recall campaign. Automakers and dealers generally take a restrictive view of what constitutes a safety or emissions defect and frequently charge for repairs that should be free under federal safety or emissions legislation. To counter this tendency, look at the following list of typical defects that are clearly safety related. If you experience similar problems, insist that the automaker fix the problem at no expense to yourself, including a car rental:

- airbag malfunctions
- corrosion affecting safe operation
- disconnected or stuck accelerators
- electrical shorts
- faulty windshield wipers
- fuel leaks
- problems with original axles, drive shafts, seats, seat recliners, or defrosters
- seat belt problems
- stalling or sudden acceleration
- sudden steering or brake loss
- suspension failures
- trailer coupling failures

In the U.S., recall campaigns force automakers to pay the entire cost of fixing a vehicle's safety-related defect for any vehicle purchased up to eight years before the recall's announcement. A reasonable period beyond that time is usually a slam-dunk in small claims court. Recalls may be voluntary or ordered by the U.S. Department of Transportation. Canadian regulation has an added twist: Transport Canada can only order automakers to notify owners that their vehicles may be unsafe; it can't force them to correct the problem. Fortunately, most U.S.-ordered recalls are carried out in Canada, and when Transport Canada makes a defect determination on its own, automakers generally comply with an owner notification letter.

Voluntary recall campaigns, frequently called Special Service or Safety Improvement Campaigns, are a real problem, though. The government doesn't monitor the notification of owners; dealers and automakers routinely deny there's a recall, thereby dissuading most claimants; and the company's so-called fix, not authorized by any governing body, may not correct the hazard at all. Also, the voluntary recall may leave out many of the affected models or unreasonably exclude certain owners.

Safety defect information

If you wish to report a safety defect or want recall info, you may access Transport Canada's website at *www.tc.gc.ca/roadsafety/recalls/search_e.asp*. You can get recall information in French or English, as well as general information relating to road safety and importing a vehicle into Canada. Web surfers can now access the recall database for 1970–2004 model vehicles but, unlike NHTSA's website, owner complaints aren't listed, defect investigations aren't disclosed, voluntary warranty extensions (secret warranties) aren't shown, and service bulletin summaries aren't provided. You can also call Transport Canada at 1-800-333-0510 (toll-free within Canada) or 613-993-9851 (within the Ottawa region or outside Canada) to get additional information.

If you're not happy with Ottawa's treatment of your recall inquiry, try NHTSA's website. It's more complete than Transport Canada's (NHTSA's database is updated daily and covers vehicles built since 1952). You can search the database for your vehicle or tires at *www.nhtsa.dot.gov/cars/problems*. You'll get immediate access to four essential database categories applicable to your vehicle and model year: The latest recalls, current and closed safety investigations, defects reported by other owners, and a brief summary of TSBs.

NHTSA's fax-back service provides the same info through a local line that can be accessed from Canada—although long-distance charges will apply. (Most calls take 5–10 minutes to complete.) The following local numbers get you into the automatic response service quickly and can be reached 24 hours a day: 202-366-0123 (202-366-7800 for the hearing impaired).

"Black box" recorders

Forget privacy rights. If your car has an airbag, it's probably spying on you.

Event data recorders (EDRs) the size of a VCR tape have been hidden under the seat or in the centre consoles of about 30 million airbag-equipped Ford and GM vehicles since the early 1990s. Presently, about 30 percent of all domestic and imported cars carry them.

Vetronix Crash Data Retrieval System
pictured above sells for $2,495 U.S.
(Courtesy: Vetronix.)

The data recorders operate in a similar fashion to flight data recorders used in airplanes: Recording data during the last five seconds before impact, including the force of the collision, the airbag's performance, when the brakes were applied, engine and vehicle speed, gas pedal position, and whether the driver was wearing a seat belt.

Apart from the "invasion of privacy" aspect of hiding recorders in customers' vehicles, Ford and GM have systematically hidden their collected data from U.S. and Canadian vehicle safety researchers investigating thousands of complaints relating to airbags that don't deploy when they should (or deploy when they shouldn't) and anti-lock brakes that don't brake.

This refusal to voluntarily share data with customers and researchers is unfortunate, because the recorders are collecting critical information that could lead to better-functioning safety devices. In fact, experts say that highway safety could be vastly improved if black boxes that record information about car crashes were installed in all cars, just as similar devices are placed in all airplanes.

To find out if your car or truck carries an EDR, go to: *www.cbc.ca/consumers/ market/files/cars/blackboxes.*

Fortunately, it has become impossible for automakers to hide recorder data now that Vitronix Corporation sells a $2,500 (U.S.) portable download device that accesses the data and stores it on any PC. It's presently marketed to accident reconstructionists, safety researchers, law enforcement agencies, and insurance companies. Furthermore, litigants can subpoena the info through an automaker's dealer, if the data is needed in court.

Car owners who wish to dispute criminal charges, oppose their insurer's decision, or hold an automaker responsible for a safety device's failure (airbags, seat belts, or brakes) will find this data invaluable.

Safety benefits

Enthusiastically promoted by government and law enforcement agencies around the world, these data recorders have actually had a positive effect in accident prevention: A 1992 study by the European Union cited by the Canada Safey Council found that EDRs reduced the collision rate by 28 percent and costs by 40 percent in police fleets where drivers knew they were being monitored.

The recorders are also sending people to jail, helping accident victims reap huge court awards, and prompting automaker recalls of unsafe vehicles. In January of 2004, South Dakota Congressman Bill Janklow was convicted of manslaughter for speeding through a stop sign—they used his EDR readout to prove he was driving faster than the speed limit, but slower than police estimated. In October of 2003, Montreal police won their first dangerous driving conviction using EDR data (*R. v. Gauthier*, (2003-05-27) QCCQ 500-01-013375-016, *www.canlii.org/qc/jug/qccq/2003/ 2003qccq17860.html*). In June of 2003, Edwin Matos of Pembroke Pines, Florida was sentenced to 30 years in prison for killing two teenage girls after crashing into their car at more than 160 km/h (100 mph). The recorder's speed data convicted him. Two months earlier, an Illinois police officer received a $10 million (U.S.) settlement after data showed the driver of an empty hearse, who was supposedly unconscious from a diabetes attack, actually accelerated and braked in the moments before slamming into the officer's patrol car. In July of 2002, New Brunswick prosecutors sent a dangerous driver to jail for two years based on his car's EDR data. (*R. v. Daley*, 2003 NBQB 20 Docket(s): S/CR/7/02, *www.canlii.org/nb/cas/nbqb/2002/ 2003nbqb20.html*). GM was forced to recall more than 850,000 Cavaliers and Sunfires when its own data recorders showed that the cars' airbags often deployed inadvertently. Incidentally, California is the only jurisdiction where EDR data cannot be downloaded unless the car owner agrees or a court order is issued.

A chronological list of dozens of Canadian and American court cases related to automotive Event Data Recorders has been prepared by Harris Technical Services (traffic accident reconstructionists) and is available at *www.harristechnical.com.*

By the way, 25 percent of rental cars have tracking devices that can be remotely monitored by computers. They can tell if you have violated your rental agreement by speeding, driving off-road, or crossing into another state or province. In extreme circumstances they can disable the car.

Three Steps to a Settlement

Step 1: Informal negotiations

If your vehicle was misrepresented, has major defects, or wasn't properly repaired under warranty, the first thing you should do is give the seller (the dealer and automaker or a private party) a written summary (by registered mail or fax) of the outstanding problems and stipulate a time period in which they will need to be corrected or your money refunded. Keep a copy for yourself, along with all your repair records. Be sure to check all of the sales and warranty documents you were given to see if they conform to provincial laws. Any errors, omissions, or violations can be used to get a settlement with the dealer in lieu of making a formal complaint.

At the beginning, try to work things out informally and, in your attempt to reach a settlement, keep in mind the cardinal rule: Ask only for what is fair and don't try to make anyone look bad.

Speak in a calm, polite manner and try to avoid polarizing the issue. Talk about how "we can work together" on the problem. Let a compromise slowly emerge—don't come in with a hardline set of demands. Don't demand the settlement offer in writing, but make sure that you're accompanied by a friend or relative who can confirm the offer in court if it isn't honoured. Be prepared to act upon the offer without delay so your hesitancy won't be blamed for its withdrawal.

Dealer/service manager

Service managers have more power than you may have realized. They make the first determination of what work is covered under warranty or through post-warranty "goodwill" programs and are directly responsible to the dealer and manufacturer for that decision (dealers hate manufacturer audits that force them to pay back questionable warranty decisions). Service managers are paid to save the dealer and automaker money and to mollify irate clients—almost an impossible balancing act. Nevertheless, when a service manager agrees to extend warranty coverage, it's because you've raised solid issues that neither the dealer nor automaker can ignore. All the more reason to present your argument in a confident, forthright manner with your vehicle's service history and *Lemon-Aid*'s "How Long Should Parts/Repairs Last?" chart. Also bring as many technical service bulletins and owner complaint printouts as you can find, from websites like NHTSA's. It's not important that they apply directly to your problem; they establish parameters for giving out after-warranty assistance or "goodwill."

Don't use your salesperson as a runner, since the sales staff are generally quite distant from the service staff and usually have less pull than you do. If the service manager can't or won't set things right, your next step is to convene a mini-summit with the service manager, the dealership principal, and the automaker's rep. By getting the automaker involved, you run less risk of having the dealer fob you off on the manufacturer and you can often get an agreement where the seller and automaker pay two-thirds of the repair cost. Independent dealers and dealers who sell a brand of used vehicle that they don't sell new give you less latitude. You have to make the case that the vehicle's defects were present at the time of purchase or should have been known to the seller, or that the vehicle doesn't conform to the representations made when it was purchased. Emphasize that you intend to use the courts if necessary to obtain a refund—most independent sellers would rather settle than risk a lawsuit with all the attendant publicity. An independent estimate of the vehicle's defects and cost of repairs is essential if you want to convince the seller that you're serious in your claim and stand a good chance of winning your case in court. Come prepared with an estimated cost of repairs to challenge the dealer who agrees to pay half the repair costs and then jacks up the costs 100 percent so that you wind up paying the whole shot.

Step 2: Sending a registered letter, fax, or email

This is the next step to take if your claim is refused. Send the dealer and manufacturer a polite registered letter or fax that asks for compensation for repairs that have been done or need to be done; insurance costs while the vehicle is being repaired; towing charges; supplementary transportation costs like taxis and rented cars; and damages for inconvenience.

Specify five days (but allow 10) for either party to respond. If no satisfactory offer is made, file suit in small claims court. Make the manufacturer a party to the lawsuit, especially if the emissions warranty, a secret warranty extension, a safety recall campaign, or extensive chassis rusting is involved.

New Vehicle Complaint Letter/Fax/Email
Without Prejudice

Date:
Name and address of dealer:
Name and address of manufacturer:

Please be advised that I am not satisfied with my _____ (indicate year, make, model, and serial number of vehicle). The vehicle was purchased on (indicate date) and currently indicates _____ km on the odometer. The vehicle presently exhibits the following defects:
     1. Premature rusting
     2. Paint peeling/discoloration
     3. Water leaks
     4. Other defects (explain)

(List previous attempts to repair the vehicle. Attach a copy of a report from an independent garage, showing cost of estimated repairs and confirming the manufacturer's responsibility.)

I hereby request that you correct these defects free of charge under the terms of the implied warranty provisions of provincial consumer protection statutes as applied in *Kravitz v. General Motors* (1979), I.S.C.R., and *Chabot v. Ford* (1983), 39 O.R. (2d).

If you do not correct the defects noted above to my satisfaction and within a reasonable length of time, I will be obliged to ask an independent garage to _____ (choose [a] estimate or [b] carry out) the repairs and claim the amount of $_____ (state the cost, if possible) by way of the courts without further notice or delay.

I have dealt with your company because of its competence and honesty. I close in the hope of hearing from you within five (5) days of receiving this letter, failing which I will exercise the alternatives available to me. Please govern yourself accordingly.

Sincerely,

(signed with telephone or fax number)

Used Vehicle Complaint Letter/Fax/Email
Without Prejudice

Date: _____
Name: _____

Please be advised that I am dissatisfied with my used vehicle, a (state model), for the following reasons:

1. _____
2. _____
3. _____
4. _____
5. _____

In compliance with the provincial consumer protection laws and the "implied warranty" set down by the Supreme Court of Canada in *Donoghue v. Stevenson, Wharton v. GM,* and *Sharman v. Ford Canada,* I hereby request that these defects be repaired without charge.

This vehicle has not been reasonably durable and is, therefore, not as represented to me.

Should you fail to repair these defects in a satisfactory manner and within a reasonable period of time, I shall get an estimate of the repairs from an independent source and claim them in court, without further delay. I also reserve my right to claim up to $1 million for punitive damages, pursuant to the Supreme Court of Canada's February 22, 2002, ruling in *Whiten v. Pilot.*
I have dealt with your company because of its honesty, competence, and sincere regard for its clients. I am sure that my case is the exception and not the rule.

A positive response within the next five (5) days would be appreciated.

Sincerely,

(signed with telephone number, fax number, or email address)

Step 3: Mediation and arbitration

If the formality of a courtroom puts you off or you're not sure that your claim is all that solid and don't want to pay legal costs to find out, consider using mediation or arbitration. These services are sponsored by the Better Business Bureau, the Automobile Protection Association, the Canadian Automobile Association, the Canadian Automobile Manufacturers Vehicle Arbitration

Program at *www.camvap.ca* (if you bought your vehicle new), small claims court (mediation is often a prerequisite to going to trial), and consumer mediation services set up by provincial and territorial governments.

> I just won my case with Chrysler Canada over my 2003 Ram SLT 4X4 quad cab truck. I've been having PCV valves freezing up (5 PCVs in 9000 km). After one month in the shop, I went to CAMVAP to put in my claim, went to arbitration and won. They have agreed to buy back my truck.

Getting outside help

Don't lose your case due to poor preparation. Ask government or independent consumer protection agencies to evaluate how well you're prepared before going to your first hearing. Also, use the Internet to ferret out additional facts and gather support (*www.lemonaidcars.com* is a good place to start, and Ontario consumers may file an online claim with the Ontario Motor Vehicle Industry Council at *ewconsumers.omvic.on.ca/complaint/complaint.asp*). By the way, OMVIC is the dealer's self-defense lobby. It's made up of 9,000 registered dealers and 20,000 registered salespersons and has a mandate to maintain a fair, safe, and informed marketplace in Ontario by protecting the rights of consumers, enhancing industry professionalism, and ensuring fair, honest, and open competition for registered motor vehicle dealers.

Online services/Internet/websites

America Online is a good online service provider with active consumer forums that use experts to answer consumer queries and to provide legal and technical advice. The Internet offers the same information using a worldwide database. If you or someone you know is able to create a website, you might consider using this site to attract attention to your plight and arm yourself for arbitration or court. You may wish to follow the example of some existing websites I've listed in Appendix I.

Classified ads and television exposés

Put an ad in the local paper describing your plight and ask for data from others who may have experienced a problem similar to your own. This alerts owners to the potential problem, helps build a base for a class action or group meeting with the automaker, and puts pressure on the local dealer and manufacturer to settle. Sometimes the paper's news desk will assign someone to cover your story after your ad is published.

Television producers and their researchers need articulate consumers with issues that are easily filmed and understood. If you want media coverage, you must summarize your complaint and have visual aids that will hold the viewer's interest. Paint delamination? Show your car. Bought a lemon car? Show your bills along with the car. Holding a demonstration? Make it a "lemon" parade: Target one of the largest dealers; give your group a nifty name, like CLOG or

FFLOG (Chrysler Lemon Owners Group or Ford Focus Lemon Owners Group); and make sure the vehicles are decorated with signs and lemons.

In tailoring your story for TV, keep in mind that the viewers should be able to understand the issues with the sound turned off.

Federal and provincial consumer affairs

The wind left the sails of the consumer movement over two decades ago, leaving consumer agencies understaffed and unsupported by the government. This has created a passive mindset among many staffers, who are tired of getting their heads kicked in by businesses, deadwood bosses, and budget cutters.

Consumer affairs offices can still help with investigation, mediation, and some litigation. Strong and effective consumer protection legislation has been left standing in most of the provinces, and resourceful consumers can use these laws in conjunction with media coverage to prod provincial consumer affairs offices into action. Furthermore, provincial bureaucrats aren't as well shielded from criticism as their federal counterparts. A call to your MPP or MLA, or to their executive assistant, can often get things rolling.

Federal consumer protection is a government-created PR myth. Don't expect the staffers in the reorganized Office of Consumer Affairs to be very helpful—they've been de-fanged and de-gummed through budget cuts and a succession of ineffective ministers. Although the beefed-up Competition Act has some bite with regards to misleading advertising and a number of other illegal business practices, the federal government has been more reactive than proactive in applying the law.

Nevertheless, you can lodge a formal complaint with Ottawa for misleading advertising, odometer tampering, or price fixing at *https:strategis.ic.gc.ca/ sc_mrksv/competit/complaint/form.html.* An online complaint sent to the address above made Toyota cease its ACCESS price-fixing practices (though rumour has it, the company's dealers may try it on their own).

Invest in protest

You can have fun and put additional pressure on a seller or garage by putting a lemon sign on your car and parking it in front of the dealer or garage; creating a "lemon" website; or forming a self-help group like the Chrysler Lemon Owners Group (CLOG), or the Ford Lemon Owners Group (FLOG).

After forming your group, you can then have the occasional parade of creatively decorated cars visit area dealerships as the local media are convened. Just remember to keep your remarks pithy and factual, don't interfere with traffic or customers, and remain peaceful.

Use your website to gather data from others who may have experienced a problem similar to your own. This alerts others to the potential problem, helps build a base for a class action or group meeting with the automaker, and puts pressure on the dealer or manufacturer to settle. Sometimes the news media will assign someone to cover your story after the website is set up.

One other piece of advice from this consumer advocate with hundreds of picketing and mass demonstrations under his belt over the past 34 years: Keep a sense of humour and never break off negotiations.

Finally, don't be scared off by threats that it's illegal to criticize a product or company. Unions, environmentalists, and consumer groups do it regularly ("informational" picketing) and the Supreme Court of Canada in *R. v. Guinard* reaffirmed this right in February, 2002. In that judgment, an insurance policy-holder posted a sign on his barn claiming the Commerce Insurance Company was unfairly refusing his claim. The municipality of St-Hyacinthe told him to take the sign down. He refused, maintaining that he had the right to state his opinion. The Supreme Court agreed.

This judgment means that consumer protests, signs, and websites that crit-icize the actions of corporations cannot be banned simply because they say unpleasant things.

The Art of Complaining

Sudden acceleration, chronic stalling, and ABS and airbag failures

Incidents of sudden acceleration or chronic stalling are quite common. However, they are very difficult to diagnose and are treated quite differently by federal safety agencies.

Sudden acceleration is considered to be a safety-related problem—stalling isn't. Never mind that a vehicle's sudden loss of power on a busy highway puts everyone's lives at risk (2001–03 VW and Audi ignition coil failures). The same problem exists with engine and transmission powertrain failures, which are only occasionally considered to be safety related. ABS and airbag failures are universally considered to be life-threatening defects. If your vehicle mani-fests any of these conditions, here's what you need to do:

1. Get independent witnesses to the fact that the problem exists. This includes verification by an independent mechanic, passenger accounts, downloaded data from your vehicle's data recorder (see pages 112–114) and lots of Internet browsing using *www.lemonaidcars.com* and Google's browser as your primary tools. Notify the dealer/manufacturer by fax, email, or registered letter that you consider the problem to be a factory-induced, safety-related defect. Make sure you address your correspondence to the manufacturer's product liability or legal affairs department. At the dealership's service bay, make sure that every work order clearly states the problem, as well as the number of previous attempts to fix it. (This should result in you having a few complaint letters and a handful of work orders confirming that this is an ongoing deficiency.) If the dealer won't give you a copy of the work order because the work is a warranty claim, ask for a copy of the order number "in case your estate wishes to file a claim, pur-suant to an accident." (This will get the service manager's attention.) Leaving this kind of paper trail is crucial for any claim you may have later on because it shows your fear and persistence, and clearly indicates that the dealer and manufacturer had ample time to correct the defect.

2. Note on the work order that you expect the problem to be diagnosed and corrected under the emissions warranty or a "goodwill" program. It also wouldn't hurt to add the phrase on the work order or in your claim letters that any deaths, injuries, or damage caused by the defect will be the dealer's and manufacturer's responsibility since this work order (or letter, fax, or email) constitutes you putting them on formal notice.

3. If the dealer does the necessary repairs at little or no cost to you, send a follow-up confirmation that you appreciate the assistance. Also, emphasize that you'll be back if the problem reappears, even if the warranty has expired, because the repair renews your warranty rights applicable to that defect. In other words, the warranty clock is set back to its original position. Understand that you won't likely get a copy of the repair bill, either, because dealers don't like to admit that there was a serious defect present. Keep in mind, however, that you can get your complete vehicle file from the dealer and manufacturer by issuing a subpoena (the cost is about $50) if the case goes to small claims or a higher court. This request has produced many out-of-court settlements when the internal documents show extensive work was carried out to correct the problem.

4. If the problem persists, send a letter, fax, or email to the dealer and manufacturer saying so, look for ALLDATA service bulletins to confirm your vehicle's defects are factory related, and call Transport Canada or NHTSA or log onto NHTSA's website (*www.nhtsa.dot.gov*) to report the failure. Also, call the Nader-founded Center for Auto Safety in Washington, D.C., (202-328-7700) for a lawyer referral and an information sheet covering the problem. For tire complaints, also notify researchers at the Strategic Safety website (*www.strategicsafety.com*).

5. Now come two crucial questions: Repair the defect now or later? Use the dealer or an independent? Generally it's smart to use an independent garage if you know the dealer isn't pushing for free corrective repairs from the manufacturer; weeks or months have passed without any resolution of your claim; the dealer keeps repeating it's a maintenance item; and you know an independent mechanic who will give you a detailed work order showing the defect is factory related and not due to poor maintenance. Don't mention that a court case may ensue, since this will scare the dickens out of your only independent witness. An added bonus is that the repair charges will be about half of what a dealer would demand. Incidentally, if the automaker later denies warranty "goodwill" because you used an independent repairer, use the argument that the defect's safety implications required emergency repairs, carried out by whomever could see you first.

6. Dashboard-mounted warning lights usually come on prior to airbags suddenly deploying, ABS brakes failing, or engine glitches causing the vehicle to stall out. (Sudden acceleration usually occurs without warning.) Automakers consider these lights to be critical safety warnings and generally advise drivers to *immediately* have the vehicle serviced to correct the problem (advice found in the owner's manual) when any of the above lights come on. This bolsters the argument that your life was threatened,

emergency repairs were required, and your request for another vehicle or a complete refund isn't out of line.

7. Sudden acceleration can have multiple causes, isn't easy to duplicate, and is often blamed on the driver mistaking the accelerator for the brakes or failing to perform proper maintenance. Yet NHTSA data shows that with the 1992–2000 Explorer, for example, a faulty cruise control or PCV valve and poorly mounted pedals are the most likely causes of the Explorer's sudden acceleration. So how do you satisfy the burden of proof showing the problem exists and is the automaker's responsibility? Use the legal doctrine called "the balance of probabilities" by eliminating all of the possible dodges the dealer or manufacturer may employ. Show that proper maintenance has been carried out, you're a safe driver, and the incident occurs frequently and without warning.

8. If any of the above defects causes an accident, the airbag fails to deploy, or you're injured by its deployment, ask your insurance company to have the vehicle towed to a neutral location and clearly state that neither the dealer nor automaker should touch the vehicle until your insurance company and Transport Canada have completed their investigation. Also, get as many witnesses as possible and immediately go to the hospital for a check-up, even if you're feeling okay. You may be injured and not know it because the adrenalin coursing through your veins is masking your injuries. Plus, a hospital exam will easily confirm that your injuries are accident related, which is essential in court or for future settlement negotiations.

9. Peruse NHTSA's online accident database to find reports of other accidents caused by the same failure.

10. Don't let your insurance company settle the case if you're sure the accident was caused by a mechanical failure. Even if an engineering analysis fails to directly implicate the manufacturer or dealer, you can always plead the aforementioned balance of probabilities. If the insurance company settles, your insurance premiums will probably be increased.

Treacherous tires

Tires aren't usually covered by car manufacturers' warranties (except for GM and Ford), and are instead warranted by the tiremaker on a pro-rated basis. This isn't such a good deal, because the manufacturer is making a profit by charging you the full list price. If you were to buy the same replacement tire from a discount store, you'd likely pay less, without the pro-rated rebate.

But consumers have gained additional rights following Bridgestone/ Firestone's massive 2001 recall of its defective ATX II and Wilderness tires. Due to the confusion and chaos surrounding Firestone's handling of the recall, Ford's 575 Canadian dealers stepped into the breach and replaced the tires with any equivalent tires dealers had in stock, no questions asked.

This is an important precedent that tears down the traditional wall separating tire manufacturers from automakers in product liability claims. In essence, whoever sells the product can now be held liable for damages. In the future, Canadian consumers will have an easier time holding the dealer, automaker, and tire manufacturer liable, not just for recalled products, but for any defect that affects the safety or reasonable durability of that product.

This is particularly true now that the Supreme Court of Canada (*Winnipeg Condominium v. Bird Construction* [1995] 1S.C.R.85) has ruled that defendants are liable in negligence for any designs that resulted in a risk to the public for safety or health. The Supreme Court reversed a long-standing policy and provided the public with a new cause of action that had not existed before in Canada. Tire companies are far easier to deal with than automobile manufacturers because, under the legal doctrine of *res ipsa loquitor* (liability is shown by the failure), tires aren't supposed to fail. It's for this reason that tire companies try to avoid liability by imputing blame to someone or something else, like punctures, impact damage, overloading, over-inflating, or under-inflating. If you have a premature tire failure, consider the 10 steps outlined previously, and include the following:

1. Access NHTSA and Strategic Safety websites on the Internet (see Appendix I) for current data on which tires are failure prone and which companies are under investigation, conducting recalls, or carrying out "silent recalls."
2. Keep the tire. If the tiremaker says an analysis must be done, permit only a portion of the tire to be taken away.
3. Plead the balance of probabilities, using friends and family to refute the tire company's contention that you caused the failure.
4. Ask for damages that are adequate for the replacement of all the tires on your vehicle, including mounting costs.
5. Include in your damage claim any repairs needed to fix body damage caused by the tire's failure.

Paint and body defects

Chrysler blamed bird excrement and the sun for its paint problems.

The following settlement advice applies mainly to paint defects, but you can use these tips for any other vehicle defect that you believe is the automaker's or dealer's responsibility. If you're not sure that the problem is a factory-related deficiency or a maintenance item, have it checked out by an independent garage or get a technical service bulletin summary for your vehicle. The summary may include specific bulletins relating to the diagnosis, correction, and ordering of upgraded parts needed to fix your problem.

1. If you believe the paint problem is factory related, take your vehicle to the dealer and ask for a written, signed estimate of what the service manager feels needs to be done. When you're handed the estimate, ask if the paint job can be covered by some "goodwill" assistance. (Ford's euphemism for this secret warranty is "Owner Notification Program" or "Owner Dialogue Program," GM's term is "Special Policy," and Chrysler simply calls it "Owner Satisfaction Notice" or "goodwill." Don't use the term "secret warranty" yet; you'll just make everyone angry and evasive.)

2. Your request will probably be met with a refusal, an offer to repaint the vehicle for half the cost, or (if you're lucky) an agreement to repaint the vehicle free of charge. If you accept half the costs, make sure that it's based on the original estimate you have in hand, since some dealers jack up their estimates so that your 50 percent is really 100 percent of the true cost.

3. If the dealer or automaker has already refused your claim and the repair hasn't been done yet, get an additional estimate from an independent garage that shows the problem is factory related.

4. Again, if the repair has yet to be done, mail or fax a registered claim to the automaker (send a copy to the dealer), claiming the average of both estimates. If the repair has been done at your expense, mail or fax a registered claim with a copy of your bill.

5. If you don't receive a satisfactory response within a week, deposit a copy of the estimate or paid bill and claim letter/fax before the small claims court and await a trial date. This means that the automaker/dealer will have to appear, no lawyer is required, and costs should be minimal (under $100). Usually, an informal pretrial mediation hearing with the two parties and a court clerk will be scheduled in a few months, followed by a trial a few weeks later (the time varies among different regions). Most cases are settled at the mediation stage.

Things that you can do to help your case: Collect photographs, maintenance work orders, previous work orders dealing with your problem, and technical service bulletins; and speak to an independent expert (the garage or body shop that did the estimate or repair is best, but you can also use a local teacher who teaches automotive repair). Remember, service bulletins can be helpful, but they aren't critical to a successful claim. Concentrate on what you can prove happened to your vehicle, not what may have occurred as outlined in the TSB.

Other situations

- If the vehicle has just been repainted but the dealer says that "goodwill" coverage was denied by the automaker, pay for the repair with a certified cheque and write "under protest" on the cheque. Remember, though, that if the dealer does the repair, you won't have an independent expert who can affirm that the problem was factory related or that it was a result of premature wearout. Plus, the dealer can say that you or the environment caused the paint problem. In these cases, technical service bulletins can make or break your case.
- If the dealer/automaker offers a partial repair or refund, take it. Then sue for the rest. Remember, if a partial repair has been done under warranty, it counts as an admission of responsibility, no matter what "goodwill" euphemism is used. Also, the repaired component/body panel should be just as durable as if it were new. Hence, the clock starts ticking from the beginning until you reach the original warranty parameter—again, no matter what the dealer's repair warranty limit says.
- It's a lot easier to get the automaker to pay to replace a defective part than it is to be compensated for a missed day of work or a ruined vacation. Manufacturers hate to pay for consequential expenses—apart from towing bills—because they can't control the amount of the refund. Fortunately, Canadian courts have taken the position that all expenses (damages) flowing from a problem covered by a warranty or service bulletin are the manufacturer's/dealer's responsibility under negligence and product liability provisions found in provincial consumer protection statutes, common law jurisprudence, Quebec civil law, and federal consumer protection legislation. Nevertheless, don't risk a fair settlement for some outlandish claim of "emotional distress," "pain and suffering," etc., unless your case is similar to *Sharman v. Ford*. If you have invoices to prove actual consequential damages, then use them. If not, don't be greedy.

Very seldom do automakers contest these paint claims before small claims court, opting instead to settle once the court claim is bounced from their customer relations people to their legal affairs department. At that time, you'll probably be offered an out-of-court settlement for 50–75 percent of your claim.

Stand fast and make reference to the service bulletins you intend to subpoena in order to publicly contest in court the unfair nature of this "secret warranty" program. (Automaker lawyers cringe at the idea of trying to explain why consumers aren't made aware of these bulletins.) One hundred percent restitution will probably follow.

Three good examples of favourable paint judgments are *Shields v. General Motors of Canada, Bentley v. Dave Wheaton Pontiac Buick GMC Ltd and General Motors of Canada,* and the most recent, *Maureen Frank v. General Motors of Canada Limited.*

Shields v. General Motors of Canada, No. 1398/96, Ontario Court (General Division), Oshawa Small Claims Court, 33 King Street West, Oshawa,

Ontario L1H 1A1, July 24, 1997, Robert Zochodne, Deputy Judge. The owner of a 1991 Pontiac Grand Prix purchased the vehicle used with over 100,000 km on its odometer. Commencing in 1995, the paint began to bubble and then flake and eventually peel off. Deputy Judge Robert Zochodne awarded the plaintiff $1,205.72 and struck down every one of GM's environmental/acid rain/UV rays arguments. Other important aspects of this 12-page judgment that GM did not appeal:

1. The judge admitted many of the technical service bulletins referred to in *Lemon-Aid* as proof of GM's negligence.
2. Although the vehicle had 156,000 km when the case went to court, GM still offered to pay 50 percent of the paint repairs if the plaintiff dropped his suit.
3. Deputy Judge Zochodne ruled that the failure to protect the paint from the damaging effects of UV rays is akin to engineering a car that won't start in cold weather. In essence, vehicles must be built to withstand the rigours of the environment.
4. Here's an interesting twist: The original warranty covered defects that were present at the time it was in effect. The judge, taking statements found in the GM technical service bulletins, ruled the UV problem was factory related, and therefore it existed during the warranty period and thereby represented a latent defect that appeared once the warranty expired.
5. The subsequent purchaser was not prevented from making the warranty claim, even though the warranty had long since expired from a time and mileage standpoint and he was the second owner.

Bentley v. Dave Wheaton Pontiac Buick GMC Ltd and General Motors of Canada, Victoria Registry No. 24779, British Columbia Small Claims Court, December 1, 1998, Judge Higinbotham. This small claims judgment builds upon the Ontario *Shields v. General Motors of Canada* decision and cites other jurisprudence as to how long paint should last on a car. If you're wondering why Ford and Chrysler haven't been hit by similar judgments, remember that they usually settle.

Maureen Frank v. General Motors of Canada Limited, No. SC#12 (2001), Saskatchewan Provincial Court, Saskatoon, Saskatchewan, October 17, 2001, Provincial Court Judge H.G. Dirauf.

On June 23, 1997, the Plaintiff bought a 1996 Chevrolet Corsica from a General Motors dealership. At the time the odometer showed 33,172 km. The vehicle still had some factory warranty. The car had been a lease car and had no previous accidents.

During June of 2000, the Plaintiff noticed that some of the paint was peeling off from the car and she took it to a General Motors dealership in Saskatoon and to the General Motors dealership in North Battleford where she purchased the car. While there were some discussions with the GM dealership about the peeling paint, nothing came of it and the Plaintiff now brings this action claiming the cost of a new paint job.

During 1999, the Plaintiff was involved in a minor collision causing damage to the left rear door. This damage was repaired. During this repair some scratches to the left front door previously done by vandals were also repaired.

The Plaintiff's witness, Frank Nemeth, is a qualified auto body repairman with some 26 years of experience. He testified that the peeling paint was a factory defect and that it was necessary to completely strip the car and repaint it. He diagnosed the cause of the peeling paint as a separation of the primer surface or colour coat from the electrocoat primer. In his opinion no primer surfacer was applied at all. He testified that once the peeling starts, it will continue. He has seen this problem on General Motors vehicles. The defect is called delamination.

Mr. Nemeth stated that a paint job should last at least 10 years. In my opinion most people in Saskatchewan grow up with cars and are familiar with cars. I think it is common knowledge that the original paint on cars normally lasts in excess of 15 years and that rust becomes a problem before the paint fails. In any event, paint peeling off, as it did on the Plaintiff's vehicle, is not common. I find that the paint on a new car put on by the factory should last at least 15 years.

Counsel for the defendant submitted that any award I should make should be reduced because of betterment. While betterment was discussed at trial, I am not persuaded that any award for damages should be reduced in this case. See *Scheeler v. C.M. Holdings Inc.* (1997) 183 Sask R (Q.B.) and *Nan v. Black Pine Manufacturing Ltd.* (1991) 5WWR172 (B.C.C.A.). I have reviewed *Pitch Snyder, Damages for Breach of Contract,* 2nd edition, pages 2-14.3 to 2-22 and read *Betterment Before Canadian Common Law Courts* by J. Berryman, (1993) 72 *Canadian Bar Review.*

It is clear that the onus to show and calculate any betterment is on the Defendant. He has not done so. In any event, I doubt that any betterment in this case would be significant.

The repair cost given by Mr. Nemeth of Superior Auto Body Ltd., Exhibit P-7 shows the repair cost (including minor dents) to be $3,679.90. I reduce the sum by $267.52 for the repair cost of the dents.

There will be judgment for the Plaintiff in the amount of $3,412.38 plus costs of $81.29.

Some of the important aspects of the *Frank* judgment:

1. The judge accepted that the automaker was responsible, even though the car was bought used. The subsequent purchaser was not prevented from making the warranty claim, even though the warranty had long

since expired from a time and mileage standpoint and she was the second owner.

2. The judge stressed that the provincial warranty can kick in anytime the automaker's warranty has expired or isn't applied.
3. By awarding full compensation to the plaintiff, the judge didn't feel there was a significant "betterment" or improvement added to the car that would warrant reducing the amount of the award.
4. The judge decided that the paint delamination was a factory defect.
5. The judge also concluded that, without this factory defect, a paint job should last up to 15 years.
6. GM offered to pay $700 of the paint repairs if the plaintiff dropped the suit; the judge awarded five times that amount.
7. Maureen Frank won this case despite having to confront GM lawyer Ken Ready, a lawyer who has argued other paint cases for GM and Chrysler.

Other paint/rust cases

Martin v. Honda Canada Inc., March 17, 1986, Ontario Small Claims Court (Scarborough), Judge Sigurdson. The original owner of a 1981 Honda Civic sought compensation for the premature "bubbling, pitting, cracking of the paint and rusting of the Civic after five years of ownership." Judge Sigurdson agreed and ordered Honda to pay the owner $1,163.95.

Thauberger v. Simon Fraser Sales and Mazda Motors, 3 B.C.L.R., 193. This Mazda owner sued for damages caused by the premature rusting of his 1977 Mazda GLC. The court awarded him $1,000. Thauberger had previously sued General Motors for a prematurely rusted Blazer truck and was also awarded $1,000 in the same court. Both judges ruled that the defects could not be excluded from the automaker's express warranty or from the implied warranty granted by ss. 20, 20(b) of the B.C. Sale of Goods Act.

Whittaker v. Ford Motor Company (1979), 24 O.R. (2d), 344. A new Ford developed serious corrosion problems in spite of having been rustproofed by the dealer. The court ruled that the dealer, not Ford, was liable for the damage for having sold the rustproofing product at the time of purchase. This is an important judgment to use when a rustproofer or paint protector goes out of business or refuses to pay a claim, since the decision holds the dealer jointly responsible.

See also:
- *Danson v. Chateau Ford* (1976) C.P., Quebec Small Claims Court, No. 32-00001898-757, Judge Lande.
- *Doyle v. Vital Automotive Systems*, May 16, 1977, Ontario Small Claims Court (Toronto), Judge Turner.
- *Lacroix v. Ford*, April 1980, Ontario Small Claims Court (Toronto), Judge Tierney.
- *Marinovich v. Riverside Chrysler*, April 1, 1987, District Court of Ontario, No. 1030/85, Judge Stortini.

Going to Court

When to sue

If the seller you've been negotiating with agrees to make things right, give him or her a deadline and then have an independent garage check the repairs. If no offer is made within 10 working days, file suit in court. Make the manufacturer a party to the lawsuit only if the original, unexpired warranty was transferred to you; your claim falls under the emissions warranty, a TSB, a secret warranty extension, or a safety recall campaign; or there is extensive chassis rusting due to poor engineering.

Choosing the right court

You must decide what remedy to pursue; that is, whether you want a partial refund or a cancellation of the sale. To determine the refund amount, add the estimated cost of repairing existing mechanical defects to the cost of prior repairs. Don't exaggerate your losses or claim for repairs that are considered routine maintenance.

A suit for cancellation of sale involves practical problems. The court requires that the vehicle be "tendered" or taken back to the seller at the time the lawsuit is filed. This means you are without transportation for as long as the case continues, unless you purchase another vehicle in the interim. If you lose the case, you must then take back the old vehicle and pay storage fees. You could go from having no vehicle to having two, one of which is a clunker.

Generally, if the cost of repairs or the sales contract amount falls within the small claims court limit (discussed later), file the case there to keep costs to a minimum and get a speedy hearing. Small claims court judgments aren't easily appealed, lawyers aren't necessary, filing fees are minimal (about $125), and cases are usually heard within a few months.

Watch what you ask for. If you claim more than the small claims court limit, you'll have to go to a higher court—where costs quickly add up and delays of a few years or more are commonplace.

Small claims courts

Small claims courts are scary to most businesses. Not because they can issue million-dollar judgments, or force litigants to spend millions in legal fees (they can't), but because they can award sizeable sums to small plaintiffs and make jurisprudence that other judges on the same bench are likely to follow.

For example, in *Dawe v. Courtesy Chrysler*, Dartmouth Nova Scotia Small Claims Court SCCH #206825, July 30, 2004, Judge Patrick L Casey, Q.C., rendered an impressive 21-page decision citing key automobile product liability cases, over the past 80 years. He awarded $5,037 to the owner of a new 2001 Cummins-equipped Ram pickup that wandered all over the road; lost power, or jerked and bucked; shifted erratically; lost braking ability; bottomed out when passing over bumps; allowed water to leak into the cab; produced a burnt-wire and oil smell in interior as lights would dim; and produced a rear-end whine and windnoise around the doors and under the dash.

Dawe had sold the vehicle and reduced his claim to meet the small claims threshold.

Interestingly, small claims court is quickly becoming a misnomer, now that Alberta allows claims of up to a limit of $25,000 and most other provinces permit $10,000 claims.

There are small claims courts in most counties of every province, and you can make a claim in the county where the problem happened or where the defendant lives and conducts business. Simply go to the small claims court office and ask for a claim form. Instructions on how to fill it out accompany the form. Remember, you must identify the defendant correctly and this may require some help from the court clerk (look for other recent lawsuits naming the same party). Crooks often change their company's name to escape liability; for example, it would be impossible to sue Joe's Garage (1999) if your contract is with Joe's Garage Inc. (1984).

At this point, it wouldn't hurt to hire a lawyer or a paralegal for a brief walk-through of small claims procedures to ensure that you've prepared your case properly and that you know what objections will likely be raised by the other side. If you'd like a lawyer to do all the work for you, there are a number of law firms around the country that specialize in small claims litigation. Small claims doesn't means small legal fees, however. In Toronto, some law offices charge a flat fee of $1,000 for the basic small claims lawsuit and trial.

Remember that you're entitled to bring to court any evidence relevant to your case, including written documents, such as a bill of sale or receipt, contract, or letter. If your car has developed severe rust problems, bring a photograph (signed and dated by the photographer) to court. You may also have witnesses testify in court. It's important to discuss a witness's testimony prior to the court date. If a witness can't attend the court date, he or she can write a report and sign it for representation in court. This situation usually applies to an expert witness, such as an independent mechanic who has evaluated your car's problems.

If you lose your case in spite of all your preparation and research, some small claims court statutes allow cases to be retried, at a nominal cost, in exceptional circumstances. If a new witness has come forward, additional evidence has been discovered, or key documents (that were previously not available) have become accessible, apply for a retrial. For example, in Ontario, this little-known provision is Rule 18.4 (1).B.

Key Court Decisions

The following Canadian and U.S. lawsuits and judgments cover typical problems that are likely to arise. Use them as leverage when negotiating a settlement or as a reference should your claim go to trial. Legal principles applying to Canadian and American law are similar; however, Quebec court decisions may be based on legal principles that don't apply outside that province. Nevertheless, you can find a comprehensive listing of Canadian decisions from small claims courts all the way to the Supreme Court of Canada at *legalresearch.org/docs/internet3.html*.

Additional court judgments can be found in the legal reference section of your city's main public library or at a nearby university law library. Ask the librarian for help in choosing the legal phrases that best describe your claim.

LexisNexis (*www.lexis-nexis.com*) and Findlaw (*www.findlaw.com*) are two useful Internet sites for legal research. Their main drawback, though, is you may need to subscribe or use a lawyer's subscription to access jurisprudence and other areas of the sites.

An excellent reference book that will give you plenty of tips on filing, pleading, and collecting your judgment is Judge Marvin Zuker's *Ontario Small Claims Court Practice 2002–2003*, Carswell, 2002. Judge Zuker's book is easily understood by non-lawyers and uses court decisions from across Canada to help you plead your case successfully in almost any Canadian court.

Product Liability

Almost three decades ago, the Supreme Court of Canada in *Kravitz v. GM* clearly affirmed that automakers and their dealers are jointly liable for the replacement or repair of a vehicle if independent testimony shows it is afflicted by factory-related defects that compromise its safety or performance. The existence of a secret warranty extension or technical service bulletins also helps prove that the vehicle's problems are the automaker's responsibility. For example, in *Lowe v. Fairview Chrysler* (see page 140), technical service bulletins were instrumental in showing an Ontario small claims court judge that Chrysler had a history of automatic transmission failures since 1989!

In addition to replacing or repairing the vehicle, an automaker can also be held responsible for any damages arising from the defect. This means that loss of wages, supplementary transportation costs, and damages for personal inconvenience can be awarded. However, in the States, product liability damage awards often exceed millions of dollars, while Canadian courts are far less generous.

Implied Warranty

Reasonable Durability

This is that powerful "other" warranty they never tell you about. It applies during and after the expiration of the manufacturer's or dealer's expressed or written warranty and requires that a part or repair will last a "reasonable" period of time. What is reasonable depends in large part on benchmarks used in the industry, the price of the vehicle, and how it was driven and maintained. Look at the reasonable durability chart on pages 108–109 for some guidelines as to what you should expect.

Judges usually apply the implied or legal warranty when the manufacturer's expressed warranty has expired and the vehicle's manufacturing defects remain uncorrected.

In the following decisions, the implied warranty forced Ford to pay for Ford's Windstar chronic engine failures.

Dufour v. Ford Canada Ltd., April 10, 2001, Quebec Small Claims Court (Hull), No. 550-32-008335-009, Justice P. Chevalier. Ford was forced to reimburse the cost of engine head gasket repairs carried out on a 1996 Windstar 3.8L engine—a vehicle not covered by the automaker's Owner Notification Program, which cut off assistance after the '95 model year.

Schaffler v. Ford Motor Company Limited and Embrun Ford Sales Ltd., Ontario Superior Court of Justice, L'Orignal Small Claims Court, Court File No. 59-2003, July 22, 2003, Justice Gerald Langlois. Plaintiff bought a used 1995 Windstar in 1998. Engine head gasket was repaired for free three years later under Ford's 7-year extended warranty. In 2002 at 109,600 km, head gasket failed again, seriously damaging the engine. Ford refused a second repair. Justice Langlois ruled that Ford's warranty extension bulletin listed signs and symptoms of the covered defect that were identical to the problems written on the second work order ("persistent and/or chronic engine overheating; heavy white smoke evident from the exhaust tailpipe; flashing 'low coolant' instrument panel light even after coolant refill; and constant loss of engine coolant.") Judge Langlois concluded "the problem was brought to the attention of the dealer well within the warranty period; the dealer was negligent." The Plaintiffs were awarded $4,941, plus 5 percent interest. This includes $1,070 for two months' car rental.

John R. Reid and Laurie M. McCall v. Ford Motor Company of Canada, Superior Court of Justice, Ottawa Small Claims Court, Claim No: #02-SC-077344, July 11, 2003, Justice Tiernay. A 1996 Windstar bought used in 1997 experienced engine head gasket failure in October 2001 at 159,000 km. Judge Tiernay awarded the Plaintiffs $4,145 for the following reasons: "A Technical Service Bulletin dated June 28, 1999, was circulated to Ford dealers. It dealt specifically with 'undetermined loss of coolant' and 'engine oil contaminated with coolant' in the 1996–98 Windstar and five other models of Ford vehicles. I conclude that Ford owed a duty of care to the Plaintiff to equip this vehicle with a cylinder head gasket of sufficient sturdiness and durability that would function trouble-free for at least seven years, given normal driving and proper maintenance conditions. I find that Ford is answerable in damages for the consequences of its negligence."

General Motors Products of Canada Ltd. v. Kravitz, [1979] 1 S.C.R. 790. The court said the seller's warranty of quality was an accessory to the property and was transferred with it on successive sales. Accordingly, subsequent buyers could invoke the contractual warranty of quality against the manufacturer, even though they did not contract directly with it. This precedent is now codified in articles 1434, 1442, and 1730 of Quebec's Civil Code.

New-Vehicle Defects

Bagnell's Cleaners v. Eastern Automobile Ltd. (1991), 111 N.S.R. (2nd), No. 51, 303 A.P.R., No. 51 (T.D.). This Nova Scotia company found that the new van it purchased had serious engine, transmission, and radiator defects. The court held that there was a fundamental breach of the implied warranty and that an exclusionary clause could not protect the seller.

Burridge v. City Motor, 10 Nfld. & P.E.I.R., No. 451. This Newfoundland resident complained repeatedly of his new car's defects during the warranty period, and stated that he hadn't used his car for 204 days after spending almost $1,500 for repairs. The judge awarded all repair costs and cancelled the sale.

Davis v. Chrysler Canada Ltd. (1977), 26 N.S.R. (2nd), No. 410 (T.D.). The owner of a new $28,000 diesel truck found that a faulty steering assembly prevented him from carrying on his business. The court ordered that the sale be cancelled and that $10,000 in monthly payments be reimbursed.

Even Chrysler's much-vaunted Hemi-equipped Ram has come under fire for defective engine valve springs and road wander.

Dawe v. Courtesy Chrysler, Dartmouth Nova Scotia Small Claims Court SCCH #206825, July 30, 2004, Judge Patrick L Casey, Q.C. Small claims doesn't mean small judgments. This recent, 21-page, unreported Nova Scotia small claims court decision is impressive in its clarity and thoroughness. It applies *Donoghue, Kravitz, Davis, et al* in awarding a 2001 Dodge Ram owner over $5,000 in damages. Anyone with engine, transmission, and suspension problems, or water leaking into the interior, will find this judgment particularly useful.

Fox v. Wilson Motors and GM, February 9, 1989, Court of Queen's Bench, New Brunswick, No. F/C/308/87. A trucker's new tractor-trailer had repeated engine malfunctions. He was awarded damages for loss of income, excessive fuel consumption, and telephone charges under the provincial Sale of Goods Act.

Gibbons v. Trapp Motors Ltd. (1970), 9 D.L.R. (3rd), No. 742 (B.C.S.C.). The court ordered the dealer to take back a new car that had numerous defects and required 32 hours of repairs.

Johnson v. Northway Chevrolet Oldsmobile (1993), 108 Sask. R., No. 138 (Q.B.). The court ordered the dealer to take back a new car that had been brought in for repairs on 14 different occasions. Two years after purchase, the buyer initiated a lawsuit for the purchase price of the car and for general damages. General damages were awarded.

Julien v. GM of Canada (1991), 116 N.B.R. (2nd), No. 80. The plaintiff's new diesel truck produced excessive engine noise. The plaintiff was awarded the $5,000 cost of repairing the engine through an independent dealer.

Magna Management Ltd. v. Volkswagen Canada Inc., May 27, 1988, Vancouver (B.C.C.A.), No. CA006037. This precedent-setting case allowed the plaintiff to keep his new $48,325 VW while awarding him $37,101—three years after the car was purchased. The problems were centred on poor engine performance.

Maughan v. Silver's Garage Ltd., Nova Scotia Supreme Court, 6 B.L.R., No. 303, N.S.C. (2nd), No. 278. The plaintiff leased a defective backhoe. The manufacturer had to reimburse the plaintiff's losses because the warranty wasn't honoured. The Court rejected the manufacturer's contention that the contract's exclusion clause protected the company from lawsuits for damages resulting from a latent defect.

Murphy v. Penney Motors Ltd. (1979), 23 Nfld. & P.E.I.R., No. 152, 61 A.P.R., No. 152 (Nfld. T.D.). This Newfoundland trucker found that his vehicle's engine problems took his new trailer off the road for 129 days during a 7-month period. The judge awarded all repair costs, as well as compensation for business losses, and cancelled the sale.

Murray v. Sperry Rand Corp., Ontario Supreme Court, 5 B.L.R., No. 284. The seller, dealer, and manufacturer were all held liable for breach of warranty when a forage harvester did not perform as advertised in the sales brochure or as promised by the sales agent. The plaintiff was given his money back and reimbursed for his economic loss, based on the amount his harvesting usually earned. The court held that the advertising was a warranty.

Oliver v. Courtesy Chrysler (1983) Ltd. (1992), 11 B.C.A.C., No. 169. This new car had numerous defects over a 3-year period, which the dealer attempted to fix to no avail. The plaintiff put the car in storage and sued the dealer for the purchase price. The court ruled that the car wasn't roadworthy and that the plaintiff couldn't be blamed for putting it in storage rather than selling it and purchasing another vehicle. The purchase price was refunded minus $1,500 for each year the plaintiff used the car.

Olshaski Farms Ltd. v. Skene Farm Equipment Ltd., January 9, 1987, Alberta Court of Queen's Bench, 49 Alta. L.R. (2nd), No. 249. The plaintiff's Massey-Ferguson combine caught fire after the manufacturer had sent two notices to dealers informing them of a defect that could cause a fire. The judge ruled under the Sale of Goods Act that the balance of probabilities indicated that the manufacturing defect caused the fire, even though there was no direct evidence proving that the defect existed.

Western Pacific Tank Lines Ltd. v. Brentwood Dodge, June 2, 1975, B.C.S.C., No. 30945-74, Judge Meredith. The court awarded the plaintiff $8,600 and cancelled the sale of a new Chrysler New Yorker with the following defects: Badly adjusted doors, water leaks into the interior, and electrical short circuits.

Used-Vehicle Defects

Fissel v. Ideal Auto Sales Ltd. (1991), 91 Sask. R. 266. Shortly after the vehicle was purchased, the car's motor seized and the dealer refused to replace it, even though the car was returned on several occasions. The court ruled that the dealer had breached the statutory warranties in s. 11 (4) and (7) of the Consumer Products Warranties Act. The purchasers were entitled to cancel the sale and recover the full purchase price.

Friskin v. Chevrolet Oldsmobile, 72 D.L.R. (3d), 289. A Manitoba used-car buyer asked that his contract be cancelled because of a chronic stalling problem. The garage owner did his best to correct it. Despite the seller's good intentions, the Manitoba Consumer Protection Act allowed for cancellation.

Graves v. C&R Motors Ltd., April 8, 1980, British Columbia County Court, Judge Skipp. The plaintiff bought a used car on the condition that certain deficiencies be remedied. They never were, and he was promised a refund, but it never arrived. The plaintiff brought suit, claiming that the dealer's deceptive activities violated the provincial Trade Practices Act. The court agreed, concluding that a deceptive act that occurs before, during, or after the transaction can lead to the cancellation of the contract.

Hachey v. Galbraith Equipment Company (1991), 33 M.V.R. (2d) 242. The plaintiff bought a used truck from the dealer to use in hauling gravel. Shortly thereafter, the steering failed. The plaintiff's suit was successful because expert testimony showed that the truck wasn't roadworthy. The dealer was found liable for damages for being in breach of the implied condition of fitness for the purpose for which the truck was purchased, as set out in s. 15 (a) of the New Brunswick Sale of Goods Act.

Henzel v. Brussels Motors (1973), 1 O.R., 339 (C.C.). The dealer sold this used car while brandishing a copy of the mechanical fitness certificate as proof that the car was in good shape. The plaintiff was awarded his money back because the court held the certificate to be a warranty that was breached by the car's subsequent defects.

Johnston v. Bodasing Corporation Limited, February 23, 1983, Ontario County Court (Bruce), No. 15/11/83, Judge McKay. The plaintiff bought a used 1979 Buick Riviera, for $8,500, that was represented as being "reliable." Two weeks after purchase, the motor self-destructed. Judge McKay awarded the plaintiff $2,318 as compensation to fix the Riviera's defects.

One feature of this particular decision is that the trial judge found the Sale of Goods Act applied, notwithstanding the fact that the vendor used a standard contract that said there were no warranties or representations. The judge also accepted the decision in *Kendal v. Lillico* (1969), 2 Appeal Cases, 31, which indicates that the Sale of Goods Act covers not only defects that the seller ought to have detected, but also latent defects that even his utmost skill and judgment could not have detected. This places a very heavy onus on the vendor and it should prove useful in actions of this type in other common-law provinces with laws similar to Ontario's Sale of Goods Act.

Kelly v. Mack Canada, 53 D.L.R. (4th), 476. Kelly bought two trucks from Mack Sales. The first, a used White Freightliner tractor and trailer, was purchased for $29,742. It cost him over $12,000 in repairs during the first five months, and another $9,000 was estimated for future engine repairs. Mack Sales convinced Kelly to trade in the old truck for a new Mack truck. Kelly did this, but shortly thereafter, the new truck had similar problems. Kelly sued for the return of all his money, arguing that the two transactions were really one.

The Ontario Court of Appeal agreed and awarded Kelly a complete refund. It stated, "There was such a congeries of defects that there had been a breach of the implied conditions set out in the Sale of Goods Act."

Although Mack Sales argued that the contract contained a clause excluding any implied warranties, the court determined that the breach was of such magnitude that the dealer could not rely upon that clause. The dealer then argued that since the client used the trucks, the depreciation of both should be taken into account in reducing the award. This was refused on the grounds that the plaintiff never had the product he bargained for and in no way did he profit from the transaction. The court also awarded Kelly compensation for loss of income while the trucks were being repaired, as well as the interest on all of the money tied up in both transactions from the time of purchase until final judgment.

Morrison v. Hillside Motors (1973) Ltd. (1981), 35 Nfld. & P.E.I.R. 361. A used car advertised to be in A-1 condition and carrying a 50/50 warranty developed a number of problems. The court decided that the purchaser should be partially compensated because of the ad's claim. In deciding how much compensation to award, the presiding judge considered the warranty's wording, the amount paid for the vehicle, the year of the vehicle, its average life, the type of defect that occurred, and how long the purchaser had use of the vehicle before its defects became evident. Although this judgment was rendered in Newfoundland, judges throughout Canada have used a similar approach for more than a decade.

Neilson v. Maclin Motors, 71 D.L.R. (3d), 744. The plaintiff bought a used truck on the strength of the seller's allegations that the motor had been rebuilt and that it had 210 hp. The engine failed. The judge awarded damages and cancelled the contract because the motor had not been rebuilt, it did not have 210 hp, and the transmission was defective.

Parent v. Le Grand Trianon and Ford Credit (1982), C.P., 194, Judge Bertrand Gagnon. Nineteen months after paying $3,300 for a used 1974 LTD, the plaintiff sued the Ford dealer for his money back because the car was prematurely rusted out. The dealer replied that rust was normal, there was no warranty, and the claim was too late. The court held that the garage was still responsible. The plaintiff was awarded $1,500 for the cost of rust repairs.

"As is" clauses

Since 1907, Canadian courts have ruled that a seller can't exclude the implied warranty as to fitness by including such phrases as "there are no other warranties or guarantees, promises, or agreements than those contained herein." See *Sawyer-Massey Co. v. Thibault* (1907), 5 W.L.R. 241.

Adams v. J&D's Used Cars Ltd. (1983), 26 Sask. R. 40 (Q.B.). Shortly after purchase, the engine and transmission failed. The court ruled that the inclusion of "as is" in the sales contract had no legal effect. The implied warranty set out in Saskatchewan's Consumer Products Warranties Act was breached by the dealer. The sale was cancelled and all monies were refunded.

Leasing

Ford Motor Credit v. Bothwell, December 3, 1979, Ontario County Court (Middlesex), No. 9226-T, Judge Macnab. The defendant leased a 1977 Ford truck that had frequent engine problems, characterized by stalling and hard starting. After complaining for one year and driving 35,000 km (22,000 miles), the defendant cancelled the lease. Ford Credit sued for the money owing on the lease. Judge Macnab cancelled the lease and ordered Ford Credit to repay 70 percent of the amount paid during the leasing period. Ford Credit was also ordered to refund repair costs, even though the corporation claimed that it should not be held responsible for Ford's failure to honour its warranty.

Salvador v. Setay Motors/Queenstown Chev-Olds, Hamilton Small Claims Court, Case No.1621/95. Plaintiff was awarded $2,000 plus costs from Queenstown Leasing. The court found that the company should have tried harder to sell the leased vehicle, and at a higher price, when the "open lease" expired.

Incidentally, about 3,700 dealers in 39 American states paid in 2004 between $3,500 and $8,000 each to settle an investigation of allegations they and Ford Motor Credit Co. overcharged customer who terminated leases early.

Schryvers v. Richport Ford Sales, May 18, 1993, B.C.S.C., No. C917060, Justice Tysoe. The court awarded $17,578.47, plus costs, to a couple who paid thousands of dollars more in unfair and hidden leasing charges than if they had simply purchased their Ford Explorer and Escort. The court found that this price difference constituted a deceptive, unconscionable act or practice, in contravention of the Trade Practices Act, R.S.B.C. 1979, c. 406.

Judge Tysoe concluded that the total of the general damages awarded to the Schryvers for both vehicles would be $11,578.47. He then proceeded to give the following reasons for awarding an additional $6,000 in punitive damages:

> Little wonder Richport Ford had a contest for the salesperson who could persuade the most customers to acquire their vehicles by way of a lease transaction. I consider the actions of Richport Ford to be sufficiently flagrant and high handed to warrant an award of punitive damages.
>
> There must be a disincentive to suppliers in respect of intentionally deceptive trade practices. If no punitive damages are awarded for intentional violations of the legislation, suppliers will continue to conduct their businesses in a manner that involves deceptive trade practices because they will have nothing to lose. In this case I believe that the appropriate amount of punitive damages is the extra profit Richport Ford endeavoured to make as a result of its deceptive acts. I therefore award punitive damages against Richport Ford in the amount of $6,000.

See also:
- *Barber v. Inland Truck Sales*, 11 D.L.R. (3rd), No. 469.
- *Canadian-Dominion Leasing v. Suburban Super Drug Ltd.* (1966), 56 D.L.R. (2nd), No. 43.
- *Neilson v. Atlantic Rentals Ltd.* (1974), 8 N.B.R. (2d), No. 594.
- *Volvo Canada v. Fox*, December 13, 1979, New Brunswick Court of Queen's Bench, No. 1698/77/C, Judge Stevenson.
- *Western Tractor v. Dyck*, 7 D.L.R. (3rd), No. 535.

Repairs

Faulty diagnosis

Davies v. Alberta Motor Association, August 13, 1991, Alberta Provincial Court, Civil Division, No. P9090106097, Judge Moore. The plaintiff had a used 1985 Nissan Pulsar NX checked out by the AMA's Vehicle Inspection Service prior to buying it. The car passed with flying colours. A month later, the clutch was replaced and numerous electrical problems ensued. At that time, another garage discovered that the car had been involved in a major accident, had a bent frame and a leaking radiator, and was unsafe to drive. The court awarded the plaintiff $1,578.40 plus three years of interest. The judge held that the AMA set itself out as an expert and should have spotted the car's defects. The AMA's defence—that it was not responsible for errors—was thrown out. The court held that a disclaimer clause could not protect the association from a fundamental breach of contract.

Secret Warranties

It's common practice for manufacturers to secretly extend their warranties to cover components with a high failure rate. Customers who complain vigorously get extended warranty compensation in the form of "goodwill" adjustments.

François Chong v. Marine Drive Imported Cars Ltd. and Honda Canada Inc., May 17, 1994, British Columbia Provincial Small Claims Court, No. 92-06760, Judge C.L. Bagnall. Mr. Chong was the first owner of a 1983 Honda Accord with 134,000 km on the odometer. He had six engine camshafts replaced—four under Honda "goodwill" programs, one where he paid part of the repairs, and one via this small claims court judgment.

In his ruling, Judge Bagnall agreed with Chong and ordered Honda and the dealer to each pay half of the $835.81 repair bill, for the following reasons:

> The defendants assert that the warranty, which was part of the contract for purchase of the car, encompassed the entirety of their obligation to the claimant, and that it expired in February 1985. The replacements of the camshaft after that date were paid for wholly or in part by Honda as a "goodwill gesture." The time has come for these gestures to cease, according to the witness for Honda. As well, he pointed out to me that the most recent replacement of the camshaft was paid for by Honda and that, therefore, the work would not be covered by Honda's usual warranty of 12 months from date of repair. Mr. Wall, who testified for Honda, told me there was no question that this situation with Mr. Chong's engine was an unusual state of affairs. He said that a camshaft properly maintained can last anywhere from 24,000 to 500,000 km. He could not offer any suggestion as to why the car keeps having this problem.
>
> The claimant has convinced me that the problems he is having with rapid breakdown of camshafts in his car is due to a defect, which was present in the engine at the time that he purchased the car. The problem first arose during the warranty period and in my view has never been properly identified nor repaired.

Automatic transmission failures (Chrysler)

Lowe v. Fairview Chrysler-Dodge Limited and Chrysler Canada Limited, May 14, 1996, Ontario Court (General Division), Burlington Small Claims Court, No. 1224/95. The following judgment, in the plaintiff's favour, raises important legal principles relative to Chrysler:

- Technical dealer service bulletins are admissible in court to prove that a problem exists and certain parts should be checked out.
- If a problem is reported prior to a warranty's expiration, warranty coverage for the problematic component(s) is automatically carried over after the warranty ends.
- It's not up to the car owner to tell the dealer/automaker what the specific problem is.
- Repairs carried out by an independent garage can be refunded if the dealer/automaker unfairly refuses to apply the warranty.
- The dealer/automaker cannot dispute the cost of the independent repair if they fail to cross-examine the independent repairer.
- Auto owners can ask for and win compensation for their inconvenience, which in this judgment amounted to $150.

Court awards quickly add up. Although the plaintiff was given $1,985.94, with the addition of court costs and prejudgment interest, plus costs of inconvenience fixed at $150, the final award amounted to $2,266.04.

False Advertising

Truck misrepresentation

Goldie v. Golden Ears Motors (1980) Ltd, Port Coquitlam, June 27, 2000, British Columbia Small Claims Court, Case No. CO8287, Justice Warren. In a well-written eight-page judgment, the court awarded plaintiff Goldie $5,000 for engine repairs on a 1990 Ford F-150 pickup in addition to $236 court costs. The dealer was found to have misrepresented the mileage and sold a used vehicle that didn't meet Section 8.01 of the provincial motor vehicle regulations (unsafe tires, defective exhaust, and headlights).

In rejecting the seller's defense that he disclosed all information "to the best of his knowledge and belief," as stipulated in the sales contract, Justice Warren stated:

> The words "to the best of your knowledge and belief" do not allow someone to be willfully blind to defects or to provide incorrect information. I find as a fact that the business made no effort to fulfill its duty to comply with the requirements of this form.... The defendant has been reckless in its actions. More likely, it has actively deceived the claimant into entering into this contract. I find the conduct of the defendant has been reprehensible throughout the dealings with the claimant.

This judgment closes a loophole that sellers have used to justify their misrepresentation and it allows for cancellation of the sale and damages if the vehicle doesn't meet highway safety regulations.

MacDonald v. Equilease Co. Ltd., January 18, 1979, Ontario Supreme Court, Judge O'Driscoll. The plaintiff leased a truck that was misrepresented as having an axle stronger than it really was. The court awarded the plaintiff damages for repairs and set aside the lease.

Seich v. Festival Ford Sales Ltd. (1978), 6 Alta. L.R. (2nd), No. 262. The plaintiff bought a used truck from the defendant after being assured that it had a new motor and transmission. It didn't, and the court awarded the plaintiff $6,400.

Used car sold as new (demonstrator)

Bilodeau v. Sud Auto, Quebec Court of Appeal, No. 09-000751-73, Judge Tremblay. This appeals court cancelled the contract and held that a car can't be sold as new or as a demonstrator if it has ever been rented, leased, sold, or titled to anyone other than the dealer.

Rourke v. Gilmore, January 16, 1928, (Ontario Weekly Notes, vol. XXXIII, p. 292). Before discovering that his new car was really used, the plaintiff drove it for over a year. For this reason the contract couldn't be cancelled. However, the appeals court instead awarded damages for $500, which was quite a sum in 1928!

Vehicle not as ordered

Whether you're buying a new or used vehicle, the seller can't misrepresent the vehicle. Anything that varies from what one would commonly expect, or from the seller's representation, must be disclosed prior to signing the contract. Typical scenarios are odometer turnbacks, accident damage, used or leased cars sold as new, new vehicles that are the wrong colour and the wrong model year, or vehicles that lack promised options or standard features.

Chenel v. Bel Automobile (1981) Inc., August 27, 1976, Quebec Superior Court (Quebec), Judge Desmeules. The plaintiff didn't receive his new Ford truck with the Jacob brakes essential to transporting sand in hilly regions. The court awarded the plaintiff $27,000, representing the purchase price of the vehicle less the money he earned while using the truck.

Lasky v. Royal City Chrysler Plymouth, February 18, 1987, Ontario High Court of Justice, 59 O.R. (2nd), No. 323. The plaintiff bought a 4-cylinder 1983 Dodge 600 that was represented by the salesman as being a 6-cylinder model. After putting 40,000 km on the vehicle over a 22-month period, the buyer was given her money back, without interest, under the provincial Business Practices Act.

Damages (Punitive)

Punitive damages (also known as exemplary damages) allow the plaintiff to get compensation that exceeds his or her losses, as a deterrent to those who carry out dishonest or negligent practices. These kinds of judgments, common in the U.S., sometimes reach hundreds of millions of dollars.

Punitive damages are rarely awarded in Canadian courts and are almost never used against automakers. When they are given out, it's usually for sums less than $100,000. In *Prebushewski v. Dodge City Auto (1985) Ltd. and Chrysler Canada Ltd.* (2001 SKQB 537; Q.B. No. 1215) the plaintiff got $25,000 in a judgment handed down December 6, 2001, in Saskatoon, Saskatchewan. It followed testimony from Chrysler's expert witness that the company was aware of many cases where daytime running lights shorted and caused 1996 Ram pickups to catch fire. The plaintiff's truck had burned to the ground and Chrysler refused the owner's claim, in spite of its knowledge that fires were commonplace.

Angered by Chrysler's stonewalling, Justice Rothery rendered the following judgment:

> Not only did Chrysler know about the problems of the defective daytime running light modules, it did not advise the plaintiff of this. It simply chose to ignore the plaintiff's requests for compensation and told her to seek recovery from her insurance company. Chrysler had replaced thousands of these modules since 1988. But it had also made a business decision to neither advise its customers of the problem nor to recall the vehicles to replace the modules. While the cost would have been about $250 to replace each module, there were at least one million customers. Chrysler was not prepared to spend $250 million, even though it knew what the defective module might do.
>
> Counsel for the defendants argues that this matter had to be resolved by litigation because the plaintiff and the defendants simply had a difference of opinion on whether the plaintiff should be compensated by the defendants. Had the defendants some dispute as to the cause of the fire, that may have been sufficient to prove that they had not wilfully violated this part of the Act. They did not. They knew about the defective daytime running light module. They did nothing to replace the burned truck for the plaintiff. They offered the plaintiff no compensation for her loss. Counsels' position that the definition of the return of the purchase price is an arguable point is not sufficient to negate the defendants' violation of this part of the Act. I find the violation of the defendants to be willful. Thus, I find that exemplary damages are appropriate on the facts of this case.
>
> In this case, the quantum ought to be sufficiently high as to correct the defendants' behaviour. In particular, Chrysler's corporate policy to place profits ahead of the potential danger to its customer's safety and personal property must be punished. And when such corporate policy

includes a refusal to comply with the provisions of the Act and a refusal to provide any relief to the plaintiff, I find an award of $25,000 for exemplary damages to be appropriate. I therefore order Chrysler and Dodge City to pay:

1. Damages in the sum of $41,969.83
2. Exemplary damages in the sum of $25,000
3. Party and party costs

Vlchek v. Koshel (1988), 44 C.C.L.T. 314, B.C.S.C., No. B842974. The plaintiff was seriously injured when she was thrown from a Honda all-terrain cycle on which she had been riding as a passenger. The Court allowed for punitive damages because the manufacturer was well aware of the injuries likely to be caused by the cycle. Specifically, the Court ruled that there is no firm and inflexible principle of law stipulating that punitive or exemplary damages must be denied unless the defendant's acts are specifically directed against the plaintiff. The Court may apply punitive damages "where the defendant's conduct has been indiscriminate of focus, but reckless or malicious in its character. Intent to injure the plaintiff need not be present, so long as intent to do the injurious act can be shown."

See also:
- *Granek v. Reiter*, Ont. Ct. (Gen. Div.), No. 35/741.
- *Morrison v. Sharp*, Ont. Ct. (Gen. Div.), No. 43/548.
- *Schryvers v. Richport Ford Sales*, May 18, 1993, B.C.S.C., No. C917060, Judge Tysoe.
- *Varleg v. Angeloni*, B.C.S.C., No. 41/301.

Provincial business practices acts cover false, misleading, or deceptive representations, and allow for punitive damages should the unfair practice toward the consumer amount to an unconscionable representation. (See C.E.D. (3d) s. 76, pp. 140–45.) "Unconscionable" is defined as "where the consumer is not reasonably able to protect his or her interest because of physical infirmity, ignorance, illiteracy, or inability to understand the language of an agreement or similar factors."

- Exemplary damages are justified where compensatory damages are insufficient to deter and punish. See *Walker et al. v. CFTO Ltd. et al.* (1978), 59 O.R. (2nd), No. 104 (Ont. C.A.).
- Exemplary damages can be awarded in cases where the defendant's conduct was "cavalier." See *Ronald Elwyn Lister Ltd. et al. v. Dayton Tire Canada Ltd.* (1985), 52 O.R. (2nd), No. 89 (Ont. C.A.).
- The primary purpose of exemplary damages is to prevent the defendant and all others from doing similar wrongs. See *Fleming v. Spracklin* (1921).
- Disregard of the public's interest, lack of preventive measures, and a callous attitude all merit exemplary damages. See *Coughlin v. Kuntz* (1989), 2 C.C.L.T. (2nd) (B.C.C.A.).

• Punitive damages can be awarded for mental distress. See *Ribeiro v. Canadian Imperial Bank of Commerce* (1992), Ontario Reports 13 (3rd) and *Brown v. Waterloo Regional Board of Comissioners of Police* (1992), 37 O.R. (2nd).

In the States, punitive damage awards have been particularly generous. Do you remember the Alabama fellow who won a multi-million dollar award because his new BMW had been repainted before he bought it and he wasn't told so by the seller?

The case was *BMW of North America, Inc. v. Gore*, 517 U.S. 559, 116 S. Ct. 1589 (1996). In this case, the Supreme Court cut the damages award and established standards for jury awards of punitive damages. Nevertheless, million-dollar awards are still quite common. For example, an Oregon dealer learned that a $1 million punitive damages award was not excessive under *Gore* and under Oregon law.

The Oregon Supreme Court determined that the standard it set forth in *Oberg v. Honda Motor Company*, 888 P.2d 8 (1996), on remand from the Supreme Court, survived the Supreme Court's subsequent ruling in *Gore*. The court held that the jury's $1 million punitive damages award, 87 times larger than the plaintiff's compensatory damages in *Parrott v. Carr Chevrolet, Inc.*, (2001 Ore. LEXIS 1 January 11, 2001) wasn't excessive. In that case, Mark Parrott sued Carr Chevrolet, Inc. over a used 1983 Chevrolet Suburban under Oregon's Unlawful Trade Practices Act. The jury awarded Parrott $11,496 in compensatory damages and $1 million in punitive damages because the dealer failed to disclose collision damage to a new car buyer.

See also:

• *Grabinski v. Blue Springs Ford Sales, Inc.*, 2000 U.S. App. LEXIS 2073 (8th Cir. W.D. MO, February 16, 2000).

VEHICLE RATINGS

4

How Bad Can You Get?

Iacocca blamed GM's downward spiral on a corporate culture top heavy with finance specialists and white-collar staff. "How did they manage to get to 28 percent (market share) from 60?" he said. "I mean how bad can you get? There again, they lost focus. It's the old story where the bean counter says don't spend a buck, and they forgot in the end you had to build good cars and trucks."

Detroit News, February 2003

Dodge's Demons

The central timer module can be short-circuited by electromagnetic interference from airports, military installations, power fields, etc. When this happens, many of your vehicle's electrical systems will go haywire. Refer to TSB #08-26-00 for 2001 Dakotas, Durangos, and Rams when you ask Chrysler to install a free revised module.

Take me, buy me, show me

It's tough rating new and used vehicles without prostituting yourself. The smooth-talking car guys come around to tell you how much they admire your work and how much better it would be with more *balance.*

Then they invite you on their trips to Japan and Europe where they give you specially prepared vehicles and hats, jackets, and interviews with the top brass. Hell, they even concoct writing prizes for the best reports.

You feel like nobility; they see you as a whore.

Rating the ratings

Lemon-Aid has managed to be both honourable and honest for over the past 33 years by following these simple rules:

- Ratings should be used primarily as a comparative database where the low-ranked or recommended models re-appear in different driving tests and owner surveys. The best rating approach is to combine a driving test with an owner's survey of past models (only *Consumer Reports* does this).

- The responses must come from a large owner pool (675,000 responses from *Consumer Reports* subscribers versus 22,000 responses from CAA members). Anecdotal responses should then be cross-referenced, updated, and given "depth and specificity" through NHTSA's safety complaint prism. Responses must again be cross-referenced through automaker internal service bulletins to determine the extent of the defect over a specific model and model year range and to alert owners to problems that are likely to occur.
- Rankings should be predicated upon important characteristics measured over a significant period of time, unlike "Car of the Year" beauty contests, owner perceived value, or J.D. Power surveys that consider only problems experienced after three months of ownership.
- Ratings must come from unimpeachable sources. There should be no conflicts of interest such as advertising, consultant ties, or self-serving tests done under ideal conditions.
- Beware of self-generated fuel-economy ratings used by automakers in complicity with the federal government. *Automotive News* recently found that Honda and Toyota hybrids get 20 percent less "real world" gas mileage (44 mpg) than advertised because hybrids require a particular style of driving to be fuel efficient, short trips penalize hybrid efficiency more so than regular cars, air conditioning penalizes hybrids more, and colder climates increase fuel consumption. *Consumer Reports* found a 4–5 percent shortfall.
- Tested cars must be bought rather than borrowed, and serviced rather than pampered as part of a journalists' fleet lent out for ranking purposes. Also, all automakers need to be judged equally (Toyota at one time did not accept weekend car journalist "roundup" tests as valid; the company refused to lend its vehicles to the events and was penalized). Automakers must not be members of the ranking body.

Key factors

A good sport-utility, van, or pickup *must* be reasonably priced, crashworthy, easy to handle, and durable (lasting 10–15 years). And don't believe for one moment that the more you spend the better the vehicle. For example, the Honda Pilot and Toyota Highlander are two great performers that rival luxury SUVs costing over $10,000 more, like the Acura MDX, BMW X5, Infiniti FX35, or Lexus RX330. The extra money only buys you more features of dubious value and newer, unproven technology, like rear-mounted video cameras and stability control.

A good choice should cost no more than about $800 a year to maintain, and should provide you with a 40–50 percent resale value after five years of use. Parts and servicing costs shouldn't be excessive, as CBC's *Marketplace* found to be the case with some Mazda dealers, and dealer servicing must be easily accessible, unlike Land Rover, Mercedes, and Kia.

Road (and off-road) performance

Off-roading requires sufficient low-range power (torque) and lots of ground clearance, which can make a vehicle more likely to tip. The suspension has to be adequate to take the punishment of off-roading challenges. ABS can be hazardous when used off-road, since you can't lock the brakes to build up a vehicle-decelerating wedge of earth in front of the wheels. Consequently, when the ABS sensors kick in to prevent wheel lock-up, it seems like you have no brakes at all. This is especially evident when descending a hill, where the driver is forced to shift into low gear and reduce speed to a crawl. Stability-control is another feature that may promise much more than it delivers.

Lemon-Aid uses mostly owner feedback and confidential service bulletins in its ratings. We don't try to curry any automaker's favour. Our guides are ad-free and don't depend upon free "loaner" vehicles. Plus, we don't play favourites, even with car companies who traditionally turn out some of the better-made vehicles, like Honda, Mazda, Nissan, and Toyota. For almost a decade we have chastised and down-rated these companies for their sliding-door, automatic transmission and engine glitches—problems now covered by generous extended warranties. Additionally, *Lemon-Aid*'s 2002 complaint led to Toyota's $2 million settlement of price-fixing charges with Ottawa a year later.

Lemon-Aid Ratings

Customer comments alone do not make a scientific sampling, and that's why they are used in conjunction with other sources of information. On the other hand, owner complaints combined with inside information found in service bulletins are a good starting point to cut through the automakers' hyperbole and get a glimpse of reality.

This guide emphasizes important new features that add to a vehicle's safety, reliability, road performance, and comfort, and points out those changes that are merely gadgets and styling revisions. Also noted are important changes to be made in the future, including the ending of a model line. In addition to the "Recommended" or "Not Recommended" rating (with the current year's rating reflected in the number of stars beside the vehicle's name), each vehicle's strong and weak points are summarized.

Recommended: This rating indicates a best buy and is the almost exclusive domain of Asian and a few GM vehicles. Interestingly, some vehicles that are identical but marketed and serviced by different automakers, like the Ford Ranger and Mazda B Series pickups, may have different ratings. This occurs because servicing and after-warranty assistance may be better within one dealer network than another.

"Recommended" vehicles combine a high level of crashworthiness with good road performance, few safety-related complaints, decent reliability, and better-than-average resale value. Servicing is readily available, and parts are inexpensive and easy to find.

Above Average: Vehicles in this class are pretty good choices. They aren't perfect, but they're often more reasonably priced than the competition. Most vehicles in this category have quality construction, good durability, and plenty of safety features as standard equipment. On the downside, they may have expensive parts and servicing, too many safety-related complaints, or only satisfactory warranty performance, one or all of which may have disqualified them from the Recommended category.

Average: Vehicles in this group have some defeciencies or flaws that make them a second choice. In many cases, certain components are prone to premature wear or breakdown, or some other positive aspect of long-term ownership is lacking. An "Average" rating can also be attributed to such factors as substandard assembly quality, lack of a solid long-term reliability record, a number of safety-related complaints, or some flaw in the parts and service network.

Below Average: This rating category denotes an unreliable vehicle that may have also had a poor safety record. Improvements may have been made to enhance durability or safety. An extended warranty is advised.

Not Recommended: Chances of having major breakdowns or safety-related failures are omnipresent. Inadequate road performance and poor dealer service, among other factors, can make owning one of these vehicles a traumatic and expensive experience.

Vehicles that have not been on the road long enough to assess, or that are sold in such small numbers that owner feedback is insufficient, are "Not Recommended" or left unrated.

Model features and model history

These sections outline the vehicle's specifications and the differences between model years. The "Model History" section provides information on the evolution of the vehicle, including redesigns and modifications. The "New for 2005" section has been omitted when the model has been carried over unchanged.

Technical data

Note that towing capacities differ depending on the kind of powertrain/ suspension package or towing package you buy. Remember that there's a difference between how a vehicle is rated for cargo capacity or payload and how heavy a boat or trailer it can pull.

In the ratings, cargo capacity is expressed in cubic feet with the rear seat up. With the rear seat folded or removed, cargo capacity becomes much larger.

Cost analysis

2005 model prices are expected to be relatively unchanged from 2004, thanks to generous customer rebates, dealer sales incentives, and low-interest financing plans. The biggest price cuts are given to large American SUVs and pickups, both new and used. Be wary, though, of "backdoor" price increases levied through outrageously high freight, PDI, and administrative fees.

Each vehicle is given a percentage markup in this guide, which includes PDI, freight, and other fees. The MSRP should be negotiated downward by about 10 percent, with 5 percent your bottom-line offer; other charges should be cut by 50 percent.

Quality/reliability

Lemon-Aid bases its quality and reliability evaluations on owner comments, confidential technical service bulletins (TSBs), and government reports from NHTSA safety complaint files, among other sources. We also draw on the knowledge and expertise of professionals working in the automotive market-place, including mechanics and fleet owners.

As you read through the quality and reliability ratings (safety is more of a mixed bag), you'll quickly discover that most Japanese automakers are far ahead of DaimlerChrysler, Ford, GM, and European manufacturers in maintaining a high level of quality control in their vehicles. Although GM quality control has improved a bit of late, you wouldn't believe it after looking over 2004 Silverado/Sierra owner complaints recorded by NHTSA at *www.odi.nhtsa.dot.gov/cars/problems/complain/*.

Warranty performance

I'm more impressed by performance than promise. A manufacturer's warranty is a legal commitment that the product it sells will perform in the normal and customary manner for which it is designed. It's an important factor in this edition's ratings and is judged by how fairly it's applied—not by what's promised. This includes warranty extensions set up by automakers to pay for defect-related failures that occur long after the original warranty has expired.

Safety summary

Some of the main features weighed in the safety ratings are a model's crash-worthiness and claims experience (as assessed by NHTSA and various insurers' groups, including the Highway Loss Data Institute and the Insurance Institute for Highway Safety), the availability of standard safety features, and front and rearward visibility. Also listed here are a summary of safety-related complaints that'll astound and worry you.

Front and side crash protection figures are taken from NHTSA's New Car Assessment Program. Vehicles are crashed into a fixed barrier, head-on, at 56 km/h (35 mph). NHTSA uses star rankings to express the likelihood of the belted occupants being seriously injured. The higher the number of stars, the greater the protection. NHTSA's side crash test represents an intersection-type collision with a 1,368 kg (3,015 lb.) barrier moving at 62 km/h (38.5 mph) into a standing vehicle. To replicate the front of a car, the moving barrier is covered with material that has "give."

IIHS rates head restraint, frontal offset, and side crash protection as "good," "acceptable," "marginal," or "poor." In the Institute's 64 km/h (40 mph) offset test, 40 percent of the total width of each vehicle strikes a barrier on the driver side. The barrier's deformable face is made of aluminum honeycomb, which makes the forces in the test similar to those involved in a frontal offset crash between two vehicles of the same weight, each going just less than 64 km/h.

The 50 km/h (31 mph) side impact test performed by IIHS is carried out at a slower speed than the NHTSA test, but uses a barrier with a front end shaped to simulate the typical front end of a pickup or SUV. The Institute also includes the degree of head injury in its ratings.

NHTSA Collision Ratings: Chance of Serious Injury

	Front	Side
*****	10% or less	5% or less
****	11% to 20%	6% to 10%
***	21% to 35%	11% to 20%
**	36% to 45%	21% to 25%
*	46% or greater	26% or greater

NHTSA Rollover Ratings: Chance of Tipping Over

	Rollover Risk
*****	Less than 10%
****	Between 10% and 20%
***	Between 20% and 30%
**	Between 30% and 40%
*	Greater than 40%

Secret warranties/Service tips

A *Lemon-Aid* exclusive, confidential technical service bulletins are listed in this section to give readers ammunition to get repairs done for free.

Some vehicles have more TSBs than others, but this doesn't necessarily mean they're lemons. It may be that the listed problems affect only a small number of vehicles or are minor and easily corrected. TSBs should also be used to verify that a problem was correctly diagnosed, the correct upgraded replacement part was used, and the billed labour time was fair.

Costs

Here we list the manufacturer's suggested retail price (MSRP) for standard models, in effect at press time; that price's negotiability; and the range of the dealer's markup, including freight and other added fees. If the dealer's price is more than 3 percent higher than the price indicated in *Lemon-Aid*, ask for a copy of the manufacturer's notice to the dealer of the MSRP increase. You can confirm the MSRP figure by accessing each manufacturer's website.

Once you discover the latest MSRP, negotiate a reduction of the MSRP by at least half the indicated markup percentage, shown in parentheses next to the MSRP, keeping in mind whether the price is "firm" or "negotiable."

SPORT-UTILITY VEHICLES

Toyota's Not So Green

Indeed, Toyota and the other Japanese automakers are putting their main engineering and marketing emphasis on challenging the Big Three's dominance of larger (and higher-profit) SUVs and pickups....

Turns out Toyota's main commitment is not to fuel efficiency, but to profits—just like any other corporation. Some environmentalists will be tricked by feel-good advertising into endorsing corporations that are getting worse, not better, at protecting the environment. But hopefully most will not.

Buzz Hargrove, President
Canadian Auto Workers
Globe and Mail, August 21, 2004

Small SUVs rule

High gasoline prices have cut deeply into full-sized SUV sales this year, while small SUV wagons remained strong, with sales up 18.9 percent in the first six months of 2004. Sport wagons like the Ford Escape, Honda CR-V, and Toyota RAV4 were hard to resist since they offer more reasonable prices, better fuel economy, and easier handling than big SUVs. Buyers have simply downsized their choices rather than switched to another kind of vehicle. Instead of scintillating 0–100 km/h performance, buyers are looking for fuel-economy bragging rights and innovative convenience and safety features.

Trucks, vans, and sport-utilities represent about half of all the vehicles sold annually in North America. And within the truck category, sport-utilities account for almost a third of annual new-car sales in Canada—five percentage points more than in the United States.

Ford's Escape had one of its best years ever, despite a history of poor quality control.

Next time you're stuck in traffic, look around at the large number of small to mid-sized SUVs that are also inching along in traffic. They're the next generation of a sport-utility stampede that has now shifted direction to smaller vehicles like the Ford Escape, GM TrailBlazer EXT/Envoy, Jeep Liberty, and a plethora of new Asian entries that include the Honda Pilot, Nissan Murano, Subaru Endeavour, and Toyota Highlander.

And don't forget the fastest growing segment of SUVs: "Crossover" car-based sport-utilities and tall wagons that take on SUV attributes and blend cargo-carrying versatility with carlike comfort and handling. Prime examples of these hybrids are the Chrysler Pacifica, Honda Pilot, Mitsubishi Outlander, Nissan Xterra, Pontiac Vibe, Subaru Forester, and Toyota Matrix.

Conversely, large SUVs are an endangered species due primarily to high fuel costs and insurance premiums. Dealers routinely give out $5,000 new-car rebates, and used prices are plummeting. Many behemoths like the Ford Excursion and GM Suburban have already been axed and others will soon be taken off the market. The Ford Expedition, GM Hummer, Lincoln Navigator and Aviator, and Mercedes M series are at the top of the hit list.

Car- or truck-based?

SUV buyers must decide whether they need the ruggedness and increased towing capability of a truck-based SUV or if they would rather have the ride comfort, more predictable handling, and increased crashworthiness of a car-based version or a crossover. For example, the car-based Chrysler Pacifica is much closer to being a station wagon than what many of us think of as an SUV. It has one of the best highway rides of any SUV, exceptional handling, and one of the lowest rollover risks among SUVs tested. Furthermore, fuel economy is almost equal to that of a minivan or large sedan (see 2004 NHTSA rollover chart on pages 17–18).

Any wonder that sales of truck-based SUVs have been flat for three years, while car-based and crossover vehicles have grown steadily?

Don't assume that all truck-based models have similar towing capabilities. The Chevy Tahoe/GMC Yukon and Ford Expedition can tow more than four tons. GM's TrailBlazer has more than double the torque of the Buick Rendezvous, whose towing capacity maxes out at 3,500 lb. with the optional towing package; the standard towing limit is just one ton.

The military made its contribution to the SUV craze with its Jeep lineup and the Hummer (now marketed by General Motors). Imagine, what was designed for use as a military vehicle during World War II and refined in Desert Storm has become the toy of well-heeled baby boomer "G.I. Joes," who miss the irony of a German company selling Jeeps. Hummer buyers throw common sense (and their money) to the wind to purchase a $60,000–$100,000 SUV that won't see off-road use 95 percent of the time.

Now, a final word for that 5 percent of us who do enjoy off-roading. Listing "adventure" as the top reason for choosing this vehicle, buyers stress that they expect it to provide outstanding off-road performance combined with good handling, a comfortable ride, good traction, and high ground clearance. But a soft suspension and precision handling are inversely proportional to true off-road capability, though some automakers are providing vehicles that offer a good compromise. Bear in mind that real off-roading takes place at about 15 km/h and can be a kidney-pounding, white knuckle experience (kinda like driving early MGs, Triumphs, and Ladas).

A buyer's market for "biggies"

Large SUVs like the Ford Expedition and Excursion, Jeep Grand Cherokees, and GM Suburban, Yukon, and Tahoe are selling for a song; three-year-old vehicles are worth less than 50 percent of their original MSRP. And, as more new products hit showrooms, used prices will continue to fall well into 2005. Other downsides for buyers, besides soaring gas prices, are the high insurance costs and increasingly complex mechanical and electronic systems associated with these goliaths.

Hatchback and wagon alternatives

Hatchbacks and wagons can be good alternatives to SUVs if you don't need to accommodate more than five passengers and carry very much cargo. Here are some pros/cons you may wish to consider:

Wagons versus SUVs

Wagon Advantages
• reasonable pricing
• low rollover risk
• good handling, braking
• many advanced safety features
• good fuel economy
• low step-in height

Wagon Disadvantages

- lower view of the road in front
- less passenger, cargo room
- difficult to access small third-row seats; limited seating flexibility
- low towing capability
- limited off-roading, even with AWD

SUV Advantages

- competitive prices and slow depreciation on smaller models
- good front visibility and predictable winter/rough-terrain driving
- seat five to nine passengers with lots of seating flexibility
- lots of cargo room and easy loading and unloading
- 2,000–5,000 lb. towing capability
- truck frame good for heavy-duty off-roading
- fuel-efficient and easy handling
- versatile performance
- post-1997 models have safety features similar to those found in cars
- impressive crashworthiness scores for car-based models

SUV Disadvantages

- overpriced, fuel-thirsty, with high insurance premiums
- accessories are expensive but essential (like running boards, roll bars, and sophisticated anti-theft systems)
- inferior handling, rough riding, moderate to very high rollover risk
- increased risk of injury to children
- inferior braking
- truck frames may be deadly to small cars in multi-vehicle crashes, and in crashes with other trucks
- awkward to enter and exit, difficult to access third row seats, smaller rear doors and high step-in height
- lower crashworthiness scores for truck-based models
- good off-road performers are poorly suited for highway/city use and vice versa

Part- or full-time 4X4?

There are two types of 4X4 vehicles: part-time and full-time 4X4s. Part-time 4X4 should be engaged when roads are wet, muddy, or snow covered. The four wheels are locked together to turn at the same speed. On dry pavement, driving in 4X4 mode may strain the drivetrain and damage the driveline components (check the owner's manual).

Full-time 4X4 (also called all-wheel drive) is a more sophisticated system that permits driving on any surface, all the time. A centre differential lets all four wheels turn at different speeds. If front or rear wheels lose traction, sensors send more power to those wheels. Most buyers prefer the convenience of all-wheel drive and most automakers are moving in that direction.

Safety

One of the main reasons buyers choose sport-utility vehicles is the safety advantages they offer. First and foremost, the large windshield and high seating give you an incredible view of the road ahead, though rear vision may be obstructed by side pillars, rear head restraints, or the spare tire hanging off the back end. As we react more slowly with age, this increased visibility comes in handy (a few extra seconds of warning can make a big difference). Improvements have also been made with three-point seat belts in the front and rear, seat belt pretensioners, optional adjustable brake and accelerator pedals, a high centre brake light, adjustable head restraints on all seatbacks, side airbags, four-wheel anti-lock brakes, side-door beams, and reinforced roofs to protect occupants in rollovers.

Most large SUVs will protect you fairly well in a frontal collision while creaming whoever hits you. But rollovers are an ever-present safety risk, particularly with early production models that were produced through the mid-1990s (we're talking Suzuki, Isuzu, and Ford Bronco) and that "poster boy" of rollovers, Ford's 1992–2004 Explorer.

Reliability and quality

In the last decade, many domestic and imported SUVs were rushed to market with serious quality and performance deficiencies. Mercedes' 1997–2000 M-Class sport-utilities, for example, are nowhere near as reliable as BMW's X5 and the SUVs produced by Asian automakers.

DaimlerChrysler, Jeep, and Ford have a long way to go to close the quality gap. Dodge's Durango has a barely acceptable reliability score; Jeep's Cherokee, Grand Cherokee, and Liberty have been afflicted by serious powertrain, AC, brake, and body defects. And don't forget the Ford Explorer, the most popular SUV ever produced (3.5 million sold). It has a terrible reputation for poor quality control and reliability, plus a plethora of safety-related factory mistakes, highlighted by sudden, unintended acceleration and rollovers (a problem first raised with the previous Bronco series).

GM's post-2000 SUVs are the best of Detroit's worst. Their relatively recent redesigns have improved overall safety and performance but reliability is still the pits with serious engine, transmission, and fit-and-finish defects. After three to five years of use (about when the warranty ends), buyers would be wise to get an extended warranty or dump these vehicles.

SPORT-UTILITY RATINGS

Recommended

Honda CR-V (2002–05)	Nissan Murano (2003–05)
Honda Pilot (2003–05)	Toyota Highlander (2001–04)
Lexus LX 450, LX 470 (1998–2004)	Toyota RAV4 (2004–05)
Lexus RX 330 (2004)	Toyota Sequoia (2001–04)

Above Average
General Motors Tracker (V6)
Honda CR-V (1997–2001)
Honda Element (2003–05)
Hyundai Santa Fe (2001–05)
Lexus GX 470, LX 450,
 LX 470 (1998–2005)
Lexus RX 300, RX 330 (1999–2005)

Infiniti FX35, FX45 (2003–05)
Infiniti QX4, QX56 (1997–2005)
Nissan Armada, Pathfinder
 (2000–05)
Nissan Xterra (2005)
Toyota 4Runner (1996–2005)
Toyota RAV4 (1997–2003)

Average
Acura MDX (2001–05)
BMW X5 (2000–04)
Chrysler Pacifica (2004–05)
Ford Escape/Mazda Tribute (2005)
General Motors Aztek, Rendezvous
 (2001–05)
General Motors Blazer, Envoy,Jimmy
 (1999–2005)
General Motors Envoy, Trailblazer,
 Rainier, (Isuzu) Ascender, (Saab)
 9–7X (2002–05)
General Motors Escalade, ESV, EXT,
 Suburban,Tahoe, Yukon, Yukon XL,
 Denali (1995–2005)

General Motors Tracker/Suzuki
 Sidekick, Vitara (1994–2005)
Jeep Cherokee, Grand Cherokee
 (2002–05)
Jeep TJ Wrangler, YJ Wrangler
 (1987–2004)
Lexus LX 450, LX 470 (1997)
Mitsubishi Endeavour (2004)
Nissan Pathfinder (1990–99)
Nissan Xterra (2003–04)
Nissan X-Trail (2005)
Subaru Forester (1994–2005)
Subaru Impreza (1997–2005)
WRX (2002–05)
Toyota 4Runner (1986–95)

Below Average
BMW X5 (2000–05)
Ford Excursion (2000–04)
Ford Expedition, Navigator
 (1997–2005)
General Motors Blazer, Envoy,
 Jimmy (1995–98)
General Motors Suburban,
 Yukon XL (1995–99)

General Motors Tracker/Suzuki
 Sidekick (1989–93)
Mitsubishi Montero (2003)
Mitsubishi Outlander (2004)
Nissan Pathfinder (1987–89)
Nissan Xterra (2000–02)

Not Recommended
BMW X3 (2005)
Dodge Durango (1998–2005)
Ford Aviator, Explorer, Explorer
 Sport Trac,
Mountaineer (1991–2004)
Ford Escape/Mazda Tribute
 (2001–04)
General Motors Equinox (2005)
General Motors Suburban, Yukon,
 Tahoe (1985–94)

Hyundai Tucson (2005)
Isuzu Ascender (2004)
Jeep Cherokee, Grand Cherokee
 (1985–2001)
Jeep Liberty (2002–05)
Jeep TJ Wrangler (2005)
Kia Sportage (2000–05)
Kia Sorento (2003–05)
Saab 9–7X (2005)
Saturn Vue (2002–05)

Acura

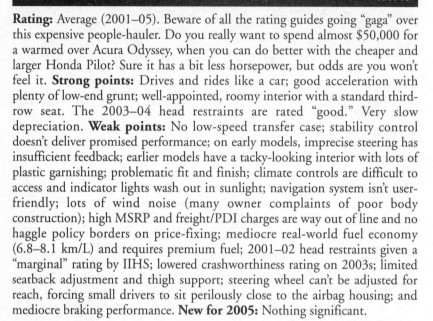

MDX   ★★★

Rating: Average (2001–05). Beware of all the rating guides going "gaga" over this expensive people-hauler. Do you really want to spend almost $50,000 for a warmed over Acura Odyssey, when you can do better with the cheaper and larger Honda Pilot? Sure it has a bit less horsepower, but odds are you won't feel it. **Strong points:** Drives and rides like a car; good acceleration with plenty of low-end grunt; well-appointed, roomy interior with a standard third-row seat. The 2003–04 head restraints are rated "good." Very slow depreciation. **Weak points:** No low-speed transfer case; stability control doesn't deliver promised performance; on early models, imprecise steering has insufficient feedback; earlier models have a tacky-looking interior with lots of plastic garnishing; problematic fit and finish; climate controls are difficult to access and indicator lights wash out in sunlight; navigation system isn't user-friendly; lots of wind noise (many owner complaints of poor body construction); high MSRP and freight/PDI charges are way out of line and no haggle policy borders on price-fixing; mediocre real-world fuel economy (6.8–8.1 km/L) and requires premium fuel; 2001–02 head restraints given a "marginal" rating by IIHS; lowered crashworthiness rating on 2003s; limited seatback adjustment and thigh support; steering wheel can't be adjusted for reach, forcing small drivers to sit perilously close to the airbag housing; and mediocre braking performance. **New for 2005:** Nothing significant.

2005 Technical Data

Powertrain
Engine: 3.5L V6 (260 hp)
Transmission: 5-speed auto.
Dimension/Capacity
Height/length/width:
69/189/77.0 in.
Headroom F/R: 4.0/4.0 in.
Legroom F/R: 41/30 in.

Wheelbase: 106 in.
Turning circle: 40 ft.
Passengers: 2/3/2
Cargo volume: 42 cu. ft.
GVWR: 5,732 lb.
Ground clear.: 5 in.
Fuel tank: 72.7L/premium
Weight: 4,555 lb.

MODEL HISTORY: Introduced as a 2001 model, the MDX initially carried a 212-hp 6-cylinder engine. It seats seven and is longer than the rival five-seat BMW X5 and Lexus RX 300 and uses second- and third-row bench seats that conveniently fold flat with the load floor (the last row is suitable for small children only). **2002**—Some noise-reduction measures. **2003**—More power, a new transmission, a standard anti-skid system, and a Honda clone, called the Pilot. **2004**—Updated styling, a tire-pressure monitor, and head-protecting curtain side airbags.

COST ANALYSIS: Priced at $49,000, the 2005 is practically identical to the 2004. **Best alternatives:** You want comparable performance for at least $10,000 less? Try a Honda Pilot (the MDX's cheaper cousin) for its additional passenger/cargo hauling capability, or a Nissan Xterra or Toyota Highlander.

The Volvo XC90, ML320/350/500, and the new Lexus RX330 have very good cargo room with all the rows down, but they don't have comparable cargo room behind the second row. **Rebates:** Look for $4,000+ rebates on the 2004 and 2005 models early next year as the competition heats up. **Delivery/PDI:** $950. **Warranty:** Bumper-to-bumper 3 years/60,000 km; powertrain 5 years/100,000 km; rust perforation 5 years/unlimited km. **Supplementary warranty:** Not needed. **Options:** Vehicle comes fully loaded, except for the non-essential navigation system, rear backup camera, and DVD player. Replace the stock Goodyear tires with Michelin Pilot LTX (245/65/17) or the equivalent for a better, quieter ride. Change only the radio speakers for improved audio quality. The roof cross rails aren't adjustable and are a bit wider than those on other SUVs, making it difficult to get roof cargo carriers that will fit. **Depreciation:** Incredibly slow. **Insurance cost:** Much higher than average. **Parts supply/cost:** Parts are reasonably priced and easily found in the Odyssey/Honda generic parts bin. **Annual maintenance cost:** Less than average. **Highway/city fuel economy:** 10.4–13.9L/100 km, but many owners say they get much less.

QUALITY/RELIABILITY: Reliability shouldn't be a problem, unless you actually believe this vehicle can go off-roading. If so, make sure you get an extended warranty and join an auto club for its towing service. **Owner complaints:** Automatic transmission failures, a rotten-egg exhaust smell, engine hesitation around 60 km/h, moon roof water leaks, squeaks and rattles (dash, door lock, and tailpipe), brake caliper clicking/clunking, gas tank sloshing, wind noise, and a high-speed harmonic drone. The auto AC mode is slow to cool the car in stop-and-go driving; AM reception is poor; Bose radio has too much bass; driver's seatback doesn't go vertical enough for some; seats have insufficient thigh and back support; and seat memory settings are gradually lost. **Warranty performance:** Average.

ROAD PERFORMANCE: Acceleration/torque: Smooth, quiet, and sustained acceleration; one of the best among V6 competitors (0–100 km/h: 8.7 seconds). 2003 model has 20 extra horses. **Transmission:** Flawless shifting with the only transaxle available, the 5-speed automatic. **Steering:** Vague, with insufficient feedback. **Routine handling:** A bit cumbersome, particularly when cornering, as body lean becomes more evident. This unsteady behaviour becomes worse as the speed increases or the steering correction is more severe. Says Consumers Union testers: "The MDX does not inspire confidence in emergency handling, even with its new stability-control." Firm suspension also jostles occupants when passing over uneven pavement (the Lexus RX 300/330 and Toyota Sequoia handle this better). The lack of a low-speed transfer case limits this SUV's off-roading prowess. **Braking:** Unimpressive; they're difficult to modulate until you adapt to their sensitivity with a lighter foot.

SAFETY SUMMARY: Airbags: Front and side. **ABS:** Standard; disc/disc. **Safety belt pretensioners:** Front. **Head restraints F/R:** *2001–02:* ***; *2003–04:* ****. **Visibility F/R:** *****. **Maximum load capacity:** 1,160 lb.

SAFETY COMPLAINTS: 2001—Chronic stalling on the highway. • Automatic transmission suddenly downshifted, causing loss of control. • Seat belts won't hold a child booster seat securely. • Airbag warning light stays lit. **2002**—Seat belts tighten progressively once buckled. **2002–03**—Transmission failures. **2003**—Airbag failed to deploy. • Front spring breakage. • Sudden acceleration. • Navigation system gives incorrect information. • Seat belt crosses at driver's neck. • Front seat belt locks up. **2004**—Tire slipped off the rim and vehicle went out of control, despite stability-control feature.

Secret Warranties/Service Tips

2001—Throttle bracket buzzing or rattling. • Clunking when braking or accelerating thought to be caused by front lower control arm. • Noisy power steering pump. • Supplementary restraint system (SRS) unit internal failure. • Product update/secret warranty relative to the seat belt harness. • Second row seat may not fold down or recline. • Water dripping from the outside mirror. • Loose rear wiper arm. • Loose or detached seatback panel covered by a TSB. **2001–02**—V6 engine oil leaks. • Missing speed sensor plug. • Brief hesitation when accelerating. • Cranks, but won't start. • Loose driver's seat. • Thumping from sloshing fuel. • Under-hood buzzing or rattling. • Booming noise from rear of vehicle at 90–100 km/h. • Squeaking noise from the middle roof area, and the moon roof. • Broken seat belt tongue stopper button. **2001–03**—Faulty remote audio controls. • Dash or front strut creaking or ticking. **2001–04**—Clunking brakes:

Rear Break Clunk Noise

Bulletin No.: 04-009   Date: March 23, 2004
2001–04 MDX

SYMPTOM: The rear brake calipers clunk when you first apply the brakes after changing the direction of the vehicle.

PROBABLE CAUSE: The outer shims on the rear brake pads do not allow the pads to slide easily when you press the brake pedal. This causes the outer pad to hit hard during a change of direction, resulting in a clunk.

2002–03—Remedy for front damper noise. **2003**—Sunroof water leaks will be fixed for free under TSB #03-018, issued June 2003.

MDX Profile

	2001	2002	2003	2004
Cost Price ($) (firm)				
MDX (19%)	47,000	48,000	49,000	50,300
Used Values ($)				
MDX ʌ	29,000	34,000	41,000	46,500
MDX v	27,000	32,000	39,000	43,000

Reliability	④	⑤	⑤	⑤
Crash Safety (F)	—	⑤	④	⑤
Side	—	⑤	⑤	⑤
Offset	⑤	⑤	⑤	⑤
Rollover	—	④	④	—

BMW

X3	★

Rating: Not Recommended (2005); this is its first year on the market. **Strong points:** High seating gives a good view of the road; costs $14,000 less than an X5; impressive power range and towing for a compact SUV; provides a full complement of high-tech safety features. **Weak points:** Highway performance not up to the 3-series standard, and Audi A4 or Infiniti G35 do just as well. Bland styling and lacks many standard features found on other $50,000 compact SUVs (would you believe optional power seats?); long shifter throws; slower and less precise steering than the competition; heavier and about 15 percent less fuel efficient than a Lexus RX 330; cargo-carrying capacity can't touch the Honda CR-V/Ford Escape crowd; doesn't project the same quality cachet as other BMWs; excessively high freight and preparation charge; no crashworthiness data yet available; and early service bulletins show serious engine and automatic transmission failures.

COST ANALYSIS: BMW's smallest SUV offers a 184-hp 2.5L or a 225-hp 3.0L inline-six engine and sells for $44,600–$49,850, depending upon the model. Power is handled in 3-series fashion via a 6-speed manual and permanent all-wheel-drive system. A 5-speed dual auto/manual shifter will only set you back $1,290 (gulp!). But that's a mere pittance when compared to the $1,595 freight/preparation fee. **Best alternatives:** The Acura MDX, Infiniti FX35, and Lexus RX 330.

Secret Warranties/Service Tips

2004—Radio reception problems. • Delayed cold automatic transmission engagement. • Engine head bolt threads pull out of block. • Engine cylinder head leaks:

Oil Leakage from Cylinder Head

Bulletin No.: B11 201 04   Date: 2/4/2004

Low Mileage Oil Leakage from Cylinder Head

All with M54 Engine

Cause: Porosity in the cylinder head casting between the oil pressure supply passage and the spark plug tubes. Replace the cylinder head.

X5   ★★

Rating: Below Average (2000–05). Sure, the X5 has lots of power and convenience features, but its high-speed performance isn't all that impressive and its quality control is still way below average. **Strong points:** Rapid acceleration with plenty of torque in all gear ranges; nimble low-speed handling; good braking; first-class interior; reasonable freight/PDI fees; a wide array of standard safety, performance, and convenience features; and a "good" crashworthiness rating from IIHS. **Weak points:** No low-range gearing for off-roading; high-speed handling seriously compromised by this wagon's choppy, tippy ride; excessive engine noise; complicated navigation system controls; tall step-up and narrow doorways; loading made difficult by the high liftover; limited rear-seat and cargo space; atrocious premium fuel economy; an unusually large number of safety-related recalls and owner complaints; confidential BMW service bulletins show manufacturing mistakes are the source of most problems. **New for 2005:** A restyled exterior, 6-speed manual and automatic transmissions, and a new AWD system.

2005 Technical Data

Powertrain
Engines: 3.0L 6-cyl. (225 hp)
• 4.4L V8 (290 hp)
• 4.6L V8 (340 hp)
Transmissions: 6-speed man.
• 6-speed auto.
Dimension/Capacity
Height/length/width:
67/184/74 in.
Headroom F/R: 4.0/4.5 in.

Legroom F/R: 42/28.5 in.
Wheelbase: 111 in.
Turning circle: 40 ft.
Passengers: 2/3
Cargo volume: 35.5 cu. ft.
GVWR: 5,860 lb.
Tow limit: 5,000 lb.
Ground clear.: 7.5 in.
Fuel tank: 93L/premium
Weight: 4,745 lb.

MODEL HISTORY: 2001—A V8-powered X5 4.4i and 6-cylinder 3.0i edition debuted in Canada after a year in the States. **2002**—A high-performance 4.6is model gave BMW a high-performance counterpunch against Mercedes-Benz's ML 500/ML55 AMG. **2004**—New front-end styling, AWD system, and V8 engine; a high-performance model was added mid-year; and a standard 6-speed transmission was added.

COST ANALYSIS: This $58,600 sport wagon isn't worth its high price, but most of the excess cost will be recovered through a higher-than-average resale value. Unless you want the fuel-thirsty 4.6L V8, stick with the 3.0L 6-cylinder. Be wary of the smaller V6 engine coupled to a manual transmission; clutch action is rough and hard to modulate. **Best alternatives:** When it comes to off-roading, the X5 is blown away by the prowess of the Toyota Land Cruiser or Lexus RX 300/330 and other less-expensive SUVs. Even Land Rover's Range Rover outperforms the X5 in off-road driving. Think seriously of getting a BMW 5 Series wagon for storage capability and performance. Forget Nissan's FX35 if you want a comfortable ride and lots of storage capacity.

Rebates: Look for $2,000 rebates on leftover 2004s by year's end. **Delivery/PDI:** $350. **Warranty:** Bumper-to-bumper 4 years/80,000 km; rust perforation 6 years/unlimited km. **Supplementary warranty:** A good idea. **Options:** Rear-obstacle warning system and 5-speed automatic transmission with manual shift capability are worthwhile investments. Sport package low-profile tires will bounce you around on rough pavement. **Depreciation:** A bit slower than average. **Insurance cost:** Much higher than average. **Parts supply/cost:** Average. **Annual maintenance cost:** Predict higher-than-average repair costs, if owner complaints already recorded and dealership servicing costs for passenger cars are any indication. Cheaper, independent garages won't touch these vehicles, adding to their servicing costs. **Highway/city fuel economy:** *6-cyl.:* 10.6–15.6L/100 km; *V8:* 11.9–16.4L/100 km.

QUALITY/RELIABILITY: Overall reliability has been quite poor, judging by owner complaints on the Internet (*roadfly.com*, among others) and by BMW's internal service bulletins. Aside from the X5's many recall campaigns, owners report a number of safety-related defects that are indicative of poor quality control. Many of the owner complaints go to the heart of the X5's reliability, as well as its overall safety. **Warranty performance:** Better than average. However, it would be comforting to see the company expend as much energy eliminating defects at the factory level.

ROAD PERFORMANCE: Acceleration/torque: Both the 6-cylinder and V8 provide exemplary acceleration unmatched by the competition. **Transmission:** Smooth and quiet shifting. **Steering:** Impressive steering is very responsive and accurate, though a bit heavy when parking. Power-adjustable steering wheel keeps small-statured drivers away from the airbag housing. **Routine handling:** Exceptional. The X5 comes closer to the carlike handling of the Lexus RX 300/330 than the more trucklike performance of the Mercedes M-Class and the less responsive Acura MDX. Emergency handling, however, is quite poor. The ride is choppy and the car seems prone to tip over despite its stability control feature. **Braking:** Excellent, with no fading after successive stops.

SAFETY SUMMARY: 2001–03 models have received a Best Pick offset crash rating from IIHS. Before you purchase this vehicle, make sure the headlight illumination is adequate. On some model years, the gas and brake pedals are poorly designed; anyone with a size 12 or larger shoe can inadvertently hit the wrong pedal. **Airbags:** Standard. There have been reports that airbags didn't deploy during a head-on collision on the 2000 models. Don't activate the side-impact airbags if you carry small-statured occupants. **ABS:** Standard; disc/disc. **Safety belt pretensioners:** Front. **Traction control:** Yes. **Head restraints F/R:** ***. **Visibility F/R:** ****/*.

SAFETY COMPLAINTS: 2000—Vehicle suddenly leaps forward or stalls. • Airbags fails to deploy. • Engine runs rough and warning light is constantly lit. • Door latch will not release; driver had to crawl out through the window. • Rear doors open while vehicle is underway. • Hooking mechanism fails to hold up shade and flies across vehicle. • Poorly designed brake pedals won't accept a large foot. **2000–03**—Headlight illumination is blinding. • Windshield shatters for no reason. **2001**—ABS brake light remains lit. • Fuel leakage into the passenger's compartment from the fuel pump seal. • Inadvertent deployment of five front airbags. • Chronic stalling problem with 3.0L engines. • Parked vehicle rolled away due to emergency brake failure. • Transmission loses First, Second, and Fifth gear due to faulty electronic chip. • Transmission often shifts into Neutral. • Bent suspension control arm caused prematurely worn-out tires. • Front door design can injure one's head. • Front door locks occupants inside vehicle. • Seat heater burns leather and occupant's skin. • Recall should be expanded to include other fire-prone fans. **2001–02**—Sudden brake failure. • Faulty electronic side-view mirrors. **2002**—X5's rear blind spot contributed to fatal accident. • While driving, driver's side door suddenly opened. • Floor mat may cause throttle to stick. • Airbag light stays lit. • Power windows won't stay up. • Wipers come on for no reason. • Fragile bumpers. **2002–03**—Frequent major electrical system failures. **2003**—Headlights may suddenly cut out while driving. **2004**—Transmission shuts down while engine is running.

Secret Warranties/Service Tips

All years: Troubleshooting tips for constantly lit engine warning light. • Intermittent electrical faults related to circuits in the upper rear hatch. • Rough running, black smoke, and starter may stay engaged. • Service action covers deburring the exhaust tail pipes. • Troubleshooting AC musty odours. • Squealing, groaning, or grinding noise when turning the steering wheel. • Steering wheel vibration at idle. • Brake pedal rattling. • Popping, clicking clutch pedal. • Front door window or door seal noise. • Outer door releases fail to operate in freezing weather. • Service action to replace the passenger-side mirror. **2000**—Window regulators produce a squeaking, clicking, and creaking noise on vehicles built before May 2000. • Some vehicles may lack the electrically adjustable steering column that is a standard feature on U.S. models. • Fuel tank vent line fitting weld may be faulty, allowing gas fumes to enter the passenger compartment; dealer will re-weld it under a product update campaign (read, secret warranty) as per TSB #16-5200. • Incorrect fuel gauge readings. • Faulty windshield wiper blades. • Generator whine on AM band. **2000–01**—Poor starting, no-starts, and erratic shifting. **2001**—Battery drain from Alpine radio hookup. • Faulty luggage compartment interior light. **2002**—Campaign to troubleshoot faulty Check Engine light. • Loose air intake boot. • Defective rear hatch switch. • Inoperative AC blower. • Brake pedal rattling. • Correcting steering squealing, grinding, or groaning. **2002–03**—Hard, no-shift condition (automatic transmission). **2004**—Defective engine cylinder head (see X3). • Engine head bolt threads pull out of block. • Hydraulic belt tensioner installation. • Campaign to troubleshoot Low Oil Level warning. • Cold weather valve cover/engine damage. • Delayed cold automatic transmission engagement. • Difficulty coding navigation system; erratic performance. • Defective keyless entry. • Telematic inspection/replacement campaign. • Rear hatch latch electrical failure campaign. • Headlamp condensation.

X5 Profile

	2000	2001	2002	2003	2004
Cost Price ($) (firm)					
X5 (12%)	—	56,960	56,900	57,800	58,500
X5 4.4i (15%)	—	—	68,900	69,800	71,400
X5 4.6is (15%)	—	—	93,900	94,500	—
Used Values ($)					
X5 ⋀	—	35,000	42,000	48,000	51,000
X5 ⋁	—	33,000	40,000	45,000	49,000
X5 4.4i ⋀	—	—	50,000	57,000	61,000
X5 4.4i ⋁	—	—	46,000	53,000	59,000
X5 4.6is ⋀	—	—	63,000	73,000	—
X5 4.6is ⋁	—	—	58,000	68,000	—
Reliability	③	③	③	④	④
Crash Safety (F)	—	—	—	⑤	⑤
Side	—	—	—	④	④
Offset	—	⑤	⑤	⑤	⑤
Rollover	—	—	—	③	—

DaimlerChrysler

JEEP TJ WRANGLER, YJ WRANGLER ★★★

Rating: Not Recommended (2005; its first year of shared production); Average (1987–2004). The only Jeep that is body-on-frame; ideal for off-roaders who won't mind living with this Jeep's many safety and performance defects. **Strong points:** Reasonably priced; slow depreciation; attractively styled; comfortable front seating; controls and displays are nicely laid out, though controls on older models aren't as user-friendly; competent low-speed handling; a versatile off-roader; and a good crashworthiness rating. **Weak points:** Base models are bereft of many standard features; rough and noisy ride; mediocre braking; cramped rear seating; little storage space; plastic windows don't stay clean for long; high step-in; chronic powertrain and body deficiencies; poor fuel economy; and many reports of engine- and steering column–related fires. **New for 2005:** Nothing significant; next redesign in 2007.

2005 Technical Data

Powertrain (4X4)
Engines: 2.4L 4-cyl. (147 hp)
• 4.0L inline 6-cyl. (190 hp)
Transmissions: 5-speed man.
• 3-speed auto.
• 4-speed auto.

Legroom F/R: 41.1/34.9 in.
Wheelbase: 93.4 in.
Turning circle: 36 ft.
Passengers: 2/2
Cargo volume: 17 cu. ft.
GVWR: 3,094–3,333 lb.

Dimension/Capacity
Height/length/width:
69.4/155/66.7 in.
Headroom F/R: 42.3/40.6 in.

Tow limit: 2,000 lb.
Fuel tank: 57L/76L/reg.
Weight: 3,510 lb.

MODEL HISTORY: Early CJs and YJs were equipped with a wimpy, fuel-thirsty 4.2L straight 6-cylinder motor mated to either a 4- or 5-speed manual or a 3-speed automatic transmission. **1991**—A powerful, better-running 180-hp 4.0L engine replaced the 4.2L 6-cylinder. For off-roading use, skip the 6-cylinder—you are much better off with a 4-cylinder engine, particularly on later models. Unfortunately, the 3-speed automatic shifts harshly and saps power from the engine. Not the best vehicle for everyday use: Pre-1997 versions have good low-speed manoeuvrability that is compromised by dismal crashworthiness scores; mediocre high-speed handling; a rough, noisy ride; and worse-than-average braking. **1997**—YJ replaced by the TJ and is much improved from safety, quality, comfort, and performance perspectives. The chassis, steering, and suspension refinements make the Wrangler more carlike in its handling and much more stable on the road. **1999**—Upgraded rotary climate controls and a larger standard fuel tank. **2000**—Sport and Sahara got a more refined, quieter 6-cylinder power plant, along with an upgraded 5-speed manual shifter. **2003**—SE models use the Liberty's 147-hp 2.4L 4-cylinder engine and the X, Sport, Sahara, and Ruibicon versions now carry a 190-hp 4.0L inline 6-cylinder power plant. **2004**—Unlimited gets a wheelbase that's 25 cm (10 in.) longer than other Wranglers and 38 cm (15 in.) longer overall, adding 5 cm (2 in.) of rear leg room and more cargo volume. A tilt steering wheel is standard.

COST ANALYSIS: Priced at $21,500 before generous rebates and discounts are applied, this is the smallest, least expensive (we're talking bare bones here), and most primitive Jeep you can find. Prices are relatively firm and almost all of the equipment that's standard on other vehicles is optional on the Wrangler. Fortunately, a base model without too many options should suit most driving needs. The 2003–05 versions with their longer powertrain warranty and base engine and automatic transmission improvements should be better buys than earlier versions, though internal service bulletins still bemoan the Wrangler's powertrain defects. **Best alternatives:** Other comparable sport-utilities worth a look are the GM Tracker (V6) or Suzuki Sidekick, Honda CR-V, and Toyota RAV4. Remember, none of these other models can follow the Wrangler off-road. **Rebates:** $1,500–$2,000 on the 2004s. **Delivery/PDI:** $860. **Warranty:** Bumper-to-bumper 7 years/115,000 km; powertrain 5 years/100,000 km; rust perforation 5 years/160,000 km. **Supplementary warranty:** Not needed with Chrysler's new 7-year warranty. An extended warranty is a must for older vehicles. **Options:** For serious off-roading, opt for the 6-cylinder power plant and 5-speed manual transmission. Keep an eye out for the optional suspension system, which includes larger shock absorbers and heavy-duty springs. An aftermarket anti-theft system is also a plus. **Depreciation:** Much slower than average. **Insurance cost:** Above average. **Parts supply/cost:** Above-average supply. Servicing from dealers can get expensive, so you'll want to frequent independent service agencies after the warranty expires. **Annual maintenance cost:** Higher than average without the 7-year warranty. A spotty service record at Jeep dealerships inflates maintenance costs. **Highway/city fuel economy:** The 5-speed manual and 6-cylinder engine give you the best fuel economy. *2.5L 4-cyl. and auto.:* 12–14.8L/100 km; *4.0L 6-cyl. and auto.:* 12.1–15.7L/100 km.

QUALITY/RELIABILITY: Factory-related defects have always plagued these vehicles, but they have improved over the years. This year, Chrysler will be building a new Wrangler with three new suppliers taking over production. This is a recipe for disaster. Shoppers would be wise to give these vehicles a wide berth until the new production system can put out quality vehicles, sometime next year. Overall quality control has remained worse than average for over a decade, with an increase in complaints about manual and automatic transmission/transfer-case failures (sometimes within the first 1,000 km). Watch out for transfer-case malfunctions, piston knocking on 1991–96 models, engine and transfer-case oil leaks, worn-out suspension and steering components, and ignition-component malfunctions.

Body welds and seams are susceptible to premature rusting, and there have been frequent complaints about peeling paint and water leaks. The worst leaks occur at the bottom of the windshield frame. An easy way to check for this is to examine the underside of the frame and see if there's excessive rust. This has been a problem area for Jeeps for what seems like forever; hence all of the ads for aftermarket windshield frames. The good news is that you can replace the windshield frame and all of the seals relatively cheaply. **Warranty performance:** Average.

ROAD PERFORMANCE: Acceleration/torque: Off-road capability is impressive with the 4-cylinder engine, thanks to gobs of low-end torque when shifted into low range (torque lb.-ft.: 140@3500 rpm). Smooth, above-average acceleration and torque with the 6-cylinder engine (0–100 km/h: 10.5 sec.). The 2.5L 4-cylinder engine is noisy and lacks the power for serious hauling; it's especially sluggish when hooked to the automatic transmission. Says one owner: "This Jeep loses power at 100 km/h and, even when the accelerator pedal is floored, won't increase speed." **Transmission:** The 3-speed automatic shifts harshly and saps power from the engine. **Steering:** Tends to wander on the highway. **Routine handling:** The ride is harsh and bouncy on all but the smoothest roads, and there's considerable body roll when cornering. Handling is mediocre on the highway, but outstanding off-road. P225/75R tires cause the vehicle to wander. **Emergency handling:** Does not take curves very well, owing to the short wheelbase and high centre of gravity. Good ground clearance and stiff suspension for off-roading. **Braking:** Unacceptably long braking distance (100–0 km/h: 47 m) with or without ABS.

SAFETY SUMMARY: Insurance industry figures show a much higher-than-average number of accident injury claims, aggravated by a high incidence of sudden rollovers caused by drivers exceeding the Jeep's very low tolerance for sporty driving. In fact, Jeeps, along with the Ford Bronco and Suzuki Samurai, have always been among the SUVs most frequently cited in rollover deaths. There are lots of recall campaigns to check out. There have also been reports of front seat belts that fail to retract and interfere with the door latch, as well as seat belts that failed to restrain occupants in a collision. **Airbags:** Front airbags are standard; no side airbags. Many complaints that the airbags fail to deploy or are late deploying; airbag light stays on. **ABS:** Optional; disc/drum. Usually, I'd suggest that you shop for an ABS-equipped model (first made available with the 1993 models), especially considering the Wrangler's poor braking performance. Upgraded a few years ago, brakes continue to be problematic. **Head restraints F/R: **. Visibility F/R: *****/*.**

SAFETY COMPLAINTS: Owners say the manual transmission doesn't shift smoothly; it constantly grinds when shifting (possibly the clutch-release/throw-out bearing) or when in Neutral when clutch is depressed; the shifter won't come out of or go into gear; it may suddenly pop out of gear; it sticks in Second gear when hot, or when accelerating in First or Second; and the Fifth gear suddenly disengages. One owner of a 2000 model said, "There have now been four transmissions in my Jeep, and all have had problems with noise, shifting into and out of gear, and getting stuck in gear." Another owner had to replace the transmission at 600 km. Reports of engine problems—almost stalling when decelerating; bucking, backfiring, and stalling when accelerating; and chronic engine overheating—are also common.

Owners report lots of clutch master and slave cylinder leaks, premature brake wear, and brake failure—there have been several incidents of sudden brake loss (master cylinder replaced) where the pedal goes all the way to the floor with no braking effect. Other brake complaints include a seal leak in the power brake booster that might cause a brake failure; brake drum not keeping its shape; vehicle pulling to left when braking; rear brakes suddenly locking up while driving in the rain and approaching a stop sign; and vehicle going into open throttle position when brakes are applied. There have also been many instances where drivers mistook the accelerator for the brake, due to the close proximity of the pedals.

Owners also report airbag failures, fuel tank leaks, fuel pump failures, and malfunctioning fuel gauges (see "Secret Warranties/Service Tips"). **1995–2003**—Manual and automatic transmission failures. • Gas and brake pedals are too close together. **1997**—Inadequate space for right knee. • Sudden acceleration with foot firmly on brake. • Sudden steering wheel lock-up. • Bolts that hold up the body mounts, engine, and transmission may be missing. **1998**—Dash and fuel line fires. • Loss of all electrical power in damp or rainy weather. • Lights and gauges function erratically. • Shift lever separated from transmission housing. • Very poor rear braking. • **1999**—Exhaust manifold leaks. • Vehicle rolls back when in gear. **2000**—Under-hood fire. • Right rear wheel separated from vehicle. • Vehicle went into Reverse after being shifted into Drive. **2001**—Many engine-related steering column fires. • Sudden, unintended acceleration in Reverse gear. • Rear brakes often fail to engage. • Sudden steering lock-up. • Camshaft sensor binding and breaking, causing vehicle to stall. • Broken rear axle seal. • Manual tranny pops out of

Third gear and grinds as the clutch is let out. • Premature wearout of the rear brake pads. • Faulty catalytic converter. **2002**—Manual transmission shifts poorly between Fourth and Fifth gear. • Defective dash cluster. • Intermittent stalling and rough running. • Vehicle accelerates when foot is taken off of gas pedal. **2003**—Transmission breakdown. • Driveshaft fell out while driving. • Vehicle slips into Neutral from Drive. • Sudden axle and steering failure. • Seat belts unlatch too easily. **2004**—Gas line leaks cause fumes to enter the cabin. • Chronic stalling. • Seized front brakes.

Secret Warranties/Service Tips

1996–99—A noisy cold transmission may signal the need to replace the transmission regulator valve. **1997**—Install an AC evaporator drain hose to stop water from leaking onto the front passenger floor. • A rough-running engine may require an upgraded crank position sensor. • In hot weather, the door may refuse to open; install a revised door latch and actuator rod. • The vehicle may run out of fuel with the gauge reading one-quarter full; replace the fuel tank sending unit. **1997–98**—Tips on silencing front-brake and front-seat clicks, heater and AC actuator squeaks, and a steering column boot squawk. **1997–99**—Measures to reduce disc brake rotor pulsation, transfer-case shifter and universal joint noise, tailgate rattles or knocks, and diagnostic tips for plugging water leaks. • AC evaporator freeze-up tips. **1997–2002**—Water leaks under the passenger-side carpet. **1997–2004**—Engine rear main oil seal leak:

Rear Main Seal Oil Leak

Bulletin No.: 09-010-04   Date: March 16, 2004

4.0L Engine—Dirt and Debris Accumulation at Rear Main Seal

OVERVIEW: This bulletin involves the application of a small amount of sealer where the top of the transmission bellhousing mates to the engine.

1997–2004 Wrangler

SYMPTOM/CONDITION: The customer may experience engine oil seepage from the area of the rear main bearing seal. If debris accumulation becomes significant, damage to the rear main seal may occur.

1999—Reprogramming the PCM (power control module) will cure hard starts, hesitation, stalling, and overall poor engine performance. **1999**—Reprogram the JTEC PCM if the Check Gauges light comes on or if it falsely indicates the engine is overheating. **1999–2000**—An interior roof sag and water accumulation can be corrected through the installation of foam blocks under warranty. **1999–2001**—Tips for correcting windshield/cowl water leaks. **1999–2004**—A rough idle may require the installation of a fuel-injector insulator sleeve. **2000–01**—If the engine runs hot, you may need to replace the cooling fan and fan drive. **2001**—Driveline clunk can be silenced by reprogramming the JTEC PCM. • A rough idle can be cured by selectively erasing and reprogramming the PCM with new software. • Difficult to remove fuel cap. **2001–03**—If the vehicle tends to drift, install upgraded ball joints. **2003**—Delayed or temporary loss of transmission engagement and harsh 4–3 downshift (NHTSA TSB #2100503, June 20, 2003). • Manual transmission may have defective Third gear weld. • 4.0L engine crankshaft burr. • Faulty fuel-injector wiring connections. **2003–04**—Automatic transmission leaks:

Automatic Transmission Fluid Leak

Bulletin No.: 21-003-04   Date: March 09, 2004

Fluid Seepage From Area of Rear Output Shaft Retainer

OVERVIEW: This bulletin involves the replacement of the NV-241 transfer case rear output shaft retainer/extension housing and related seals.

2003–04   (TJ)   Wrangler

Jeep TJ Wrangler, YJ Wrangler Profile

	1997	1998	1999	2000	2001	2002	2003	2004
Cost Price ($) (firm)								
TJ, YJ (14%)	17,725	18,575	19,205	19,445	20,355	21,000	21,340	21,995
Used Values ($)								
TJ, YJ ⋀	6,500	9,000	10,000	11,500	12,500	13,500	15,000	16,500
TJ, YJ ⋁	5,500	8,000	9,000	10,000	11,500	12,500	13,500	15,000
Reliability	③	③	③	③	③	④	④	④
Crash Safety (F)	④	—	④	④	④	④	④	④
Side	—	—	③	—	—	③	③	③
IIHS Side	❷	❷	❷	❷	❷	❷	❷	❷
Offset	③	—	③	③	③	③	③	③
Rollover	—	—	—	③	③	③	③	—

JEEP CHEROKEE, GRAND CHEROKEE   ★★★

RATING: Average (2002–05); Not Recommended (1985–2001). For highway cruising or city use, the Grand Cherokee is a better choice. The Cherokee's forte is its superior off-roading capability; it was replaced in 2002 by the Liberty. **Strong points:** Powerful V8 (Grand Cherokee), easy handling, plenty of cargo space (Grand Cherokee), a comfortable ride, and smooth-shifting transmission, when it's not in the shop for repairs. Good fuel economy and smooth, integrated drivetrain performance with the 6-cylinder. Excellent base warranty on 2002 through 2005 versions, and Jeep says 2005 prices will be cut by several thousand dollars. **Weak points:** Abrupt throttle tip-in, restricted rear visibility, high fuel consumption with the Grand Cherokee, an unreliable powertrain and fuel system, cheap, rattle-prone interior trim, low door openings make for difficult entry/exit, uncomfortable rear seating, and an unusually high number of safety-related complaints. *Cherokee:* The high step-up and narrow rear doors make entry and exit difficult. Back-seat access is also problematic. **New for 2005:** A major redesign will yuppify the Grand Cherokee's road manners in favour of on-road comfort without sacrificing its off-road prowess. A re-engineered suspension will improve the ride via three 4X4 systems and a longer and wider platform. The new models will offer three engines, including the new Hemi, with cylinder deactivation.

2001 Cherokee Technical Data

Powertrain
Engine: 4.0L 6-cyl. (190 hp)
Transmissions: 5-speed man.
• 3-speed auto.
• 4-speed auto.
Dimension/Capacity (4-door)
Height/length/width:
63.9/167.5/69.4 in.
Headroom F/R: 37.8/38.5 in.

Legroom F/R: 41.4/35 in.
Wheelbase: 101.4 in.
Turning circle: 38 ft.
Cargo volume: 36.5 cu. ft.
Passengers: 2/3
GVWR: 4,550–4,900 lb.
Tow limit: 5,000 lb.
Fuel tank: 76L/reg.
Weight: 3,150 lb.

2005 Grand Cherokee Technical Data

Powertrain (rear-drive or 4X4)
Engines: 3.7L 6-cyl. (210 hp)
• 4.7L V8 (235 hp)
• 5.7L V8 (325 hp)
Transmissions: 4-speed auto.
• 5-speed auto.
Dimension/Capacity
Height/length/width:
70.3/181.6/72.3 in.
Headroom F/R: 38.9/39 in.

Legroom F/R: 40.9/35.7 in.
Wheelbase: 105.9 in.
Turning circle: 40 ft.
Passengers: 2/3
Cargo volume: 37 cu. ft.
GVWR: 4,889–6,200 lb.
Tow limit: 5,000–6,500 lb.
Fuel tank: 87L/reg.
Weight: 3,800 lb.

MODEL HISTORY: Cherokee and its early partner, the Wagoneer, were the first four-door Jeeps designed under the tutelage of American Motors (boy, do I miss the straight-talking Bill Pickett, AMC Canada's former prez). Intended as downsized and upgraded replacements for the old full-sized wagons, they were an instant success. They kept AMC afloat until the Chrysler buyout.

Transmission choices include 4- and 5-speed manuals, and 3- or 4-speed automatics. The 3-speed automatic is the most reliable; the manuals have heavy clutches and notchy shifting. The smaller engines are jokes in such large vehicles, most of which come with optional, larger engines. These Jeeps wander at highway speeds (now a Dodge truck/SUV problem; see *Dawe v. Courtesy Chrysler* in Part Three), which isn't helped by the numb power steering. They are not a pleasure to manoeuvre or park around town. Interiors are spacious—although the spare tire reduces interior space—and will easily and comfortably accommodate five people on long rides.

Early Cherokees and Wagoneers have very poor repair histories. Buyers should be especially wary of the 4-cylinder engine; electrical system; fuel system; and the failure-prone, expensive-to-repair 4X4 system.

The 1995–2001 Cherokees provide a smoother, more integrated drivetrain performance (later models offered full-time AWD) and give better fuel economy. However, interior room is still limited, standard features are few, and rear visibility is restricted. These later models are apparently less failure-prone, although long-term reliability remains questionable.

Grand Cherokee

Early Grand Cherokees are just as failure-prone as other early Jeeps. The 1995–98 Grand Cherokees are easier to handle, give a more comfortable ride, and are equipped with an optional 5.9L V8. On the minus side, you'll still find limited rear seating, a difficult entry/exit, high fuel consumption, and uncertain powertrain reliability. Since the Grand Cherokee is afflicted with the same failure-prone parts as the Cherokee, we see chronic engine and transmission failures, poor-quality hardware, sloppy assembly, oil leaks, electrical system glitches, and brakes that frequently fail and are in need of frequent servicing. Selec-Trac continues to be expensive to maintain and glitch-prone (this has dramatically worsened over the past few years). **1999**—Grand Cherokee is longer, wider, roomier, and generally more refined. A new optional 235-hp 4.7L V8 replaced the base 4.0L 6-cylinder, used since the early '60s in American Motors' Ramblers. A Dana-built Quadra-Trac transmission was added and a re-styled exterior gives this upscaled Cherokee a more modern look. Brakes and steering components were upgraded as well. **2003–04**—Improved steering and brake feel, and additional storage space. These models still suffer from poor quality control, afflicting the engine, transmission, brakes, AC, and body fit and finish.

COST ANALYSIS: Pay the $500 to $1,000 premium and get the upgraded 2005. **Best alternatives:** *Cherokee:* A used 2001 (its last model year) offers more base power than the Liberty and sells for thousands less. *Grand Cherokee:* The 2003 and 2004 Grand Cherokee returned heavily discounted with some important upgrades like a longer warranty that make it a better choice than earlier models. Other 4X4s worth a look are the Honda CR-V, Hyundai Santa Fe, Nissan Xterra, or Toyota RAV4 and 4Runner. **Rebates:** $2,000–$3,500 on last year's leftovers; a $2,000 price cut on the 2005s. **Delivery/PDI:** $875. **Warranty:** Bumper-to-bumper 3 years/60,000 km; powertrain 7 years/ 115,000 km; rust perforation 5 years/160,000 km. **Supplementary warranty:** A good idea for any model not covered for seven years. **Options:** Get an anti-theft system or kiss your vehicle goodbye. Choose your tires carefully. Off-road rubber with an aggressive tread isn't conducive to comfortable highway driving. *Grand Cherokee:* Get the 4.7L V8 for the best overall performance. **Depreciation:** A bit slower than average. **Insurance cost:** Average; higher than average for the Grand Cherokee. **Parts supply/cost:** Moderately priced parts that are usually easily found. Owners report waits of several months for recall campaign parts. **Annual maintenance cost:** Higher than average without the 7-year warranty. Spotty service record at Jeep dealerships. The drivetrain is particularly expensive to repair. **Highway/city fuel economy:** *Cherokee: 2.5L 4-cyl. and auto.:* 10–13.4L/100 km; *4.0L 6-cyl. and auto.:* 10.2–15L/100 km; *4.0L 6-cyl. and 4X4:* 10.4–14.9L/100 km. *Grand Cherokee: 4.0L 6-cyl.:* 10.4–14.7L/100 km; *4.0L 6-cyl. and 4X4:* 10.4–14.9L/100 km; *4.7L V8 and 4X4:* 11.6–16.1L/100 km.

QUALITY/RELIABILITY: Although not as badly built as the Ford Explorer, quality control is unacceptably poor. Transmission and fuel system problems continue to dog Chrysler—and its customers. An inadequate base warranty and a spotty service record at Jeep dealerships compound a poor overall reliability record for the Cherokee. Long-term reliability doesn't look good for the Grand Cherokee either, despite its recent makeover. AWD components are expensive to maintain after the fourth year of use.

The transfer cases and axles are unreliable, noisy, and prone to early wearout. A misalignment of the gears produces a loud humming noise, emanating from the ring gear and pinion gear. Although dealers have attempted to fix the problem by realigning the gears, the noise continues to this day (see "Secret Warranties/Service Tips").

Another quality problem is the binding of the wheels in the Quadra-Trac system when the outer wheel can't rotate faster than the inner wheel during a turn, causing excessive noise and premature wear. Electrical system and body deficiencies continue to plague these redesigned models, and everything points toward these vehicles being hazardous, underperforming, and costly to maintain as they age. **Owner-reported problems:** *Cherokee:* Knocking connecting rods on 6-cylinder engines. Selec-Trac 4X4 often requires expensive servicing after a few years of use or high mileage. Transmission bangs (clunks) when shifting. Steering failures. Engine and ABS warning lights stay on. Frequent and expensive brake repairs due to warped rotors, cracked shoes, etc. Excessive vibration and pulling when brakes are applied. Electrical system shorts, power windows fail, and rear wipers won't work. Premature shock absorber and tie-rod wearout, resulting in uneven tire wear. Alloy wheels can fuse to the drums. AC leaks and failures, and engine and transfer case oil leaks. *Grand Cherokee:* Engine difficult to start when hot and acts as if it's starved for fuel. Chronic automatic transmission failures. Rear-end whine upon acceleration. Excessive steering wander and noisy operation (honking). Premature wearout of original equipment tires and ball joints, fuel and electrical system glitches, poorly performing and expensive-to-maintain brakes, and subpar body hardware and paint. Hard to secure loads to the roof rack. Premature rusting of the undercarriage, steering spindle, brake lines, and exhaust. **Warranty performance:** Very tight-fisted in handling warranty claims.

ROAD PERFORMANCE: Acceleration/torque: *Cherokee:* The 6-cylinder engine provides a smooth and powerful performance with brisk acceleration (0–100 km/h: 9 sec.). The 2.5L 4-cylinder engine is noisy and lacks the power for serious hauling, and it is especially sluggish when hooked to the automatic transmission. *Grand Cherokee:* Plenty of power with the inline 6-cylinder and V8 engines. The V8s accelerate to 100 km/h about as fast as the Ford Explorer. Excellent engines for off-roading. **Transmission:** *Cherokee:* Smooth-shifting automatic, but it's the 5-speed manual gearbox that gives the best performance. *Grand Cherokee:* Usually shifts smoothly in all gear ranges (if working properly). Occasional abrupt throttle response can cause jerky shifting. **Steering:** *Cherokee:* Precise, with good road feedback. Many reports that the steering will suddenly veer to the right at highway speeds. *Grand Cherokee:*

Fairly good, as a result of the 2000's enhancements. Suspension geometry requires constant steering corrections to keep vehicle on the highway. **Routine handling:** *Cherokee:* Average at moderate speeds. The ride is harsh and bouncy when the going gets rough. Does not take curves graciously and likes to wander on the highway. *Grand Cherokee:* Ride comfort is augmented by a three-link rear axle. Handling is precise, with improved high-speed cornering stability. The Quadra-Trac system has a "Vari-Lok" feature that provides a mechanical lock in the low-range position for extra traction. Many complaints that the vehicle tends to wander all over the road. **Emergency handling:** *Cherokee:* Average. Good ground clearance and stiff suspension for off-roading. *Grand Cherokee:* Good. Cornering is well controlled, and handling is predictable and precise. Little body roll. **Braking:** *Cherokee:* Average (100–0 km/h: 41 m.). *Grand Cherokee:* Very good (100–0 km/h: 132 ft. with the V8). Some plowing in hard stops. Braking upgrades have followed years of criticism related to sudden brake failure, poor braking performance, and the premature wearout of expensive, major brake components.

SAFETY SUMMARY: Location of fuel tank makes it vulnerable, leading to fires in rear-end collisions. In *Rolf v. Winger* (Jackson County, Missouri, October 2001), lawyers obtained a $5.7 million verdict in a wrongful death case where the driver was killed when his Jeep Cherokee was rear-ended by a drunk driver. The collision caused the gas tank on the Cherokee to explode on impact. Confidential settlements were reached before trial with DailmerChrysler and the pub where the drunk driver became intoxicated. The case was tried against the remaining defendants, including the drunk driver's employer. There are also many complaints that the low-beam headlights give insufficient illumination. Be wary of tow figures given out by salespeople. They are often wrong, particularly in not divulging a lower rating for manual transmissions. **Airbags:** *Grand Cherokee:* Side airbags are standard. There have been many reports of airbags not deploying when they should and deploying when they shouldn't. **ABS:** 4W optional on Cherokee; standard on Grand Cherokee. ABS failures characterized by pedal going to the floor with no braking action and extended stopping distances. **Traction control:** Optional on Grand Cherokee. **Head restraints F/R:** *Cherokee: 1997: *; 1998–99: **/*; 2001: *. Grand Cherokee: 1996–97: *; 1999: *; 2001: *; 2002–04: **/*.* **Visibility F/R:** *Cherokee: *****/*; Grand Cherokee: *****/**.* **Maximum load capacity:** *1999 Grand Cherokee Limited V8:* 1,150 lb.

SAFETY COMPLAINTS: All years: Under-hood fires. • Ignition switch and steering column overheated. • Fuel leakage from the gas tank. • Transfer-case leakage causes fire to ignite in exhaust system area. • Engine mount bolts shear off, causing the engine to fall down. • Brake rotors corrode, crack, and warp. • Brake pads wear out prematurely. • Frequent replacement of the master cylinder and proportioning valve. • Sudden acceleration caused by faulty cruise control or by going into Reverse. • Transfer-case grinding, fluid leakage, and failure. • Transmission allows vehicle to roll away even though it's in Park. • Power-steering bracket shears off, causing steering loss. • Complete electrical failure and sudden stalling. • Airbag, ABS, and Check Engine lights come on for no reason. • Erratically functioning interior and exterior lights. • Headlights dim when the AC engages. • Frequent AC malfunctions. • Water leakage through improperly welded seam near dash causes chronic electrical shorts. • Water leaks from dash and doors. • Doors fall off due to defective hinges. **1998**—Dash panel fire. • Driver-side mat jams the accelerator. • Tire jack platform is too small. • Right rear wheel fell off. • Stabilizer bar broke. • Left rear axle shaft failed. • Warped door. • Fuel gauge reads one-quarter tank when it's empty. **1999**—Engine fire. • Rear seat belt won't secure a child safety seat. **2000**—Many reports of under-hood fires. • Right rear door latch caught on fire while driving. • One fire in the under-hood area, believed to be caused by the headlight switch shorting out. • Leaking gas comes out of hoses (appear to be dry-rotted) between gas tank filler and fuel tank. • Fuel leakage from tailpipe and fumes entered passenger compartment; dealer replaced fuel injectors and PCM. • While braking, vehicle suddenly accelerated. • Another report of sudden, unintended acceleration when driving slowly (10–15 km/h) uphill. • Check Engine light comes on all the time (often it's a loose gas cap, defective #5 spark plug, or ignition coil). • Sudden stalling with loss of brakes and steering. • Premature transmission failure. • Rear axle misalignment causes vehicle to sway to the side of the road. • Excessive steering wheel vibrations. • Steering lock-up while driving in a parking lot. • Brake rotor failure causes extended stopping distance and vibration when braking. • Report that rear secondary brake pads and shoes were cracked down the middle. • Goodyear tire tread separation, blowout, and premature wear. • Plastic fuel tank is located too close to the rear bumper. • Headlights work intermittently. • Rear tailgate glass shattered for unknown reason. **2001**—Suspension, steering, and driveline fell off vehicle. • Engine surging and sudden acceleration. • Cam sensor failures cause vehicle to lose all power. • Brake failures. • Airbag didn't deploy during collision. • Headlights suddenly went out. • Sudden, unintended acceleration while vehicle was parked with engine running. • Transmission often slips from Park into Reverse or from Drive into Reverse. • Warped brake rotors and cracked brake shoes (7,000 km). • Excessive vibration; vehicle pulls to one side when braking. • Seat belt abraded from catching on door latch. • Horn is hard to access. • Incorrect speedometer readings. • Brake and gas pedal too close together. **2002**—Waits of several months for recalled parts. • Airbags fail to deploy. • Check Engine light comes on and vehicle suddenly stalls in traffic • Sudden acceleration while braking. • Brake goes to the floor without any braking effect. **2002–03**—Many incidents where transmission jumped from Park to Reverse and vehicle rolled downhill. • Premature brake rotor warpage after only a couple thousand kilometres. **2003**—Sudden acceleration. • Frequent automatic transmission failures. • Automatic transmission jumped from Park to Reverse. • Vehicle rolled downhill into a tree. • Differential failure. • Rear axle mounting bolt snapped. • Rear end sways left and right while driving. • Dashboard reflects into windshield at night. • Driver's seat instability. **2004**—Sudden, unintended acceleration. • Faulty ECM causes chronic stalling. • Transmission jumped from Park into Reverse. • Tire sidewall blew out. • Complete brake failure. • Warped brake rotors. • Imprecise steering. • Sunroof exploded while driving. • Power outlet wiring can easily overheat under a 20-amp load.

1993–2003—Paint delamination, peeling, or fading (see Part Three page 123). **1995–99**—Transfer-case noise correction. **1996–99**—Transmission noise when in Reverse can be corrected by replacing the regulator valve. **1997–98**—Excessive driveline vibration and the presence of a droning noise at speeds over 100 km/h may require the installation of upgraded transmission components under warranty. • Measures to silence front-brake clicks, front-seat click, heater and AC actuator squeak, steering-column boot squawk, transfer-case shifter, and universal-joint noise. • Troubleshooting erratic instrument panel and ABS light operation. • Likely causes for engine compartment noises and air and water leaks. • How to prevent the fan viscous drive from contacting the radiator. **1997–99**—Disc brake rotor pulsation (a persistent problem) is tackled in TSB #05-03-98 Rev A. • AC evaporator freeze-up can be prevented by installing a low-pressure cycling switch. **1998–99**—Corrective measures to take if the airbag warning light comes on for no reason, or the instrument lights and gauges operate erratically. **1999**—Reprogramming the power control module (PCM) will cure hard starts, hesitation, stalling, and overall poor engine performance. **1999–2000**—Harsh upshifts or downshifts may require the reprogramming of the TCM or PCM, under the emissions warranty, says TSB #21-09-00, published September 15, 2000. • Front axle whining or moaning, a rear-end whine at speeds greater than 65 km/h, long cranking time to start, steering gear honk noises on turns, slow to retract seat belts, an intermittent bump felt when stopping, front seat binding or sticking, brake roughness or pedal pulsation when brakes are applied, and cold air leaking into the passenger footwell are all addressed in Jeep's bulletins for these two model years. • A worn-out O-ring (quad ring) in the fuel module assembly may be the cause of long cranking before starts. **1999–2001**—A front axle whine may require extensive repairs to correct, says TSB # 03-001-01 Rev A. **1999–2003**—Many anecdotal reports of Chrysler paying for brake caliper and rotor replacement after the warranty has expired. **1999–2004**—Rough-running engine:

Hot Start Misfire, Rough Idle

Bulletin No.: 18-031-03   Date: Sep. 05, 2003
4.0L Rough Engine Idle After Restart Following A Hot Soak
This bulletin involves the installation of a fuel injector insulator sleeve.
2000–04 (TJ) Wrangler
1999–2004 (WJ) Grand Cherokee
2000–01 (XJ) Jeep Cherokee

• Front door wind noise. • Suspension noise:

Suspension – Stabilizer Bushing Squeak/Squawk

Bulletin No.: 02-002-04   Date: March 16, 2004

Suspension Squeak/Squawk - Stabilizer Bushing

This bulletin involves the disassembly and lubrication of the bushings on the front and rear stabilizer bars.

1999–2004 Grand Cherokee

A squeak or squawk-like sound may be present in the front or rear sspension. Closer investigation may reveal that the sound is coming from one or more of the vehicle stabilizer bar bushings. The sound may occur most often when the ambient temperature is around 0°C (32°F).

2001—Harsh upshifts; a clunk or shudder noticed when accelerating. • Exhaust boom when idling. • Honking noise when turning. • Front axle whine. • Troubleshooting geartrain sound that enters into the passenger compartment. • Remedy for climate control setting that may be too warm or too cool. **2001–02**—Vehicle runs rough or exhibits a bucking or hesitation. • Excessive vibration and brake pedal pulsation. **2001–03**—Steering wheel pop/tick noise. • **2002**—Engine compartment ticking. • 4.7L engine crankshaft problems. • Brake roughness; front brake pulsation. • Premature fuel-nozzle shutoff when fuelling. • Faulty seat cushion heater. • Inadvertent activation of panic alarm. **2002–03**—Front door wind noise. • False intrusion alarm. • Shift/speed control improvements. • Transmission may only operate in Second gear. **2003**—Crankshaft burr. • Erratic-shifting automatic transmission may require a re-calibrated PCM or transmission control module (TCM). • Automatic transmission may overheat. • A "customer satisfaction" program will fix for free the automatic transmission's torque converter. • Power-steering moan/whine. **2003–04**—Liftgate glass lifts up in wet conditions. **2004**—Rough cold engine operation.

Cherokee, Grand Cherokee Profile								
	1997	1998	1999	2000	2001	2002	2003	2004
Cost Price ($) (negotiable)								
Base 4X2 (18%)	21,615	21,425	22,460	22,460	—	—	—	—
Cherokee 4X4 (19%)	23,835	23,645	24,680	24,680	28,550	—	—	—
Gr. Cherokee (20%)	34,670	34,980	36,295	38,860	—	—	—	—
Gr. Cherokee 4X4 (20%)	35,570	35,880	37,195	43,300	39,790	39,005	40,230	39,775
Used Values ($)								
Base 4X2 ⋏	5,500	6,500	7,500	9,500	—	—	—	—
Base 4X2 ⋎	4,500	5,000	6,000	8,000	—	—	—	—
Cherokee 4X4 ⋏	6,500	7,500	10,500	13,500	14,500	—	—	—
Cherokee 4X4 ⋎	5,500	6,500	9,500	13,000	13,000	—	—	—
Gr. Cherokee ⋏	7,000	9,000	11,000	14,000	—	—	—	—
Gr. Cherokee ⋎	6,000	8,000	10,000	13,000	—	—	—	—
Gr. Cherokee 4X4 ⋏	8,500	11,000	12,000	14,000	18,000	22,000	26,000	30,000
Gr. Cherokee 4X4 ⋎	7,500	9,500	10,500	13,000	16,000	20,000	24,000	27,000

Reliability	③	③	③	③	③	③	④	④
Crash Safety (F)	③	—	③	③	③	—	—	—
Grand Cherokee	③	③	③	③	③	③	③	③
Side	—	—	④	④	④	—	—	—
Grand Cherokee	—	—	③	③	④	④	④	④
Offset	❷	❷	❷	❷	❷	—	—	—
Grand Cherokee	—	—	❷	❷	❷	❷	❷	—
Rollover	—	—	—	—	❷	❷	❷	—

JEEP LIBERTY ★

RATING: Not Recommended (2002–05). This heavier, more versatile successor to the Cherokee has too many reliability and quality problems. **Strong points:** Reasonable base price and comprehensive 7-year powertrain warranty; good towing capability for a V6; very comfortable ride; generous interior volume; practical, versatile interior; well appointed and offers a nice array of standard and optional safety features. A tight turning circle, low-range gearing, load-levelling shocks, a front skid plate, and good visibility enhance off-road performance (while mediocre quality control compromise safety and performance). **Weak points:** The 2001 Jeep Cherokee came with a standard 190-hp inline 6-cylinder engine; Liberty's base engine is a 150-hp, underpowered Cirrus-sourced 4-cylinder. There's little V6 reserve power for passing, merging; Selec-Trac 4X4 not as user-friendly as rivals' AWD; excessive swaying, rocking, and jiggling on uneven roads; steering is less responsive than that of the RAV4; and independent front suspension can limit off-roading prowess. 2001 Cherokee also offered an extra inch of ground clearance and a heavy-duty suspension for serious off-roading; the Liberty has compromised rear-seat comfort; rear visibility blocked by spare tire; driver's seat is positioned closer to the door than usual and could use additional lumbar and lateral support; high step-in and narrow door openings; a bulging heater box protrudes into the cabin area; no folding centre rear armrest; 4X4 gear whine (a Jeep trademark for years) and excessive engine, tire, and wind noise; cheap-looking plastic interior trim; and surprisingly poor fuel economy for a compact SUV. **New for 2005:** A 148-hp, 2.8L 4-cylinder diesel engine will be offered in late 2004.

2005 Technical Data

Powertrain
Engines: 2.4L 4-cyl. (150 hp)
• 3.7L (210 hp)
• 2.8L 4-cyl. diesel (148 hp)
Transmissions: 5-speed man.
• 4-speed auto.
Dimension/Capacity
Height/length/width:
73.2/174.4/71.6 in.
Headroom F/R: 40.7/42.1 in.
Legroom F/R: 40.8/37.2 in.

Wheelbase: 104.3 in.
Turning circle: 35.9 ft.
Passengers: 2/3
GVWR: N/A
Cargo volume: 29.2 cu. ft.
Load capacity: 1,150 lb.
Tow limit (V6): 5,000 lb.
Ground clear.: 9.6 in.
Fuel tank: 70L/reg.
Weight: 3,857 lb.

MODEL HISTORY: Introduced as a 2002 model, Liberty is offered as a four-door that's longer, wider, taller, and generally roomier than the Cherokee it replaced. It has less cargo space and ground clearance, though. It also weighs a lot more than its predecessor, which eats into its fuel economy figures.

Stay away from the little 4-banger. It's the same failure-prone beastie used on the Cirrus (someone mention biodegradable head gaskets?). It's completely overwhelmed by the Liberty's extra weight, although it does manage to eke out a 900 kg (2,000 lb.) tow rating. On the other hand, if you choose the V6, you get a fairly powerful and versatile drivetrain that's got plenty of low-end grunt and is able to tow up to 2,265 kg (5,000 lb.) when equipped with the optional towing package. **2002**—Given larger, stronger brake rotors and drums than the Cherokee (brake problems remain a constant complaint) and a new ABS system with electronic brake force distribution. **2003**—Standard 4-wheel disc brakes.

COST ANALYSIS: Selling for $25,000, the 2005 Sport still seems overpriced; try a cheaper 2004 version. The $30,000 Limited is basically the same price as last year's model. **Best alternatives:** A new Honda CR-V, Nissan Xterra, or Toyota RAV4. The 2001 Jeep Cherokee isn't a bad choice, either. **Rebates:** Look for $2,000 rebates, or low-financing deals. **Delivery/PDI:** $860, about twice what it should be, but a quarter less than what Toyota profiteers charge. **Warranty:** Bumper-to-bumper 3 years/60,000 km; powertrain 7 years/ 115,000 km; rust perforation 5 years/160,000 km. **Supplementary warranty:** A comprehensive extended warranty is a wise buy since this vehicle is so poorly made. **Options:** Get the V6 engine, 4-speed automatic transmission, and Selec-Trac full-time 4X4. Larger 16-inch tires are a performance plus. Two worthwhile, though overpriced, option packages worth considering: a trailer towing package ($480), which includes engine oil cooler, Class 3 trailer hitch, and 7-pin wiring harness; and a convenience package ($2,485), which includes air conditioning, CD changer, roof rack, deluxe steel wheels, full-sized spare tire, power front windows with one-touch-down feature, and a tilt steering wheel. **Depreciation:** Slower than average. **Insurance cost:** Average. **Parts supply/cost:** Expect high parts costs and month-long waits until the parts supply line gets filled. **Annual maintenance cost:** Average, thanks to the 7-year extended powertrain warranty. **Highway/city fuel economy:** *4-cyl.:* 9.4–11.8L/100 km; *V6:* 10.7–12.4L/100 km.

QUALITY/RELIABILITY: Owner complaints: Ongoing reliability problems compromise the Liberty's safety and performance. **Warranty performance:** DaimlerChrysler's warranty performance stinks. The new extended powertrain protection is pretty straightforward, though.

ROAD PERFORMANCE: Acceleration/torque: Plenty of power with the V6, although it could use more high-end grunt for highway cruising. **Transmission:** Quite versatile over a variety of roads. For ordinary day-to-day driving on dry roads, 4X2 is fine; on wet or snow-covered roads, full-time 4X4 enhances stability and traction; for gravel and dirt roads, part-time 4X4 provides more traction; and for steep, slippery inclines, 4X4 Low gives you lots of engine braking and pulling power. **Steering:** Fairly accurate and predictable, though outclassed by the Japanese. **Routine handling:** A firm but comfortable ride. Drivetrain and body are more vibration-prone and noisy than the Cherokee's. Unibody construction and independent front suspension provide more carlike handling than a body-on-frame design. But the independent suspension may limit off-road capability. **Braking:** Works quite well. Off-roaders will appreciate that the ABS system is defeated when the transfer case is placed in Low and has been redesigned to limit false activation on bumpy surfaces.

SAFETY SUMMARY: Airbags: Front. **ABS:** Optional; disc/drum. **Head restraints F/R:** *****/***. **Safety belt pretensioners:** Front. **Traction control:** No. **Visibility F/R:** *****/***. **Maximum load capacity:** 1,150 lb.

SAFETY COMPLAINTS: You would think this newly designed, Mercedes-backed SUV would avoid most of the factory-related mistakes that have plagued so many Chrysler/Jeep vehicles.

Think again. There are 436 safety complaints logged by government probers on the 2002 model alone. This is an astounding figure given that the Liberty was Mercedes' first chance to show it could produce a top-quality vehicle in cooperation with Chrysler. This raises the question: How could Mercedes bosses allow such poorly designed junk to be rushed into production? Because they're turning out junk themselves. In fact, Mercedes' own product quality has been judged to be unacceptable by J.D. Power and the U.S. National Automobile Dealers Association (NADA).

> My son hit a 50ft [15 m] tree head on and the air bags did not deploy. He and his passenger were both injured and Chrysler is telling me that he wasn't going fast enough or hit hard enough to deploy air bags. Passenger's head broke windshield and my son't tooth is loosened by hitting steering wheel. The front end frame of jeep is bent. Not hard enough?

All years: Many complaints of electrical fires, faulty airbags, no brakes, sudden acceleration, chronic stalling, transmission failures, excessive on-road vibration, and recall snafus with owners not being notified, parts not available (sudden airbag deployment), and the correction not fixing the problem (dash recall campaign). **2002**—Fire ignited at right side of vehicle. • Vehicle tips over quite easily. • Transmission went from Park to Reverse and rolled over when started. • Vehicle easily rolled over from a side impact. • Vehicle rolled over when wheel/axle suddenly collapsed. • Side airbags deployed while driving. • Low suspension allows underside to be easily damaged; makes off-roading unsafe. • Part of steering wheel fell off while driving. • Front seats propelled forward when braking. **2002–03**—Sudden unintended acceleration. **2003**—Vehicle suddenly shuts down due to chronic fuel pump failures. • Front ball joint/strut mount failures. **2004**—Airbag-induced injuries:

> While driving at 25 mph [40 km/h], the driver side air bag deployed for no logical reason. The consumer lost control of the vehicle and collided with an embankment. The vehicle never ran over anything or hit anything before the mishap. The consumer suffered a sprained wrist, a concussion and trauma to his back. The consumer also reported that before the air bag deployed, electrical currents from the steering wheel were shocking whoever drove the vehicle.

Fuel smell in cabin, then fire igniting. • Hood latch failure. • Goodyear Wrangler tire tread separation.

Secret Warranties/Service Tips

2002—Skunk-like odour remedy. • Front engine compartment harness may have an intermittent loose ground. • Loss of crankshaft position sensor signal. • Troubleshooting 45RFE transmission solenoids. • Radiator oil cooler contamination. • Longer-than-normal crank time prior to start. • Reduced power steering assist when steering wheel is turned quickly. • Excessive wind buffeting. • Software improvement for unlatching flip-up glass. • Flickering panel lights or display. • Difficulty refuelling the fuel tank. • Exhaust rattle caused by flange bolt springs. • Front-end creaking noise. • Wind whistle from Mopar brushguard or front air deflector. • AC drain water leaks under passenger side carpet are caused by a factory mistake, says TSB #24-012-01. **2003**—An erratic-shifting automatic transmission may require a re-calibrated PCM or TCM. • Harsh-shifting countermeasures. • Scored 3.7L engine crankshaft. • Insufficient body sealer in cowl area. **2003–04**—Liftgate glass lifts up. • AC won't cool/heat properly. • Harsh downshifts. • Excessive brake noise:

Brake Moaning

Bulletin No.: NUMBER: 05-001-04   Date: January 13, 2004
Rear Disc Brake Moan
This bulletin involves the replacement of the rear disc brake pads and rotors.
2003–04 Liberty (Domestic Market)
The customer may experience a rear brake moan-like sound during light or no brake application pressure. This condition is more likely to occur when the brakes are cool (first use) and ambient temperatures are below 50°F. The moan-like sound may be intermittent.

2004—Slow gear engagement after a cold start requires reprogramming of the PCM.

Jeep Liberty Profile

	2002	2003	2004
Cost Price ($) (negotiable)			
Liberty Sport (15%)	22,800	24,490	25,695
Liberty Limited (17%)	28,680	29,790	30,675

Used Values ($)			
Liberty Sport A	16,000	19,000	21,000
Liberty Sport V	14,500	17,000	19,000
Liberty Limited A	18,000	22,000	24,000
Liberty Limited V	17,000	21,000	23,000
Reliability	④	④	④
Crash Safety (F)	⑤	⑤	⑤
Side	⑤	⑤	⑤
Offset	❷	❷	—
Rollover	❷	③	③

DODGE DURANGO ★

RATING: Not Recommended (1998–2005). **Strong points:** Powerful V8 engines provide brisk acceleration, with plenty of low-end torque for trailering heavy loads; lots of passenger and cargo room; an extended powertrain warranty; and a comfortable ride. **Weak points:** Poor acceleration with the V6, emergency handling unacceptable, unsteady road manners, vehicle jerks suddenly when passing over bumps, harsh and abrupt downshifts, obstructed rear visibility, difficult rear entry/exit, insufficient rear seat padding, climate control system won't blow air on the floor and your face at the same time (earlier models), problematic drivetrain durability, biodegradable ball joints (also a Dakota failing), fuel-thirsty, and a painfully loud pounding noise heard while cruising with the rear windows down. **New for 2005:** Nothing important. **Likely failures:** Transmission, steering, and ball joints and control arms:

> 2003 Dodge Durango upper ball joint failed on interstate at 65 mph [105 km/h]. Right front wheel and assembly seperated from vehicle causing single car accident. Skidded into guard rail. Damage estimated at $10,000 plus.

Brake rotors and pads, centre wheel caps may fly off, AC compressor and evaporator, and water leaks.

2005 Technical Data

Powertrain (front-drive or 4X4)
Engines: 4.8L V8
5.9L V8 (245 hp)
Transmission: 5-speed auto.
Dimension/Capacity
Height/length/width:
72.9/193.3/71 in.
Headroom F/R1/R2: 39.8/40.6/37.9 in.
Legroom F/R1/R2: 41.9/35.4/30.7 in.
Wheelbase: 115.9 in.
Turning circle: 41 ft.
Passengers: 3/3/2
Cargo volume: 39.5 cu. ft.
GVWR: 6,050–6,400 lb.
Tow limit: 7,300 lb.
Fuel tank: 87L/reg.
Weight: 4,750 lb.

MODEL HISTORY: Essentially a re-badged Dakota pickup, the Durango is touted as a compact even though it's larger than the Jeep Grand Cherokee but shorter than the Ford Expedition.

Redesigned last year, a 4.7L V8 is the base power plant and a 5.9L V8 is optional. Buyers can choose either 4X2 or part- or full-time 4X4. Interestingly, the Durango's 5.9L V8 has a 3,310–3,450 kg (7,300–7,600 lb.) towing capacity, giving this mid-sized truck as much hauling power as some costlier full-sized sport-utilities.

A few 1998–99 models carry the standard 3.9L V6, but most Durangos were ordered with the more robust 5.2L and 5.9L optional V8 engines. **1999**—Added rear-wheel drive, a rear power outlet, steering wheel-mounted radio controls, and heated mirrors. **2000**—The standard V6 was replaced by the 4.7L V8, suspension was upgraded, and a sporty R/T package was introduced. **2001**—A standard electronic transfer case, interior upgrades, 15-inch wheels, and a tilt steering column. The 5.2L V8 was dropped. **2003**—An upgraded 5-speed automatic transmission; standard 4-wheel disc brakes. **2004**—A reworked chassis and improved ride and handling; the interior got additional luxury features and the front end was slightly re-styled.

COST ANALYSIS: Go for a heavily discounted second-series 2004 model, since it's practically identical to this year's version. **Best alternatives:** Check out a Chevrolet Blazer, Jeep Grand Cherokee, Nissan Xterra, or a Toyota Highlander. **Options:** Get the 5.2L V8 (on used models) or 5.9L V8 engine and Quadra-Drive permanent AWD for best overall performance. An anti-theft system is a must-have. **Rebates:** $3,000+ rebates likely by year's end. **Delivery/PDI:** $875. **Depreciation:** Much slower than average. **Insurance cost:** Above average. **Parts supply/cost:** Parts have been moderately priced and plentiful, due to the large availability of competitively priced parts from the Dakota parts bin. Expensive brake and drivetrain servicing. **Annual maintenance cost:** Average. **Warranty:** Bumper-to-bumper 3 years/60,000 km; powertrain 7 years/115,000 km; rust perforation 5 years/160,000 km. **Supplementary warranty:** An extended warranty isn't needed. **Highway/city fuel economy:** *3.9L V6:* 11.0–15.9L/100 km; *4.7L V8:* 12.0–17.4L/100 km; *5.9L V8:* 13.2–18.9L/100 km.

QUALITY/RELIABILITY: Quality control has declined markedly. Body components and trim items still seem to be "blue-light specials." For additional uncensored owner comments, go to *www.durangoclub.com.* **Owner-reported problems:** Engine crankshaft, drive shaft, differential, motor mount, ball joint, and wheel bearing failures; chronic drivetrain whine and howl; electrical system and brake defects (spongy brakes, warped rotors); chronic AC failures, dash rattles, and premature differential bearing failure. **Warranty performance:** Average.

ROAD PERFORMANCE: Acceleration/torque: Although the V6 may look like a bargain, it's not powerful enough for a vehicle this large. The 4.7L V8 is the best compromise for most driving chores. If you intend to tow a trailer or carry a full load of passengers, move up to the huskier 5.9L. **Transmission:** Automatic transmission downshifts can be abrupt at times. The floor-mounted transfer-case lever can be a stretch for some drivers. **Routine handling:** 2004 models provide easier handling and a more pleasant ride. Some body lean and front-end plowing in fast turns. **Emergency handling:** Acceptable. Not as ponderous as most vehicles this size. Cornering is well controlled and handling is more crisp and predictable on the 2004 version. **Steering:** Good, most of the time. Very responsive, with lots of road feedback. **Braking:** Mediocre (100–0 km/h: 43 m with the V8).

SAFETY SUMMARY: Side-view mirror is too large to see through and blocks view when making turns. **Airbags:** Reports of airbags failing to deploy. **ABS:** Standard; on rear wheels only. **Head restraints F/R: *. Visibility F/R: *. Maximum load capacity:** 1,619–1,887 lb.

SAFETY COMPLAINTS: All years: Sudden acceleration and frequent stalling. • Vehicle wanders all over the road. • Transmission/differential break-downs. • Collapsing ball joints. • Loss of brakes. • Electrical fires. • Violent shaking. **1998–99**—Child accidentally moved shift lever out of Park, causing vehicle to roll into lake. • Horn failure. • Power windows go down by themselves and won't go back up. • Brakes slow, but won't completely stop vehicle when vehicle's in Reverse on an incline. • Rear-liftgate support rod broke. **2000**—Accelerator tends to stick. • Loss of all electrical power. • Vehicle can be put into gear without pressing the brake pedal; child placed transmission into Drive and vehicle took off. • Goodyear tire blowouts and tread separation. • Defective brake retainer spring caused loss of braking ability and cracked the rim. • Steering wheel lock-up while driving, which had to be jerked free; dealer suggested that the clock spring broke. • Steering wheel fell off. • Seat belt fails to release when release button is fully depressed. **2001**—Left front wheel flew off vehicle. • Suspension causes vehicle to go out of control over uneven roads. • Steering will suddenly pull to the left or right. • Surging when cruise control is engaged. • Child pulled vehicle out of gear, without touching brakes. • Middle fold-down rear seat doesn't lock properly; when applying brakes it hit driver in head, causing a concussion. • Second-row seat leaves a sharp edge exposed when it's tumbled forward for rear access. • Cracked fuel tank. **2002**—Vehicle slips into gear without keys in the ignition. • Passenger-side window suddenly shattered. • Exhaust fumes come in through back door. **2003**—Early engine failure due to oil system defect. • Faulty ABS braking pump results in extended stopping distance. • Erratically performing cruise control. • Door locks and unlocks for no reason. **2004**—Instrument cluster fire. • Misfiring caused by water getting into the spark plug area. • Complete loss of steering. • Polymer bumper cracks in cold weather. • Rear wiper fell out. • Unsafe speed control on Hemi-equipped models causes engine to race when going downhill. • Rearview mirror creates a serious blind spot.

Secret Warranties/Service Tips

All years: Internal service bulletins cover the following problems: Engine knocking, stalling, poor performance, vehicle bucking during wide-open throttle operation, and transmission and suspension defects. **1998–2003**— Upper and lower ball joints, control arm, and bushing failures. Sometimes Chrysler offers a 50 percent replacement refund, which doesn't help when applied to the full retail charge, as this owner of a 2001 Durango SLT discovered (*www.cox-internet.com/coffee/dodge.htm*):

> I was finally able to find replacements online at Advanced Auto Parts. Here are the online ordering pages for each bushing (note: there are two different bushings on each control arm): TRW 12357 ($7.33 ea.) and TRW 12505 ($6.04 ea.). I had a tire & alignment shop install the bushings (I used this type of business opposed to a general mechanic as they are usually specialists in fixing suspension problems). They charged me $45 an hour labor X 2 mechanics X 2 hours = **$180**.... The mechanic also performed a front end alignment on the Durango and said the dealership could not have done a proper alignment after replacing the ball joints because the bushings were bad....

1999—Engine overheating. • Hard starts and stalling. • Poor AC performance. • Faulty rear AC. • Front-end squeaking or creaking. • Brake grinding or growling. **2000**—The central timer module can be short-circuited by electromagnetic interference from airports, military installations, power fields, etc. When this happens, many of your vehicle's electrical systems will go haywire. Ask Chrysler to install a free revised module. • Harsh upshifts or downshifts can be smoothed out by reprogramming the PCM or TCM under the emissions warranty. • A front axle noise upon acceleration may be fixed by replacing the right-side front axle bearing. • Driveline noise, vibration:

Noise/Vibration in Drivetrain

Bulletin No.: 03-07-00   Date: Sep. 8, 2000

Noise/Vibration in Drivetrain and/or Front Propeller Shaft Constant Velocity Boot Integrity
This bulletin involves the replacement of the front propeller shaft.

2001 Dakota, Durango

SYMPTOM/CONDITION: Loss of lubricant may occur at the front propeller shaft constant velocity joint boot. One possible cause of this condition may be a partially crimped boot to the joint housing. Another cause of this condition may be a damaged (punctured) boot.

2000–01—If the malfunction indicator light (MIL) comes on, indicating a TCC/OD solenoid performance problem, consider replacing the transmission pressure boost valve cover plate. **2001**—Spark knock when accelerating. • Prohibition against oil additives. • Drivetrain noise and vibration. • Constant velocity joint boot integrity. • Troubleshooting transmission warning lamps. •

Silencing a noisy suspension. • Steering column pop or snap. **2000–04**—AC water leak into passenger area. **2002–2003**—An erratic-shifting automatic transmission may require a re-calibrated PCM or TCM. • Automatic transmission may overheat. • A "customer satisfaction" program will fix for free the automatic transmission's torque converter. • Brake pads will be replaced for free to cure excessive vibration (Bulletin No.: 05-007-03). • Water leak at the B-post seam and roof. **2004**—AC/heater fluttering. • Suspension squawk/Screech. • Campaign to correct left front door flange rusting. • Exhaust system drone.

Durango Profile

	1998	1999	2000	2001	2002	2003	2004
Cost Price ($) (negotiable)							
4X2 (21%)	—	36,705	37,750	—	—	—	—
4X4 (21%)	36,560	38,070	39,115	38,410	38,060	38,765	41,975
Used Values ($)							
4X2 ⋏	—	13,500	16,500	—	—	—	—
4X2 ⋎	—	12,000	14,500	—	—	—	—
4X4 ⋏	12,500	15,500	18,000	22,000	26,000	30,000	32,000
4X4 ⋎	10,500	14,500	16,000	20,000	24,000	28,000	30,000
Reliability	③	③	③	④	④	④	④
Crash Safety (F)	❷	❷	❷	④	④	④	⑤
Offset	③	③	③	③	③	③	—
Rollover	—	—	—	③	③	③	③

PACIFICA ★★★

RATING: Average (2004–05). Don't be misled: This is neither a performance nor an off-road vehicle; it's more like your dad's luxury station wagon—or a mini-minivan. **Strong points:** A comfortable ride and quiet interior; lots of front and middle-row seating space and storage areas; easily accessible seat controls; cargo floor is low enough for easy loading and unloading; excellent front and side crashworthiness scores and three-point seat belts for all six seats; impressive ventilation system; and an extended powertrain warranty. **Weak points:** Seriously overpriced; V6 engine provides mediocre acceleration; second-row seats only accommodate two occupants, making it necessary for whoever picks the shortest straw to sit in the cramped third-row seat bereft of a seatback head restraint; restricted rear visibility; unproven body and mechanicals; and excessive fuel consumption.

2005 Technical Data

Powertrain (front-drive or AWD)
Engine: 3.5L V6 (250 hp)
Transmission: 4-speed auto.
Dimension/Capacity
Height/length/width:

Wheelbase: 116.3 in.
Turning circle: 39.8 ft.
Passengers: 2/2/2
GVWR: N/A
Cargo volume: 79.5 cu. ft.

66.5/198.9/79.3 in.
Headroom F/R1/R2: N/A
Legroom F/R1/R2: N/A

Tow limit: 3,500 lb.
Fuel tank: 87L/reg.
Weight: 4,675 lb.

MODEL HISTORY: The $38,600 ($42,500 for AWD models) six-passenger Pacifica is an SUV, miniwagon, and station wagon all rolled into one. It's a big, tall vehicle that appears much lower and longer than it really is. Second- and third-row seats fold flat and those in the third row split 50/50.

Built in Windsor, Ontario, on the same production line as Chrysler's minivans, Chrysler calls it a "sports tourer" and cringes every time it's referred to as a mini-minivan. It is actually wider, heavier, and almost as long as the Chrysler Town and Country minivan.

Pacifica's V6, also featured in the 300M sedan, uses both a front-drive and all-wheel-drive powertrain (an on-demand 4X4 system, transferring power to the rear wheels when the front wheels lose traction). The 4-speed automatic transmission includes an AutoStick manual-shift feature. DaimlerChrysler Canada expects 70 percent of Pacificas to be all-wheel-drive models.

Handling and ride are enhanced through a strut-type suspension in front and a multi-link independent suspension in the rear, featuring automatic load levelling.

Safety features include standard four-wheel disc brakes with ABS, a tire-pressure monitoring system, three-row head-curtain airbags, adjustable pedals, and driver-side inflatable knee-bolsters.

COST ANALYSIS: Buy a model made late in 2004 to distance yourself as far as possible from the Pacifica's first-year production glitches (did you see the "offensive odour" 2004 bulletin on page 95) and over-priced intro models. With just a few options, the Pacifica's price tag can hit $50,000, the price for an AWD Town and Country or his and hers entry-level Caravans. **Best alternatives:** Try the Audi Allroad, BMW X5, Honda Pilot, Lexus RX 300, Nissan Murano, or Toyota Highlander. **Options:** The most expensive and non-essential include a $1,140 video system, a navigation system with its small screen located in the instrument cluster (bright sunlight washes out the navigation map), a hands-free communication system that recognizes up to five individual cell phones, chrome wheels, and a power liftgate. Traction control is not available for all-wheel-drive Pacificas, but comes standard on front-drive models. $35 will get you a cigarette lighter and two ashtrays. **Rebates:** Expect huge rebates of $3,000+ early in the new year when GM's planned dealer/customer sales incentives take their toll on the competition. **Delivery/PDI:** $995. **Depreciation:** Faster than average. **Insurance cost:** Fairly costly. **Parts supply/cost:** Parts aren't easily found and are relatively expensive. **Annual maintenance cost:** Predicted to be costlier than average. **Warranty:** Bumper-to-bumper 3 years/60,000 km; powertrain 7 years/ 115,000 km; rust perforation 5 years/160,000 km. **Supplementary warranty:** An extended warranty would be a wise buy until long-term reliability has been established. **Highway/city fuel economy:** 9.8L–14.2L/100 km. Owners say fuel economy is much less than advertised due to the car's heft, rather high drag coefficient, and overworked engine.

QUALITY/RELIABILITY: Quality control should be much better than Chrysler's other sport-utilities, yet we thought the same of the Liberty, and it still turned out to be a pig. Cheap-looking plastic centre console, small backlit gauges. **Warranty performance:** Predicted to be below average.

ROAD PERFORMANCE: Acceleration/torque: The V6 performs reasonably well, but may not be powerful enough for a 2,100 kg (4,675 lb.) vehicle when pushed; it can be annoyingly loud when climbing long grades or passing at high speeds. **Transmission:** Some gear-hunting and occasional abrupt shifts. The 4-speed automatic also kicks down for long periods, when the vehicle is fully loaded or going uphill. **Routine handling:** Fairly nimble. **Emergency handling:** Feels top-heavy; some body lean in hard cornering. Fairly wide turning circle. **Steering:** Not much steering feel; road feedback is limited. **Braking:** Large four-wheel disc brakes perform quite well, with little fade, even under heavy use.

SAFETY SUMMARY: NHTSA-rated five-star occupant protection in front and side collisions. Rear visibility is seriously compromised by the car's high beltline and the thick rear side pillars. Backing up and lane changing can be scary. **Airbags:** Front and side curtain. **ABS:** Standard; on all four wheels. **Visibility F/R:** *.

SAFETY COMPLAINTS: 2004—Glass roof exploded.

Secret Warranties/Service Tips

2004—An erratic-shifting automatic transmission may require a re-calibrated PCM or TCM. • Rattling front splash shield. • Interior materials may give off an offensive odour.

Pacifica Profile

	2004
Cost Price ($) (negotiable)	
Base (20%)	39,995
Used Values ($)	
Base ⋀	30,000
Base ⋁	27,000
Reliability	④
Crash Safety (F)	⑤
Side	⑤
Offset	⑤
Rollover	④

Ford

RATING: Not Recommended (1991–2005). Particularly prone to rolling over through the 2001 model year (and up until the 2004 Sport Trac). The Lincoln Aviator is essentially a baby Navigator spun off from the Explorer 4X4. Mountaineers are 1997 Mercury spin-offs with chrome and standard luxury features. Not quite a pickup truck, not quite an SUV, the Sport Trac takes elements from both to create an SUV able to transport five passengers and carry tall objects in the small rear bed. **Strong points:** The redesigned 2002–04 Explorers are a big improvement from a performance point of view, though quality is still abysmally low. Well appointed; with many standard safety features; good 4.6L V8 powertrain matchup that gives you much-needed power without too severe a fuel penalty (when compared with the thirsty V6); stable and forgiving handling when performing routine and emergency manoeuvres; steering is accurate and smooth; comfortable ride; permanent, full-time 4X4; versatile seven-passenger seating; attractively styled. Redesigned model has larger doors for easier entry/exit and a lower step-up. Lots of cargo space (more than Chevrolet Blazer or Jeep Cherokee). Impressive crashworthiness scores and insurance injury claim data except for head restraint performance. **Weak points:** Base warranty is inadequate to deal with chronic factory defects. Unacceptable off-road performance: Slow, noisy acceleration with the base power plant, hard riding over rocky terrain at slow speeds, and slow steering response. Excessive road noise and fuel consumption with the V6 engine (11.5–16.8L/100 km, or 17–25 mpg). Power driver seat and seat heater controls are hard to access; short drivers may have trouble reaching the pedals due to the driver seat cushion; interior takes a while to warm up on very cold days; inconveniently located passenger-side fuel-filler door. **New for 2005:** Standard roll stability control. When it senses the vehicle starting to tilt, this device slows the engine speed and activates the brakes (yikes!). Aviator will be dropped in early 2005 and the Explorer/Mountaineer won't be freshened up until the 2006 model year. *Sport Trac:* Essentially a previous-generation Explorer, Sport Trac will likely bite the dust at the end of the 2004 model year.

2005 Technical Data

Powertrain (4X2 or 4X4)
Engines: 4.0L V6 (210 hp)
• 4.6L V8 (240 hp)
Transmissions: 5-speed man. OD
• 5-speed auto. OD
Dimension/Capacity
Height/length/width:
67.7/188.5/70.2 in.
Headroom F/R: 39.9/39.3 in.
Legroom F/R: 42.4/37.7 in.

Wheelbase: 101.7/113.7 in.
Turning circle: 39 ft.
Passengers: 2/3; 2/3/2
Cargo volume: 45.5 cu. ft.
GVWR: 4,425–4,648 lb.
Load capacity: 1,325 lb.
Tow limit: 3,500–7,000 lb.
Ground clear.: 9.2 in.
Fuel tank: 79L/reg.
Weight: 4,339 lb.

MODEL HISTORY: The Explorer was introduced over a decade ago as a compact sport-utility that combined the solidity of a truck with carlike handling. Despite its Firestone and quality woes, it remains the top-selling sport-utility in North America. It is available in two or four doors and 4X2 or 4X4 modes. The V6 engine can be hooked to a 5-speed manual with Overdrive or a 5-speed automatic with Overdrive. The Control-Trac 4X4 system is controlled by a dial on the instrument panel and has three modes. Unlike a traditional 4X4 system, Control-Trac can be left in 4X4 all the time. 4X4 High is a constant 50/50 front/rear split, and should be used only on loose or slippery road surfaces. 4X4 Low is a low-range gear for climbing steep hills or travelling on very poor roads. The vehicle must be stopped and the transmission put into Neutral to engage or disengage the low range.

Generous cargo space, large doors, and lots of rear headroom and legroom make the Explorer a top contender in the sport-utility "space" race. The 4.0L V6 engine does a respectable job in pulling the Explorer's hefty weight, but passing power is underwhelming. **1995**—Dual airbags, four-wheel ABS, and Control-Trac 4X4. **1996**—Four-door versions were given a V8 engine, and a new SOHC V6 mated to a redesigned 5-speed automatic. **1999**—An improved braking system, a 5-hp boost for the 4.0L V6 (210 hp), optional side airbags, a sonar-sensing system that warns drivers of objects behind the vehicle when backing up, a slight revamping of the exterior, and the addition of a new four-door XLS series.

Overall, 1995–2001 models are good performers, although they still have some of their traditional quirks. For example, the 160-hp 4.0L V6 is slow to accelerate and even slower hauling a full passenger load. It's noisy and not as refined as the new V6—or the old V8, for that matter. The 210-hp 4.0L V6, on the other hand, is a smoother-running engine that gives better fuel economy, but much less than one would expect. Expect impressive acceleration with the V8 engine. Though smoother than the Jeep Grand Cherokee's 5.2L, it's not quicker and, again, you will pay a huge fuel penalty.

Year 2002–04 models have a split personality: The Sport and Sport Trac were carried over unchanged, which means they remain tippy and unreliable, while the four-door 4X4 was substantially improved for 2002, making it safer, more powerful, roomier, and more carlike in its comfort and handling. Its "smart" airbags deploy at different speeds, depending upon the severity of the crash and whether or not the occupants are wearing seat belts. Buyers also get a more powerful standard 4.0L V6 engine and, for the first time, an optional 4.6L V8. Although it's 1.2 inches shorter than the 2001, width and wheelbase were increased by 1.9 and 2.1 inches, respectively. The cargo area behind the second row seat is 7 percent bigger, and the new optional third-row seating makes the Explorer a seven-seater. Suspension, steering, and drivetrain improvements also reduce rollover risk, but the risk is still serious.

COST ANALYSIS: The 2005 models with standard stability control are worth a few extra loonies, but even this modest price increase will fall once competition heats up in early 2005. Some competitors worth checking out: the Nissan Pathfinder and Xterra, a second-series Hyundai Santa Fe, Toyota 4Runner,

Sequoia, and Highlander. Forget about the luxury European SUVs: BMW and Mercedes' M-Class have a worse quality control record, and a much heftier sticker price. **Rebates:** Look for zero percent financing and $3,000+ rebates on 2004 and 2005 models. **Delivery/PDI:** $895; *Aviator:* $1,045. **Warranty:** Bumper-to-bumper 3 years/60,000 km; rust perforation 5 years/unlimited km. **Supplementary warranty:** An extended warranty is essential; don't leave home without it. **Options:** Order the 260-hp 4.6L V8; the base 210-hp V6 engine's lacklustre performance isn't worth the fuel economy trade-off. Shorter drivers will want the power-adjustable brakes and accelerator pedals. Stay away from Bridgestone, Goodyear Wrangler, and Continental tires. Michelin Cross Terrain tires are an excellent alternative. The $700 side curtain airbags add head protection to those in the first two rows, but their safety is questionable. The Reverse-Sensing system, which includes an audible warning system when backing up too close to another vehicle or obstacle, has been glitch-prone; learn to turn your head. **Depreciation:** Higher than average. **Insurance cost:** Unusually high. **Annual maintenance cost:** Average during the warranty period. Driveline, fuel system, brake, suspension/steering, and electrical defects cause maintenance costs to rise after the third year of ownership. **Parts supply/cost:** Parts are expensive but easily found. **Highway/city fuel economy:** *4.0L V6 and auto.:* 11.5–16.8L/100 km; *4.6L V8 with 4X4:* 12.5–17.8L/100 km.

QUALITY/RELIABILITY: Reliability record is dismal, particularly with the V6 and V8 engines. St. Louis Ford employees say the optional 4.6L V8 engine "has been blowing head gaskets and overheating big time." Furthermore, according to the sources, cars and trucks equipped with 4.6L and 5.4L V8 engines are burning oil due to engine blocks that were improperly cast, causing the number-two cylinder bore to fail. The powertrain control modules (PCM) on early 2002 Explorers were allegedly programmed with corrupted software. Some Explorers have been repaired up to five times to correct driveline defects.

> Ford just replaced the differential on my 2002 4X2 Explorer. I took it in with gear howling and clunking. When I tried to get more specifics about what happened and why, I was stonewalled by "It was worn out." The SUV is one year old, [with] 16,000 miles [25,600 km], [and] used like a family car. As I was leaving, the service writer quietly confided she didn't know what happened but I was the fourth such replacement this week. This is not a large dealership so the repair ratio sounds really bad.

Owner-reported problems: A perusal of owner comments confirms that these SUVs will likely continue to have serious factory-related defects that will probably include automatic transmission failures, fuel system glitches, air conditioning system malfunctions, premature brake wear and noise, and brake failures. **Warranty performance:** Much worse than average. The company's staff is overwhelmed by complaints and owners who are poorly served by an inadequate base warranty. Chrysler went back to their 7-year/115,000 km warranty in mid-2002, and Ford needs to adopt a similar warranty or risk losing more sales and owner relations staffers disgusted by Ford Canada's tight-fisted attitude.

1995–97 defects

The main problems targeted in service bulletins or reported by owners are automatic transmission failures, including water ingestion through the transfer-case vent tube; engine surging, causing sudden acceleration; a failure to decelerate when exiting a highway; airbag malfunctions; loss of braking and expensive brake maintenance; windshield wiper failures; chronic electrical shorts; defective AC compressors; poorly fitted doors, windows, and windshields; and inoperative locks and handles.

A major concern is the poor durability of the SOHC 4.0L V6.

1998–2004 defects

Components with a high failure history include the engine, cooling, fuel, and electrical systems; automatic transmission; brakes; AC; suspension; and body hardware. Specific problem areas: AC remains on a high setting; airbag service light stays on for no reason; transmission lacks power upon acceleration; a faulty speed sensor; excessive drivetrain vibration throughout vehicle; automatic transmission fluid leakage at the radiator; premature fuel pump failure; steering binding; and engine knocking. One owner replaced the engine at 15,000 km but the new engine makes the same knocking noise, which the dealer now describes as normal. **Other problem areas:** Defective 4X4 electronic module, roof shakes and ear-piercing sound occurs when rear windows are lowered while cruising; overwhelming "rotten egg," sulphur, fuel, and oil-burning smells; horn muffled in snow; flimsy front bumper; cracked moulding under the rear light; sticking rear door handle; door handles are easily broken; ice and slush enter the door panels, causing the doors to freeze shut; and water leaks into the interior. Running board cracks and paint peeling. Mouldy AC and defroster.

ROAD PERFORMANCE: Acceleration/torque: The overhead cam 210-hp V6 is an adequate all-around performer that puts the rougher 2001 base V6 to shame. The V8 engine, however, provides a more versatile power supply. The engine is smoother—though not quicker—than the Jeep Grand Cherokee's 4.7L V8, but you'll pay a fuel penalty. With the standard Class 2 towing package on models equipped with the V6 or V8 engines, towing capacity is 1,588 kg (3,500 lb.). Add a Class 3 or 4 towing package, and V6-equipped models will tow 2,495 kg (5,500 lb.); V8-equipped Explorers max out at 3,175 kg (7,000 lb.). **Transmission:** Mostly smooth-shifting, until about the third year or 100,000 km. **Routine handling:** Handles like a large sedan and rides better as the load is increased. The V8 handles better, owing to the engine being positioned lower and farther back in the frame, improving steering responsiveness, reducing wallowing, and making the Explorer less nose-heavy.

Emergency handling: Good on dry highways. The tendency to fishtail when cornering under speed or upon hard acceleration has been reduced with the new independent rear suspension. Ford engineers have raised the ground clearance without raising the ride height. **Steering:** Precise and predictable. Some steering column noise. **Braking:** Very good (100–0 km/h: 137 ft.). The suspension could be stiffer, to reduce body roll in turns. With a light load, the ride gets choppy on bumpy roads; off-road, the suspension frequently bottoms out. Owners report vehicle has a propensity for hydroplaning on wet roads. Automatic transmission low-speed driveline vibration and occasional jerky shift when changing from Second to Third under light acceleration. Inadequate ground clearance and excessive front and rear overhangs preclude serious off-roading. On-road handling is not as responsive as the Jeep Grand Cherokee. Redesigned Explorer needs to go on a diet and lose about 180 kg (400 lb.).

SAFETY SUMMARY: Now, a question everyone's asking: Is the Explorer more dangerous than other vehicles if it has a blowout? Absolutely. Just look at NHTSA's latest 2004 rollover ratings: Sport Trac, virtually unchanged post-Firestone, got an "Unacceptable" two-star ranking, while the re-engineered Explorer (with steering and suspension upgrades) scored three stars. In August 2004, a Fort Meyers, Florida, jury rendered a $2 million negligence judgment against Ford, after seeing internal Ford documents that showed Ford was aware of a stability problem with Explorers manufactured through the 2001 model year.

Ford's PR mantra is that Explorer owners are being killed and injured *only* because of faulty Firestone tires, while Firestone maintains that the Explorer's faulty design *sends* the vehicle out of control. Firestone's finger pointing has been buttressed by the *Washington Post*'s October 9, 2000, analysis of 27,000 fatal and non-fatal sport-utility accidents from 1997 to 1999. The study's conclusions:

> The Explorer has a higher rate of tire-related accidents than other sport-utility vehicles—even when equipped with Goodyear tires; the Explorer was 53 percent more likely than other compact SUVs to roll over when an equipment failure such as faulty brakes, bald tires, or blowouts caused an accident; in 187 fatal blown-tire accidents, the Explorer rolled over 95 percent of the time, compared with 83 percent for other SUVs.

Many owners report excessive engine knocking and premature engine replacement in vehicles that have yet to reach 10,000 km. When the Explorer stalls, brakes and steering are lost, the Check Engine light comes on, and the driver has to wait a few minutes before the vehicle can be restarted. Automatic transmission malfunctions and failures are still quite common with low-mileage Explorers. Poor braking or no brakes are a frequent complaint. Other safety-related complaints include fires erupting in the rear of the vehicle and within the rear-view mirror wiring harness; no seat belt for the rear middle seat; seat belts that fail to retract or detach from wall anchor; power steering locks up or leaks fluid; wheel may separate when backing up; front brake rotor warping; the emergency brake won't stop the vehicle; and tail lights fill with water when it rains. **Airbags:** Side airbags are optional. Many reports of airbags failing to deploy or deploying for no reason. **ABS:** 4W is standard; disc/disc. **Safety belt pretensioners:** Standard. **Traction control:** Standard. **Head restraints F/R:** *2002: **/*; 2003-04: *.* **Visibility F/R:** *******. **Maximum load capacity:** 1,325 lb.

SAFETY COMPLAINTS: All years: Explorer lacks stability on the highway, as it tends to bounce around and veer off to one side or the other and is excessively prone to hydroplane on wet roadways. • Due to the absence of rear leaf springs, the Explorer becomes even more unsteady when engaged for towing. • Sudden acceleration or stalling, often related to erratic cruise control operation. • Sticking accelerator pedal and throttle linkage. • Engine overheating. • After driving the vehicle through water, engine died when water was sucked into engine due to air intake being located on bottom of vehicle. • Fuel, water pump, and ignition module failures. • Transmission slips in forward gears, Overdrive light comes on, and vehicle loses power. • Overdrive failures. • Repeat transmission failures caused by defective planetary gear. • Repeated transfer-case failures. • Excessive drive-shaft vibration. • Brake master cylinder and fluid-line failures. • Emergency parking brake won't stay engaged. • Brake pedal sticks. • Repeat brake failures. • Brake lock-up. • Power-steering pump fluid leakage. • Steering lock-up. • Front-end suspension failure. • Faulty rear liftgate support assembly allows hatch to fall. • Horn pad failure. • Driver seat belt fails to retract. • Rear seat belts are hard to unbuckle. • Driver's seat frame breaks. • Inside rear door handles break. • Power door lock and antenna failures. • Electric door locks will disengage while driving. Steering wheel came off steering column due to missing bolt. • Power-steering failure. • Steering column failure. • Gas gauge failure. • Under-dash wiring short caused a fire to ignite. • Fire erupted in the centre console. • Overheated ignition electronic control unit caught fire. • Engine fire. • Engine failure. • Power seat switch failure. • Aluminum wheels cause tires to go flat. • Spare tire is too small. • Speed control failure. • Rear-view mirror sits too low; obstructs forward vision. • Fuel spews out of fuel-filler tube, no matter how slowly it is filled. • Antisway bar pulled loose from suspension when vehicle was pulling into a parking lot. • Axle bearing assembly failure. **2000**—Firestone tire failures are paramount, with new allegations that the wheel rims aren't symmetrically round, making for difficult tire mounting. • A number of tires have failed that weren't in the Firestone recall. • **2001**—Rear-view mirror sparked a fire in the dash wiring. • Exhaust fumes invade the passenger compartment. • While driving, gas line exploded. • Driver's side window shattered while cruising at 100 km/h. • Reports of windshield suddenly shattering. • Vehicle rolled over when turning to avoid another vehicle. • Hitting a water puddle causes vehicle to flip and roll onto its side. • When driving 110 km/h, 4X4 suddenly kicked in, causing transmission to downshift, and vehicle suddenly accelerated. •

Gearshift sticks in Park; vehicle can roll backward even though transmission is engaged in Drive or Park. • Wheel fell off when backing out of the driveway. • Lug nuts loosen while driving. • Sudden steering loss. • Rear suspension unsafe for towing a boat. • Sudden brake lock-up while driving 35–40 km/h. • When brakes were applied during a panic stop, pedal went to the floor without braking. • Excessive rear-end sag and rear axle jumps when load is placed in the cargo area. • Bolt that attaches the seat belt for the integrated child safety seat comes apart. • During rear impact, driver's seat frame broke, causing seat to collapse backward. • Front and rear shoulder belts ride up on occupants' necks and slip off small-statured persons. • Sudden loss of all electrical power. • Windshield wiper failure; wipers are activated when you hit a bump or use the turn signal or may stop suddenly in rainy weather. • Inadequate defrosting. • Brake lights don't work during gentle braking. • Overheated CD player melts CD. • Sudden loss of power to lights, odometer, speedometer, wipers, and power windows. • Incorrect fuel gauge reading. • Key hard to turn in the ignition. **2001–02**—Almost 1,100 written safety-related complaints found in NHTSA's on-line database relating to the same failures listed repeatedly above. • Tail light fire. • No airbag deployment. • Hydraulic liftgate cylinder arm often comes off, window explodes and blows out the rear door:

> Four hours after new 2002 Explorer was picked up from the dealer, glass tailgate exploded on being closed gently. Rear window shattered with such force that metal components of the door were badly bent and scratched. Glass was scattered over a radius of 20 feet, including into the back seats and onto the roof. My right leg was cut in three places ....The entire door was replaced by the dealer. Unless recalled, this apparently common defect will result in serious injury.

Ford has a "Safety Improvement Program," NHTSA #01I010000 (secret warranty), that will fix the defect for free. It is not a recall. • Vehicle rolls away while in Park. • Three out of five wheel lug nuts were sheared off. • Intermittent steering lock-up while driving. • Head restraints sit too low; could snap one's neck in a rear-end collision. • Door handles are easily broken. • Smoky rear-view mirror. • Message Center dash light is too dim. • Headlights suddenly fail. • Rear-view mirror obscures forward vision. **2003**—Same old complaint patterns. • Sudden unintended acceleration in Drive as well as in Reverse gear. • Driver's airbag deployed when key was put into the ignition. • Airbags failed to deploy. • Fire ignited in the engine compartment's front right side. • ABS brakes perform poorly. • Many complaints that the rear lift glass shatters for no reason; right-side window has a history of shattering as well. • Liftgate window frequently pops open. • Defective engine, transmission, drive shaft, and steering clock spring. • Faulty sensor module causes the ignition, seats, and other electrical features to fail. **2004**—Underhood fire. • Sudden acceleration when parking. • No start, stalling. • Running board broke when stepped upon. • Excessive vibration. • Steering wheel sticks when turning; power steering suddenly disengages. • Misleading fuel gauge.

Secret Warranties/Service Tips

All years: Press Ford for "goodwill" warranty coverage if your AC fails within 5 years/80,000 km. **1991–97**—Transmission slippage may be caused by a damaged fluid pump support seal. **1993–97**—Premature wearout of the clutch slave cylinder calls for the installation of a revised slave cylinder. **1993–2002**—Paint delamination, peeling, or fading (see Part Three). • A buzzing or rattling noise coming from underneath the vehicle indicates the need to secure the heat shield. **1994–98**—TSB #98-18-5 has lots of tips on eliminating side-door wind noise. **1995–99**—Service the blend door if AC doesn't cool the interior. **1995–2002**—Automatic transmission defects:

No 2nd, 3rd Gear/No Engine Braking

Bulletin No.: 03-22-10   Date: 11/10/03

1995–2001 EXPLORER
1995–2002 RANGER
1996–97 AEROSTAR
2000–02 EXPLORER SPORT
2001–02 EXPLORER SPORT TRAC
1997–2001 MOUNTAINEER

ISSUE: Some vehicles may exhibit the following shift and engagement conditions:

^ No 2nd Gear

^ No 3rd Gear

^ No Engine Braking In Manual 1st.

ACTION: The main control valve body separator plate may need to be updated to the latest level.

1996–2000—A rubbing sound heard from the rear during right-hand turns may be caused by insufficient clearance between the muffler hanger rod and the rear drive shaft. **1997–98**—Troubleshooting tips for tracking down and eliminating side-door wind noise. • Sticking throttle, surging, and hesitation can be corrected by installing a new throttle body assembly, says TSB #98-21-22. • To eliminate a front-end suspension clunk, replace the stabilizer bar and insulators. • Restore loss of electrics and 4X4 capability. **1997–99**—Excessive vibration at idle or boom, or hearing a grunt, groan, or moan noise at idle, may require the installation of an exhaust system y-brace. • Cold condensate dripping from the AC system onto the heated exhaust gas oxygen sensor could be the cause of backfiring, stalling, or a rough idle. **1997–2000**—Transmission fluid may leak between the radiator transmission oil cooler and the transmission oil cooler fitting, due to insufficient thread sealer on the transmission oil cooler fitting; install o-ring #W705181-S onto the oil cooler fitting. **1997–2001**—Hesitation on acceleration or when turning may be caused by fuel pump cavitation; install a revised fuel pump and sender assembly, says TSB #00-20-1. **1997–2002**—Troubleshooting a constantly lit MIL light. **1998–2000**—A buzzing or grinding noise heard during a shift from Second to Third gear with a manual transmission usually signals the need to replace the 3–4 synchronizer assembly. **1998–2001**—4X4 front axle squealing, whistling countermeasures. **1999**—Automatic transmission slipping, delayed shifting, or no engagement may need a new EPC solenoid and bracket. **1999–2001**—Vibration, shake, or a resonance noise at speeds in excess of 72 km/h may be due to an imbalance in one or more of the driveline components.

Engine Timing Chain Rattling

Bulletin No.: 02-8-1   Date: 04/29/02

ENGINE - 4.0L SOHC - RATTLE NOISE FROM PRIMARY CHAIN DRIVE AREA BETWEEN 2000–3000 RPM - COLD ENGINE OPERATION ONLY

1999–2002 EXPLORER, SPORT TRAC, SPORT, RANGER, MOUNTAINEER

ISSUE: The noise is audible during hot and cold engine operation (but predominantly found on cold engines) under acceleration, typically at 2400–2500 rpm. This may be caused by a defective Primary Timing Chain Tensioner system.

ACTION: Replace the Primary Timing Chain Tensioner, Chain Guide, Jackshaft and Crankshaft Sprockets with a Primary Timing Chain Tensioner Kit.

2001—AC stays on high setting. • Manual transmission buzzing or grinding. • Automatic transmission fluid leakage at the radiator. • Rear rubbing noise when making right-hand turns. **2001–03**—Stinky exhaust:

Engine Controls/Emissions – Exhaust Sulfur Smell

Article No.: 02-21-6   Date: 10/28/02

2001–02 EXPLORER SPORT
2002 EXPLORER SPORT TRAC
2002–03 EXPLORER
2002–03 MOUNTAINEER

ISSUE: Some vehicles may exhibit excessive sulfur smell from the exhaust under certain drive modes. This may be due to the highly active state of a new catalyst, calibration factors, underbody catalyst temperature, and amount of sulfur present in the fuel.

WARRANTY STATUS: Eligible under the provisions of bumper-to-bumper warranty coverage and emissions warranty coverage.

OASIS CODES: 403000, 499000

1999–2002—Engine timing chain rattling. **2002**—Engine coolant seepage. Harsh shifting and shuddering may simply require that the PCM be re-calibrated. Automatic transmission ticking, whine, or howl. **2002–2004**—4.6L engine ticking (replace the cylinder head and cam assembly with Part Number 4L3Z-6049-AA (RH) or 4L3Z-6049-BA (LH). **2003**—Incorrectly installed gear driven camshaft position sensor synchronizer assemblies can cause engine surge, loss of power, a lit MIL light. • Front axle leaks fluid from the vent tube. • Rear driveline click, creak, or pop. • Squeaking accelerator pedal.

Aviator, Explorer Profile

	1997	1998	1999	2000	2001	2002	2003	2004
Cost Price ($) (negotiable)								
Explorer 4X2	26,095	28,995	28,995	29,995	27,750	28,600	30,540	31,150
4X4	28,795	30,095	30,095	29,995	35,400	37,700	37,795	39,140
Aviator	—	—	—	—	—	—	58,950	59,240
Used Values ($)								
Explorer 4X2 ▲	6,500	8,000	10,500	13,500	15,000	17,500	21,500	25,000
Explorer 4X2 ▼	5,500	6,500	9,000	12,000	14,000	16,000	20,000	23,000
4X4 ▲	8,000	10,000	11,000	14,500	17,500	21,000	22,000	28,000
4X4 ▼	6,500	9,000	10,000	12,500	16,000	19,000	22,000	26,000
Aviator ▲	—	—	—	—	—	—	35,000	41,000
Aviator ▼	—	—	—	—	—	—	33,000	38,000
Reliability	❷	❷	❷	❷	❷	❷	❷	❷
Crash Safety (F)	④	④	④	④	④	④	④	④
Side	—	—	⑤	⑤	⑤	⑤	⑤	⑤
Offset	③	③	③	③	③	⑤	⑤	⑤
Rollover	—	—	—	—	❷	③	③	③
Sport Trac	—	—	—	—	—	❷	❷	❷

Note: Sport Trac models cost a few thousand less than their Explorer equivalent; Mountaineers aren't sold in Canada.

EXPEDITION, NAVIGATOR ★★

RATING: Below Average (1997–2005). The Lincoln Navigator is a re-badged Expedition carrying tons of chrome and plastic cladding. **Strong points:** Powerful engines suitable for heavy hauling; excellent ride and visibility; lots of passenger room; and a luxury carlike interior. **Weak points:** Hard to park or drive in the city; lethargic steering; limited rear-seat access and cargo space; slow to heat or cool; entry is hampered by a high step-in and lack of grab handle on the driver's side; poor fuel economy; problematic quality control and an unusually large number of performance- and safety-related complaints. Insurance claims show these vehicles are frequently stolen. **New for 2005:** Optional roll stability control (see Explorer).

2005 Technical Data

Powertrain (4X4)
Engines: 4.6L V8 (240 hp)
• 5.4L V8 (260 hp)
Transmission: 4-speed auto.
Dimension/Capacity
Height/length/width:
74.3/204.6/78.6 in.
Headroom F/R1/R2: 39.8/39.8/35.1 in.
Legroom F/R1/R2: 40.9/38.9/28.8 in.
Wheelbase: 119.1 in.
Turning circle: 42 ft.
Passengers: 3/3/3
Cargo volume: 70 cu. ft.
GVWR: 8,000 lb.
Tow limit: 8,000 lb.
Ground clear.: 8.5 in.
Fuel tank: 98/113L/reg.
Weight: 4,850 lb.

MODEL HISTORY: Based on the F-150 pickup and offered only as a four-door, the Expedition and Navigator handle serious trailer towing with more comfort than a pickup or a van. They have a nine-passenger potential if you use the optional third-row bench seat. The full-time 4X4 is taken from the Explorer, along with four-wheel ABS disc brakes. Both the 4.6L and 5.4L V8s are peppy, even though they can't match the torque and fuel economy of the Tahoe's diesel engines. On the other hand, both V8 engines experience a similar delay when accelerating, as do the Tahoe and Yukon. Keep in mind that these vehicles have many serious safety-related problems reported time and again to NHTSA. Ditch the Firestone tires; many tires that were not on the recall list have been defective.

1999—A small power boost, an upgraded Command Trac 4X4 system that provides 4X4 when needed, and optional power-adjustable gas and brake pedals. **2000**—Standard power-adjusted foot pedals, a rear sonar backing up alert system, a revised centre console, and optional side airbags. **2003**—An independent rear suspension, stiffer chassis, increased towing capabilty of 4,035 kg (8,900 lb.), improved braking and stability, and a third-row, foldable seat. Third-row passengers gained lots of legroom but lost some shoulder room. The 4.6L V8 gets a bit more horsepower. Navigators were given exceptionally large seats and tweaks to reduce vibrations and noise. Optional power-deployed running boards that pop out when the door is opened and a remote-controlled aluminum liftgate were also added. **2004**—Wider availability of last year's new features.

COST ANALYSIS: Go for the 2005 with stability control; the $43,300 base price is quite soft, so haggle aggressively. **Best alternatives:** GM's large SUVs, like the Tahoe and Yukon (with an extended warranty) are far more nimble and reliable. Toyota's Highlander and 4Runner are also worth a look. If they won't do, consider a Nissan Pathfinder or the Lexus LX 450 and 470. **Rebates:** Look for $4,000+ rebates on the 2004 models and on this year's version early in the new year. **Delivery/PDI:** $980. **Warranty:** Bumper-to-bumper 3 years/60,000 km; rust perforation 5 years/unlimited km. **Supplementary warranty:** An extended warranty is a good idea. **Options:** Stay away from any Firestone or Continental tires; both the 16- and 17-inch Firestone tires have a history of sudden tread separation; Continental tires simply lose chunks of tread. Bridgestone tires should be boycotted as well. Be wary of the moon roof option; many complaints of water leaks and wind noise have been reported. Consider the 5.4L power plant with its sturdier transmission (the E40D instead of the 4R70W), 20 additional horses, and extra torque. Other recommended options: adjustable accelerator and brake pedals and running boards. **Depreciation:** Much faster than average. **Insurance cost:** Higher than average. A 2003 IIHS study says the Expedition and Navigator are two of the 10 most frequently stolen vehicles—despite their sophisticated anti-theft features. **Parts supply/cost:** Body parts are often back-ordered, but moderately priced mechanical parts are easily found either in the Explorer or F-Series bins. **Annual maintenance cost:** Costlier than average. **Highway/city fuel economy:** *4.6L V8:* 12.2–17.6L/100 km; *5.4L V8:* 13.6–19.7L/100 km; *4.6L V8 and 4X4:* 13.4–19.1L/100 km.

QUALITY/RELIABILITY: Overall quality control and reliability are way below average. There's also a disturbingly high rate of safety-related complaints that show a "What, me worry?" attitude among Ford engineers. After all, how much engineering prowess does it take to prevent wheels from falling off or the rear hatch from falling on one's head? Or, reducing the enormous amounts of brake dust buildup on the front and back wheels after driving only a few kilometres? Continental General and Firestone tires have a history of tread retention problems. The website *www.blueovalnews.com* reports that Ford upgraded the 4R100 transmission for 2001 by using a new mechanical diode in the forward clutch area. The new diode was expected to save Ford $4 per transmission, but now the diode is the cause of the transmission's failure. If a diode fails, it could damage the transmission and/or disable Second gear. 4R100 transmissions are found in the 5.4L V8-powered Expedition, Navigator, Excursion, Econoline van, and F-Series truck. **Owner-reported problems:** Inadequate troubleshooting of sudden acceleration or stalling; 4.6L engine piston slap noise with cold starts; rough idling due to a faulty throttle cable; excessive steering play requires constant correction; chronic electrical shorts for all model years, affecting everything from gauges and lights to engine and transmission performance; transmission failure; excessive rear differential noise; engine oil leaks lead to engine replacement within first year of ownership; defective fuel pump sensors; poor braking, high brake maintenance costs (chronic rotor warpage and brake dust everywhere), and excessive brake noise; automatic-adjusting side mirrors constantly re-adjust themselves to the wrong setting; and assorted clunks, rattles, and wind noise. **Warranty performance:** Average. Powertrain problems are ignored if you bought your SUV used:

After two weeks of ownership I had to have my '99 Navigator towed to the dealer because it would not go into gear. I also complained that there was knocking while driving; they found that the motor mounts were also bad.

After much protesting, Ford decided that this was a warranty issue that they could cover. But I would still have to pay $800, and they would give me a powertrain warranty good for 100,000 miles [160,000 km] or seven years. I was not happy about having a vehicle with serious issues at 45,000 miles [72,000 km].

ROAD PERFORMANCE: Acceleration/torque: 0–100 km/h: 9.9 seconds (about a second slower than the Tahoe) with the 2000's base engine; expect much better acceleration with the 2001 model's additional horses. **Transmission:** Well-spaced gearing shifts imperceptibly, without any gear hunting when traversing hilly terrain. **Steering:** Over-sensitive at lower speeds. **Routine handling:** Smooth, comfortable ride that's above average for a sport-utility. The variable-assist steering is fairly precise at lower speeds and gives adequate feedback from the road. Leaving the Expedition in AWD improves handling considerably. Parking is more like docking. **Emergency handling:**

Above average. The Expedition's tight chassis and supple suspension keep the vehicle on track, without the wallowing and nose-diving evident in many other sport-utilities in its class. **Braking:** Adequate, but not impressive (100–0 km/h: 149 ft.).

SAFETY SUMMARY: An Ontario law firm (*www.willbarristers.com*) has filed a class-action petition against Ford for defective door latches on 1997–2000 model year Expeditions, Navigators, and F-series trucks. It will cost about $994 per four-door vehicle to replace the door latches, which could open in a side-impact crash or rollover accident. There have been many cases where the wheel lug nuts sheared and the wheel flew off (recalled). But the kicker is that even the spare tire is dangerous: Several reports state the spare tire cable broke while turning a corner, causing the spare tire to fly away. Also, an inaccurate fuel gauge indicates a quarter tank full when you are actually out of gas. Many incidents have been reported of unintended, sudden acceleration, which has been blamed on a variety of causes. Horn design makes it hard to activate in an emergency. Some complaints of insufficient low-beam illumination. **Airbags:** Side airbags are optional. There have been reports of airbags failing to deploy and the airbag light staying on for no reason. **ABS:** 4W is standard; disc/disc. ABS failure or lock-up often caused by faulty sensor or ABS module. **Traction control:** Optional. **Head restraints F/R:** **/*; *2003-04:* ****/***. **Visibility F/R:** *****. **Maximum load capacity:** 1,349 lb.

SAFETY COMPLAINTS: All years: Fire ignites while vehicle is parked. • Cruise control fails to disengage when brakes are applied. • Chronic engine head gasket failures and oil leaks; Check Engine light comes on as coolant leaks onto plugs and #3 and #4 coil packs. • Too much steering play. • Excessive front-end wandering. • Tie-rod end and torsion bar failures. • Excessive suspension vibration. • Transmission failures. • Slips while in gear. • Rear axle failure. • Seat belt failures. • Slippery plastic running board. • Rear hatch latch cylinders fail, allowing hatch to fall on driver's head. • Inoperative power windows. • Windows shatter for no reason. • Defective gas cap causes engine warning light to go off and makes for poor driveability. **1999**—Vehicle exploded while getting gas. • Pitman arm suddenly detached from the steering gear. • Rear door hinge cut off child's finger as door was opened. • Incredible but true—the vehicle started twice on its own without the key in the ignition. • Rear brake caliper seizure scored rotor: $1,000 repair. • Rear-view mirror backing (silver) peels off. • Cracked hood welds. **2000**—Sudden loss of engine power when accelerating, especially when fuel tank is less than one-quarter full. • Suspension and steering combination makes the vehicle wander over the road. Over-sensitive steering also makes vehicle hard to control; one report that it almost tipped over. • Three bolts that hold the steering gearbox came apart. • In some cases, the steering assist may cut on and off. • Plastic fuel tank is quite vulnerable to leakage from road debris punctures. • Jack failures. • Driver-side seat belt clip won't go into buckle, apparently a national problem. **2001**—Sudden, unintended acceleration when brakes were applied. • Stalling and unable to restart. • Child shifted vehicle into Neutral without touching brake pedal. • Vehicle surges forward, despite brakes being applied. • Brake pedal fell to the floor when brakes were applied. • Adjustable gas pedal will sometimes get stuck under floor mat. • Vibration, moan at highway speeds. • Door lock is easily thwarted. • Driver-side seat belt unlatches. • Wheel lug nuts won't stay tight; wheel flew off vehicle. • Passengers sickened by white powder coming out of air vents. • Vehicle stalls and won't start when vehicle is on an incline with only a quarter tank of fuel left. **2002**—Airbags failed to deploy. • Vehicle fishtailed out of control. • Sudden acceleration when braking. • Steering wheel lock-up. **2003**—Serious tire defects (Continental). • Early failure of powertrain components. • Brake failures. **2004**—Sudden, unintended acceleration:

> The vehicle transmission was in the Park position while waiting on a slow train. When engaging the transmission into the Drive position, after the train had passed, the vehicle uncontrollably fully accelerated on it's own. To avoid a serious collision with oncoming traffic, the driver turned the vehicle on to the railroad tracks where it came to a stop after damaging two wheels and high centering on the tracks. This is a very dangerous vehicle.

Steering wheel sticks when turning. • Still excessive brake wear and brake dust everywhere (TSB covers this problem). • Faulty tire pressure monitor. • Throttle sticks, especially when the cruise control is engaged. • Total brake loss.

Secret Warranties/Service Tips

All years: Free fuel gauge/sender replacement under ONP #97B17, Supplement 1 (secret warranty). • Front engine cover oil leaks. • No-starts in cold weather. **1997–98**—Troubleshooting tips for tracking down and eliminating side-door wind noise. • Fuel may leak from the spring lock couplings at the fuel rail. **1997–99**—A buzzing or rattling noise coming from underneath the vehicle indicates the need to secure the heat shield. • Vibration or shimmy above 70 km/h may require an upgraded drive shaft. • Diagnostic tips for correcting a front differential moaning, whining, or buzzing in the speakers and a whistling noise when driving with the AC off. • An exhaust system crack/break between the muffler and tailpipe may require a new drive shaft, muffler, and tailpipe assembly. **1997–2000**—A hesitation upon acceleration or while turning may be caused by fuel pump cavitation, due to fuel sloshing away from the filter sock in the fuel tank reservoir. Ford TSB #00-20-1 says a new fuel pump should be installed if other possible causes have been eliminated. **1997–2001**—Under a little-known extended warranty, Ford will repair or replace 5.4L engines with faulty headgaskets on the 1999–2001 F-150 and Super Duty F-Series pickups, Econoline, Expedition, and Lincoln Navigator. **1997–2002**—Throttle sticks in very cold weather. **1998**—Erratic speedometer readings require the installation of an upgraded unit. • A free service kit is available to add an extra 25 mm to the narrow running boards. • TSB #98-17-21 gives a comprehensive listing of the probable causes of rattles and squeaks. • Electrical accessories that short out may be contaminated by water leaks, says TSB #98-9-13. **1999–2000**—Install a clutch pack kit under warranty to silence rear axle chattering (vehicles with a limited slip rear axle) on turns or when cornering, says TSB #00-8-4. **2000**—A new side intake manifold gasket will correct a coolant leak from the passenger-side intake manifold. **2001**—No-starts, stalling with the 7.3L engine. • Engine stalls when vehicle is shifted into Reverse. • A buck or jerk may be felt with cruise control engaged. • Turbo hooting. • Ford admits investigating cam sensor failures (leads to loss of power, engine shutdown, and no-starts). • Sudden loss of Second gear; vehicle won't move. • Delayed shifts. • Sway bar clunk and popping. • Front shaft seal leakage. • Water pump shaft seal leakage. • Higher than normal steering effort at low speed, or stopped with the brakes applied. • Incorrect oil pressure readings. **2002**—Engine cylinder head leaks. • 5.4L engine power loss. • Engine vibration at idle and droaning noise when accelerating. • Lack of fuel pressure. • Driveline vibration at 100 km/h. • Loose axle bearing; axle tube seal leakage. • Excessive braking when decelerating. • Front suspension noise. • Heater core leaks. • Faulty ignition switch lock cylinder. • Air suspension air leak. • Excessive wind noise. **2003**—Frequent no-starts. • Front axle groan, hum, or vibration. • Powertrain fluid leaks from the rear halfshaft seal. • Transmission fluid leaks at the transmission oil cooler. • Rear axle whine. • Electrical shorts may cause gauge, alarm, radio/DVD, and door lock failures. • Power steering leaks, noise, vibration. **2003–04**—Axle seal leaks:

Rear Axle Seal Leaks

Bulletin No.: 04-10-5   Date: 05/25/04
AXLE SEAL LEAKS
2003–04 EXPEDITION, NAVIGATOR

ISSUE: Some vehicles may exhibit fluid leaks from the rear halfshaft axle seal. This may occur when the halfshaft spline comes in contact with the inner diameter of the axle seal. The leak may be more pronounced in cold weather.

ACTION: To service order and install Axle Seal Kit 3L1Z-4A109-BA. Review the revised instruction sheet and obtain the required tools before beginning any repairs. Also refer to the following installation service tips.

Intermittent loss of cooling. • Excessive brake dust on wheels:

Excessive Brake Dust on Wheels

Bulletin No.: 04-5-2   Date: 03/22/04
REVISED BRAKE LININGS
2003–04 EXPEDITION, NAVIGATOR

Ford Motor Company recognizes that some customers may object to brake dust for appearance reasons. Effective 12/18/03, the brake linings have been revised. The revised linings will generate less dust. The revised linings are also being made available for service, as Service Kit 4L1Z-2001-BA.

Expedition, Navigator Profile

	1997	1998	1999	2000	2001	2002	2003	2004
Cost Price ($) (very negotiable)								
Expedition 4X2 (24%)	35,395	36,495	37,495	—	—	—	—	—
Expedition 4X4 (24%)	38,495	39,595	40,595	41,195	40,855	41,255	43,270	46,800
Navigator	—	52,548	63,765	68,690	66,425	66,425	69,995	72,625
Used Values ($)								
Expedition 4X2 ⋏	9,000	11,000	15,000	—	—	—	—	—
Expedition 4X2 ⋎	8,000	10,000	13,000	—	—	—	—	—
Expedition 4X4 ⋏	10,000	12,500	16,000	21,000	23,000	27,000	32,000	36,000
Expedition 4X4 ⋎	8,500	11,000	14,000	19,000	21,000	25,000	30,000	33,000
Navigator ⋏	—	17,000	21,000	25,000	31,000	37,000	46,000	52,000
Navigator ⋎	—	15,000	19,000	23,000	29,000	34,000	43,000	50,000
Reliability	❷	❷	❷	❷	❷	❷	③	④
Crash Safety (F)	④	④	④	④	⑤	⑤	⑤	⑤
Rollover	—	—	—	—	❷	❷	—	—

Note: A used 4X2 Navigator is worth about $2,000 less than a 4X4.

EXCURSION   ★★

RATING: Below Average (2000–04). This Godzilla SUV has been felled by the Sierra Club; Ford will pull the plug on the Excursion early into the 2005 model year. **Strong points:** Well appointed, good optional powertrain match for highway cruising or city commuting, automatic 4X4, versatile, good passenger room, comfortable seating, and attractive styling. **Weak points:** Slow acceleration with the base 5.4L power plant, unacceptable off-road performance, excessive engine noise, mediocre handling, obstructed rear visibility, poor head restraint protection, no crashworthiness data, and non-existent fuel economy. An unusually high number of safety-related complaints are recorded by government safety investigators.

2005 Technical Data

Powertrain
Engines: 5.4L V8 (255 hp)
• 7.3L V8 D (250 hp)
• 6.8L V10 (310 hp)
Transmission: 4-speed auto.
Dimension/Capacity
Height/length/width:
77/227/80 in.
Legroom F/R: 41.5/31 in.
Headroom F/R: 41/41.1 in.

Wheelbase: 137 in.
Turning circle: 52 ft.
Passengers: 3/3/3
Cargo volume: 84 cu. ft.
GVWR: 8,835–8,887 lb.
Tow limit: 6,200–12,500 lb.
Ground clear.: 8.1 in.
Fuel tank: 166L/reg.
Weight: 7,270 lb.

MODEL HISTORY: The Excursion is a re-styled version of Ford's three-quarter-ton Super Duty pickup, equipped with a standard 260-hp 5.4L V8 engine on its 4X2s and a choice of a 300-hp 6.8L V10 or a 235-hp 7.3L turbo-diesel V8 power plant on the 4X4 versions. A dash-mounted switch permits shifting "on the fly"; however, unlike the GM competition, Ford's 4X4 system can't be used on dry pavement.

First launched in 1999 to compete against GM's full-sized Chevrolet Suburban SUV, the 2001 Excursion got a beefed-up 250-hp 7.3L diesel power plant, and additional entertainment and convenience features. Since then it has returned each model year relatively unchanged.

COST ANALYSIS: Dealers are quite willing to bargain down the $46,950 base price by almost 20 percent. **Best alternatives:** The redesigned Suburban looks to be a better choice, due to its better quality and handling and performance refinements. **Rebates:** Look for $5,000–$7,000 rebates early in 2005. **Delivery/PDI:** $980. **Warranty:** Bumper-to-bumper 3 years/60,000 km; rust perforation 5 years/unlimited km. **Supplementary warranty:** An extended warranty is essential. **Options:** Nothing worth the extra money, unless you absolutely need running boards. Stay away from Firestone and Bridgestone tires. **Depreciation:** Much faster than average. **Insurance cost:** Higher than average. **Annual maintenance cost:** Average during the warranty period; fairly costly once the warranty expires. **Parts supply/cost:** Parts should be fairly inexpensive and easily found, since they all come from Ford's truck parts bin. **Highway/city fuel economy:** N/A.

QUALITY/RELIABILITY: Amazingly bad for a vehicle this expensive. Next time someone suggests that you "get what you pay for" in vehicle quality, show the service bulletin references for luxury SUVs like the Excursion, Expedition/ Navigator, Liberty, X5, and Mercedes' M-Series. **Owner-reported problems:** Steering instability and poor handling; drive shaft, differential, motor mount, and wheel bearing failures; chronic drivetrain whine and howl; electrical system; poor braking, high brake maintenance costs (chronic rotor warpage), and excessive brake noise; and assorted clunks, rattles, and wind noise. Excessive vibration at cruising speed (not tire related); vehicle bounces all over the road and nose-dives as front shocks bottom out. **Warranty performance:** Average, but likely to decline when Ford abandons the model by the end of 2004.

SAFETY SUMMARY: No head restraints or shoulder belts on centre rear seats. Vehicle has yet to be crash-tested by NHTSA. **Airbags:** Side airbags are optional. Front and side airbags have failed to deploy in collisions. **ABS:** Standard; disc/disc. **Head restraints F/R:** *. **Visibility F/R:** *****/**. **Maximum load capacity:** 1,630 lb.

SAFETY COMPLAINTS: 2000—A plethora of Firestone tire failures. • Cracked fuel tank leaked gasoline. • Passenger-side airbag light stays lit, due to a short-circuit in the system. • Transmission fluid leaked onto drive shaft, causing a fire. • Transmission popped out of gear while vehicle parked (a common Ford failure seen over the past three decades). • Sudden breakage of the right front tie-rod end. • Turbocharger malfunctions cause oil leaks and stalling. • Drive shaft fell out due to loose bolts. • Complete brake failure when approaching intersection. • Brakes pulsate violently. • Poor steering and handling compromise safety. • Poorly designed suspension causes vehicle to move laterally on dry pavement. • Severe shaking and vibrating while driving over 90 km/h. • Excessively sharp seat tracks injured two people. • Jack won't align with suspension pins and may suddenly fail. • If you close the rear tri-doors in the wrong order, the rear window glass may explode. **2001**—Rear-end instability when passing over uneven terrain. • Cruise control surges when set at 110 km/h. • Driver-side seat belts unlatch. **2002**—No airbag deployment. • Sudden acceleration. • Chronic stalling. • Rough roads cause sudden loss of steering control. • Steering binds. • Excessive vehicle shake when rear windows are open while underway. **2003**—Vehicle (gas and diesel) suddenly shuts down. • Diesel fuel leaks from the fuel filter onto the engine. • Total automatic transmission failure. • Hatchback window shattered for no reason. • High-intensity headlights blind other drivers. **2004**—Engine surges while cruising. • Cruise control goes on and off when descending a hill. • Vehicle frequently goes out of alignment. • Firestone sidewall blowout saga continues. • Limited spring travel causes suspension to "bottom out" easily • Passenger window suddenly exploded.

Secret Warranties/Service Tips

All years: Front brake caliper rattling. **2000**—Engine knocking. • Due to low fuel pressure, diesel engine may produce a loud knocking or cackle noise. • The Reverse Park Aid may sound a false alarm if contaminated by debris in the system. **2000–03**—Rough idle or hesitation when accelerating is covered in TSB #03-9-11. **2001**—No-starts, stalling with the 7.3L engine. • Engine stalls when vehicle is shifted into Reverse. • Ford admits investigating cam sensor failures (leads to loss of power, engine shutdown, and no-starts). • Sudden loss of Second gear; vehicle won't move. • Delayed shifts. • Turbo hooting. • Sway bar clunk and popping. • Front shaft seal leakage. • Water pump shaft seal leakage. • A buck or jerk may be felt with cruise control engaged. • Higher-than-normal steering effort at low speed, or when stopped with the brakes applied. • Incorrect oil pressure readings. **2002**—Heater core leaks. • Faulty ignition switch lock cylinder. • Engine cylinder heads leak oil or coolant. • Oil contamination in the cooling system. • Vehicle pulls to one side when braking. • Popping noise from the floorboard area. • Increased steering effort. • Hard starts, battery won't charge. **2003**—Special Customer Satisfaction Program to enhance cold weather engine performance (reduce rough idle). • Special Customer Satisfaction Program #03B05 to replace ICP sensor. • Loss of power and exhaust noise. • Remedy for faulty adjustable pedals. • Correction for starter failures. **2003–04**—Poor diesel engine performance requires a revised computer module calibration (TSB # 03-20-12) and the following counter-measures:

Diesel Engine – Driveability/Oil Fuel Dilution

Bulletin No.: 04-9-3   Date: 05/11/04

DRIVEABILITY - RUNS ROUGH, LOW POWER

2003–04 EXCURSION, F SUPER DUTY
2004 ECONOLINE

ISSUE: Some vehicles equipped with the 6.0L diesel engine may exhibit engine oil diluted with fuel (OIL LEVEL MAY APPEAR OVER FULL), runs rough and/or a low power condition.

Diesel Engine – Turbo-Induced Exhaust Drone/Moan

Bulletin No.: 04-9-4   Date: 05/11/04

ENGINE - EXHAUST - TURBO-INDUCED EXHAUST
MOAN/DRONE- VIBRATION-6.0L

2003–04 EXCURSION, F SUPER DUTY

ACTION: To service, neutralize the exhaust system. It may also be necessary to install a revised turbocharger pedestal mounting bracket if it is not already installed. Refer to the following Service Procedure.

Excursion Profile

	2000	2001	2002	2003	2004
Cost Price ($) (very negotiable)					
4X4 XLT (21%)	47,795	47,645	49,885	50,150	48,945
Used Values ($)					
4X4 XLT ʌ	23,000	28,000	28,000	33,000	38,500
4X4 XLT v	21,000	26,000	26,000	31,000	36,000
Reliability	❷	❷	❷	❷	❸

Note: A 4X2 Excursion is worth about $5,000 less than the 4X4 version.

Ford/Mazda

ESCAPE, TRIBUTE ★★

RATING: Average (2005); Not Recommended (2001–04). Escape's latest iteration targets the power and performance lacunae of its predecessor. Question is: Has the abysmally bad quality also been addressed? Up to this year, the Escape/Tribute has promised a lot, but delivered a low-quality, dangerous SUV that may stall or suddenly accelerate at any time. Interestingly, Mazda dealers generate fewer servicing complaints. **Strong points:** *2005:* A smoother driveline; more powerful base engine; an automatic tranny is now available with the base engine; a quieter cabin; less V6 engine noise and vibration; and more standard equipment. *Pre-2005 models:* Quick 6-cylinder acceleration; good manoeuvrability; plenty of passenger space and cargo room, almost equal to the Explorer; well laid-out and easy-to-read instruments and controls; good visibility; easy-to-fold rear seatbacks; and rear liftgate's flip-up glass gives quick access to cargo. **Weak points:** *2005:* Only rated "Acceptable" for offset crash-worthiness by the IIHS. Outrageously high freight and PDI charges ($1,095). *Pre-2005 models:* Poorly equipped and underpowered, with unimpressive snow traction; historically poor-quality Ford-designed engines and transmissions. There's a sluggish 4-cylinder and a V6 that needs more high-end grunt for long upgrades; you won't find a base 4-cylinder, front-drive model with an automatic transmission; no low-speed transfer case; bumps can be jolting; entry/exit compromised by high step-in; side mirrors are on the small side; excessive engine and road noise; and an unusually large number of safety- and performance-related complaints filed with NHTSA. **New for 2005:** Foremost, you get a quieter engine and 26 more horses with the new 2.3L Duratec 4-banger, which raises towing capability from 454 kg (1,000 lb.) to 680 kg (1,500 lb.). The V6 engine has one less horse (200 hp), but uses upgraded engine mounts and computers to smooth out the idle and improve throttle response. Safety is also enhanced this year with "smart" seat sensors that can prevent airbag deployment if a child or small adult is seated; dual-stage airbags; head restraints and three-point safety belts for all seats; side curtain air bags; larger diameter four-wheel disc and anti-lock brakes. By year's end, the Escape's front structure will be reinforced to better protect occupants in offset frontal crashes. Other enhancements include an improved 4X4 system that is fully automatic (it no longer needs to be switched on); larger diameter front shocks; a new stabilizer system; a floor-mounted shifter; new headlights, fog lamps, grille, front and rear ends; different gauges; upgraded seat cushions; more storage space; additional sound-absorbing materials (though it still lets in excessive wind noise); and alloy wheels. A gasoline-electric hybrid will use Ford's 2.3L 4-cylinder engine, a 65-kilowatt electric motor, and a 28-kilowatt generator. The vehicle will have off-road and towing capability and accelera-tion comparable to the 201-hp Escape V6 engine. The 2005 Mariner, a Mercury version of the Escape (sold only in the States), will debut in the fall of 2004.

2005 Technical Data

Powertrain
Engines: 2.3L 4-cyl. (153 hp)
• Hybrid (130 hp)
• 3.0L V6 (200 hp)
Transmissions: 5-speed man.
• 4-speed auto.
• CVT Hybrid

Dimension/Capacity
Height/length/width:
69.7/174.9/70.1 in.
Headroom F/R: 3.5/3.5 in.

Legroom F/R: 41.6/36.3 in.
Wheelbase: 103.1 in.
Turning circle: 39 ft.
Passengers: 2/3
Cargo volume: 29.3 cu. ft.
GVWR: 4,120–4,520 lb.
Tow limit: 3,500 lb.
Ground clear.: 8 in.
Fuel tank: 58L/reg.
Weight: 3,065 lb.

MODEL HISTORY: Launched as 2000 models, both vehicles combine a car-like ride and handling, thanks to an independent rear suspension and front MacPherson struts, with the ability to go in the snow and carry up to five passengers and their luggage. Neither vehicle is an upsized car or a downsized truck—they're actually totally new four-doors that sip fuel, look like a sport-utility, and drive like a sedan.

COST ANALYSIS: Get the 2005 model for the upgrades. Upgrading the 2005 Escape and Tribute to an Average rating is like betting "on the come" after rolling "snake eyes" four times in a row. Still, it's hard to ignore the 2005's many enhancements. MSRP is $22,795 for the XLS with 2.3L, manual transmission, and front-drive, to $28,195 for the XLT with standard V6, automatic transmission, and front-drive, and $35,895 for the fully loaded Limited 4X4. 4X4 models start at $28,125 for the XLS automatic. **Best alternatives:** Roughly the size of a Ford Focus sedan, the base Escape XLS 4X2 targets the low-priced, compact sport-utility market presently dominated by the Honda CR-V, Jeep Cherokee, Nissan Xterra, Pontiac Vibe, and Toyota RAV4/Matrix. It costs considerably less than a V6-equipped Ford Explorer 4X4, yet the Escape is nearly the same width and height as the Explorer. **Rebates:** These compact SUVs are hot, so expect only modest $1,000 rebates and low financing rates. **Delivery/PDI:** *Escape:* $860; *Tribute:* $1,095 (That's sneaky, Mazda). **Warranty:** Bumper-to-bumper 3 years/80,000 km; powertrain 5 years/ 100,000 km; rust perforation 5 years/unlimited km. **Supplementary warranty:** A wise buy, unless you trust Ford's quality control; I don't. **Options:** AWD, if you really need it; 1588 kg (3500 lb.) towing package; sunroof reduces headroom considerably. Convenient snap-in pet barrier and mountain-bike hauler from Ford Outfitters. **Depreciation:** So far, depreciation has been quite low. **Insurance cost:** Higher than average, but about average for a small SUV. **Parts supply/cost:** Few complaints so far. Generic powertrain parts aren't hard to find, though electronics can be expensive and hard to troubleshoot. Long delays for parts needed for recall campaigns. **Annual maintenance cost:** Expected to be higher than average, once first-year models lose base warranty protection. **Highway/city fuel economy:** *2.0L:* 8.4–10.2L/100 km; *V6:* 9.8–11.8L/100 km.

QUALITY/RELIABILITY: Both companies have a poor record for quality control during the first few years their vehicles are on the market. Numerous "secret warranty" programs (Ford now calls this "Special Service Instruction," or SSI) are used to correct problems like chronic stalling, a sticking cruise control, steering wheel and rear wheels falling off, and leaking fuel lines. Off-roading compromised by the profusion of dust and dirt that works its way into the cabin. **Owner complaints:** Vehicle out of service 36 days while dealer looked for cause of raw fuel smell entering cabin; chronic stalling and hard starts; transmission refuses to go into gear; automatic transmission won't upshift at 85 km/h; lost Reverse gear; automatic transmission gearshift handle gets stuck halfway down when changing gears, due to a design flaw; excessive front brake dust turns wheels black; frequent short circuits; rear defogger won't shut off; alternator light comes on intermittently; cruise control turns itself off; faulty side windows; ice forming on front wheels cause excessive vibrations; poor fuel economy; lots of squeaks, rattles, and wind noise; poor fit and finish; rear passenger door internal support beam contracts and pulls the door panel inward causing a dimpling effect at six separate areas; tires make a humming noise; engine hesitates when AC is engaged; AC makes a loud, cyclic sound; mildew odour from AC and vents; can't remove key from ignition. **Warranty performance:** Doesn't look good. Ford's SSI secret warranty programs are a giant step backward from its ONPs, where all owners were notified.

ROAD PERFORMANCE: Acceleration/torque: Good 2005 performance, but previous year 4-cylinders were overwhelmed by the wagon's heft. V6 performs well, though it's a bit rough and could use a bit more power for passing and merging. **Transmission:** Smooth and quiet shifting, though long-term automatic transmission's reliability is still worrisome. Automatic transmission lever blocks access to controls for the rear defogger, parking lights, and radio; transmission lever often knocked inadvertently into Neutral when adjusting the radio. Dial-up 4X4 engagement a pain on 2004 and earlier versions. **Steering:** Above average. Not as tippy or vague as others in this group. **Routine handling:** Surprisingly good for a wagon. Easy to manoeuvre in tight places. Corners very well at high speeds, with only a bit of body lean. Taut four-wheel independent suspension may be too firm for some, but it enhances handling considerably. **Braking:** Brakes perform very well, with little fading after successive stops; some nose-dive, however.

SAFETY SUMMARY: A class-action petition has been filed by Ontario lawyer Harvin Pitch on behalf of a Toronto couple injured when their 2003 Tribute rolled over in New Mexico. The ensuing rollover caused brain damage to the seat-belted passenger. Two issues are raised: That SUVs are unsafe because they have a propensity to rollover, and that the Tribute's passenger roof is not strong enough to absorb the rollover crush. (Harvin Pitch may be reached at *hpitch@teplitskycolson.com.*)

Five three-point seat belts and five height-adjustable head restraints. **Airbags:** Front and side. Owners have reported that airbags may go off without warning or have failed to deploy in a collision. **ABS:** Optional; disc/drum. **Safety belt pretensioners:** Front. **Head restraints F/R:** *2001:* *; *2002–04:* *****/***. **Visibility F/R:** *****. **Maximum load capacity:** 900 lb.

SAFETY COMPLAINTS: Chronic stalling, sudden unintended acceleration (gas pedal sticking), airbag and brake malfunctions, and frequent transmission replacements are major problems through the 2003 model year. **2001–04—** Engine misfire troubleshooting tips. • Rear wiper arm failure. • Headliner sagging. **Escape: 2001—**Fuel vapours enter passenger compartment via ventilation ducts (tighten bolts on the left side intake manifold). • Fuel leakage around fuel injectors. • Fuel line clip failed, causing loss of power, and fuel was sprayed onto hot engine. • Vehicle rolled over unexpectedly while doing

25–40 km/h. • CV joints and front axle fell off vehicle. • Transmission failures. • Clutch cable often comes off when driving. • Automatic transmission pops out of Drive into Neutral while underway. • Sudden, unintended acceleration when shifting into Reverse or First gear, or when taking foot off the accelerator. • When going downhill, vehicle often suddenly loses all electrical power and shuts down on the highway with loss of steering and brake assist (faulty EGR valve suspected). • Chronic electrical problems. • Left rear wheels suddenly locked up, pulling vehicle into traffic. • Vehicle pulls randomly to the right or left when steering wheel is let go. • Steering too tight. • Sometimes steering tugs a bit to one side, then freezes, brakes won't work, and Check Engine light comes on (engine still running). • Part of power-steering system fell out of car when it was put into Park. • Rear seats don't lock properly. • Car seatback collapsed in collision. • Left rear seat belt frequently jams. • Windshield wiper failures; six-week delay for recall fix. **Tribute: 2001**—Fuel smell still enters cabin (after recall). • Wiring harness fire. • Erratic shifting. • Transmission will slip if vehicle has been sitting for an extended period of time. • Faulty rear differential seal caused differential to self-destruct. • Sudden loss of steering and brakes. • Power steering cuts out when making a left turn; steering often locks up. • Loss of steering due to a broken tensioner belt. • Steering linkage fell off vehicle while underway. • Frequent brake failures; brake master cylinder replaced. • Windshield wiper failures (after recall). • Headlights collect moisture. • Power windows and sunroof quit working. • Excessive side mirror vibration. **2002**—Over 400 complaints reported to federal investigators (50–100 would be normal). • Sudden acceleration. • Brake and steering failures. • Reports of water entering the passenger compartment. • Transmission fluid and engine oil leaks. • Wipers that skip over the windshield. **2003**—Prone to roll over; roof cannot support crush forces (see lawsuit info in "Safety Summary"). • Brake/accelerator pedals placed too close together. • Suspension failure while driving. • Driver's door hinge failure, allowing door to fall off. • Tire tread separation (Continental Conti-Trac). **2004**—Sudden, unintended acceleration. • Automatic transmission failure:

> The "needle bearings" in the "planetary bearing" had failed. They disintegrated. Small metal fragments worked throughout the transmission, resulting in excessive internal damage.

Window short-circuits. • Vehicle may pull sharply to one side or gain speed when descending a hill with the cruise control engaged. • Rolls backwards when stopped on an incline.

Secret Warranties/Service Tips

All years: Engine hydromount insulator and rear drive shaft replacement. • No forward transmission engagement (yes, the forward clutch piston, the cause of so many Windstar and Taurus/Sable failures, once again rears its ugly head). • Rear axle pinion seal leak. • Driveline grinding and clicking. • Possible leak in the transmission converter housing near the cooler line. • Intermittent loss of First and Second gear. • Manual transmission gear shifter buzz or rattle in Third or Fourth gear is being investigated by Ford technicians. • Possible causes for a lit MIL warning lamp. • EGR failures. • Fuel pump whine heard through speakers (a Ford problem since 1990). • Vehicles with 3.0L engines may show a false "low coolant" condition. • ABS light may stay lit. • AC temperature control knob may be hard to turn or adjust. **2001–02**—Harsh, delayed upshifts • Defective door latches. • Power steering leaks. **2001–03**—3.0L engine stalling remedy:

Engine Controls/Emissions – Idle Dip/Intermittent Stall

Article No.:02-23-1   Date:11/25/02

2001–03 ESCAPE

ISSUE: Some vehicles equipped with the 3.0L Duratec engine may exhibit an intermittent engine quit and restart condition. This is usually a one-time event during closed throttle deceleration with no Diagnostic Trouble Codes (DTCs) and no Malfunction Indicator Lamp (MIL). Due to the intermittent nature of the condition and the multiple potential causes of the condition, the complete bulletin checklist, and all appropriate part replacements should be performed regardless of whether the condition can be duplicated by the technician. Otherwise, customers may experience the intermittent condition and be forced to return to the dealership. If the vehicle is no longer eligible for warranty coverage, discuss this service with the customer before performing.

2002—Coolant, oil leakage from engine cylinder head area. • Defective Duratec engines. • Heater core leaks. • Brake squealing. • Wheels make a clicking sound. **2003**—Automatic transmission shudder and whine. • Powertrain throttle body service replacement. • Front wheel-bearing noise. • Rear shock leak/noise. **2003–04**—False activation of Parking Assist ("Stop! Stop! There's something behind you! Just kidding."). You know what's most worrisome? Ford says this device may be operating as it should:

Parking Assist False Activation

Bulletin No.: 04-7-1   Date: 04/19/04

FALSE ACTIVATION OF WARNING TONE

1999–2003 WINDSTAR
1999–2004 EXPLORER
2000–04 EXCURSION AND EXPEDITION
2001–04 F SUPER DUTY
2003–05 ESCAPE
2004 F-150, FREESTAR
2000–04 NAVIGATOR
2002–03 BLACKWOOD
2003–04 AVIATOR
1999–2004 MOUNTAINEER
2004 MONTEREY

ISSUE: Various 1999–2005 vehicles equipped with the Parking Aid reverse sensing system (RSS) may sound a warning tone when the vehicle is in reverse, even though there are no objects behind the vehicle. This condition may also occur on vehicles equipped with the forward sensing system (FSS) when vehicle is in reverse or drive.

ACTION: The condition MAY NOT be due to proximity sensor(s) malfunction but may be a normal operation characteristic, or due to sensor contamination (sensor being covered with dirt).

Escape, Tribute Profile

	2001	2002	2003	2004
Cost Price ($) (negotiable)				
XLS 4X2 (15%)	21,310	21,510	21,595	21,895
XLS 4X4 (16%)	23,960	24,190	27,495	27,825
Tribute 4X2 (15%)	22,150	22,415	22,790	22,790
Tribute 4X4 (16%)	24,800	25,065	25, 575	25,445
Used Values ($)				
XLS 4X2 ▲	12,500	14,000	15,000	17,500
XLS 4X2 ▼	11,500	13,000	14,000	16,000
XLS 4X4 ▲	14,500	18,000	20,000	22,000
XLS 4X4 ▼	13,000	17,000	18,000	20,000
Tribute 4X2 ▲	14,000	16,000	16,500	18,500
Tribute 4X2 ▼	13,000	14,500	15,000	16,000
Tribute 4X4 ▲	16,000	18,500	19,000	21,500
Tribute 4X4 ▼	14,500	17,500	18,000	19,500
Reliability	❷	❷	❷	③
Crash Safety (4X4) (F)	⑤	⑤	⑤	⑤
Side	⑤	⑤	⑤	⑤
Offset (Tribute)	❷	❷	❷	❷
Rollover	③	③	③	—

General Motors

AZTEK, RENDEZVOUS ★★★

RATING: Average (2001–05). More luxury minivans than sporty SUVs; neither vehicle is any match for the Asian competition. **Strong points:** Quiet, comfortable ride; one of the more affordable seven-passenger SUVs; tight steering; lots of passenger and storage room; low step-in and large doors; uses regular fuel; and relatively few reliability complaints. **Weak points:** 3.4L V6 lacks kick of GM's new inline-six; interior materials don't say "Buick luxury"; one-piece tailgate. Very expensive for what little you get. If you want four-wheel discs, for example, you have to get the higher-end AWD version. Rear hatch is often coated with road grime that can't be removed because there's no rear wiper. Over-the-shoulder visibility is hampered by the thick side roof pillars and front body corners are hard to see. Large doors could be a problem when parking in tight spaces. Poor acceleration; mediocre handling and road holding; and no low-range gearing and low ground clearance make off-roading a no-no. The Rendezvous has a more jiggly ride and its additional seating isn't that comfortable; plus, to access the more-than-ample storage areas, you have to remove the seats. Imprecise steering has insufficient feedback; marginal head restraint and offset crash scores; excessive road, tire, and engine noise; mediocre fuel economy; and spotty quality control. **New for 2005:** Nothing important.

2005 Technical Data

Powertrain
Engines: 3.4L V6 (185 hp)
• 3.6L V6 (245 hp)
Transmission: 4-speed auto.
Dimension/Capacity (Aztek)
Height/length/width:
67/182/74 in; 69/186.5/74 in.
Headroom F/R: 39.7/39.1 in.
Legroom F/R: 40.8/38 in.

Wheelbase: 108/112 in.
Turning circle: 40 ft.
Passengers: 2/3; 2/3/2
Cargo volume: 49 cu. ft.
GVWR: 4,986–5,218 lb
Tow limit: 3,500 lb.
Ground clear.: 6.7; 7.5 in.
Fuel tank: 70L/reg.
Weight: 3,900 lb.

MODEL HISTORY: Essentially minivan/SUV crossovers, the Aztek and Rendezvous, are practically identical except for the Rendezvous' 4-inch-longer wheelbase that accommodates third-row seating.

Aztek is built on a shorter Montana minivan platform while the Rendezvous' larger wheelbase allows for more, but not as comfortable, seating. The Aztek is especially roomy, with more cargo room than a Ford Explorer, and is capable of carrying a bicycle upright. Rendezvous excels in storage capacity too, once you remove the seats. These vehicles are also full of innovative features like a centre console that doubles as a portable cooler and three special packages for biking, camping, and hiking. Aztek's stiff suspension makes for an uncomfortable ride, though, and is likely to cause more severe rattling as the vehicle ages. Rendezvous provides a more forgiving, gentler ride. Driving performance is minivan-boring, though, with considerable understeer, sluggish steering, and mediocre handling; it takes almost 11 seconds to reach 100 km/h.

Rendezvous comes with standard ABS and four-wheel disc brakes, only found on the Aztek AWD. Second-row seating is provided by a three-person split bench or twin-bucket seats. The optional two-passenger third-row seat folds flush with the floor. **2002**—A revised front end and a spoiler added to the Aztek. **2003**—A rear-seat DVD player, upgraded wheels, and a tire-inflation monitoring system. **2004**—An all-new, plush AWD Rendezvous Ultra equipped with a 245-hp 3.6L aluminum, V6. 2004 is the Aztek's last model year.

COST ANALYSIS: Best alternatives: 2004s and 2005s are equally good buys. Prices changed little, with the 2004 base Aztek and Rendezvous costing $30,000 and $32,000, respectively (4X4 versions go for $37,000–$36,000). If you can downsize a bit to save fuel and insurance costs, consider the Honda CR-V, Hyundai Santa Fe, and Toyota RAV4. **Rebates:** These mid-sized SUVs attract hefty $3,000+ rebates and zero percent financing. Wait at least a year for the newly launched GM Equinox to prove itself. **Delivery/PDI:** $850. **Warranty:** Bumper-to-bumper 3 years/60,000 km; powertrain 3 years/60,000 km; rust perforation 5 years/unlimited km. **Supplementary warranty:** For the powertrain only. **Options:** AWD, if you really need it. Stay away from the distracting and not always accurate rear obstacle detection feature, as well as the head-up instrument display. **Depreciation:** Faster than average. **Insurance cost:** Higher than average. **Parts supply/cost:** Few complaints so far. These SUVs use generic Montana parts that are found everywhere and are usually reasonably priced. **Annual maintenance cost:** Expected to be just a bit higher than average, once the warranty expires. **Highway/city fuel economy:** 8.3–12.3L/100 km.

QUALITY/RELIABILITY: Owner complaints: Incredibly few complaints. Would you believe only a couple dozen owner complaints have been recorded in the NHTSA database (versus over 400 for the 2002 Ford Escape/Mazda Tribute)? Predicted engine and AC problems:

> I currently have a 2001 Aztek. At 64,000 km the AC went. The dealer did pay for half, however .... I walked out of there with a $700 bill. Just recently, the head gasket went at 93,000 km. An independent garage is fixing it at a high cost, after talking with the mechanic at the dealership, he simply told me the cost was reasonable and I should go with that garage.

Warranty performance: Good.

SAFETY SUMMARY: Airbags: Front and side. **ABS:** Standard; disc/drum. **Safety belt pretensioners:** Yes. **Traction control:** Optional. **Head restraints F/R:** *Aztek: **; 2003 Aztek: ***/**; Rendezvous: ***/***. **Visibility F/R:** *Aztek: ***/*; Rendezvous: ******.

SAFETY COMPLAINTS: All years: Gas tank fill hose enters tank at a very vulnerable location. • Rear spoiler obstructs vision. • Water leaks or heavy condensation in the tail lights. **2001**—Numerous reports of rollover accidents where occupants were ejected. Vehicle fire caused by shorted wiring harness. • Steering tie-rod/drive bar failed sending vehicle out of control. • Delayed automatic transmission shifts, slippage, extended shifts, or flaring during cold operation. • Transmission grinding. • Growling noise when sitting in Park on a hill or slope with the engine running and parking brake not applied. • Rear brake failure. • Excessive vibration while driving. • Instrument panel may be warped rearward of the defroster outlet. • Water may enter the passenger compartment near the H-back module. • GM says windshield distortion could be caused by car washes. • Rear liftgate will not release the secondary latch position when opened automatically. • Wiper blades hit each other. • Airbag light comes on intermittently. • Shock absorber rattling. **Aztek: 2001**—Rear brake failures. • Stalling. • Excessive vibration above 100 km/h, said to be caused by faulty driveshaft. • Dealer says front wheels cannot be realigned without bending the frame. • Rear wipers are hard to find. • Faulty rear door security-lock lever. **2002**—Engine surges when braking. • Brakes work intermittently. **2003**—ABS control unit failure. • Vehicle rear end skips about when passing over highway bumps. **Rendezvous: 2002**—Chronic differential leak. • Vehicle won't stay in gear while stopped on an incline. • Car stalls when changing gears. • Sudden loss of all electrical power. • Loss of steering when right axle spindle gear broke. • Parts for airbag recall aren't available. • Faulty sending unit causes inaccurate fuel gauge readings. • Water enters and soaks the front carpet. • Wind blows door back, breaking hinge. **2003**—Engine, transmission, and brake failures. • Electrical shorts, blown fuses. **2004**—Speedometer readings hard to read. • Gas tank neck snapped off. • Chronic stalling. • Transmission failure. • Horn failed to blow. • Radio and horn would self-activate. • Unable to open windows and rear doors. • Middle seat belt securing baby seat suddenly unlatched.

Secret Warranties/Service Tips

All years: Harsh transmission shifts while Check Engine Soon warning lamp is lit. • Poor engine and transmission performance. • Rear axle seal leaks. • Hard start, no-start, stalling, and fuel gauge fluctuation. • Muffler heat shield rattle. **2001**—No forward, delayed forward, or the automatic transmission may lock in Reverse. **2001–02**—Customer Satisfaction Program (secret warranty) regarding the brake booster power piston, valve springs replacement, and dead battery replacements. • Grinding noise or failure of 4-speed automatic transmission to engage when shifting into Drive or Reverse. **2001–03**—Faulty intake manifold may cause coolant/oil loss (TSB #03-06-01-O10A). • Defective AC, compressor. • Exhaust rattle, buzz. • Radio speaker static. **2002**—Hard shifting, shuddering with automatic transmission (TSB #02-07-30-039B). **2002-03**—Engine exhaust manifold defect correction:

Intake Manifold Oil/Coolant Leak

Engine Oil or Coolant Leak (Install New Intake Manifold Gasket)

Bulletin No.: 03-06-01-010B   Date: 10/24/2003

2000–03 Buick Century
2002–03 Buick Rendezvous
1996 Chevrolet Lumina APV
1997–2003 Chevrolet Venture
1999–2001 Chevrolet Lumina
1999–2003 Chevrolet Malibu, Monte Carlo
2000–03 Chevrolet Impala
1996–2003 Oldsmobile Silhouette
1999 Oldsmobile Cutlass
1999–2003 Oldsmobile Alero
1996–99 Pontiac Trans Sport
1999–2003 Pontiac Grand Am, Montana
2000–03 Pontiac Grand Prix
2001–03 Pontiac Aztek with 3.1L or 3.4L V-6 Engine.

Condition: Some owners may comment on an apparent oil or coolant leak. Additionally, the comments may range from spots on the driveway to having to add fluids.

Correction: Install a new design intake manifold gasket. The material used in the gasket has been changed in order to improve the sealing qualities of the gasket. When replacing the gasket, the intake manifold bolts must also be replaced and torqued to a revised specification. The new bolts will come with a pre-applied threadlocker on them.

2003—Long, hard starts, rough idle, and clogged fuel injectors. **Rendezvous: 2002**—Wet carpet in the passenger footwell produces a foul odour. • Water enters passenger compartment at the area of the H-back module.

Aztek, Rendezvous Profile

	2001	2002	2003	2004
Cost Price ($) (very negotiable)				
Aztek (19%)	29,255	29,255	29,500	28,180
GT 4X4 (22%)	36,185	36,185	36,985	34,060
Rendezvous (19%)	—	30,995	31,545	32,440
Rendezvous 4X4 (21%)	—	34,995	35,595	36,415
Used Values ($)				
Aztek ⋀	12,500	16,000	18,500	20,000
Aztek ⋁	11,500	14,500	17,000	18,000
GT 4X4 ⋀	14,500	16,500	21,000	24,000
GT 4X4 ⋁	13,000	15,000	19,500	23,000
Rendezvous ⋀	—	18,500	21,000	24,000
Rendezvous ⋁	—	17,000	20,000	22,000
Rendezvous 4X4 ⋀	—	20,000	28,000	27,000
Rendezvous 4X4 ⋁	—	19,000	26,000	25,000
Reliability	❷	③	③	③
Crash Safety (4X4) (F)	③	③	③	③
Side (4X2)	⑤	⑤	⑤	—
Rendezvous	—	③	③	—
Side	—	⑤	⑤	⑤
Offset	❷	❷	❷	❷
Rendezvous	—	③	③	③
Rollover	③	③	③	—

BLAZER, ENVOY, JIMMY ★★★

RATING: Average (1999–2005); Below Average (1995–98). **Strong points:** Reasonably well appointed; full-time AutoTrac 4X4 shifts on the fly and can be used on dry pavement; strong engine; comfortable ride; nice handling; comfortable seating and sufficient headroom and legroom for all but the last row of passengers; plenty of cargo space; expanding the cargo room by folding the rear seat is a snap; low noise levels; and average depreciation. **Weak points:** Thick centre and rear roof pillars and the tinted rear windows compromise rear visibility; restricted rear access; short, hard rear seats; and a gas-guzzler. **New for 2005:** Nothing; 2005 will be the Blazer's last model year.

2005 Technical Data

Powertrain (4X2/4X4)
Engine: 4.3L V6 (190 hp)
Transmissions: 4-speed auto.

Wheelbase: 100.5 in.
Turning circle: 34.8 ft.
Passengers: 2/2

OD 5-speed man.
Dimension/Capacity (2d)
Height/length/width:
64/177/68 in.
Headroom F/R: 39.6/38.2 in.
Legroom F/R: 42.4/35.6 in.

Cargo volume: 30.2 cu. ft.
GVWR: 5,000–5,300 lb.
Tow limit: 3,900–5,400 lb.
Ground clearance: 8 in.
Fuel tank: 71L/reg.
Weight: 3,885 lb.

MODEL HISTORY: These are identical, two-door and four-door, mid-sized sport-utility vehicles, incorporating 4X2 and 4X4 drive and based on the GM S-series pickup platform. Part-time 4X4 (InstaTrac) is standard with all models, while the optional AutoTrac system delivers full rear-drive power until road conditions require it to automatically readjust the power ratio to other wheels. The only available engine is a 4.3L V6, rated at 190-hp, hooked to a 4-speed automatic transmission with Overdrive. Only two-door manuals come with a 5-speed manual gearbox.

The compact Blazer and Jimmy were first launched in 1983, as spin-offs of the full-sized GM Blazer and Jimmy—1970 SUV offshoots of GM's full-sized trucks. Although the Blazer and Jimmy are identical, they are marketed by separate GM divisions. The Envoy, a Jimmy clone with some styling twists and more standard features, was launched in 1998, dropped for the 2001 model year, and revived as a 2002 model.

The redesigned 1995–98 models aren't really all that different—GM didn't want to cannibalize sales of its full-sized Blazer, Yukon, and Tahoe. Nevertheless, interior noise was muffled, and cargo room was increased by mounting the spare tire beneath the rear end. **1996**—A Vortec V6 with five fewer horses became the standard power plant. **1999**—An upgraded 4L60-E automatic transmission and optional AutoTrac transfer case that automatically engages 4X4 when needed. **2000**—Some engine, exhaust system, manual transmission, and ABS enhancements, but horsepower remained the same. Vehicles equipped with the ZR2 package were given an upgraded axle ratio to improve shifting and acceleration. Watch the payload rating though; some vehicles were sold with incorrect payload ratings.

The Jimmy got the axe in June 2001 to make way for the 2002 TrailBlazer and redesigned Envoy (see "TrailBlazer, Envoy, Bravada"). Blazer continues as a cheaper alternative to Chevrolet's larger, more powerful TrailBlazer. **2001**—GM offered an Extreme package that includes a low-riding suspension and a slight re-styling. **2003**—A new fuel injection system and some trim changes. **2004**—Arrival of the Envoy XUV, an SUV with a number of pickup features. It's basically an XL Envoy with a sliding rear roof and a small pickup bed.

COST ANALYSIS: Best alternatives: The 2004 and 2005 Blazer are equally good buys, particularly since this year's model shouldn't cost much more. Also check out the Nissan Xterra or X-Trail and Toyota Highlander, Sequoia, or 4Runner. **Rebates:** Look for $3,500+ rebates as we get closer to the Blazer's 2004 model phase-out. **Delivery/PDI:** $875. **Warranty:** Bumper-to-bumper 3 years/60,000 km; rust perforation 6 years/160,000 km. **Supplementary warranty:** An extended warranty is a good idea. **Options:** Rear window defroster, remote keyless entry, power door locks, engine block heater, and an upgraded sound system are worth considering. Have a transmission oil cooler installed. Choose a suspension and traction package to suit your needs (I recommend the "Premium" package). Get a sophisticated anti-theft system or you'll keep your Blazer only a few days. **Depreciation:** Average. **Insurance cost:** Average. **Annual maintenance cost:** Higher than average. **Parts supply/cost:** Parts are inexpensive from independent suppliers and widely available. **Highway/city fuel economy:** High fuel consumption in city driving. *V6 4X2:* 10.4–14.4L/100 km; *V6 4X4:* 10.8–14.7L/100 km.

QUALITY/RELIABILITY: Average. **Owner-reported problems:** Fuel-injection glitches; noisy and rough-shifting transmissions; electrical system shorts causing blown fuses, brake light, hazard lights, and turn signal failures; excessive steering wheel play makes vehicle wander all over the road and difficult to control at times; excessive engine knocking; front suspension noise; body assembly and paint application have been below standard. **Warranty performance:** Average. Don't get your hopes up if you're beyond the warranty. GM is tight-fisted in allocating after-warranty compensation, unless you file a small claims action. Plus, it's not interested in "coddling" owners of a model that will soon disappear.

SAFETY SUMMARY: These vehicles have registered an extraordinarily large number of accident injury claims. **Airbags:** Standard side. Reports of airbags failing to deploy. **ABS:** Standard 4W; disc/disc. **Head restraints F/R:** *1996:* ***/**/*; *1997:* *; *1999:* ***/**/*; *2001–02:* ***/*. **Visibility F/R:** ****/*. **Maximum load capacity:** *1998 Blazer LT:* 1,040 lb.; *2003 Blazer LT:* 838–2,000 lb.

SAFETY COMPLAINTS: 1995–97—Frequent reports of complete loss of braking; when the brakes are applied, they suddenly lock up or the pedal goes to the floor without any braking effect. In some cases, there is limited braking, but stopping distance is lengthened considerably. • Windshield wiper failure (even after their recall) is another frequent complaint over the years. • Engine (camshaft and bearing) and transmission failures (leaks and slippage). • Inner tie-rod and ball joint collapse. • Tire rubs against the sway bar, subframe, and wheel weld when turning, causing vehicle to jump out of control. • Sudden acceleration and stalling. • Cruise control malfunctions. • Intermittent loss of electrical power (car plays out a scene in *Close Encounters of the Third Kind* with all the lights, gauges, and other electrical systems going on and off). • Excessive vibration when cruising. • Faulty fuel gauge (vehicle stalls out for lack of fuel though the gauge reads tank is one-quarter full). • Inoperative door locks, rear hatch/liftgate pops open while driving. • Loss of power steering. • Front driver's seat moves forward when stopping. • Seat belt failures. **1998**—The three most frequent complaints: ABS don't brake, or *do* break. • Transmission sticks in Park, slips when in gear, and is noisy. • Steering wheel suddenly pulls to the right or vehicle generally wanders to the right. • Transfer case engagement causes vehicle to jump out of control. • Sudden power loss to engine and electrical system. • Dash lights and gauges suddenly shut on and off. • Tailgate glass pops open while vehicle is underway. • Poor rear-view mirror design allows mirror to vibrate excessively, spoiling rear view. **1999–2000**—Wiring harness and non-specific under-hood fires. • Plastic fuel tank is easily punctured. • Accelerator pedal sticks. • Cruise control still engaged when brakes are applied. • Chronic stalling when decelerating (likely fuel pump failure). • Premature automatic transmission failure; leaks, delayed and harsh shifting are the first signs of eventual breakdown. • Transfer case gets stuck in 4X4 High and Low. • Jumps out of First gear when accelerating. • Right wheel came off due to a missing cotter pin that locked the spindle in place. • Spare tire cable broke, allowing tire to fly off. • Defective locking nut on the steering shaft allows the steering wheel to come off in the driver's hands. • Inner tie-rod and ball joint failure. • ABS light remains lit for no apparent reason. • Complete loss of braking. • Brake pedal went to floor with little braking effect. • On bumpy and rough surfaces, brake pedal goes soft and then stiffens. • When applying brakes while going downhill, vehicle fishtails out of control. • Driver and passenger seats slide back and forth while driving due to a weak spring. • Bad switch causes sudden headlight failure. • Windshield wipers work poorly. • Exhaust fumes invade cabin. • Driver seat belt retractor failed to restrain driver in a collision. • Horn goes off by itself. • In cold weather, driver-side window shattered as passenger door was closed. • Liftgate may suddenly fall due to support struts collapsing. • Interior and exterior light failures. **1999–2004**—Transmission debris may cause poor performance:

A/T - 4L60-E/4L65-E MIL ON/DTC P0757/Slipping

Bulletin No.: 01-07-30-038B   Date: January 26, 2004

DTC P0757 Set, SES Lamp Illuminated, Poor Performance of Transmission, Transmission Slipping (Clean Transmission Valve Body and Case Oil Passages of Debris)

1999–2004 Passenger Cars and Light Duty Trucks
2003–04 HUMMER H2 with 4L60-E/4L65-E Automatic Transmission

Condition: Some customers may comment on any of the following conditions:

^ The SES lamp is illuminated.

^ No 3rd and 4th gear.

^ The transmission does not shift correctly.

^ The transmission feels like it shifts to Neutral or a loss of drive occurs.

The vehicle freewheels above 48 km/h (30 mph). High RPM needed to overcome the freewheeling.

The most likely cause is chips or debris plugging the bleed orifice of the 23 shift solenoid (367). This will cause the transmission to stay in 2nd gear when 3rd gear is commanded and return to 1st gear when 4th gear is commanded.

2001—Airbags failed to deploy. • Power-steering hose fell off. • Malfunctioning brakelights said to be covered by a "silent" recall. • Theft-deterrent alarm goes off for no reason. • Brake pedal hits floor without activating brakes. • Faulty rear hatch actuator. • Vehicle accelerates when foot is taken off the accelerator. **2002**—Sudden acceleration. • Extreme buffeting when driving with rear window open. • 4X4 suddenly engages, locking up wheels. • 4X4 fails to engage. • Sudden tie-rod failure. • Faulty electronic mirror memory. • Seat belt continually retracts while worn. • Faulty camshaft position sensor. • Fuel tank leak, fuel line fell off, and incorrect fuel gauge readings. **2003**—Airbags didn't deploy. • Manual and automatic transmission fall into Neutral when driving. • Incorrect fuel gauge readings. • Fuel splashes outside of tank when refuelling. • Unacceptably long braking distance.

Secret Warranties/Service Tips

1993–2002—Paint delamination, peeling, or fading (see Part Three). **1996–2000**—If the Service Engine light comes on or there's a rough idle, consider using a new injector unsticking and cleaning process detailed in TSB #00-06-04-003. **1997–98**—A variety of service bulletins outline steps to correct the following: Engine high idle/flare when shifting gears; excessive ticking noise in ambient temperature; a blower fan that runs continuously with the ignition off; rough idling after vehicle has sat overnight; and instrument panel rattles. **1999**—If the front wheels slip while in 4X4, consider replacing the transfer case clutch plates and front-drive axle lubricant. • An inoperative CD changer may simply have a defective trip latch mechanism. • A steering column squeak noise may be silenced by replacing the steering wheel SIR module coil assembly. **1999–2000**—Before spending big bucks for engine head gasket repairs or the replacement of costly emissions components to fix a hot-running engine or stop coolant loss, first replace the radiator cap and polish the radiator filler neck. • GM's infamous "driveline clunk" has been carried over in another "don't worry about it" bulletin sent to dealers. **1999–2001**—TSB #01-07-30-038B indicates transmission malfunctions likely caused by debris plugging the bleed orifice of the 2–3 shift solenoid. • A faulty ignition switch may cause the transmission to stick in Third gear. **2000–03**—Hard to close doors. **2001**—Harsh shift remedies. • Premature wearout of automatic transmission and clutch components. • Automatic transmission 2–4 band or 3–4 clutch damage. • Transmission sticks in Third gear, MIL light comes on, and instrument cluster is inoperative. • Transmission slips when placed in 4X4. • Transmission sticks in Third gear, instrument cluster failure, and MIL light stays on. • No-starts, hard starts, and stalling while Security lamp flashes. • Rear suspension popping noise. • Rear roof corrosion or perforation. • Corroded trailer pre-wire harness. • Muffler rattling. • Light flickering. **2001–02**—Poor engine performance and erratic shifting. • Service Engine light comes on and transmission feels like it has slipped into Neutral. **2002**—Diagnostic tips for loss of Third or Fourth gear. • Wet carpet and mildew odour in the front passenger seat area.

Blazer and Envoy Profile

	1997	1998	1999	2000	2001	2002	2003	2004
Cost Price ($) (negotiable)								
Blazer 4X2 (18%)	27,160	28,800	26,899	28,305	—	—	—	—
Blazer 4X4 (18%)	29,015	30,655	28,750	31,005	32,085	28,770	29,270	29,350
Envoy (20%)	—	43,805	45,185	45,185	—	—	—	—

Used Values ($)

Blazer 4X2 Λ	7,000	8,500	10,000	11,000	—	—	—	—
Blazer 4X2 V	6,000	7,000	8,500	10,000	—	—	—	—
Blazer 4X4 Λ	7,500	10,000	11,500	12,500	14,500	16,000	18,000	19,500
Blazer 4X4 V	6,500	8,500	10,500	11,000	13,500	14,500	17,000	18,000
Envoy Λ	—	11,500	14,000	17,000	—	—	—	—
Envoy V	—	10,500	12,500	15,500	—	—	—	—
Reliability	❶	❷	③	③	③	③	③	③
Crash Safety (F)								
Blazer 4d	③	④	③	③	③	③	③	③
Envoy 4d	—	—	—	—	—	③	③	③
Side	—	—	⑤	⑤	⑤	⑤	⑤	⑤
Envoy 4d	—	—	—	—	—	⑤	⑤	⑤
Offset	❶	❶	❶	❶	❶	❷	❷	❷
Rollover	—	—	—	—	❷	❷	❷	—
Envoy	—	—	—	—	—	③	③	③

ENVOY, TRAILBLAZER, RAINIER, (ISUZU) ASCENDER, (SAAB) 9-7X ★★★

RATING: Average (2002–05). These mid-sized sport-utilities are bigger, wider, and roomier than the Jimmy they replace. The TrailBlazer is the least luxurious; Buick's Rainier, the newest and cushiest; the Ascender, Isuzu's last-gasp product sold only in the States; and the 9-7X, a Saab facsimile that offers little that is new or innovative. **Strong points:** Good acceleration in all gear ranges; high tow rating; AutoTrac 4X4 can be left engaged on dry pavement and has low-range gearing for off-road use; comfortable ride; easy city manoeuvring thanks to the relatively tight turning radius; less tippy than competitors with a higher centre of gravity; plenty of headroom and legroom, plus ample cargo space; rear seating for three adults; and supportive seats. **Weak points:** Over-priced MSRP; trucklike handling (vague steering, excessive body lean in turns) despite the increased dimensions; excessive vibration and droning with six-cylinder engine; white-knuckle braking due to numb and spongy brakes; sudden stops lead to severe nose-dive and steering instability; ground clearance that's 1.2 or 1.3 inches lower than the competition (Explorer, Grand Cherokee) compromises off-road prowess; front seats lack lateral support (GMC Envoy has better seats); climate controls are hard to adjust by feel; rear visibility blocked by head restraints and rear pillars; tacky-looking interior with plastic as the dominant theme; excessive wind noise; awkward loading due to the rear hatch's high sill; mediocre fuel economy; early-production brakes or calipers allow debris to lodge in assembly, causing excessive noise when braking; and no crashworthiness or reliability data. **New for 2005:** The Buick Rainier and Saab 9-7X. **Likely failures:** Automatic transmission; transfer case; brake rotors (excessive rusting and scoring), linings, and ABS module; electrical (shorts); and fuel systems leaks. Fit and finish deficiencies include water leakage at the driver-side B-pillar (seat belt will be wet), excessive wind noise, and constant clicks and rattles.

2005 Technical Data

Powertrain
Engine: 4.2L 6-cyl. (275 hp)
Transmission: 4-speed auto.
Dimension/Capacity
Height/length/width:
71.9/191.8/74.6 in.
Headroom F/R: 40.2/39.6 in.
Legroom F/R: 44.6/37.1 in.

Wheelbase: 113 in.
Turning circle: 36.4 ft.
Passengers: 2/3
Cargo volume: 39.8 cu. ft.
Tow limit: 6,400 lb.
Ground clear.: 8 in.
Fuel tank: 70.8/reg.
Weight: 4,442 lb.

MODEL HISTORY: With the debut of these four-door, five-passenger wagons, GM repositions the Blazer as an entry-level, smaller SUV. In fact, each of these models is larger than the model it replaces, although they all share the same styling details, rear-drive, 4X4 platform, and mechanical components. These vehicles also offer lots of passenger and cargo room. **2003**—Seven-passenger stretched version (the Yukon's only size advantage is its 4 inches of extra width, and its optional 5.3L 285-hp V8). **2004**—TrailBlazer returned unchanged; Envoy was joined by an XUV variant that arrived with an electrically operated sliding roof over the cargo area.

Rainier

Selling for $49,245, Buick's mid-sized Rainier has hit the the market just as buyers begin downsizing their SUV choices to compact SUVs in the $30,000 range. Look for heavy discounting and rapid depreciation.

COST ANALYSIS: The 2005 TrailBlazer's $35,900 base price is quite soft this year. Prices and features are practically identical to the 2004 models; choose whichever is cheapest in the long run. **Best alternatives:** Also consider the Lexus RX 300/330, and Toyota Highlander or 4Runner. **Rebates:** Look for $3,000+ rebates and low-financing rates. **Delivery/PDI:** $875. **Warranty:** Bumper-to-bumper 3 years/60,000 km; powertrain 3 years/60,000 km; rust perforation 6 years/160,000 km. **Supplementary warranty:** A wise buy. **Options:** Air suspension makes for a less jolting ride, but degrades handling. Dual exhausts will give you 30 extra horses, and skid plates are essential to counteract undercarriage damage from excessive suspension dive. **Depreciation:** Likely to be much faster than average. **Insurance cost:** Higher than average. **Parts supply/cost:** Most parts seem to be reasonably priced and easy to find. **Annual maintenance cost:** Expected to be higher than average, once these models go off warranty. **Highway/city fuel economy:** 10.6–15.6L/100 km.

SAFETY SUMMARY: Airbags: Front. **ABS:** Standard; disc/disc. **Traction control:** Optional. **Head restraints F/R:** *2002:* **; *2003:* ***. **Visibility F/R:** *****/**. **Maximum load capacity:** 1,090 lb.

SAFETY COMPLAINTS: 2002—Detached fuel lines. • Airbag failed to deploy. • Transfer case and 4X4 failures. • Stalling caused by oil seeping onto the camshaft position sensor wiring harness. • Loss of steering, loose steering. • Sudden tie-rod failure. • Horn doesn't blow. • Faulty brake light switch. • Wind blows lightweight hood away. • Front passenger window suddenly shattered. • Side-view mirrors change position at random. • Dash lights and gauges go blank. • Seat belt locks up too easily; has no slack. **2003**—Transfer case failure. • Brake failure. • Wiper motor works erratically. • Rear window shattered for no reason. • Seat belts pin occupants against the seat. • Jack handle is too short to safely change the tire. **2004**—Engine surging. • Temporary loss of steering control when passing over bumpy terrain. • Tie-rod steering arm adjusting sleeve may rust out prematurely. • Loose plastic running board cut driver's leg. • Security and dome lights remain lit.

Secret Warranties/Service Tips

1999–2004—TSB #01-07-30-038B indicates transmission malfunctions likely caused by debris plugging the bleed orifice of the 2–3 shift solenoid. **2002**—4.2L engine cylinder bore liner cracking will be repaired under a Special Policy (Bulletin # 03019; June 2003) up to 7 years/160,000 km (100,000 miles). • Service Engine light comes on and transmission feels like it has slipped into Neutral. • Delayed transmission shift, harsh shift, and shudder. • Transfer case may be poorly calibrated, causing erratic operation. • Poor engine performance and transmission slips. • Diagnostic tips for loss of Third or Fourth gear. • Surging in First gear. • Campaign (secret warranty) to replace the left and right front lower control arm brackets. • Excessive fan and side mirror noise. • Service Engine or Service 4X4 light stays on. • Loss of electrical power to dash. • Front axle seal high-pitched noise emanating from the front of vehicle. • Roof rack howling. • Heater may not warm driver's feet. **2002–03**—Rear axle whine. • Drivetrain shudder or binding. Faulty ignition switch may cause transmission to stick in third gear. • Front drive axle noise. • AC blows warm air. • Inoperative AC. • Steering column noise remedies. • Adjust striker on hard to close doors. • Wet front carpet due to poor weather-stripping. **2002–04**—Liftgate unlatches on bumpy roads. • Front hood rattles. • Jammed seat belt retractor. • Inoperative 4WD/AWD:

AWD/4WD System Inoperative

Bulletin No.: 02-04-21-006D   Date: March 24, 2004

Inoperative 4WD/AWD Lamps, Inoperative 4WD/AWD System (Reprogram Transfer Case Control Module)

2004 Buick Rainier
2002–04 Chevrolet TrailBlazer, TrailBlazer EXT
2003–04 Chevrolet Avalanche, Silverado, Suburban, Tahoe
2002–04 GMC Envoy, Envoy XL
2003–04 GMC Sierra, Yukon, Yukon XL
2004 GMC Envoy XUV
2002–04 Oldsmobile Bravada

2003—Transmission slippage. **2003–04**—GM will replace the fuel-tank fill-up pipe and lower hose under "goodwill" to prevent "spit back" when refuelling. **2004**—Harsh transmission shifts:

Harsh A/T Shifts From PARK to DRIVE

Bulletin No.: 04-07-30-022 Date: April 29, 2004

Harsh Garage Shift from PARK to DRIVE or from PARK to REVERSE with Transmission Fluid at Cold Ambient Temperatures (Reprogram PCM)

2004 Buick Rainier
2004 Chevrolet TrailBlazer, TrailBlazer EXT
2004 GMC Envoy, Envoy XL
2004 Oldsmobile Bravada

Envoy, TrailBlazer Profile

	2002	2003	2004
Cost Price ($) (negotiable)			
Envoy 4X2 (20%)	37,995	37,195	41,475
Envoy AWD (20%)	37,995	37,195	41,820
Rainier AWD	—	—	49,245
Trailblazer 4X2 (20%)	34,600	37,500	39,705
Trailblazer AWD (20%)	37,455	38,500	40,120
Used Values ($)			
Envoy 4X2 ⋀	21,000	26,000	30,000
Envoy 4X2 ⋁	19,000	24,000	28,000
Envoy AWD ⋀	22,000	30,000	32,000
Envoy AWD ⋁	20,000	29,000	30,000
Rainier AWD ⋀	—	—	37,000
Rainier AWD ⋁	—	—	35,000
Trailblazer ⋀	20,000	28,500	30,000
Trailblazer ⋁	19,000	27,500	29,000
Trailblazer 4X4 ⋀	25,000	30,500	32,500
Trailblazer 4X4 ⋁	23,000	28,500	30,500
Reliability	④	④	④
Crash Safety (F)	③	③	③
Side	⑤	⑤	⑤
Offset	❷	❷	❷
Envoy	❶	❶	❶
Rollover	③	③	③

Note: Ascenders aren't sold in Canada.

ESCALADE, ESCALADE ESV, EXT, SUBURBAN, TAHOE, YUKON, YUKON XL, DENALI   ★★★

RATING: Average (2001–05); Average with an extended warranty (1995–2000); *Suburban, Yukon, Tahoe:* Not Recommended (1985–94).

Strong points: Strong engine, great for trailering, lavishly appointed, good array of instruments and controls, a large and comfortable cabin, high ground clearance, a rattle-resistant body, and a slow rate of depreciation. **Weak points:** Insufficient front passenger legroom (ventilation housing blocks the footwell); cramped third-row seating; high step-up; premature brake wear; excessive suspension and steering vibrations; vague steering; a suspension that provides a too-compliant, wandering ride; and excessive road and engine noise. **New for 2005:** Restyled gauges, new interior trim, upgraded cooling system, and standard chrome exhaust tips. Also, the optional navigation system will hereafter use a touch screen.

2005 Technical Data

Powertrain (4X2/4X4)
Engines: 4.8L V8 (275 hp)
• 5.3L V8 (285 hp)
• 6.0L V8 (320 hp)
• 8.1L V8 (340 hp)
Transmission: 4-speed auto.
Dimension/Capacity
Height/length/width:
74/198.9/78.9 in.
Headroom F/R: 40.7/39.4 in.

Legroom F/R: 41.3/38.6 in.
Wheelbase: 116 in.
Turning circle: 45 ft.
Passengers: 3/3/3
Cargo volume: 108 cu. ft.
GVWR: 6,500–7,000 lb.
Tow limit: 6,500–7,000 lb.
Ground clearance: 10.6 in.
Fuel tank: 114L/reg.
Weight: 5,465 lb.

MODEL HISTORY: These full-sized, four-door, rear-drives and 4X4s haven't lost much of their popularity over the last few years in spite of their large size, excessive fuel consumption, so-so reliability, and atrocious fit and finish. Except for a wimpy base 275-hp V8 power plant, there's a full array of engines capable of hauling almost any load, towing a trailer, or carrying up to nine passengers.

The GMC Yukon 4X4 (and its twin, the Tahoe) came on the scene in 1992 when GMC gave the Jimmy name to its smaller sport-utility wagon line and re-badged the big one as the Tahoe/Yukon.

During the 1995 model year, Blazers became Tahoes and a four-door version with standard driver-side airbags was added. The base V8 engine lost 10 horses (210 hp), but this was made up in the following year when the 5.7L V8s got 50 more horses (250 hp) and a 4-speed automatic transmission became standard (no more manual). **1997**—A standard passenger-side airbag. **1998**—An optional full-time 4X4 system called AutoTrac that can be used on any surface. **1999**—Luxury trappings were added to the Yukon, which was designated the Denali. **2000**—Tahoe, Yukon and Suburban totally redesigned based upon the reworked Silverado pickup. Wider and taller vehicles, the Tahoe and Yukon adopted a new V8 engine, front side airbags, and a seating capacity that grew from six to nine passengers. The familiar two-door version was dropped. **2001**—New engine cylinder heads. The 6.0L V8 gained 20 horsepower. An 8.1L 340-hp V8 for the Suburban 2500. **2002**—More standard features, such as AC, power windows, power front seats, heated power mirrors, and rear climate controls. **2003**—New entertainment options, an antiskid system, 4-wheel steering, and adjustable pedals. **2004**—A tire-pressure monitor.

Pre-2000 models are set on GM's C/K truck platform and have been available with a variety of V8s over the years. The best choice, though, is the 5.7L gas engine mated to an electronic 4-speed automatic. This match-up provides gobs of torque at low rpm, making these part-time 4X4s great for towing, stump pulling, or mountain climbing.

Transmission alternatives include a 4-speed manual or a 4-speed automatic. Standard-equipment hubs must be locked manually before shifting into 4X4 on early models. The diesel provides a good compromise between power and economy, although it has been plagued by malfunctions for decades and has never been the equal of Cummins. Overall reliability is only average, and declining.

Suburban, Yukon XL

Although it's classed as a full-sized SUV, the Suburban is really a cross between a station wagon, van, and pickup. It can carry nine passengers, tow just about anything, and go anywhere with optional 4X4.

These vehicles hadn't changed much until the launch of the 2000 models. **1995**—A four-door version and standard driver-side airbag. **1996**—5.7L V8s got 50 more horses (250 hp), and the 7.4L gained 60 horses (290 hp) and push-button 4X4. **1997**—Standard passenger-side airbag and upgraded, middle-seat height-adjustable shoulder belt anchors.

2000—Chevrolet re-styled the Suburban by setting it on the Silverado/Tahoe/Yukon platform and using generic parts from the same parts bin. With the changeover, GMC's Suburban name was swapped for the Yukon XL, while the Chevrolet division soldiered on, keeping the Suburban name alive.

Both the Suburban and Yukon XL are GM's largest sport-utilities: 14.7 inches longer than the Ford Expedition, but 7.4 inches shorter than the Excursion. Handling was improved considerably, but fuel economy remains atrocious. Improvements include a wider and taller body; new 5.3L and 6.0L V8 engines that replace the 5.7L and 7.4L engines, and turbocharged diesel V8; an automatic transmission with tow/haul mode for smoother shifting; standard front side airbags; and four-wheel disc brakes. Rear leaf springs have been replaced by rear coil springs.

2001—Suburban got an upgraded 6.0L V8 in addition to a totally new 340-hp 8.1L V8. The upscale Yukon Denali (the Cadillac Escalade's big brother) moved to GM's new full-sized platform. Until the changeover, when it became the Yukon XL, the Suburban was a Hummer in civilian garb, and like the Hummer, it's far less sturdy than it looks.

Cadillac Escalade

Cadillac's first truck, the 1999 Escalade 4X4 was nothing more than a warmed-over GMC Yukon Denali covered with ugly, poorly designed side cladding in an effort to disguise its parentage. The redesigned 2002 Escalade got many improvements, including an EXT version (a Suburban/Avalanche clone with additional luxury features), a 6.0L V8, and a more refined AWD system. **2003**—A longer ESV and Escalade EXT, an all-dressed version of the Chevrolet Avalanche SUV/pickup truck. Other changes include standard power-adjustable gas and brake pedals and second-row bucket seats for the wagons.

COST ANALYSIS: Best alternatives: GM says it is holding the line on 2005 prices, so choose the 2004 model that gives you the best deal. If looking for a used vehicle, try to find a Suburban with the 7.4L V8 engine—the 5.7L is barely adequate for this behemoth. When looking for other choices, remember that few other similar-class vehicles equal the Suburban for sheer size. Alternatively, a full-sized van or extended minivan might be a better choice if off-road capability isn't a priority. If size isn't your primary concern, look to other more reliable SUVs that are less costly to operate, like a late-model Chevrolet, full-sized Tahoe or Yukon, and Toyota 4Runner. **Rebates:** $3,000 rebates and zero percent financing should continue well into 2004. **Delivery/PDI:** $1,000. **Warranty:** Bumper-to-bumper 3 years/60,000 km; rust perforation 6 years/160,000 km. **Supplementary warranty:** An extended warranty is a good idea, but not critical. **Options:** You won't find many bare-bones models, because dealers want the extra profit gained from selling these SUVs fully loaded. Transmission oil cooler, rear window defogger, engine block heater, and upgraded sound system are all worthy add-ons. Consider buying running boards ($300) if you plan to carry people who will have difficulty stepping up into the vehicle. **Depreciation:** Slower than average. **Insurance cost:** Insurance industry statistics indicate that these full-sized vehicles have a substantially lower-than-average number of accident injury claims, yet the cost of insurance is way above average. Surprised? **Annual maintenance cost:** Higher than average. The early Suburban's many mechanical and body deficiencies boost its upkeep costs way above average. One saving grace, however, is that it can be serviced practically anywhere. Escalade's redesign will probably result in higher maintenance costs, once the warranty expires. **Parts supply/cost:** Good supply and inexpensive. There have been long waits for transfer-case replacements. Competition from independent suppliers keeps prices down. **Highway/city fuel economy:** *Tahoe and Yukon: 4.8L with or without 4X4:* 12.7–16.9L/100 km; *Tahoe, Suburban, Yukon, Yukon Denali, and Yukon XL: 5.3L 4X4:* 12.6–17.1L/100 km. There is no fuel mileage data on the 6.0L or 8.1L V8s.

QUALITY/RELIABILITY: The best of the Detroit Big Three; ho-hum. **Owner-reported problems:** Lots of driveability complaints relating to excessive wander and vibrations. Other complaints pertain to the brakes, electrical, fuel, and exhaust systems (popping and pinging). A loose O_2 sensor connection is the reason why Check Engine light is often activated. Body assembly and paint application is below standard. **Warranty performance:** Average.

SAFETY SUMMARY: The vehicle will wander, requiring constant steering correction, particularly when buffeted by crosswinds. The Suburban is too large for safe off-road use. Braking is terrible—one of the worst in the sport-utility class (100–0 km/h: 165 ft.). Although standard four-wheel ABS first appeared on 1992 models, it has been failure-prone and not very effective. NHTSA reports 1,755 complaints, 604 accidents, and 142 injuries related to ABS failures on 1992–98 versions. In spite of the above findings, injury claim rates reported by insurance companies have been judged to be much better than average. **Airbags:** Standard side airbags. **ABS:** Standard four-wheel; disc/disc. **Traction control:** Optional. **Head restraints F/R:** *. **Visibility F/R:** *****. **Maximum load capacity:** 950–1,610 lb.

SAFETY COMPLAINTS: All years: Sudden, unintended acceleration. • Engine head gasket and exhaust manifold, transmission, steering, ABS brake and brake drums, tire, doorlocks, and airbag failures. • Vehicle wanders, vibrates excessively, and jerks to one side when braking. • Seat belt tightens progressively. • Gas tank leaks fuel. • Gas fumes permeate the interior. **Tahoe, Yukon: 1997**—Long stopping distance after pedal goes all the way to the floor. • Vehicle fails to slow down sufficiently when driver takes foot from accelerator pedal. • Engine misses when AC is engaged. • Lack of rear stabilizer bar results in poor high-speed stability. • Faulty differential pinion gear seal. • Rear axle failure. • Chassis fluid leaks onto brake rotors. **1998**—Steering bolt failed, leading to steering loss. • Excessive vibrations when braking, usually caused by premature rotor and pad wearout. • Brakes suddenly grab in rainy weather. • Poor fuel-tank design allows fuel to leak out the filler spout whenever vehicle is parked on an incline. • Electrical problems cause AC surging, flickering lights and switches, and an instrument panel that's hot to the touch. • Rear middle seat belt failure. **2000**—Steering broke loose and caused complete loss of steering control. • Tie-rod fell off, causing serious steering difficulties. • Child had to be cut free from locked up seat belt. • Windshield wipers don't stay in contact with the windshield. • Factory roof rack came off vehicle while hauling a lightweight kayak. • Passenger windows don't operate properly. • Fuel smell invades the interior. • Driver's seat rocks back and forth while accelerating and decelerating. • Mirror is mounted in such a way that it blocks visibility. **2000–04**—Steering wheel clunk. **2001**—Erratic shifting, slipping, jerking, and clunking. • Sudden stalling. • Catalytic converter glowing red. • Stones lodge between the brake calipers and wheel rims. • Finger cut from lowering head restraint. **2002**—Loose steering feels unstable, causes vehicle to wander. • Faulty transmission; delayed shifts. **2003**—Faulty steering linkage. • Vehicle can be shifted out of Park without pressing the brake pedal. • Rear passenger doors don't lock properly. • Leaking gas tank. • High beam light is too bright. Suburban, Yukon XL: **1997**—Steering is too sensitive and doesn't tighten up as speed increases. • Side door doesn't lock/close. **1998**—Sudden steering loss. • Engine oil leak caused by oil plug failure. • AC compressor failure. • Electrical components stay on when ignition is turned off. • Power window regulator failure causing window to stick and rattle. • **1999–2000**—Emergency brake failed, allowing vehicle to roll downhill. • Battery acid ran down the negative cable and caused the brake line to rupture. • Loss of rear braking due to brake cylinder fluid leakage. • Fuel leakage from fuel injector and regulator. • All lights (including headlights) go off intermittently. • Driver-side door handle broke. • Rear power windows often fail in the up or down position. • Window may shatter for no reason. • Rear left shoulder belts don't stay connected. • Unable to secure child safety seat into the middle position due to seat belt location. • Driver seat caught fire. • Driver seat rocks back and forth upon acceleration and deceleration. • Several cases where rear wheel flew off after lug nuts failed. • Cracked trailer hitch. • Spare tire jack won't hold vehicle. **2001**—Total electrical shutdown. • Simultaneous failure of steering and brakes. **2002**—Headlights are aimed too high. • Dash lights reflect into mirror. • Dashboard lights are too bright. • Gas tank hard to refuel, causes premature shutoff. • Liftgate window exploded. **2003**—Excessive shoulder belt tension. • Cab reverberation causes ear pain. **2004**—Sharp pull to the right when accelerating, then vehicle snaps to the left when foot is taken off the accelerator. • Complete transmission replacement. • While driving, tailgate window fell inward. • Inoperative emergency brake.

Secret Warranties/Service Tips

Tahoe, Yukon: 1992–99—Upgraded rear brake shoes will eliminate brake lead and pull and reduce front brake wear. **1993–2002**—Paint delamination, peeling, or fading (see Part Three). **1994–99**—Hard starts on vehicles equipped with a 6.5L diesel engine may signal the need to replace the shutoff solenoid. **1995–2000**—No-starts or hard starts can be eliminated by replacing the crankshaft position sensor. **1996–97**—Excessive engine noise can be corrected by installing upgraded valve stem oil seals. **1996–98**—Diagnosing causes of fluid leak near front wheels or front engine area. • Vehicles equipped with a 6.5L diesel engine that experience hard upshifts may need to reprogram the PCM/VCM. **1996–99**—Engine bearing knocking on vehicles equipped with a 5.7L V8 may be silenced by using a special GM countermeasure kit. **1996–2000**—Hard starts, backfires, or an unusual grinding sound when starting can all be addressed by replacing the crankshaft position sensor. **1998**—Engine stalling or surging and a slipping transmission may signal the need to repair the auxiliary oil cooler or replace the transmission torque converter. • Tips for fixing water leak at the driver-side windshield or just below the instrument panel. **1998–2000**—GM, at no charge, will repaint the outside rear-view mirror housing if it turns a chalky, dull colour. • Stalling or surging following a stop may be corrected by re-calibrating the PCM settings. • A transfer-case bump or clunk on acceleration is usually caused by a slip-stick condition between the rear propeller shaft slip yoke and the transfer-case output shaft. It can be eliminated by using a new transfer-case fluid that contains a better friction modifier, says TSB #99-04-21-004. **1999**—If the front wheels slip while in 4X4, consider replacing the transfer case clutch plates and front-drive axle lubricant. • A steering-column squeak noise may be silenced by replacing the steering-wheel SIR module coil assembly. **Tahoe, Yukon, Cadillac Escalade: 1999–2000**—Engine may misfire, water may mix with fuel, or the Service Engine light may come on if water has entered through the EVAP canister. Correct the problem by installing a new EVAP canister vent solenoid. **1999–2004**—Transmission failure caused by debris in the 2–3 shift solenoid bleed orifice. **2000**—If the steering column makes a clunking noise, it may signal the need to change the upper intermediate steering-shaft assembly. **2000–03**—Excessive engine noise:

Engine – Knocking or Lifter Noise

Bulletin No.: 02-06-01-038   Date: December 2002

Engine Knock or Lifter Noise (Replace o-ring)

2001–02 Chevrolet Camaro
2001–03 Chevrolet Corvette
2001–02 Pontiac Firebird
2002–03 Cadillac Escalade, Escalade EXT
2000–03 Chevrolet Suburban, Tahoe
2001–03 Chevrolet Silverado
2002–03 Chevrolet Avalanche
2000–03 GMC Yukon, Yukon XL
2001–03 GMC Sierra
with 4.8L, 5.3L, 5.7L or 6.0L V8 Engine (VINs V, T, Z, G, S, N, U - RPOs LR4, LM7, L59, LS1, LS6, LQ9, LQ4)

Condition: Some customers may comment on an engine tick noise. The distinguishing characteristic of this condition is that it likely will have been present since new, and is typically noticed within the first 161–322 km (100–200 mi.). The noise may often be diagnosed as a collapsed lifter. Additionally, the noise may be present at cold start and appear to diminish and then return as the engine warms to operating temperature. This noise is different from other noises that may begin to occur at 3,219–4,828 km (2,000–3,000 mi.).

2000–04—Remedies for a steering wheel clunk and inoperative power windows. **2001**—Fuel tank leakage. • Harsh shifts. • 2–4 band or 3–4 clutch damage. • Rear heater puts out insufficient heat. • Carpet may be wet or have a musty odour. **2003–04**—Inoperative AWD. • Noisy, inoperative power window. • Faulty heated seats. **Suburban, Yukon XL: 1992–99**—Upgraded rear brake shoes will eliminate brake lead and pull and reduce front-brake wear. **1996–99**—Engine bearing knocking on vehicles equipped with a 5.0L or 5.7L V8 may be silenced by using a special GM countermeasure kit to service the crankshaft and select-fit undersized connecting rod bearings. **1998**—Tips for fixing a water leak at the driver-side windshield or just below the instrument panel. • Engine stalling or surging and a slipping transmission may signal the need to repair the auxiliary oil cooler or replace the transmission torque converter. • **1998–99**—If you can't engage the 4X4 mode, it may be necessary to replace the transfer-case actuator/shift detent plunger. **1999**—If the front wheels slip while in 4X4, consider replacing the transfer-case clutch plates and front-drive axle lubricant. • AC blows hot air due to faulty inlet actuator. **1998–2000**—If only all the Suburban's problems were this easy to resolve: A transfer-case bump or clunk on acceleration is usually caused by a slip-stick condition between the rear propeller shaft slip yoke and the transfer-case output shaft. It can be eliminated by using a new transfer-case fluid that contains a better friction modifier, says TSB #99-04-21-004. • Increased accelerator pedal effort can be fixed by replacing the throttle body. • Silence front- door rattling by replacing the door window regulator bolts. • **2000–04**—Remedies for a steering wheel clunk and inoperative power windows. **2001**—Fuel tank leakage. • Harsh shifts. • 2–4 band or 3–4 clutch damage. • Rear heater puts out insufficient heat. • Carpet may be wet or have a musty odour. **2002–03**—Second-row footwell carpet may be wet with dirty water. GM will seal the rear wheelhouse under warranty (Bulletin #03-08-57-001; May 2003). **2002–04**—Suspension clunk, slap. GM will replace the spring insert and insulator for free (see Silverado "Service Tips"). **2003—** Harsh automatic transmission 1–2 shifting, slipping due to a faulty pressure control solenoid (Bulletin #03-07-30-020; May 2003). **2003–04—** Inoperative front power window.

Escalade, Suburban, Tahoe, Yukon Profile

	1997	1998	1999	2000	2001	2002	2003	2004
Cost Price ($) (negotiable)								
Escalade (21%)	—	—	63,055	63,805	63,805	72,700	74,970	70,675
Suburban (21%)	33,335	33,965	34,620	34,620	37,905	45,875	46,670	46,680
Tahoe, Yukon (20%)	30,595	31,155	31,555	33,305	31,715	42,680	42,530	44,105
4X4 (21%)	33,365	34,155	34,555	36,715	35,010	46,895	50,385	42.530
Yukon XL (21%)	—	—	—	34,620	35,760	46,895	47,290	44,720
Used Values ($)								
Avalanche ⋀	—	—	—	—	—	26,000	30,000	34,000
Avalanche ⋁	—	—	—	—	—	24,000	27,000	32,000
Escalade ⋀	—	—	27,000	32,000	38,000	40,000	48,000	52,000
Escalade ⋁	—	—	25,000	30,000	36,000	38,000	45,000	50,000
Suburban ⋀	12,500	15,000	18,500	21,000	24,000	33,000	34,000	37,000
Suburban ⋁	10,500	13,000	17,000	19,000	22,000	31,000	32,000	35,000
Tahoe, Yukon ⋀	11,500	13,500	16,500	22,000	24,000	35,000	32,000	36,000
Tahoe, Yukon ⋁	10,000	12,000	15,000	20,000	23,000	33,000	30,500	34,000
4X4 ⋀	13,000	13,500	18,500	24,500	23,000	33,000	36,000	39,000
4X4 ⋁	11,000	12,000	17,000	23,000	22,000	31,000	34,000	36,000
Yukon XL ⋀	—	—	—	22,500	25,500	34,000	43,000	39,000
Yukon XL ⋁	—	—	—	21,000	24,500	30,000	41,000	37,000
Reliability								
Tahoe, Yukon	②	③	③	③	③	③	③	③
Suburban, Yukon XL	❶	❷	③	③	③	③	③	③
Crash Safety (F)								
Suburban, Yukon XL	—	—	④	—	④	—	—	④
4X4	—	④	④	—	—	④	④	—
Denali 4d	④	—	④	④	④	—	④	④
Tahoe/Yukon	④	—	④	④	③	③	④	④
4X4	④	—	④	③	③	③	④	—
Escalade	—	—	—	—	—	③	③	④
4X4	—	—	④	④	—	③	④	—
Rollover								
Tahoe/Yukon	—	—	—	—	③	③	❷	③
Yukon	—	—	—	—	③	③	③	③
4X4	—	—	—	—	③	③	③	—
Escalade	—	—	—	—	—	③	③	—
Suburban	—	—	—	—	—	③	③	—
EXT	—	—	—	—	—	—	❷	—

General Motors/Suzuki

TRACKER/SIDEKICK, VITARA, GRAND VITARA ★★★

RATING: Average (1994–2005); Below Average (1989–93). Acceptable for commuting and Saturday night cruising, but stay on the asphalt unless your definition of off-roading is visiting the city park. **Strong points:** Shift-on-the-fly capability and average reliability record. The Grand Vitara is the better performer, with its minimal body lean when cornering, good emergency handling, and braking. Lots of front and rear passenger space, but three in the rear is a real squeeze. **Weak points:** The 4-cylinder engine is weak and rough-running; part-time 4X4 not suitable for dry pavement; stiff riding; sluggish automatic transmission; frequent downshifting with the base Vitara; skimpy interior appointments; heater is slow to warm interior on sub-freezing days and employs a noisy fan; the AC struggles to keep the Vitara cool; accelerator is placed too far left; seats feel cheap and inadequately padded and lack thigh support; seatbacks lack shoulder and lower back support; driver's seat doesn't adjust for height, making it hard for short drivers to get a clear view; spare tire further restricts rear visibility; and lots of road, wind, axle whine, and engine noise invade the cabin. **New for 2005:** Tracker and Vitara get axed.

2005 Technical Data (base Vitara/Tracker)

Powertrain (rear-drive/part-time 4X4)
Engines: 2.0L 4-cyl. (127 hp)
• 2.5L V6 (165 hp)
• 2.7L V6 (183 hp)
Transmissions: 5-speed man.
• 3-speed auto.
• 4-speed auto.
Dimension/Capacity (Vitara)
Height/length/width:
67.3/152/64.8 in.
Headroom F/R: 39.9/39.6 in.

Legroom F/R: 41.4/35.9 in.
Wheelbase: 97.6 in.
Turning circle: 37 ft.
Passengers: 2/3/2
Cargo volume: 30 cu. ft.
GVWR: 3,373–3,593 lb.
Tow limit: 1,000 lb.
Ground clearance: 7.2 in.
Fuel tank: 66L/reg.
Weight: 2,450 lb.

MODEL HISTORY: Introduced as a GM/Suzuki co-venture in 1989, these vehicles have been quite successful as entry-level 4X4s for city dwellers wanting off-roading allure. They will provide some off-road thrills (if not pushed too hard) but are "more show than go."

The Tracker and Sidekick, available as a two-door convertible and a four-door wagon, come with a standard 1.6L 4-cylinder power plant. The 1997 Sport version, sold only by Suzuki, carries a 1.8L 4-cylinder with dual overhead camshafts, rated at 120 hp.

The GM Tracker and Vitara are built in Ontario and use similar designs and components. The Grand Vitara carries a 6-cylinder engine and is made in Japan.

The Vitara is longer, wider, taller, and handles much better (read: is less tippy) than the Sidekick it replaced. It's essentially an entry-level version of the Grand Vitara and carries a smaller 2.0L 127-hp, 4-cylinder engine and less standard equipment. Nevertheless, it projects a more solid appearance, has a more refined interior, and exhibits less noise and vibration than its primitive predecessor.

Suzuki's top-line Grand Vitara, is wider, longer, and taller, and gives a more supple ride than its predecessor, the Sidekick Sport. It comes with a competent, though not very powerful, 24-valve 2.5L 165-hp V6 power plant, shared with GM's Tracker. Other standard features include a full-sized spare tire and four-wheel ABS on any "+" model. Peppy in the lower gears (good for off-roading), the engine quickly loses steam in the higher gear ranges (a drawback to highway cruising). It has competent road holding and handling, though it doesn't provide as much carlike handling as the Honda CR-V and Toyota RAV4.

Inside, there's plenty of headroom, arm room, and legroom, but the interior is somewhat narrow. The rear seats and seatbacks fold flat, adding to cargo capacity, and there are plenty of small trays, bins, and compartments to store things.

Tracker/Vitara: 1999–2000—The four-door carried a standard 2.0L 16-valve 120-hp 4-cylinder engine, shift-on-the-fly 4X4, rack-and-pinion steering, and revised interior and exterior styling. **2002**—Standard air conditioning, AM/FM cassette stereo, and child seat tethers. The base 1.6L engine was dropped in favour of the more powerful 127-hp 2.0L version. The Tracker also got the Suzuki V6 it had been lusting for, since many buyers found the 4-banger inadequate. **2003**—An upgraded dash and centre console. **2004**—Tracker's last model year. **Grand Vitara: 2000**—First year on the market. **2002**—V6 engine gets 10 more horses. **2003**—Given a new dash, aluminum wheels, smaller rear head restraints, and interior upgrades.

COST ANALYSIS: Best alternatives: Go for the 2004 models; they are identical to the 2005s and should cost much less. For off-roading, look to the 2004 Jeep Wrangler (the 2005 model will be built by a consortium of three suppliers). For pretend off-roading, consider the Honda CR-V, Subaru Forester, and Toyota RAV4, or, if you really want to splurge, a Toyota Highlander. **Rebates:** $1,500 to $2,000 on 4-cylinder models; low-interest financing plans worth about $2,000. **Delivery/PDI:** $995. **Warranty:** *Suzuki:* Bumper-to-bumper 3 years/80,000 km; rust perforation 5 years/unlimited km. *GM:* Bumper-to-bumper 3 years/60,000 km; rust perforation 6 years/160,000 km. **Supplementary warranty:** An extended warranty is a good idea. **Options:** An automatic transmission will give you snail-like acceleration and eat into fuel economy. **Depreciation:** Average. **Insurance cost:** Average. **Annual maintenance cost:** Average repair costs; easily repaired at independent garages and Chevrolet or Suzuki dealerships. **Parts supply/cost:** Good supply. Parts can be expensive. **Highway/city fuel economy:** *2.0L:* 8.4–10.3L/100 km; *V6:* 10.2–12.6L/100 km.

QUALITY/RELIABILITY: Quality control is average. Defects haven't led to a lot of shop downtime or rendered these cars unreliable. Repairs are usually quite simple and relatively easy. **Owner-reported problems:** Most owners' complaints target poor handling due to under-performing brakes, steering, and suspension components. Other failure-prone components: serpentine belt, electrical system, catalytic converter, and muffler/exhaust system. Some early transmission failures reported. Poor body fit and finish allows water and wind to enter the cabin. **Warranty performance:** Average. Although warranty performance and dealer servicing are unimpressive, these vehicles aren't very dealer dependent, so it doesn't matter a great deal.

SAFETY SUMMARY: These lightweights are very vulnerable to side-wind buffeting. **ABS:** Optional 4W. Later models have standard rear ABS; disc/drum. **Head restraints F/R:** *Tracker 2d: 1997: *; 1999: ***; 2001: *****/***; 2002–03: ***; Tracker 4d: 2001: *****/***; 2002–03: *****; Grand Vitara: 1999–2002: ***; 2003: *****; Grand Vitara XL-7: 2003: *****.* **Visibility F/R:** ****/**. **Maximum load capacity:** *1999 2.0L Tracker:* 870 lb.; *Vitara, Grand Vitara:* 895 lb.

SAFETY COMPLAINTS: All years: Airbags failed to deploy. • Lots of road wander. • Premature tire wearout and poor tire/wheel design compromises handling. **Sidekick/Tracker: 1996–99**—Airbag light lit for no reason. • Engine EGR valve failures. • Frequent automatic transmission breakdowns, electrical shorts, chronic stalling, sudden brake loss, and emergency brake and AC failures. • Water leaking through the AC assembly causes chronic window fogging and blows the turn signal indicator fuse. **2000**—Rear side window air vents allow exhaust fumes to enter cabin. • Sudden steering linkage failure when turning. • Complete brake failure. • Continuously low brake-fluid level causes failure of front and rear calipers. • Brake and accelerator pedals are too close together. • Right front plastic inner fender came loose, caught tire, and damaged the inner fender. • Inadequate peripheral visibility. • GM's wiper blade material takes the shape of the windshield in its rest position and doesn't clean the windshield when needed. • Weather stripping doesn't clear rain from windows when they're rolled up or down. • Headlights don't adequately light up the road. • Hard to stay in lane when driving with the top off. • Automatic light sensor is designed to turn on the lights when it gets dark; however, it seldom works properly. **2001**—Driveshaft failure. • Driver tapped brakes to disengage cruise control, brakes locked up, and vehicle went out of control. • Extended braking stopping distance. **Vitara, Grand Vitara: 1999**—Excessive vibration at 100 km/h. • Electrical shorts (a common Suzuki failing). • Excessive brake fade. • Stalling and surging (stuck accelerator). • Defective motor mounts. **2000**—Vehicle pulls right when accelerating and vibrates excessively. **2001**—Blown oil line dripped oil on hot exhaust and caused a fire. • Vehicle is tippy when cornering. **2002**—Brake grinding when stopping. **2003**—Grand Vitara XL-7 automatic transmission slips between Second and Third gear. **2004**—Accelerator stuck after recall for sudden acceleration.

Secret Warranties/Service Tips

All years: 4X4 may not fully engage or pop out of gear. • Get rid of an annoying engine ticking noise by purging the air from the valve lifters. • **Tracker: 1989–2003**—Troubleshooting automatice transmission slipping. **1999–2003**—Engine ticking. • Serpentine belt frayed or squealing. • Brake pulsation, vibration. **Vitara: 1999**—Vitaras equipped with 2.0L engines may not start in cold temperatures due to a faulty ECM/PCM program (TSB #TS06-01-03099). **Tracker and Vitara: 1999–2000**—On vehicles equipped with a manual transmission, the engine may idle poorly until it warms up; reprogram the PCM under the emissions warranty. • Manual transmission gears that clash when shifting may require a new synchronizer spring kit. • If the transmission won't upshift after downshifting with cruise control engaged, chances are the cruise control module is at fault. • An inoperative or malfunctioning (blows warm air) AC may simply require a new o-ring. **1999–2002**—Windows bind and tip forward. **1999–2003**—Oil level reads low. **2001**—Excessive driveline vibration. • Frayed serpentine belt. • Instrument panel squeaks and rattles. • Heating, ventilation system may not work properly. • Ignition key sticks in the ignition. **2002**—Air leaks out of dash vents; AC air leaks. • Windows bind. **2003**—Oil seepage from left front of engine.

Tracker/Sidekick, Vitara, Grand Vitara Profile

	1997	1998	1999	2000	2001	2002	2003	2004
Cost Price ($) (negotiable)								
Tracker 4X2 (15%)	16,855	—	—	—	—	—	—	—
Tracker 4X4 (15%)	18,130	18,630	19,400	19,710	21,395	21,395	21,500	25,605
Sidekick S/T (15%)	15,595	16,495	—	—	—	—	—	—
Sidekick H/T (15%)	17,996	18,295	—	—	—	—	—	—
Vitara (13%)	—	19,995	20,795	18,695	18,695	18,695	20,295	21,995
Grand Vitara (15%)	—	23,495	23,995	24,495	23,995	23,995	23,995	28,595
Used Values ($)								
Tracker 4X2 Λ	2,500	—	—	—	—	—	—	—
Tracker 4X2 V	2,000	—	—	—	—	—	—	—
Tracker 4X4 Λ	4,100	6,500	8,500	10,000	11,000	13,000	15,000	18,000
Tracker 4X4 V	3,000	5,500	7,000	8,500	10,000	12,000	14,000	17,000
Sidekick S/T Λ	4,500	6.500	—	—	—	—	—	—
Sidekick S/T V	3,000	5,000	—	—	—	—	—	—
Sidekick H/T Λ	5,000	7,000	—	—	—	—	—	—
Sidekick H/T V	4,000	6,000	—	—	—	—	—	—
Vitara Λ	—	—	8,000	9,000	10,000	12,000	15,000	15,500
Vitara V	—	—	7,000	8,000	9,000	10,500	13,500	14,000
Grand Vitara Λ	—	—	9,500	11,500	13,000	15,000	17,500	21,500
Grand Vitara V	—	—	8,500	10,000	11,500	14,000	16,500	19,500

Reliability								
Sidekick, Tracker	③	③	④	④	④	④	④	④
Vitara, Grand Vitara	—	—	④	④	④	④	④	④
Crash Safety (F)								
Sidekick, Tracker 2d	❷	—	—	—	④	④	④	④
Vitara	—	—	—	—	④	④	④	④
Grand Vitara	—	—	—	—	④	④	④	④
Side (Vitara)	—	—	—	—	④	④	④	④
Grand Vitara	—	—	—	—	—	⑤	⑤	⑤
Tracker	—	—	—	—	④	④	④	④
Offset (all)	—	—	③	③	③	③	③	③
Rollover (Tracker)	—	—	—	—	③	③	③	—
Vitara	—	—	—	—	③	③	③	—
Grand Vitara	—	—	—	—	③	③	③	—

Note: Almost identical Suzukis usually cost less than the GM version.

EQUINOX ★

RATING: Not Recommended (2005); this is its first year on the market **Strong points:** Well-equipped and reasonably priced, this is one of the largest, most powerful, compact SUVs available. Other pluses are its versatile drivetrain, carlike unibody frame, and a fully independent suspension that smoothes out the ride. A unique sliding rear seat slides fore and aft to accommodate long-legged passengers, and an adjustable shelf behind the rear seats can be used as a picnic table. Received a five-star rating for front and side occupant crash protection. **Weak points:** Uses a GM-bred V6, instead of the more reliable and peppy Honda 3.5L V6 used in the 2004 Vue. Mediocre handling; suspension bottoms out noisily when passing over bumps; no low-range gearing for off-roading; rear drum brakes, instead of better-performing discs; wide turning circle makes for tough handling in tight areas; power window controls are found on the centre console instead of the doors; seats could use more side support and may be too firm for some; no third-row seat available; rear hatch doesn't have separate-opening glass; rear suspension housings intrude into rear cargo space; and uses many of the Saturn Vue's quality-challenged mechanical components. **New for 2005:** Everything. **Likely failures:** Engines and engine head gaskets, automatic transmission, AC condenser, rear-drive clutch unit, electrical, and fit and finish (water leaks, squeaks, and rattles).

2005 Technical Data

Powertrain (4X2/4X4)
Engine: 3.4L V6 (185 hp)
Transmissions: 5-speed auto. OD
Dimension/Capacity (4d)
Height/length/width:
67/188.8/71.4 in.
Headroom F/R: 40.9/40.1 in.
Legroom F/R: 41.2/40.2 in.

Wheelbase: 112.5 in.
Turning circle: 42 ft.
Passengers: 2/3
Cargo volume: 32.2 cu. ft.
GVWR: 5,700 lb.
Tow limit: 3,500 lb.
Ground clearance: 8 in.
Fuel tank: 75L/reg.
Weight: 3,776 lb.

MODEL HISTORY: A replacement for GM's Suzuki *cum* Chevrolet Tracker, the five-passenger Equinox distinguishes itself from the rest of the SUV pack by offering standard V6 power, a 5-speed automatic transmission, and a comfortable ride. Although it uses many of the Vue's underpinnings (without the plastic body panels), it has a longer wheelbase and wider body.

COST ANALYSIS: The Equinox LS FWD costs $26,560; the LT FWD: $28,565; the LS AWD: $29,170; and the LT AWD: $31,275. **Delivery/PDI:** $960. **Highway/city fuel economy:** 8.6–12.7L/100 km. **Best alternatives:** Honda CR-V, Hyundai Santa Fe, Mazda Tribute, Nissan X-Trail, Subaru Forester, and Toyota RAV4.

Honda

CR-V   ★★★★★

RATING: Recommended (2002–05); Above Average (1997–2001). The CR-V is a compact SUV that's both fun and functional. **Strong points:** The small power boost and improved chassis added in 2002 give additional interior room (interior volume has grown by 8 percent) and provide improved functionality. Lots of interior room and standard features; impressive steering and handling, particularly around town; easy front entry/exit; top-quality fit and finish; plastic cargo floor panel *cum* picnic table; outstanding NHTSA front crashworthiness scores; good fuel economy; and superior reliability. **Weak points:** Acceleration is somewhat compromised on vehicles equipped with an automatic transmission; reduced steering feedback; jittery ride on less-than-perfect roadways; excessive road noise; latest redesign reduced front legroom slightly; problematic rear entry/exit and only room for two in rear; not suitable for true off-roading; and may be tippy in a side impact (1999–2001 models), according to NHTSA crash results. "Marginal" IIHS offset crash rating, and head restraints scored poorly as well. **New for 2005:** Nothing important; next redesign is scheduled for the 2007 models.

2005 Technical Data

Powertrain (front-drive/4X4)	Wheelbase: 103.1 in.
Engine: 2.4L 4-cyl. (160 hp)	Turning circle: 34.1 ft.
Transmissions: 5-speed man.	Passengers: 2/3
• 4-speed auto.	Cargo volume: 33.5 cu. ft.
Dimension/Capacity	GVWR: 4,165 lb.
Height/length/width:	Tow limit: 1,500 lb.
66.2/178.6/70.2 in.	Ground clear.: 8.1 in.
Headroom F/R: 40.9/39.1 in.	Fuel tank: 58L/reg.
Legroom F/R: 41.3/39.1 in.	Weight: 3,375 lb.

MODEL HISTORY: The 2002–05 models don't look that different from their predecessors, although they are a bit longer, wider, and higher. The interior, though, has undergone a major change, with more space for both passengers and cargo, and more user-friendly features and controls.

The CR-V's Civic-based platform incorporates a four-wheel independent suspension that shortens the nose and frees up more rear cargo room. Steering components have also been modified. The base 160-hp 2.4L I-VTEC 4-cylinder engine is offered with either a 5-speed manual or a 4-speed automatic transmission—both redesigned for the 2002 model.

The CR-V is offered in two trim levels, both with full-time 4X4. Combining sport-utility styling with minivan versatility, this SUV is essentially a re-styled Civic with 4X4 capability added. Since its '97 launch, the car changed little until the revamped 2002 came out. **1998**—Front-drive comes equipped with either a standard 5-speed manual transmission or optional automatic. **1999**—picked up 20 more horses and an Overdrive On-Off switch. **2001**—Standard-issue ABS and user-friendly child-seat tether anchors added to the EX and SE. **2002**—Restyled and given more power, interior room, and features, like a side-hinged tailgate and new interior panels. **2004**—A front-passenger power door lock switch.

COST ANALYSIS: Best alternatives: Honda's 2005 model will cost about $500 more this year and probably be discounted due to slow sales; 2004s will likely be discounted by at least ten percent before the end of the year and represent the better buy. In theory, a used, upgraded, second-series 2002 would be the best buy from a quality/price perspective, but there aren't many available. 2001 or earlier CR-Vs are acceptable, but they are poor second choices, underpowered and overpriced for what they offer. Take solace in knowing that, even if you pay too much for a Recommended model, you can drive this bantam 4X4 until you outgrow it and trade it in for almost as much as you paid originally. Good second choices: Hyundai Santa Fe, Subaru Forester, and Toyota RAV4. **Rebates:** Mostly low-financing programs. **Delivery/PDI:** $895.

Warranty: Bumper-to-bumper 3 years/60,000 km; powertrain 5 years/ 100,000 km; rust perforation 5 years/unlimited km. **Supplementary warranty:** Honda's impressive quality control makes an extended warranty unnecessary. **Options:** Make sure a moon roof doesn't reduce your headroom to an uncomfortable degree. Be wary of the cruise control—it's quirky, and when it's engaged you may find that the car won't hold its speed over hilly terrain. One other bit of advice: Due to their design, CR-Vs tend to sandblast the paint off the side door bottoms. Invest in a pair of $25 mudflaps. Also, steer clear of the original-equipment Bridgestone and Firestone tires. Owners report poor performance on wet roads and premature failures. Try Michelin, Yokohama, or Pirelli instead. **Depreciation:** Much slower than average. **Insurance cost:** Average. **Parts supply/cost:** Parts are easily found and reasonably priced (they come mostly from the Civic parts bin). **Annual maintenance cost:** Well below average; easily repaired at independent garages. **Highway/city fuel economy:** Estimated to be 8.9–10.9L/100 km.

QUALITY/RELIABILITY: Traditionally beyond reproach, quality has slipped a bit lately. **Owner-reported problems:** Harsh shifting on the 1997–99 models, and high-rev shifting, slipping, pulsing, and surging on the 2000 version. Other reported problems include minor body trim defects, premature front brake wear and vibrations, drive shaft popping noise, accessories that malfunction (particularly the sound system and AC), and electrical glitches. **Warranty performance:** Like most other automakers, Honda frequently extends its warranty through "goodwill" policies that cover generic factory-related defects. The company denies this is the case, but, interestingly enough, almost all of its service bulletins include a paragraph stating that post-warranty goodwill compensation will be considered if requested by the dealer.

ROAD PERFORMANCE: Acceleration/torque: The more powerful, upgraded engine is faster accelerating from a standing start and is less prone to hunt for the right gear when pressed. Manual transmissions need to downshift less frequently, as well. Generally, though, the CR-V is slow to accelerate—add passengers and an automatic transmission and you're likely to get passed by bicycling seniors. Nevertheless, increased low-end torque adds 227 kg (500 lb.) to the towing rating (680 kg/1,500 lb.). **Transmission:** The 5-speed manual is precise, with short throws and easy shifting, while the automatic is quick and smooth. The full-time 4X4 disengages under braking, allowing the ABS system to engage. **Steering:** Variable-assisted steering is nimble, accurate, and provides just the right boost for highway and city driving. On the downside, the 2002 modifications have reduced road "feel." **Routine handling:** Although there are 8 inches of ground clearance, the CR-V isn't tippy and handles remarkably well. Excellent ride over smooth surfaces. The car's small size doesn't handle road imperfections well, making for a bumpy, jittery ride. Forget about off-roading: there's no locking feature for the centre differential and no low-range 4X4 capability. **Emergency handling:** Very good, partly because of the four-wheel independent suspension and precise steering. Little body lean when cornering under power. **Braking:** Better than average, with good directional control and little fading after repeated application.

SAFETY SUMMARY: When compared with Toyota, Honda has had fewer safety-related defects reported to NHTSA. One recurring complaint, though, is that large occupants can't use the original equipment seat belts. Note also that the CR-V flipped over in 1999 side-impact tests carried out by NHTSA. **Airbags:** There's a concern that the steering wheel design is on an angle, which could result in an injury if airbag deploys at an angle. There have been reports of airbags failing to deploy or deploying inadvertently. In one incident, vehicle was going about 25 km/h when the driver's airbag suddenly exploded. Vehicle went off the road, flipped over, and injured driver. **ABS:** Standard; disc/disc. **Seat belt pretensioners:** Standard. **Head restraints F/R:** *1997: ***; 1998: **; 2001: ***/**; 2002–03: *****.* **Visibility F/R: *****.** **Maximum load capacity:** 850 lb.

SAFETY COMPLAINTS: All years: Sudden acceleration. • Chronic stalling. • ABS lock-up. • Bridgestone tire blowouts. **1997**—Seatback collapsed. • ABS lock-up. • Cruise control doesn't maintain speed going up or down hill. • Cruise control activates without warning at highway speeds. **1998**—Low-speed rear-ender pushed tailpipe into the fuel tank. • Accelerator sticks. • Knuckle arm broke, causing left front tire to come off. • Loss of steering while driving. • Steering locked up while making a right turn. • Cruise control often malfunctions. • Vehicle pulls to the right at any speed. • Front brake rotors need replacing after only 5,000 km. • Seat belt unlatched when brakes were applied. **1999**—Engine cylinder failure causes excessive vibration and stalling. • Automatic transmission slams into First gear. • Hatch window blew out while driving. **2000**—Bumper assembly caught fire. • Vehicle rolled over, A-pillar collapsed and killed driver. • Automatic transmission takes an inordinate amount of time to go into First gear and doesn't hold car when stopped in traffic on an incline. • Unacceptable slippage, poor traction of Bridgestone tires on wet pavement. • Excessive shimmying and front suspension vibration when accelerating. • Chronic steering wheel vibrations. **2001**—Chronic stalling. • Short drivers find airbag points toward face. • Rear wheel lock-up while turning caused head-on collision (clutch failure suspected). • Driver's seatback collapsed in rear-ender. • Seat belt tightens uncomfortably. **2002**—Hood suddenly flew open while cruising. • Loud popping noise when braking and changing direction (replacing the brake pads doesn't fix the problem). • Vehicle hesitates when accelerating or surges and then stalls. • Dim driver-side headlight. **2003**—Hood flew up. • Airbags failed to deploy. • Driver and rear centre seat belts unbuckled when car was rear-ended. • Steering wheel doesn't return to normal position after making a turn. **2004**—Many reports of engine fires after oil has been changed. • Gas pedal stuck. • Wheel froze while making a turn. • Stress fractures in windshield. • Airbag failed to deploy. • Wheel lug bolt broke off. • Constantly stalling. • Removable picnic table caused serious head injuries in a rollover accident. • Gas spews out of filler tube when refuelling. • Water can enter the fuel tank from gas-cap vent. • Door lock doesn't function with key as indicated in the owner's manual. • No seat belt extender available.

Secret Warranties/Service Tips

All years: Keep in mind that Honda service bulletins almost always mention that "goodwill" extended warranties may be applied to any malfunction. **1997–98**—If the ABS light remains lit, check first for a faulty wheel-speed sensor, says TSB #98-041. • Tips on correcting a noisy driver's seat. • Replace the AC expansion valve under a "goodwill" warranty as a possible cure for dashboard noise (hissing, moaning, or whistling) when the AC is engaged. • Wind whistling from the top of the windshield may be corrected by applying additional sealant to the windshield moulding. Another "goodwill" claim. **1997–99**—Harsh shifting caused by faulty solenoid; subject to free "goodwill" repair. • Front suspension clunking can be corrected by replacing the upper arm flange bolts. • Cargo-cover end-caps come off. **1997–2001**—Differential noise:

Rear Differential – Screech/Whine Noise

Bulletin No.: 01-079   Date:October 30, 2001
1997–01 CR-V (4X4)

SYMPTOM: A screech or whine from the rear differential when making a tight turn at low speed (for example, in a parking lot when 4X4 engages).

PROBABLE CAUSE: The differential fluid is contaminated or broken down, providing insufficient lubrication.

CORRECTIVE ACTION: Replace the dual pump fluid, and test-drive the vehicle. If necessary, replace the rear differential clutch, replace the oil pump assembly (1997 model only), and add a flow collar.

1998—Correcting wind noise coming from the door mirror area and a clunking noise from the power-window motor. **2000**—Information regarding shudder or vibration upon hard acceleration. • The remedy for differential moan during turns. • Malfunctioning Low Fuel light. **2001**—Rear differential noise. • Water leaks into the interior. **2002**—Rattling from the passenger grab handle area and above the doors. **2002–03**—A front brake clicking noise is due to faulty front brake pad lower retaining clips that may be replaced for free under a "goodwill" program. • Engine stumbles/stalls after a stop:

Engine Stumbles/Stalls After a Stop Notes

Bulletin No.:02-075   Date:December 10, 2002
2002–03 HONDA CR-V

SYMPTOM: When the fuel tank is about three-quarters full, the engine may stumble or stall after the vehicle comes to a stop.

PROBABLE CAUSE: Fuel sloshing in the tank causes a purge of fuel vapors to enter the engine.

CORRECTIVE ACTION: Update the vehicle's ECM/PCM software from your December 2002 or later Interactive Network (IN) CD.

• Misaligned door glass. **2003**—Coolant in the oil pan. **2002–04**—Troubleshooting a rear brake grinding noise. • Remedy for a rattle, grind, or growl coming from the A-pillar of the right front side of the vehicle when turning left.

CR-V Profile

	1997	1998	1999	2000	2001	2002	2003	2004
Cost Price ($) (negotiable)								
Base (14%)	26,800	25,800	26,000	26,000	26,300	26,900	27,300	27,200
Used Values ($)								
Base ⋀	9,000	11,000	13,500	15,500	17,500	20,000	23,000	25,000
Base ⋁	8,000	9,500	12,000	14,500	16,500	18,500	21,500	23,000
Reliability	④	④	④	⑤	⑤	⑤	⑤	⑤
Crash Safety (F)	—	④	④	④	④	⑤	⑤	⑤
NHTSA Side	—	—	⑤	⑤	⑤	⑤	⑤	⑤
IIHS Side	—	—	—	—	—	❷	❷	❷
Offset	❷	❷	❷	❷	❷	⑤	⑤	⑤
Rollover	—	—	—	—	③	③	③	—

Note: You don't get much off the price until the fourth model year.

PILOT   ★ ★ ★ ★ ★

Rating: Recommended (2003–05). A bigger and cheaper alternative to the Acura MDX. It's not as stylish as the MDX, but it's not as expensive, either, and you'll appreciate the savings. **Strong points:** Roomier and more powerful than most of the mid-sized competition; good acceleration with the AWD V6 powertrain; drives and rides like a car (less bounce and jerk); seating for eight with three-point seat belts for all; reasonably equipped, versatile, and roomy interior with lots of cargo space; can tow a small trailer or boat (1,588–2,040 kg/ 3,500–4,500 lb.); strong resale value; NHTSA five-star front and side crashworthiness rating. **Weak points:** A bit drab-looking; steering is a bit heavy during parking manoeuvres; no low-speed transfer case for off-road use; transmission shifts a bit slowly when accelerating at 100 km/h; no transmission On-Off Overdrive button, nor a manual shift mode; average fuel economy; rear hatch door doesn't lift up high enough and doesn't have a convenient, separate rear liftglass; third-row seat isn't large enough for three adults. Think of the Pilot as a different minivan with higher ground clearance and all-wheel drive. Limited production and no V8 engine option. **New for 2005:** Carried over unchanged. **Likely failures:** Quite a few first-year glitches were reported to government safety agencies, but things seem to have settled down with the latest models. Still, watch out for sudden loss of power steering, intolerable cabin wind noise, and an annoying thunking gas tank noise.

2005 Technical Data

Powertrain
Engine: 3.5L V6 (240 hp)
Transmission: 5-speed auto.

Wheelbase: 106.3 in.
Turning circle: 39 ft.
Passengers: 2/3/3

Dimension/Capacity
Height/length/width:
70.6/188/77.3 in.

Cargo volume: 90.3 cu. ft.
Ground clear.: 8 in.
Fuel tank: 72.7L/reg.
Weight: 4,436 lb.

MODEL HISTORY: Introduced as a 2003 model, Pilot borrows its chassis's basic design and powertrain from the MDX. It differs from its upscale brother with more conservative styling, a softer suspension, larger wheels, and a shorter body that's slightly wider and taller than the Acura. Overall performance is enhanced by the Odyssey-sourced V6 240-hp engine, coupled to a full-time, all-wheel-drive unit. Four-wheel independent suspension ensures fairly good handling and a comfortable ride.

Built in Alliston, Ontario, along with the Honda Odyssey, Honda Civic, Acura 1.7EL, and Acura MDX, the Pilot EX base model sells for full list at $41,000 ($5,000 more than the Odyssey; $7,000 *less* than the MDX).

COST ANALYSIS: Go for last year's 2004 model ($41,500) if you can get a 10 percent discount. **Best alternatives:** BMW X5, Infiniti QX4, Jeep Grand Cherokee Laredo, Lexus RX 300/330, and Toyota Highlander AWD or Toyota Sequoia. If towing is your thing, you may wish to consider a GM Envoy or Trailblazer (2,812 kg/6,200 lb.). **Rebates:** Few rebates available because Honda knows they're not needed. **Delivery/PDI:** $975. **Warranty:** Bumper-to-bumper 3 years/60,000 km; powertrain 5 years/100,000 km; rust perforation 5 years/unlimited km. **Supplementary warranty:** Not needed. **Options:** Nothing that's necessary. **Depreciation:** Predicted to be much less than average. **Insurance cost:** Will likely be higher than average. **Parts supply/cost:** Parts have been reasonably priced and easily found in the MDX/Odyssey generic parts bin. **Annual maintenance cost:** Much less than average. **Highway/city fuel economy:** 9.6–13.8L/100 km.

SAFETY SUMMARY: Airbags: Front and side. **ABS:** Standard; disc/disc. **Safety belt pretensioners:** Front. **Head restraints F/R:** ***/**. **Visibility F/R:** *****.

SAFETY COMPLAINTS: 2003—Vehicle rolled over after driver made a small steering correction. • Small road imperfections make the Pilot suddenly veer left or right. • Airbags failed to deploy. • Engine oil leakage caused by damaged timing belt and valves. • Intermittent hard starts. • ABS brake lock-up. • Power-steering pulley breakage. • Head restraints are too low for tall occupants. • Shoulder straps cut across neck. • Intolerable noise and turbulence is produced when cruising with the windows open. • Weak headlights. **2004**—Automatic transmission suddenly downshifted on its own. • Transmission recall parts aren't available. • Hard starting due to poor electrical connection. • Alarm goes off whenever car is started. • Airbag constantly disables itself. • Weak low beam headlights. • Plastic fuel tank is easily punctured. • Interior cabin light flickers on and off, door locks cease to function, and window won't go down. • Passenger window shattered after a drop in temperature.

• Severe wind buffeting when driving with the rear windows down. • Excessive vibration when driving over 100 km/h (see *www.honda-pilot.org*). • Sunroofs are failure-prone, leak, and create wind and vibration noise.

Secret Warranties/Service Tips

2003—V6 engine oil leaks. • Power-steering pump, front strut and damper, hood air deflector, dash, and sloshing fuel tank noise. • Security system won't arm. • Steering vibration. • Power-window failure. • Homelink can't be programmed. • Row seat won't fold, tilt, slide, or recline. **2003**—Rear brake clunk. • Right rear suspension clicking. **2003–04**—Rear brake clunk. • Right rear suspension clicking.

Pilot Profile

	2003	2004
Cost Price ($) (negotiable)		
Base (14%)	41,000	38,800
Used Values ($)		
Base Λ	33,000	34,000
Base V	31,000	32,000
Reliability	⑤	⑤
Crash Safety (F)	⑤	⑤
Side	⑤	⑤
IIHS Side	⑤	⑤
Offset	⑤	⑤
Rollover	④	—

Note: Look for soaring fuel prices and competition to speed up depreciation a bit.

ELEMENT ★★★★

RATING: Above Average (2003–05). Honda launched this oddly styled SUV as a youth magnet, but has only succeeded in giving soccer moms and baby boomers a minivan alternative. **Strong points:** It's the same size as a CR-V, with a better package, and it costs thousands less. Other notable features include a limited though adequate powertrain; roomy, versatile interior; unusually large cargo door opening; low liftover; a sliding roof partition that permits the carrying of bulky items like kayaks, fishing poles, and surfboards; interior tie-down hooks; dash allows for Internet access; predicted slow depreciation; first-year Honda defects usually aren't that serious. **Weak points:** No 6-cylinder option; engine is noisy when pushed; mediocre passing performance; doesn't corner very well; unusual driving position; gauges are sometimes difficult to see; the front windshield is more vertical than most and seems far away from the driver; lack of a third seat in rear; side windows don't roll down; poor stereo sound; some high-speed wind noise; side crashworthiness rated "poor" by the IIHS; 8 inches shorter than the Civic coupe; looks a bit like the 2003 Hummer H2. **New for 2005:** Nothing significant. **Likely failures:** Minor fit and finish, electrical system, AC, and sound system glitches.

MODEL HISTORY: A CR-V clone based on the Civic platform, the tall, square-looking Element is a crossover sport wagon SUV launched in early 2003 and priced in the $24,000–$29,000 range. Aimed at the youth market with its rugged exterior styling, buyers get the versatility of an SUV, the cargo-hauling capability of a pickup, and the interior access of a minivan.

Campers are well served by front- and second-row seats that fold flat for sleeping. Plus, the second-row seats can be folded away to the side, or removed to make more room for sports equipment and other toys.

Powered by a 160-hp 2.4L 4-cylinder engine coupled to a 4-speed automatic transmission or a 5-speed manual, the Element's powertrain and light weight make it a good all-around performer. Nonetheless, the lack of a V6 engine compromises its sporty pretensions.

COST ANALYSIS: The 2005 model sells for $24,000–$29,000, with minimal discounting. **Best alternatives:** The Honda CR-V, Hyundai Santa Fe GLS, Nissan Xterra, Subaru Forester, and Toyota Highlander AWD. **Rebates:** Few rebates because Honda is limiting Canadian sales. **Delivery/PDI:** $975. **Warranty:** Bumper-to-bumper 3 years/60,000 km; powertrain 5 years/ 100,000 km; rust perforation 5 years/unlimited km. **Supplementary warranty:** Not needed. **Options:** Nothing that's necessary. **Depreciation:** Should be much slower than average. **Insurance cost:** Likely to be higher than average. **Parts supply/cost:** Body parts may not be easily found. **Annual maintenance cost:** Likely to be less than average. **Highway/city fuel economy:** 10.2–11.2L/100 km.

SAFETY SUMMARY: The driver and front passenger's shoulder belts are attached to the rear doors. This means they must unbuckle their seat belts before the rear passengers can open their rear doors (assuming the front door is open). Windshield pillars are quite thick, and occasionally obscure vision when turning. **Airbags:** Front and side. **ABS:** optional; disc/disc. **Safety belt pretensioners:** Front. **Head restraints F/R:** ***. **Visibility F/R:** ***/*. **Side Crashworthiness:** Here's an interesting dilemma: NHTSA gives the Element top marks, while IIHS insurance safety group gives its lowest marks.

SAFETY COMPLAINTS: 2003—Many complaints related to windshield cracking (covered by a "goodwill" policy on a case-by-case basis). • Extensive low-speed collision damage. • Loose rear torsion bar nut.

Secret Warranties/Service Tips

2003—Windshield cracks in the lower corners due to an uneven flange surface (TSB #03-028, issued May 6, 2003). • Driver's seat rocks back and forth. • Troubleshooting ABS problems. **2003**—What to do when the tailgate rattles, Hatch Open indicator is on, and interior light is lit. **2003–04**—What to do when the tailgate rattles, Hatch Open indicator is on, and interior light is lit.

Element Profile

	2003	2004
Cost Price ($) (negotiable)		
Base (14%)	23,900	23,900
Used Values ($)		
Base Λ	19,000	21,000
Base V	17,500	19,500
Reliability	⑤	⑤
Crash Safety (F)	⑤	⑤
Side	⑤	⑤
IIHS Side	❶	❶
Offset	⑤	⑤
Rollover	③	—

Hyundai

SANTA FE   ★★★★

RATING: Above Average (2001–05). Japanese refinement at Korean prices.
Strong points: Smooth-shifting automatic transmission; very comfortable
ride; generous occupant space; practical, versatile interior; well appointed;
and good build and finish quality. **Weak points:** Underpowered with the
4-cylinder; little V6 reserve power; engine struggles with too-tall second
gearing; no low-range gearing; mediocre braking (rear drum brakes); excessive
engine noise; and thirsty around town. **New for 2005:** Tucson has anchored
the entry-level spot, meaning Santa Fe models will go a bit upscale in price and
equipment. Don't get overly impressed. **Likely failures:** The automatic transmission, electrical system, cruise control, catalytic converter, speedometer,
alternator, and fit and finish (water leaks). In rainy weather, air intake sucks
water into the engine and shorts out the mass air sensor (MAS).

2005 Technical Data

Powertrain
Engines: 2.4L 4-cyl. (150 hp)
• 2.7L (185 hp)
Transmissions: 5-speed man.
• 4-speed auto.
Dimension/Capacity
Height/length/width:
60/177/73 in.
Headroom F/R: 39.6/39.2 in.
Legroom F/R: 41.6/36.8 in.

Wheelbase: 103 in.
Turning circle: 40 ft.
Passengers: 2/3
Cargo volume: 30.5 cu. ft.
GVWR: 5,240 lb.
Tow limit: 2,000–2,700 lb.
Ground clear.: 8.1 in.
Fuel tank: 65L/reg.
Weight: 3,700 lb.

MODEL HISTORY: Hyundai's first sport-utility is essentially a Sonata with SUV amenities. It's about the same size as the Honda CR-V and the Ford Escape, but a bit wider and its interior room is slightly larger than either of the aforementioned vehicles. It's attractively styled, with a user-friendly cockpit, comfortable seating, and lots of storage areas.

Overall, the car's 1,678 kg (3,700 lb.) and puny 150-hp 2.4L 4-cylinder engine hamper performance considerably. The 185-hp V6 power plant's additional 35 horses still don't give this SUV wannabe sufficient power to overcome its heft. Handling is good, with responsive steering and a comfortable ride. The 4X4 system works efficiently, without any harshness or undue noise. There isn't any low-range gear; instead, a limited-slip rear differential does the job.

This small SUV has lots of potential because of its attractive styling, reasonable price, and comprehensive warranty. The powertrain shortcomings may not be very important if your driving requirements don't demand more performance than what this little SUV offers. **2003**—Front side airbags, an upgraded optional CD changer, and a garage door opener.

COST ANALYSIS: A 2005 Santa Fe GL sells for $21,050 and is likely to carry big discounts. **Best alternatives:** A used 2002 is a good buy, unless you really want the 2003's side airbag. Check out the Honda CR-V, Toyota RAV4, and Subaru Forester. Ford's pre-2005 Escape doesn't make the grade, and the Jeep Liberty is scary from a reliability perspective. **Rebates:** Rebates and discounting will remain strong due to a sharp downturn in sales during the first half of 2004. Look for $2,000 rebates early in the new year. **Delivery/PDI:** $505. **Warranty:** Bumper-to-bumper 3 years/60,000 km; powertrain 5 years/ 100,000 km; rust perforation 5 years/unlimited km. **Supplementary warranty:** Not necessary. **Options:** The GL option is a must for the V6 engine. **Depreciation:** Expected to be slower than average. **Insurance cost:** Average. **Parts supply/cost:** Santa Fe shares the compact Sonata platform, so parts should be easily found and reasonably priced. **Annual maintenance cost:** Predicted to be lower than average. **Highway/city fuel economy:** 9.3–12.6L/100 km with the V6; no data for the 2.4L.

QUALITY/RELIABILITY: Hyundai's quality control is a heck of a lot better than Detroit's Big Three and practically as good as Honda and Toyota. **Owner-reported problems:** Remarkably few complaints reported so far although there is a smattering of engine and transmission complaints. Owners also complain of a "rotten-egg" exhaust smell (yes, the catalytic converter is a prime suspect). **Warranty performance:** Much better than average, but as sales increase the company has become more insensitive to customer claims. We have now come full-circle since Hyundai angered Pony, Stellar, and Excel owners by denying warranty claims in the '70s, '80s, and '90s.

SAFETY SUMMARY: For some drivers, the rear-view mirror obstructs the right-side view. **Airbags:** Front. **ABS:** Optional; disc/drum. **Safety belt pretensioners:** Front. **Traction control:** Optional. **Head restraints F/R:**

****/***. **Visibility F/R:** Vision is clear in the front and rear. **Maximum load capacity:** 880 lb.

SAFETY COMPLAINTS: All years: Engine hesitates, then surges, causing unintended acceleration. • Windshield cracking. • Alternator failures drain battery and cause instruments and gauges to malfunction. • Check Engine light is constantly lit. **2001**—Fire ignited in the starter. • Airbags failed to deploy. • Steering wheel locks up while driving. • Sudden, unintended acceleration. • Chronic stalling and hesitation when accelerating. • Accelerator and pedal set too close together. • Power steering belt shredded repeatedly. • Refuelling made difficult because gas pump shuts off prematurely. • Defective speedometers and alternators replaced under a secret "'goodwill'" warranty. **2002**—Coolant leak onto engine caused fire. Premature failure of the transmission and engine. Passenger window suddenly shattered. • Loose wheel lug bolts. **2003**—Engine camshaft and axle failures. • Steering wheel wouldn't lock. **2004**—Vehicle will suddenly pull to the left while underway. • Complete brake failure; vehicle out of service for a month. • Sudden, unintended acceleration. • Airbag deployed for no reason. • Jerky automatic transmission engagement.

Secret Warranties/Service Tips

2001—A faulty automatic transaxle oil temperature sensor or solenoid may be the cause of poor shifting or no shifts. • Harsh or delayed Park-Reverse or Park-Drive engagement. • Engine runs and idles roughly. • Inoperative or intermittent operation of the sport mode switch. • Noise from rear wheels. • Front door wind noise. • Poor AM reception. **2001–02**—Delayed, erratic, and harsh shifts. • Front suspension knocking. **2001–03**—Cruise control disengages on its own. • Automatic transmission erratic performance or whining. • Headlight dimming. **2003**—Cruise control doesn't downshift. • 2.7L V6 engine oxygen sensor upgrade.

Santa Fe Profile

	2001	2002	2003	2004
Cost Price ($) (negotiable)				
GL	25,250	21,050	21,050	22,595
GLS	29,250	29,500	29,950	30,195
Used Values ($)				
GL ⋀	12,500	13,500	15,000	17,500
GL ⋁	11,500	12,500	13,500	16,000
GLS ⋀	15,500	18,000	20,000	24,500
GLS ⋁	14,000	16,500	18,000	23,500
Reliability	④	④	④	⑤
Crash Safety (F)	—	⑤	⑤	⑤
Side	—	⑤	⑤	⑤
IIHS side	—	③	③	③

Offset	⑤	⑤	⑤	⑤
Rollover	—	③	③	—

Note: Santa Fe prices are much more reasonable than those of Honda and Toyota models.

TUCSON ★

RATING: Not recommended (2005); this was its first year on the market. Choose the manual gearbox to avoid constant gear shifting **Strong points:** Reasonably priced; quiet and efficient 4X4 system; very comfortable ride. **Weak points:** Underpowered and undergeared; bland interior; no crashworthiness ratings; likely to be beset with numerous first-year factory-related deficiencies. **New for 2005:** Everything. **Likely failures:** The automatic transmission, electrical system, radio and AC accessories, and fit and finish.

2005 Technical Data

Powertrain
Engines: 2.0L 4-cyl. (140 hp)
• 2.7L (173 hp)
Transmissions: 5-speed man.
• 4-speed auto.
Dimension/Capacity
Height/length/width:
66.1/170.3/70.7 in.
Headroom F/R: 40.2/38.8 in.
Legroom F/R: 42.1/37.2 in.
Wheelbase: 103.5 in.
Turning circle: 35.6 ft.
Passengers: 2/3
Cargo volume: 28 cu. ft.
GVWR: N/A.
Tow limit: N/A.
Ground clear.: 8.1 in.
Fuel tank: 55L/reg.
Weight: 3,250 lb.

MODEL HISTORY: Hyundai's second and smallest sport-utility is built on a strengthened and stretched Elantra platform and provides two more cubic feet of passenger space than its bigger brother, the Santa Fe (cargo volume is less). The interior looks fairly low-tech and uses cheap-looking plastics everywhere. The powertrain is also borrowed from the Elantra, with the addition of four-wheel drive. This little SUV is in dire need of an engine or transmission transplant. The optional 2.7L V6 is harnessed to a "manumatic" 4-speed automatic transmission, a setup that leads to excessive gear-hunting, imprecise automatic-to-manual shifting, and compromised fuel economy. What's really needed is a conventional 5-speed or the Santa Fe's 3.5L, 200-hp V6 to handle the Tucson's heft.

While we're on the subject of weight, the Tuscon is heavier than the CR-V and Toyota RAV4, but this doesn't lead to a mushy ride or degrade handling inordinately, Nevertheless, true handling enthusiasts will throw their lot in with the RAV4 or Escape/Tribute to get their performance thrills.

Infiniti

FX35, FX45 ★★★★

RATING: Above Average (2003–05). A luxury SUV for buyers secretly wanting a sports sedan. **Strong points:** The FX35 rivals BMW's X5 in its car-like handling. Excellent acceleration, steering response, and braking; good fuel economy; and predicted to be more reliable than the competition. Few safety-related complaints. **Weak points:** The AWD lacks low-range gearing and is not intended for off-roading. An uncomfortable, stiff, jerky ride when going over road imperfections. Annoying tire noise and excessive exhaust roar. The sports sedan driving position isn't for everyone with its low driving position, sloping rear hatch, and high window line creating a claustrophobic feeling. Sporty interior limits cargo space and impairs visibility through the narrow rear windshield. Power front seat, dash- and steering-mounted controls are confusing and not user-friendly. Premium fuel is required. **New for 2005:** Nothing important.

2005 Technical Data

Powertrain (4X4)
Engine: 3.5L V6 (280 hp)
4.5L V8 (315 hp)
Transmission: 5-speed man./auto.
Dimension/Capacity
Height/length/width:
65/188.5/76.7 in.
Headroom F/R: 40.8/39.5 in.
Legroom F/R: 43.9/35.2 in.
Wheelbase: 112 in.

Turning circle: 42 ft.
Passengers: 2/3
Cargo volume: 29 cu. ft.
GVWR: 5,164/5,462 lb.
Payload: 1,100 lb.
Tow limit: 3,500 lb.
Ground clearance: 7.0 in.
Fuel tank: 79L/prem.
Weight: 4,295 lb.

MODEL HISTORY: Launched in 2003, this crossover model is a high-performance, 5-passenger, 4-door wagon spin-off of Infiniti's G35 sedan. The FX35 comes with a 3.5L V6 and rear- or all-wheel drive, while the FX45 has a 4.5L V8 and comes only with AWD. Every FX has ABS, anti-skid/traction control, front torso side airbags, head-protecting curtain side airbags, and xenon headlights. The FX35 comes with 18-inch wheels. A sport suspension with 20-inch wheels is standard for the FX45, optional for FX35.

COST ANALYSIS: Best alternatives: Go for a discounted 2004, since the 2005s are practically the same and plenty of 2004s remain in stock. The FX beats BMW's X5 in almost every category. The Lexus RX 300 and Toyota Highlander are good alternatives because they are more highway-proven and dealers will have more choices available. **Rebates:** Not likely due to the popularity and limited availability of these models. **Delivery/PDI:** $1,160 (Talk about greed!). **Warranty:** Bumper-to-bumper 4 years/100,000 km; powertrain 6 years/100,000 km; rust perforation 7 years/unlimited km. **Supplementary warranty:** Not necessary. **Options:** A sunroof and roof rails. **Depreciation:** Much slower than average. **Insurance cost:** Higher than average. **Parts supply/cost:** Average parts supply but relatively costly. **Annual maintenance cost:** Lower than average, so far. **Highway/city fuel economy:** 11.9–15.6L/100 km; real world experience is much less.

QUALITY/RELIABILTY: No serious reliability problems have been reported during the first year on the market. **Owner-reported problems:** Some body trim defects and premature front brake wear and noise. **Warranty performance:** Better than average.

SAFETY SUMMARY: Airbags: Side airbags are standard. Reports of airbags failing to deploy. **Child safety seat hard to install. ABS:** Standard 4W; disc/disc. **Safety belt pretensioners:** Standard. **Traction control:** Standard. **Head restraints F/R:** *2003:* *****. **Visibility F/R:** ***/**. **Maximum load capacity:** 950 lb.

FX35/FX45 Profile

	2004
Cost Price ($) (firm)	
FX35 (20%)	52,700
FX45 (20%)	60,200
Used Values ($)	
FX35 ↑	45,000
FX35 ↓	43,000
FX45 ↑	52,000
FX45 ↓	50,000
Reliability	⑤
Crash Safety (F)	⑤
Side	⑤
Offset	⑤

QX4, QX56 ★★★★

RATING: Above Average (1997–2005). With its more powerful engine, the QX4 became a real competitor; too bad 2003 was its last model year. **Strong points:** Impressive acceleration on 2001 and later models; attractively styled;

mostly posh interior; front seats are especially supportive; reasonably priced, with a long list of standard features; automatic 4X4; cargo bay has a low, wide opening; and a slow rate of depreciation. Excellent front and side crashworthiness scores, and few safety-related complaints. **Weak points:** Feeble acceleration with earlier models; rear-wheel-only ABS; rear drum brakes; limited rear legroom; no third-row seat; fake wood interior trim; interior door handles are too small; rear windows don't roll all the way down; small, narrow rear door openings; useless running boards; the cargo area is long and rather shallow; and a gas guzzler. Average reliability. Low ground clearance and large bumpers limit off-road capabilities. Below-average offset crashworthiness and head restraint scores. QX56 models are way overpriced for what you get and depreciate rather dramatically. **New for 2005:** Nothing important.

2005 Technical Data

Powertrain (4X4)
Engine: 3.5L V6 (240 hp)
Transmission: 4-speed auto.
Dimension/Capacity
Height/length/width:
70.7/183.1/72.4 in.
Headroom F/R: 38.1/37.5 in.
Legroom F/R: 41.7/31.8 in.
Wheelbase: 106.3 in.

Turning circle: 42 ft.
Passengers: 2/3
Cargo volume: 34.5 cu. ft.
GVWR: 4,934 lb.
Tow limit: 5,000 lb.
Ground clearance: 8.3 in.
Fuel tank: 79L/reg.
Weight: 4,300 lb.

MODEL HISTORY: In 1997, Nissan waved its magic wand and created another Infiniti out of what was once a Nissan—in this case, a Nissan Pathfinder with about 130 extra kilos (288 lbs.). Don't be surprised—it has been done before with the Altima/G20 and Maxima/I30. What is surprising, though, is that people are likely to buy these high-priced clones simply because they carry the Infiniti moniker.

2001—A larger 240-hp, 3.5L V6 engine and reworked instrument panel; improved power window controls; xenon headlights (you'll love 'em; your neighbours won't); minor exterior re-styling; a new roof rack; and a redesigned grille. The previous model had only a 3.3L, 170-hp V6 with lower torque. It barely provided adequate performance for the 1,810+ kg (4,000+ lb.) truck. **2004**—The QX56 was spun off the Nissan Titan platform, and will target Lexus LX 470 and Lincoln Navigator buyers.

COST ANALYSIS: A 2004 QX4 goes for $48,800; get it, rather than spending more for an identical 2005 version. **Best alternatives:** Pre-2001 models changed little over the years, so look for the cheapest model available. If you want 40 extra horses with the V6 and convenience upgrades, a second-series 2001 would be the best choice. Credible alternatives would be the Lexus RX 300, Nissan Xterra, and Toyota Highlander. **Rebates:** Look for $3,000–$4,000 rebates or zero percent financing programs. **Delivery/PDI:** $1,160 (wow!). **Warranty:** Bumper-to-bumper 4 years/100,000 km; powertrain 6 years/100,000 km; rust perforation 7 years/unlimited km.

Supplementary warranty: Not needed. **Options:** Save your money. **Depreciation:** A bit slower than average. **Insurance cost:** Higher than average. **Parts supply/cost:** Good parts supply but relatively costly. Body parts may be back-ordered. **Annual maintenance cost:** Lower than average, so far. **Highway/city fuel economy:** 11.9–15.6L/100 km.

QUALITY/RELIABILTY: Infiniti quality control is better than average—as good as Honda and Toyota. **Owner-reported problems:** Some body trim defects; automatic transmission slippage; premature front brake wear and noise; minor electrical glitches; windshield wiper fluid discolours paint; lift-gate sensor beeps for no reason; and headliner squeaks and rattles. **Warranty performance:** Better than average.

SAFETY SUMMARY: Airbags: Side airbags are standard. Reports of airbags failing to deploy. **ABS:** Standard 4W; disc/drum. **Safety belt pretensioners:** Standard. **Traction control:** Optional. **Head restraints F/R:** *1997:* *; *1999:* **; *2001–03:* ****. **Visibility F/R:** *****. **Maximum load capacity:** 860 lb.

SAFETY COMPLAINTS: All years: Hesitation, followed by sudden acceleration. • Airbags failed to deploy. **1997**—While driving, driver-side rear wheel fell off. • Defective coil springs cause the vehicle to lean to the left. • Cracked exhaust manifold. **1998**—Complete brake failure. • Rear shock failure. • Frequent emission system repairs. **1999**—Sudden loss of steering control, steering lock up, excessive vibration. • Excessive drive shaft vibration. • Distorted front windshield. **2000**—Under-hood fire. **2001**—Airbags failed to deploy. • Stalling when going uphill. • Early automatic transmission replacement. • Complete brake failure. **2002**—Rear suspension bottoms out with four passengers in the car. • Inaudible turn signal indicator. **2003**—Severe rear brake pulsation. **2004**—Passenger's airbag turns off intermittently due to passenger's "light" weight (120 lb. is not light!).

Secret Warranties/Service Tips

1997—Improvement of brake pedal feel. • Reducing A-pillar wind noise. • Causes of poor AC cooling and excessive noise coming from the AC idler pulley bearing. **1997–98**—Fixing a high-pitched squeal or whistle from the front hub or brake area. • Silencing wind noise or rattling coming from the roof rack area. • Remedies for excessive pull to one side and too much play in the front and rear suspension. **1997–2000**—Remedy for steering wheel vibration, brake pedal pulsation. • Service tips to silence a rear hatch that squeaks or rattles. **1998–2000**—Tips on troubleshooting hard starts at high elevation or low temperatures after vehicle has been parked a few hours. **2001**—Automatic transmission flares on the 1–2 shift when accelerating from a hard stop and then backing off on the throttle. • Engine won't start, or fails to start intermittently. • Incorrect engine idle speed. • Steering fluid leak near the pump hose fitting. **2001–02**—Transfer-case oil leak, clunk, or stuck in Low gear. • Steering column noise. • Speaker static. • Navigation system freezes. **2002–03**—Roof rack whistle. **2003–04**—Vibration/shudder may be related to low engine oil.

QX4, QX56 Profile

	1997	1998	1999	2000	2001	2002	2003	2004
Cost Price ($) (negotiable)								
Base (20%)	47,900	45,000	45,700	45,500	48,000	48,000	48,800	—
QX56	—	—	—	—	—	—	—	69,550
Used Values ($)								
Base ▲	10,500	13,000	16,000	20,000	24,000	30,000	35,000	—
Base ▼	8,500	11,500	14,000	18,000	22,000	28,000	33,000	—
QX56 ▲	—	—	—	—	—	—	—	56,000
QX56 ▼	—	—	—	—	—	—	—	51,000
Reliability	⑤	⑤	⑤	⑤	④	④	⑤	⑤
Crash Safety (F)	③	—	④	④	④	④	—	—
Side	—	—	⑤	⑤	⑤	⑤	⑤	—
Offset	❷	❷	❷	❷	❷	❷	❷	—
Rollover	—	—	—	—	③	③	③	—

Kia

SPORTAGE ★

RATING: Not Recommended (2000–05). Only for city use; lacks refinement; minimally acceptable performance. There was no 2003 or 2004 model. The 2005 is pretty much an unknown, though it is expected to be more Hyundai than Kia. Nevertheless, wait at least a year before investing in this new Sportage. **Strong points:** Reasonably priced, with lots of discounting. Plenty of headroom for six-footers but insufficient rear legroom unless riding in a wagon. Good fuel economy. Very few real-world consumer complaints on previous-year models. **Weak points:** Slow, hard riding, clumsy, unstable, unimpressive crashworthiness and quality control scores, and an uncertain future. As if that's not enough, there are other deficiencies, including less-effective rear drum brakes, a constantly shifting automatic transmission, part-time 4X4 that's not suited for dry pavement use, uneven interior ventilation, a noisy engine and fan, obstructed rear visibility with raised convertible top, and tight rear seating. **New for 2005:** A more carlike and refined Sportage will return. Essentially a twin of the Hyundai Tucson sport wagon, it will use the Elantra/Spectra platform.

2002 Technical Data

Powertrain (4X4)
Engine: 2.0L 4-cyl. (130 hp)
Transmission: 4-speed auto.
Dimension/Capacity
Height/length/width:
65/156.4/68.1 in.
Headroom F/R: 39.6/39.8 in.
Legroom F/R: 44.5/31.1 in.
Wheelbase: 92.9 in.

Turning circle: 37 ft.
Passengers: 2/3
Cargo volume: 30 cu. ft.
GVWR: 4,156 lb.
Tow limit: 2,000 lb.
Ground clearance: 7.9 in.
Fuel tank: 60L/reg.
Weight: 3,365 lb.

MODEL HISTORY: The Sportage is a rudimentary compact sport-utility that's an unimpressive performer. Although it was once rated the "worst" choice among small sport-utilities by Consumers Union, owner complaints aren't that numerous and technical service bulletins are fairly benign.

Sportage is offered as a five-passenger, four-door wagon or a four-passenger, two-door convertible. The only engine available is an anemic 130-hp 2.0L 4-cylinder, attached to either a rear-drive or 4X4 system.

Kia has only been in Canada a few years, yet it has sold an impressive number of cars, thanks to its extensive warranty and low prices. Recently bought out of bankruptcy by Hyundai, Kia now has the money to bring out new products and expand its North American dealer network. As fuel prices continue to rise, sales of Kia's entry-level cars and SUVs should continue to be strong.

COST ANALYSIS: Best alternatives: Consider Honda's CR-V, Hyundai's Santa Fe, or the Toyota RAV4. Nissan's Xterra or Toyota's Highlander are good second choices. **Rebates:** Not applicable until production starts again. **Supplementary warranty:** A good idea, judging by the poor quality record. **Depreciation:** A bit slower than average. **Insurance cost:** Higher than average. **Annual maintenance cost:** Much higher than average due to the simple fact that dealers aren't investing in parts and service for a model that's not being sold. **Parts supply/cost:** Parts aren't easily found, but they are reasonably priced. **Highway/city fuel economy:** 10.3–11.9L/100 km with an automatic transmission.

QUALITY/RELIABILITY: Although Hyundai owns Kia and has received impressive quality-control ratings for its own models, poor quality scores continue to dog Kia's entire model lineup. The J.D. Power and Associates Initial Quality Study has placed Kia at or near dead last in its annual survey every year since 1993, forcing the company's American COO to admit that "up until 1999, the company wasn't focused on quality." **Owner-reported problems:** Fuel and electrical system malfunctions, transmission glitches, AC water leaks, premature catalytic converter, brake pad and rotor replacement, and poor body fit and finish (rattles, paint peeling, and doors often ajar, wind noise from all doors). **Warranty performance:** Average.

SAFETY SUMMARY: Airbags: Kia includes a unique knee-level airbag to protect the lower extremities. **ABS:** Optional 4W; disc/drum. **Head restraints F/R:** *1997:* ***; *1999:* ***; *2001–02:* **. **Visibility F/R:** *****/*. **Maximum load capacity:** *1999 EX:* 860 lb. **Front crashworthiness**: Although there's no recent NHTSA frontal crash tests, the 1997 model (not sold in Canada) garnered three stars.

SAFETY COMPLAINTS: All years: Fumes enter passenger compartment when driving. • Defective front hub assembly won't let drive shift into 4X4 "on-the-fly." • During highway driving, vehicle vibrates excessively. • Vehicle veers from right to left due to faulty suspension. • When driving, 4X4 comes on and off on its own, leading to vehicle almost going off the road. • Brake lights won't turn off • Sudden failure of the turn signals and flashers. • Seat belts tighten uncomfortably on their own. • Gears grind as they shift into Third or Fourth. • Excessive shaking when braking. • Airbag and ABS lights stay on. • Driver-side shoulder belt doesn't work. • Water leaks through the door frame. **2001**—Chronic stalling. Complete brake failure. • Low-speed rear-ender caused seatback to collapse. • Vehicle pulls to one side upon acceleration, or rocks side to side when turning. • Dash indicators fail from blown fuse. • Fuel tank hard to refuel. **2001–02**—Airbags failed to deploy. • Very loose steering. • Check Engine light is constantly lit. • Doors won't latch unless pulled up when closing. **2002**—Airbags failed to deploy. Airbag light is constantly lit. • Panel lights go out intermittently. • Steering locked up. • Prematurely worn brake rotors. • Rear seats move backward or forward when accelerating or braking. • Fuel tank filler spout spits out fuel when refuelling.

Secret Warranties/Service Tips

2001–02—Free catalytic converter replacement under emissions campaign #022. • Front windows won't close at freeway speeds. • Airbag warning light stays lit.

Sportage Profile

	2001	2002
Cost Price ($) (negotiable)		
Sportage (17%)	20,995	22,095
Used Values ($)		
Sportage ⋀	10,500	13,000
Sportage ⋁	9,000	11,500
Reliability	③	③
Crash Safety (Offset)	❷	❷

SORENTO ★

RATING: Not Recommended (2003–05). The Sorento's a particularly risky buy during its first two years on the market, due to Kia's history of poor quality control with early-years models and of "bailing out" when the model doesn't sell. **Strong points:** Reasonably priced with lots of standard features, handles well, true off-road capability, and comprehensive warranty coverage. **Weak points:** Engine needs more power, mediocre braking, poor fuel economy, cheap-looking seat upholstery, and a tacky plastic dash. **New for 2005:** Nothing significant. **Likely failures:** Fuel and electrical systems.

2005 Technical Data

Powertrain (4X4)
Engine: 3.5L 4-cyl. (192 hp)
Transmission: 4-speed auto.
Dimension/Capacity
Height/length/width:
69.3/179.8/74.6 in.
Headroom F/R: 38.38 in.
Legroom F/R: 42.6/36.1 in.
Wheelbase: 106.7 in.

Turning circle: 36.4 ft.
Passengers: 2/3
Cargo volume: 31.4 cu. ft.
GVWR: 5,644 lb.
Tow limit: 3,500 lb.
Ground clearance: 8.2 in.
Fuel tank: 80L/reg.
Weight: 4,255 lb.

MODEL HISTORY: This SUV crossover and Honda Pilot look-alike carries passenger-car genes in a compact SUV body. Although the "torque on demand" 4X4 system is better suited for slippery surfaces than off-road cavorting, the Sorento's full- and part-time low range gearing gives it a decided off-road advantage over Honda. Other off-road assets: a wide track, fully independent suspension, high ground clearance, and short front and rear overhangs.

The Sorento's wheelbase is within half an inch of the Pilot's wheelbase, and it has a similar 3.5L V6 power plant. You won't find the Pilot's third-row seating, though, nor the fuel-saving 5-speed automatic transmission. **2004—** Engine and transmission upgrades

COST ANALYSIS: Best alternatives: Choose the 2004 version ($29,900) if it's discounted enough. The Honda CR-V and Pilot, Hyundai Santa Fe, Nissan Murano, or Toyota Highlander are also good choices. **Rebates:** Look for $3,000 rebates or zero percent financing programs. **Delivery/PDI:** $610. **Warranty:** Bumper-to-bumper 5 years/100,000 km; powertrain 5 years/100,000 km; rust perforation 5 years/100,000 km. **Supplementary warranty:** Always a good idea with Kia. **Options:** Side running boards. **Depreciation:** Slower than average. **Insurance cost:** Higher than average. **Parts supply/cost:** Not easily found (only 5,000 units will be shipped to Canada and dealers loath huge parts inventories), reasonably priced. **Annual maintenance cost:** Average. **Highway/city fuel economy:** 13.1–15.7L/100 km.

QUALITY/RELIABILITY: Average. **Owner-reported problems:** Excessive drive shaft vibration and fuel and electrical system malfunctions (chronic starting problems). **Warranty performance:** Average.

SAFETY SUMMARY: Thick roof pillars cut visibility; large side mirrors compensate somewhat. **Airbags:** Standard front and side airbags. **ABS:** Optional 4W; disc/disc. **Head restraints F/R**: ****/***. **Visibility F/R:** ***. **Maximum load capacity:** 1,213 lb.

SAFETY COMPLAINTS: 2003—Airbags failed to deploy. • Power-steering failures. • Defective front axle (gear oil leakage).

Secret Warranties/Service Tips

2003—Enhanced power-steering feel. • Hood anti-corrosion treatment. • Rattling heard from the jack compartment. • Service campaign to inspect and re-position the driver seat belt buckle wire harness.

Sorento Profile

	2003	2004
Cost Price ($) (negotiable)		
Sorento (17%)	29,795	29,845
Used Values ($)		
Sorento ⋀	21,500	25,000
Sorento ⋁	20,000	23,000
Reliability	③	④
Crash Safety	④	④
Side	⑤	⑤
Offset	⑤	—
IIHS offset	③	③
Rollover	③	—

Lexus

GX 470, LX 450, LX 470 ★★★★

RATING: Above Average (1998–2005); Average (1997). An overpriced Toyota 4Runner. **Strong points:** Strong, smooth V8 engine performance, carlike handling, an adjustable suspension, hill descent control, user-friendly instrumentation and controls, lots of passenger and cargo room, comfortable seating, pleasant ride, excellent fit and finish, and exceptional reliability. "Good" head restraint crashworthiness score (LX 470). **Weak points:** Acceleration is only fair, brakes are overly sensitive, and the ride can be busy.

Difficult middle-row entry/exit, antiquated rear-seat folding system (Honda's Pilot gets it right), cramped third-row seats, side-opening tailgate can be inconvenient, lots of tire and wind noise, poor fuel economy, requires premium fuel. Head restraints and roof pillars may obstruct rear vision. "Poor" head restraint crashworthiness score (LX 450). No front, side, or offset crashworthiness data. Tell the dealer to take a hike with his $1,500 freight charge. **New for 2005:** A roll-detection sensor for the head-protecting curtain side airbags.

2005 LX 470

Powertrain (4X4)	Turning circle: 39.7 ft.
Engine: 4.7L V8 (235 hp)	Passengers: 2/3/3
Transmission: 5-speed auto.	Cargo volume: 18 cu. ft.
Dimension/Capacity	GVWR: 6,100 lb.
Height/length/width:	Ground clearance: 9.8 in.
72.8/192.5/76.4 in.	Tow limit: 6,500 lb.
Headroom F/R1/R2: 39.1/39.4/38.9 in.	Fuel tank: 96L/prem.
Legroom F/R1/R2: 42.3/34.3/34.3 in.	Weight: 6,860 lb.
Wheelbase: 112.2 in.	

MODEL HISTORY: Launched in early 1998, the 230-hp 4.7L V8-equipped LX 470 still has all of its Land Cruiser trappings and a few additional features all its own, including a 2,903 kg (6,400 lb.) towing capacity, adaptive variable suspension, automatic height control, rear air conditioning, side running boards, and an in-dash CD changer. The 470 comes with only an automatic transmission, however.

The V8 engine, based on that of the Lexus LS 400, uses an iron block instead of aluminum and is modified to provide lots of low- and mid-range torque, essential to propel the 470's extra heft to 100 km/h in less than 10 seconds. Off-roading is no problem either, thanks to the transfer case's low-range gearing and a centre differential that locks in low range for better traction. These SUVs can seat up to six passengers in creature comfort, or seven with one drawing the short straw for the rear seat. Other sport-utilities have more room but not as much off-road capability.

2003 models were given additional airbags, a small horsepower boost, a new gated shifter for the 5-speed automatic, improved steering and brakes, a voice-controlled navigation system, 18-inch wheels, rain-sensing windshield wipers, radio controls on the steering wheel, and a new grille, bumper, headlights, and lower rear hatch.

Even though it was only around for the 1997 model year, the LX 450 offered a full array of safety, comfort, and convenience features that included full-time 4X4 and a nicely appointed interior. Additionally, owners were attracted to the SUV's benchmark quality, first-class assembly, and slow rate of depreciation. On the other hand, many buyers have been a bit reluctant to buy what is essentially a Land Cruiser with extra side cladding and prominent wheel arches. Other minuses: the LX 450 has ponderous handling and is a gas-guzzler equipped with a small fuel tank. The 450's 212-hp 4.5L inline 6-cylinder is hooked to an electronically controlled 4-speed automatic transmission.

The LX 470 version replaced the LX 450 for the 1998 model year and remained unchanged over the next several model years.

GX 470

Having made its debut in early 2003, the GX 470 is a mid-sized, four-door luxury SUV that bridges the price and performance gap between the RX 300 series and the LX 470. With promised seating for eight adults (don't be too hopeful), this new entry has a minivan's passenger-carrying capability without minivan "mommy-mobile" cachet.

Overall, it's slightly shorter, wider, taller, and heavier than a Ford Explorer, with a bit less cargo space: 4.78 metres (188.2 inches) long, 1.88 metres (74 inches) wide, 1.89 metres (74.6 inches) tall, on a 2.79-metre (109.8-inch) wheelbase, and weighing 2,120 kg (4,675 lb.) Towing capability is rated as 2,268 kg (5,000 lb.).

Set on a modified truck platform and lacking an independent rear suspension, the GX 470 doesn't have as comfortable a ride nor is it as manoeuvrable as its car-based brethren. A new feature called Downhill Assist Control helps drivers maintain control on very steep descents (I still think independent rear suspension would be more useful). Power is supplied by Toyota's 292-hp 4.7L V8, which is also used in the Sequoia and the LX 470.

Sold only in the United States since January 2003, Canadian buyers would be wise to shy away from this SUV until it has been on the market a few more years. Canadian dealers will then be more familiar with its care and feeding, and prices will likely moderate.

COST ANALYSIS: Best alternatives: Since a new LX 470 costs $100,400, try to find a cheaper and practically identical 2004 for about $10,000 less. Some credible Toyota alternatives: a 4Runner or Sequoia. **Rebates:** Expect $3,000 rebates and low-financing programs to kick in by early 2005. **Delivery/PDI:** An excessive $1,520. **Warranty:** Bumper-to-bumper 4 years/80,000 km; power-train 6 years/110,000 km; rust perforation 6 years/unlimited km. **Supplementary warranty:** Not necessary. **Options:** None. **Depreciation:** Much slower than average. **Insurance cost:** Above average. **Annual maintenance cost:** Average. **Parts supply/cost:** Good parts supply, but parts can be costly. **Highway/city fuel economy:** 11.6–15.7L/100 km.

SAFETY SUMMARY: Airbags: Standard front and side airbags. Reports of airbags failing to deploy. **ABS:** Standard 4W; disc/disc. **Safety belt pretensioners:** Standard. **Traction control:** Standard. **Head restraints F/R:** *1997 LX 450:* *; *1999:* ***; *2001–03 LX 470:* ****; *GX 470:* ***. **Visibility F/R:** ****/**. **Maximum load capacity:** 1,459 lb. **Crashworthiness:** Amazingly, these luxo-toys have never been crash-tested by the NHTSA.

SAFETY COMPLAINTS: LX 450: 1997—Many complaints that vehicle suddenly accelerated. • At highway speeds, the front of the car becomes unstable, with the left and right side alternately rising and falling. • Sudden deceleration when the cruise control is shut off. • Odometer and gauges can't be seen well in daylight. • Alternator and Michelin tire failures. **LX 470: 1998**—The brake pedal needs to be pumped to reach a satisfactory pedal height. • Automatic height adjustment failure. **1999**—Airbag failed to deploy. **2000**—Unintended sudden acceleration. • Premature Michelin tire wear. **2003**—Airbags failed to deploy. **2004**—Engine surges when the AC compressor is activated. • Gas tank will only fill up two-thirds of the way.

Secret Warranties/Service Tips

LX 450: 1997—Troubleshooting tips for correcting delayed engagement from Park to Reverse or Neutral to Reverse. **LX 470: 1998**—Tips on reducing front and rear brake rattles and cabin squeaks and rattles. • Tips on troubleshooting excessive wind noise. • A front suspension buzz noise can be corrected by replacing the lower control arm ball-joint snap ring. **1998–99**—AC noise can be silenced by replacing the expansion valve. • Roof-rack wind noises may be caused by improperly installed crossbars. **1998–2000**—If the AC fan continues to run after the ignition has been turned off, it's likely caused by a corroded relay. Lexus has a repair kit that will correct the problem. • To eliminate a transfer-case buzzing at moderate speeds, TSB #NV008-00 suggests installing an upgraded high-speed output gear and shift lever assembly. • The in-dash CD player and changer may work erratically. Lexus will replace it under warranty. **1998–2003**—Booming sound at idle. • Steering column noise/roughness. **2001–02**—Front brake vibration. • Continuous alarm chime noise. • Upgrade to reduce telescopic steering wheel noise and enhance smoothness. **2002**—Brake vibration. • Noisy, rough telescopic steering. • Upgraded rear-view mirror.

GX470, LX 450, LX 470 Profile

	1997	1998	1999	2000	2001	2002	2003	2004
Cost Price ($) (negotiable)								
GX 470	—	—	—	—	—	—	—	66,800
LX 450, 470 (23%)	72,300	82,000	83,265	83,265	90,100	90,600	98,200	99,950
Used Values ($)								
GX 470 ⋀	—	—	—	—	—	—	—	60,000
GX 470 ⋁	—	—	—	—	—	—	—	57,800
LX 450, 470 ⋀	20,000	25,000	34,000	39,000	47,000	56,000	69,000	77,000
LX 450, 470 ⋁	17,000	22,000	31,000	36,000	43,000	53,000	65,000	74,000
Reliability	④	⑤	⑤	⑤	⑤	⑤	⑤	⑤
IIHS Offset (GX)	—	—	—	—	—	—	—	⑤

RX 300, RX 330 ★★★★

RATING: Above Average (1999–2005). The rating has been lowered due to Toyota's engine sludge problems and delayed automatic transmission shifts that have yet to be resolved. Both vehicles are ideal for light-duty chores and driving in inclement weather, but not for serious off-roading. Consider the Highlander as a cheaper, more refined alternative. **Strong points:** *RX 300:* Strong powertrain performance; handles well; fully equipped; top-quality mechanical components and fit and finish; pleasant riding (better than the Acura MDX and Mercedes' M series); plenty of passenger room; very comfortable seating; lots of small storage areas; easy entry/exit; slow depreciation. Reliability has been its strong suit over many years. *RX 330:* A bit more powerful and quieter, longer, wider, slightly taller, and uses a longer wheelbase than its predecessor. Comfortable rear seats are adjustable for rake, and easily folded out of the way. Better interior ergonomics, and ride comfort doesn't deteriorate with a full load. Much better emergency handling than with the RX 300. Improved fuel economy; can take regular unleaded fuel. Predicted to be quite reliable. **Weak points:** *RX 300:* Pricey, and too big and heavy for sporty handling. No low-range gearing for off-roading, and traction control is optional. Thick roof pillars obstruct outward visibility. Instrument displays wash out in direct sunlight. Tilt steering wheel may not tilt sufficiently for some drivers. Expect some wind noise, squeaks, and rattles, in addition to wind roar from the moon roof. Limited rear storage area, with a high liftover and excessive wind noise. Takes premium fuel. *RX 330:* Additional power undermined by added kilos. Dangerous shift delay when downshifting with the automatic transmission. Considerable body lean when cornering, suspension bottoms out easily, and steering could be more sensitive. Front and rear seat cushions lack thigh support. Thick rear roof panels obstruct visibility. No third-row seating and sloping rear end cuts into cargo space. Power rear door is slow to open and moon roof takes too much headroom. Reduced ground clearance. The optional navigation system screen washes out in sunlight. High freight charges would make Tony Soprano proud. Overpriced when compared to the Toyota Sienna or Highlander. **New for 2005:** A hybrid RX 400H will go on sale in December 2004.

2005 Technical Data

Powertrain (4X4)
Engine: 3.0L V6 (220 hp)
Transmission: 4-speed auto.
Dimension/Capacity
Height/length/width:
70.7/180.1/71.5 in.
Headroom F/R: 40.4/39.6/38.6 in.
Legroom F/R: 39.4/55.6/42.5 in.

Wheelbase: 103.1 in.
Turning circle: 43 ft.
Passengers: 2/3
Cargo volume: 37.8 cu. ft.
GVWR: 4,950 lb.
Ground clearance: 7 in.
Tow limit: 3,500 lb.
Fuel tank: 73L/prem.
Weight: 3,925 lb.

2004 RX 330 Technical Data

Powertrain (4X4)	Wheelbase: 106.9 in.
Engine: 3.3L V6 (230 hp)	Turning circle: 37.4 ft.
Transmission: 5-speed auto.	Passengers: 2/3
Dimension/Capacity	Cargo volume: 38.3 cu. ft.
Height/length/width:	GVWR: 5,245 lb.
66/186/73 in.	Ground clearance: 5.9 in.
Headroom F/R: 39.4/NA/38.6 in.	Tow limit: 3,500 lb.
Legroom F/R: 42.5/NA/36.4 in.	Fuel tank: 65L/reg.
	Weight: 4,065 lb.

MODEL HISTORY: The RX 300 is a compact luxury sport-utility, based partly on Toyota's passenger-car platform. It's a bit longer and wider than a Jeep Grand Cherokee, and is sold as either a front-drive or permanent all-wheel drive. Available only with a 4-speed automatic transmission and a Camry/Lexus ES 300-derived, upgraded 220-hp V6, the RX 300 handles competently on the highway, but isn't suitable for off-roading due to its lack of low-range gearing and tall, four-door wagon body.

First launched in Canada as a 1999 model, the RX 300 was a pioneer "crossover" SUV that combined minivan versatility with the practicality of a 4X4 drivetrain, suitable for light tasks. And, as practically the only game in town for its first several years on the market, many critics ignored this Lexus' many shortcomings and aging design. Now that's all changed, with Acura, Ford, Nissan, Hyundai, and Toyota raising the bar with their cutting-edge SUVs, and in Toyota's case, a revamped Sienna minivan that offers the same features and performs as well, for lots less money.

RX 330

Introduced as a 2004 replacement for the RX 300, Lexus calls the RX 330 a "luxury utility vehicle." And, yes, it does eclipse the old model with its many luxury features and extra-cost gadgets, extra interior room, and an upgraded powertrain. But, in many ways, competing minivans have more utility, more room inside, more seats, and even, as in the new 2004 Toyota Sienna, 4X4 drive. All they lack is the RX 330's luxury cachet.

The RX 330 offers a good ride, a plush and innovative interior, great all-around visibility, plenty of power, all-wheel drive, and predicted top-notch quality and reliability. Not bad for a bestselling SUV cobbled together from ES 330, Camry, and Sienna parts.

COST ANALYSIS: Best alternatives: *RX 330:* Consider buying a 2004 second-series base model for $49,900; you'll get fewer first-year glitches and pay less than what a 2005 costs. Any used RX 300 is also a good buy, if you can find one that's sufficiently discounted. However, the RX 330 is by far the better buy, if you stay away from its many frivolous and costly optional gadgets. Other vehicles worth considering are the Nissan Murano and the Toyota 4Runner, Sienna, or Highlander. **Rebates:** Not likely. **Delivery/PDI:**

$1,535. **Warranty:** Bumper-to-bumper 4 years/80,000 km; powertrain 6 years/ 110,000 km; rust perforation 6 years/unlimited km. **Supplementary warranty:** Not necessary. **Options:** The $7,000+ Premium Package bundled options is a waste of money. On the RX 300, the moon roof has generated many complaints of excessive wind noise entering the cabin. **Depreciation:** Value practically stands still. **Insurance cost:** Above average. **Parts supply/cost:** Parts are taken from the Camry bin and are reasonably priced. **Annual maintenance cost:** Average. **Highway/city fuel economy:** *RX 300:* 9.7–13L/100 km; *RX 330:* 9–12.8L/100 km. Incidentally, putting regular fuel in your RX 330 should save you at least $200 annually, wiping out the car's price premium in just a few years.

QUALITY/RELIABILITY: Good quality control, although some powertrain reliability-related defects and sudden acceleration incidents reported. **Owner-reported problems:** The automatic transmission lurches between gears and lags in shifting at low speeds, making the car vulnerable to being rear-ended. The fuel gauge gives inaccurate readings, and there have been some minor electrical shorts, excessive brake noise, and a variety of interior squeaks and rattles. Also, there are some body trim defects and the instrument panel display may be too dim. **Warranty performance:** Fair. Toyota and Lexus stupidly blamed owners for costly engine sludge defects and haven't effectively tackled the lurching transmission problem:

> My 2004 Lexus RX 330 AWD has a problem with the transmission "hanging" on the 2–3 upshift. The car hesitates then roughly shifts into the next gear. It has never shifted as smoothly in any gear as other Lexus and Toyota products I've driven. I went to the dealer and the dealer reprogrammed the engine management control. The net result has been that the engine shifts at a higher rpm than it did before, but is still not smooth. The hesitation between gears was less frequent for a week or two after the reprogram, but has now returned and there is an increasing lag or hesitation in shifting in the 2–3 and 3–4 upshift.

SAFETY SUMMARY: Airbags: Standard front and head-protection side airbags; a driver's knee airbag. There have been reports of airbags failing to deploy. **ABS:** Standard; disc/disc. **Safety belt pretensioners:** Standard. **Traction control:** Standard. **Head restraints F/R:** *1999: ***; 2001–03: *****.* **Visibility F/R:** *****/**.* **Maximum load capacity:** *1999:* 880 lb.; *2001:* 840 lb.; *2003 (RX 330):* 925 lb.

SAFETY COMPLAINTS: All years: Sudden, unintended acceleration. • Airbags failed to deploy. **1999**—Engine overheating and under-hood fires. • Car suddenly accelerated when shifted from Reverse to Drive. • Right rear axle sheared in two, causing the wheel to fall off and vehicle to roll over. **2000**— During hard acceleration from a standing start on dry pavement, the left front tire loses traction and spins free, causing vehicle to veer to the left. • A power distribution problem in the transfer case causes the wheels to lock up at 100 km/h. • Displays on the instrument panel are too dim. • If the wireless remote entry is used to lock the vehicle with an occupant inside, that person may be trapped inside if the vehicle isn't exited within 30 seconds. • When vehicle is travelling at 70–100 km/h, air entering through the open sunroof makes the whole vehicle shake and produces a horrendous noise. • Original equipment tires aren't acceptable for off-roading. **2001**—Engine compartment burst into flames after slowly accelerating from a stop. • Transmission jumped from Park to Reverse. • Defective jack. **2002**—Vehicle rolls backward when stopped on a hill. • Sunroof doesn't offer pinch protection. • Cupholders are too shallow. **2003**—Dash lights illuminate without headlights on, creating confusion. • Major rear blind spot. **2004**—Automatic transmission lurching. • Poor headlight illumination. • Dash reflects onto the windshield. • Wipers don't clean effectively.

Secret Warranties/Service Tips

All years: Free engine sludge repairs. • Lexus blames "rotten-egg" exhaust smells on fuel, not its vehicles. **1999**—If the MIL alert comes on, you may have to install an improved air/fuel ratio sensor under the emissions warranty. • A 2–3 shift shudder can be corrected by installing an upgraded transaxle valve body. • Tips on driver's door master switch improvement. • To reduce noise and vibration at idle speeds, a dynamic damper has been added to the centre exhaust pipe. • There are dozens of bulletins that address the correction of various squeaks and rattles found throughout the vehicle. • Countermeasures are outlined to reduce wind-rushing noise from the moon roof wind deflector panel. **1999–2000**—Glove box rattling and front suspension noise. **1999–2001**—Measures to silence front brake squeal:

Brakes – Front Squeal Noise

Bulletin No.:BR001-02   Date: March 22, 2002

1999–2001 RX 300

To reduce brake squeal noise, which may occur during brake application while backing up and/or while turning, the front brake disc rotor, the anti-squeal shim, the pad support plate, ** and the brake pad ** have been modified. This warranty is in effect for 48 months or 50,000 miles [80,000 km], whichever occurs first, from the vehicle's in-service date.

2000—Front wheel bearing noise correction. Low-speed drivetrain noise and vibration will be corrected for free up to 6 years/72,000 miles (116,000 km), says TSB #SU007-02, dated November 22, 2002. • More glove box rattles. • Outside mirror stress cracks. **2001–03**—Front seatback popping or clicking. • Inoperative mirror compass. **2002**—Drivetrain vibration. **2002–03**—Troubleshooting front brake vibration. **2003**—Remedy for ABS brake noise. **2004**—AC groaning; diminished blower speed. • Inoperative power back door. • Deceleration hump/thump. • Front suspension creaking/knocking. • Hatch area creak/tick. • Glove box and instrument panel rattles.

RX 300/330 Profile

	1999	2000	2001	2002	2003	2004
Cost Price ($) (negotiable)						
Base (21%)	46,000	46,640	53,000	51,250	51,600	49,900
Used Values ($)						
Base Λ	20,000	24,000	28,000	35,000	40,000	45,000
Base V	18,000	22,000	25,000	33,000	37,000	42,000
Reliability	⑤	⑤	⑤	⑤	⑤	⑤
Crash Safety (F)	—	—	④	④	④	⑤
Side	—	—	⑤	⑤	⑤	⑤
Offset	⑤	⑤	⑤	⑤	⑤	⑤
Rollover	—	—	③	③	③	—

Mitsubishi

MONTERO ★

RATING: Below Average (2003). No one knows if the 2005s will make it to our shores in any great number. There is nothing fundamentally wrong with Mitsubishi SUVs. The problem is the company itself. It's one step away from bankruptcy, and DaimlerChrysler has already cut back its investment in the company. As a result, warranty claims and servicing will certainly suffer. **Strong points:** Low-range gearing for off-roading; traction control; and ABS on four-wheel disc brakes. Seats seven, and features lots of passenger and cargo room. A good reliability record and average depreciation. Frontal crashworthiness for the 2001–04 rated fours stars and side protection five stars (2002–04 models) by NHTSA. IIHS says 2001–03 Monteros give Average offset crash protection and have head restraints that are also Average. *Montero Sport:* Rated Good in providing offset crash protection. **Weak points:** Overpriced at $32,497, with quickly declining resale value (a plus for buyers of used models). The 2003 is a case in point with a resale price that varies between $18,000 and $20,000, or at least 10 percent less than what it should be. A high propensity for rollovers: *Consumer Reports* magazine found the 2001–03 models have a tendency to roll over under hard cornering, a conclusion also reached by NHTSA in its two-star rollover rating given to the 2001–03 models. The V6 is adequate for highway use, but requires a full throttle for passing and merging, hurting fuel economy. Rear head restraints block rearward vision. A tightly sprung chassis degrades handling and ride comfort. Lots of body lean in turns, and steering isn't as precise as the Japanese competition. Problematic rear seat access. Buttressing *CR*'s findings, rollover resistance has been rated below average by NHTSA. *Montero Sport:* More trucklike than the Montero which results in poor handling, an uncomfortable ride, considerable wind and engine noise, and excessive fuel consumption. Entry/exit is made difficult by the low roofline and high floor. The narrow rear bench seat is uncomfortable. Head restraints have been ranked Below Average, and like the Montero, the Sport doesn't come with standard side airbags. The model is likely to be phased out by 2005. **Likely failures:** Owner complaints have targeted airbag (failure to deploy), tie-rod, brake (rotors and pads), Bridgestone tire, and electrical system failures. Chronic stalling is also a common complaint. 1999–2003 Sport models are noted for costly speedometer failures covered in TSB #03-23-002.

MODEL HISTORY: Going into its 10th year in the States, with sales down 50 percent this year, five of its executives facing felony charges, and a comatose administration, Mitsubishi isn't likely to invest much money into improving its lineup or creating its own dealer body in Canada. So, after paying top dollar for an average-performing SUV, with rollover tendencies, you run the risk of buying what may become an auto "orphan."

OUTLANDER ★★

RATING: Below Average (2004). Mitsubishi's shaky finances and chaotic administration are hobbling an average product that could use some power-train and handling enhancements. **Strong points:** Twenty more horses and a quieter cabin for 2004 is a good start, but more power is needed and steering/suspension geometry needs more refining. Stable handling. Longer than most SUVs in the compact class, so there's plenty of cargo room. Base price that's often deeply discounted, nice styling, and tight handling. NHTSA gives the 2003–04 versions a four-star frontal and five-star side rating. Three stars were given to the 2003 for rollover risk. IIHS rates head restraint protection and offset crash protection for 2001–03 models as Good. **Weak points:** Weak, noisy engine; fuel-thirsty; automatic transmission constantly downshifts. Not suitable for off-roading; steering is way too light and there's too much body lean. Other minuses: A narrow body, excessive road noise, a weak dealer network, and side crashworthiness rated Poor by IIHS. **New for 2005:** A manual transmission, upgraded airbags, four-wheel disc brakes, updated styling, and new Limited features. **Likely failures:** Brake pads and rotors, and interior and exterior trim.

MODEL HISTORY: Priced at $27,000, this compact SUV is a spin-off of Mitsubishi's Lancer, which explains its carlike handling and ride. Unfortunately, the Lancer's 140-hp 2.4L 4-banger is no match for the larger and heavier Outlander, even with its transmission set in manual mode. Plus, a lack of low-range gearing compromises its off-road capability. Smart buyers will opt for the 2004 version with its 20 extra horses and other improvements.

The Outlander seats five comfortably, though tall occupants may wish for a bit more legroom. It also offers good all-around visibility and is easy to enter and exit.

ENDEAVOUR ★★★

RATING: Average (2004). A decent performing mid-sized SUV that was spun off the 2004 Galant sedan platform, giving it carlike handling and a comfortable ride. Wait another year to see if Mitsubishi stays in business. **Strong points:** A strong 225-hp 3.5L V6, a liftgate with separate opening glass; and a NHTSA five-star rating for front- and side-impact crashworthiness. **Weak points:** 2005 models may not be sold in Canada. Off-roading is compromised by lack of low-range gearing; cornering produces excessive body lean; fuel-thirsty; curtain side airbags are unavailable. Depreciation is more rapid than usual due to Mitsubishi's fragile financing and a trend toward smaller SUVs. **Likely failures:** Brake pads and rotors.

MODEL HISTORY: Selling for $35,000, this mid-size SUV carries five passengers and offers front- or all-wheel drive. The 3.8L V6 is coupled to a four-speed automatic that lacks low-range gearing, thereby making it more suitable for highway cruising than off-roading. Towing capacity is 1,590 kg (3,500 lb.).

Safety features include 4-wheel disc brakes, a tire-pressure monitor, 17-inch alloy wheels, standard front side airbags (XLS and Limited), traction control (2WD XLS and 2WD Limited), and ABS (optional on the 2WD LS). **Best alternatives:** Chevrolet TrailBlazer, GMC Envoy, Honda Pilot, Nissan Pathfinder, and Toyota Highlander or Toyota 4Runner.

Nissan

MURANO ★★★★★

RATING: Recommended (2003–05). A tall Altima 4X4 that has performed much better than expected, with fewer factory-related defects than other recently launched Nissan models. **Strong points:** Powerful, responsive engine, carlike handling, an easily accessed interior, and plenty of passenger and cargo room. Few production glitches reported. **Weak points:** Poor rear visibility, and unsuitable for off-roading. Fit and finish may disappoint. **New for 2005:** Nothing significant.

2005 Technical Data

Powertrain (Permanent AWD)
Engine: 3.5L V6 (245 hp)
Transmission: CVT.
Dimension/Capacity
Height/length/width:
66.5/187.6/74 in.
Headroom F/R: 40.7/39.7 in.
Legroom F/R: 43.4/36.1 in.
Wheelbase: 111.2 in.

Turning circle: 37.4 ft.
Passengers: 2/3
Cargo volume: 35 cu. ft.
GVWR: 3,801 lb.
Tow limit: 3,500 lb.
Ground clearance: 7 in.
Fuel tank: 82L/reg.
Weight: 3,955 lb.

MODEL HISTORY: This is a stylish five-passenger, mid-sized SUV crossover wagon that is essentially a tall wagon with 4X4 capability. Built on the Altima sedan's platform, the $39,900 Murano uses a permanently engaged all-wheel-drive system as well as front-drive; only the AWD is sold in Canada. Wearing huge 18-inch wheels and equipped with a continuously variable transmission hooked to a 245-hp 3.5L V6, the Murano combines performance with comfort. It features standard four-wheel disc brakes with Brake Assist (BA) and Electronic Brakeforce Distribution (EBD).

With its 245 horses and CVT transmission, the Murano accelerates effortlessly, posting some of the fastest times in its class. The car rides comfortably with little jostling of passengers when passing over uneven terrain. The SE's sport-tuned suspension adds very little to ride quality.

On the downside, the CVT is relatively unproven and takes some getting used to (it slips rather than shifts) and third-row seating isn't available. The body feels cheap. There's lots of wind buffeting with the windows or sunroof open, first-year models were plagued by a variety of squeaks and rattles, and the doors don't sound solid when closed. The optional navigation system is complicated to operate. Furthermore, despite the Murano's rugged looks, it can't handle serious off-roading, and its towing ability is quite limited.

QUALITY/RELIABILITY: Better than average quality, all the more surprising considering that recent Altima, Maxima, and Quest versions have been plagued by unreliable components and poor fit and finish. **Owner-reported problems:** Poor fuel economy, CVT transmission won't hold vehicle stopped on an incline, transmission and alternator failures, a variety of interior squeaks and rattles, and shock absorber thunking. **Warranty performance:** Good.

COST ANALYSIS: Best alternatives: The Honda Pilot or Toyota Highlander. **Rebates:** Not likely. **Warranty:** Bumper-to-bumper 3 years/60,000 km; powertrain 5 years/100,000 km; rust perforation 5 years/unlimited km. **Supplementary warranty:** Not needed. **Options:** Power adjustable pedals are a good idea to distance you from the airbag housing. Navigation system and cold package (heated seats and mirrors) add $3,000 to the price with little benefit. Inadequate seat side bolstering means you'll have even less support. **Depreciation:** Predicted to be slower than average. **Insurance cost:** Much higher than average. **Annual maintenance cost:** Predicted to be lower than average. **Parts supply/cost:** Parts aren't easily found, and can be expensive. **Highway/city fuel economy:** 8.9–11.9L/100 km, but owners complain they get much less.

SAFETY SUMMARY: Airbags: Front, rear, and side. **ABS:** Standard 4W; disc. **Head restraints F/R:** *****. **Visibility F/R:** *****/*. **Maximum load capacity:** 860 lb.

SAFETY COMPLAINTS: All years: Airbags failed to deploy. **2003—** Sudden, unintended acceleration. • Complete loss of power steering when turning steering wheel rapidly. • Vehicle vibrates violently when driven with the rear windows down. • Front seat rocks, causing driver's seat belt to tighten progressively. • Suspension is hard and stiff; with a full load, the Murano tends to bounce about. • Doors randomly lock themselves. • Rear roof pillars block view rearward. • Wipers clog easily; can't be raised to wipe off accumulated snow and ice without opening the hood. • Ineffective defroster system. • False Open Door alert. **2004**—Stalling. • Automatic transmission loses all power. • Shifts out of Park without the keys in the ignition. • Gas tank is vulnerable to puncture from road debris.

Secret Warranties/Service Tips

2002–03—Engine fails to start. • Automatic transmission clicking noise. • ABS or airbag light may remain lit. • Doors lock and unlock intermittently, front window rolls down, and alarm sounds. • Centre console lid is hard to close. • Inoperative interior courtesy lamps. **2003–04**—Defective sunroof. • Door glass ticking.

Murano Profile

	2003	**2004**
Cost Price ($) (negotiable)		
Murano (17%)	39,500	37,700
Used Values ($)		
Murano ▲	29,000	32,000
Murano ▼	26,000	30,000
Reliability	③	③
Crash Safety (F)	④	—
Side	⑤	⑤
Offset	❷	❷
Rollover	④	④

PATHFINDER, ARMADA ★★★★

RATING: Above Average (2000–05); Average (1990–99); Below Average (1987–89). Performance wasn't the early Pathfinder's strong suit, and you still have to pay big bucks for the LE's more refined drivetrain and performance enhancements. **Strong points:** Impressive acceleration, pleasant ride, little road or wind noise, plenty of cargo room, and very slow depreciation. Nicely finished, quiet interior, with plenty of standard convenience and comfort features. The attractive and user-friendly dashboard is at the head of the class in terms of clear instrumentation and easily accessed controls. SE and LE transmissions have low-range gearing on recent models. Standard side airbags on the LE. The Armada is a tremendous performer that's getting cheaper as gas prices soar. **Weak points:** Lethargic early models. Part-time 4X4 isn't to be used on dry pavement, subpar emergency handling, and unimpressive braking. Difficult entry/exit, due to a high step-up and doors that aren't wide enough to permit easy access. Barely adequate rear leg space and restricted rear visibility. Rear seats lack sufficient back support and aren't easily folded out of the way. Standard running boards on the LE are more decorative than practical. Side airbags are optional on the SE. No third-row seating. A history of sudden, unintended acceleration. Poor fuel economy. **New for 2005:** Redesigned as a larger, more luxurious version of the Xterra, the 2005 Pathfinder has been given a 250-hp 4.0L V6, independent double wishbone front and rear suspensions, and a standard third-row seat for seven-passenger seating. A 5-speed automatic is the only transmission available.

2005 Technical Data

Powertrain (rear-drive/4X4)
Engine: 4.0L V6 (250 hp)
Transmission: 4-speed auto. OD
Dimension/Capacity
Height/length/width:
67.9/182.7/69.7 in.
Headroom F/R: 39.5/37.5 in.
Legroom F/R: 41.7/31.8 in.

Wheelbase: 106.3 in.
Turning circle: 40 ft.
Passengers: 2/3
Cargo volume: 33 cu. ft.
GVWR: 5,050–5,300 lb.
Tow limit: 5,000 lb.
Ground clearance: 8.3 in.
Fuel tank: 80L/prem.
Weight: 4,090 lb.

MODEL HISTORY: Introduced in 1987, the Pathfinder has developed slowly over the years. Originally based on the Nissan pickup, it was seriously underpowered until 1990, when the 3.0L V6 added multipoint fuel injection which boosted horsepower from 153 to 180 horses. **1991**—A four-door body came on the scene. **1993**—Better side-impact protection. **1994**—The LE 4X4 luxury model debuts and a new instrument panel is introduced. **1995**—Debut of a 4X2 version of the LE. **1996**—Redesigned model is more powerful, longer, taller, wider, and 91 kg (200 lb.) lighter. The new engine is a 3.3L 168-hp V6 hooked to a part-time four-wheel drive powertrain (not for dry pavement) with shift-on-the-fly, a unibody platform, dual airbags, and standard 4-wheel ABS. **1997**—Door map pockets and an Infiniti QX4 clone. **1999**—A mid-year facelift. **2001**—Given a 3.5L V6 (240-250 hp). The QX4's on-demand All-Mode drivetrain given to the LE (okay for dry pavement), though the SE system can't be used on dry pavement. Other new features: standard cruise control and a restyled interior. **2002**—A slight restyling and larger wheels. **2003**—Traction control, front side/curtain airbags, and user-friendly child-seat anchors were offered for the first time.

The four-door Pathfinder, introduced in 1990, gives a bit better access to the rear seat, but entry/exit is still problematic, with a high step-up and doors that are still not wide enough to permit easy access, though they are larger than in previous years. Recent models have the spare tire mounted under the vehicle, where it's more vulnerable to premature corrosion and highway contaminants.

The base engine until 1996 is a wimpy 3.0L V6 developed for passenger cars; it does a respectable job in pulling the Pathfinder's substantial weight but lacks the low-end torque of an Explorer or Cherokee.

Handling isn't the Pathfinder's strong suit, either. There's lots of body roll in turns and braking distance is unacceptably long. Some people will find the ride harsh, owing to the stiffer suspension and Nissan's adoption of a unibody frame instead of the separate body-on-frame construction used in most large sport-utilities.

The 3.3L V6 delivers so-so acceleration and it's noisy when pushed; a more refined and efficient 3.5L V6 replaced it in March 2000. It was replaced by the 4.0L V6 on 2005 models.

Armada

A new Pathfinder Armada arrived in 2004 and ditched the Pathfinder name for 2005. Built on the Nissan Titan pickup platform, it's a larger, meaner-looking SUV with more angular lines and a 305-hp 5.6L DOHC V8 and 5-speed automatic it shares with the Titan. Armada's long wheelbase gives it enhanced stability and handling and a longer interior with plenty of cargo room. The short front and rear overhangs add to the Armada's maneuverability. Interior amenities provide exceptional versatility, roominess and flexibility—including standard fold-flat second and third row seats, the most second row leg room in the full-sized, light duty SUV class, and a full-length overhead console.

A bit larger than Ford's Expedition with a 3.12-metre (123-inch) wheelbase, 5.26-metre (206.9-inch) overall length, and 2.0-metre (78.8-inch) width, the Armada competes against the Chevy Tahoe, GMC Yukon, and Toyota Sequoia. The Dodge Durango, Ford Expedition, and Jeep Grand Cherokee are in the size class, but aren't as well-made. Buyers will likely see lots of discounting and rebates as GM fights back with generous sales incentives.

COST ANALYSIS: Best alternatives: The 2004s can't compete with the features on the 2005, but if you wait until mid-2005 you'll get a much better made vehicle that'll be heavily discounted. Consider the QX4 instead of the uplevel LE Pathfinder. Other alternatives are the Lexus RX 300/330, Nissan Murano, X-Trail, or Xterra, and Toyota Highlander. **Rebates:** $2,000 rebates on the 2004s (not worth it) and zero percent financing. **Delivery/PDI:** $986. **Depreciation:** Slower than average. **Warranty:** Bumper-to-bumper 3 years/ 60,000 km; powertrain 5 years/100,000 km; rust perforation 5 years/ unlimited km. **Supplementary warranty:** Not needed. **Options:** Worthwhile options include the remote keyless entry, theft-deterrent system, rear window defroster and wiper, and air conditioning. Not recommended: Fender flares (standard on the LE), and large tires that will make turning in tight corners more difficult. Don't take original equipment Firestone or Bridgestone tires. **Insurance cost:** Higher than average. **Annual maintenance cost:** Average; easily repaired by independent garages. **Parts supply/cost:** Parts are widely available and of average cost. **Highway/city fuel economy:** *3.5L engine:* 11.1–14.2L/100 km.

QUALITY/RELIABILITY: Good quality control. Although paint and trim are acceptable, body hardware quality has been below average for some time.

The Pathfinder's overall reliability is about average. Reports of transmission failures are the only other dark cloud on the reliability horizon. **Owner-reported problems:** The automatic transmission, electrical and cooling systems, brakes, and exhaust components. **Warranty performance:** Base warranty, service, and customer relations are average.

ROAD PERFORMANCE: Acceleration/torque: The 4.0L V6 transforms the Pathfinder into an impressively powerful SUV, although the 3.5L is no slouch. Power is delivered smoothly with little engine noise. **Transmission:** Usually functions smoothly but some reports of delayed downshifts when passing. Long-term durability may be a problem. LE's 4X4 is more useful and refined than the SE's system. **Steering:** A bit vague and over-assisted at times. Turning radius is a bit larger than the competition. **Routine handling:** Very nice, well-controlled ride, though a bit more jarring than that of the QX4. **Emergency handling:** Not good. Moderate body lean in turns. **Braking:** Average.

SAFETY SUMMARY: Airbags: Optional side airbags. **ABS:** Standard 4W. **Safety belt pretensioners:** Standard. **Traction control:** Optional. **Head restraints F/R:** *1997:* *; *1999:* ***/**; *2001–03:* **/*. **Visibility F/R:** *****/*. **Maximum load capacity:** *1996:* 1,060 lb.; *2001:* 1,030 lb.

SAFETY COMPLAINTS: All years: Many reports of sudden, unintended acceleration after coming to a stop. • Airbag failures. • Sudden loss of steering control, lock-up. • ABS brake lock-up and failure. • Transmission failure. • Gas and brake pedals are set too close. **1998**—While travelling at 100 km/h on the highway, with the standard shift in Fifth gear, the vehicle suddenly went into Reverse, causing a collision. • Sudden loss of steering. • Vehicle suddenly stopped in traffic and lost all power. • Transmission design allows vehicle to roll backward when in gear. • Seat belts won't accommodate a child safety seat securely. **1999**—Electrical arcing beneath hood at right front fender, along wiring harness from ABS actuator to fuse block, caused wiring insulation to ignite while vehicle was parked. • Steering wheel lock-up caused driver to lose control. • Complete engine and brake failure on a hill with no guardrail. • When in 4X4 High, 4X2 High won't engage. • Excessive vibration felt throughout vehicle while driving 70 km/h, and then a severe front-end shimmy kicks in around 100 km/h. • Sudden steering lock-up. • Premature tread wear, blowouts with Bridgestone tires. • Front driver-side strut, housing, and bearings self-destructed. **2000**—Excessive steering wheel vibration (steering rack replaced). • ABS doesn't work properly on wet pavement. **2001**—Brake pedal takes too much effort to stop vehicle; extended stopping distances are the result. • All gauges and instruments fail intermittently. • Steering pull and excessive body vibration at 100 km/h. • Passenger-side window suddenly exploded. • Strut tower bolt broke. • Although rated to pull 2,250 kg (5,000 lb.), vehicle flipped while pulling a 1,400 kg (3,100 lb.) trailer. **2002**—Stuck throttle. • Rear window fell out. **2003**—Excessive shaking when brakes are applied. **2004**—Automatic "roll-up" windows can be dangerous to children. • Both side curtain airbags deployed for no reason. • Faulty anchor bolt for driver's seat belt. • Spontaneous shattering of the rear hatch glass. • Multiple brake problems include early wearout of rotors and pads, grinding, and vibration.

Secret Warranties/Service Tips

All years: Brake pedal slowly drops to the floor. • Vehicle wanders. **1996–98**—A defective front hub dust shield may cause a high-pitched squeal or whistle in the front hub or axle area. TSB #NTB97-014a shows how a countermeasure baffle plate should be installed. **1996–99**—If the MIL light comes on, it may be due to poor grounding between the intake manifold and the engine cylinder head. • TSB #96-032 addresses hard starting and no-starts. **1996–2002**—Transfer case noise or hard shifting. **1999–04**—Engine over-heating or coolant problems traced to a faulty radiator cap. **2000–02**—Rear suspension bottoms out. **2001**—Computer module may have incorrect idle setting. • Power-steering fluid leak near the pump hose fitting. **2001–02**—Transfer case stuck in 4X4 Low. • Troubleshooting navigation system malfunctions. • Steering column noise when turning. **2001–03**—Transfer case oil leak. • Front brake problems:

Front Brake Vibration/Pulsation/Judder

Bulletin No.: NTB03-091   Date: October 8, 2003
BRAKE JUDGER FROM FRONT BRAKES
2001–03 Pathfinder (R50)
While braking, a steering wheel shake, body vibration, or brake pedal pulsation (also known as "brake judder"), especially during high speed braking. Actions:
ACTIONS:
^ Check front wheel bearing axial end play.
^ "Turn" the front brake rotors using an On-Car Brake Lathe.
^ Install the new front brake pads and hardware kit (see Parts Information).
^ Burnish the brake pads.

2002—Roof rack noise or poor appearance. **2003**—ABS light stays lit. • Roof rack whistling. • Tire pressure monitor stays lit.

Pathfinder Profile

	1997	1998	1999	2000	2001	2002	2003	2004
Cost Price ($) (soft)								
Pathfinder 4X4 (19%)	30,898	30,898	33,800	34,700	34,700	34,700	34,200	34,200
Armada (21%)	—	—	—	—	—	—	—	53,500
Used Values ($)								
Pathfinder ▲	9,000	11,500	16,000	20,000	23,000	22,000	25,000	29,000
Pathfinder ▼	8,000	10,000	14,000	18,500	22,000	20,000	23,000	27,000
Armada ▲	—	—	—	—	—	—	—	45,000
Armada ▼	—	—	—	—	—	—	—	42,000

Reliability	③	③	③	④	④	④	④	⑤
Crash Safety (F)	③	—	④	④	④	④	—	—
Side	—	—	⑤	⑤	⑤	⑤	⑤	⑤
Offset	❷	❷	❷	❷	❷	❷	❷	❷
Rollover (2X4)	—	—	—	❷	❷	❷	❷	—
4X4	—	—	—	—	③	③	③	—

Note: The 1998 and 1999 Pathfinders offer the better deal. High fuel costs and poor sales have hit Armada new and used prices particularly hard.

XTERRA ★★★★

RATING: Above Average (2005); Average (2003–04); Below Average (2000–02). **Strong points:** Reasonably priced, a competent off-roader and highway cruiser (V6), smooth-shifting automatic transmission, good braking, interior space for five adults, well laid-out instruments and controls, elevated rear seats, and good handling and ride. Engine and transmission skid plates and a short front overhang enhance its off-road prowess. Depreciation is practically nil and first-year quality control problems were minimal. **Weak points:** The underpowered 4-cylinder is most suitable for off-road use, and the 2004 and earlier 6-cylinder could use a few more horses as well. Supercharged V6 doesn't impress and requires premium fuel. All three engines are noisy when pushed. The part-time 4X4's low-range gearing could be lower, steering is a bit over-assisted for highway driving, and the pre-2002 knee-banging handbrake is an irritant. Early model dash gauges are hard to read and small rear-door openings complicate entry/exit. To get more cargo space with 2004 and earlier versions, you must first remove flimsy blocks of foam that are passed off as the rear seat cushions. Seats are hard and lack thigh support. There's insufficient rearward seat travel for tall drivers. Some engine, wind, and road noise. **New for 2005:** Redesigned as a smaller version of the Titan pickup, the new Xterra drops the 4-banger in favour of a more powerful V6, coupled to new transmissions that equip the 350Z. In addition to being wider and taller, the wheelbase has been stretched a couple of inches, enhancing ride comfort and interior room, most of which is given to rear-seat passengers. Seats are more practical and comfortable; there's a newly available fold down front passenger seat (great for skis); the instrument panel has been revised; and the radio and climate controls in the centre console have been made more user-friendly. The roof rack has a latching lid, ground clearance is higher, and the Off-Road model now uses high-performance gas shocks.

2005 Technical Data

Powertrain (rear-drive/4X4)
Engine: 4.0L V6 (250 hp)
Transmissions: 5-speed auto.
   Cargo volume: 44.5 cu. ft.
• 6-speed manual
• 5-speed auto.

Legroom F/R: 41.7/31.8 in.
Wheelbase: 106.3 in.
Turning circle: 35.4 ft.
Passengers: 2/3
GVWR: 5,000 lb.
Tow limit: 5,000 lb.

Dimension/Capacity
Height/length/width:
71.4/178.7/72.8 in.
Headroom F/R: 39.6/40.5 in.

Ground clearance: 10.2 in.
Fuel tank: 73L/reg.
Weight: 3,589 lb.

MODEL HISTORY: Essentially a $29,900 Frontier spin-off, the 2005 Xterra is a four-door, five-passenger sport-utility vehicle that's larger and more powerful than previous versions. Xterra is longer and wider than the Jeep Cherokee, and its fully loaded top price is less than what one would begin to pay for an unadorned Pathfinder.

2004 and earlier models came with a base 2.4L 4-cylinder (XE version) and an optional 3.3L V6 or supercharged variant. Top-line models offer rear-drive or 4X4, however, the 4X4 isn't to be used on dry pavement.

2001—Minor revisions. **2002**—An optional supercharged V6 and limited-slip differential. **2003**—An additional 10 horses, optional head-protecting curtain side airbags, an antiskid system, 16-inch alloy wheels, optional tire pressure monitoring, side step rails, 90 more watts for the entertainment system, a new driver's seat height and lumbar support adjuster, and dual 12-volt power outlets. **2004**—15-inch wheels replaced by 16-inchers.

COST ANALYSIS: Best alternatives: Get the larger, more powerful 2005. Other vehicles worth considering: The Honda CR-V, Toyota RAV4 and Highlander. **Rebates:** $1,500 rebates and zero percent financing. **Delivery/PDI:** $986. **Warranty:** Bumper-to-bumper 3 years/60,000 km; powertrain 5 years/100,000 km; rust perforation 5 years/ unlimited km. **Supplementary warranty:** Not necessary. **Options:** The roof rack generates excessive wind noise and interferes with the sunroof's operation, and the step rails can get hung up in sand or mud. Stay away from the dealer-ordered Firestone tires. **Depreciation:** Very slow. **Insurance cost:** Above average. **Annual maintenance cost:** Less than average. **Parts supply/cost:** Good supply of relatively inexpensive parts (after all, this is mostly a Frontier pickup). **Highway/city fuel economy:** *2.4L:* 9.2–12.6L/ 100 km with a manual transmission; *3.3L:* 11.4–14.2L/100 km with a manual transmission, 11.1–14.8L/100 km with an automatic transmission; *3.3L and 4X4:* 11.9–14.5L/100 km with a manual transmission, 11.7–15.6L/100 km with an automatic transmission. No supercharger data.

QUALITY/RELIABILITY: Owner-reported problems: Complaints of transmission failures; oil, transmission fluid, and coolant leaks; cooling system problems; assorted squeaks and rattles; steering clunk or rattle; front bumper rattling; AC idler pulley whine and compressor continuing to run when defogger is switched off; electrical short circuits; engine warning lamp comes on due to a faulty fuel tank, canister, or valve assembly; airbag warning light stays lit; erratic speedometer performance; excessive fuel consumption; paint chipping and blisters; grille stains from the windshield wiper fluid; and the premature rusting of the front wheel spindles. **Warranty performance:** Average.

ROAD PERFORMANCE: Acceleration/torque: Sluggish 4-cylinder performance, though the non-supercharged V6 is an adequate performer.
Supercharged version is peppier, but no more so than larger V6 engines offered
by the competition. **Transmission:** Smooth and quiet shifting with the auto-
matic gearbox; manual transmissions only offered with a 4-cylinder engine.
Steering: Competent steering that's a bit vague on-centre. **Routine handling:**
Corners well, with minimal body lean; however, the Xterra's truck platform
doesn't react well to sudden steering corrections. **Emergency handling:**
Acceptable, though the steering feels too loose at higher speeds. **Braking:**
Quite good; some fading after successive stops.

SAFETY SUMMARY: Airbags: Standard side airbags. Reports of airbags
failing to deploy. **ABS:** Standard 4W; disc/drum. **Safety belt pretensioners:**
Standard. **Traction control:** Standard. **Head restraints F/R:** *2000: ***/**;
2001: ****; 2002–03: ***/**.* **Visibility F/R: *****. Maximum load
capacity:** *2000:* 885 lb.

SAFETY COMPLAINTS: All years—Sudden acceleration. • Airbag malfunctions. • Vehicle pulls sharply when braking. **2000**—Vehicle parked, with
engine running, suddenly took off. • On one wheel, three of the six studs
failed, and on the other wheel, five of the six studs failed. • Rear end suddenly
goes out of control. • Stalling at full throttle. • Driver's seat belt doesn't buckle.
• ABS light comes on for no reason. **2001**—Fuel splashes out of filler tube
when refuelling (Nissan will replace the tank for free, if pushed). • Right rear
wheel and axle flew off vehicle. • Centre-seat seat belt won't adequately accommodate a child safety seat. • Windshield wipers stop intermittently. • Dash
lights are way too dim. **2002**—Sudden loss of power and stalling. • Vehicle
wanders all over the road. • When keyless remote entry was activated, airbag
deployed. • Axle bearing inner seal failure. **2003**—Vehicle suddenly went out
of control when brakes were lightly applied. • General Grabber tire blowout. •
Complete brake loss. • Driver's side upper ball joint collapsed, leading to loss
of steering. • Brake and gas pedals are mounted too close together.

Secret Warranties/Service Tips

All years—Cracked right-hand exhaust manifold. **1999–2004**—Coolant
problems may be due to a defective radiator cap. **2000**—If the MIL light
comes on, it may be due to poor grounding between the intake manifold and
the engine cylinder head. • Idle fluctuation can be eliminated by updating the
ECM program. • Tips on troubleshooting Xterra squeaks and rattles.
2000–02—Transfer case noise and hard shifting troubleshooting. • Bearing
noise. • Coolant leak from intake manifold water outlet. **2001**—Idle fluctuation when coasting to a stop with the clutch depressed. • Roof paint damage at
lower edge of roof rack air dam. • Paint chipping at the rear of the hood or top
of the fender area. • Water may have entered the distributor assembly. • V6
engines may experience a rough idle or engine vibration at idle. **2001–02**—
Goodwill warranty will replace free of charge faulty window regulators:

Window Regulator Replacement

Bulletin No.: NTB03-118   Date: December 10, 2003
VOLUNTARY SERVICE CAMPAIGN CAMPAIGN I.D. #: PU306 & PU307

2001   Altima
2001–02 Frontier
2001–02 Xterra

Nissan has identified that certain models may experience unexpected or difficult operation of the windows. The primary cause is extended high temperature conditions affecting the window regulator system. Nissan has initiated a Voluntary Service Campaign to replace the affected window regulators with the improved design. In other areas where this incident in not expected to occur, Nissan is extending the warranty on the vehicles should a future repair be needed.

Cruise control, engine, and transmission malfunctions:

Cruise Control, Engine Surging/No A/T Upshift

Bulletin No.: EC02-032   Date: April 15, 2003

2001–02 Frontier–with A/T
2001–02 Xterra–with A/T

When using the Automatic Speed Control Device (ASCD – "Cruise Control" ON) at highway speeds of 55–75 mph, the vehicle shows either of the following symptoms:

^ "surge" – a vehicle speed fluctuation as if the ASCD is "hunting" to set the speed, OR

^ after going uphill, Automatic Transmission upshift does not occur.

ACTIONS:

^ Adjust the ASCD Wire.

^ Remove and Replace the ASCD Control Unit.

2001–04—Nissan says headlamp condensation is normal. **2002**—Engine knocking noise. • Coolant leak from intake manifold water outlet. • Steering pull during braking. • Airbag warning light continually flashes. • Malfunctioning engine MIL warning light. • Bearing noise from transfer case area. • Oil leak from the front transfer case oil seal. **2002–04**—Cold engine rattle or clatter. **2003**—ABS light stays lit. • All lights shut down. • AC won't turn off.

Xterra Profile

	2000	2001	2002	2003	2004
Cost Price ($) (negotiable)					
Xterra (12%)	29,998	28,498	29,498	29,798	29,798
Used Prices ($)					
Xterra ∧	14,000	17,500	20,000	23,000	26,000
Xterra ∨	13,000	16,000	18,500	21,500	24,000
Reliability		④	⑤	⑤	⑤	⑤
Crash Safety (F)		④	④	④	④	④
Side		④	④	④	④	⑤
Offset		③	③	③	③	③
Rollover		—	❷	❷	❷	—

X-TRAIL ★★★

RATING: Average (2005). Crashworthiness and dependability are still to be determined. Nissan's X-Trail isn't all that new, nor is it very high-tech or as refined as the Honda and Toyota competition. Actually, the five-passenger small SUV has been on sale in the rest of the world (excluding the United States) since the end of 2000, which means that Nissan's engineers should have had ample time to work out the early-production bugs (a problem still afflicting recent Altimas, Maximas, and Quests).

European crash tests faulted the side-impact head-protecting airbags, warned of risks to the driver's and front passengers' knees, and concluded that the rear-facing child restraint didn't provided sufficient chest and neck protection. Since the X-Trail isn't sold in the States, no NHTSA crash tests will be carried out.

MODEL HISTORY: The X-Trail is based on the Nissan C (compact) car platform used by the Sentra. Equipped with a fully independent suspension and all-wheel drive, it sells for $25,900 for a front-drive XE and $28,200 for the midsized XE AWD with automatic transmission. A 5-speed manual is available, but only on the all-wheel-drive versions. It competes in the small SUV niche that includes the Honda CR-V, Ford Escape, Mazda Tribute, Jeep Liberty, Subaru Forester, Toyota RAV4, Hyundai Santa Fe, Mitsubishi Outlander, Saturn VUE, Suzuki Vitara/Grand Vitara, and Chevrolet Tracker and Equinox.

It is powered by a peppy, though sometimes growly, 165-hp 2.5L 4-cylinder Sentra/Altima engine that'll give the Honda and Toyota a run for their money. Both the 5-speed manual and 4-speed automatic transmission work effortlessly.

This is a fun car to drive, with a bias toward cruising rather than off-roading. Handling is enhanced by a fully independent suspension, responsive steering, and exceptionally well-performing four-wheel vented disc brakes with ABS. A Snow-Mode switch, standard on all front-drive models, is particularly useful in that it retards engine power to provide extra traction in slippery conditions.

The X-Trail's unusually tall and boxy styling takes a little getting used to, but it does provide a surprisingly large amount of easily-accessed interior room (more cargo space than the Mazda Tribute, Toyota RAV4, or the Jeep Liberty), many cleverly located storage compartments, plenty of leg- and headroom, a low step-in height, and a nice view of the road, though the extra-wide rear D-pillars obstruct the view somewhat. On the downside, the rear window doesn't open. **Best alternatives**: Honda CR-V, Hyundai Santa Fe, Mazda Tribute, Subaru Forester, and Toyota RAV4.

Saab

9-7X ★

RATING: Not Recommended (2005). GM is killing the Saab cachet, while Saab continues to drain GM's resources with vehicles nobody wants. You want proof? Take Saab's latest SUV, the $45,000 9-7X, a warmed-over GM TrailBlazer built in Ohio. This is the second Saab neither assembled in Sweden nor sold in Europe (the recently launched 9-2X AWD sports compact is the first). GM figures that a European SUV serviced by an atrophied dealer body and not even built or sold in Europe and is just the ticket to "goose" American sales. Proves corporate leaders can exhibit just as much arrogance and stupidity as politicians.

Saab's 9-7X is a TrailBlazer with a console-mounted ignition. (Hey, Anna Mae, get the dog off the ignition!!)

Who wants to buy a TrailBlazer from Saab? Plus, the name is a major turn-off for buyers who are used to names that depict something, and aren't just a jumble of letters and numbers for the "wink, wink, nudge, nudge" car *cognoscenti*. Reminds one of the departed and unlamented Ford/Merkur XR4Ti of a few decades ago. Apparently, those whom the gods wish to destroy, they first give unintelligible nameplates.

MODEL HISTORY: The 9-7X retains some Saab features, like the centre console ignition key, the distinctive air vents, and cockpit. It has a wheelbase of 2.87 metres (113 inches), is 4.91 metres (193.4 inches) long, and can carry up to 1.16 cubic metres (41 cubic feet) of luggage in the trunk with the seats up. There's a standard 60/40 split rear seat and a trailer hitch receiver and cover. The V-8 model is estimated to have a maximum towing capacity of 2,950 kg (6500 lb.).

For a dash of European performance, the 9-7X uses a double A-arm front suspension with coil springs and a multi-link, electronically controlled rear air suspension, a low ride height, thick front stabilizer, and stiff rear upper control arm bushings in the rear. The front has been stiffened, and steering response and precision have also been enhanced.

Two engines are available: A 275 hp 4.2L in-line 6-cylinder and a 300 hp 5.3L V-8—both engines are teamed to a 4-speed automatic transmission, standard all-wheel drive, and a limited-slip differential.

Saturn

VUE   ★

RATING: Not Recommended (2002–05); you couldn't buy a worse SUV and that includes the Ford Explorer and defunct Lada Nivea. Honda gave a new heart to this dying patient with its V6, while GM cut if off at the knees with its soon-to-be-dropped failure-prone CVT transmission. **Strong points:** Honda's 3.5L V6 and 5-speed automatic transmission work well in the Odyssey and Pilot and should do just as well with the lighter Vue. Last year's GM-bred 3.0L V6 was adequate, but had a history of factory-induced glitches that compromised performance and overall powertrain reliability. Dent-resistant plastic side body panels; 4-cylinders use a CVT automatic transmission touted for its smoothness and fuel efficiency; average handling and comfortable ride; instruments and controls are generally easily accessible and clearly marked; low step-in height and trunk liftover; and an adequate, versatile interior that includes a split-folding seat to accommodate long objects. **Weak points:** Mediocre acceleration with the base 2.2L engine; excessive torque steer (twisting) when accelerating; excessive body roll and rocking in turns; lots of nose plow when stopping; vague steering; excessive engine noise when accelerating; lots of road noise, too; driver's visor is too low; seats don't appear as comfortable as those offered by competitors; liftgate doesn't have separate opening glass; CVT automatic transmission still unproven for durability and serviceability; not a serious off-roader (no low-range gearing, for example); no ceiling-mounted grab handles for easier entry and exit; second-row seats are firmer than and not as comfortable as front seats; rear seats are too low; cheap-looking interior and plastic trim; and average to below-average quality control. **New for 2005:** Red Line handling and cosmetic improvements.

MODEL FEATURES: The part-time 4X4 Vue is a conventionally styled, late-arriving (midway through the 2002 model year) compact SUV that targets cars in the Ford Escape and Honda CR-V class. The Vue runs in the middle-rear of the SUV pack and uses as its chief selling point the mantra that Saturn is a "different" car company that cares about its customers.

Don't you believe it. When the warranty expires, it's "goodbye, Charlie."

2003—Expanded powertrain combination. **2004**—Honda's 250-hp V6 engine replaces the unreliable GM-bred powerplant. It delivers lots of power on regular fuel and offers a high degree of reliability and durability. A new Red Line "high-performance" version sits an inch lower, uses a tighter suspension, offers better-performing 18-inch wheels, and sports a racier appearance. Horsepower remains the same, no matter what the salesman says.

2005 Technical Data

Powertrain (Front, AWD)
Engines: 2.2L 4-cyl. (143 hp)
• 3.5L V6 (250 hp)
Transmissions: 5-speed man.
Dimension/Capacity
Passengers: 2/3
Height/length/width:
66.3/181.8/71.5. in.
Headroom F/R: 39.2/37.4 in.

Legroom F/R: 43.1/32.4 in.
Wheelbase: 106.6 in.
Turning circle: 38 ft.
Cargo volume: 31.3 cu. ft.
GVWR: 4,598–4839.
Tow limit: 1,500–2,500 lb.
Ground clearance: 8 in.
Fuel tank: 59L/reg.
Weight: 3,590 lb.

COST ANALYSIS: Best alternatives: Go for a leftover $27,795 2004 Vue: Its Honda powertrain makes all the difference. Other vehicles worth considering: Buick Rendezvous, Chevrolet Blazer, Honda CR-V, Honda Element, Hyundai Santa Fe, Jeep TJ, Mitsubishi Outlander, Nissan Xterra, Subaru Forester, Subaru Outback, Toyota Highlander, and Toyota RAV4. **Rebates:** $3,000 rebates to clear out the 2004s. **Delivery/PDI:** $830. **Warranty:** Bumper-to-bumper 3 years/60,000 km; powertrain 5 years/100,000 km; rust perforation 5 years/unlimited km. **Supplementary warranty:** Absolutely. **Options:** I recommend the "Power Package," which includes power windows, Saturn Security System (power door locks with remote keyless entry, content theft, anti-lockout, and theft deterrent system), auto-dimming rear-view mirror with compass and temperature, power remote-controlled side mirrors, cruise control, and overhead console light. **Depreciation:** Average. **Insurance cost:** Average. **Parts supply/cost:** Parts can be costly. **Annual maintenance cost:** Average. **Highway/city fuel economy:** 7.6–10.6L/100 km with the 2.2L; 8.4–12L/100 km with the 3.0L V6. Owners say real-world fuel economy is much less than what is advertised.

QUALITY/RELIABILITY: Below average, with unreliable powertrain, brake, and body components, plus service bulletins that cast doubt on the Vue's long-term dependability. Honda engines in later models are more dependable. **Owner-reported problems:** Engine knocking, automatic transmission failures, hard downshifts, horn is hard to operate, steering column thumping, a plethora of electrical malfunctions, anti-lock brakes hammer excessively, cupholder so low as to be useless, water collects in the roof rack pin wells, chronic rattling and squeaking, **Warranty performance:** GM Canada offers a 30-day/2,500 km exchange warranty, which usually runs out before the Vue's chronic powertrain problems appear. After-warranty assistance is parsimonious, at best.

SAFETY SUMMARY: Airbags: Side airbags aren't offered; optional for head protection. Numerous reports of airbags failing to deploy. **ABS:** Optional. Front disc/rear drum. There have been many complaints of ABS failure and premature wearout of brake components. **Head restraints F/R:** *2002–03:* *****. **Visibility F/R:** ****. **Maximum load capacity:** *2002:* 825 lb.

SAFETY COMPLAINTS: All years: Loss of steering, transmission failure, airbag malfunction, chronic stalling and surging, and horn is hard to activate. **2002**—Transmission fluid lines vulnerable to road debris. • A steering column thump sounds like something is loose in the steering assembly. **2002–03**— Airbags failed to deploy. • Reduced power light comes on and vehicle shuts down. • Torque steer jerks car to the right when accelerating. **2003**—Almost 200 complaints, double what would be normal. • Transmission breakdown (variable drive unit). • Vehicle slides backward when stopped on a hill. • Inside door latches couldn't open the door. • Incorrect speedometer readings. • Electrical short-circuit in the signal/headlight control stalk. • Headlight and daylight driving lights burn out, and vehicle stalls when it rains. **2004**—Rear suspension collapsed from a rear fender-bender and when another car veered off the road. • Corrosion from bolt holes in roof rail mounting.

Secret Warranties/Service Tips

2002—Engine flare during 2–3 upshifts. • Timing belt coolant contamination. • Rattle or tapping noise from steering column shroud area. • Creaking noise may come from left or right rear of vehicle while driving. • Front seat squeaking. • Troubleshooting a defective MIL light. • Rear seat cushion cover is baggy or loose along the bottom edge. Horn design makes it difficult to activate at night. AC and lower condenser are exposed to road debris. **2002–03**—No-starts, stalling, a rough-running engine, and a poor idle may all be caused by a stuck engine intake manifold pressure relief valve. • A history of faulty valve seals and poor cold weather engine performance:

Blue Smoke at Start-Up

Bulletin No.: 04-06-01-010 Date: April, 2004
(Inspect Valve Stem Seal Color and Perform Service Procedure)
2000–04 Saturn L-Series
2002–03 Saturn VUE with 3.0L V6

This condition may be caused by leaking valve seals (on engines with brown seal color) or excessive clearance between valve stem and valve guide.

Oil Leaks In Sub-Freezing Temps.

Bulletin No.: 04-06-01-001 Date: January, 2004

Oil Leaks from Engine After Sub-Freezing Temperatures (Remove Ice/Water from Positive Crankcase Ventilation (PCV) Hose and Re-route Hose) 2002–03 Saturn VUE Vehicles with 3.0L V6 Engine

---

Powertrain vibration with AC activated. • A moan, growl noise, and vibration from rear of vehicle can be corrected by replacing the rear drive module limited-slip clutch drum. • Torque converter shudder, vibration. • Shudder, vibration in Reverse. • Transaxle whine. • Starter stays engaged after start-up. • Electrical accessories fail intermittently. • Fluid leak caused by loose VTI transaxle converter housing bolts. • Transmission won't go into gear:

No Shift/No Gear Engagement

Bulletin No.: 03-07-30-023 Date: November, 2003

Vehicle Does Not Shift or Move After Running For a Period of Time and/or Check Engine Light is ON and DTC P0741 is Set (Replace Torque Converter, Valve Body, Clean Out Transaxle and Install New Flex Plate Bolts and Washers)

2002–03 Saturn VUE

Upper steering column noise. • Incorrect speedometer, fuel gauge readings. • Insufficient AC cooling and heating. • Instrument panel condensation. • Fluid dripping onto driver's floormat. • Engine compartment whistling, chirping. • Front-end squeaking. • Buzzing, grinding, growling from rear of vehicle when fuel pump is activated. • Clunk, pop, or click when accelerating or decelerating. • Upgraded liftgate latching system. **2004**—Special warranty policy adjustment for the CVT transmission. • Hard starts. • Moan, growl, and vibration when turning. • Steering rattle. • Suspension pop, clunk noise. • AC hissing. • Exhaust system rattle or buzz. • Drone noise between 80 and 120 km/h. • Outside rearview mirror cracking.

Vue Profile			
	2002	**2003**	**2004**
Cost Price ($) (negotiable)			
Base Vue (18%)	21,565	21,980	22,745
4X4 (19%)	26,055	27,595	26,390
Used Values ($)			
Base Vue ʌ	13,000	15,000	17,000
Base Vue v	11,000	13,000	15,000
4X4 ʌ	15,000	18,000	20,000
4X4 v	13,000	16,000	18,000

Reliability	❷	③	③
Crash Safety (F)	⑤	⑤	⑤
Side	❶	❶	❶
Offset	⑤	⑤	⑤
Rollover	③	③	—

Note: The Vue's rear wheel collapsed on two different models during the rollover test; 246,000 2002–04 Vues were recalled.

Subaru

FORESTER, IMPREZA, WRX ★★★

RATING: *Forester:* Average (1994–2005). *Impreza:* Average (1997–2005). *WRX:* Not Recommended (2002–05). The Forester and WRX have been downgraded this year mainly because the competition has raised the performance bar while Subaru simply coasts. There is nothing remarkable about Subaru except for its use of AWD and Australian "Survivor" chic to stave off bankruptcy in the mid-90s.

Now, these ordinary little AWD sedans and wagons have priced themselves out of the market. Quality control has declined and customer service is barely an after-thought. Choose a cheaper Asian or South Korean SUV. **Strong points:** A refined AWD drivetrain; a powerful WRX engine and impressive acceleration with the base 2.5L; competent handling, without any torque steer; well-appointed base models; lots of storage space with the wagons; nice control layout; and average quality control. **Weak points:** Recent models are overpriced. Problematic entry/exit; the coupe's narrow rear window and large rear pillars hinder rear visibility; heater is insufficient and air distribution is inadequate; comfort compromised by WRX's short wheelbase, suspension, and 16-inch tires; front- and rear-seat legroom may be insufficient for tall drivers; small doors and entryways restrict rear access; WRX requires premium fuel; and a surprisingly large number of safety-related complaints that include complete brake loss, chronic surging, and stalling. **New for 2005:** A cosmetically enhanced L.L. Bean edition.

2005 Technical Data

Powertrain (AWD)
Engines: 2.5L 4-cyl. (165 hp)
• 2.5L turbo (210 hp)
• 2.0L turbo (227 hp)
Transmissions: 5-speed man.
• 4-speed auto.
Dimension/Capacity
Passengers: 2/3
Height/length/width:
60/172.2/67.1 in.
Headroom F/R: 39.2/37.4 in.
Legroom F/R: 43.1/32.4 in.
Wheelbase: 99.2 in.
Turning circle: 36 ft.
Cargo volume: 19.5 cu. ft.
GVWR: 4,120 lb.
Tow limit: 2,000 lb.
Ground clearance: 7.5 in.
Fuel tank: 50L/reg.
Weight: 2,900 lb.

MODEL HISTORY: The full-time 4X4 Impreza is essentially a shorter Legacy with additional convenience features. It comes as a four-door sedan, a wagon, and an Outback Sport Wagon, all powered by a 165-hp 2.5L flat-four engine. The rally-inspired WRX models have a more powerful 227-hp 2.0L turbocharged engine, lots of standard performance features, a sport suspension, aluminum hood with functional scoop, and higher-quality instruments, controls, trim, and seats. 2003 Impreza and WRX were carried over unchanged.

Another Subaru spin-off, the Forester, is a cross between a tall wagon and a sport-utility. Based on the shorter Impreza, the Forester uses the Legacy Outback's 2.5L 165-hp engine coupled to a 5-speed manual transmission or an optional 4-speed automatic. Its road manners are more subdued and its engine provides more power and torque for off-roading.

1995—Entry-level Imprezas got a coupe and an Outback model, and optional AWD. **1996**—A mix of front-drives and all-wheel drives, along with a new sport model, a new Outback Wagon (for light off-roading), and larger engines. **1997**—Additional power and torque, a re-styled front end, and a new Outback Sport Wagon. **1998**—Imprezas got a revised dash and door panels. The Brighton was dropped and the high-end 2.5 RS was added. **1999**—Stronger engines, more torque, and upgraded transmissions. **2002**—2.2L 4-cylinder was dropped, along with Subaru's pretensions for making affordable entry-level cars. Totally redesigned models include the 2.5 TS Sport Wagon, 2.5 RS sedan, Outback Sport Wagon, the WRX sporty sedan, and the Sport Wagon. There is no longer a two-door version available. **Impreza: 2004**—Fewer entry-level models. **Forester: 1999**—A quieter, torquier engine; a smoother-shifting transmission; and a more solid body. **2000**—Standard cruise control (L) and limited-slip differential (S). **2003**—improved interior materials, an upgraded suspension, and enhanced handling and ride quality. You'll also find larger tires and fenders, and revised head restraints and side-impact airbags. **2004**—A turbocharged 210-hp 2.5L 4-banger that includes a variable valve control system and a racier appearance to make the 2.5XT stand out. **WRX: 2003**—An AWD car for the high-performance crowd, the WRX is a goofy-looking, squat little wagon/SUV with a large rear end and a 227-hp 2.0L 4-cylinder engine mated to a high-boost turbocharger. **2004**—A 300-hp engine.

COST ANALYSIS: The 2005 Impreza 2.5TS Sport Wagon starts at $22,995. **Best alternatives:** Buy cheaper 2002 entry-level Imprezas, or go for an upgraded 2003 Forester. WRX versions are expensive Imprezas that equal the sporty performance of the Audi A4 and BMW 3 Series—cars costing $10,000 more. But, can you handle the brake failures? An excellent alternative is the Toyota Matrix/Pontiac Vibe front-drive and AWD models. If you really don't need a 4X4, here are some front-drives worth considering: Honda Civic, Hyundai Elantra, Mazda3, and Toyota Corolla. The AWD models are way overpriced. Furthermore, you may wish to budget an extra $500 or more for an extended powertrain warranty to protect you from premature and repeated clutch failures. **Rebates:** $2,000 rebates to clear out last year's models.

Delivery/PDI: $550. **Warranty:** Bumper-to-bumper 3 years/60,000 km; powertrain 5 years/100,000 km; rust perforation 5 years/unlimited km. **Supplementary warranty:** Not needed. **Options:** Larger tires smooth out the ride. **Depreciation:** Slower than average. Foresters hold their value best of all. WRX versions depreciate rapidly. **Insurance cost:** Higher than average. **Parts supply/cost:** Parts aren't easy to find and can be costly; delayed recall repairs. **Annual maintenance cost:** Higher than average. Mediocre, expensive servicing is hard to overcome because independent garages can't service key AWD components. **Highway/city fuel economy:** 7.7–10.5L/100 km with the 2.5L.

QUALITY/RELIABILITY: Fair quality control; Subaru reps sometimes cop too much of an attitude when faced with serious safety-related complaints:

> While attempting to slow my 2003 WRX for a corner on a well groomed, dry gravel road the ABS system of the car initiated a mode that would not allow the car's brakes to function at all. During the episode (which has been and can be recreated) pedal pressure and pedal height was maintained as during normal braking operations. The brakes would not work despite the fact that I was standing with both feet on the brake pedal. I am in the process of disconnecting my ABS. Subaru North America claims that I'm nuts.

A history of premature powertrain, fuel system, and brake failures, and some body panel and trim fit and finish deficiencies. Servicing quality is spotty. **Owner-reported problems:** Poor engine idling, cooling; frequent cold weather stalling; manual transmission malfunctions (mostly clutch chatter and shudder); rear wheel bearing failures; alloy wheels cause excessive vibration; premature exhaust system rust-out and early brake wear; minor electrical short circuits; catalytic converter failures; doors don't latch properly; water leaks and condensation problems from the top of the windshield or sunroof; windshield scratches too easily; paint peeling. **Warranty performance:** Has declined markedly during the past couple of years (especially in relation to brake and clutch complaints).

SAFETY SUMMARY: Huge fold-away side mirrors. Front shoulder belts can uncomfortable and rear seat belts may be hard to buckle up. **Airbags:** Side airbags are optional. Numerous reports of airbags failing to deploy; also reports of airbags injuring passengers or deploying but not inflating. Subaru has been slow to install de-powered airbags. **ABS:** Standard. There have been many complaints of ABS failure and premature wearout of brake components. **Head restraints F/R:** *Forester: 1999: **/*; 2001–02: ***/**; 2003: *****. Impreza: 1995: **; 1997: **/*; 2001: **; 2002–03: ***.* **Visibility F/R:** *Coupe: *****/**.* **Maximum load capacity:** *1998–2003 Forester:* 900 lb.

SAFETY COMPLAINTS: All years: Sudden acceleration, stalling, transmission failures, steering loss, airbag malfunctions, brake and engine lights continually on, and front seats move fore and aft. **1997**—Cruise control failed to disengage when brakes were applied. • Igniter failed, allowing unburned fuel to flow into catalytic converter. • AC blew fumes into interior, causing driver to black out. • Complete engine failure due to defective valves and pistons. • Transmission surges when cold, or shifts into Neutral at low speed or when descending a small hill. • Frequent electronic control unit failures. • Rear seat belts are too long to properly secure child safety seat, and the locking mechanism doesn't lock properly. • Alternators frequently quit while vehicle is under power. **1998**—Oil leak from oil filter seam caused fire. • Sudden brake loss after linings, calipers, and master cylinder had been replaced. • Cruise control failed to disengage when brakes were applied. • Excessive shaking at highway speeds. • Seatback collapsed when vehicle was rear-ended. **1999**—Engine failure due to cracked #2 piston. • When accelerating or decelerating, vehicle will begin to jerk due to excessive play in the front axle. • Front bumper skirt catches on parking blocks, resulting in bumper twisting and being ripped off. • The centre rear seat belt's poor design prohibits the installation of many child safety seats. **Forester: 2000**—Driver burned from airbag deployment. • Sudden loss of transmission fluid. • Driver's seatback may suddenly recline because seat belt gets tangled up in the recliner lever. • Frequent wheel bearing failures. • Fuel filler cap design is too complicated for gas station attendants to put on properly. Driver, therefore, has to pay dealer to reset Check Engine light. **2001**—Breakage of rear wheel bearings. • Brake and accelerator pedals are too close together. • In a collision, airbags failed to deploy and seat belt didn't restrain occupant. • In a similar incident, shoulder belt allowed driver's head to impact the windshield. • Headlights don't illuminate the edge of the road and are either too bright on High or too dim on Low. • Alarm system self-activated trapping baby inside of car until fire rescue arrived. **2002**—Dangerous delay, then surging when accelerating forward or in Reverse. • Surging at highway speeds and stalling at lower rpms. • Transmission failure; gears lock in Park intermittently. • Intermittent backfire when shifting manual transmission. • Open wheel design allows snow and debris to pack in the area and throw wheel out of balance, creating dangerous vibration. • High hood allows water onto the engine. (Note: The preceding comments apply to the Forester but can be relevant to Impreza owners, too.) **2003**—When backing vehicle into a parking space, the hill holder feature activates, forcing the driver to use excessive throttle in Reverse. • Brake pedal went to floor without braking. • Heater, defroster failure. • Five doors but only one keyhole makes for difficult access when the keyless entry fails. **WRX: 2002–03**—Windshield cracking. • Chronic ABS brake failures.

Secret Warranties/Service Tips

All years: Bulletins relate to automatic transmission popping out of gear. • At least three bulletins deal with manual transmission malfunctions. • Diagnostic and repair tips are offered on transfer clutch binding and/or bucking on turns. • Troubleshooting tips on a sticking anti-lock brake relay are offered. This problem is characterized by a lit ABS warning light or the ABS motor continuing to run/buzz when the ignition is turned off. • A rotten-egg smell could be caused by a defective catalytic converter. It will be replaced, after a bit of arguing, free of charge, up to five years under the emissions warranty. **1999**—Air intake chamber box breakage will cause start-up stall and Check Engine light to remain lit. **1999–2002**—Sliding seat belt latch. **2000**—Growling noises from the engine area. • Automatic transmission light flashing. • Low brake pedal adjustment procedure. **2000–01**—Front oxygen air/fuel sensor cracking. **2001–03**—Uneven brake application:

Uneven Disc Brake Pad Wear

Bulletin No.: 06-33-04 Date: 01/15/04

2001–03 Subarus

The purpose of this bulletin is to address unevenly or prematurely worn brake pads. There is the possibility that the pads are too tight in the caliper and have insufficient clearance as a result of rust buildup and dirt. If that is the case, the backplate of the disc brake pads will need to be slightly filed no more than 0.1 mm (0.0039") on each end to remove the rust.

2003—Defective 4EAT transmission parking pawl rod. • Clutch pedal sticking.

Forester, Impreza, WRX Profile

	1997	1998	1999	2000	2001	2002	2003	2004
Cost Price ($) (negotiable)								
Forester (18%)	—	26,695	26,695	26,895	28,395	28,395	27,995	27,995
Base/Brighton (17%)	16,991	16,240	17,795	—	—	—	—	—
Sedan 4X4 (17%)	21,395	21,395	21,995	21,995	22,196	21,995	26,995	26,996
WRX (18%)	—	—	—	—	—	34,995	34,995	35,495
Used Values ($)								
Forester ▲	—	8,000	11,000	13,000	16,000	18,500	22,000	24,000
Forester ▼	—	7,000	9,500	12,000	14,500	17,000	20,500	22,500
Base/Brighton ▲	5,000	6,500	8,000	—	—	—	—	—
Base/Brighton ▼	4,500	5,000	6,500	—	—	—	—	—
Sedan 4X4 ▲	5,500	7,000	8,000	10,500	12,000	16000	17,000	18,000
Sedan 4X4 ▼	4,500	6,000	7,000	9,500	11,000	14,500	16,000	16,000
WRX ▲	—	—	—	—	—	21,000	26,000	30,000
WRX ▼	—	—	—	—	—	19,000	24,000	28,000
Reliability	③	③	③	③	③	④	④	④
Crash Safety (F)								
Forester	—	—	④	④	④	④	⑤	⑤
Impreza	④	—	—	—	—	④	④	—
Side (Forester)	—	—	—	—	⑤	⑤	⑤	⑤
Impreza	—	—	—	—	—	④	④	—
IIHS Side	—	—	—	—	—	⑤	⑤	⑤
Offset	—	—	—	—	—	④	⑤	⑤
Forester	—	—	⑤	⑤	⑤	⑤	⑤	⑤

| Rollover (Forester) | — | — | — | — | ③ | ③ | ③ | — |
| Impreza | — | — | — | — | — | ④ | ④ | — |

Toyota

RAV4 ★★★★★

RATING: Recommended (2004–05); Above Average (1997–2003). An impressive all-around performer suitable for limited off-road tasks, with an impressive array of long-awaited 2004 enhancements. **Strong points:** Full-time 4X4; much-improved acceleration (may still be too tame for some), handling, and riding; the four-door has a handling advantage over the two-door version; all passengers have more than enough head and legroom; the four-door has more cargo space than most passenger cars, though the two-door version reduces that cargo capacity by half; the split rear bench seat folds for extra cargo space; easy access and a low liftover; the four-door is nicely equipped; the two-door is spartan, though adequate; incredibly high resale value; and legendary reliability. **Weak points:** Automatic gearbox and 4X4 reduces engine performance (front-drive is faster); excessive road and engine noise; rearward visibility is seriously compromised by the RAV4's convertible top, high headrests, and spare tire placement. **New for 2005:** No major changes.

2005 Technical Data

Powertrain (front-drive/4X4)
Engine: 2.4L 4-cyl. (161 hp)
Transmissions: 5-speed man.
• 4-speed auto. OD
Dimension/Capacity
Height/length/width:
64.9/166/68.3 in.
Headroom F/R: 40.3/39 in.
Legroom F/R: 39.5/33.9 in.

Wheelbase: 98 in.
Turning circle: 35.4 ft.
Passengers: 2/3
Cargo volume: 29.2 cu. ft.
GVWR: 3,946–3,990 lb.
Tow limit: 1,500 lb.
Ground clearance: 6.3 in.
Fuel tank: 56L/reg.
Weight: 3,070 lb.

MODEL HISTORY: Selling for a bit over $25,000, the 2005 RAV4 is a cross between a small car and an off-road wagon with a tall roof, and marks Toyota's entry into the mini-sport-utility market. "RAV4" stands for "Recreational Active Vehicle with four-wheel drive." It has attractive lines, a high profile, and two drivetrains: permanent 4X4 or front-drive.

The RAV4 is based on the Camry platform and features four-wheel independent suspension and unibody construction; it rides and handles like a stiffly sprung, small-wheelbase car.

The RAV4, like Honda's CR-V, is an upsized car that has been made more rugged with the addition of AWD, larger wheels, more ground clearance, and a boxy body.

Although the RAV4s have been around for a few years, you won't find many on the used-car market. Those that are for sale aren't cheap either. However, the reworked 2001 RAV4 is exerting some downward price pressure on the less-refined older used versions. Don't spend extra bucks opting for the 1999 or 2000 versions; they're not much different than the earlier models except for a minor face-lift, the addition of a two-door softtop, and a full-sized spare tire. The two-door convertible was dropped from the year 2000 models. **2001**—Completely redesigned, growing in size and getting a more powerful engine, upgraded suspension, a more rigid body, and new, aggressive styling. **2004**—The Highlander's 2.4L engine, rear disc brakes, vehicle skid control, a revised suspension and steering, a tire pressure monitor, and optional side curtain airbags.

COST ANALYSIS: Best alternatives: Get the upgraded 2004, rather than a more expensive 2005. Even at a $500 premium, ($25,000) it's still the best buy with all the additional features. When compared with the Honda CR-V, Honda has a slight edge from a quality perspective. Also take a look at the Isuzu Rodeo, Nissan Xterra, Subaru Forester, and Toyota Highlander. **Rebates:** Expect $1,500 rebates and zero percent financing throughout the year. **Delivery/PDI:** $1,245. **Warranty:** Bumper-to-bumper 3 years/60,000 km; powertrain 5 years/100,000 km; rust perforation 5 years/unlimited km. **Supplementary warranty:** An extended warranty isn't needed. **Options:** All-wheel drive. **Depreciation:** Very slow. **Insurance cost:** Above average. **Parts supply/cost:** Parts are moderately priced and fairly easy to find from independent suppliers. **Annual maintenance cost:** Below average, owing to the proven reliability of Camry and Corolla components used in the RAV4. **Highway/city fuel economy:** 8.0–10.6L/100 km.

QUALITY/RELIABILITY: Better-than-average quality control. **Owner-reported problems:** Many reports of frequent stalling or hesitation, brake noise, and throttle body whine between 2700 and 3000 rpm. Owners note that the brakes screech, squeal, or grind even after the pads have been replaced. Other noises: Dash and cowl rattling (worse in low temperatures), rear suspension creaking when accelerating from a stop, and windshield cowling rattles (particularly in cold weather). To a lesser degree, owners tell of rear-view mirror and windshield cowling vibration, as well as minor electrical shorts. **Warranty performance:** Above average.

ROAD PERFORMANCE: Acceleration/torque: Brisk acceleration with the manual gearbox, with an acceptable amount of low-end torque, makes the RAV4 a competent performer for most daily chores, while giving it the power for traversing hilly terrain and doing some light off-roading. **Transmission:** Smooth shifting and particularly well suited for off-roading when mated to the AWD. With the 5-speed manual transmission, the 4X4 mode can be engaged by a push of a button on the dashboard. With the 4-speed automatic transmission, the standard centre differential is controlled by a hydraulic multi-plate clutch. Large 16-inch wheels provide stability. The high ground clearance, wide track, short overhangs, and four-wheel independent suspension make it more suitable for off-roading than some other "light" sport-utilities lacking these features. The automatic transmission, however, saps too much power. **Steering:** Power steering is much more precise than with the 2003 version. **Routine handling:** Good. Minimal body lean, a smooth ride, and less trucklike handling. **Emergency handling:** Despite the vehicle's high centre of gravity, its handling feels sure and responsive. **Braking:** Good. Less fade than before.

SAFETY SUMMARY: Airbags: Dual front; optional side. **ABS:** Optional; disc/disc. **Safety belt pretensioners:** Standard. **Traction control:** Optional. **Head restraints F/R:** *1997:* ***; *1998:* **; *1999:* ***; *2001–03:* *****. **Visibility F/R:** *****/*. **Maximum load capacity:** *1996:* 910 lb; *1997:* 895 lb.; *2001:* 760 lb.

SAFETY COMPLAINTS: 1990–2000—A new brake caliper grease will reduce front brake clicking when the brakes are applied. **1997**—Vehicle stalls in rainy weather. • Middle rear seat belt tightens uncomfortably. • Sudden stalling in traffic. • Shoulder belt failed to hold occupant in a side collision. • Door locks won't lock unless key is used, and then it locks driver in. • Manual transmission shifter boot came off, jamming the shifter. **1998**— Firewall cracked, causing gas pedal to move side to side and literally pushing through the floor with no support structure to hold it in position. • Accelerator pedal sticks when accelerating. • Drive shaft freezes in cold weather. • Transmission won't hold vehicle stopped on an incline. • Power-assisted front brake discs and rear brake drums failed. • Intermittent brake malfunctions that result in extended stopping distances. • Reports that the braking system is ineffective on wet pavement, leading to brake lock-up. • Shift lock jammed, preventing any operation of the vehicle. • Brakes constantly need new rotors, pads, and calipers. **1999**—Fire ignited in the engine compartment (electrical wires) and fuse box (insulation). • Spot welds broke away from frame, causing trailer hitch to separate. • Alternator short caused sudden loss of power. • Uneven pavement caused the vehicle to flip over. • Cruise control causes a power loss when it engages, or won't disengage when the brakes are applied. • When driver applies the brakes gently, cruise control doesn't disengage; instead, it kicks in harshly when vehicle speeds up. • Fuel tank is easily punctured by rocks thrown up by the front wheels. • Premature failure of the rear shocks. • Frequent brake pad replacement. **2000**— Windshield is easily chipped. • Sudden tire blowout. **2001**—Airbag deployed when key was inserted into the ignition. • Sudden, unintended acceleration. • Vehicle suddenly accelerated when coming to a stop by applying ABS brakes. • Vehicle pulls to one side when accelerating; alignment and tires eliminated as cause. • Intermittent hesitation when accelerating. • Engine hesitates when making a slow turn, or when accelerating from a stop. • Rear brake problems. • Brakes squeal or grind when braking. • Rear window suddenly shattered. • Excessive mirror vibration. • Front brake groan noise. **2002**—Fire ignited in the engine compartment. • Airbags failed to deploy. • Fuel throttle linkage failure causes abnormally high engine revs, sudden acceleration. • Excessive noise and vibration when driving with rear window lowered halfway. • Brake pedal is too small. **2003**—Airbags failed to deploy. **2004**—Sudden acceleration in Reverse, accompanied by brake failure.

Secret Warranties/Service Tips

All years: Remedy for front brake clicking found in TSB #BR004-00. Loose, poorly fit trim panels. **1997–98**—Front door lock knob improved operation. • Free seat belt extenders will be made available. • Correct front fender liner vibration noise with Toyota's wind noise kit. **1997–99**—Fifth gear engagement improvement campaign is covered under Toyota's powertrain warranty. **1998**—To minimize moisture retention and improve driveability, the length of the connecting vacuum line has been shortened. **1998–2000**—Delayed upshift to Overdrive with cruise control engaged. • Troubleshooting a lit MIL light. **2001**—Ticking noise at base of windshield. • Windshield creak noise. • Upgraded brake pads to reduce front brake noise. • Diagnosing noises in passenger-side dash and the A- and C-pillar areas. • Headlight retainer tab broken. • Improvement to the rear wiper washer nozzle. • Exhaust fumes enter into the interior. • Roof rack rattle or buzz. **2001–02**— Troubleshooting rear brake squeal; Toyota will replace the rear drums free of charge. • Backdoor rattles. • Noise from top of instrument panel. • Measures to remedy a MIL illumination. **2001–03**—Cowl noise troubleshooting tips. **2002**—Service campaign to inspect or repair the cruise control switch. • The MIL light stays lit due to a damaged fuel tank vent. • Wind whistle from front edge of hood. • Steering wheel may be off-centre. • Speedometer fluctuations. **2004**—Stinky exhaust countermeasure converter:

Excessive Sulfur Dioxide Odors

Bulletin No.: EG010-04   Date: May 7, 2004
2004 RAV4
Some customers may complain of excessive sulfur dioxide odour under the following conditions:
^ Stop and go driving.
^ Heavy acceleration.
In order to reduce the sulfur dioxide odor, a new catalytic converter has been developed.

RAV4 Profile

	1997	1998	1999	2000	2001	2002	2003	2004
Cost Price ($) (firm)								
4X2 (17%)	20,348	20,628	22,150	—	—	—	—	—
4X4 (17%)	23,078	22,048	22,500	24,185	23,260	24,420	24,485	24,485

Used Values ($)								
4X2 ⋏	5,000	6,500	7,000	—	—	—	—	—
4X2 ⋎	4,500	5,500	6,000	—	—	—	—	—
4X4 ⋏	7,000	8,000	9,000	12,000	15,500	17,500	19,000	22,000
4X4 ⋎	6,000	7,000	8,000	11,000	14,500	16,500	17,000	20,000

Reliability	④	⑤	⑤	⑤	⑤	⑤	⑤	⑤
Crash Safety (F)	③	④	④	④	④	④	④	④
Side	—	—	⑤	⑤	—	⑤	⑤	⑤
IIHS Side	—	—	—	—	❶	❶	❶	❶
Offset	❷	❷	❷	❷	③	③	③	③
Rollover	—	—	—	—	③	③	③	—

4RUNNER ★★★★

RATING: Above Average (1996–2005); Average (1986–95). Beefed up considerably for the 2003 model year, the new version looks like an on- and off-road winner. Previous models had been yuppified so much that their off-roading capability was seriously compromised. **Strong points:** Part-time 4X4 system allows the driver to shift on the fly and can be used on dry pavement. Instrument panel features easy-to-read gauges and user-friendly controls. Plenty of leg and headroom. Three can sit in the back as long as the road isn't rough. Seats are generally quite comfortable, though rear seat feels too low, rear passengers especially may feel cramped. Good off-road performance, high ground clearance, top-quality mechanical components and body construction, legendary reliability, and incredibly slow depreciation. **Weak points:** This SUV stinks (exhaust system rotten-egg smell). It vibrates excessively and assaults the ears when driven with a rear window or sunroof open. It's much less practical than the Highlander on-road; underpowered (especially when compared with Nissan's Pathfinder); has no manual gearbox for a safer and more thrilling off-roading experience; hard riding; somewhat numb steering; a cramped interior; a serious lack of head room with sunroof option; difficult entry/exit due to the narrow doors and steep step-in height; ventilation controls aren't easily accessed; excessive road and wind noise; and a gas guzzler. The optional differential lock has been discontinued, a serious blow to hardcore off-roaders. **New for 2005:** No significant changes.

2005 Technical Data

Powertrain (rear-drive/4X4)
Engines: 2.7L 4-cyl. (150 hp)
• 3.4L V6 (183 hp)
Transmission: 4-speed auto. OD
Dimension/Capacity
Height/length/width:

Wheelbase: 105.3 in.
Turning circle: 39 ft.
Passengers: 2/3
Cargo volume: 44 cu. ft.
GVWR: 5,250 lb.
Tow limit: 3,500–5,000 lb.

68.5/183.3/66.5 in.   Ground clearance: 10.2 in.
Headroom F/R: 39.2/38.7 in.   Fuel tank: 70L/reg.
Legroom F/R: 43.1/34.9 in.   Weight: 4,070 lb.

MODEL HISTORY: One of the most rugged compact sport-utilities on the market, the 4Runner is powered by a 3.4L V6—the same engine that powers Tacoma 4X4 pickups.

What can you expect after paying top dollar for a used 4Runner? Excellent off-road performance, better-than-average reliability, and incredibly slow depreciation. What you overspend in buying one, you'll likely recoup when you sell. On the other hand, be wary of early 4Runner "bargains"; they are hard riding, have mediocre highway handling, use biodegradable head gaskets up to 1997 (see "Secret Warranties/Service Tips"), and guzzle fuel. Whatever you do, don't try to save money by purchasing an underpowered, 4-cylinder-equipped version. Also ditch the Bridgestone, Firestone, or Goodyear tires (have them replaced with Michelin or Pirelli tires).

If the most recently redesigned 2003 and later models are too rich for your blood, consider a cheaper 1996–2001 version that underwent a previous revamping. They are lower, wider, and longer; have much more passenger room; are easier to enter and exit; use dual airbags and four-wheel ABS; and offer a user-friendly one-piece tailgate. Both the 4- and 6-cylinder engines were upgraded and fully independent suspension was added, along with rack-and-pinion steering. Channel your savings into a model equipped with the more versatile 6-cylinder engine.

Handling wasn't the 4Runner's strong suit until the redesigned 1996 models came along. The slow steering response and excessive body roll on previous models didn't exactly inspire confidence. Although a bit harsh, the ride is relatively civilized for a truck-based sport-utility, but you should expect lots of cabin vibration. Despite the stronger V6, the 4Runner is no tire burner. Transmission engagement isn't smooth or very precise, either, and the absence, until 1998, of full-time 4X4 in such a pricey vehicle is disappointing.

Interiors are acceptably appointed and finished, though one would expect a bit more luxury and some additional features, considering the 4Runner's cost. The body on pre-1996 4Runners is also fairly narrow, and rear-seat passengers especially may feel cramped. Entry/exit is also difficult for many, who find the step-in height too steep when compared to the Ford Explorer or GM Blazer and Jimmy.

1999—Both the grille and bumper were re-styled, along with the addition of a new 4X4 system that allows for full-time 4X4 as well as two-high, four-high, and four-low modes. Inside amenities include a new cupholder and centre console along with an overhead console that houses a garage door opener. **2001**—Base models were killed, leaving only the Limited and SR5 versions, with all 4Runners coming with an automatic transmission. **2003**—Completely redesigned, it's larger than the outgoing model and features a more powerful V6 and V8 borrowed from the Tundra pickup.

COST ANALYSIS: Best alternatives: Off-roaders will want a discounted second-series 2004 for the enhanced 4X4 capability and additional torque. Be wary of used models equipped with the 4-cylinder engine; it's only suitable for the lighter rear-drive versions. Also look at the Lexus LX 470, RX 300/330, or Toyota Sequoia. The Jeep Grand Cherokee is more agile, but nowhere near as reliable. **Rebates:** $2,000 along with zero percent financing by mid-2004. **Delivery/PDI:** $1,245 (yikes!). **Warranty:** Bumper-to-bumper 3 years/60,000 km; powertrain 5 years/100,000 km; rust perforation 5 years/unlimited km. **Supplementary warranty:** Don't waste your money. **Options:** Four-wheel ABS, V6 supercharger, air conditioning, a good anti-theft system, remote key-less entry, full-sized spare tire, oversized tires (they include larger brakes), and an upgraded sound system. **Depreciation:** Incredibly slow rate of depreciation beats out most vehicles in its class. **Insurance cost:** Average. **Annual maintenance cost:** Average. **Parts supply/cost:** Good, owing to a strong dealer network. Expensive parts. **Highway/city fuel economy:** 11.4–14.4L/100 km.

QUALITY/RELIABILITY: Better than average, but why in heck does it take Toyota five years to clean up its exhaust and how can they ignore the overpowering noise and vibration produced when their SUVs and pickups are driven with an open window? **Owner-reported problems:** Frequent owner complaints of stalling under all driving conditions, electrical shorts, premature brake wear, excessive driver seat and seat track creaking (covered by a TSB), foul-smelling exhaust, harmonic vibration, engine ticking, and accessories and trim items that don't hold up. **Warranty performance:** Much better than average.

SAFETY SUMMARY: Handling is steady at low speeds, but the rear end can swing out unexpectedly on slippery surfaces and when cornering at high speeds. All versions have built-in roll bars and a removable roof. **Airbags:** There have been reports of airbags failing to deploy. **ABS:** Standard 2W. Some later models may have optional four-wheel ABS. **Safety belt pretensioners:** Standard. **Head restraints F/R:** *1996:* **/*; *1997:* **; *1999:* **/*; *2001–02:* **/*; *2003:* ****/***. **Visibility F/R:** *****. **Maximum load capacity:** *1996:* 1,320 lb.; *2001:* 1,115 lb.; *2003:* 1,035 lb.

SAFETY COMPLAINTS: All years: Sudden acceleration. • Intermittent stalling, especially when braking or decelerating. • Fuel, ammonia, or rotten-egg exhaust smell. • Brake failures. • Warped front rotors. • Tire sidewall blowouts. • Excessive engine/drivetrain vibration and harmonic humming, felt initially through the gas pedal between 1400 and 2000 rpm (worst in Fifth gear). Painful noise produced when vehicle is driven with the rear window down or the sunroof opened. **1997**—Cruise control won't disengage and brakes failed. • Steering shaft failure caused the sudden loss of steering. • Rear suspension drops more than it should when rear of vehicle is occupied. • Anti-rattling spring in the ABS failed, causing excessive brake noise. • In emergency, the ABS didn't engage at first, then the front wheels locked up. • Brake pedal takes excessive effort and results in extended stopping distance. • Vehicle suddenly stalled and all electrical power was lost. • Jack supplied with vehicle may be inadequate for size of tires. • Rear seat belts are too short. **1998**— Cruise control malfunctioned, causing the vehicle to suddenly stall. • Brakelight comes on for no reason. **1999**—Fuel line leak sprayed gasoline all over the engine. • Incorrect fuel gauge readings; Low Fuel warning light comes on way too early. **2000**—Wheel came off and vehicle rolled over. • Gas gauge reads empty when the tank is half full. • Driver's door-mounted rear-view mirror gives a distorted image due to warping of the mirror. **2001**—When applying brakes, driver has to turn foot sideways. • Emergency braking causes vehicle to slide or skid. **2003**—Insufficient heating, defrosting. • Faulty Dunlop Grand Trek tire. **2004**—Loose driver's seat. • Instrument panel is washed out in daylight.

Secret Warranties/Service Tips

All years: Loose, poorly fitting trim panels. **1999–2000**—An inaccurate fuel gauge may require a new fuel sender. **1999–2001**—Power windows activate on their own. **2000**—On vehicles equipped with a supercharger, a squeaking or rattling noise coming from the idler pulley is likely caused by an out-of-tolerance idler pulley shaft. **2003**—Sunroof and headliner rattles. • Front-seat squeaks covered by TSB #00403; issued April 2003. • Free replacement of the fuel pulsation damper. **2003–04**—Replace deformed, warped windshield moldings with a free, new service part to correct the condition (TSB #BO005-04). • Second row passenger side seat noise.

4Runner Profile

	1997	1998	1999	2000	2001	2002	2003	2004
Cost Price ($) (firm)								
4Runner 4X4 (20%)	28,998	29,828	30,800	30,800	36,670	36,250	39,100	39,220
Used Values ($)								
4Runner 4X4 ʌ	12,000	14,500	15,500	18,000	21,000	24,000	28,000	34,000
4Runner 4X4 v	11,000	13,000	14,000	17,000	19,000	22,500	26,500	33,000
Reliability	④	④	④	⑤	⑤	⑤	⑤	⑤
Crash Safety (F)	③	③	④	④	④	④	④	④
Side	—	—	⑤	⑤	⑤	⑤	⑤	⑤
Offset	③	③	③	③	③	③	⑤	⑤
Rollover	—	—	—	—	❷	❷	③	③

HIGHLANDER ★★★★★

RATING: Recommended (2001–05). Beats out all truck-based SUVs and is a top contender among the five-passenger unibody competiton. **Strong points:** Good acceleration with the V6; impressive manoeuvrability; comfortable, though firm, ride; well equipped; plenty of passenger space and cargo room; well laid-out and easy-to-read instruments and controls; little engine or road noise; offset crashworthiness and head restraint protection rated Good by IIHS; reasonably priced; slow depreciation; base engine uses regular fuel; and high-quality components and fit and finish. **Weak points:** 4-cylinder engine is adequate but has little reserve power; audio and climate system graphics aren't intuitive; high step-in; unbelievably high freight and PDI charges ($1,245); poor fuel economy; no low-speed transfer case; and V6 requires premium fuel. **New for 2005**: No major changes.

2005 Technical Data

Powertrain
Engines: 2.4L 4-cyl. (160 hp)
• 3.3L V6 (230 hp)
Transmission: 4-speed auto.
• 5-speed auto.
Dimension/Capacity
Height/length/width:
60.5/184/72 in.
Headroom F/R: 40/39.8 in.
Legroom F/R: 40.7/36.4 in.

Wheelbase: 107 in.
Turning circle: 40 ft.
Passengers: 2/3
Cargo volume: 41.5 cu. ft.
GVWR: 4,985 lb.
Tow limit: 3,500 lb.
Ground clear.: 7.3 in.
Fuel tank: 75L/reg./prem.
Weight: 3,915 lb.

MODEL HISTORY: The Highlander is a Camry-based sport-utility that's similar to the RX 330, though roomier and cheaper. It comes with either a 4-cylinder engine or optional V6, mated to a 4- or 5-speed automatic. Serious off-road performance is compromised by the absence of a transfer case for low-range gearing.

Although not as powerful as the Sequoia, the $32,500 Highlander is quiet-running and comfortably accomodates five passengers. With its responsive handling, user-friendly controls, full-time all-wheel-drive, smooth powertrain, and folding third-row seat (for kids only), this is the ideal SUV for folks who want to step up from the RAV4, but don't want to shell out about $20,000 more for an RX 330.

2004—A 5-hp boost for the 4-banger and a new 3.3L V6 used by the 2004 Sienna and Lexus RX 330. Other improvements: A re-styled front end and more entertainment options.

COST ANALYSIS: Best alternatives: Get a discounted second-series 2004, since the 2005 is essentially the same car. Other good buys: The Honda CR-V, Hyundai Santa Fe, Subaru Forester, and Toyota RAV4. **Rebates:** $2,000 rebates, and low-financing rates early in the new year. **Delivery/PDI:** $1,245. **Warranty:** Bumper-to-bumper 3 years/60,000 km; powertrain 5 years/ 100,000 km; rust perforation 5 years/unlimited km. **Supplementary warranty:** Not necessary. **Options:** The V6 is essential for passing and merging with traffic; the sunroof, however, eats up valuable headroom. **Depreciation:** Quite low. **Insurance cost:** Higher than average. **Parts supply/cost:** Generic parts also used by the RX series are easy to find and moderately priced. **Annual maintenance cost:** Much lower than average. **Highway/city fuel economy:** 7.9–10.7L/100 km with the 2.4L; 9.7–13L/100 km with the 3.0L (V6).

QUALITY/RELIABILITY: Owner-reported problems: Excessive vibrations; painful pulsating pressure felt in the ears caused by wind noise when vehicle is driven with the rear windows down; poor acceleration; hard gear shift; erratic speedometer; AC and door lock glitches; and faulty automatic transmission and computer control unit. **Warranty performance:** Better than average. Toyota is usually efficient and fair in its customer relations dealings, except for its recent engine sludge debacle.

SAFETY SUMMARY: Cupholders are positioned too close to the gear shift lever—making it easy to inadvertently bump the lever into Neutral when reaching for a drink (Lexus RX 300 has the same problem). **Airbags:** Front; optional side. **ABS:** Standard; disc/disc. **Safety belt pretensioners:** Front. **Traction control:** Optional limited-slip differential. **Head restraints F/R:** *****. **Visibility F/R:** *****. **Maximum load capacity:** 925 lb.

SAFETY COMPLAINTS: All years: Brakes applied and pedal went to the floor without braking. • If the back window is opened while underway, the vehicle vibrates wildly and creates a vacuum, painful to the ears; rolling down the front window or opening the moon roof eliminates the problem. **2001**—Airbags failed to deploy. • Automatic transmission failure. • Transmission bangs into gear. • Speedometer is unreadable with sunglasses and tinted windows. • Plastic fuel tank shield is ineffective. • Centre cupholders are poorly designed; when you remove a drink, it's easy to knock gearshift lever, taking vehicle out of gear. **2002**—ABS failure. The top of the dash panel reflects sunlight, blinding the driver. **2003**—Brake failures; overheating. **2004**—Sudden, unintended acceleration. • Jack is inadequate, particularly with 16-inch wheels. • Daytime running lights blind on-coming drivers (2004 Sienna has the same problem).

Secret Warranties/Service Tips

All years: Poorly fitted trim panels. • Sulfur smell (Toyota will change the catalytic converter). **2001**—Goodwill extended warranty to correct engine oil sludge problem. • Check Engine light troubleshooting. • Wind noise at the A-pillar. **2002**—Excessive brake noise and increased pedal stroke when applying brakes. • Malfunctioning MIL light. • Moon roof moulding creak. • Squeak and rattle remedies. • Reducing front seatback noise. **2001–03**—Drive axle squeak.

Squeak from Right Rear of Vehicle

Bulletin No.: DL001-03   Date: May 23, 2003
2001–03 Highlander (4WD)
The right rear inner oil seal has been improved to correct this condition.

2001–04—Hood protector wind noise countermeasures. **2004**—Install improved catalytic converter to clean up smelly exhaust (TSB #EG009-04).

Highlander Profile				
	2001	**2002**	**2003**	**2004**
Cost Price ($) (firm)				
Highlander FWD (18%)	33,000	31,990	32,330	32,900
Highlander AWD (19%)	36,100	36,190	34,530	36,900
Used Values ($)				
Highlander FWD ⋀	18,000	22,000	25,000	27,000
Highlander FWD ⋁	16,000	22,500	23,000	26,000
Highlander AWD ⋀	22,000	24,000	27,000	32,000
Highlander AWD ⋁	20,000	23,000	25,500	30,000
Reliability	④	⑤	⑤	⑤
Crash Safety (F)	—	④	④	⑤
Side	—	④	⑤	⑤
Offset	⑤	⑤	⑤	⑤
Rollover	—	③	③	—

SEQUOIA	★★★★★

RATING: Recommended (2001–05). A refined, well-equipped, and reliable best buy. In exchange for less towing and payload capability, you get a smooth-running, dependable powertrain and a spacious, versatile interior. **Strong points:** Potent V8 performance on the 2005, though earlier V8 was a decent performer. Plenty of torque and low-end grunt; acceptable big-truck manoeuvrability; comfortable ride; lots of passenger space and cargo room; well appointed, with a nice array of easy-to-understand and access instruments and controls; a 3,000 kg (6,500 lb.) towing capacity (without 4X4); high-quality mechanical components and body construction; and runs on regular fuel. **Weak points:** *2001–04 models:* Sequoia's heft compromises acceleration needed for passing and merging; large turning radius; right rear quarter vision is obstructed by the second-row head restraint; tough to parallel park; due to the high ground clearance, step-in may be difficult for some; rear-seat access a bit awkward; vehicle shakes when driven with the rear window open; high freight and PDI charges; and poor fuel economy. **New for 2005:** A more powerful engine (42 more horses), a new 5-speed electronically-controlled (ECT) automatic transmission with lock-up torque converter, Overdrive cancel switch and cooler, tire pressure monitoring system, a standard TRD OffRoad Sport package for the SR5, a standard Luxury Package for the Limited, and a JBL Premium Sound system added to the entire lineup.

2005 Technical Data	

Powertrain
Engine: 4.7L 4-cyl. (282 hp)

Turning circle: 42.3 ft.
Passengers: 2/3/3

Transmission: 5-speed auto.   Cargo volume: 73.6 cu. ft.
Dimension/Capacity   GVWR: 6,500 lb.
Height/length/width: Tow limit: 6,200 lb.
75.8/203.9/78.9 in.   Ground clear.: 10.6 in.
Headroom F/R: 40.4/38.8/36.9 in.   Fuel tank: 100L/reg.
Legroom F/R: 41.6/38.7/29.8 in.   Weight: 5,280 lb.
Wheelbase: 118 in.

MODEL HISTORY: A Tundra pickup-based sport-utility introduced in 2001, the Sequoia is a full-sized SUV that targets the GM Tahoe, Yukon, and Suburban, and the Ford Expedition. A bit narrower than the above-mentioned vehicles, the Sequoia nevertheless offers eight-passenger, third-row seating, and generous interior dimensions A ground clearance of 11 inches allows for some off-roading; however, the rear suspension has been modified to prioritize comfortable cruising. Safety features include Vehicle Stability Control, standard four-wheel disc brakes with ABS, curtain-shield side airbags, and three-way seat belts for all passenger positions.

2003s were given a rear load-levelling suspension, a centre differential lock button, Brake Assist, a seven-pin towing connect, larger wheels and tires, and an electrochromic mirror.

COST ANALYSIS: Best alternatives: The upgraded 2005 is the better buy, even though last year's $53,650 MSRP has jumped to $59,530 (oh, what a feeling, Toyota!). Even with additional features, it's doubtful these kind of price increases will withstand $5,000+ rebates and discounts proffered by Ford, GM, and Chrysler. For more brawn than reliability, you'll want the GM Tahoe or Yukon. Ford's reworked 2002 or later Explorer 4X4 is no bargain when its poor reliability is taken into account. **Rebates:** $2,500 rebates, plus other discounts and zero percent financing. **Delivery/PDI:** $1,245 (shame on you, Toyota!). **Warranty:** Bumper-to-bumper 3 years/60,000 km; powertrain 5 years/100,000 km; rust perforation 5 years/unlimited km. **Supplementary warranty:** Not needed. **Options:** Nothing worth the extra money. **Depreciation:** Much slower than average. **Insurance cost:** Higher than average. **Parts supply/cost:** Tundra-sourced parts aren't expensive and are easily found. **Annual maintenance cost:** Much lower than average. **Highway/city fuel economy:** 12.4–15.9L/100 km.

QUALITY/RELIABILITY: Better than average. **Owner-reported problems:** Premature brake wear and vibration; rotten-egg exhaust smell (Toyota service bulletins recommend replacing the catalytic converter under warranty); pungent ammonia smell. **Warranty performance:** Better than average.

ROAD PERFORMANCE: Acceleration/torque: Acceleration is quick, smooth, and quiet. Even though the Sequoia's 2001–04 engine surpasses the Ford Expedition's basic 215-hp engine, it lags 35 horses behind the Chevy Tahoe's 275 hp. Payload also trails the Ford and GM competition. **Transmission:** Flawless performance. **Steering:** Precise and responsive; less trucklike than the Tahoe or Expedition. **Routine handling:** Pleasant ride quality and handling, except in tight spots and twisty roads, where the Sequoia's size and large turning radius compromise handling. Very effective Active Traction Control and Vehicle Stability Control, an automatic anti-skid system that regulates the throttle and selectively applies the brakes to individual wheels to correct understeer or oversteer. **Braking:** Braking is exceptional.

SAFETY SUMMARY: Airbags: Front; optional side. **ABS:** Standard; disc/disc. **Safety belt pretensioners:** Front. **Traction control:** Yes. **Head restraints F/R:** *****. **Visibility F/R:** *****/**. **Maximum load capacity:** 1,320 lb.

SAFETY COMPLAINTS: All years: Inconsistent braking; brake warning light constantly lit. • If the back window is opened while underway, the vehicle vibrates wildly and creates a vacuum, painful to the ears; rolling down the front window or opening the moon roof eliminates the problem; loose or poorly-fitted trim panels. **2001**—Airbags failed to deploy. • Sudden stalling. • Chronic hesitation when accelerating. • Windshield is easily cracked by road debris. • Anti-skid system activates when it's not needed. • Passengers slip on running board non-slip strip. **2001–02**—Excessive vibration when braking. **2002**—Vehicle will suddenly drift across the highway. **2003**—Transmission may slip from Park to Drive or Park to Reverse. • Anti-skid control engaged when it shouldn't. • Vehicle surges from a stop or when accelerating out of a turn. • Engine drops to idle for about 6–10 seconds when completing a turn. • Rear-view mirror is too small. • Noxious gas fumes enter the cabin. • Door latch failure allowed door to open when turning.

Secret Warranties/Service Tips

2001—Inoperative high beam indicator light. • Fog lamp moisture. • Front seat cover damage. **2001–02**—Hard starts, or no starts. • Vibrating front brakes can be corrected by installing improved front brake calliper assemblies. • Upgraded back door pull strap. **2001–03**—AC compressor durability improvement:

Poor AC Compressor Durability

Bulletin No.: AC001-04   Date: February 11, 2004

2001–03 Sequoia

To improve the durability and integrity of repairs on 2001–03 model year Sequoia vehicles with rear AC, a new suction tube and in-line filter system is now available. Please follow the procedures in this bulletin if the compressor is being replaced because of a noise concern and/or has seized.

2001–04—If the AC doesn't sufficiently cool the cabin, TSB #AC004-04 says the water control valve is the likely culprit. • Faulty oil pressure gauge:

Oil Pressure Gauge Reads Low

Bulletin No.: EL017-03   Date: December 23, 2003

2001–04 Sequoia
2000–02 Tundra

Some customers with Sequoia or Tundra vehicles may encounter an oil pressure gauge that reads
abnormally low at idle. An updated oil pressure sender has been created to address this condition.

Sequoia Profile

	2001	2002	2003	2004
Cost Price ($) (firm)				
SR-5 (20%)	45,400	45,670	48,100	53,650
Limited (20%)	57,900	58,205	52,150	63,500
Used Values ($)				
SR-5 Λ	28,000	32,000	38,000	45,000
SR-5 V	25,000	30,000	35,000	42,000
Limited Λ	34,000	38,000	40,000	55,000
Limited V	32,000	36,000	38,000	52,000
Reliability	⑤	⑤	⑤	⑤
Crash Safety (F)	—	④	⑤	⑤
Rollover	—	③	③	—

MINIVANS AND VANS

GM Silhouette Intake Manifolds

I have filed a claim in Ontario Small Claims Court with regards to a 1998 Oldsmobile Silhouette that we have had since the beginning. The problem, which will be no surprise to you, is the intake manifold gasket, which has now brought the need to replace the whole engine!

S. B.

Four Odyssey Transmissions

You are already aware of the transmission problems with the 1999–2001 models (mine is a base Odyssey 2000 model with about 67,000 km). Well, my van is currently in the shop to get its 4th transmission (!). It is covered by the warranty, which as you know is now extended to 7 years/160k.

The service response has been good but I do not want to be replacing transmissions every 9 months (my current average) or worrying in-between about when it is going to fail again (ie. on vacation etc.). The last transmission lasted only 2 months!

L. M.

Minivans

Like sport-utilities, minivans fall into two categories: upsized cars and downsized trucks. The upsized cars are "people-movers." They're mostly front-drives, handle like a car, and get great fuel economy. The Honda Odyssey and Toyota Sienna are the best examples of this kind of minivan. In fact, following Toyota's upgrades last year and Honda's 2005 Odyssey improvements, their road performance and reliability surpass the front- and rear-drive minivans built by DaimlerChrysler, Ford, and General Motors.

GM's Astro and Safari, and Ford's Aerostar, on the other hand, are downsized trucks. Using rear-drive, 6-cylinder engines, and heavier mechanical components, these minivans handle cargo as well as passengers. On the negative side, fuel economy is no match for the front-drives, and highway handling is more trucklike. Interestingly, rear-drive GM and Ford minivans are much more reliable performers than the front-drive Ford Windstar or Chrysler minivans. As AWDs, though, they'll keep you in the repair bay for weeks.

Rear-drive vans are also better suited for towing trailers in the 1,600–2,950 kg (3,500–6,500 lb.) range. Most automakers say their front-drive minivans can pull up to 1,600 kg (3,500 lb.) with an optional towing package (often costing almost $1,000 extra), but don't you believe it. Owners report white-knuckle driving and premature powertrain failures caused by the extra load. It just stands to reason that Ford and Chrysler front-drives equipped with engines and transmissions that blow out at 60,000–100,000 km under normal driving conditions are going to meet their demise much earlier under a full load.

Declining quality

Quality control has always been a serious problem with minivans and vans. In the '60s, VW minivans were unreliable, rust-catching boxes that spent more time in the service bay than on the road. And to this day, the VW EuroVan is more a curiosity than a credible transporter.

Chrysler

But Chrysler minivans did catch on from their debut in 1984, when they were seen as fairly reliable and efficient people-haulers. Since they were backed by Chrysler's 7-year bumper-to-bumper warranty, much of the sting was taken out of repair costs. Since then, these minivans have dominated the market, despite their biodegradable engines, automatic transmissions, brakes, and air conditioners. In fact, it's amazing how little Chrysler's defect patterns have changed during the past two decades.

Ford

Ford's minivans have gone from bad to worse. Its first minivan, the 1985–97 Aerostar, was fairly dependable, although it did have some recurring tranny, brake, and coil spring problems. Collapsing coil springs may cause tire blowouts on all model years, although 1988–90 models are covered by a regional recall. Other years fall under a "goodwill" program, as this *Lemon-Aid* reader reports:

> On vacation in Washington, our 1995 Aerostar blew a tire that was worn right through from the left rear coil spring (broken in two places). The right rear coil spring is broken, as well. I showed Dams Ford in Surrey, B.C. the broken spring and they have "graciously" offered to replace the tire or repair the right side at no cost to us.

Ford's quality decline continued with the Mercury Villager, a co-venture that also produced the Nissan Quest. The Villager/Quest duo lasted through the 2000 model year, until Nissan brought out its completely redesigned 2004 Quest—a minivan that has been greeted by underwhelming enthusiasm (first year models were so glitch-prone that Nissan sent over 200 engineers to the States to correct the factory-related deficiencies).

Then Ford brought out the 1995 Windstar—one of the poorest quality, most dangerous minivans ever built. Renamed the Freestar, its failure-prone powertrain, suspension (broken coil springs), electrical, fuel, and braking systems can put both your wallet and your life at risk.

Ford has compounded the Windstar's failings by its hard-nosed attitude in treating customer complaints and refusing warranty coverage for what are clearly factory-induced defects. Fortunately, a flood of Canadian small claims court decisions have come to the aid of Ford owners when Ford wouldn't. These Canadian courts say Ford and its dealers must pay for engine and transmission repairs, even if the original warranty has expired (see page 132).

General Motors

GM's minivans and vans have also been seriously "bug afflicted." Plagued by faulty engine intake manifolds and diesel engine injectors, clunky, failure-prone automatic transmissions, defective brake and fuel systems, and subpar fit and finish, they are no better than Detroit's other contenders.

Asian

Asian competitors aren't perfect machines, either, as a quick perusal of NHTSA-registered safety complaints, service bulletins, and online complaint forums will quickly confirm. Asian companies, looking to keep costs down, have also been bedevilled by chronic engine and automatic transmission failures, sliding door malfunctions, catastrophic tire blowouts, and electrical malfunctions.

A word of warning about Nissan. Yes, the company has made fairly dependable vehicles for the past three decades—minivans being among them. However, the newly redesigned Quest minivan has been the exception, along with recent Altimas and Maximas, which all use similar components. Interestingly, the Murano and Titan have so far escaped a large number of factory-related glitches.

European

And finally we come back to where we started—Volkswagen. Its Vanagon (1979) and EuroVan/Camper (1993) have never been taken seriously since they came to North America in 1950 as a Transporter cargo van or nine-seat, 21-window Microbus. A reputation for poor overall quality, puny engines, and insufficient parts and servicing support continues to drive buyers away.

Getting more for less

Most minivans are overpriced for what is essentially an upgraded car or down-sized truck, and motorists needing a vehicle with large cargo- and passenger-carrying capacity should consider a Chrysler, Ford, or GM full-sized van, even if it means sacrificing some fuel economy. You just can't beat the excellent forward vision and easy-to-customize interiors that these large vans provide. Furthermore, parts are easily found and are competitively priced, due to the large number of independent suppliers.

Please remember that the following minivan ratings may differ somewhat from those in *Lemon-Aid Used Cars and Minivans* due to the use of more current data and an additional review of the ratings by the author. Also, some minivans that are no longer built, like the Ford Aerostar and Nissan Axxess, are given mini-ratings in Appendix II.

Full-Sized Vans

The North American full-sized van is a venerable institution. Contractors, electricians, and plumbers have turned these vans into portable tool boxes. Campers have customized full-sized vans to travel the country in comfort— canoe on top and trailer in tow. And retirees are cruising our nation's highways with large vans chock-full of every safety and convenience feature imaginable, literally turning their vehicles into mobile condos. Extended family? Hockey mom? No problem—an extended van can seat up to 15. Whatever the need, the full-sized van can accommodate.

"Geezer-mobiles?"

C'mon. Sure, they may not be sleek or sexy (neither am I, for that matter), their styling is likely decades old, and their popularity has certainly waned, but large vans are versatile carriers that have more "grunt" than front-drives and are more reliable as well. Okay, they *are* fuel-thirsty. But I'll bet that'll be the last thought in your mind when you pass more fuel-efficient minivans stuck on the side of the road with cooked engines or burned-out transmissions. There are also some safety reasons for choosing a large van, including superb forward visibility and plenty of room to sit away from the airbag housing. As well, SUVs and other vehicles are less likely to run up over the frame and crash into the van's passenger compartment.

Handling, though, is definitely not carlike (no matter the hype to the con-trary); expensive suspension modifications may be needed to produce a reasonable ride and manoeuvrability. Rear visibility is also problematic. They are susceptible to crosswinds, wander at highway speeds, and demand greater driving skills simply to corner safely and for parking in the city. They are also not cheap; and in base form, all you get is a steel box on four wheels.

Fifteen-passenger vans are particularly hazardous. Often used to shuttle sports teams, church groups, and airport passengers, they are prone to roll over when fully loaded. In fact, they are three times more likely to roll over when carrying 10 or more passengers, says NHTSA. This is because the van's centre of gravity shifts up and to the back unexpectedly, and excess baggage adds to this instability. Ford paid $37.5 million in a 2004 Kentucky van crash case, after a Scott County jury found the automaker's 15-passenger van responsible for two deaths.

GM and Chrysler have substantially redesigned their full-sized vans within the past few years to improve both the handling and the ride, and to add important safety features like ABS and additional airbags. Following this redesign, GM has led the Detroit pack with better-handling and smoother-riding models than those available from Ford and Chrysler.

But quality has been forgotten.

Chrysler's full-sized, rear-drive vans are more reliable than its front-drive minivans. But this isn't saying much when you consider the expensive repair bills generated by blown transmissions and collapsed ball joints. On the other hand, the problems are well-known and easily fixed. These vans were replaced by the Mercedes-bred, rear-drive 2004 Dodge Sprinter in the fall of 2003.

Ford's Econoline joins GM in the rear of the pack from a warranty performance standpoint. Both companies are sticking with 5-year guarantees through 2005, even though they are in serious need of a 7-year powertrain warranty to restore confidence in their lineup.

GM van quality hasn't improved much over the years and right now isn't any better than Ford and Chrysler offerings. Some of the more common problems shared by all three automakers: Engine and drivetrain breakdowns, brake failures, premature brake and suspension/steering wearout, AC failures, electrical and computer module glitches, and both manual- and sliding-door defects.

The reason why there's such similarity in the defect trending among Asian and Detroit van builders is that they all get their key components from a small band of suppliers. And, as they cut supplier profits, quality goes down the drain. Hence, as Toyota and Honda become more skinflint in their supplier payouts they, too, see a corresponding quality decline, evidenced by engine and transmission defects and sliding-door failures.

The important difference lies in how each automaker responds to these quality problems. Chrysler brought back its 7-year base powertrain warranty in 2001; Toyota and Honda set up publicly disclosed 7- and 8-year "goodwill" extended warranties, and Ford and GM pay repair costs on a case-by-case basis, through secret warranties and small claims court settlements.

Van advantages

- lots of reasonably priced, converted, used models available
- gasoline and diesel versions available
- easy to repair, with excellent parts availability at reasonable prices
- huge network of independent converters
- versatile people- and cargo-haulers
- easily converted to carry physically challenged occupants
- commanding view of the road
- excellent front and side crash protection
- much lower-than-average collision repair costs

Van disadvantages

- depreciated prices are still higher than what many people can afford
- homeowners' association may prohibit vans not garaged
- base models require costly options for comfortable performance
- inadequate standard suspension needs expensive modification
- lack of power with base engines
- uncomfortable seats in base models
- expensive interior upgrades are necessary
- poor-performing, standard-issue tires (try replacing them with Michelin or Yokohama instead)
- poor handling at highway speeds and in winter conditions
- difficult engine access
- excessive road and tire noise resonates in cabin

- large interior volume requires extra AC and defroster
- washing and waxing can be an all-day affair
- clunky transmission noise amplified by "echo chamber" styling
- sliding side doors usually rust out at the bottom and top runners. Body panels rust out at the left and right upper-front welds, just above the windshield, and water pours off the roof into the power-window housing or onto front-seat exiting passengers (add extra waterproofing to the window motor assembly, or expect to replace the motors every few years)

Safety-related problems

- inadequate acceleration
- lateral winds affect driveability
- unforgiving, risky handling
- trucklike manoeuvrability
- uneven braking and loss of directional stability
- high-speed instability
- poor rearward visibility
- poor heating, defrosting, and ventilation systems
- poor frontal crash protection (improved with airbag technology)
- few vans come with de-powered airbags
- hazardous sliding doors

Full-sized van tips

Car washes spray directly into door panel window channels, which plays havoc with the electrically operated windows, requiring at least $400 per door to correct. Side mirrors are extremely hazardous. Objects are much closer than they appear in the side-view mirrors. Smart owners soon learn to rely on the rear windshield mirror, instead—pulling back into traffic only when they can see a full profile of the following car. Built-in ice coolers are of minimal value; they're hard to clean, and don't carry much. Heavy doors need oiling and adjusting periodically. Large front windshield tends to leak water through the top molding and surrounding metal panels rust-out early. Roof leaks are legion and are best plugged by adding a "hi-top" roof. A good idea is to buy a light-coloured van: Dirt doesn't show as much, they're cooler in the summer (reflecting, rather than absorbing the sun's rays), and colour is easier to match when repainting.

Conversion vans

A conversion van feels good. With dual captain's chairs (large, plush seats with arm supports), lots of power accessories, TV, sofa/bed, and window shades…hey, it meets all our fantasies (or at least mine).

GM has one-half of a dying conversion van market, Ford has about a third, and Dodge has the rest.

Generating from $3,500 to $5,500 in profits, these vans are under fire from more fuel-efficient SUVs and minivans. GM bought most of the conversion van companies in 2004, following a dismal decade of poor conversion sales. Since 1988, conversions declined by more than 90 percent and have yet to recover. In fact, during the first half of 2004, consumers bought only about 15,000 conversion vans—compared with 204,000 units sold in 1988.

MINIVAN, VAN RATINGS

Recommended
Honda Odyssey (2005)

Above Average
Ford Villager/Nissan Quest
  (1997–2003)
Honda Odyssey (2003–2004)

Mazda MPV (2002–05)
Toyota Sienna (1998–2003; 2005)

Average
DaimlerChrysler Caravan, Voyager,
Grand Caravan, Grand Voyager,
 Town & Country (2002–05)
DaimlerChrysler Ram Van, Ram
 Wagon (1980–2003)
Ford Econoline (2004)
Ford Villager/Nissan Quest (1997–2003)
General Motors Astro, Safari
 (1996–2005)

General Motors Cargo Van,
 Chevy Van, Express, Savana,
 Vandura (1980–2005)
Honda Odyssey (1996–2002)
Kia Sedona (2002–05)
Mazda MPV (2000–01)
Toyota Previa (1991–97)
Toyota Sienna (2004)

Below Average
DaimlerChrysler Caravan, Voyager,
 Grand Caravan, Grand Voyager,
 Town & Country (1998–2001)
Ford Econoline (1980–90)
Ford Freestar (2004–05)
Ford Villager/Nissan Quest (1995–96)
General Motors Astro, Safari
 (1985–95)

General Motors Astro, Safari
 (1985–95)
General Motors Lumina, Lumina
 APV, Montana, Montana SV6,
 Silhouette, Trans Sport,
 Uplander, Venture (1997–2005)
Mazda MPV (1988–98)
Nissan Quest (2004–05)

Not Recommended
DaimlerChrysler Caravan, Voyager,
 Grand Caravan, Grand Voyager,
 Town & Country (1984–97)
DaimlerChrysler Sprinter (2004–05)
Ford Econoline Cargo Van,
 Club Wagon (1991–2003)
Ford Villager/Nissan
 Quest (1993–94)

Ford Windstar (1995–2003)
General Motors Astro, Safari
 (1985–95)
General Motors Lumina, Lumina
 APV, Silhouette, Trans Sport
 (1990–96)

DaimlerChrysler

CARAVAN, VOYAGER, GRAND CARAVAN, GRAND VOYAGER, TOWN & COUNTRY ★★★

RATING: Average (2002–05); Below Average (1998–2001); Not Recommended (1984–97). Let's get this straight: Chrysler, Ford, and GM minivans are at the bottom of the heap as far as quality and dependability are concerned. Chrysler, however, has the best warranty for engines and transmissions and only its transmissions are seriously defective. Ford and GM, on the other hand, have serious transmission *and* engine problems, covered by a much shorter warranty. Therefore, the Chrysler lineup has been given a one-notch higher rating than the other two Detroit automakers. **Strong points:** A comprehensive powertrain warranty; failure-prone AWD to be dropped; discounted 2004–05 prices and rapid depreciation bring down ownership costs; quiet and plush ride, excellent braking, lots of innovative convenience features, user-friendly instruments and controls, driver-side sliding door, and plenty of interior room. **Weak points:** Seven-year powertrain warranty isn't available on 2001 and earlier models and the chintzy base warranty is inadequate to deal with serious powertrain, ABS, and body defects. Resale value plummets due to new minivan discounting. Poor acceleration with the base engine and mediocre handling with the extended versions. Both automatic transmissions perform poorly in different ways, but the 3-speed is decidedly the worst of the two. Headlight illumination may be inadequate. Skimpy storage compartments. Get used to a cacophony of rattles, squeals, moans, and groans, caused by the vehicle's poor construction and subpar components. Crashworthiness has declined. **New for 2005:** Curtain side airbags and second- and third-row seats that fold flush with the floor; AWD will be dropped.

2005 Technical Data

Powertrain (front-drive)
Engines: 2.4L 4-cyl. (150 hp)
• 3.3L V6 (180 hp)
• 3.8L V6 (215 hp)
Transmissions: 3-speed auto.
• 4-speed auto.
Dimension/Capacity (base)
Height/length/width:
68.5/186.3/76.8 in.

Headroom F/R1/R2: 39.8/40.1/38.1 in.
Legroom F/R1/R2: 41.2/36.6/35.8 in.
Wheelbase: 113.3 in.
Turning circle: 39.5 ft.
Passengers: 2/2/3
Cargo volume: 146.7 cu. ft.
GVWR: 5,800 lb.
Tow limit: 2,700–3,500 lb.
Fuel tank: 76L/reg.
Weight: 3,985 lb.

MODEL HISTORY: These versatile minivans offer a wide array of standard and optional features that include AWD (dropped for 2005), anti-lock brakes, child safety seats integrated into the seatbacks, flush-design door handles, and front windshield wiper/washer controls located on the steering column lever for easier use. Childproof locks are standard, and the front bucket seats incorporate vertically adjustable head restraints. The Town & Country, a luxury version of the Caravan, comes equipped with a 3.8L V6 and standard luxury features that make the vehicle more fashionable for upscale buyers.

Chrysler's minivans continue to dominate the new- and used-minivan market, though they're quickly losing steam, due to a cooling of the market and better product quality from Japanese and South Korean automakers. Nevertheless, they offer pleasing styling and lots of convenience features at used prices that can be very attractive. They can carry up to seven passengers in comfort and also ride and handle better than most truck-based minivans. The shorter-wheelbase minivans also offer better rear visibility and good ride quality, and are more nimble and easier to park than truck-based minivans and larger front-drive versions. Cargo-hauling capability is more than adequate.

Caravans also give you a quiet and plush ride, excellent braking, lots of innovative convenience features, user-friendly instruments and controls, a driver-side sliding door, and plenty of interior room. Depreciation is much faster than pickups, SUVs, and Japanese minivans.

Don't make the mistake of believing that Chrysler's Mercedes connection means you'll get a top-quality minivan. You won't. In fact, owner complaints and service bulletins tell me that the 2004–05 minivans will likely have powertrain, electrical system, brake, suspension, and body deficiencies similar to previous versions. The following *Lemon-Aid* reader's email is rather typical:

> My 2003 Dodge Caravan is a piece of garbage. My new Caravan had a recall for a part in the transmission. It is noisy, rough running, and it doesn't get the 21–27 mpg [13.5–10.5 L/100 km] as advertised. 12 mpg [23.0 L/100 km] is more realistic.

These minivans pose maximum safety risks, due to their chronic electronic, mechanical, and body component failures. Owners report bizarre "happenings" with their minivans, like seat belts that may strangle children, airbags that deploy when the ignition is turned on, transmissions that jump out of gear, or sudden stalling and electrical short-circuits when within radar range of airports or military installations.

Astoundingly, recently launched minivans continue to exhibit an array of serious mechanical deficiencies that belie Chrysler's so-called commitment to quality improvement. Some of the more serious and most common problems include the premature wearout of the engine tensioner pulley, automatic transmission speed sensors, engine head gaskets, motor mounts, starter motor, steering column glitches, front brake discs and pads (the brake pad material crumbles in your hands), front rotors and rear drums, brake master cylinder, suspension components, exhaust system components, ball joints, wheel bearings, water pumps, fuel pumps and pump wiring harnesses, radiators, heater cores, and AC units. Fuel injectors on all engines have been troublesome, the differential pin breaks through the automatic transmission casing, sliding doors malfunction, engine supports may be missing or not connected, tie-rods may suddenly break, oil pans crack, and the power-steering pump frequently leaks. Factory-installed Goodyear tires frequently fail prematurely at 40,000–65,000 km.

Since 1996, Chrysler's V6 engines have performed quite well—far better than similar engines equipping Ford and GM minivans. Nevertheless, some owners have reported engine oil sludging and head gasket failures, hard starts, stalling, serpentine belt failures, and power-steering pump hose blowouts (causing loss of power steering).

Chrysler's A604, 41TE, and 42LE automatic transmissions phased in with the 1991 models are a reliability nightmare that can have serious safety consequences (see "Safety Complaints"): Imagine having to count to three in traffic before Drive or Reverse will engage, "limping" home in Second gear at 50 km/h, or suddenly losing all forward motion in traffic.

Catastrophic transmission failures are commonplace due to poor engineering, as the following reader discovered:

> My '99 Grand Voyager had a complete differential failure at 104,000 km. The retaining pin sheared off, which allowed the main differential pin to work its way out and smash the casing and torque converter.
>
> In our case this is what happened. The gear bit, the pin spun, shearing the retaining pin off. With the centrifugal force the main pin worked its way out of the housing and smashed a 2″ x 4″ [4 cm x 10 cm] hole through the bell housing and nearly punctured the torque converter. In my opinion this is a design flaw that should have been corrected 10 years ago. From my research I have determined that the transaxle identification number matches the original A604 transaxle. I was shocked that they would still use these in 1999.

Fit and finish has gotten worse over the past two decades. Body hardware and interior trim are fragile and tend to break, warp, or fall off (door handles are an example). Premature rust-out of major suspension and steering components is a major safety and performance concern. Plus, paint delamination often turns these solid-coloured minivans into two-tone models with chalky white stripes on the hood and roof. Chrysler knows about this problem and often tries to get claimants to pay half the cost of repainting (about $1,500 on a $3,000 job), but will eventually agree to pay the total cost if the owner stands fast, or threatens small claims court action.

And as the minivan takes on its albino appearance, you can listen to a self-contained orchestra of clicks, clunks, rattles, squeaks, and squeals as you drive. Giving new meaning to the phrase "surround sound," this noise usually emanates from the brakes, suspension and steering assemblies, poorly anchored bench seats, and misaligned body panels.

1991—Restyled second-generation models offered all-wheel drive, ABS, and a driver-side airbag (all optional); body was rounder and the glass area was increased. **1992**—Standard driver-side airbag. **1993**—Upgraded front shoulder belts; bucket seat tilts forward to ease entry/exit. **1994**—Passenger-side airbag, side door guard beams, a redesigned dash, new bumpers, and mouldings. **1996**—Third generation models have more aerodynamic styling, a driver-side sliding door, roll-out centre and rear seats, a longer wheelbase, standard dual airbags and ABS (ABS later became optional on base models), and a more powerful 150-hp 2.4L 4-cylinder engine. **1998**—The 3.0L V6 engine was paired with a better-performing 4-speed automatic transmission and the 3.8L V6 got 14 additional horses (180 hp). **2000**—A new AWD Sport model (it was a sales flop) and standard cassette player and AC. **2001**—A small horse-power boost for the V6s, front side airbags, adjustable pedals, upgraded headlights, and a power-operated rear liftgate. **2002**—Fuel tank assembly redesigned to prevent post-collision fuel leakage, a tire air-pressure monitor, and a DVD entertainment system. **2003**—AutoStick transmission dropped; standard power liftgate on the Grand EX and ES models.

COST ANALYSIS: A new Caravan will cost you about $26,000, before sub-stantial fall and winter rebates kick in. If you can get a discounted (20 percent) 2004 version, do so. There's not much difference between the two. **Best alter-natives:** The 2005 Honda Odyssey should be your first choice, but earlier versions will do quite nicely. Toyota's 2003 or earlier models are the best choice. Mazda's 2002–03 MPV is also a good used alternative. GM and Ford front- and rear-drive minivans aren't credible alternatives due to their failure-prone powertrains; brake, suspension, and steering problems; electrical short circuits; and subpar bodywork. Full-sized GM and Chrysler rear-drive cargo vans, though, are a more affordable and practical buy if you intend to haul a full passenger load, do some regular heavy hauling, are physically challenged, use lots of accessories, or take frequent motoring excursions. Don't splurge on a new luxury Chrysler minivan: Its upscale Town & Country may cost up to $15,000 more than a base Caravan, yet only be worth a few thousand more after five years on the market. The 2000 model is a bargain, until you notice that it's not covered by an extended powertrain warranty. **Options:** As you increase body length you lose manoeuvrability. Don't even consider the 4-cylinder engine—it has no place in a minivan, especially when hooked to the inadequate 3-speed automatic transmission. It lacks an Overdrive and will shift back and forth as speed varies, and it's slower and noisier than the other choices. The 3.3L V6 is a better choice for most city-driving situations, but don't hesitate to get the 3.8L if you're planning lots of highway travel or car-rying four or more passengers. Since its introduction, it's been relatively trouble-free, plus it's more economical on the highway than the 3.3L, which strains to maintain speed. The sliding side doors may expose occupants to traffic and may not be very dependable. Child safety seats integrated into the rear seatbacks are convenient and reasonably priced, but Chrysler's versions have had a history of tightening up excessively or not tightening enough, allowing the child to slip out. Try the seat with your child before buying it. Power-adjustable pedals are an important upgrade, especially for short drivers. Other important features to consider are the optional defroster, power mir-rors, power door locks, and power driver's seat (if you're shorter than 5'9" or expect to have different drivers using the minivan). You may wish to pass on the tinted windshields; they seriously reduce visibility. Town & Country buyers should pass on the optional all-wheel drive coupled with four-wheel disc brakes (instead of the standard rear drums). Although the disc brakes have been improved, Chrysler's large number of ABS failures is worrisome. Ditch

the failure-prone Goodyear original equipment tires and remember that a
night drive is a prerequisite to check out headlight illumination, called inadequate by many. **Rebates:** 2004 and 2005 models will get $2,500–$3,000
rebates and zero percent financing throughout the year. **Delivery/PDI:** $995.
Warranty: Bumper-to-bumper 3 years/ 60,000 km; powertrain 7 years/
115,000 km; rust perforation 5 years/ 160,000 km. **Supplementary warranty:**
The 7-year powertrain warranty is a must-have. If buying the warranty separately, bargain it down to about one-third of the $1,500 asking price. Forget
the bumper-to-bumper extended warranty; it's simply too expensive.
Depreciation: Slightly slower than average, but not as slow as pickups and
SUVs. **Insurance cost:** Higher than average. **Parts supply/cost:** Easy to find
reasonably priced parts. **Annual maintenance cost:** Repair costs are average
during the warranty period. Chrysler says that its 3.3L and 3.8L engines won't
require tune-ups before 160,000 km. Prepare to be disappointed.
Highway/city fuel economy: *Caravan:* 9–13L/100 km; *Grand Caravan
AWD:* 10–14L/100 km; *Town & Country:* 9–14L/100 km; *Town & Country
AWD:* 10–15L/100 km.

QUALITY/RELIABILITY: Below average, but Chrysler's comprehensive warranty will go a long way toward keeping transmission repair costs down.
Owner-reported problems: Owners say these minivans are a hoot (and a
howl, moan, squeal, chirp, and thunk) as they age. Powertrain failures are
increasingly found to be caused by defective or poorly calibrated computer
modules, rather than the hardware deficiencies seen a decade ago. Owner
complaints focus on electrical glitches, erratic AC performance (compressor
clutch burnout), rapid brake wear, and accumulation of brake dust.

The following parts wear out quickly and are expensive to repair or replace:
Cooling system, clutches, front suspension components, wheel bearings, AC,
and body parts (trim; weather stripping becomes loose and falls off; plastic
pieces rattle and break easily). A word about brakes: The front brakes need
constant attention, if not to replace the pads or warped rotors, then to silence
the excessive squeaks. Premature wearout of the front brake rotors within two
years or 30,000 km is common and has serious safety implications. **Warranty
performance:** Average, but better than Ford and GM. Hit-or-miss warranty
compensation can't replace better quality control.

SAFETY SUMMARY: Dual airbags include knee bolsters to prevent front
occupants from sliding under the seat belts. Side-impact protection has been
increased with steel beams in door panels. An innovative engine compartment
layout also makes for a larger "crumple zone" in the event of collision.

Much like Ford and GM, Chrysler continues to downplay the implications
of its minivan safety defects, whether in the case of ABS failures, inadvertent
airbag deployments, or sudden transmission breakdowns. Seat belts are
another recurring problem: They may become unhooked from the floor
anchor, buckles jam or suddenly release, and the child safety seat harness easily
pulls out or over-retracts, trapping children. **Airbags:** De-powered front
airbags. Side airbags are standard. NHTSA has recorded numerous complaints
of airbags failing to deploy in an accident or deploying unexpectedly—when

passing over a bump in the road, or simply turning on the vehicle. **ABS:** Optional. **Traction control:** Standard. **Head restraints F/R:** *Caravan:* *; *Grand Caravan 1995:* *; *1996:* **/*; *1997:* *; *1999:* **/*; *2001–04:* ****/***. *Voyager 2001–03:* **/*; *Town & Country 1995:* *; *1997:* *; *1999:* *; *2001–04:* ***/**/*. **Visibility F/R:** ***/*****. **Maximum load capacity:** *2001 Grand Caravan Sport:* 1,150 lb.

SAFETY COMPLAINTS: All models/years: Sudden, unintended acceleration; owners report that cruise control units often malfunction, accelerating or decelerating the vehicle without any warning. • Airbag malfunctions. • Get used to the term "clock spring." It's an expensive little component that controls some parts within the steering wheel and, when defective, can lead the airbag warning light to come on or cause the airbag, cruise control, or horn to fail. It has been a pain in the butt for Chrysler minivan owners since the 1996 model year. Chrysler has extended its warranty for 1996–2000 model year minivans in two separate recalls and replaced the clock spring at no charge. Apparently, the automaker has found that the part fails because it was wound too tightly or short-circuited from corrosion. • Defective engine head gaskets, rocker arm gaskets, and engine mounts. • Engine sags, hesitation, stumble, hard starts, or stalling. • No steering/lock-up. • Carbon monoxide comes through air vents. • Brakes wear out prematurely, or fail completely. • Transmission fails, suddenly drops into low gear, won't go into Reverse, delays engagement, or jumps out of gear when running or parked. • One can move automatic transmission shift lever without applying brakes. • Several incidents where ignition was turned and vehicle went into Reverse at full throttle, although transmission was set in Park. • ABS failure caused an accident. • Front suspension strut towers rusting, then cracking at the weld seams; jig-positioning hole wasn't sealed at the factory. • Brakes activated by themselves while driving. • Prematurely warped rotors and worn-out pads cause excessive vibrations when stopping. • Seatbacks fall backward. • Rear windows fall out or shatter. • Power window and door lock failures. • Sliding door often opens while vehicle is underway, or jams, trapping occupants. • Weak headlights. • Horn often doesn't work. • Several incidents where side windows exploded for no apparent reason. • Adults cannot sit in third-row seat without their head smashing into roof as vehicle passes over bumps. **1996–97**—U.S. Supreme Court says an Oklahoma jury must decide if faulty passenger airbags are unsafe. • When driving through water, air breather intake ingests water and engine seizes. • Loss of steering control after running through a puddle. • No standard head restraints on the second- and third-row seats. • Right front door latch failures. • Distorted windshields and exterior rear-view mirror. • Inadequate windshield defrosting caused by poor design. **1996–2002**—Steering may emit a popping or ticking noise. **1997**—Engine sags, hesitates, stumbles, stalls, or is hard to start. • Faulty speed control. • Smooth-road shake, vibration, or wobble. • Wipers won't park or wipe in intermittent mode. • Water leaks onto floor from HVAC housing. **1998**—Engine overheating. • Right rear tail light caught fire. • Frequent replacement of the steering column and rack and pinion; in one incident, the steering wheel separated from the steering column. • Front suspension strut failure. • Many reports of defective liftgate gas shocks. • Many incidents reported of electrical short circuits and total electrical system failure. • Difficult to see through windshield in direct sunlight. • Defroster vent reflects in the windshield, obscuring driver's vision. • Poor steering-wheel design blocks the view of instruments and indicators. • Rear-view mirror often falls off. • Horn hard to find on steering hub. **1999**—Instrument panel fire. • Faulty speed sensors cause the automatic transmission to shift erratically and harshly. • Five-year-old child was able to pull shift lever out of Park into Drive without engaging brakes. • Sudden tie-rod breakage, causing loss of vehicle control. • Chronic steering-pump and rack failures. • Poor braking performance; brake pedal depressed to the floor with little or no effect; excessive vibrations or shuddering when braking. • Rusted-through front brake rotors and rear brake drums. • Power side windows fail to roll up. • Dash gauges all go dead intermittently. **2000**—Gas tank rupture. • Engine camshaft failure. • Although the owner's manual says vehicle should have a transmission/brake interlock, the feature is lacking (see "Secret Warranties/Service Tips/TSBs"). • Cruise control malfunctions. **2000–01**—Sudden loss of engine power, accompanied by fuel leakage from the engine compartment. • Emergency parking brake may not release, due to premature corrosion. • Right front brake locked up while driving, causing the vehicle to suddenly turn 90 degrees to the right; same phenomenon when braking. • Transmission shift lever blocks the driver's right knee when braking. • Fifth-wheel assembly fell off while vehicle was underway. • Instruments are recessed too deep into the dash, making it hard to read the fuel gauge and speedometer, especially at night. **2001–02**—Engine camshafts may have an improperly machined oil groove. • Snow and water ingestion into rear brake drum. • Inaccurate fuel tank gauge drops one-quarter to one-half while driving. • Faulty power seat adjuster. **2002**—Adults cannot sit in third-row seat without neck smashing into roof as vehicle passes over bumps. • Airbags deployed for no reason. • Airbag light comes on randomly and clock spring defect disabled the airbag. • Middle-seat seat belt unbuckles on its own. • Headlights come on and off on their own. **2003**—Exposed electrical wires under the front seats. • Excessive steering vibration. • Seat belts unlatch themselves. • Missing suspension bolt caused the right side to collapse. • Wiper blades stick together. **2004**—Chronic stalling. • Airbag clock spring failed causing cruise control to also malfunction. • Seat belts don't latch properly.

Secret Warranties/Service Tips

All models/years: If pressed, Chrysler will replace the AC evaporator for free up to seven years. Other AC component costs are negotiable. **1993–2002**—Paint delamination, peeling, or fading (see Part Three). • A rotten-egg odour coming from the exhaust may be the result of a malfunctioning catalytic converter, probably covered under the emissions warranty. **1995–98**—Possible causes of delayed transmission engagement (TSB #21-07-98). **1996**—Poor engine performance near military installations or airports is caused by radar interference. Correct by installing a "hardened" crankshaft position sensor and/or reprogramming (flashing) the PCM with new software calibrations.

1996–99—A serpentine belt that slips off the idler pulley requires an upgraded bracket. • Upgraded engine head gasket. • Oil seepage from the cam position sensor. **1996–2000**—Strut tower corrosion:

Brake Drums (Rear) – Snow/Water Ingestion

Number: 05-001-02   Date: Mar. 4, 2002

OVERVIEW: This bulletin involves installing a revised rear drum brake support (backing) plate and possible replacement of the rear brake shoes and drums.

MODELS: 1996–2003 (RS) Town & Country/Voyager/Caravan

SYMPTOM/CONDITION: While driving through deep or blowing snow/water, the snow/water may enter the rear brake drums causing rust to develop on the rear brake drum and shoe friction surfaces. This condition can lead to temporary freezing of the rear brake linings to the drums. This symptom is experienced after the vehicle has been parked in below freezing temperatures long enough for the snow/water to freeze inside of the rear brake drums. When the parking brake has been applied the symptom is more likely to occur.

• Cruise control that won't hold the vehicle's speed when going uphill may have a faulty check valve. • Countermeasures detailed to correct a steering column click or rattle. • Airbag warning light stays lit. **1996–2001**—AWD models *must* be equipped with identical tires; otherwise, the power transfer unit may self-destruct. • A suspension squawk or knock probably means the sway bar link needs replacing under Chrysler's "goodwill" policy (5 years/ 100,000 km). **1996–2005**—Rusted, frozen rear brake drums:

Rear Drum Water/Snow Ingestion/Freezing

Bulletin No.: 05-002-04   Date: February 17, 2004

Snow/Water Ingestion Into Rear Brake Drum

This bulletin involves installing a revised rear drum brake support (backing) plate and possible replacement of the rear brake shoes and drums.

2001–05 Town & Country/Voyager/Caravan
1996–2000 Town & Country/Caravan/Voyager
1996–2000 Chrysler Voyager (International Markets)

SYMPTOM/CONDITION: While driving through deep or blowing snow/water, the snow/water may enter the rear brake drums causing rust to develop on the rear brake drum and shoe friction surfaces. This condition can lead to temporary freezing of the rear brake linings to the drums. This symptom is experienced after the vehicle has been parked in below freezing temperatures long enough for the snow/water to freeze inside of the rear brake drums. When the parking brake has been applied the symptom is more likely to occur.

• Roof panel is wavy or has depressions. **1997–98**—Engines that run poorly or stall may need the PCM reprogrammed under the emissions warranty. **1997–2000**—If the ignition key can't be turned or cannot be removed, TSB #23-23-00 proposes four possible corrections. **1997–2001**— Rear brake noise:

AC Compressor – Locks Up At Low Mileage

Number: 24-15-99   Date: Jul. 9, 1999

OVERVIEW: This bulletin involves determining the extent of AC compressor lock-up and either working the compressor loose or replacing it.

MODELS: 1998– **2000** (NS) Town & Country/Caravan/Voyager
1998– **2000** (GS) Chrysler Voyager (International Market)
1998– **2000** (PL) Neon

SYMPTOM/CONDITION: The AC compressor may lock up, causing the drive belt to slip in the AC clutch pulley, producing a squealing noise at initial start-up.

1998—A faulty radiator fan relay may cause the engine to overheat; replace it with a new relay and reprogram the powertrain control module under Customer Satisfaction Notice #771. **1998–99**—Front brakes continue to wear out quickly on front-drive minivans. Owners report that Chrysler pays half the cost of brake repairs for up to 2 years/40,000 km. • Silence a chronic squeaking noise coming from underneath the vehicle by installing a new strut pivot bearing. **1998–2000**—Troubleshooting AC compressor failure. **1999–2000**—Measures to prevent the right-side sliding-door trim panel from hitting the quarter panel when the door is opened. **2000**—Delayed shifts. **2000–01**—Poor starting, • Rear disc brake squeal. • AC compressor failure, loss of engine power when switching on the AC, serpentine belt chirping, and spark knock can all be traced to a miscalibrated PCM. • No heat on front right side, due to a defective blend air door. • AC compressor squeal. • Rear bench seat rattle or groan. • Hood hinge rattle. • Inoperative overhead reading lamp and rear wiper. • Noisy roof rack and power-sliding door. **2001–02**—Engine surging at highway speeds. • Engine knocking. • Engine sag and hesitation caused by a faulty throttle position sensor (TPS). • Engine mount grinding or clicking. • Steering wheel shudder; steering column popping or ticking. • Poor rear AC performance. • AC leaks water onto passenger-side carpet. • Wind or water leaks at the rear quarter window. • High-pitched, belt-like squeal at high engine rpms. • Sliding door reverses direction. • Incorrect fuel gauge indicator. • Loose tail light. • Flickering digital display. • Difficult to remove fuel cap (install a new seal); this free repair applies to all of the 2002 vehicle lineup. **2001–03**—Rear brake rubbing sound. • Oil filter leaks with 3.3L and 3.8L engines (confirmed in TSB # 09-001-03):

> On February 25, 2003, my 2002 Grand Caravan lost almost all of its engine oil, which resulted in engine failure. At no time did the vehicle's warning sensors indicate any problem with the engine. The failure was the result of a leak in the filter gasket of the FE292 Mopar oil filter. Documentation from the oil filter manufacturer indicates that the oil filter gasket overhangs the inside diameter of the adapter head by .1 cm/side [.045 in./side].

2001–04—AC water leaks. **2002**—Transmission slips in First or Reverse gear. • Airbags deployed for no reason. • Airbag light comes on randomly and clock spring defect disabled the airbag. • Power-steering fluid leakage. • Middle-seat

seat belt unbuckles on its own. • Rear side vent window exploded while driving. • Erratically operating power sliding door or liftgate. • Headlights come on and off on their own. • Noisy engine and transmission. **2002–03**—Sliding door or liftgate malfunctions. **2003**—Troubleshooting water leaks. • Three bulletins relating to automatic transmission malfunctions: Delayed gear engagement; harsh 4–3 downshift; and excessive vibration and transfer gear whine. **2004**—Rough idle, hesitation, and hard starts. • Accessory drivebelt chirping. • Front suspension rattling. **2004–05**—Warm engine rough idle. • Transmission ticking.

Caravan, Voyager, Grand Caravan, Grand Voyager, Town & Country Profile

	1997	1998	1999	2000	2001	2002	2003	2004
Cost Price ($) (very negotiable)								
Caravan (16%)	19,885	20,255	24,230	24,970	24,885	25,430	25,430	27,620
Grand Caravan (17%)	21,465	23,160	25,890	26,665	29,505	28,875	29,295	30,190
Town & Country (21%)	40,350	41,040	41,260	41,815	41,150	40,815	42,705	44,095
Used Values ($)								
Caravan ⋀	5,500	6,500	8,000	10,000	13,000	15,000	16,500	19,500
Caravan ⋁	4,000	5,500	6,500	9,000	11,000	13,000	15,000	17,500
Grand Caravan ⋀	6,000	7,500	8,500	11,000	13,500	16,000	18,000	21,000
Grand Caravan ⋁	4,500	6,500	7,500	9,500	12,000	14,500	17,000	19,500
Town & Country ⋀	7,000	8,500	11,000	13,500	17,500	22,000	24,000	27,000
Town & Country ⋁	6,000	7,500	9,000	12,000	16,000	20,500	23,000	25,000
Reliability	❶	❷	❷	❷	❷	③	③	③
Crash Safety (F)								
Caravan	④	③	—	④	④	④	④	④
Grand Caravan	③	③	④	④	④	④	④	④
Town & Country	④	③	—	—	—	—	④	④
Town & Country LX	③	③	④	④	④	④	④	④
Side								
Caravan	—	—	⑤	⑤	④	④	④	④
Grand Caravan	—	—	⑤	⑤	④	⑤	⑤	⑤
Town & Country LX	—	—	⑤	⑤	④	⑤	⑤	⑤
Offset (G. Caravan)	❷	❷	❷	❷	❶	❷	❷	❷
Town & Country	❷	❷	❷	❷	❶	❷	❷	❷

Note: Voyager and Grand Voyager prices and ratings are almost identical to the Caravan and Grand Caravan.

RAM VAN, RAM WAGON, SPRINTER ★★★

RATING: Average (1980–2003); *Sprinter:* Not recommended (2004–05). Fuel economy and cargo capacity trumps performance and dealer support is questionable. **Strong points:** *2003:* Powerful engines; lots of passenger/cargo space; airbag cut-off switch; and quiet running. **Weak points:** *2003:* Old tech; sparsely equipped; ponderous manoeuvring; excessive fuel consumption; and rear-wheel ABS with a history of failures. **New for 2005:** Nothing significant.

Likely failures: *Sprinter:* Likely to be quirky and highly dealer-dependent for parts and servicing. Electronics, fuel system, and brakes are likely trouble spots. *2003:* Automatic transmission, fuel system, brakes, and AC.

2005 Technical Data

Powertrain (rear-drive)
Engines: 2.7L 5-cyl. (154 hp)
Transmissions: 5-speed auto.
Dimension/Capacity
Height/length/width:
93.5/196/74 in.
Headroom: 73 in.
Legroom: N/A
Wheelbase: 118./158 in.

Turning circle: 42 ft.
Passengers: 2/10
Cargo volume: 247 cu. ft.
GVWR: 8,550–9,990 lb.
Tow limit: 5,000 lb.
Ground clear.: 7.4 in.
Fuel tank: 132L/reg.
Weight: 8,550 lb.

MODEL HISTORY: Chrysler's full-sized van has an extended chassis to allow for a more forward engine placement that increases interior passenger room and gives the van rounder lines, in keeping with the redesign of Chrysler's truck line. Body style changes aside, this is one of the oldest designs on the market. The full-sized van shares the same strengths and weaknesses as all of Chrysler's rear-drive trucks. Chrysler says they are used commercially 97 percent of the time, mostly as small school buses, car rental shuttles at airports, and delivery vehicles. The Ram Van is the commercial truck; the Ram Wagon is the people-hauler. Base 1500s are about the size of a short GM Astro van.

Both versions aren't hard to find and are generally reasonably priced. Make sure to take a test-drive at night to test headlight illumination—inadequate, say some owners.

It's hard to get excited about the basic Chrysler van; its seats are uncomfortable and the lack of interior trimmings makes it essentially a shipping container on wheels. The sturdy 175-hp 3.9L V6 engine first appeared in the Dakota truck series and is adequate for most uses, but one of the optional V8s would be a better all-around choice, without much more of a fuel penalty. If you do get a used van with the V6, keep in mind that multi-point fuel injection, added in 1992 on both the V6 and V8 power plants, makes for smoother engine performance (and more expensive troubleshooting). For 1993, the 5.9L V8 received the same upgrades as its 3.9L and 5.2L cousins—revised cylinder heads and fuel injection—boosting horsepower from 205 to 230.

Putting all of its cash into minivans, Chrysler didn't make any major improvements to these rear-drive trucks disguised as vans until the spring of 1993; even then, the changes weren't all that dramatic. Five years later, Chrysler redesigned the 1998 version by restyling the interior and exterior, de-powering the airbags, adding a passenger-side airbag, and providing more front legroom and footroom. The 1999 models returned unchanged except for a larger fuel tank on vehicles equipped with 5.2L and 5.9L natural gas V8 engines. Since then, these vans have been carried over without any major changes.

Dodge Sprinter

The new $38,000 Sprinter is actually an old rear-drive Mercedes-Benz model that's been tooting around Europe and foreign markets since 1995. Freightliner first sold it in the States as a 2001 commercial hauler. Henceforth, the Sprinter will have a passenger and separate cargo van distributed by DaimlerChrysler dealers throughout Canada and the United States.

The Sprinter offers a large load capacity and a fuel-sipping, 154-hp Mercedes-Benz 5-cylinder turbo diesel engine hooked to a 5-speed automatic transmission. Three wheelbase models are available, 118 inch, 140 inch, and 158 inch; cargo area ranges from 7 cubic metres (247 cubic feet) to 13 cubic metres (473 cubic feet); and GVWR is between 3,878 kg (8,550 lb.) and 4,531 kg (9,990 lb.).

In its favour, the Sprinter offers impressive refinement, many body configurations, slightly better fuel economy than other vans, and class-leading passenger and cargo capacity. On the minus side, it's much more expensive than the competition, overweight, underpowered for everyday tasks, and lacks a V8 for towing, hauling, and high-speed cruising.

In summary, it's a loser.

COST ANALYSIS: Best alternatives: Look for an off-lease 2003 traditional Chrysler van. There is insufficient owner feedback regarding the Sprinter's long-term viability. Ford and GM full-sized vans are good alternatives, but their warranties fall short. **Rebates:** Expect zero percent financing, rebates, and dealer incentives for the Sprinter. **Delivery/PDI:** $995. **Warranty:** 7 years/ 115,000 km; rust perforation 5 years/160,000 km. **Supplementary warranty:** Yes, on the powertrain, if it has expired. **Options:** None. The Sprinter comes well-equipped. **Depreciation:** Faster than average. **Insurance cost:** Above average. **Annual maintenance cost:** Higher than average. Maintenance is a breeze, as is the case with most rear-drive vans; any garage can repair these vehicles. However, ABS, transmission, or AC repairs can easily wipe out your maintenance savings. **Parts supply/cost:** Good supply. Parts are a little less expensive than the competition's. **Highway/city fuel economy:** *N/A.*

QUALITY/RELIABILITY: *2003:* Competent servicing by dealers or independent garages is easy to find, and troubleshooting most problems is easy. Quality control is below average, however, and each redesign seems to carry over the same problem components. Sloppy assembly and poor-quality parts, in addition to fragile hardware, make the bodies rattletraps and allow for lots of air and water leaks. Paint peeling and delamination isn't as bad as on Ford and GM vans, but rusting is a problem. Be sure to inspect a potential purchase for premature rust, especially around the front suspension attachment points, doors, and exhaust/catalytic converter (stainless-steel exhaust systems excepted). **Owner-reported problems:** *2003:* Owners complain of air conditioning, electrical system, fuel system, brake, and transmission failures. Paint delamination is also a common gripe, which Chrysler will often remedy for free up to six years of ownership. Owners also cite excessive brake pulsation (caused by premature front disc wear around 40,000 km). Corroded parking brake cables may also cause the brakes to seize. **Warranty performance:** Average.

SAFETY SUMMARY: Remarkably few NHTSA complaints; nevertheless, complaints about airbags, brakes, door locks, seat belt failures, and chronic stalling when turning are quite common throughout the past decade of production. **Airbags:** Airbag cut-off switch. No side airbags. Severe injuries have been caused by airbag deployment, and there have been reports of airbags that deployed when the key was put into the ignition and airbags that did not deploy. **ABS:** Two-wheel ABS is standard. **Head restraints F/R:** *1997 Van:* *. **Visibility F/R:** *****/**. Some owners report annoying dash reflection onto the front windshield (corrected by placing a dark-coloured drop sheet onto the dash).

SAFETY COMPLAINTS: 1997—Steering jams because cotter pin pulls out from nut. • Steering pump failure. • Hydraulic brake reservoir gasket failure. • Fuel tank hangs by one strap. • Transmission failure. • Van caught fire from overheated brake fluid. • Headlight switch is also known to overheat and catch fire. • Faulty brake rotors cause vehicle to pull to one side when braking. • Incorrect fuel gauge readings. • Weight of the diesel engine causes premature brake wear and a loosening of the tie-rods. • Poor headlight illumination. **1998**—Fuel leakage from cracked fuel tank. • Brakes, steering, and transmission lock up. • Shoulder lapbelt rides too high and the windshield wiper motor fails frequently. • Faulty cruise control causes sudden acceleration and stalling. **1999**—Several wire harness fires under the dash. • Passenger-side wheel locked up and sheared off. • Tire studs frequently shear off. • Excessive road wander. • Cracked trailer hitch. • Cruise control self-activates. • Vehicle pulls unexpectedly to one side when braking. • Brakes lock up with light pressure. **2000**—Many complaints of excessive wandering over the highway. • When brakes applied, pedal went to floor, extending stopping distance. • Transmission seal leaks continuously due to previous driveshaft failures. • Transmission popped out of gear while pulling a load uphill. **2001**—Faulty latch can cause seatback to collapse. • Child can put vehicle in gear without depressing brake pedal. **2002**—Not enough seat belts for the number of passengers that can be seated.

Secret Warranties/Service Tips

1993–2000—Paint delamination, peeling, or fading (see Part Three). **1994–99**—TSB #23-43-90 gives lots of tips on locating water leaks through the dual cargo doors. **1994–2000**—Noisy rear leaf springs can be silenced by replacing the spring tip liners and installing new spring clinch clip isolators. **1995–97**—A front suspension clunk is likely caused by a poorly seated front upper coil spring isolator. **1996–97**—Chrysler has developed a repair kit to correct a buzzing sound that occurs when one shifts into Reverse in cold weather. **1996–98**—If Overdrive won't engage in cold climates, Chrysler may install a free bypass kit. • If your van bucks during wide-open throttle acceleration, TSB #18-19-98 says you may need to replace the governor pressure sensor. **1996–99**—If the MIL light comes on, you may have to reprogram the JTEC powertrain control module (PCM). **1997–98**—If the remote keyless entry transmitter batteries discharge prematurely, Chrysler may replace and reprogram the transmitters under warranty. **1998**—If your van shudders and vibrates whenever the brakes are applied, TSB #05-07-98 lists a number of remedies. **1998–99**—A knocking noise in the front suspension signals the need to install an upgraded stabilizer bar. • Measures to eliminate wind noise at the upper A-pillar area. **1998–2000**—If the side or rear doors open beyond their normal travel, replace the check arm pin and bumper. • In cases where the sliding door won't open or close, consider installing a revised sliding door rear latch assembly and latch rods and modifying the rear latch opening. **1998–2001**—Hard starts, no-starts, and stalling may be caused by a malfunctioning central timer module. **2000**—Excessive engine knock upon acceleration may be silenced by reprogramming the PCM. • Harsh transmission engagement can be fixed by replacing the transmission valve body upper housing separator plate and the valve body check ball. Plus, you may need to reprogram the JTEC PCM. **2000–01**—If the MIL light comes on with a TCC/OD alert, consider replacing the transmission pressure boost valve cover plate. • A likely cause for sudden, widespread electrical failures may be a locked up central timer module. • If the engine won't start or crank, you may have a blown starter relay; install a starter solenoid and circuit fuse. **2000–03**—Doors lock/unlock on their own. **2001**—Remedies for hard starts, no-starts, and stalling. • Radiators may leak between the filler neck and the cap. **2002**—Indicated 9.25-axle vehicle speed may be inaccurate.

Ram Van, Ram Wagon, Sprinter Profile								
	1997	1998	1999	2000	2001	2002	2003	2004
Cost Price ($) (very negotiable)								
Ram Van	22,600	24,480	25,120	25,695	26,250	26,008	26,100	—
Ram Wagon	26,345	28,000	28,845	29,080	29,720	31,000	31,300	—
Sprinter (22%)	—	—	—	—	—	—	—	38,180
Used Values ($)								
Ram Van ⅄	4,500	6,000	8,500	11,000	13,500	15,500	18,000	—
Ram Van ⱴ	3,500	5,000	7,000	10,000	12,500	14,000	16,500	—
Ram Wagon ⅄	6,000	8,000	10,500	13,000	15,500	16,500	21,500	—
Ram Wagon ⱴ	5,000	6,500	9,000	11,500	14,000	15,000	20,000	—
Sprinter ⅄	—	—	—	—	—	—	—	30,000
Sprinter ⱴ	—	—	—	—	—	—	—	29,000
Reliability	❷	❷	❷	③	③	③	③	③
Crash Safety (F)	—	—	—	—	④	④	④	—
Rollover	—	—	—	—	③	③	③	—

Ford

WINDSTAR, FREESTAR   ★

RATING: *Windstar:* Not Recommended (1995–2003). Infamous for atrocious quality control, stonewalled complaints, and life-threatening defects. *Freestar:* Below Average (2004–05). Freestar is a warmed over Windstar, with its own serious quality control problems. Windstars have similar transmission, brake, and AC failures to the Chrysler and GM competition, and their engines aren't very reliable. Unfortunately, Ford doesn't protect its owners with a 7-year powertrain warranty, as Chrysler does. Hence the different ratings for the two vehicles. **Strong points:** *Windstar:* Comfortable and well-appointed interior; comfortable ride; good instrument/controls layout; plenty of passenger space; lots of small storage spaces, in addition to the large amount of space for larger items; low floor improves cargo handling; and a five-star crashworthiness rating. *Freestar:* A 4.2L V6 engine, new cabin appointments, optional side curtain airbags, easier rear access; flat-folding third-row seats, and larger four-wheel disc brakes. **Weak points:** *Windstar:* Mediocre handling and restricted side and rear visibility. Driver's seat isn't comfortable for big, tall drivers, who complain of the lack of legroom, seat contouring, and lower back support. An abundance of clunks, rattles, and wind and road noise. These minivans have maxi-failures that include failure-prone engines, transmissions, brakes, electrical systems, and suspension components. Sure, the Windstar combines an impressive five-star safety rating, plenty of raw power, an exceptional ride, and impressive cargo capacity. But self-destructing automatic transmissions, defective engine head gaskets and bearings, and "do you feel lucky today?" brakes and front coil springs can quickly transform your dream minivan into a nightmare. And, as a counterpoint to Ford's well-earned Windstar crashworthiness boasting, take a look at the summary of safety-related complaints recorded by the U.S. Department of Transportation: Coil spring breakage blowing the front tire, sudden acceleration, stalling, steering loss, windows exploding, wheels falling off, horn failures, sliding doors that open and close on their own, and vehicles rolling away while parked. **New for 2005:** Nothing significant.

2005 Technical Data

Powertrain (front-drive)
Engines: 3.9L V6 (193 hp)
• 4.2L V6 (202 hp)
Transmission: 4-speed auto.
Dimension/Capacity
Height/length/width:
68.8/201/76.6 in.
Headroom F/R1/R2: 38.8/39.7/37.9 in.
Legroom F/R1/R2: 40.7/38/35.6 in.

Wheelbase: 120.8 in.
Turning circle: 42 ft.
Cargo volume: 136.4.
GVWR: N/A.
Passengers: 2/2/3
Tow limit: 2,000 lb.
Fuel tank: 75/94L
Weight: 4,275 lb.

MODEL HISTORY: Ford can call it the Windstar or the Freestar; the fact remains, car shoppers want no part of it. In 2003, it competed as the Windstar and posted 70,404 sales in the first half. In 2004 it was reincarnated unchanged, and renamed the Freestar. Sales fell off about 22 percent as soon as shoppers saw through the masquerade.

It features upgrades in safety, interior design, steering, ride and performance, but still lags behind the Japanese competition for performance and dependability. An optional "safety canopy" side curtain airbag system offers protection in side-impact collisions and rollovers for all three rows of seating. There's also better access to the third-row seat, which now folds flat into the floor.

Entry-level LX models came with a 200-hp 3.9L V6, based on the Windstar's current 3.8L engine. Uplevel SE and top-line Limited models got a new 201-hp 4.2L V6, also derived from the 3.8L.

1996—45 more horses added to the 3.8L engine, a smaller 3.0L V6 powers the GL, upgraded seat belts, and a tilt-slide driver-side seat to improve rear seat access. **1998**—A wider driver's door, easier rear seat access, and new front styling. **1999**—A bit more interior space; the third-row bench got built-in rollers; improved steering and brakes (compromised by rear drums, though); ABS; an anti-theft system; new side panels; a new liftgate; larger headlights and tail lights; and a revised instrument panel. **2001**—No more 3.0L V6, an upgraded automatic transmission, a low-tire-pressure warning system, "smart" airbags, new airbag sensors, and a slight restyling. **2002**—Dual sliding doors. **2003**—Freestar debuts as a 2004 model; in the States, Mercury will sell an upscale Freestar called Monterey to replace that brand's defunct Nissan-based Villager.

Engine and transmission failures

Engine and transmission failures are commonplace. The 3.0L engine is overwhelmed by the Windstar's heft and struggles to keep up, but opting for the 3.8L V6 may get you into worse trouble. Even when it's running properly, the 3.8L knocks loudly when under load and pings at other times. Far more serious is the high failure rate of 3.8L engine head gaskets shortly after the 60,000 km mark. Ford's 7-year/160,000 km Owner Notification Program only covers '95s, so owners are asked to pay $1,000 to $3,000 for an engine repair, depending upon how much the engine has overheated. Transmission repairs seldom cost less than $3,000.

Early warning signs are few and benign: The engine may lose some power or overheat; the transmission pauses before downshifting or shifts roughly into a higher gear. Owners may also hear a transmission whining or groaning sound, accompanied by driveline vibrations. There is no other prior warning before the transmission breaks down completely and the minivan comes to a sudden banging, clanging halt.

> Phil, I just want to thank you for saving us at least $1,500. The transmission in our '98 Windstar went *bang* with only 47,300 miles

[75,700 km]. After reading about Ford's goodwill adjustment, we were told by our local Ford dealer that owner participation would be $495. We received a new rebuilt Ford unit installed. Believe it or not, I am a fairly good mechanic myself and this came with no warning! We even serviced the transmission at 42,000 miles [67,200 km] and found no debris or evidence of a problem.

Ford admits automatic transmission glitches may afflict its 2001 Taurus, Sable, Windstar, and Continental. In a March 2001 Special Service Instruction (SSI) #01T01, Ford authorized its dealers to replace all defective transaxles listed in its TSB, which describes the defect in the following manner:

The driver may initially experience a transaxle "slip" or "Neutral" condition during a 2–3 shift event. Extended driving may result in loss of Third gear function and ultimately loss of Second gear function. The driver will still be able to operate the vehicle, but at a reduced level of performance.

Ford's memo states that owners weren't to be notified of the potential problem (they obviously didn't count on *Lemon-Aid* getting a copy of their memo).

Brakes are another Windstar worry. They aren't reliable, and calipers, rotors, and the master cylinder often need replacing. Other frequent Windstar problems concern no-starts and chronic stalling, believed to be caused by a faulty fuel pump or powertrain control module (PCM); electrical system power-steering failures; hard steering at slow speeds; excessive steering wheel vibrations; sudden tire tread separation and premature tread wear; advanced coil spring corrosion, leading to spring collapse and puncturing of the front tire (only 1997–98 models were recalled); rear shock failures at 110 km/h; left-side axle breakage while underway; exploding rear windshields; power-sliding door malfunctions; and failure-prone digital speedometers that are horrendously expensive to replace. There have also been many complaints concerning faulty computer modules; engine oil leaks; AC failures; and early replacement of engine camshafts, tie-rods, and brake rotors and calipers.

Getting compensation

Since 1997, I've lobbied Ford to stop playing "Let's Make a Deal" with its customers and set up a formal 7-year/160,000 km engine and transmission warranty similar to its 1994–95 model 3.8L engine extended warranty and emission warranty guidelines (see "Service Tips" internal bulletin on page 377). I warned the company that failure to protect owners would result in huge sales losses by Ford as word spread that its vehicles were lemons.

In the ensuing three years, under the capable leadership of Bobbie Gaunt, President of Ford Canada, hundreds of engine and transmissions claims were amiably settled using my suggested benchmark. But it didn't last.

Ford USA got wind of it and squashed the Canadian initiative. Interestingly, the three top Ford Canada executives who pleaded the Canadian case have since left the company. And Jac Nasser, the Ford USA CEO who rejected additional protection for owners, was fired shortly thereafter, after he tried a similar move with Firestone claimants.

No, Nasser isn't one of my favourite auto executives.

And as I predicted, Ford sales have plummeted, small claims court judgments are pummelling the company, and owners are vowing to never again buy any Ford product.

> Hi Phil: I just wanted to let you know that I did have to go to small claims court to nudge Ford into action. In pretrial settlement proceedings, the Ford representative at first gave me an offer of $980 for my troubles. I countered with the actual cost of $2,190 to replace my '96 Windstar's transmission. He did not like that idea, and we went back into the court setting. After instruction from the judge, I began to copy my 200+ pages (for the judge as evidence) of documentation for why this is a recurring problem with Ford transmissions (thank you, by the way, for all the great info).
>
> I think it made him a little scared, so I asked if he would settle for $1,600 (a middle ground of our original proposals) to which he accepted. My transmission costs were $2,190, so I basically paid about $600 for a new transmission (*not* a Ford replacement, either).
>
> Anyway, I figured a guaranteed $1,600 was better than not knowing what would happen in court. Thanks for your help!

Ford's denial of owner claims has been blasted in small claims court judgments across Canada during the past few years. Judges have ruled that engines and transmissions (*and* power-sliding doors) must be reasonably durable long after the warranty expires, whether the vehicle was bought new or used, notwithstanding that it was repaired by an independent, or had the same problem repaired earlier for free. The three most recent engine judgments supporting Ford owners are:

Dufour v. Ford Canada Ltd., Quebec Small Claims Court (Hull), No. 550-32-008335-009, April 10, 2001, Justice P. Chevalier. Money refunded for 1996 Windstar engine repairs (see page 132 or download from *www.lemonaidcars.com*).

Schaffler v. Ford Motor Company Limited and Embrun Ford Sales Ltd., Ontario Superior Court of Justice, L'Orignal Small Claims Court, Court File No. 59-2003, July 22, 2003, Justice Gerald Langlois. Plaintiff bought a used 1995 Windstar in 1998. Engine head gasket was repaired for free three years later under Ford's 7-year extended warranty. In 2002 at 109,600 km, head gasket failed, again, seriously damaging the engine. Ford refused a second repair. Justice Langlois ruled that Ford's warranty extension bulletin listed signs and symptoms of the covered defect that were identical to the problems written on the second work order ("persistent and/or chronic engine overheating; heavy white smoke evident from the exhaust tailpipe; flashing 'low coolant' instrument panel light even after coolant refill; and constant loss of engine coolant.") Judge Langlois concluded "the problem was brought to the attention of the dealer well within the warranty period; the dealer was negligent." The plaintiffs were awarded $4,941, plus 5 percent interest. This includes $1,070 for two months' car rental.

John R. Reid and Laurie M. McCall v. Ford Motor Company of Canada, Superior Court of Justice, Ottawa Small Claims Court, Claim No: #02-SC-077344, July 11, 2003, Justice Tiernay. A 1996 Windstar bought used in 1997 experienced engine head gasket failure in October 2001 at 159,000 km. Judge Tiernay awarded the plaintiffs $4,145 for the following reasons: "A Technical Service Bulletin dated June 28, 1999, was circulated to Ford dealers. It dealt specifically with 'undetermined loss of coolant' and 'engine oil contaminated with coolant' in the 1996–98 Windstar and five other models of Ford vehicles. I conclude that Ford owed a duty of care to the Plaintiff to equip this vehicle with a cylinder head gasket of sufficient sturdiness and durability that would function trouble-free for at least seven years, given normal driving and proper maintenance conditions. I find that Ford is answerable in damages for the consequences of its negligence."

The Ford TSB that Judge Tiernay cited is found in the Windstar's "Secret Warranties/Service Tips/TSBs" section.

Automatic transmission lawsuits have also been quite successful. They are often settled out of court because Ford frequently offers 50–75 percent refunds, if the lawsuit is dropped. Alan MacDonald, a *Lemon-Aid* reader who won his case in small claims court, gives the following tips on beating Ford:

I want to thank you for the advice you provided in my dealings with the Ford Motor Company of Canada, Limited and Highbury Ford Sales Limited regarding my 1994 Ford Taurus wagon and the problems with the automatic transmission (Taurus and Windstar transmissions are identical). I also wish to apologize for not sending you a copy of this judgment earlier that may be beneficial to your readers. (*MacDonald v. Highbury Ford Sales Limited,* Ontario Superior Court of Justice in the Small Claims Court London, June 6, 2000, Court File #0001/00, Judge J. D. Searle).

In 1999, after only 105,000 km, the automatic transmission went. I took the car to Highbury Ford to have it repaired. We paid $2,070 to have the transmission fixed, but protested and felt the transmission failed prematurely. We contacted Ford, but to no avail: Their reply was we were out of warranty period. The transmission was so poorly repaired (and we went back to Highbury Ford several times) that we had to go to Mr. Transmission to have the transmission fixed again nine months later at a further $1,906.02.

It is at that point that I contacted you, and I was surprised, and somewhat speechless (which you noticed) when you personally called me to provide advice and encouragement. I am very grateful for your call. My observations with going through small claims court involved the following: I filed in January of 2000, the trial took place on June 1, and the judgment was issued June 6.

At pretrial, a representative of Ford (Ann Sroda) and a representative from Highbury Ford were present. I came with one binder for each of the defendants, the court and one for myself (each binder was about three inches thick—containing your reports on Ford Taurus automatic transmissions, ALLDATA Service Bulletins, Taurus Transmissions Victims (Bradley website), Center for Auto Safety (website), Read This Before Buying a Taurus (website), and the Ford Vent Page (website).

The representative from Ford asked a lot of questions (I think she was trying to find out if I had read the contents of the information I was relying on). The Ford representative then offered a 50 percent settlement based on the initial transmission work done at Highbury Ford. The release allowed me to still sue Highbury Ford with regards to the necessity of going to Mr. Transmission because of the faulty repair done by the dealer. Highbury Ford displayed no interest in settling the case, and so I had to go to court.

For court, I prepared by issuing a summons to the manager at Mr. Transmission, who did the second transmission repair, as an expert witness. I was advised that unless you produce an expert witness you won't win in a car repair case in small claims court. Next, I went to the law school library in London and received a great deal of assistance in researching cases pertinent to car repairs. I was told that judgments in your home province (in my case Ontario) were binding on the court; that cases outside of the home province could be considered, but were not binding, on the judge.

The cases I used for trial involved *Pelleray v. Heritage Ford Sales Ltd.*, Ontario Small Claims Court (Scarborough) SC7688/91 March 22, 1993; *Phillips et al. v. Ford Motor Co. of Canada Ltd. et al.*, Ontario Reports 1970, 15th January 1970; *Gregorio v. Intrans-Corp.*, Ontario Court of Appeal, May 19, 1994; *Collier v. MacMaster's Auto Sales,* New Brunswick Court of Queen's Bench, April 26, 1991; *Sigurdson v. Hillcrest Service & Acklands* (1977), Saskatchewan Queen's Bench; *White v. Sweetland,* Newfoundland District Court, Judicial Centre of Gander, November 8, 1978; *Raiches Steel Works v. J. Clark & Son*, New Brunswick Supreme Court, March 7, 1977; *Mudge v. Corner Brook Garage Ltd.*, Newfoundland Supreme Court, July 17, 1975; *Sylvain v. Carroseries d'Automobiles Guy Inc. (1981)*, C.P. 333, Judge Page; *Gagnon v. Ford Motor Company of Canada, Limited et Marineau Automobile Co. Ltée.* (1974), C.S. 422–423.

In court, I had prepared the case, as indicated above, had my expert witness, and two other witnesses who had driven the vehicle (my wife and my 18-year-old son). As you can see by the judgment, we won our case and I was awarded $1,756.52, including prejudgment interest and costs.

Dangerous doors

Ford has been slammed by the courts for allowing dangerously defective sliding doors to go uncorrected year after year. Here are some rather typical scenarios reported by owners and concerned parents: Sliding door slammed shut on child's head while vehicle was parked on an incline; passengers are often pinned by the door; door reopens as it is closing; door often pops open while vehicle is underway; driver's finger broken in closing manual sliding door; handle is too close to the door jamb and the hazard has been reported on the Internet since 1999 (*www.cartrackers.com/Forums/live/Ford*).

> I am writing about our 2003 Ford Windstar. Our passenger automatic sliding door frequently pops open after it appears to have latched shut. It has opened by itself on three occasions while the van was in Drive. Recently my three-year-old daughter almost fell out of the van headfirst onto concrete because the door popped back open as soon as it "latched" shut. The van has been in to repair this problem seven times without success. We first started having problems with both doors within the first two weeks of purchase. The times the door has popped back open are way too numerous to count.
>
> The 2003 Windstar automatic sliding door opens by itself—no command; door will not power open; door lock assembly freezes. The door has opened itself while the vehicle is in motion—very scary and dangerous for my children. This is a problem Ford has known about but has not been proactive about fixing (see Ford TSB article 03-6-8).

Mental distress (door failures)

In *Sharman v. Formula Ford Sales Limited, Ford Credit Limited, and Ford Motor Company of Canada Limited*, Ontario Superior Court of Justice, No: 17419/02SR, 2003/10/07, Justice Sheppard awarded the owner of a 2000 Windstar $7,500 for mental distress resulting from the breach of the implied warranty of fitness, plus $7,207 for breach of contract and breach of warranty. Problem: The Windstar's sliding door wasn't secure and leaked air and water after many attempts to repair it. Interestingly, the judge cited the *Wharton* decision (see page 97), among other decisions, as support for his award for mental distress.

> The plaintiff and his family have had three years of aggravation, inconvenience, worry, and concern about their safety and that of their children. Generally speaking, our contract law did not allow for compensation for what may be mental distress, but that may be changing. I am indebted to counsel for providing me with the decision of the British Columbia Court of Appeal in *Wharton v. Tom Harris Chevrolet Oldsmobile Cadillac Ltd.*, [2002] B.C.J. No. 233, 2002 BCCA 78. This decision was recently followed in *T'avra v. Victoria Ford Alliance Ltd.*, [2003] B, CJ No. 1957.

In *Wharton*, the purchaser of a Cadillac Eldorado claimed damages against the dealer because the car's sound system emitted an annoying buzzing noise and the purchaser had to return the car to the dealer for repair numerous times over two-and-a-half years. The trial court awarded damages of $2,257.17 for breach of warranty with respect to the sound system, and $5,000 in non-pecuniary damages for loss of enjoyment of their luxury vehicle and for inconvenience, for a total award of $7,257.17....

In the *Wharton* case, the respondent contracted for a "luxury" vehicle for pleasure use. It included a sound system that the appellant's service manager described as "high end." The respondent's husband described the purchase of the car in this way: "[W]e bought a luxury car that was supposed to give us a luxury ride and be a quiet vehicle, and we had nothing but difficulty with it from the very day it was delivered with this problem that nobody seemed to be able to fix.... So basically we had a luxury product that gave us no luxury for the whole time that we had it."

It is clear that an important object of the contract was to obtain a vehicle that was luxurious and a pleasure to operate. Furthermore, the buzzing noise was the cause of physical, in the sense of sensory, discomfort to the respondent and her husband. The trial judge found it inhibited listening to the sound system and was irritating in normal conversation. The respondent and her husband also bore the physical inconvenience of taking the vehicle to the appellant on numerous occasions for repairs....

In my view, a defect in manufacture that goes to the safety of the vehicle deserves a modest increase. I would assess the plaintiff's damage for mental distress resulting from the breach of the implied warranty of fitness at $7,500.

Judgment to issue in favour of the plaintiff against the defendants, except Ford Credit, on a joint and several basis for $14,707, plus interest and costs.

COST ANALYSIS: Buyers should steer away from both the Windstar and Freestar; however, if you must make a choice, get the Freestar for its upgrades. The 2004 Freestar sells for $23,775 and Ford says the 2005 version will be similarly priced, making it the better buy. Be wary of a used upscale Windstar SEL; like the Chrysler Town & Country, it loses its value quicker than other versions. **Best alternatives:** The Honda Odyssey, Mazda MPV, and pre-2004 Toyota Sienna are recommended alternatives. Other, more reliable, used minivans you may wish to consider: A late-model Ford or GM rear-drive, a Nissan Axxess (see Appendix II) or pre-2004 Quest. **Rebates:** $3,000 rebates or zero percent financing on 2004 and 2005 Freestars. **Delivery/PDI:** $1,025. **Depreciation:** Much faster than average. **Warranty:** Bumper-to-bumper 3 years/60,000 km; rust perforation 5 years/unlimited km. **Supplementary**

warranty: An extended bumper-to-bumper warranty is a good idea. **Options:** Dual integrated child safety seats for the middle bench seat and adjustable pedals are worthwhile options. Sliding side doors are an overpriced convenience feature and are failure-prone, as well. The Parking Assist beeper's false warnings will drive you crazy. **Insurance cost:** Above average. **Parts supply/ cost:** Reasonably priced parts are easy to find, mainly due to the entry of independent suppliers. Digital speedometers are often defective and can cost almost $1000 to repair. **Annual maintenance cost:** Average while under warranty; outrageously higher than average thereafter, due primarily to powertrain breakdowns not covered by warranty or insufficiently covered by parsimonious "goodwill" gestures. **Highway/city fuel economy:** *Windstar:* 9.5–13.3L/100 km.

QUALITY/RELIABILITY: Worst quality control among all other minivans. "Goodwill" payouts, with owners paying over one-third the cost, have been used as a substitute for better quality control. **Owner-reported problems:** Engine, transmission, suspension (coil springs), and power sliding door malfunctions lead the list of factory-related problems, but there have also been many complaints concerning computer modules, engine oil leaks, timing cover gasket leaking coolant, early engine camshaft replacement, AC failures, premature brake rotor and caliper wear, and excessive brake noise. Poor body seam sealing causes excessive interior wind noise and allows water to leak into cabin. Owners also report a smattering of paint delamination complaints (see Part Three) and a windshield glare from the dash. **Warranty performance:** Incredibly bad. Customer reps read a script that says there's no more warranty protection and that requested repairs are the owner's responsibility. This is particularly sad because Ford was improving progressively over the past couple of years. Now, owners are once again complaining that Ford is unusually tight-fisted and duplicitous in giving out refunds for the correction of factory-related deficiencies.

SAFETY SUMMARY: Base models may not have head restraints for all seats, and the digital dash can be confusing. Optional adjustable pedals help protect drivers from airbag injuries. Be careful, though; some drivers have found that they are set too close together and say they often feel loose. Other nice safety features: Airbags that adjust deployment speed according to occupant weight, and a sliding door warning light. **Airbags:** Standard. **ABS:** Standard. **Traction control:** Optional. **Head restraints F/R:** *1995–97:* *; *1999:* ***/*; *2001–03:* ****/***/**; *2004 Freestar:* *****. **Visibility F/R:** *****/**. **Maximum load capacity:** *2001 SE Sport:* 1,360 lb.

SAFETY COMPLAINTS: All models/years: These are the most dangerous minivans on the market. 1998 Windstar owners, for example, have logged over 1,549 safety-related complaints in the NHTSA database, compared to 708 incidents registered against Chrysler's 1998 Caravan, which had more than double the sales. And it gets worse the further back you go. The good news is that the 2004 Freestar, a revamped Windstar, has only generated 19 reports of safety-related failures. **1995–98**—The following is a short summary of problems carried over, year after year; unfortunately, I don't have the space to list many other reported defects. Nevertheless, you can easily access NHTSA's website (see Appendix I) for the details of thousands of other Windstar complaints: Airbag failed to deploy. • Severe injuries caused by airbag deployment. • Sudden acceleration and chronic stalling. • Control arm and inner tie-rod failures cause the wheel to fall off. • Sudden steering lock-up or loss of steering ability. • Engine head gasket failures. • Loose or missing front brake bolts could cause the wheels to lock up or a loss of vehicle control. • Chronic ABS and transmission failures. • Almost a dozen reports that the vehicle jumps out of Park and rolls away when on an incline, or slips into Reverse with the engine idling. • Transmission and axle separation. • Faulty fuel pump, sensor, and gauge. • Built-in child safety seat is easy to get out of, yet securing seat belts are too tight; child almost strangled. • Faulty rear liftgate latches; trunk lid can fall on one's head. • Horn doesn't work properly. **1999**—This is a faithful summary of the several hundred complaints in the NHTSA database. Keep in mind that many of these defects have been found in previous model-year Windstars, but may not have been included due to space limitations. • Airbag failed to deploy. • While parked, cruising, turning on the ignition, or when brakes are applied, vehicle suddenly accelerates. • Stuck accelerator causes unintended acceleration. • Chronic stalling caused by fuel vapour lock or faulty fuel pump. • Check Engine light constantly comes on, due to a faulty gas cap or over-sensitive warning system. • Front passenger-side wheel fell off when turning at a traffic light; in another reported incident, dealer found the five lug nuts had broken in half. • Vehicle pops out of gear while parked and rolls away. • Frequent transmission failures, including noisy engagement, won't engage forward or Reverse, slips, or jerks into gear. • Transmission jumped from Park to Reverse and pinned driver against tree (this is a common problem affecting Ford vehicles for almost three decades). • Sudden loss of power steering, chronic leakage of fluid, and early replacement of steering components, like the pump and hoses. • Excessive brake fade after successive stops. • When brake pedal is depressed, it sinks below the accelerator pedal level, causing the accelerator to be pressed as well—particularly annoying for drivers with large feet. • ABS module wire burned out. • Complete electrical failure during rainstorm. • Horn button "sweet spot" is too small and takes too much pressure to activate; one owner says, "Horn doesn't work, unless you hit it with a sledgehammer." • Windshield suddenly exploded when car was slowly accelerating. • Sliding door opens and closes on its own, sticks open or closed, or suddenly slams shut on a downgrade. • Sliding door closed on child's arm. • Door locks don't stay locked; passenger-side door opened when turning, causing passenger to fall out. • Many complaints that the side or rear windows suddenly exploded. • Rear defogger isn't operable (lower part of windshield isn't clear) in inclement weather when windshield wipers are activated. • Windshield wipers fail to clear windshield. • Water pours from dash onto front passenger floor. • Floor cupholder trips passengers. • Continental General tires lose air and crack between the treads. • Unspecified original equipment tires have sudden tread separation. • Large A-pillar (where windshield attaches to door) seriously impairs forward visibility, hiding pedestrians. • Seat belts aren't as described in owner's manual (supposed to be automatic retractable). • Two incidents where flames shot up out of fuel tank filler spout when gassing up. **2000**—Vehicle caught on fire while parked. • Sudden, unintended acceleration while stopped. • Chronic stalling; engine shuts down when turning. • Sometimes cruise control won't engage or engages on its own. • Right passenger-side wheel came off due to lug nut failure. • One Ingersoll, Ontario, owner of a year 2000 Windstar recounts the following harrowing experience:

> Last week, as my wife was running errands, the support arm that goes from the rear crossmember (not an axle anymore) up under the floor, broke in half. The dealer replaced the whole rear end as it is one welded assembly. If she had been on the highway going 80 km/h she would probably have been in a bad accident.

• Check Engine light constantly comes on for no reason. • Driver heard a banging noise and Windstar suddenly went into a tailspin; dealer blamed pins that "fell out of spindle." • Transmission jumped out of gear while on highway. • Many reports of premature transmission replacements. • Transmission lever can be shifted without depressing brake pedal (unsafe for children). • After several dealer visits, brakes still spongy, pedal goes to floor without braking, and emergency brake has almost no effect. • When braking, foot also contacts the accelerator pedal. • Emergency brake is inadequate to hold the vehicle. • Dealers acknowledge that brake master cylinders are problematic. • Joints aren't connected under quarter wheel weld; one weld is missing and three aren't properly connected. • Passenger door opened when vehicle hit a pothole. • While underway, right-side sliding door opens on its own and won't close (see "mental distress" judgment on pages 332–333). • When parked on an incline, sliding door released and came crashing down on child. • Hood suddenly flew up on the freeway. • Steering failed three times. • Power-steering pump whines and lurches. • Steering wheel is noisy and hard to turn. • Rear side windows, liftgate window, and windshield often explode suddenly. • When the interior rear-view mirror is set for Night Vision, images become distorted and hard to see. • Windshield wipers are unreliable. • Second-row, driver-side seat belt buckle wouldn't latch. • Original equipment tire blowouts and sidewall bulging. • Driver must hunt for right place to push for horn to work. **2000–01**—Harsh 3–2 shifting when coasting then accelerating. • Transmission fluid leakage. • 3.8L engine hum, moan, drone, spark knock, and vibration. • Power-steering grunts or shudders during slow turns; fluid leaks. • Faulty self-activating wipers and door, trunk, and ignition locks. **2001**—Airbag may suddenly deploy when the engine is started. • Transmission shudder during 3–4 shifts. • Transmission fluid leaks from the main control cover area. • Power-steering grunt or notchy feel when turning; leaks. • Drifting or pulling while driving. • Rear drum brakes drag or fail to release properly. • Fogging of the front and side windows. • Twisted seatback frame. **2002**—Airbags failed to deploy. • Sudden automatic transmission failure. • Gas and brake pedal are set too close. • Back door won't open or close properly. • Both sliding doors won't retract. • Child can shift transmission without touching brake pedal. **2003**—Wheel suddenly broke away. • Airbags failed to deploy. • Sudden, unintended acceleration when braking. • Engine surging. • Chronic stalling from blown fuel pump fuses. • Coolant leaks from the timing cover gasket. • Advanced tracking system engages on its own, causing vehicle to shake violently. • Automatic transmission suddenly seized. • Steering wheel locked up. • Interior windows always fogged up due to inadequate defrosting. • Brake and gas pedals are mounted too close together. • Gas pedal arm pivot causes the pedal to flip almost horizontally, exaggerating any pedal pressure. • Body seams not sealed; water intrudes into floor seat anchors. • Driver's seat poorly anchored. Dashboard glare onto the windshield. • Check Tire warning light comes on for no reason. • Tire jack collapsed. **Freestar: 2004**—Sudden loss of steering. • Airbag light stays on, may not deploy. • Driver heard a bang, then felt like vehicle was running on a flat tire: A-frame had dropped out of the tie-rod collar. • Front axle suddenly broke while underway. • Left inner brake pad fell apart and locked up brake. • Dealer had to change pads and rotor. • Sliding door closed on a child, causing slight injuries. • Broken plastic running board broke, blocking sliding door operation, locking occupants inside the vehicle. • Headliner-mounted DVD screen blocks rear-view mirror.

Secret Warranties/Service Tips

All models/years: Engine intake manifolds: Engine oil mixed with coolant or coolant loss signals the need for revised engine lower intake manifold side gaskets and/or front cover gaskets. The internal bulletin below can go a long way in getting a repair refund for any Ford model up to 7 years/160,000 km, since it shows the defect is factory-related, an upgraded part has been devised, and the problem is covered by the much-longer emissions warranty:

Engine Coolant Loss/Oil Contamination

Bulletin No.: 99-20-7   Date: 10/04/99

3.8L and 4.2L engine—Loss of coolant; engine oil contaminated with coolant

1996–97 THUNDERBIRD
1996–98 MUSTANG, WINDSTAR
1997–98 E-150, E-250, F-150
1996–97 COUGAR

This may be caused by the lower intake manifold side gaskets and/or front cover gaskets allowing coolant to pass into the cylinders and/or the crankcase.

ACTION: Revised lower intake manifold side and front cover gaskets have been released for service.

WARRANTY STATUS: Eligible under the provisions of bumper to bumper warranty coverage and emissions warranty coverage

---

• An exhaust buzz or rattle may be caused by a loose catalyst or heat shield. • Sliding door malfunctions. • Buzzing noise in speakers caused by fuel pump. A malfunction indicator light (MIL) lit for no reason may simply show that the gas cap is loose. • If the power-sliding door won't close, replace the door controller; if it pops or disengages when fully closed, adjust the door and rear striker to reduce closing resistance. • Front wipers that operate when switched off need a revised multi-function switch (service program and recall). **1995–98**—A parking brake that won't release needs a new parking pawl actuating rod. • Power door locks that grind or won't work may need a new front door lock actuator. • Tips on finding and silencing instrument panel buzzing, rattling, squeaking, chirping, and ticking. • The front-end accessory drive belt (FEAD) slips in wet weather, causing a reduction in steering power-assist. • Water leakage onto carpet or headliner in rear cargo area is a factory-related defect covered in TSB #98-5-5. **1995–99**—Tips for correcting excessive noise, vibration, and harshness while driving; side door wind noise; and windshield water leaks. **1995–2000**—A harsh 3–2 downshift/shudder when accelerating or turning may simply mean the transmission is low on fluid. • Diagnostic tips on brake vibration, inspection, and friction material replacement. **1995–2002**—Silencing suspension noise. **1995–2003**—Engines that have been repaired may have an incorrectly installed gear driven camshaft position (CMP) sensor synchronizer assembly. This could cause poor fuel economy, loss of power, and engine surge, hesitation, and rough running. **1996–98**—Harsh automatic 1–2 shifting may be caused by a malfunctioning electronic pressure control or the main control valves sticking in the valve body. • Unwanted airflow from the AC vents can be stopped by replacing the evaporator case baffle. • An intermittent Neutral condition when coming to a stop signals the need to replace the forward clutch piston and the forward clutch cylinder. • Black soot deposits on the right rear quarter panel can be avoided by installing an exhaust tailpipe extension. **1996–2003**—Tips on troubleshooting automatic transmission faulty torque converters. **1997–98**—A rattling or clunking noise coming from the front of the vehicle may be caused by a loose front tension strut bushing retainer. **1998**—Lack of AC cooling may be caused by refrigerant leak at the P-nut fitting. • AC may have a loose auxiliary climate control fan switch. • A Low Fuel light lit for no reason signals the need for an upgraded fuel tank and sender assembly. • An inaccurate metric speedometer requires a new speedometer gear. • Squeaks and creaks from the left rear of the driver's seat can be silenced by lubricating the lateral stability bracket. • Chronic stalling can be corrected by reprogramming the PCM. • Excessive vibration at highway speeds may require new rear brake drums. **1998–99**—Tips on spotting abnormal ABS braking noise, although Ford says some noise is inevitable. **1999**—No Reverse engagement may be caused by torn Reverse clutch lip seals. • To improve the defogging of the driver-side door glass, install a revised window de-mister vent. **1999–2003**—Things that go beep in the night:

Parking Assist – False Activation

Bulletin No.: 04-7-1   Date: 04/19/04

FALSE ACTIVATION OF WARNING TONE

1999–2003 WINDSTAR
1999–2004 EXPLORER
2000–04 EXCURSION, EXPEDITION
2001–04 F SUPER DUTY
2003–05 ESCAPE
2004 F-150; FREESTAR

```
2000–04 NAVIGATOR
2002–03 BLACKWOOD
2003–04 AVIATOR
1999–2004 MOUNTAINEER
2004 MONTEREY
```
Various 1999–2005 vehicles equipped with the Parking Aid reverse sensing system (RSS) may sound a warning tone when the vehicle is in Reverse, even though there are no objects behind the vehicle. This condition may also occur on vehicles equipped with the forward sensing system (FSS) when vehicle is in Reverse or Drive.

ACTION: The condition MAY NOT be due to proximity sensor(s) malfunction but may be a normal operation characteristic, or due to sensor contamination (sensor being covered with dirt).

Huh? It's a "normal operating characteristic?"

• Bulletin No. 04-2-3, published 02/09/04, goes into excruciating detail on finding and fixing sliding door's many failures. • Inoperative rear window defroster. **2001**—Ford admits automatic transmission defects (slippage, delayed shifts) in Special Service Instruction #01T01. **2001–02**—Service tips for reports of premature engine failures. • Vacuum or air leaks in the intake manifold or engine system causing warning lamps to light. • Concerns with oil in the cooling system. • Engine cylinder heads that have been repaired may still leak coolant or oil from the gasket area. • Hard starts; rough-running engines. • Shudder while in Reverse or during 3–4 shift. • Transmission fluid leakage. • Power-steering fluid leaks. • Brake roughness and pulsation. • Rear brake-drum drag in cold weather. • Fogging of the front and side windows. • False low tire warning. • Repeated heater core failures. • Troubleshooting MIL warning light. **2001–03**—Remedy for a slow-to-fill fuel tank. **2002**—Automatic transmission fluid leaking at the quick connect for the transmission cooler lines. • MIL light comes on, vehicle shifts poorly, or vehicle won't start. • Instrument panel beeping. • Buzz, groan, or vibration when gear selector lever is in Park. • Some vehicles may run roughly on the highway or just after stopping. • Defective ignition switch lock cylinders. • Anti-theft system operates on its own. • Battery may go dead after extended parking time. • Sliding doors rattle and squeak. • Steering system whistle/whine. • Loose rear wiper arm. **2003**—Front-end grinding popping noise when passing over bumps or making turns. • Airbag warning light stays lit. • Inoperative rear window defroster. **Freestar: 2004**—Transmission has no 1–2 upshift (TSB #04-15-12). • False activation of parking assist. (Remember, I said this optional safety device would drive you nuts with false warnings.) • Bulletin No. 04-2-3, published 02/09/04, lists ways to find and fix sliding door's many failures. • Loose rear door trim.

Freestar, Windstar Profile

	1997	1998	1999	2000	2001	2002	2003	2004
Cost Price ($) (very negotiable)								
Freestar	—	—	—	—	—	—	—	27,295
Windstar/Base	23,495	24,495	24,295	—	—	—	—	—
LX (19%)	28,995	28,995	28,195	25,995	26,750	25,995	26,195	—
SEL (20%)	—	—	36,195	36,195	33,190	33,685	37,015	—

Used Values ($)								
Freestar ▲	—	—	—	—	—	—	—	17,500
Freestar ▼	—	—	—	—	—	—	—	16,000
Windstar/Base ▲	3,000	4,500	6,000	—	—	—	—	—
Windstar/Base ▼	2,500	6,500	5,000	—	—	—	—	—
LX ▲	4,500	5,500	7,500	10,000	11,500	14,500	16,500	—
LX ▼	3,500	4,500	6,500	8,500	10,500	13,000	15,500	—
SEL ▲	—	—	8,000	10,500	13,500	16,500	21,000	—
SEL ▼	—	—	7,000	9,500	12,000	15,000	19,500	—
Reliability	❶	❶	❶	❶	❷	❷	❷	③
Crash Safety (F)	⑤	⑤	⑤	⑤	⑤	⑤	⑤	⑤
Side	—	—	⑤	④	④	④	④	④
Offset	⑤	⑤	③	③	③	③	③	⑤
Rollover	—	—	—	—	④	④	④	④

ECONOLINE CARGO VAN, CLUB WAGON ★★★

RATING: Average (2004–05); Below Average (1980–2003). **Strong points:** Good base warranty and more reliable than any Detroit front-drive. Reasonably well equipped; more-refined powertrain and brakes on the 2004s; good control/instrument layout; adequate interior room, and an acceptable ride. **Weak points:** Huge and heavy with sloppy handling, similar to the Ram lineup. With earlier vehicles, excessive braking distance and harsh transmission shifting and hunting. Limited second-row legroom and excessive engine, wind, and road noise. Quality control isn't the best. **New for 2005:** Nothing major.

2005 Technical Data

Powertrain (rear-drive)
Engines: 4.6L V8 (225 hp)
• 5.4L V8 (255 hp)
• 6.8L V10 (305 hp)
• 6.0L turbo diesel (325 hp)
Transmissions: 4-speed auto.
• 5-speed auto.
Dimension/Capacity (XLT)
Height/length/width:
80.7/211.8/79.3 in.
Headroom F/R1/R2: 42.5/40.2/40.1 in.
Legroom F/R1/R2: 40.0/39.2/40.1 in.
Wheelbase: 138 in.
Turning circle: 46.7 ft.
Passengers: 7–15
Cargo volume: 257 cu. ft.
GVWR: 10,000–20,000 lb.
Tow limit: 3,700–10,000 lb.
Ground clear.: 10.7 in.
Fuel tank: 132L/reg./diesel
Weight: 5,150 lb.

MODEL HISTORY: The rear-drive Econoline has long been a fixture in the commercial delivery market, primarily because of its 4,536 kg (10,000 lb.) carrying capacity. Like Chrysler, Ford has made few changes over the last several decades, figuring that a good thing is best left alone. The Ford Club Wagon, which is an Econoline dressed up for passenger duty, offers lots of room with capacity to spare for luggage.

Easily found at reasonable prices, Econolines don't possess any glaring virtues or vices; they all perform in a manner similar to that of the Chrysler and GM large vans. Overall reliability is on par with similar Chrysler and GM full-sized vans.

2004 models got a 4.6L V8 base engine; the 7.3L diesel was ditched for a problematic 6.0L turbocharged variant; and a new 5-speed automatic transmission was added (turbo models, only) along with rear disc brakes on larger wheels.

Econolines have had fewer quality-control deficiencies than Chrysler and GM, but they are merely the best of an old-tech, bad lot. Admittedly, Ford engine defects are legion. Electrical, fuel, and ignition systems are constantly on the fritz. The 3- and 4-speed automatic transmissions, steering and suspension components (lower steering shaft/tie-rods), and brakes (calipers, pads, rotors, and torn rear caliper boots) have also come under considerable criticism.

Econolines equipped with the 4.9L inline-six engine were offered with a 3- or 4-speed manual, or a 3-speed automatic transmission. All recent V8-equipped vans come with a 4-speed automatic. It would be best to find an Econoline or Club Wagon with the more refined and reliable 4-speed automatic and 5.0L V8, until we see how the base 4.6L handles long-term use. If heavy-duty hauling is your métier, then you'll be interested in getting an Econoline equipped with the optional 7.5L V8, capable of moving a gross combined weight rated at 8,392 kg (18,500 lb.).

Body fit and finish, typically, are below average and have been that way for the past several decades. Still, squeaks and rattles have been notably reduced on the more recent models. Premature rusting hasn't been a serious problem either since the mid-1980s (except for rusted-out oil pans), but water leaks through the windshield and doors and paint delamination and peeling are quite common.

COST ANALYSIS: Best alternatives: Go for a second-series $27,940 upgraded 2004 or a 2005, depending upon the discount. **Rebates:** $3,500 rebates on the 2004s and half as much on the 2005s. **Delivery/PDI:** Unacceptedly high at $1,025. **Warranty:** Bumper-to-bumper 3 years/60,000 km; rust perforation 5 years/unlimited km. **Supplementary warranty:** An extended warranty is a must. **Options:** Running boards, upgraded sound system, heavy-duty alternator, remote keyless entry, power windows and door locks, and rear air conditioning. A transmission oil cooler for the Overdrive transmission, particularly if you plan to do some trailering. **Depreciation:** Faster than average. **Insurance cost:** Higher than average. **Parts supply/cost:** Good supply. Cheap parts. **Annual maintenance cost:** Higher than average. **Highway/city fuel economy:** *E-150 with a 4.2L engine:* 11.7–16.6L/100 km; *4.6L:* 12.2–17.6L/100 km; *5.4L:* 12.3–17.4L/100 km.

QUALITY/RELIABILITY: Mediocre quality control and average reliability. With Ford's constant management reorganizations, the deck chairs get shuffled around, but the ship is still sinking. Many "goodwill" programs cover owner problems listed below. However, this approach is mostly hit or miss and is no solution for Ford's poor quality control. **Owner-reported problems:** Poor engine performance, automatic transmission breakdowns, electrical glitches, sudden failure of key suspension or steering components, AC malfunctions, brakes that are noisy or wear out prematurely, and excessive creaks, squeaks, rattles, buzzing, and whining from body and mechanical components. **Warranty performance:** Quite poor.

SAFETY SUMMARY: Insurance industry statistics show that Ford vans have had a lower-than-average frequency of accident injury claims when compared to all vehicles on North American roads. Many Econolines don't have front-seat head restraints; Club Wagons may have head restraints for the two front seats, depending on the trim level. **Airbags:** There have been reports of airbags failing to deploy. **ABS:** Four-wheel; standard. **Safety belt pretensioners:** Standard. **Head restraints F/R:** *2004:* *. **Visibility F/R:** *****/**.

SAFETY COMPLAINTS: All models/years: Airbag malfunctions. • Chronic stalling. • Exhaust fumes enter into the vehicle. • Film covers inside of windshield, causing poor visibility. • Steering tie-rod end failures. • Tire tread separation. **1998**—Windshield stress crack at base of wiper arm. • Fuel fumes permeate the interior. • Horn doesn't work. • Wheel rubs against the torsion bar when turning left. • Driver's seat moves forward when stopping. **1998–99**—Still lots of complaints of road wander, vibration, and premature brake rotor warpage and pad wearout, leading to extended stopping distances and front brake lock-up. **1998–2002**—Sticking or binding ignition lock cylinder. **1999**—Sudden acceleration when idling or when cruise control is activated. • Van rolled away while parked with emergency brake engaged. • Electrical shorts cause fuses to blow and makes brakes, turn signals, and transmissions malfunction. • Vehicle tends to pull to one side when cruising. **2000**—Vehicle is equipped with non-adjustable camber bushings, causing premature outer tire wear in both front tires. • Child trapped between sofa bed and captain's chair. **2001**—Flat mirrors create a large blind spot. **2002**—Engine damaged because water entered through the intake. • Engine surges at idle. • Loss of power steering. • Brake failure caused by brake pads sticking to the rotor. • Vehicle pulls to the right when brakes are hot. • Fuel tank won't fill up completely. • Jammed rear seat belt. **2003**—Engine stalled and then exploded. • Transmission slipped out of Park into Reverse. • Loss of power steering. • Excessive on-road shake. **2004**—5.4L slow throttle response. • Loss of power steering; steering gearbox failure. • Excessive highway wander; loose steering. • Fuel pump failure due to misrouted electrical harness. • Seat belts may be too short.

Secret Warranties/Service Tips

All models: 1992–98—A misaligned shift column shaft bushing will make the ignition key hard to turn or difficult to remove. **1993–99**—A buzzing or rattling noise coming from underneath the vehicle indicates the need to secure the heat shield. **1993–2000**—Paint delamination, peeling, or fading (see Part Three). **1994–97**—An erratic or prolonged 1–2 shift is likely caused by premature accumulator seal wear. Replace the piston and top accumulator spring. **1995–96**—On vehicles equipped with a 5.8L engine, check the secondary air injection pump as the source of chronic engine knocking. • Hard starts and stalling with all engines may be caused by a sticking idle air control valve. **1996–97**—If the automatic transmission causes the van to stall when engaged, install an upgraded fluid filter and seal assembly. **1996–98**—Water leaking onto the rear door power lock switch may cause inoperative or self-activating power door locks, or an inoperative remote keyless entry. **1996–2000**—A rear axle whine on E450 Super Duty with a Dana 80 can be silenced by putting in a dampened rear driveshaft. **1997**—Inoperative power windows may need a non-cycling circuit-breaker in the window motor circuit. **1997–98**—On vehicles equipped with a 7.3L engine, consider reprogramming the power control module (PCM) if the van stalls, burns excessive gas and oil, or loses power. • Troubleshooting tips for tracking down and eliminating side-door wind noise. **1998**—Harsh 1–2 shifts or stalling when put into gear. • A squeaking steering column may be caused by an improperly seated rubber seal. • Seat belts may be slow to retract. • Loss of temperature control. • **1998–2003**—7.3L diesel engine turbocharger pedestal may leak oil around the exhaust backpressure actuator; high pressure oil pump may leak. **1999–2000**—To prevent the lower rear brake caliper boots from being damaged from driving over gravel roads, Ford will install a brake caliper shield kit. **1999–2001**—Ford admits to faulty 5.4L engines with defective head gaskets. The April 1, 2002, edition of *Automotive News* says the automaker budgeted up to $4,500 (U.S.) to replace affected engines and $800 to replace the cylinder heads and head gasket. **1999–2003**—Models with the 7.3L diesel engine may have premature oil pan corrosion, or a high-pressure oil pump leak (TSB #04-4-4). **2000**—Replace the intake manifold gasket if leakage is evident. **2000–03**—Poor engine performance:

Engine Controls – Rough Idle/Hesitation

Article No.: 03-9-11   05/12/03

2000–03 E-350, E-450, EXCURSION, SUPER DUTY F-SERIES

ISSUE: Some F250-F550 Super Duty and Excursion vehicles equipped with a 5.4L or 6.8L engine, and some E350/450 vehicles equipped with a 6.8L engine may exhibit a rough idle and/or hesitation when accelerating. This may occur intermittently within the first 2–3 minutes after start when engine is not warmed up (i.e., conditions other than hot restart). The condition is more likely to occur at ambient temperatures of approximately 60°F (160°C) and higher, and may be aggravated by an unmetered air leak or exhaust leak.

2001—Owner Notification Program says automatic transmission could have internal damage, may lose Second gear, or be unable to engage any gear. • Front shaft seal leakage. • An automatic transmission ticking or clicking may be heard when First gear is engaged. • Water pump shaft seal leakage. **2002**—Repeat heater core leaks. **2003**—Incorrectly machined engine crankshaft. • Exhaust air rush noise and reduced power. **2003–04**—6.0L diesel engine runs rough, loses power, or has fuel in the oil (Bulletin #04-9-3, published 05/11/04).

Econoline Cargo Van, Club Wagon Profile

	1997	1998	1999	2000	2001	2002	2003	2004
Cost Price ($) (very negotiable)								
Cargo Van (19%)	23,295	23,695	24,295	26,295	25,970	27,200	—	28,480
Club Wagon (18%)	27,395	27,795	28,195	29,295	28,615	29,000	30,050	31,120
Used Values ($)								
Cargo Van ʌ	4,500	6,000	9,500	11,500	13,500	16,500	—	22,000
Cargo Van v	3,500	5,000	8,000	10,000	12,500	15,500	—	21,000
Club Wagon ʌ	6,500	8,000	11,000	13,000	15,500	19,000	22,500	25,000
Club Wagon v	5,000	7,000	9,500	11,500	14,500	18,000	21,000	24,000
Reliability	②	②	②	③	③	③	③	③
Crash Safety (F)	③	—	④	④	④	④	④	—
Side	—	—	—	—	—	—	—	—
Rollover	—	—	—	—	②	②	②	—

Ford/Nissan

VILLAGER, QUEST

RATING: *Quest:* Below Average (2004–05). Even though it's larger, more powerful, and better-appointed, factory defects are legion. *Villager and Quest:* Average (1997–2003); Below Average (1995–96); Not Recommended (1993–94). Best used for city commuting, rather than fully loaded, long highway journeys. **Strong points:** Wide side sliding doors; third-row seats fold into the floor; small handgrips easily accessed by children; hefty discounts. *2003:* Impressive highway performance (as long as you're not carrying a full load) and easy, no-surprise, carlike handling; highway stability is above reproach; occupants get a comfortable ride with lots of seating choices; the 4-speed automatic transmission is particularly smooth and quiet; braking performance is quite good (when it's working properly); plenty of passenger and cargo room (these vans are nearly a foot longer and two inches wider and higher than Chrysler's short-wheelbase minivans); and mechanical components have been tested for years on the Maxima. *Quest:* Carlike handling, lots of interior room, and well appointed. **Weak points:** Quirky dash and interior styling. *2003:* These fuel-thirsty minivans are quite heavy, and the 3.0L and 3.3L engines have to go all out to carry the extra weight. Surprisingly, GM's 2.8L engines produce more torque than what the Villager and Quest can deliver. Powertrain set-up trails the Odyssey in acceleration and passing. Other minuses: A cheap-looking interior; the control layout can be a bit confusing; suspension is too soft; and rear-seat access can be difficult. Some wind and road noise, and excessive engine noise under heavy throttle. *Quest:* High priced, suspension bottoms out on rough roads, and instrument panel produces windshield glare. **New for 2005:** Engineering upgrades that will hopefully correct last year's mistakes; rating will be upgraded when this is evident.

2002 Technical Data

Powertrain (front-drive)
Engine: 3.3L V6 (170 hp)
Transmission: 4-speed auto.
Dimension/Capacity
Height/length/width:
64.2/194.8/74.9 in.
Headroom F/R1/R2: 39.7/39.9/37.6 in.
Legroom F/R1/R2: 39.9/36.4/36.3 in.
Wheelbase: 112.2 in.

Turning circle: 39.9 ft.
Passengers: 2/2/3
Cargo volume: 127 cu. ft.
GVWR: 5,445 lb.
Tow limit: 2,000–3,500 lb.
Ground clear.: 5.8 in.
Fuel tank: 75L/reg.
Weight: 3,850 lb.

2005 Quest Technical Data

Powertrain (front-drive)
Engine: 3.5L V6 (240 hp)
Transmissions: 4-speed auto.
• 5-speed auto.
Dimension/Capacity
Height/length/width:
70/204.1/77.6 in.
Headroom F/R1/R2: 41.9/41.7/37.7 in.
Legroom F/R1/R2: 41.6/41.3/41.2 in.
Wheelbase: 124 in.

Turning circle: 40 ft.
Passengers: 2/2/3
Cargo volume: 148.7 cu. ft.
GVWR: 5,732 lb.
Tow limit: 3,500 lb.
Ground clearance: 5.8 in.
Fuel tank: N/A
Weight: 4,012 lb.

MODEL HISTORY: Smaller and more carlike than most minivans, the pre-2004 Villager and Quest are sized comfortably between the regular and extended Chrysler minivans.

These minivans' strongest assets are a 170-hp 3.3L V6 engine that gives them carlike handling, ride, and cornering; modular seating; and reliable mechanical components. Nissan borrowed the powertrain, suspension, and steering assembly from the Maxima, mixed in some creative sheet metal, and left the job of outfitting the sound system, climate control, dashboard, steering column, and wheels to Ford. This has resulted in an attractive, not overly aero-styled minivan.

1996—Motorized shoulder belts are dropped, a passenger-side airbag is added, and the dash and exterior are slightly restyled. **1997**—Buyers of the entry-level GS model may order captain's chairs. **1998**—Carried over unchanged in preparation for the redesigned '99 version. **1999**—The Pathfinder's 3.3L V6 replaced the 3.0L V6, giving the Villager and Quest an additional 19 horses. **Villager: 1999**—A fourth door, more interior room, a revised instrument panel that's easier to reach, restyled front and rear ends, and improved shifting, acceleration, and braking (ABS takes less effort and is supposedly more durable). The suspension was retuned to give a more carlike ride and handling, the old climate control system was ditched for a more sophisticated version with air filtration, and optional ABS was made available with all models. Mercury's top-of-the-line model, the Nautica, was dropped. **Quest: 1999**—An additional 4.6 inches in length and 1.2 inches in width, standard ABS brakes, and a driver-side sliding rear door. The second row of seats can now be removed and the third row is set on tracks. Upgraded headlights and rear leaf springs. Owners gain an extra 10 cubic feet of storage space, due to the addition of a cargo shelf behind the rear seats. **2001–02**—An improved child safety seat anchoring system; performance, suspension, and comfort upgrades; a stabilizer bar on the GLE; freshened exterior styling; and a standard entertainment centre with a larger screen.

2004–05 Quest

A totally different minivan than its predecessor, the $33,895–$50,000 2004 Quest is one of the largest and priciest minivans on the road. Based on the Altima/Murano platform, it offers a more powerful engine, and all the standard high-tech safety, performance, and convenience features one could want. Its long wheelbase allows for the widest opening sliding doors among front-drive minivans, rear seating access is a breeze, and a capacious interior allows for flexible cargo and passenger configurations that can easily accommodate 4' x 8' objects with the liftgate closed. Standard fold-flat third-row seats and fold-to-the-floor centre-row seats allow owners to increase storage space without worrying about where to store the extra seats, although third row headrests must be removed before the seats can be folded away.

Although it feels a bit heavy in the city, the Quest is very carlike when driven on the highway. Ride and handling are enhanced by a new four-wheel independent suspension, along with front and rear stabilizer bars, and upgraded anti-lock brakes.

Safety features include standard head curtain supplemental airbags for outboard passengers in all three rows, supplemental front-seat side-impact airbags, standard traction control, and ABS brakes with brake assist.

COST ANALYSIS: Unless your needs require all the newest bells and whistles, save thousands by getting a fully loaded 1999–2003 Quest. Give the 2005s another year to work out the dozens of production glitches found this year and allow a few months for prices to fall by about 15 percent.

Classification: BT04–014   Reference: NTB04–053   Date: June 23, 2004
Customer Satisfaction Initiative   Applied Vehicle: 2004 Quest (V42)
Service Information

As part of Nissan's commitment to continually improve both the quality and durability of our products, Nissan is offering owners of 2004 Quests the opportunity to have their vehicle upgraded with a number of production changes that have been incorporated in Quests manufactured after their vehicle was produced. With this Quest Customer Satisfaction Initiative, all Nissan dealers are authorized to perform these service upgrades at no cost to the customer. This Customer Satisfaction Initiative is intended to address any related symptoms a Quest customer may currently be experiencing and, to maximize the driving experience of Quest owners by preventing the related symptoms from occuring in the future.

In order to take advantage of Nissan's Quest Customer Satisfaction Initiative, Nissan Quest owners must contact their Nissan dealer and schedule a service appointment. This initiative will expire on June 30, 2005, and all related service and upgrades must be completed no later than June 30, 2005.

These upgrades fall into three areas: squeaks and rattles; ease of component operation; and an air conditioning label replacement. The upgrades will include the installation of a noise reduction kit for the sliding doors and structural insulation in the body above the rear door. Additionally, the driver power window switch; shifter lever; 2nd row seat lever; throttle pedal; and ball studs that mount the rear door support struts will be replaced. The reading lamps will be modified to improve operation and an AC servicing label will be replaced with a new one.

Nissan says its many 2004 Quest defects were caused by inexperienced American plant workers and a rush to get new models to market.

Best alternatives: Other minivans worth considering are the Honda Odyssey, the 2002–04 Mazda MPV, or a Toyota Sienna. **Options:** Nothing really worthwhile. **Rebates:** Not likely. **Delivery/PDI:** $1,100. **Depreciation:** Predicted to be average. **Insurance cost:** Should be higher than average. **Parts supply/cost:** Good supply and reasonably priced, although the 2004 model will likely have some body part delays. **Annual maintenance cost:** Should be less than average. **Warranty:** Bumper-to-bumper 3 years/80,000 km; powertrain 5 years/100,000 km; rust perforation 5 years/unlimited km. **Supplementary warranty:** An extended warranty isn't needed unless you buy a 1993–96 model. **Maintenance/Repair costs:** Higher than average. **Highway/city fuel economy:** *Villager/Quest:* 8.9–13.8L/100 km; *2004 Quest:* 8.2–12.4L/100 km.

QUALITY/RELIABILITY: Body integrity has always been subpar, with doors opening and closing on their own and poor fit and finish, allowing lots of wind noise to enter the interior. There have also been some reports of panel and paint defects and premature rusting on the inside sliding door track. Later models have improved quality control and better fit and finish. **Owner-reported problems:** Most owner-reported problems involve excessive brake noise and premature brake wear, door lock malfunctions, interior noise, and driveline vibrations. There have also been many reports of engine exhaust manifold and crankshaft failures costing up to $7,000 to repair. Other problems include electrical shorts; brake failures due to vibration, binding, or overheating; premature wear of the front discs, rotors, and pads; chronic stalling, possibly due to faulty fuel pumps or a shorted electrical system; and loose steering and veering at highway speeds. Other common problems include film buildup on windshield and interior glass; a sulfur smell from the exhaust system; poor AC performance or compressor failures, accompanied by musty, mildew-type AC odours; and recurring fuel pump buzzing heard through the radio speakers. **Warranty performance:** Average.

SAFETY SUMMARY: Interestingly, front passenger protection in a frontal collision for the 1999–2000 models only rated three stars, compared to the Windstar, Odyssey, and Toyota five-star awards. **ABS:** Standard. **Safety belt pretensioners:** Standard. **Head restraints F/R:** *1995: ***; 1997: **; 1999–2002: *. Quest 2004: **.* **Visibility F/R:** *****/**. **Maximum load

capacity: *1999 base Mercury Villager and similarly equipped Nissan Quest:* 1,450 lb.

SAFETY COMPLAINTS: All models/years through to the 2003 model: Airbags fail to deploy. • Inadvertent airbag deployment. • Vehicle suddenly accelerated forward. • Sudden stalling due to faulty fuel pump. • Steering wander and excessive vibration. • Chronic ABS failures; brake pads and rotors need replacing every 5,000 km. • Brake failures (extended stopping distance, noisy when applied). Brake and accelerator pedals are the same height, so driver's foot can easily slip and step on both at the same time. • Cycling or self-activating front door locks failures; occupants have been trapped in their vehicles. **1997–99**—Gas fumes leak into the interior. • Gas pedal sticks. **2000**—Vehicle tends to lurch forward when the AC is first engaged. • Weak tailgate hydraulic cylinders. • Instrument panel's white face hard to read in daylight hours. **2000–01**—Missing seat belt latch plate stopper button. • Broken shift lock cable plate causes shift indicator to be misaligned. • 22-month-old child was able to pull the clasp apart on integrated child safety seat. • Seat belts don't retract properly. • Rear window on liftgate door shattered for unknown reason (replaced under warranty). • Power steering fluid leakage due to o-ring at rack gear splitting. **2002**—Stuck accelerator pedal. • Excessive vibration at highway speeds. • Leaking front and rear struts degrade handling. • Steering wheel is off-centre to the left. • Continental tire tread separation. **2004**—Sudden, unintended acceleration. • Sliding door trapped child; adults also trapped; door continuously pops open. • Bad reflection of dash on windshield. • Automatic transmission won't downshift. • Dome light fuse blows continuously. • Ineffective windshield washers.

Secret Warranties/Service Tips

1993–97—Front door windows that bind may have the glass rubber improperly installed in the door sheet metal channel. **1993–98**—Automatic transmission whining when accelerating may be caused by a faulty transaxle support bracket and insulators. **1993–2002**—Paint delamination, peeling, or fading (see Part Three). • Repeat heater core failure. **1995–99**—Tips for correcting windshield water leaks and excessive noise, vibration, and harshness. **1996–2002**—Power door locks that intermittently self-activate are covered in TSB #98-22-5. **1997–98**—Tips on silencing rattles and creaks. • Hard starts, no-starts, stalling, or an exhaust rotten-egg smell can all be corrected by replacing the power control module (PCM) under the emissions warranty. **1997–99**—An exhaust buzz or rattle may be caused by a loose catalyst or muffler heat shield. **1999–2004**—Troubleshooting abnormal shifting. • Side windows pop open. **2004**—No-start, hard start remedies. • Silencing a ticking engine/exhaust noise. • Tips on correcting an abnormal shifting of the automatic transmission. • Skyroof water leaks (TSB #BT03-045). • AC blows out warm air from floor vents. • Leaks, overheating cooling system. • Guidelines on troubleshooting brake complaints.

Villager, Quest Profile

	1997	1998	1999	2000	2001	2002	2003	2004
Cost Price ($) (negotiable)								
Villager GS	24,295	24,595	24,595	24,595	—	—	—	—
Villager LS	29,195	29,495	29,495	29,495	—	—	—	—
Quest GXE/S (20%)	30,898	30,898	27,798	30,498	30,498	30,698	32,600	32,900
Used Values ($)								
Villager GS ▲	5,500	7,500	9,500	11,000	—	—	—	—
Villager GS ▼	4,000	6,500	8,000	9,500	—	—	—	—
Villager LS ▲	7,000	9,000	10,500	12,500	—	—	—	—
Villager LS ▼	5,500	8,000	9,000	11,500	—	—	—	—
Quest GXE ▲	6,000	7,500	9,500	11,500	15,000	19,500	22,000	25,000
Quest GXE ▼	5,500	6,500	8,500	10,000	13,500	18,000	20,000	23,500
Reliability	④	④	④	④	④	④	④	③
Crash Safety (F)	④	—	—	④	⑤	⑤	—	⑤
Side	—	—	—	⑤	⑤	⑤	—	⑤
Offset	❷	❷	❶	❶	❶	❶	—	⑤
Rollover	—	—	—	—	④	④	—	④

General Motors

ASTRO, SAFARI ★★★

RATING: Average (1996–05); Below Average (1985–95). These vehicles are more mini-truck than minivan and they are beginning to look quite good when compared to the problem-plagued Chrysler and Ford minivans and the overpriced Asian competition. They have fewer safety-related problems reported to the government, are easy to repair, and cost little to acquire. Stay away from the unreliable AWD models; they're expensive to repair and not very durable. **Strong points:** Brisk acceleration, trailer-towing capability, lots of passenger room and cargo space, well laid-out instrument panel with easy-to-read gauges. Very low ground clearance enhances this minivan's handling, but precludes most off-roading. Good brakes. Rock-bottom used prices, and average reliability and quality control. **Weak points:** Driving position is awkward for many; some drivers will find the pedals too close; obtrusive engine makes for very narrow front footwells that give little room for the driver's left foot to rest. Difficult entry/exit due to the high step-up and the intruding wheelwell. Harsh ride, limited front seat room, interior noise levels rise sharply at highway speeds, and excessive fuel consumption made worse by the AWD option. **New for 2005:** Nothing significant.

2005 Technical Data

Powertrain (rear-drive)
Engine: 4.3L V6 (190 hp)
Transmissions: 4-speed auto.
• AWD
Dimension/Capacity
Height/length/width:
74.9/189.8/77.5 in.
Headroom F/R1/R2: 39.2/37.9/38.7 in.
Legroom F/R1/R2: 41.6/36.5/38.5 in.

Wheelbase: 111.2 in.
Turning circle: 45 ft.
Passengers: 2/3/3
Cargo volume: 170.4 cu. ft.
GVWR: 5,600 lb.
Tow limit: 5,500 lb.
Ground clearance: 6.8 in.
Fuel tank: 95L
Weight: 4,520 lb.

MODEL HISTORY: More a utility truck than a comfortable minivan, these boxy, rear-drive minivans are built on a reworked S-10 pickup chassis. As such, they offer uninspiring handling, average-quality mechanical and body components, and relatively high fuel consumption. Both the Astro and Safari come in a choice of either cargo or passenger van. The cargo van is used either commercially or as an inexpensive starting point for a fully customized vehicle.

1991—A more powerful V6; and lap/shoulder belts. **1993**—Base engine gained 15 hp. **1994**—Driver-side airbag and side-door guard beams, plus a centre-mounted rear stop lamp was installed in the roof. **1995**—Lightly restyled front end, extended bodies, and a 190-hp engine. **1996**—Passenger-side airbag, a new dash, engine torque cut by 10 pound-feet, and more front footroom. **1997**—Upgraded power steering. **1998**—An improved automatic transmission. **1999**—A reworked AWD system. **2000**—Only seven- and eight-passenger models available; engine made quieter and smoother, while the automatic transmission was toughened up to shift more efficiently when pulling heavy loads; and a larger fuel tank was installed. **2001**—A tilt steering wheel; cruise control; CD player; remote keyless entry; power windows, mirrors, and locks. **2002**—A rear heater on cargo models. **2003**—Upgraded four-wheel disc brakes.

The 1985–95 versions suffer from failure-prone automatic transmissions, poor braking systems, failure-prone AC compressors, and fragile steering components. The early base V6 provides ample power, but also produces lots of noise, consumes excessive amounts of fuel, and tends to have leaking head gaskets and failure-prone oxygen sensors. These computer-related problems often rob the engine of sufficient power to keep up in traffic. While the 5-speed manual transmission shifts fairly easily, the automatic takes forever to downshift on the highway. Handling isn't particularly agile on these minivans, and the power steering doesn't provide the driver with enough road feel. Unloaded, the Astro provides very poor traction, the ride isn't comfortable on poor road surfaces, and interior noise is rampant. Many drivers find the driving position awkward (no left legroom) and the heating/defrosting system inadequate. Many engine components are hidden under the dashboard, making repair or maintenance awkward. Even on more recent models, highway performance and overall reliability aren't impressive. Through the 2000 model year, the 4-speed automatic transmissions are clunky and hard shifting, though they're much more reliable than Ford or Chrysler gearboxes.

Other owners report that the front suspension, steering components, computer modules, and catalytic converter can wear out within as little as 60,000 km. There have also been lots of complaints about electrical, exhaust, cooling, and fuel system bugs; inadequate heating/defrosting; failure-prone wiper motors; and axle seals wearing out every 12–18 months.

Body hardware is fragile, and fit and finish is the pits. Water leaks from windows and doors are common, yet hard to diagnose. Squeaks and rattles are legion and hard to locate. Sliding-door handles often break off and the sliding door frequently jams in cold temperatures. The hatch release for the Dutch doors occasionally doesn't work, and the driver-side vinyl seat lining tears apart. Premature paint peeling, delamination, and surface rust are fairly common.

The 1995–99 models are a bit improved, but they still have problems carried over from earlier years, with stalling, hard starts, and expensive and frequent automatic transmission, power-steering, wheel bearing, brake pad, caliper, and rotor repairs heading the list.

Year 2000–04 models are a bit more reliable and better performing, inasmuch as they underwent considerable upgrading by GM. Nevertheless, buyers should be aware that extra attention is merited in the following areas: Excessive vibration transmitted through the AWD; automatic transmission clunk; poor braking performance (brake pedal hardens and brakes don't work after going over bumps or rough roads) and expensive brake maintenance; electronic computer modules and fuel system glitches that cause the Check Engine light to remain lit; hard starts, no-starts, or chronic stalling, especially when going downhill; heating and AC performance hampered by poor air distribution; electrical system shorts; and sliding door misalignment and broken hinges.

COST ANALYSIS: Get a discounted 2004; the $27,600 MSRP can be cut by almost $5,000 the further you get into 2005. The 2005 doesn't cost much more, but it doesn't offer more either. **Best alternatives:** Most front-drive minivans made by Nissan and Toyota have better handling and are more reliable and economical people-carriers; unfortunately, they lack the Astro's considerable grunt, essential for cargo-hauling and trailer towing. Also consider getting a later-model Ford Aerostar (check for tranny and coil spring damage, though). **Rebates:** About $3,000 on the 2004 and half that amount on 2005 models by midsummer. **Delivery/PDI:** $995. **Warranty:** Bumper-to-bumper 3 years/60,000 km; rust perforation 6 years/160,000 km. **Supplementary warranty:** A toss-up. Individual repairs won't cost a lot, but those nickels and dimes can add up. A powertrain-only warranty is a wise choice. **Options:** Integrated child safety seats and rear AC. Be wary of the AWD option; it exacts a high fuel penalty and isn't very dependable. **Depreciation:** Average. **Insurance cost:** Slightly higher than average. **Parts supply/cost:** Good supply of cheap parts. A large contingent of independent parts suppliers keeps repair costs down. **Annual maintenance cost:** Average. Any garage can repair these rear-drive minivans. **Highway/city fuel economy:** 10.6–14.6L/100 km for rear-drive and 11.3–15.3L/100 km with AWD.

QUALITY/RELIABILITY: Average; most of the Astro's and Safari's defects are easy to diagnose and repair leading to a minimum of downtime. Early rear axle failures. Mechanics say the rear axle is a "light-duty" axle not suitable for a vehicle of this type (*www.bigclassaction.com/automotive.html*). **Owner-reported problems:** Some problems with the automatic transmission, rear axle whine, steering, electrical system, heating and defrosting system, premature brake wear, faulty suspension components, and glitch-prone sliding doors. **Warranty performance:** Average.

SAFETY SUMMARY: NHTSA has recorded numerous complaints of dashboard fires. Power steering locks up or fails unexpectedly, components wear out quickly, and steering may bind when turning. Seat belt complaints are also common: Seat belts tighten up unexpectedly, cannot be adjusted, or have nowhere to latch. **Airbags:** Standard front. Reports of driver's airbag failing to deploy in a collision. **Seat belt pretensioners:** Not offered. **Anti-lock brakes:** Standard; disc/disc. Reports of ABS failure, brakes hesitating when applied, brakes engaging for no reason, and premature brake wear. **Traction control (AWD):** Optional. **Head restraints F/R:** *1995:* *; *1996–97:* **/*; *1999:* **; *2001–02:* **; *2003-04:* *. **Visibility F/R:** *****/**.

SAFETY COMPLAINTS: 1995–98—Vehicle continues to accelerate after foot is removed from accelerator. • Frequent stalling. • Erratic engine performance due to blocked catalytic converter. • Vehicle jerks to one side when braking. • Front wheels lock up when turning the steering wheel to the right from a stop while in gear. • Steering stuck when turning. • Fresh-air ventilation system allows fumes from other vehicles to enter interior compartment. • With jack almost fully extended, wheel doesn't lift off ground. • Spare tire not safe for driving over 60 km/h. • Horn buttons require excessive pressure to activate. • Driver-side window failure. • Sliding door suddenly fell off. • Front passenger door won't close. • Passenger-side door glass fell out. • Rear hatch latch release failed. • Rear hatch hydraulic rods are too weak to support hatch. • Front passenger's seat reclining mechanism failed. • Poor traction. • Parked in gear and rolled downhill. • Transmission failures. • Left rear axle seal leaks, causing lubricant to burn on brake lining. • Sudden wheel bearing failure. • AC clutch fell apart. • Alternator bearing failure. **1999**—Very few safety-related complaints, compared with most other minivans. Many of the 1999 model problems have been reported by owners of earlier model years. • Hard shifting between First and Second gear; transmission slippage. • Delayed shifting or stalling when passing from Drive to Reverse. • Leaking axle seals. • Rear cargo door hinge and latch slipped off, and door opened 180 degrees. • Floor mat moves under brake and accelerator pedals. • Brake pedal set too close to the accelerator. • Fuel gauge failure caused by faulty sending unit. **2000**—Brake and gas pedals are too close together. • When brakes are applied, rear wheels tend to lock up while front wheels continue to turn. • Vehicle stalls when accelerating or turning. • Astro rolls back when stopped on an incline in Drive. • Sliding door slams shut on an incline or hinges break. • Extensive damage caused to bumper and undercarriage by driving over gravel roads.

2001—Sudden acceleration. • Chronic stalling. • Sudden total electrical failure, especially when going into Reverse. • Brake pedal set too high. • Differential in transfer case locked up while driving; defective axle seals. • Vehicle rolls backward on an incline while in Drive (dealer adjusted transfer case to no avail). • Fuel gauge failure. • Faulty AC vents. • Water can be trapped inside the wheels and freeze, causing the wheels to be out of balance. **2002**—Airbag failed to deploy. • Sticking gas pedal. • Brake pedal goes to floor without braking. • Seat belts in rear are too long; don't fit children or child safety seats. • Driver-side window failures. • Sliding-door window blew out. • Uniroyal spare tire sidewall cracks. **2003**—Harsh, delayed shifting. • On a slight incline, sliding door will unlatch and slam shut. • Intermittent windshield wiper failure. **2004**—Rear driver-side window exploded.

Secret Warranties/Service Tips

1993–99—Tips on getting rid of AC odours. • Defective catalytic converters may cause a rotten-egg smell eligible for an emissions warranty refund. **1993–2005**—GM says that a chronic driveline clunk can't be silenced and is a normal characteristic of its vehicles. • Paint delamination, peeling, or fading (see Part Three). **1995–2000**—Dealer guidelines for brake servicing under warranty. **1995–2004**—Booming interior noise at highway speeds. **1996–98**—Rough engine performance may be caused by a water-contaminated oxygen sensor, and a rough idle shortly after starting may be caused by sticking poppet valves. **1996–2000**—Hard start, no-start, backfire, and kickback when starting may be corrected by replacing the crankshaft position sensor. • A rough idle after start and/or a Service Engine light that stays lit may mean you have a stuck injector poppet valve ball that needs cleaning. **1996–2001**—Poor heat distribution in driver's area of vehicle (install new heat ducts). • Exhaust rattle noise. **1996–2003**—Engine noise remedy:

Engine Rattle

Bulletin No.: 03-06-01-024B   Date: March 04, 2004

Rattle Noise In Engine (Install Timing Tensioner Kit)

1996–2003 Chevrolet Astro, Blazer, Express, S-10, Silverado
1996–2003 GMC Jimmy, Safari, Savana, Sierra, Sonoma
1996–2001 Oldsmobile Bravada with 4.3L V6 Engine

Condition: Some customers may comment on a rattle-type noise coming from the engine at approximately 1800 to 2200 RPMs.

Cause: The spark, rattle-type noise may be caused by torsional vibration of the balance shaft.

Correction: Install a new tensioner assembly kit.

1996–2004—Silence a boom-type noise heard during engine warm-up by installing an exhaust dampener assembly (TSB #00-06-05-001A). **1997–98**—An engine ticking noise that appears when the temperature falls may require an EVAP purge solenoid valve. **1997–99**—A hard start, no-start, and rough idle can be fixed by replacing the fuel tank fill pipe assembly and cleaning the SCPI poppet valves. **1999**—Steering column squeaking can be silenced by replacing the steering wheel SIR module coil assembly. **1999–2000**—If the engine runs hot, overheats, or loses coolant, try polishing the radiator filler neck or replacing the radiator cap before letting any mechanic convince you that more expensive repairs are needed. • A popping or snapping sound may emanate from the right front door window area. **1999–2004**—Automatic transmission malfunctions may be caused by debris in the transmission (Bulletin No.: 01-07-30-038B). **2001**—Harsh automatic transmission shifts. • 2–4 band and 3–4 clutch damage. • Steering shudder felt when making low-speed turns. • Excessive brake squeal. • Wet carpet/odour in passenger footwell area (repair evaporator case drain to cowl seal/open evaporator case drain). • Delayed shifts, slips, flares, or extended shifts during cold operation (replace shift solenoid valve assembly). **2002**—Automatic transmission slips, incorrect shifts, and poor engine performance. • Service Engine light comes on, no Third or Fourth gear, and loss of Drive. • Slipping or missing Second, Third, or Fourth gear. • Inadequate heating. • Roof panel has a wavy or rippled appearance. • Water leak in the windshield area. **2002–03**—Engine runs rough or engine warning light comes on. • Sliding door difficult to open. **2003**—Hard starts, rough idle, and intermittent misfiring. • Transfer case shudder. • Right rear door handle breakage. **2004**—Silencing a suspension pop.

Astro, Safari Profile

	1997	1998	1999	2000	2001	2002	2003	2004
Cost Price ($) (very negotiable)								
Cargo (17%)	25,110	25,110	23,290	24,015	24,465	—	—	26,390
CS/base (17%)	26,920	23,839	25,675	25,675	26,440	27,255	27,600	27,615
Used Values ($)								
Cargo ⋀	4,500	5,500	7,500	9,000	10,500	—	—	19,000
Cargo ⋁	4,000	4,000	6,000	7,500	9,500	—	—	17,500
CS/base ⋀	5,000	6,000	8,500	10,000	12,000	15,500	18,000	20,000
CS/base ⋁	4,500	5,000	7,000	8,500	10,500	14,500	16,500	19,000
Reliability	❷	③	③	③	④	④	④	④
Crash Safety (F)	③	③	③	③	③	③	③	③
Side	—	—	—	—	—	—	⑤	⑤
Offset	❶	❶	❶	❶	❶	❶	❶	❶
Rollover	—	—	—	—	③	③	③	—

MONTANA, MONTANA SV6, SILHOUETTE, TRANS SPORT, UPLANDER, VENTURE ★★

RATING: Below Average (1997–2005); Not Recommended (1990–96). These minivans have been down-rated this year for three reasons: Serious automatic transmission and engine head gasket failures; deteriorating reliability combined with an inadequate warranty (Chrysler's warranty is better); and safety defects that include sliding doors injuring and crushing children. These minivans are almost as bad as Ford's Windstar/Freestar, and actually make

Chrysler's minivans look good. *Montana SV6/Uplander:* These 2005 replacements for the Montana and Venture aren't recommended during their first year on the market. Furthermore, while Honda, Toyota, and Nissan push the envelope in engineering and styling, these restyled GM minivans join the Ford Freestar and Kia Sedona as also-ran, *pseudo-nouveau* entries. **Strong points:** A comfortable ride, easy handling, dual sliding doors, plenty of comfort and convenience features, flexible seating arrangements, good visibility fore and aft, lots of storage bins and compartments, and good crash scores. One of the quietest minivans in its class. **Weak points:** Average acceleration with a light load; unproven AWD; less effective rear drum brakes and excessive brake fading; tall drivers will find insufficient headroom, and short drivers may find it hard to see where the front ends; low rear seats force passengers into an uncomfortable knees-up position; narrow cabin makes front-to-rear access a bit difficult; seat cushions on the centre and rear bench seats are hard, flat, and too short, and the seatbacks lack sufficient lower back support; cargo may not slide out easily, due to the rear sill sticking up a few inches; a high number of safety-related failures and engine exhaust manifold defects; and disappointing fuel economy. **New for 2005:** The Montana SV6 and Uplander are GM's old minivans dressed up to look new. Powered by 15 more horses than previous versions, there's still ample cargo room thanks to removable second and third-row seats, and flat folding third-row seats. Equipped with a 3.5L V-6 engine and an electronically controlled 4-speed automatic transmission, the Uplander and Montana are loaded with standard features like 17-inch wheels, ABS, strut-type front suspension/non-independent rear suspension, an OnStar security system, and dual-stage driver and passenger front airbags. Important options include AWD, a vehicle stability enhancement system, side-impact airbags, and "smart" front airbags. Unfortunately, these new-styled minivans don't have flip-and-fold rear seats or side-curtain airbags.

2005 Technical Data

Powertrain (front-drive)
Engine: 3.4L V6 (185 hp)
Engine: 3.5L V6 (200 hp)
Transmissions: 4-speed auto.
• AWD
Dimension/Capacity (Silhouette;
Montana and Venture)
Passengers: 2/2/3; 2/3/3
Height/length/width:
 67.4/186.9/72 in.;
 68.1/187.3/72.7 in.
Headroom F/R1/R2: 39.9/39.3/38.8 in.;
 F/R1/R2: 39.9/39.3/38.9 in.

Legroom F/R1/R2: 39.9/36.9/34 in.;
F/R1/R2: 39.9/39/36.7 in.

Wheelbase: 112 in.
Turning circle: 42 ft.
Tow limit: 3,500 lb.
Cargo volume: 126.6 cu. ft.
GVWR: 5,357 lb.
Ground clearance: 8.5 in.
Fuel tank: 94.6L
Weight: 3,699 lb.

MODEL HISTORY: These minivans have more carlike handling than GM's Astro and Safari. Seating is limited to five adults in the standard models (two up front and three on a removable bench seat), but this can be increased to seven if you find a vehicle equipped with optional modular seats. Seats can be folded down flat, creating additional storage space.

As with most minivans, be wary of vehicles equipped with a power-assisted passenger-side sliding door; it's both convenient and dangerous—despite an override circuit that should prevent the door from closing when it is blocked, a number of injuries have been reported. Furthermore, the doors frequently open when they shouldn't, and can be difficult to close securely.

All models and years have had serious reliability problems—notably, engine head gasket and intake manifold defects; electronic module (PROM) and starter failures; premature front brake component wear, brake fluid leakage, and noisy braking; short circuits that burn out alternators, batteries, power door lock activators, and the blower motor; AC evaporator core failures; premature wearout of the inner and outer tie-rods; automatic transmission breakdowns; abysmal fit and finish; chronic sliding door malfunctions; and faulty rear seat latches. Other problems include a fuel-thirsty and poor-performing 3-speed automatic transmission; a poorly mounted sliding door; side door glass that pops open; squeaks, rattles, and clunks in the instrument panel cluster area and suspension; and wind buffeting noise around the front doors. The large dent- and rust-resistant plastic panels are robot-bonded to the frame, and they absorb engine and road noise very well, in addition to having an impressive record for durability.

1994—A shortened nose, APV designation is dropped, driver-side airbag arrives. **1996**—3.4L V6 debuts, and the Lumina was replaced by the Venture at the end of the model year. **1997**—Dual airbags and ABS. **1998**—The sliding driver-side door is available on more models. **1999**—A 5-hp boost to the base V6 engine (185), de-powered airbags, an upgraded automatic transmission, a rear-window defogger, and heated rear-view mirrors. **2000**—Dual sliding rear side doors. **2001**—Slightly restyled, a fold-flat third-row seat, driver-side power door, and a six-disc CD player added; cargo version dropped. **2002**—Nothing major; optional AWD and DVD entertainment centre. **2003**—Optional ABS and front side airbags.

By the way, don't trust the towing limit listed in GM's owner's manual. Automakers publish tow ratings that are on the optimistic side—and sometimes they even lie. Also, don't be surprised to find that the base 3.1L engine doesn't handle a full load of passenger and cargo, especially when mated with the 3-speed automatic transmission. The ideal powertrain combo would be the 4-speed automatic coupled to the optional "3800" V6 (first used on the 1996 versions). These minivans use a quiet-running V6 power plant similar to Chrysler's top-of-the-line 3.8L 6-cylinder, providing good mid-range and top-end power. The GM engine is hampered by less torque, however, making for less grunt when accelerating and frequent downshifting out of Overdrive when climbing moderate grades. The electronically controlled 4-speed automatic transmission shifts smoothly and quietly—one advantage over Chrysler and Ford.

The 1997 and later models are less rattle-prone, due to a more rigid body structure than that of their predecessors. However, fit and finish quality is still wanting. The front windshield is particularly prone to leak water from the top portion into the dash instrument cluster (a problem affecting rear-drive vans as well and covered by a secret warranty). Owner-reported problems on post-'97s include chronic plastic intake manifold/head gasket failures (covered by a 6-year/100,000 km secret warranty), EGR valve failures, transmission fluid leaks, electrical glitches shorting out dash gauges and causing difficult starting, excessive front brake noise and frequent repairs (rotors and pads), and assorted body deficiencies, including water leaks in the jack well:

> Our 2002 Venture has a poorly fitted windshield and a misaligned dash and hood, as well as quarter panels, front doors, and the sliding rear door on the passenger side. I have inspected other 2002 and 2003 Chevrolet Ventures and have seen the same windshield fit errors.

COST ANALYSIS: The 2004 Venture goes for $26,000; buy it at a discounted price of about 20 percent, until the upgraded 2005 Montana and Uplander prove their worth. **Best alternatives:** A 1999 or later Honda Odyssey, 2002 or later Mazda MPV, a 1998–2003 Nissan Quest or Toyota Sienna. Full-sized Chrysler, GM, or Ford vans are also good choices. **Rebates:** $3,000 rebates and zero percent financing. **Delivery/PDI:** $995. **Warranty:** Bumper-to-bumper 3 years/60,000 km; rust perforation 6 years/160,000 km. **Supplementary warranty:** Not needed, but if you do buy a warranty, a cheaper powertrain-only policy will do. **Options:** $5,000 (U.S.) "Sit-N-Lift" electrically powered second seats for the physically challenged (see page 28) have performed well. Be wary of the AWD option; it's unreliable. Many of these vans are equipped with Firestone tires—have them removed by the dealer or ask for a $400 rebate. Integrated child safety seats are generally a good idea, but make sure your child can't slip out. Don't get the power-assisted passenger-side sliding door; it's a wrist-breaker and can crush a child. Consider the $235 load-levelling feature—a must-have for front-drive minivans. It keeps the weight on the front wheels, giving you better steering, traction, and braking. Other options that are worth buying: The extended wheelbase version (provides a smoother ride), traction control, power side windows, a firmer suspension, self-sealing tires, and a rear air conditioner, defroster, and heater. **Depreciation:** Average. **Insurance cost:** High, but about average for a minivan. **Parts supply/cost:** Engine parts are generic to GM's other models, so they should be reasonably priced and not hard to find. **Annual maintenance cost:** Average during the warranty period. Engine, transmission, ABS, and electrical malfunctions will likely cause maintenance costs to rise after the third year of ownership. **Highway/city fuel economy:** 9.3–13.5L/100 km.

QUALITY/RELIABILITY: 1996–2004 models have chronic powertrain problems highlighted by engine manifold, head gasket, and camshaft failures along with frequent automatic transmission breakdowns and clunky shifting.

> Our '97 Venture has less than 100,000 km and the engine has seized, with broken camshafts. I am looking at paying $4,000.

Owner-reported problems: EGR valve failures, electrical glitches, excessive front brake noise and frequent repairs (rotors and pads), early wheel bearing failure, blurry front windshield, air constantly blown through the centre vent, assorted body deficiencies, including paint peeling and blistering and poor fit and finish. Failure-prone AC condensers may also be part of a larger scam run by GM, says this *Lemon-Aid* whistle-blower:

> I must remain anonymous as I am employed by GM, but what GM is doing is wrong.
>
> A problem exists with GM's Montana, Venture and Silhouette mini-vans. The AC condensers are cracking and causing a loss of refrigerant and the AC becomes inoperative.
>
> The proper repair for these vehicles (we are talking about new car warranty here) would be to replace the AC condenser with a new part. (I'm pretty sure that this is what most customers would expect). The warranty cost for this part would be $441.
>
> To save money General Motors is having these condensers welded by local radiator repair shops at a significant cost savings. The repaired condenser costs about $90.00....

Warranty performance: Very bad; the company still denies it has serious engine problems and often makes payouts only on the courthouse steps.

SAFETY SUMMARY: Sudden steering loss in rainy weather or when passing over a puddle (serpentine belt slippage); ABS brake failures; ABS light stays on for no reason; airbags fail to deploy; sliding doors suddenly open, close, come off their tracks, jam shut, stick open, injure children, and rattle (1997–2001 models recalled); fire may ignite around the fuel filler nozzle or within the ignition switch; tie-rod failures may cause loss of control; during highway driving, transmission slips from Drive into Neutral. Some front door-mounted seat belts cross uncomfortably at the neck, and there's a nasty blind spot on the driver's side that requires a small stick-on convex mirror to correct. **Anti-lock brakes:** Standard; disc/drum. **Seat belt pretensioners:** Standard. **Airbags:** Side airbags are standard. **Traction control:** Optional. **Head restraints F/R:** *1997: *; 1999: ***/*; 2001–04: ***.* **Visibility F/R: *****. Maximum load capacity:** *2001 Chevrolet Venture LS and similarly equipped Montana and Silhouette:* 1,365 lb.

SAFETY COMPLAINTS: All years: Fire may ignite around the fuel-filler nozzle or within the ignition switch. • Tie-rod failures may cause loss of steering control. • Sudden steering loss in rainy weather or when passing over a puddle (serpentine belt slippage). • Chronic brake failures or excessive brake fade. • Airbags malfunction. • Sliding doors suddenly open, close, come off their tracks, jam shut, stick open, injure children, and rattle during highway driving. • Transmission failures; slips from Drive into Neutral; and won't hold gear on a grade. • Some front door-mounted seat belts cross uncomfortably at the neck, and there's a nasty blind spot on the driver's side that requires a small stick-on convex mirror to correct. **1995–99**—Headlight assembly collects moisture, burns bulb, or falls out. • Seatback suddenly collapses. • Windshield wipers fail intermittently. • Accelerator and brake pedals are too close together • Fuel slosh/clunk when vehicle stops or accelerates (new tank useless). • Self-activating door locks lock occupants out or in. • Door handles break inside the door assembly. • Horn is hard to access. • Window latch failures. **2000–2001**—Fire ignited under driver's seat. • Windshield suddenly exploded outward while driving with wipers activated. • Firestone tire blowout. • Faulty fuel pump causes chronic stalling, no-starts, surging, and sudden acceleration. • Snapped rear control arm:

> In May we were driving our 2002 Pontiac Montana with six adults inside (luckily), on a small two-lane road, doing about 50 or 60 km/h. Suddenly, the right rear control arm snapped and the rear axle rattled and shook.
>
> Our mechanic said in 28 years he had never seen such a thing happen. If we'd been going 120 km/h on a 400 highway we'd be dead.
>
> The dealer we bought it from paid all the costs for a used part to be installed, even thought there was no warranty, but our mechanic suggested we photograph the parts he had removed. He was surprised at the thinness of the metal of the control arm. Also that the control arm is welded to the axle, so it can't be replaced without replacing the entire component. New, they are $2000!
>
> Kitchener, Ontario

• Steering idler arm fell off due to missing bolt. • Brakes activate on their own, making it appear as if van is pulling a load. • Loose fuel tank due to loose bolts/bracket. • Fuel tank cracked when passing over a tree branch. • Plastic tube within heating system fell off and wedged behind the accelerator pedal. • Bracket weld pin that secures the rear split seat sheared off. • Centre rear lap seat belt isn't long enough to secure a rear-facing child safety seat. • Children can slide out of the integrated child safety seat. • Electrical harness failures result in complete electrical shutdown. • Headlights, interior lights, gauges, and instruments fail intermittently (electrical cluster module is the prime suspect). • Excess padding around horn makes it difficult to depress horn button in an emergency. • Weak-sounding horn. • Frequent windshield wiper motor failures. • Heater doesn't warm up vehicle sufficiently. • Antifreeze smell intrudes into interior. • Premature failure of the transmission's Fourth clutch. • Delayed shifts, slips, flares, or extended shifts in cold weather. • Poorly performing rear AC. • Flickering interior and exterior lights. • Airbag warning lamp stays lit. • Windshield glass distortion. **2002**—Rear hatch handle broke, cutting driver's hand. • Vehicle jumped out of Park and rolled downhill. • Vehicle suddenly shuts off in traffic. • Windshield water leaks short out dash gauges. **2003**—Rear seat belts failed to release. • Weld holding the lift wheel pin is not adequate to support weight of trailer. **2004**—Engine surging, stalling. • Loss of coolant, engine overheating. • Two incidents where child's wrist was fractured after elbow and hand caught between the seat and handle. • Tail lights fail intermittently. • Door opens and closes on its own while vehicle is underway. • Door doesn't lock into position; slides shut and crushes all in its path:

> We are very concerned that another child, or adult, is going to be injured in this van's automatic sliding door. We were curious just how far the 2004 Venture's door would go before it would bounce back open so we put a stuffed animal in the door and hit the auto door close button. I have to say, the stuffed animal did not fare well. We also put a large carrot and a banana in the door, in an attempt to simulate a small child's arm. The carrot was sliced right in half, and the banana was smashed and oozing out of its peel. I will never purchase a Chevrolet Venture after our experience with the van.

Secret Warranties/Service Tips

1990–98—An oil odour coming from the engine compartment may be eliminated by changing the crankshaft rear main oil seal. **1993–2000**—GM says that a chronic driveline clunk can't be silenced and is a normal characteristic of its vehicles. • Paint delamination, peeling, or fading (see Part Three). **1995–2000**—Dealer guidelines for brake servicing under warranty. **1996–2001**—Poor heat distribution in driver's area of vehicle (install new heat ducts). **1996–2003**—Engine intake manifold/head gasket failures:

> I just wanted to let you know that after contacting you back in January regarding our 2001 Chevy Venture head gasket problem, I have just received my judgment through the Canadian Arbitration Program.
>
> I used the sample complaint letter as well as the judgment you have posted in the *Ford Canada vs. Dufour* court case. This combined with an avalanche of similar Chevy Venture complaints that are posted on the Internet helped us to win a $1,700 reimbursement of the $2,200 we were looking for.
>
> The reason for us not receiving the full amount is that the arbitrator stated that GM Canada would have only replaced one head gasket instead of replacing both as we had done, and that a dealer would have supplied us with a car free of charge and therefore did not allow us the car rental expense we incurred.
>
> We are still extremely happy with the results and thank you for your books and website, you have a fan for life.

1997—Brakes that don't work, drag, heat up, or wear out early may have a variety of causes, all outlined in TSB #73-50-27. • A rear suspension thud or clunk may be silenced by installing upgraded rear springs. **1997–98**—A fuel tank thud or clunk noise may require new fuel tank straps and insulators. •

Loose lumber noise coming from the rear of the vehicle when it passes over bumps means upgraded rear shock absorbers are required. • Poor rear windshield wiper performance may require that the fluid line be purged. • Windshield wiper blade chatter can be reduced by changing the wiper arm. • Insufficient windshield clearing in defrost mode requires the installation of new seals. **1997–99**—Upgraded front disc pads will reduce brake squeal. **1997–2000**—Front door windows that are inoperative, slow, or noisy may need the window run channel adjusted or replaced, in addition to new weather stripping. **1997–2001**—Pssst! GM minivans may show premature hood corrosion and blistering. A dealer whistle-blower tells me that dealers have been authorized to repair the hoods free of charge (refinish and repaint) up to six years under a GM "goodwill" program:

Blistering, Bubbling Paint

Bulletin No.: 01-08-51-004 Date: October, 2001

Premature Aluminum Hood Corrosion/Blistering (Refinish)

1997–2001 Trans Sport (export only)
1997–2001 Venture
1997–2001 Silhouette
1997–98 Trans Sport
1999–2001 Pontiac Montana

Some vehicles may have the appearance of blistering or bubbling paint on the top of the hood or under the hood.

1997–2002—Mildew odour; water leaks. • Wind noise at base of windshield. **1997–2004**—Defective catalytic converters that cause a rotten-egg smell in the interior may be replaced free of charge under the emissions warranty. • Second-row seat belt won't release. • Windshield wind noise. **1998**—No-start, engine miss, and rough idle may indicate that melted slush has contaminated the fuel system. **1998–99**—An inoperative sliding door may have a defective control module. **1998–2000**—Poor AC performance in humid weather may be caused by an undercharged AC system. **1999**—Diagnostic tips for an automatic transmission that slips, produces a harsh upshift and garage shifts, or causes acceleration shudders. **1999–2000**—If the engine runs hot, overheats, or loses coolant, try polishing the radiator filler neck or replacing the radiator cap before considering more expensive repairs. • Before taking on more expensive repairs to correct hard starts or no-starts, check the fuel pump. • An automatic transmission that whines in Park or Neutral, or a Service Engine light that stays on, may signal the need for a new drive sprocket support bearing. **1999–2002**—Transmission noise/no movement:

Transmission Noise/No Movement in 'D' or 'R'

Bulletin No.: 03-07-30-017 Date: May, 2003

Grind Noise or No Vehicle Movement when Shifting into Drive or Reverse (Inspect Transaxle, Replace Various Transaxle Components)

1999–2002 Century, LeSabre, Park Avenue
2002 Rendezvous
1999–2002 Monte Carlo, Venture
2000–02 Impala
1999–2002 Intrigue, Silhouette
1999–2002; Bonneville, Grand Prix, Montana
2001–02 Aztek

Important: If the vehicle DOES NOT exhibit a grinding condition but DOES exhibit shifting concerns, refer to Corporate Bulletin #00-07-30-002

1999–2003—Incorrect fuel gauge readings caused by a contaminated fuel-tank sensor/sender. If a fuel "cleaner" doesn't work, GM says it will adjust or replace the sensor/sender for free, on a case-by-case basis (*Toronto Star*, June 13 and 14, 2003, and December 20, 2003). This failure afflicts GM's entire lineup and could cost up to $800 to repair. **2000–02**—Service Engine light comes on and automatic transmission is harsh shifting. • Hard start, no-start, stall, and fuel gauge inoperative. **2000–04**—Tail light/brake light and circuit board burns out from water intrusion. Repair cost covered by a "goodwill" policy (TSB #03-08-42-007A). **2001**—Customer Satisfaction Program (read: secret warranty) to correct the rear HVAC control switch. **2001–02**—Poor engine and automatic transmission operation. **2001–03**—Water in jack compartment. **2001–04**—Inability to shift out of Park after installation of Sit-N-Lift device. • Slipping automatic transmission. **2003**—Shudder, chuggle, hard shifting, and transmission won't downshift. **2003–04**—Power sliding door binding. • Windshield whistle.

APV, Montana, Silhouette, Trans Sport, Venture Profile

	1997	1998	1999	2000	2001	2002	2003	2004
Cost Price ($) (negotiable)								
Montana (20%)	—	—	25,130	26,625	26,755	27,870	28,520	29,380
Silhouette (20%)	—	29,410	29,955	30,630	31,105	33,060	35,695	36,290
Trans Sport/SE (20%)	23,690	24,650	—	—	—	—	—	—
Venture (20%)	23,185	24,145	24,725	24,895	25,230	25,195	25,865	26,680
Used Values ($)								
Montana ▲	—	—	8,000	10,000	13,000	15,500	18,500	21,000
Montana ▼	—	—	6,500	8,500	11,000	14,000	17,000	19,500
Silhouette ▲	—	7,500	9,000	11,500	14,500	17,000	21,500	25,000
Silhouette ▼	—	6,000	7,500	9,500	13,000	15,500	19,500	23,500
Trans Sport/SE ▲	5,000	6,500	—	—	—	—	—	—
Trans Sport/SE ▼	3,500	5,000	—	—	—	—	—	—
Venture ▲	5,000	6,500	8,000	9,500	12,000	15,000	17,500	20,000
Venture ▼	3,500	5,500	7,000	8,000	11,000	13,500	16,500	18,500
Reliability	③	③	③	③	③	③	③	③
Crash Safety (F)	④	④	④	④	④	④	④	④
Side	—	—	⑤	⑤	⑤	⑤	⑤	⑤
Offset	❶	❶	❶	❶	❶	❶	❶	❶
Rollover	—	—	—	—	③	③	③	—

CARGO VAN, CHEVY VAN, EXPRESS, SAVANA, VANDURA

RATING: Average (1980–2005). These rear-drive, full-sized vans are about as good as the Ford Econoline; Chrysler's Sprinter doesn't have enough time on the market to evaluate. 2003 and earlier Ram Vans have an edge over Ford and GM vans, if the 7-year powertrain warranty is in effect. **Strong points:** A large array of powerful engines, de-powered airbags, improved ride and handling, transmission and brake upgrades, plenty of interior room, and more fuel efficient than its rivals, even with larger engines. **Weak points:** Spartan base model, difficult to enter and exit, serious powertrain, brake, and body fit and finish deficiencies. No crashworthiness data. **New for 2005:** Nothing significant. **Likely failures:** Engine, diesel injectors, turbocharger, and cracked head; automatic transmission 6.5L diesel oil cooler lines, electrical system, starter, EMC fuses, fuel pump (black and gray wires fused together inside the fuel tank), and fuel sending unit; catalytic converter, suspension, steering gearbox and power steering pump; brake pads and rotors, ABS sensors, AC, tire tread separation, sidewall splitting, and fit and finish (broken door hinges, paint flakes off of mirror, bumpers, and trim, etc.).

2005 Technical Data

Powertrain (rear-drive)
Engines: 4.3L V6 (200 hp)
• 4.8L V8 (270 hp)
• 5.3L V8 (285 hp)
• 6.0L V8 (300 hp)
Transmissions: 4-speed auto. OD
• 4-speed heavy-duty auto. OD
Dimension/Capacity (Base)
Height/length/width:
81.6/224/79.4 in.
Headroom F/R1: 40.2/38.5 in.

Legroom (5.0L) F/R1: 41.2/38.6 in.
Wheelbase: 135/155 in.
Turning circle: 45–47 ft.
Passengers: 8–15
Cargo volume: 267–316 cu. ft.
GVWR: 6,100–9,500 lb.
Tow limit: 4,000–10,000 lb.
Ground clear.: 7.2–8.7 in.
Fuel tank: 117L/reg.
Weight: 5,015–5,985 lb.

MODEL HISTORY: These vans are easily found at reasonable prices that are getting even more reasonable as fuel costs chase insurance premiums into the stratosphere. Passenger versions are usually heavily customized and can mean great savings if you don't pay top dollar for accessories you're not likely to use, or if you get a used model.

The Chevy Van and GMC Vandura (both dropped for the '96 model year) are big steel cocoons—without a separate frame—to which a subframe is attached for the independent front suspension and leaf springs that support the live rear axle.

The Chevy versions cost about the same as the GMC variants and have a similar rate of depreciation, which hovers around 75 percent after seven years. Extended warranty coverage is a toss-up, inasmuch as most of the quality deficiencies can be diagnosed and remedied inexpensively.

The 3- and 4-speed automatics and manual transmissions are on the pre-1993 equipment list, after which the recommended 4-speed automatic is standard. The 3-speeds are jerky, fuel-thirsty, and overwhelmed by the van's heft. Overall reliability is average, as owners report serious problems with early 5.7L diesels and V8s, as well as with cooling, electrical, and braking systems, front suspension, and steering components. Interior accommodations are primitive on cargo models. Body assembly quality and paint application are particularly bad, so watch out for premature rust, paint delamination, and peeling. Water/air leaks and rattles are also commonplace.

1996–2005 Express and Savana

The product of GM's 1996 redesign of the Chevy Van and GMC Vandura, these full-sized cargo-haulers and people-movers moved sideways, rather than forward.

Powered by Vortec engines and a turbocharged diesel, these vans are built on longer wheelbases and use a ladder-type frame, as opposed to the unit-body construction of their predecessors. This has improved ride quality somewhat, but serious performance deficiencies remain.

1999—De-powered airbags and an upgraded transmission. **2001**—A powerful 8.1L V8 replaced the 7.4L. **2003**—New features included optional all-wheel drive, four-wheel disc brakes, a stiffer box frame, enhanced ride and handling, dual side doors that open outwardly, and a minor face-lift. Engines and transmissions were revised and the suspension retuned. Although the engine-gasket-challenged 200-hp remained the base engine, GM added the GEN III V8 engines used in full-sized trucks since 1999. **2004**—Standard stability control on 15-passenger models.

COST ANALYSIS: Choose an identical 2004 Express or Savana Cargo/Passenger version for $25,810–$29,965, plus a 20 percent discount (prices are easily bargained down). **Best alternatives:** Stay away from the AWD; it has a high failure rate. The Ford Econoline is an okay second choice, but it also has chronic factory-related defects. Your best Detroit choice is one of the Chrysler-warranteed variants. **Rebates:** Look for $3,000 rebates early in the new year, as GM continues its rebate offensive in order to capture a market share. **Delivery/PDI:** $1,000. **Warranty:** Bumper-to-bumper 3 years/ 60,000 km; rust perforation 6 years/160,000 km. **Supplementary warranty:** A good idea. **Options:** Running boards, rear air conditioning, power windows and door locks, and heavy-duty alternator. You'll find the SLE garnish creates a much cozier interior. Don't go for the base V6 engine; it's not that much more fuel efficient than the 5.0L or 5.3L V8 (the most engine you will need for everyday driving). If you plan to load up on power-draining optional equipment or do some heavy hauling, choose a model equipped with the 5.7L or 6.0L V8. **Depreciation:** Higher than average. **Insurance cost:** Much higher than average. **Parts supply/cost:** Average supply and cost for generic mechanical and body parts. **Annual maintenance cost:** Less than average; any independent garage can repair these vans. **Highway/city fuel economy:** *Express model with a 4.3L engine and an automatic transmission:* 11.4–16.0L/100 km; *5.0L and automatic:* 12.5–16.9L/100 km; *5.7L and automatic:* 11.9–17.3L/100 km.

QUALITY/RELIABILITY: Quality control and overall reliability have declined since these vehicles were redesigned less than a decade ago. **Owner-reported problems:** Engine and transmission malfunctions, electrical shorts, excessive brake wear and pull, and some accessories fail to operate properly. **Warranty performance:** Average.

SAFETY SUMMARY: For 1993, four-wheel ABS was added as a standard feature along with variable-ratio power steering. **Airbags:** Standard front and side. **ABS:** Standard; disc/disc. **Head restraints F/R:** ***. **Visibility F/R:** *****/*.

SAFETY COMPLAINTS: All models/years: Front wheel flew off. • PCM/VCM computer module shorts from water intrusion. • Vehicle won't decelerate when gas pedal is released. • Power-steering and ABS brake failures. • Premature brake pad/rotor wear • Broken power seat anchor/brackets; seats come off their tracks, costing $900 to repair. • Broken/weak side door hinges. • Fuel gauge failure. • Excessive side mirror vibration. • Tire tread separation. **1999**—Airbags deployed for no reason. • Gas pedal sticks when accelerating. • Differential failure. • Loose power-steering line leaks steering fluid. • Nut on steering column fell off, causing loss of steering. • Excessive brake fade after successive stops, and pedal will sometimes go to the floor without stopping the vehicle. • Rear-wheel seal leaks coat rear brakes with oil. • Sticking speedometer needle. • Positive post pulled out of battery. **2000**—Dashboard fire. • Unnecessary 4–3 downshifts. • Upper ball joint suddenly collapsed. • Chronic stalling. • Loose steering wheel. • Braking malfunctions and brake lock-up. • ABS performs erratically. • Rear shoulder belts cross too high on the torso. • Seat belt retractor doesn't lock properly. • Broken/stiff door hinges. **2001**—Under-hood fire caused by electrical short under dash on passenger side. • Chronic stalling caused by moisture in the distributor. • Delayed 2–3 transmission shifts. • Windshield tinted strip cuts visibility for tall drivers. • Brake pedal goes to floor without stopping vehicle. • Vehicle wanders all over the road at 100 km/h. • Firestone tread separation. • Faulty tire valve stems leak air. **2002**—Fire ignited at the bottom of driver's door. • Fuel leak. • 5.7L engine loses power when AC is engaged. • Cruise control won't decelerate vehicle when going downhill. • Leaking axle tube seals. • Leaking front grease seals contaminate the front inner disc brake pads, causing loss of braking effectiveness. • Front wheel speed sensor melted. • Tail lights blow when headlights are turned on. • AC Delco battery acid leaked out from broken positive cable post. • Door opened while vehicle was underway. **2003**—Extended stopping distance when brakes are applied; sometimes they fail to hold. • Fire ignited from a short in the right rear door lock motor. • Tailpipe exhaust leak where it fits into converter. • Horn and wiper failure.

Secret Warranties/Service Tips

All models/years: GM bulletins say automatic transmission clunks are "normal." **All models: 1992–96**—If the engine won't start or is hard to start, check the fuel pump pulsator. **1993–2002**—Paint delamination, peeling, or fading (see Part Three). **1994–99**—Hard starts on vehicles equipped with a 6.5L diesel engine may signal the need to replace the shut-off solenoid. **1996–99**—Engine bearing knocking on vehicles equipped with a 5.0L or 5.7L V8 may be silenced by using a special GM countermeasure kit to service the crankshaft and select-fit undersized connecting rod bearings. **1996–2000**—Poor starts, no-starts, and backfire on starting all point to the need to replace the crankshaft position sensor. • A rough idle or constantly lit Service Engine light may require that a cleaner be used to unstick and clean the central sequential fuel injection poppet valves. **1996–2002**—Cargo door binding requires new hinge pins and bushings (covered by a "goodwill" policy on a case by case basis). **1997–98**—Vehicles equipped with a 6.5L diesel engine with hard upshifts may need to reprogram the PCM/VCM. **1997–2001**—Diagnostic procedures to fix AC performance problems and leaks. **1998**—Engine stalling or surging and a slipping transmission may signal the need to repair the auxiliary oil cooler or replace the transmission torque converter. **1998–2000**—Stalling or surging can be corrected by installing updated transmission software. **1999–2000**—List of procedures to follow in correcting door wind noise. • An inexpensive cure for an overheated engine or coolant loss may be as simple as replacing the radiator cap or polishing the radiator filler neck. **2001**—Automatic transmission harsh shifting. • Reports of automatic transmission 2–4 band or 3–4 clutch damage. • Inaccurate fuel gauge. **2002**—Check Engine light comes on, followed by poor engine and automatic transmission performance; transmission feels like it has slipped into Neutral. • Leaking engine oil cooler lines. **2003**—Hard starts, rough idle and intermittent engine misfiring. • Driveshaft may fracture; a free repair under Customer Satisfaction #03040. • Thumping noise/feel in brake pedal • Voluntary emission recall to replace spark plugs. • Vehicle difficult to fill with fuel. **2003–04**—Suspension clunk, slap. GM will replace the spring insert and insulator for free (see Silverado "Service Tips"). **2004**—Overdrive gear may fail due to lack of lubrication at the factory; a free Customer Satisfaction repair (#04019).

Express, Savana Profile

	1997	1998	1999	2000	2001	2002	2003	2004
Cost Price ($) (very negotiable)								
Savana Cargo (21%)	24,700	25,315	25,330	25,495	24,905	25,025	25,125	26,465
Express (21%)	28,455	29,140	29,155	29,330	30,885	29,105	29,215	30,000
Used Values ($)								
Savana Cargo ▲	4,500	6,500	9,500	11,000	13,500	16,500	19,500	22,000
Savana Cargo ▼	3,000	5,000	8,000	10,000	12,500	15,000	18,000	20,500
Express ▲	6,000	8,000	10,500	13,500	16,500	19,000	21,500	24,000
Express ▼	5,000	6,500	9,500	12,000	15,000	17,500	20,000	22,000
Reliability	③	③	③	④	④	④	④	④

Honda

ODYSSEY ★★★★★

RATING: Recommended (2005); Above Average (2003–04); Average (1996–2002). The upgraded 2005 model passes the Sienna in safety, perform-ance, and convenience features. Nevertheless, there are some reports of safety- and performance-related failures on previous year Odysseys, hence their down-grade. Of particular concern are airbag malfunctions, automatic-sliding door failures, engine failures, transmission breakdowns and erratic shifting, and sudden brake loss. Early Odysseys get only an Average rating due to their small engine and interior—identical shortcomings to those of Mazda's early MPV minivan. **Strong points:** *2005:* More power, room, and safety/convenience features. Additional mid-range torque means less shifting when engine is under load; uses regular gas (Sienna can burn regular, but needs pricier high-octane to get the advertised horsepower and torque). *2004:* Strong engine perform-ance; carlike ride and handling; easy entry/exit; second driver-side door; quiet interior; most controls and displays are easy to reach and read; lots of passenger and cargo room; low step-up facilitates entry/exit; an extensive list of standard equipment, and a willingness to compensate owners for production snafus. **Weak points:** *2005:* Unlike with the Sienna, all-wheel drive isn't available; middle-row seats don't fold flat like other minivans, thus they need to be stowed somewhere else; second row head restraints block visibility. *2004:* A high base price; front-seat passenger legroom is marginal due to the restricted seat travel; you can't slide your legs comfortably under the dash; some passen-gers bump their shins on the glove box; third-row seat is only suitable for children; the narrow back bench seat provides little legroom, unless the middle seats are pushed far forward, inconveniencing others; radio control access is blocked by the shift lever, and it's difficult to calibrate the radio without taking your eyes off the road; power-sliding doors are slow to retract; some tire rumble, rattles, and body drumming at highway speeds; premium fuel is required for optimum performance; a decline in quality; poor head restraint crashworthiness rating; and rear-seat head restraints impede side and rear visi-bility. The storage well won't take any tire larger than a "space saver"—meaning you'll carry your flat in the back. **New for 2005:** A bigger Odyssey with a torquier 255-hp 3.5L V6, which has 15 more horses than last year's version and more horsepower than any other minivan. The new engine uses variable cylinder de-activation to increase fuel economy up to 10 percent by automatically switching between 6-cylinder and 3-cylinder activation, depending upon engine load. Other features: Eight-passenger seating (EX), less road noise, upgraded rear shocks, an upgraded driver's seat, easier access to the back seats, a new power tailgate, more interior volume than the Sienna, interior lengthened by two inches; second-row middle seats can be folded down as an armrest or removed completely, much like the middle-row cap-tain's chairs, which can slide fore or aft by 10 inches, in unison or separately; second-row power windows; and floor-stowable, 60:40 split, third-row seats with three more inches of legroom. Convenience upgrades include climate, radio and optional navigation controls that are easier to reach (and navigation voice recognition is bilingual, yippee!), air conditioning toggles with raised lips for easy flipping, and a more accessible dash-mounted gearshift. Safety has been enhanced with a more crashworthy body, vehicle stability assist to prevent rollovers, side curtain airbags with rollover sensors for all rows, and adjustable brake and accelerator pedals. Run-flat tires may be used in Canada at a later date. **Likely failures:** *2005:* Judging by the redesigned Quest misadventures, expect problems with the electrical system, electronics, accessories, and trim. *2004:* V6 engine and automatic transmission (both covered by a goodwill warranty), brakes, accessories, and trim (one pre-production tester had a wind whistle around the driver's door, creaks near the driver's-side sliding door, and a balky latch on one side of the third-row seats).

2005 Technical Data

Powertrain (front-drive)
Engine: 3.5L V6 (255 hp)
Transmission: 5-speed auto.
Dimension/Capacity
Height/length/width:
68.8/201/77.1 in.
Headroom F/R1/R2: 40.9/40/38.4 in.
Legroom F/R1/R2: 40.8/39.6/41.1 in.

Wheelbase: 118.1 in.
Turning circle: 36.7 ft.
Passengers: 2/3/3
GVWR: 5,567 lb.
Cargo volume: 147.4 cu. ft.
Tow limit: 3,500 lb.
Fuel tank: 65L/reg.
Ground clear.: 6.4 in.
Weight: 4,378 lb.

MODEL HISTORY: When it was first launched in 1995, the Odyssey was a sales dud, simply because Canadians and *Lemon-Aid* saw through Honda's ruse in trying to pass off an underpowered, mid-sized, four-door station wagon with a raised roof as a minivan. However, in 1999 and again this year, the Odyssey was redesigned, and it now represents one of the better minivans on the Canadian market.

It's easy to see what makes the Odyssey so popular: Strong engine performance; carlike ride and handling; easy entry/exit; a second driver-side door; quiet interior; most controls and displays are easy to reach and read; there's lots of passenger and cargo room; an extensive list of standard equipment; and a willingness by Honda to compensate owners for production snafus.

This minivan does have its drawbacks, though, foremost being a recent decline in quality and a high resale price, making bargains rare. Owners report that front-seat passenger legroom is marginal due to the restricted seat travel; third-row seating is only suitable for children; power sliding doors are slow to retract; there's some tire rumble, rattles, and body drumming at highway speeds; premium fuel is required for optimum performance; and rear-seat head restraints impede side and rear visibility.

One can sum up the strengths and weaknesses of the 1996–98 Odyssey (and its American twin through the 1998 model, the Isuzu Oasis) in three words: Performance, performance, performance. You get carlike performance and handling, responsive steering, and a comfortable ride, offset by slow-as-molasses-in-January acceleration with a full load, a raucous engine, and limited passenger/cargo space due to the narrow body.

1997—Small improvements. **1998**—A new 2.3L engine adds 10 horses (not enough!), and a restyled grille and instrument panel debut. **1999**—A new, more powerful engine and increased size make this second-generation Odyssey a more versatile highway performer; still, steering requires fully extended arms, and power sliding doors operate slowly. **2001**—User-friendly child safety seat tether anchors, upgraded stereo speakers, and an intermittent rear window wiper. **2002**—A slight restyling, 30 additional horses, disc brakes on all four wheels, standard side airbags, and additional support for front seats.

COST ANALYSIS: A 2005 Odyssey sells for about $34,000, and is really the only game in town. A discounted 2004 model would be a poor second choice, considering all of the 2005 upgrades. **Best alternatives:** The redesigned 2002 or later Mazda MPV, Nissan's 1999–2003 Quest, or a Toyota Sienna. If you're looking for lots of towing "grunt," then the rear-drive GM Astro, Safari, or full-sized vans would be best. **Rebates:** Don't expect any substantial incentives before the fall of 2005, if then. **Delivery/PDI:** $850. **Warranty:** Bumper-to-bumper 3 years/60,000 km; powertrain 5 years/100,000 km; rust perforation 5 years/ unlimited km. **Supplementary warranty:** Not needed. **Options:** Traction control is a good idea. Remember, if you want the gimmicky video entertainment and DVD navigation system, you also have to spring for the expensive (and not-for-everyone) leather seats. Ditch the original equipment Firestone tires: You don't need the extra risk. **Depreciation:** Slower than average. **Insurance cost:** Higher than average. **Parts supply/cost:** Moderately priced parts; availability is better than average because the Odyssey uses many generic Accord parts. **Annual maintenance cost:** Average; any garage can repair these minivans. **Highway/city fuel economy:** *2005:* 8.6–12.3L/100 km; *2004:* 8.5–13.2L/100 km. 2005s will run on regular fuel, earlier models will lose about five horses with regular.

QUALITY/RELIABILITY: Reliability is much better than average. Failure-prone sliding doors continue to be a hazard to children through the 2004 model year. Imagine, they open when they shouldn't, won't close when they should, catch fingers and arms, get stuck open or closed, are noisy, and frequently require expensive servicing. The Check Engine light may stay lit due to a defective fuel-filler neck. There's a fuel sloshing noise when accelerating or coming to a stop, and the transmission clunks or bangs when backing uphill or when shifted into Reverse. There are also reports of rattling and chattering when put into forward gear. Owners note a loud wind noise and vibration from the left side of the front windshield, along with a constant vibration felt through the steering assembly and front wheels. Passenger doors may also require excessive force to open. And owners have complained of severe static electricity shocks when exiting. Other potential problem areas are frequent and high-cost front-brake maintenance (see "Secret Warranties/Service Tips"), and trim and accessory items that come loose, break away, or malfunction. **Owner-reported problems:** Transmission breakdowns; when shifting into Fourth gear, engine almost stalls out and produces a noise like valve clattering; transmission gear whine at 90 km/h or when in Fourth gear (transmission replaced under new "goodwill" warranty). Front-end clunking caused by welding breaks in the front subframe; exhaust rattling or buzzing; loud fuel splashing sound in the fuel tank when coming to a stop; vehicle pulls to the right when underway; premature front brake wear; excessive front-brake noise; sliding side door frequently malfunctions; electrical glitches; defective remote audio controls; leather seats split, crack, or discolour; and accessory items that come loose, break away, or won't work. Plastic interior panels have rough edges and are often misaligned. **Warranty performance:** Comprehensive base warranty that's usually applied fairly, with lots of "wiggle room" that the service manager can use to apply "goodwill" adjustments for post-warranty problems. However, after-warranty assistance and dealer servicing have come in for a great deal of criticism from *Lemon-Aid* readers. Owners complain that "goodwill" refunds aren't extended to all model years with the same defect; recall repairs take an eternity to perform; and dealers exhibit an arrogant, uncaring "take it, or leave it" attitude.

SAFETY SUMMARY: A class action petition has been filed against Honda in Quebec to recover recall costs incurred in re-connecting anti-theft devices, remote-controlled car starters, and radios (1998–2000 Odysseys and CR-Vs, Civics, 1997–99 Accords and Preludes, and 1997–2000 Acura CL, EL, and TL sedans.). Power-sliding doors a constant danger. **Airbags:** Standard side airbags. **ABS:** Standard 4W; disc/disc. **Head restraints F/R:** *1995–97:* **; *1999:* **/*; *2001-04:* **. **Visibility F/R:** *****/*. **Maximum load capacity:** 1,160 lb.

SAFETY COMPLAINTS: All years: Passenger seatbacks collapsed when vehicle was rear-ended. • Airbag malfunctions. • Sudden, unintended acceleration when slowing for a stop sign. • Minivan was put in Drive, and AC was turned on; vehicle suddenly accelerated, brakes failed, and the minivan hit a brick wall. • Stuck accelerator. • V6 engine oil leaks. • Automatic transmission failures. • Transmission doesn't hold when stopped on a hill; gas or brakes have to be constantly applied. **1999**—Fire erupted in the electrical harness. • Another fire erupted as vehicle was getting fuel. • Plastic gas tank cracks, leaks fuel. • Gasoline smell when transmission is put into Reverse. • Side window exploded while driving. • Check Engine light comes on and vehicle loses all power. • When driving, all the instrument panel lights will suddenly go out (faulty multiplex controller suspected). • When parked on a hill, vehicle may roll backward; transmission doesn't hold vehicle when stopped at a light on a hill and foot is taken off accelerator or brake. • Complete loss of power steering due to a pinhole in the power-steering return hose. • Poor power-steering performance in cold weather. • Power door locks lock and unlock on their own. • Design of the gear shifter interferes with the radio controls. • Child unable to get out of seat belt due to buckle lock-up. • Faulty fuel gauge. • Inconvenient cell phone jack location. **2000**—Almost 400 safety complaints recorded by NHTSA; a hundred would be normal. During fuelling, fuel tank burst into flames. • Many incidents where driver-side sliding door opened onto fuel hose while fuelling, damaging gas flap hinge and tank. • On cold days, accelerator pedal is hard to depress. • Catastrophic failure of the right-side suspension, causing wheel to buckle. • Vehicle continually pulls to the right; dealers unable to correct problem. • Excessive steering wheel vibration at 105+ km/h. • Electric doors often inoperative. • As child slept in safety seat, seat belt tightened progressively to point that fire department had to be called; other similar incidents. • Chronic automatic transmission problems: Won't shift into lower gears, suddenly loses power, torque converter failure, makes a loud popping sound when put into Reverse. • Two incidents where vehicle rear-ended due to transmission malfunction. • Power seatback moves on its own. • Dash lights don't adequately illuminate the dash panel. • Driver's seat-back suddenly reclines, hitting rear passenger's legs, even though power switch is off. • Protruding bolts in the door assembly are hazardous. • Seat belt buckle fails to latch. • Driver-side mirror breaks away; mirror glass fell out due to poor design. • Easily-broken sliding door handles. **2001**—While fuelling, fuel tank exploded. • In a frontal collision, van caught fire due to a cracked brake fluid reservoir. • Chronic stalling (transmission replaced). • Many reports of sudden transmission and torque converter failure. • When Reverse is engaged, car makes a popping or clunking sound. • Cracked wheel rim. • Check Engine light constantly on (suspect faulty gasoline filler neck). • Entire vehicle shakes excessively at highway speeds and van pulls to the right (dealer said bar adjust-ment was needed). • Passenger-side door window suddenly exploded while driving on the highway. • Driver's seatback collapsed from rear-end collision. • Driver's power seat will suddenly recline on its own, squeezing rear occupant's legs and falling on child. • Rear seat belt tightened up so much that a child had to be cut free. • Too much play in rear lapbelts, which won't tighten ade-quately, making it difficult to install a child safety seat securely. • Inoperative driver seat belt buckle. • Faulty speedometer and tachometer. • Remote wouldn't open or lock vehicle. • Placement of the gear shift lever interferes with the radio's controls. • Unable to depress accelerator pedal on cold days. • Can hear gasoline sloshing in tank while driving. • Frequent static electricity shocks. • Many owners report that the rear head restraints seriously hamper rear and forward visibility and that it was difficult to see vehicles coming from the right side. **2002**—Over 232 complaints registered, where normally 50 would be expected. Only 66 complaints recorded against the 2002 Toyota Sienna. • Owners say many engines have faulty timing chains. • Loose strut bolt almost caused wheel to fall off. • Axle bearing wheel failure caused driver-side wheel to fall off. • Left to right veering and excessive drivetrain vibration. • Loud popping sound heard when brakes are applied. • Many complaints that the brake pedal went to floor with no braking capability. • Sticking sliding door. • Head restraints are set too low for tall occupants. • Rear windshield shattered from area where wiper is mounted. • Rear seat belt unlatched during emergency braking. • Brake line freezes up in cold weather. • Abrupt down-shift upon deceleration. • Driver-side door came off while using remote control. • Dashboard lights come on and off intermittently. • Passenger window exploded. • Airbag light comes on for no reason. **2003**—Fire ignited in the CD player. • Child injured from a side collision because second-row seat belt failed to hold her in due to gap caused by door attachment. • Rear seat belts lock for no reason. • Seat belt extenders aren't offered. • Defective speed sensor caused vehicle to suddenly lose power when merging into traffic. • Vehicle suddenly shut down in traffic. • Hard starts and engine misfiring. • Faulty steering causes wander. • Sudden brake failure. • Driver often shocked when touching door handle. • Fuel spits out when refuelling. • Inaccurate fuel gauge readings. • Sliding door closed on driver's hand.

Secret Warranties/Service Tips

All models/years: Most of Honda's TSBs allow for special warranty consideration on a "goodwill" basis by the company's District Service Manager or Zone Office, even after the warranty has expired or the vehicle has changed hands. Referring to this euphemism will increase your chances of getting some kind of refund for repairs that are obviously factory defects. • There's an incredibly large number of sliding door problems covered by a recall and a plethora of service bulletins that are simply too numerous to print here. Ask Honda politely for the bulletins or "goodwill" assistance. If refused, subpoena the documents through small claims court, using NHTSA's summary as your shopping list. **1999**—Poor engine performance may fall under a free service campaign whereby the company will replace, at no charge, the rear intake manifold end plate and gasket, the PCV hose, and the intake manifold cover. • Problems with the fuel tank pressure sensor are covered in TSB #99-056 and could call for the installation of an in-line orifice in the two-way valve vacuum hose. • AC knocking may require the installation of a new compressor clutch set. • Front windows that bind or are noisy. • An inaccurate fuel gauge is likely caused by a faulty sending unit. **1999–2001**—Extended warranty coverage on Odysseys with defective 4- and 5-speed automatic transmissions to 7 years/ 100,000 miles (160,000 km) to fix erratic or slow shifting. **2000–01**—Third-row seat won't unlatch. • Clunk or bang when engaging Reverse. • Bulletin confirms Honda USA is currently investigating complaints of pulling or drifting (Service Bulletin Number: 99165, Bulletin Sequence Number: 802, Date of Bulletin: 9909, NHTSA Item Number: SB608030). • Excessive front brake noise. • Dash ticking or clicking. **1999–2003**—Engine oil leaks will be corrected under a "goodwill" policy. • Deformed windshield moulding. **2002**—Hesitation when accelerating. • Diagnosing automatic transmission problems. • No-starts; hard start in cold weather. • Driver's seat heater may not work. • Thump at cold start. • Loose rear wiper arm. • AC can't be turned off while in defog setting. **2002–03**—Free replacement of the engine timing belt auto-tensioner and water pump under both a recall and "product update" campaign:

Recall

DEFECT: On certain minivans, sedans, coupes, and sport utility vehicles equipped with V6 engines, a timing belt tensioner pulley on the water pump is misaligned and could cause the timing belt to contact a bolt on the cylinder head. Eventually the belt could be damaged and fail. If the timing belt breaks, the engine will stall, increasing the risk of a crash. REMEDY: Dealers will inspect the water pump, and if it is one of the defective pumps, the water pump and timing belt will be replaced.

> **Product Update**
>
> Bulletin No.: 03-081 Date: October 27, 2003
>
> BACKGROUND: The timing belt tensioner is filled with oil to dampen oscillation. Due to a manufacturing problem, the tensioner oil can leak. If enough oil is lost, the timing belt loosens and causes engine noise.
>
> **MODELS:** 2002–03 Odyssey
> 2003 Pilot
>
> **CORRECTIVE ACTION:** Replace the timing belt auto-tensioner.

2002–04—Free tranny repair or replacement for insufficient lubrication that can lead to heat buildup and broken gears. Transmission noise will signal if there is gear breakage; transmission may also lock up. • Rear brake noise:

> **Rear Brake Clunk**
>
> Bulletin No.: 04-019 Date: March 23, 2004
>
> 2002–04 Odyssey
> 2003–04 Pilot
>
> The rear brake calipers clunk when you first apply the brakes after changing the direction of the vehicle. The outer shims on the rear brake pads do not allow the pads to slide easily when you press the brake pedal. This causes the outer pad to hit hard during a change of direction, resulting in a clunk.
>
> **CORRECTIVE ACTION:** Replace the rear brake pad shims.

2003—Engine cranks, but won't start. • ABS problems. • Power-steering pump noise. • Warning lights blink on and off. • Exhaust rattling. • Remote audio control troubleshooting. • Leather seat defects. • HomeLink range is too short; hard to program. • Factory security won't arm. • Faulty charging system; electrical shorts. • Front door howls in strong crosswind. • Squealing from rear quarter windows and motors. • Fuel tank leak. • Front damper noise. • Steering wheel bent off-centre. • Manual sliding door is difficult to open.

Odyssey Profile

	1997	1998	1999	2000	2001	2002	2003	2004
Cost Price ($) (negotiable)								
LX (18%)	28,995	29,800	30,600	30,600	30,800	31,900	32,200	32,400
EX (18%)	—	—	33,600	33,600	33,800	34,900	35,200	35,400
Used Values ($)								
LX ▲	8,000	10,000	11,000	16,500	19,500	22,500	26,000	29,000
LX ▼	6,500	8,500	9,500	14,500	17,000	21,000	24,000	27,000
EX ▲	—	—	12,500	17,500	20,500	23,500	27,500	31,000
EX ▼	—	—	11,000	15,500	18,500	22,000	26,000	29,500
Reliability	③	③	③	❷	❷	❷	③	④
Crash Safety (F)	④	—	⑤	⑤	⑤	⑤	⑤	⑤
Side	—	—	—	—	⑤	⑤	⑤	⑤
Offset	❷	❷	⑤	⑤	⑤	⑤	⑤	⑤
Rollover	—	—	—	—	④	④	④	—

Kia

SEDONA

RATING: Average (2002–05). Sedona is a very user-friendly, roomy, practical, versatile, and comfortable mid-sized minivan. **Strong points:** Reasonably priced; well appointed; transmission shifts smoothly and quietly; low ground clearance adds to stability and helps access; low step-in; comfortable ride; convenient "walk-through" space between front seats; well laid-out, user-friendly instruments and controls; lots of storage areas; good visibility; fairly well built; minimal engine and road noise; good braking; head restraints for the 2002 model are rated good up front, acceptable in the rear; acceptable crashworthiness scores; and comprehensive base warranty. **Weak points:** Engine power is drained by the Sedona's heft; 10–20 percent higher fuel consumption than V6-equipped Dodge Caravan and Toyota Sienna; subpar, vague steering and handling; excessive engine and wind noise; and weak dealer network. Quality control is its weakest link. **New for 2005:** Nothing significant. **Likely failures:** Seat belts, fuel and electrical systems, brake pads and rotors, AC compressor, windows, and fit and finish.

2005 Technical Data

Powertrain
Engine: 3.5L V6 (195 hp)
Transmission: 5-speed auto.
Dimension/Capacity
Height/length/width:
69.3/194.1/74.6 in.
Headroom F/R: 39.4/39.2/36.3 in.
Legroom F/R: 40.6/37.2/32.8 in.

Wheelbase: 114.6 in.
Turning circle: 44
Passengers: 2/3/2
GVWR: 5,959 lb.
Cargo volume: 127 cu. ft.
Tow limit: 3,500 lb.
Ground clear.: 6.7 in.
Fuel tank: 87L/reg.
Weight: 4,802 lb.

MODEL HISTORY: Embodying typically bland minivan styling, this front-drive, seven-passenger minivan comes with a good selection of standard features, including a 195-hp 3.5L V6 engine hooked to an automatic 5-speed transmission, a low step-in height, and a commanding view of the road. For convenience, there are two sliding rear side doors (automatic doors aren't available); folding, removable second- and third-row seats; a flip-up hatchback; standard front/rear air conditioning; and a large cargo bay. Other standard amenities: 15-inch tires, AM/FM/CD stereo, power steering, power windows, power door locks, power-heated mirrors, tilt steering, rear defroster and wiper, dual airbags (side airbags not offered), and six adjustable head restraints.

2003s were given new tail lights, a passenger door lock switch, and an optional trailer hitch; 2004s got a new grille.

COST ANALYSIS: 2005 Sedonas range in price from $25,000 (LX) to $31,000 (EX). **Best alternatives:** Used Sedona prices vary from $18,000 to $19,500 for the LX—several thousand dollars less than comparable minivans. It doesn't matter which year you buy, since these minivans have changed little since 2002. Make sure the base warranty is transferable or check out the Mazda MPV, Honda Odyssey, or pre-2004 Toyota Sienna instead. **Rebates:** Look for $2,500 rebates and low-financing rates in early 2005. **Delivery/PDI:** $595. **Warranty:** Bumper-to-bumper 5 years/100,000 km; powertrain 5 years/ 100,000 km; rust perforation 5 years/unlimited km. **Supplementary warranty:** A wise buy, considering Kia's previous transmission troubles. **Options:** Forget the EX option; it doesn't offer much for the extra cost. **Depreciation:** Predicted to be a bit slower than average. **Insurance cost:** Average for an entry-level minivan. **Parts supply/cost:** Predicted average cost; expect long delays for parts. **Annual maintenance cost:** Expected to be higher than average, once first-year models lose base warranty protection. **Highway/city fuel economy:** 10.9–15.6L/100 km.

SAFETY SUMMARY: Airbags: No side airbags. **ABS:** Optional; disc/drum. **Head restraints F/R:** *2002–04:* ****/***. **Visibility F/R:** *****. **Maximum load capacity:** 1,160 lb.

SAFETY COMPLAINTS: 2002—Over 100 safety incidents reported. Fuel tank design could spray fuel on hot muffler in a collision. • Oil leaks onto the hot catalytic converter. • Fuel leaks from the bottom of the vehicle. • Loose fuel line to fuel pump clamp. • Fuel tank filler hose vulnerable to road debris. • Fuel spits back when refuelling. • Vehicle continues to accelerate when brakes are applied. • Intermittent stalling. • Brake failure; pedal simply sinks to the floor. • Excessive brake shudder when slowing going downhill. • ABS brake light comes on randomly. • Power steering pulley broke. • Windshield may suddenly shatter for no apparent reason. • Windshields have distortion at eye level. • Second- and third-row seats don't latch as easily as touted. • Oil leaks onto the catalytic converter. • Electrical shorts cause lights, windows, and door locks to fail. • Sliding doors won't retract if object is in their way. • Stuck rear hatch door. • Child safety seat can't be belted in securely. • Child door safety lock failure. • Inoperative back-seat seat belts. • Seat belt holding child in booster seat tightened progressively, trapping child. • Kumho tire tread separation. **2003**—Under-hood fire ignited while car was underway. • Airbags failed to deploy. • Sudden, unintended acceleration. • Stuck accelerator pedal. • Brakes fail due to air in the brake lines. • Fuel odour in cabin. • Broken window regulator. • Rear seat removal instructions can throw your back out. • Tires peeled off the rim. • When reclined, passenger seatback is released upright and slams a young child forward. • AC condenser vulnerable to puncture from road debris. • Electrical shorts cause door lock malfunctions. **2004**—Excessive brake rotor wear. • Parking brake didn't hold vehicle on an incline. • Chronic stalling. • Windshield has a cloudy haze.

Secret Warranties/Service Tips

2002—Correction for engine hesitation after cold starts. • Free replacement of seat belt buckle anchor bolts. **2002–03**—Changes to improve alternator output to prevent hard starts or battery drain. **2004**—Engine head gasket leak.

Sedona Profile

	2002	2003	2004
Cost Price ($) (negotiable)			
LX (18%)	24,595	24,995	25,595
EX (19%)	27,595	28,295	28,995
Used Values ($)			
LX ⋀	13,000	16,000	18,500
LX ⋁	11,500	14,500	17,000
EX ⋀	15,000	17,000	21,000
EX ⋁	13,500	16,500	19,500
Reliability	③	③	④
Crash Safety (F)	⑤	⑤	⑤
Side	⑤	⑤	⑤
Offset	③	③	③
Rollover	④	④	—

Mazda

MPV   ★★★★

RATING: Above Average (2002–05); Average (2000–01); Below Average (1988–98). Mazda has accomplished an amazing turnaround in the past three years; its MPV is now smaller, sportier, and more nimble than its more space- and comfort-oriented counterparts. Early models were underpowered, lumbering, undersized, and overpriced. There was no '99 model. The redesigned 2000–01 model is still hampered by a wimpy powertrain and is just too small for most tasks. **Strong points:** Well appointed (lots of gadgets), an adequate engine, smooth-shifting 5-speed automatic transmission, comfortable ride and easy handling, good driver's position, responsive steering, and innovative storage spots. Without a doubt, the MPV manages its limited interior space far better than the competition. Remarkably few factory-related defects reported at NHTSA or in the service bulletin database. **Weak points:** Smaller than most of the competition; don't believe for a minute that the MPV will hold seven passengers in comfort—six is more like it. Elbow room is at a premium, and it takes a lithe figure to move down the front- and middle-seat aisle. Excessive engine and road noise. Transport and preparation fee is excessive. Dealer servicing and head office support have been problematic in the past. **New for 2005:** Nothing major.

2005 Technical Data

Powertrain (front-drive)
Engine: 3.0L V6 (200 hp)
Transmission: 5-speed auto.
Dimension/Capacity
Height/length/width:
68.7/187.8/72.1 in.
Headroom F/R1/R2: 41/39.3/38 in.
Legroom F/R1/R2: 40.8/37/35.6 in.

Wheelbase: 111.8 in.
Turning circle: 33 ft.
Passengers: 2/2/3
GVWR: 5,229 lb.
Cargo volume: 127 cu. ft.
Ground clear.: 5.4 in.
Tow limit: 3,000 lb.
Fuel tank: 75L/reg.
Weight: 3,796 lb.

MODEL HISTORY: Manufactured in Hiroshima, Japan, this small minivan offers a number of innovative features, like "theatre" seating (rear passenger seat is slightly higher) and a third seat that pivots rearward to become a rear-facing bench seat—or folds into the floor for picnics or tailgate parties. Another feature unique among minivans is Mazda's Side-by-Slide removable second-row seats, which move fore and aft as well as side-to-side while a passenger is seated. Sliding door crank windows are standard on the entry model and power-assisted on the LS and ES versions.

Mazda's only minivan quickly became a bestseller when it first came on the market in 1989, but its popularity fell just as quickly when larger, more powerful competitors arrived. Mazda sales have bounced back recently as a result of price-cutting and the popularity of the automaker's small cars and pickups. This infusion of cash has allowed the company (34 percent owned by Ford) to put additional money into its 2002 redesign, thus ending a sales slump that has plagued the company for over a decade. Early MPVs embodied many of the mistakes made by Honda's first Odyssey—its 170 horses weren't adequate for people-hauling and it was expensive for what was essentially a smaller van than buyers expected—a foot shorter than the Ford Windstar and a half-foot shorter than the Toyota Sienna and Nissan Quest.

1992—5-speed manual transmission deleted and the 3.0L V6 got a 5-horsepower boost. **1993**—A driver-side airbag. **1994**—A centre brake light and side-door impact beams. **1995**—Seven-passenger seating and a 155-horsepower, 3.0L engine. **1996**—A passenger-side airbag, four-wheel ABS, and four doors. **2000**—A new model with front-drive and sliding side doors. **2002**—A 200-hp V6 and 5-speed automatic transmission, power-sliding side doors, revised suspension settings, and 17-inch wheels. **2003**—More standard features (LX) that include power-sliding rear side doors, 16-inch wheels, a flip-up side table, and doormat. **2004**—Refreshed interior and exterior styling of no real consequence, except for the driver's seat additional lumbar support.

Presently, the MPV uses the Taurus 200-hp 3.0L Duratec V6. Some refinements produce a lower torque peak—3,000 rpm versus 4,400 rpm—giving the Mazda engine better pulling power at lower speed. Making good use of that power is a smooth-shifting 5-speed automatic transmission, which should cut fuel consumption a bit. One immediate benefit: The 3.0L is able to climb hills without continuously downshifting, and Mazda's "slope control" system automatically shifts to a lower gear when the hills get very steep.

Torque is still less than the Odyssey's 3.5L or the 3.8L engine in top-of-the-line Chryslers, though comparable with lesser Chrysler products and GM's Venture and Montana. The suspension has been firmed up to decrease body roll, enhancing cornering ability and producing a sportier ride than other minivans. This firmness may be too much for some.

I've been tougher on the MPV than have *Consumer Reports* and others due to the price-gouging, poor servicing, small size, underpowered drivetrain, and reliability problems (all too common on pre-2000 models). Presently it looks like most of these concerns have been met, although I'm still worried that the 3.0 Duratec may not hold up.

On more recent models, engine overheating and head gasket failures are commonplace with the 4-banger, and the temperature gauge warns you only when it's too late. Some cases of chronic engine knocking in cold weather with the 3.0L have been fixed by installing tighter-fitting, Teflon-coated pistons. Valve lifter problems are also common with this engine. Winter driving is compromised by the MPV's light rear end and mediocre traction, and low ground clearance means that off-road excursions shouldn't be too adventurous. The last couple of model years are much improved; nevertheless, expect some transmission glitches, ABS malfunctions, a rotten-egg exhaust, stalling and surging, and some oil leakage. Owners report that the electronic computer module (ECU), automatic transmission driveshaft, upper shock mounts, front 4X4 drive axles and lash adjusters, AC core, and radiator fail within the first three years. Cold temperatures tend to "fry" the automatic window motor, and the paint is easily chipped and flakes off early, especially around the hood, tailgate, and front fenders. Premature brake caliper and rotor wear and excessive vibration/pulsation are chronic problem areas (repairs are needed about every 12,000 km). Premature paint peeling afflicting white-coloured MPVs is quite common.

COST ANALYSIS: A 2005 DX costs about $26,500, but sizeable discounts are common; if you don't get an attractive price go to an identical, cheaper 2004. When the MPV is compared with Honda's latest Odyssey or the revamped pre-2004 Toyota Sienna, there's not enough savings and quality to make up for the MPV's smaller size and less powerful engine.

Also, be wary of unwarranted extra charges. Says one *Lemon-Aid* reader who just bought a 2003 MPV:

> There are far too many "extra" charges for things (like $70 for getting Scotiabank financing) that should be included in the price of the MPV. All these extra charges add up and create friction with the dealer that doesn't need to exist.... Wheel lock bolts should be standard when buying alloy wheels. It seems very petty to add $31.50 for wheel locks to the price of the $3,000 Sport Package. How can Mazda charge an extra $105 for certain paint colours on a $30,000 vehicle? This is no way to make friends.

Best alternatives: Of course, the Honda Odyssey, Nissan Quest ('93 or earlier), Axxess (see Appendix II), or Toyota Sienna. **Rebates:** Expect $3,000 rebates and zero percent financing. **Delivery/PDI:** $1,095. **Warranty:** Bumper-to-bumper 3 years/80,000 km; powertrain 5 years/100,000 km; rust perforation 5 years/unlimited mileage. **Supplementary warranty:** An extended warranty is worth having, particularly in view of the fact that powertrain problems have plagued these vehicles after the first three years of use. **Options:** Rear AC and seat height-adjustment mechanisms are recommended convenience features. Beware: Dealers pretend Mazda accessories like a roof rack don't include the labour charge. Also, the higher trim levels don't offer much of value, except for power windows and door locks and an ignition immobilizer/alarm/keyless entry system. **Depreciation:** Worse than average. **Insurance cost:** Higher than average. **Parts supply/cost:** Likely to be back ordered and cost more than average, despite Mazda's warning to dealers to keep prices in check. **Annual maintenance cost:** Average; any garage can repair these minivans. **Highway/city fuel economy:** 9.6–13.6L/100 km.

QUALITY/RELIABILITY: Below-average reliability of early models, a "take it or leave it" attitude when handling warranty claims, mediocre, expensive scheduled maintenance, and high fuel and parts costs make ownership costs higher than normal. Overheating and head gasket failures are commonplace with the 4-banger, and the temperature gauge warns you only when it's too late. Some cases of chronic engine knocking in cold weather with the 3.0L have been fixed by installing tighter-fitting, Teflon-coated pistons. Valve lifter problems are also common with this engine. Winter driving is compromised by the MPV's light rear end and mediocre traction, and low ground clearance means that off-road excursions shouldn't be too adventurous. Recent models have remarkably improved workmanship and more rugged construction. Nevertheless, expect some transmission glitches, ABS malfunctions, and premature wearout of the front and rear brakes. **Owner-reported problems:** There have been extraordinarily low numbers of engine complaints on 2001–04 models, except for a few complaints of rotten-egg exhaust, stalling and surging, and some oil leakage. Owners report that the electronic computer module (ECU), automatic transmission driveshaft, upper shock mounts, front 4X4 drive axles and lash adjusters, AC core, and radiator fail within the first three years. Cold temperatures tend to "fry" the automatic window motor, and the paint is easily chipped and flakes off early, especially around the hood, tailgate, and front fenders. Premature brake caliper and rotor wear and excessive vibration/pulsation are chronic problem areas (repairs are needed about every 12,000 km). Premature paint peeling afflicting white-coloured MPVs. **Warranty performance:** Inadequate base warranty; mediocre past servicing.

SAFETY SUMMARY: Airbags: Side airbags are optional on the LX and standard on the ES model. NHTSA has recorded several complaints of airbags failing to deploy in a collision. **ABS:** *2W; 4W:* Standard; disc/drum. **Head restraints F/R:** *1995–96:* **; *1997:* *; *2000:* ***; *2001–03:* **/*; *2004:* ***/**. **Visibility F/R:** *****/***. **Maximum load capacity:** 1,305 lb.

SAFETY COMPLAINTS: All models: 1998—Rear anti-sway bar brackets snapped off from rear axle housing. • ABS brake failure. • Defective gas cap causes the false activation of the Check Engine light. **2000**—Fixed seat belt anchors and buckle placement prevent the safe installation of child safety seats. • Vehicle windshield and side glass suddenly shattered while parked. • Excessive vibrations while cruising. • Rear hatch door flew open when rear-ended. **2000–01**—Engine valve failure. • Cupholders will spill drink when making a sharp turn; holders were redesigned in 2002. **2000–03**—Airbags failed to deploy. **2001**—Engine surging. • Malfunctioning #1 spark plug causes chronic engine hesitation. • Tranny lever can be shifted out of Park without key in ignition; sometimes it won't shift out of Park when you want it to. • Brake failure. • Brake caliper bolt fell off, causing vehicle to skid. • Sliding doors don't lock in place. • Rear visibility obstructed by high seatbacks. **2002–03**—Engine oil leakage. • Sudden stalling. • Shifter obscures dash and is easily knocked about. **2003**—Child's neck tangled in seat belt. **2003–04**—Rotten-egg exhaust smell. **2004**—Engine seized when connecting rod failed. • Transmission failure due to worn shaft solenoid. • Blown tire sidewall. • Tread separation on Dunlop tires.

Secret Warranties/Service Tips

All models/years: TSB #006-94 looks into all the causes and remedies for excessive brake vibrations, and TSB #11-14-95 gives an excellent diagnostic flow chart for troubleshooting excessive engine noise. • Serious paint peeling and delaminating will be fully covered for up to six years under a Mazda secret warranty, say owners. • Troubleshooting tips for correcting wind noise around doors. • Tips for eliminating a musty, mildew-type AC odour. **1996–98**—Tips for correcting water leaks from the sliding sunroof. • Brake pulsation repair tips. • Front power window noise. • Wind noise around doors. • Steering wheel a bit off-centre. **1997–98**—Front power window noise can be silenced by installing a modified window regulator. **2000–01**—Hard starts caused by inadequate fuel system pressure, due to a fuel pressure regulator that's stuck open. • Front brake clunking can be silenced by replacing the eight brake guide plates under warranty (TSB #04-003/00). • Insufficient airflow at bi-level setting. • Door key difficult to insert or rotate. **2000–03**—Rotten-egg exhaust smell. • Remedy for a mildew odour. • A corroded rear heater pipe may leak coolant; Mazda will fix it for free (see TSB #07-004/03). **2001**—Rear brake popping, squealing, or clicking. • Tips for eliminating a musty, mildew-type odour from the AC. **2002**—Engine tappet noise. **2002–03**—Cargo net hooks detach. **2002–04**—Remedies for shift shock (transmission slams into gear).

MPV Profile

	1997	1998	2000	2001	2002	2003	2004
Cost Price ($) (negotiable)							
DX/GX (18%)	—	—	25,505	25,095	25,975	26,090	26,600
LX/GS (18%)	27,845	25,200	29,450	29,450	29,150	29,090	29,995

Used Values ($)							
DX/GX ▲	—	—	11,000	13,000	16,000	19,000	21,000
DX/GX ▼	—	—	9,500	11,500	14,500	17,500	19,500
LX/GS ▲	5,000	7,500	12,500	15,500	17,500	21,000	23,000
LX/GS ▼	3,500	6,000	11,500	14,000	16,000	19,500	22,000
Reliability	③	③	④	④	④	④	⑤
Crash Safety (F)	④	④	④	④	⑤	⑤	⑤
Side	—	—	⑤	⑤	⑤	⑤	⑤
Offset	❷	❷	③	③	③	③	③
Rollover	—	—	—	③	③	③	—

Note: 4X4 models cost about $500 more. No prices listed for 1999 models.

Toyota

SIENNA, PREVIA ★★★★

RATING: *Sienna:* Above Average (2005); Average (2004); there has been a resurgence of safety-related defects reported with the redesigned 2004 Sienna. Above Average (1998–2003). *Previa:* Average (1991–97). The Previa has reasonable reliability, mediocre road performance, and limited interior amenities. Nevertheless, it's far better than any of Toyota's earlier LE minivans. Mazda minivans are catching up to Honda and Toyota in performance and reliability, while the less reliable and old-tech Ford and GM models are hardly in the running. Chrysler's extensive 7-year powertrain warranty, generous rebates, and innovative styling have kept its minivans in the game for the past several years. Earlier Toyotas are outclassed by the brawnier, more innovative Odyssey. The best all-around used choices are the early Toyota Sienna, Honda Odyssey, and 1999–2003 Nissan Quest. The 2002–04 Mazda MPV is a small minivan that's more reliable than some top-rated models. The GM minivans are adequate performers, but like the Ford Windstar/Freestar duo and Chrysler minivans they are plagued by serious reliability problems. **Strong points:** Incredibly smooth powertrain; a comfortable, stable ride; plenty of standard safety, performance, and convenience features; a fourth door; and a good amount of passenger and cargo room. *2004:* Takes the "mini" out of minivan; reasonable base price; acceleration second only to the Odyssey; an AWD option; a better-performing, economical 5-speed automatic transmission; a tighter turning circle; enhanced seating versatility and storage capacity; quiet interior; and uses regular fuel. **Weak points:** Unacceptably high freight and PDI charges ($1,245); V6 performance compromised by AC and automatic transmission power drain; and lacks the trailer-towing brawn of rear-drive minivans. Less-efficient rear drum brakes; rear visibility obstructed by middle roof pillars and rear head restraints; low head restraint crashworthiness rating; the wide centre pillars make for difficult access to the middle seats; removing middle- and third-row seats is a two-person chore; radio speakers are set too low for acceptable acoustics; and an unusually large number of body rattles and safety-related complaints (158 safety complaints, or three times what is considered normal). Suspect towing capability, mediocre braking, third-row head restraints are mounted too low, and expensive options. **New for 2005:** Nothing major.

2005 Technical Data	
Powertrain (front)	Wheelbase: 119 in.
Engine: 3.3L V6 (230 hp)	Turning circle: 38 ft.
Transmission: 5-speed auto.	Passengers: 2/2/3; 2/3/3
Dimension/Capacity (LE)	Cargo volume: 70.1 cu. ft.
Height/length/width:	GVWR: 5,690 lb.
69/200/77 in.	Tow limit: 3,500 lb.
Headroom F/R1: 42/40.2 in.	Ground clear.: 6.9 in.
Legroom F/R1: 42.9/39.6 in.	Fuel tank: 79L/reg.
	Weight: 4,123 lb.

MODEL HISTORY: Completely redesigned in 2004, this year's Sienna continues to provide lots more interior room that accommodates up to eight passengers, handles much better, rides more comfortably, and uses a more powerful fuel-efficient engine. Standard four-wheel disc brakes and all-wheel drive is offered for the first time.

A new 3.3L 230-hp V6 turns in respectable acceleration times under nine seconds, almost as good as the Odyssey. Handling is completely carlike, with less vulnerability to wind buffeting, and minimal road noise.

Sienna's interior and exterior have been gently restyled. The third-row seats split and fold away, head restraints don't have to be removed when the seats are stored, and second-row bucket seats are easily converted to bench seats.

The Sienna is Toyota's Camry-based front-drive minivan. It replaced the Previa for the 1998 model year and abandoned the Previa's futuristic look in favour of a more conservative Chevrolet Venture styling. The Sienna seats seven, and offers dual power sliding doors with optional remote controls and a V6 power plant. It's built in the same Kentucky assembly plant as the Camry and comes with lots of safety and convenience features that include side airbags, anti-lock brakes, and a low-tire-pressure warning system.

Sienna's strong points include standard ABS and side airbags (LE, XLE); a smooth-running V6 engine and transmission that's a bit more refined and capable than what the Odyssey offers; a comfortable, stable ride; a fourth door; a quiet interior; easy entry/exit; and better-than-average fit and finish reliability. Its weak areas: V6 performance is compromised by AC and the automatic transmission powertrain and it lacks the trailer-towing brawn of rear-drive minivans:

> Imagine our surprise when we discovered within the owner's manual a "Caution" stating that one must not exceed 72 km/hr [45 mph] while towing a trailer.... This limit is not stated in the promotional literature we were provided, or on the *Toyota.ca* website, or in any trailer-towing

rating guide. This limit was also not mentioned at any time during our purchase negotiations. Alarmingly, Toyota defines a "Caution" as a "warning against anything which may cause injury to people if the warning is ignored." As it turns out, the dealer was not aware of this speed limit....

Although the rear seats fold flat to accommodate the width of a 4' x 8' board, the tailgate won't close, the heavy seats are difficult to reinstall (a two-person job, and the centre seat barely fits through the door), and rear visibility is obstructed by the middle roof pillars and rear head restraints. There's also no traction control, less-efficient rear drum brakes, mediocre fuel economy (premium fuel), the low-mounted radio is hard to reach, and third-row seats lack a fore/aft adjustment to increase cargo space.

Reliability is still problematic on 1997–2002 models. Although mechanical and body components are generally reliable, there's been a disturbing increase in factory-related defects reported by owners during the past few years. The most serious reliability problems concern self-destructing, sludge-prone engines (1997–2002 models) and defective automatic transmissions on 1998–2004 Siennas.

Toyota Canada advises owners who notice the telltale signs of engine sludge formation to take their vehicle to their local dealer to have the engine inspected. These signs may include the emission of blue smoke from the tailpipe and/or excessive oil consumption, which may cause overheating, rough running, or the Check Engine light to come on.

Other recent model problems reported by owners include a clunk or banging in the driveline; the car jolting or creeping forward when at a stop, forcing you to keep your foot firmly on the brake; stalling when the AC engages; electrical shorts; premature brake wear and excessive brake noise (mostly screeching); a chronic rotten-egg smell; distracting windshield reflections and distorted windshields; sliding door defects; window suddenly shatters; paint is easily chipped; and various other body glitches, including a hard-to-pull-out rear seat, water leaks, and excessive creaks and rattles (seat belt, sun visor).

Previa

The redesigned 1991 Previa's performance and reliability are so much improved over its LE predecessor that it almost seems like a different vehicle. Roomier and rendered more stable thanks to its longer wheelbase, equipped with a new 2.4L engine (supercharged as of the 1994 model year), and loaded with standard safety and convenience features, 1991–97 Previas are almost as driver-friendly as the Chrysler and Mazda competition. Still, they can't match Ford, GM, or Chrysler front-drive minivans for responsive handling and a comfortable ride, and Toyota's small engine is overworked and doesn't hesitate to tell you so. Previa owners have learned to live with engine noise, poor fuel economy, premature front brake wear, excessive brake vibration and pulsation, electrical glitches, AC malfunctions, and fit and finish blemishes. The 4X4 models with automatic transmissions steal lots of power from the 4-cylinder power plant, though they have fewer reliability problems than similar drive-trains found on competitors, especially Chryslers.

1995—DX models get a supercharged engine. **1996**—Supercharged engine is the only power plant offered. **1997**—Extra soundproofing. **1998**—Introduction of the Sienna; no more Previa. **2001**—A rear defroster, some additional horsepower and torque, and a driver-side sliding door added to the Sienna. **2004**—Sienna completely redesigned.

COST ANALYSIS: Crafty Toyota is keeping most prices at last year's levels, which isn't surprising since the 2005's are essentially identical, warmed-over 2004s. Base 2005s start at $30,000 for the 7-passenger CE; the all-new CE AWD sells for $35,900; prices for the LE start at $35,420; and the AWD version fetches $39,830. The top-of-the-line Limited package will cost $49,545. **Best alternatives:** Consider a 2003 or earlier Sienna, any year Honda Odyssey, a Mazda MPV, Nissan Quest (pre-2004), or any year Axxess. Bargain hunters take note: Used cargo Siennas (year 2000 or earlier) cost thousands less than the base CE. **Rebates:** $2,000 on the '05s in early 2005. **Delivery/PDI:** $1,260 (Grrrr...). **Warranty:** Bumper-to-bumper 3 years/ 60,000 km; powertrain 5 years/100,000 km; rust perforation 5 years/ unlimited mileage. **Supplementary warranty:** Not needed. **Options:** Power windows and door locks, rear heater, and AC unit. Be wary of the power-sliding door. As with the Odyssey and GM minivans, these doors can injure children and pose unnecessary risks to other occupants. Go for Michelin or Pirelli original equipment tires. **Depreciation:** Much slower than average. **Insurance cost:** A bit higher than average. **Parts supply/cost:** Excellent supply of reasonably priced Sienna parts taken from the Camry parts bin. Only exception has been fuel tank components needed for recall repairs. Automatic transmission torque converters are frequently back ordered due to their poor reliability. Previa parts are in limited supply. **Annual maintenance cost:** For the Sienna, like the Camry, much lower than average. Previa maintenance costs are higher than average, and only Toyota dealers can repair these older mini-vans, particularly when it comes to troubleshooting the supercharged 2.4L engine and All Trac. **Highway/city fuel economy:** *3.3L V6:* 8.1–12.2L/100 km; *3.0L V6:* 8.8–12.4L/100 km.

QUALITY/RELIABILITY: Toyota dealers tell me they are ticked off with their head office. They say Toyota Canada has received marching orders from Toyota USA to improve customer relations. Dealers agree, but they say the problem is with Toyota's out-of-touch, Ontario-fixated Canadian administration, that came up with Access program no-haggle pricing, engine sludge stonewalling, and fuel-tank recall mishandling. Reliability concerns include stalling when the AC engages; electrical shorts; excessive brake noise; sliding door defects; and various other body glitches, including excessive creaks and rattles and paint that's easily chipped. **Owner-reported problems:** Premature brake wear and noisy brakes, engine replacement due to sludge buildup, auto-matic transmission failures, fuel-tank leaks, distracting windshield reflections and distorted windshields, power-sliding door malfunctions, interior squeaks and rattles, and rusting of the AC lines.

> The Sienna's front to back A/C lines rust out because they are made of aluminum and are connected to the body frame with another type of metal fastener. This combination causes extensive leakage. Toyota says it will cost $500 to correct this design defect.

Warranty performance: Average, but you have to stand your ground and ignore head office bull-crap.

SAFETY SUMMARY: Many complaints that the steering wheel locks up when making a turn, won't return to centre without extreme effort, or simply no longer responds. Owners have also complained that the vehicle pulls sharply to one side or another when driving at moderate speeds. **Airbags:** Reports of airbags failing to deploy in a collision. **ABS:** Standard; disc/drum. Numerous reports of ABS failures, loud grinding or groaning noise when braking, and brake pedal going to the floor without braking effect. **Seat belt pretensioners:** Standard. **Head restraints F/R:** *1998–99:* *; *2001–03:* **; *2004:* ****/***. **Visibility F/R:** *****/**. **Maximum load capacity:** 1,160 lb.

SAFETY COMPLAINTS: All models/years: A multiplicity of sliding door defects covered by internal bulletins. • Windshield distortion. • Reflection of the dashboard on the windshield impairs visibility. **Previa: 1996**—Poor, noisy AC compressor performance. • Windshield wipers suddenly stopped working. • Middle right bench seat lapbelt is impossible to adjust due to its poor design. **Sienna: 1998**—Sudden acceleration, due to a defective throttle cable; vehicle hit a wall. • Shape and design of the Sienna creates severe blind spots. • Headlights give poor illumination. • Rear door doesn't shut tightly. • Poor visibility due to the tinted window design. • Headrests and third-row seats are loose and vibrate. • Shoulder belts in the middle row lock up instantly when first put on and stay locked up, binding the passenger. **1999**—Wheel lug nuts broke and allowed wheel to fall off. • Window exploded at stoplight. • Rear brake drums may overheat and warp. • Faulty fuel cap causes the Check Engine light to come on. **2000**—Sudden acceleration during rainstorm. • Check Engine light continues to come on due to a defective transmission torque converter. • Chronic transmission failure due to faulty torque converter. • Wheel lug nuts sheared off. • Driver's seat belt anchor bolt on door pillar unscrewed and fell to the floor. • Premature tire blowouts (Dunlop and Firestone). • Right rear passenger window suddenly exploded. • Annoying dash/windshield reflection also impairs visibility (very bad with black and beige colours). **2001**—Sudden stalling when the AC is turned on. • Automatic transmission suddenly went into Neutral while on the highway. • Defective transmission torque converter causes the engine warning light to come on. • Sudden, unintended acceleration. • Vehicle rolled away, with shifter in Park on a hill and ignition shut off. • Rear seat belts can't be adjusted. • Centre rear seat belt doesn't tighten sufficiently when children are restrained. • Slope of the windshield makes it hard to gauge where the front end stops. • Rear window exploded as front door was closed. • Sunroof flew off when opened while Sienna was underway. **2002**—Several electrical fires in the engine compartment. • Neither front nor side airbag deployed in a collision. • Defective power steering. • Loss of steering. **2003**—Unsafe transmission Overdrive design. • Child safety seat second-row tethering is poorly designed. • Vehicle jerks to one side when accelerating or stopping. **2004**—An incredible 158 complaints versus 35 for the 2003 Sienna. • Engine surging with minimal pedal pressure. • When proceeding from a rolling stop, acceleration is delayed for about two seconds.

> While parking, accelerating no more than 5 mph [8 km/h] vehicle surged forward. Although I was applying the brake, the car would not stop until it ran into a tree trunk.

• Child knocked gearshift lever into Drive from Park, without key in the ignition. • Difficulty shifting into a higher gear. • Sluggish transmission downshift; vehicle sometimes seems to slip out of gear when decelerating. • Skid control system lock-up. • Fuel tank leakage after recall repairs; leaking fuel line. • Complete loss of brakes. • Rapid brake degradation (glazed and warped rotors). • Sliding door caught passenger's arm and child's leg; manual door doesn't latch properly (particularly when windows are open); door opens when turning, jams, or closes when vehicle is parked on an incline.

> Our two-year-old son pulled on the sliding door handle, and the door began to open (we thought the child locks were on, but this was not the case). He was surprised and was afraid of falling out of the van, so he just held onto the handle. As the door was opening, his head then was dragged between the sliding door and the side of the van. But the van door did not stop opening. It just continued opening, exerting even more force on our son's head. Fortunately we were able to grab the door and forcefully pull it back closed before our son was horribly injured.

• Second-row seat belt locks up; faulty seat belt bracket in rear passenger seat. • Seat belts won't retract. • Battery saver device doesn't work, particularly if interior lights are left on (they don't turn off, as advertised). • Small brake lights inadequate. • Foot gets stuck between pedals. • Rotten-egg smell. • Daytime running lights blind oncoming drivers (2004 Highlander has the same problem). • Long delay for fuel tank recall campaign parts.

Secret Warranties/Service Tips

All models/years: Sliding door hazards, malfunctions, and noise are a veritable plague affecting all model years and generating a ton of service bulletins.

• Owner feedback confirms that front brake pads and discs will be replaced under Toyota's "goodwill" policy if they wear out before 2 years/40,000 km. • Loose, poorly fitted trim panels (TSB # BO017-03 REVISED September 9, 2003). • Rusting at the base of the two front doors. Will be repaired at no cost, usually with a courtesy car included. According to *www.siennaclub.org*, the proper fix is: Repaint inside of doors (presumably after removing paint and rust); cover with 3M film; and replace and coat inside seals with silicone grease. **1997–2002**—Free engine overhaul or replacement due to engine sludge buildup. The program includes 1997 through 2002 Toyota and Lexus vehicles with 3.0L, V6, or 2.2L 4-cylinder engines. There is no mileage limitation, and tell Toyota to shove it if they give a song and dance about proof of oil changes. **1998**—Upgraded brake pads and rotors should reduce brake groan and squeak noises. **1998–2000**—An 8-year/160,000 km warranty extension for automatic transmission failure. Says Toyota:

> We have recently become aware that a small number of Sienna owners have experienced a mechanical failure in the automatic transaxle, drive pinion bearing. This failure could result in slippage, noise, or a complete lack of movement.
>
> To ensure the continued satisfaction and reliability of your Sienna, Toyota has decided to implement a Special Policy Adjustment affecting certain 1998–2000 Sienna models.... This Special Policy will extend the warranty coverage of the automatic transaxle to 8 years or 160,000 km, whichever occurs first, from the original warranty registration date.

• Outline of various diagnostic procedures and fixes to correct vehicle pulling to one side. • Power steering squeaks can be silenced by installing a countermeasure steering rack end under warranty. • Power steering "feel" can be improved by replacing the steering rack guide. • False activation of the security alarm can be fixed by modifying the hood latch switch. • Power window rattles can be corrected by installing a revised lower window frame mounting bracket. **1998–2003**—A new rear brake drum has been developed to reduce rear brake noise:

Rear Brake Squealing

Bulletin No.: BR003-04   Date: March 16, 2004

1998–2003 Sienna

A new rear brake drum has been developed to reduce rear brake squeal noise.

On a case-by-case basis, Toyota will pick up most of this cost under a "goodwill" policy.

• An upgraded alternator will improve charging (see TSB #EL013-03) and is also subject to "goodwill" treatment. **1999–2001**—Tips on fixing power seat motor cable to prevent a loose seat or inoperative seat adjustment. • Power sliding door transmitter improvements. **2000**—Toyota has field fixes to correct washer fluid leakage from the rear washer nozzle and eliminate moisture and odours permeating the vehicle interior. • Correction for an inoperative spare tire lift. • Speedometer or tachometer troubleshooting. **2001**—False activation of the security alarm. • Power windows rattling. • Entertainment system hum. • Faulty speedometer and tachometer. • Inoperative third-row sliding seat. • Special service campaign to inspect or replace the front subframe assembly on 2001 models. • Water leaking into the trunk area. • Troubleshooting interior moisture or odours. • Loose sun visor. • Front wheel bearing ticking. **2002**—Troubleshooting complaints that vehicle pulls to one side. **2002–03**—Steering angle sensor calibration. • Loose sun visor remedy. **2004**—New ECM calibration for a poor shifting transmission (TSB #TC007-03). • Rear disc brake groan (TSB #BR002-04). • Intermediate steering shaft noise on turns. • Front door area wind noise (TSB #NV009-03). • Power sliding door inoperative, rattles (the saga continues). • Back door shudder and water leaks. • Charging improvement at idle (TSB #RL013-03).

Sienna, Previa Profile

	1997	1998	1999	2000	2001	2002	2003	2004
Cost Price ($) (negotiable)								
Previa	36,998	—	—	—	—	—	—	—
Sienna Cargo 3d	—	24,438	24,570	24,570	—	—	—	—
Sienna CE 4d (16%)	—	26,808	26,940	27,770	29,535	29,335	29,060	30,000
Sienna LE 4d (17%)	—	29,558	29,980	30,705	31,900	32,985	31,925	35,000
Used Values ($)								
Previa ʌ	5,500	—	—	—	—	—	—	—
Previa ᴠ	4,000	—	—	—	—	—	—	—
Sienna Cargo 3d ʌ	—	8,000	10,500	12,500	—	—	—	—
Sienna Cargo 3d ᴠ	—	6,500	9,000	11,000	—	—	—	—
Sienna CE 4d ʌ	—	9,500	12,000	14,000	16,500	19,000	22,500	25,500
Sienna CE 4d ᴠ	—	8,000	11,000	13,000	15,000	17,500	21,000	24,000
Sienna LE 4d ʌ	—	10,500	13,000	15,000	18,000	21,000	24,000	27,500
Sienna LE 4d ᴠ	—	9,000	12,500	13,500	16,500	19,000	22,500	26,000
Reliability	③	④	④	④	④	④	④	③
Crash Safety (F)	④	⑤	⑤	⑤	⑤	⑤	⑤	⑤
Side	—	—	④	④	④	④	④	⑤
Offset	❶	⑤	⑤	⑤	⑤	⑤	⑤	⑤
Rollover	—	—	—	—	④	④	④	④

PICKUP TRUCKS

Dodge Hemi Hysteria
I bought my Dodge Ram 1500 Hemi on 5-26-03. Two weeks later the truck broke down: broken valve springs. Truck is still in the shop, with the replacement motor not in sight.

NHTSA Safety Complaint Database

"That thing got a Hemi? What's a valve spring?"

More than a hay hauler

This year light trucks continued to gain share from cars. And it's easy to see why. Pickups have moved uptown and joined the Saturday night party crowd. Buyers are looking more for cachet than cargo-hauling capacity and woman drivers are demanding practical features never imagined by the hay-hauling crowd. No wonder, trucks now represent about 53 percent of North America's vehicle production. And they're continuing to make inroads into the passenger car niche by offering more carlike styling, handling, comfort, and convenience. Safety features have also been added to give pickups greater stability, better braking, and improved crashworthiness.

In general, base models are less costly than cars with comparable features, but prices for full-size pickups can easily top $45,000 for all-equipped versions with crew cabs, 4X4, and a full list of amenities. All pickups are getting bigger and more expensive with the advent of extended cabs and crew cabs. Extended cabs have a small rear seat and doors, while crew cabs generally have large interiors that can sit up to six, four full-sized doors, a full-sized back seat, and windows that roll down. Even though they can cost up to $15,000 more than a regular cab, buyers are flocking to the larger pickups—over 50 percent of buyers versus 30 percent, a year ago.

So, who are the major players in this lucrative league?

Ford, to begin with. Its F-series pickup has been America's best-selling vehicle for 22 years. In fact, through April 2004, the three top-selling vehicles in the United States were the F-Series, General Motors' Chevrolet Silverado/Sierra, and the Dodge Ram, in that order.

General Motors sells a balanced mixture of trucks and cars, while Ford and Chrysler are kept on "life-support" by truck sales, augmented by a few car purchases. Asian and European carmakers are just that, car manufacturers, with trucks seen as almost an afterthought.

This year more pickups will be powered by smaller, all-aluminum engines with fuel-efficient variable-valve timing instead of the decades-old iron-block designs. Innovative power management, such as a 4-6-8-cylinder engine, and hybrid electrical/gasoline setups are also in the works. Never mind that aluminum engines in the past encountered serious sealing/durability problems, or that GM's first (and last) 4-6-8-cylinder engine used in its early '80s Cadillacs was a fiasco, providing 8-cylinder power in the city and 4-cylinder power just as you were merging on the freeway. The GM trucks' electric motor engages upon acceleration and has a stop-start system that shuts off the gasoline engine at traffic lights. A built-in generator is also standard.

Consumers looking for hybrid pickups at dealerships selling Chrysler group or General Motors brands will have a hard time finding them. GM will build only 2,500 gasoline-electric hybrid versions of the 2005 Silverado and Sierra pickups; they will be sold only in the States for about $1,500 more than a gasoline-powered version. Dodge will build just 100 diesel-electric 2005 Ram pickups and will sell them mostly to utility companies.

Depreciation

Although high fuel costs are driving down resale values, full-size trucks still keep their value longer than compacts, and extended-cabs are generally worth more than regular-cab pickups. The number of doors also determines value: A four-door pickup is worth more than one with two or three doors. And, while 4X4s maintain a resale value, commercial trucks tend to depreciate quickly.

As with cars, imports hold their value better than domestics. For example, a Ford Ranger will be worth less than 30 percent of its initial value after three years, yet a Toyota Tacoma PreRunner Double Cab will retain as much as 61 percent of its value during the same period.

Among full-size pickups, Ford's F-150 regular-cab XL retains only 36 percent of its selling price after three years, while its "plain Jane" cousin, the F-150 Heritage, is likely to be worth only 23 percent. Toyota Double Cab Tundras depreciate the slowest, keeping almost 60 percent of their value after three years.

Parking prowess

Don't buy any pickup without first seeing how easily it parks, keeping in mind that a good view is more important than the truck's size. For example, a Toyota Tundra, though wider than the GM Sierra/Silverado, is far easier to park due to its low window sills and cowl and a throttle that's not so twitchy.

With the Sierra/Silverado, small throttle corrections are hard to perform and the power-folding side mirrors don't tuck in enough. Moreover, the automatic mirror-look-down feature in Reverse makes it hard to see the rear fenders.

A high tailgate blocks your rearward view, and Ford's F-Series is one of the worst offenders. Rather than fixing its mistake, the company sells a rear-parking-distance indicator for $300. It beeps less for posts than cars, goes off when it shouldn't, and doesn't go off when it should. Drivers end up ignoring the beeps or disconnecting the device entirely.

Diesels

Diesel engines are making a comeback, with smaller GM and Ford power plants and cleaner running variants that conform to higher emissions regulations. Unfortunately, these cleaner diesels cost more and aren't as reliable as earlier versions, say industry insiders.

Trucking companies are scouring dealer lots for 2002 diesel-equipped heavy trucks, in an effort to avoid getting unproven, less-polluting 2003 and later diesels that entered the market in October 2003. A creation of the U.S. Environmental Protection Agency, seconded by Canadian regulators, these new diesels cost $3,000 to $5,000 more than previous versions, are 3–5 percent less fuel efficient, and use new technology to recirculate exhaust gases through the engine. Oil changes are more frequent and repair costs are expected to be much higher than before, because few mechanics and dealers will have the diagnostic tools and experience to correct factory-related defects that are commonplace with new designs.

Diesel defects

All three Detroit manufacturers are having injector problems with their newest diesel engines. Ford is covering repair costs through a variety of "goodwill" programs, Chrysler is using its 7-year warranty to authorize repair refunds, and General Motors has extended fuel injector warranty coverage for owners of all 2001 and 2002 model-year Chevrolet and GMC Duramax 6600 equipped pickup trucks. Special Policy #04039 was set up in June 2004 giving additional warranty protection for 7 years from the date the vehicle was placed into service or 321,870 km (200,000 miles)—whichever occurs first.

Diesel-specific service bulletins can be downloaded on a number of Internet sites: Dodge: *www.turbodieselregister.com*; Ford: *www.thedieselstop.com*; and Chevy: *www.thedieselpage.com*.

Pros and Cons of Pickup Ownership

Trucks have grown in popularity because they're stylish, fun to drive, and versatile. They'll do everything a car will and then some. They're rugged and comfortable, depreciate slowly, and are more crashworthy than earlier models, and, in an effort to attract women, have adjustable pedals, larger cabs, usable back seats, airbag cut-off switches, more user-friendly child safety seat anchors, and additional, wider doors to facilitate easy loading of kids, pets, groceries, and small pieces of luggage.

Part of the pickup's popularity is by default. The station wagons that used to haul families to the beach and the cottage are practically all gone, though Chrysler's 2005 Dodge Magnum may revive the wagon's popularity. Plus, minivans don't have the awesome towing capacity and big-engine grunt (torque) that some motorhome owners, boaters, and off-roaders require.

As much as the minivan saved Chrysler two decades ago, booming pickup and SUV sales have rescued Detroit automakers from what has been a dismal year for profits. As with sport-utilities, even though it's unlikely you'll need the 4X4 versatility or brawny V8, it is reassuring to know it's there—just in case. Consequently, despite rising fuel costs and a fragile economy, small and mid-sized pickups will remain the last vehicles to be sacrificed on the altar of fuel efficiency and rising ownership costs.

Pickup advantages

- relatively low base price for the smaller, Japanese pickups
- fuel efficient (4- and 6-cylinder engines)
- gasoline and diesel versions available
- good support network for parts and servicing
- numerous body, engine, and suspension choices
- available in 4X2, part-time 4X4, or full-time 4X4 drive
- versatile cargo- and RV-haulers
- easy to customize or convert into a recreational vehicle
- easy to repair, with excellent parts availability at reasonable prices
- rear ABS now standard (but you really need four-wheel ABS)
- commanding view of the road
- much lower-than-average collision repair costs

Pickup disadvantages

- many have full-strength airbags and are often equipped with dealer-installed, failure-prone Bridgestone, Firestone, Goodyear, or Continental tires
- accelerated depreciation on feature-laden, medium- and large-sized models
- homeowners' associations may prohibit trucks that are not garaged
- trucks used commercially lose value quickest
- chassis may be rust-cankered; box is rust-prone without a liner
- truck, tools, and cargo are easily stolen
- small pickups don't offer much cab room; underpowered
- centre front seat passenger lacks legroom
- three adults can't sit in comfort in rear seat on base models

- a bone-jarring ride unless the suspension is modified
- can't be driven with rear windows down because of deafening, painful "boom"
- tire upgrade needed on base models to improve handling
- entry/exit may be difficult without running boards or an extra door
- some compacts can't haul a 4' x 8' sheet of plywood flat on the cargo bed
- long box makes in-town parking a problem
- fuel-thirsty V6s and V8s; be wary of diesel fuel-economy claims
- GM hybrids' fuel economy may be illusory
- base models are relatively bare
- loading up on options can explode base price
- rear bench seat usually comes with an uncomfortably upright seatback
- rear doors don't always operate independently of the front doors
- 4X4 can't always be engaged while running on dry pavement
- rear wheels spin on slippery roads
- four-wheel ABS isn't always available
- rear end tends to swing out
- heaters are slow to heat the cabin
- taller, narrower trucks are more prone to rollovers
- high-mounted headlights blind other drivers

Full-sized pickups have changed considerably over the past decade, beginning with Ford's 1996 model redesign, then GM's 1999 model revamping, and last year's reworked 2004 models, highlighted by Ford's upgraded F-150 and the bold and powerful Nissan Titan. Pickups have been re-engineered to become more carlike, with better handling characteristics and more convenience features (like extra doors, interior space, padding, and carpeting) that enlarge their appeal from farmer and tradesperson trucks to vehicles for everyday transportation. Still, the half-ton full-sized pickups haven't abandoned their base clientele—they just come in a larger variety of sizes and powertrains to suit more diverse driving needs.

Nevertheless, no matter how carlike these trucks become, you'll be constantly reminded that these are trucks (especially with Dodge Rams) whenever you brake, corner, stop for fuel (which will be often), or climb on board (*climb* is used in the literal sense).

In choosing a pickup, consider reliability, cost, and size/style, in that order. Start small, with reliable entry-level Mazda, Nissan, or Toyota light-duty trucks. If you need more brawn and performance and *must* buy something Detroit-made, go for Chrysler's Ram series. Then consider Ford or GM. But be prepared for high maintenance costs and rapid depreciation on all Detroit Big Three models..

Getting the best for less

Full-sized used-truck prices are moving downward this year because of high-priced fuel, a glut of new, heavily discounted 2005 models, and an unprecedented number of used trucks coming off lease. Coopers and Lybrand's Autofacts division predicts that over the next few years the capacity for building light trucks will be far beyond what the market can absorb, leading to much lower MSRP prices, more substantial dealer incentives and customer rebates, and fierce price competition for both new and used pickups.

What do you do if all the *Lemon-Aid*–recommended full- or medium-sized pickups are either too expensive or aren't what you require? Simply downsize your needs and, if you can, go down a notch and buy a $3,000–$5,000 cheaper Japanese-made compact pickup. Or, better yet, wait another year for the market to be saturated with pickups and prices to level out.

PICKUP TRUCK RATINGS

Recommended
Nissan Frontier, Pickup (2005)   Toyota Tacoma (2005)

Above Average
DaimlerChrysler Ram 1500 (2002–05)   Nissan Titan (2004–05)
Nissan Frontier, Pickup   Toyota Tacoma (1987–2004)
  (1985–2004)

Average
DaimlerChrysler Dakota (2003–05)   General Motors Canyon,
DaimlerChrysler Ram 1500   Colorado (2004–05)
  (1986–2001); 2500, 3500   General Motors S-10, Sonoma,
  (1986–2005)   T-10 (1999–2004)
Ford Ranger/Mazda B Series   Isuzu Space Cab, Hombre
  (1984–2005)   (1997–2002)
General Motors Avalanche   Toyota Tundra (2004–05)
  (2002–05)
General Motors C/K, Sierra, Silverado
  (1988–98)

Below Average
DaimlerChrysler Dakota (1987–2002)   General Motors S-10, Sonoma,
Ford F-Series (1990–2005)   T-10 (1996–98)
General Motors C/K, Sierra,   Isuzu Space Cab, Hombre
  Silverado (1999–05)   (1989–96)
                                            Toyota Tundra (2001–03)

Not Recommended
General Motors S-10, Sonoma,   Subaru Baja (2003–05)
  T-10 (1986–95)

DaimlerChrysler

DAKOTA   ★★★

RATING: Average (2003–05); Below Average (1987–2002). **Strong points:** A stronger base V6 that's said to be more fuel frugal; the V8 also has a bit more power; either engine can be hooked to a new 6-speed manual transmission;

and the interior has been upgraded. *2004:* Brisk acceleration; available 4X4; lots of low-end torque; well-appointed, carlike interior; good visibility; lots of front head- and legroom; and attractively styled. **Weak points:** Quad Cab uses a shortened 5'3" bed. *2004:* Poor acceleration with the 4-cylinder engine; underpowered with the entry-level V6; watch out for false tow ratings on the R/T version; automatic transmission shifts erratically; awkward rear seat entry/exit (Club Cab); uncomfortable rear seats; folding rear bench seat is inadequate for three passengers, mainly due to the limited room for legs and knees; Quad truck cannot be driven with rear window down because of a deafening, painful noise created by the vacuum; sunlight glare off the gauges is distracting; inadequate headlight illumination on some versions; interior controls are from another era (Pleistocene); lousy fuel economy; poor results in offset crash tests; and an unacceptably large number of performance- and safety-related defects reported to NHTSA and other agencies. **New for 2005:** A redesigned Dakota with a more powerful base engine and less noise, vibration, and ride harshness. It will be 3.7 inches longer, 2.7 inches wider, and have a restyled interior that carries additional storage space. The 5.9L V8 equipped R/T will be dropped.

2005 Technical Data

Powertrain (rear-drive/4X4)
Engines: 3.7L V6 (210 hp)
• 4.7L V8 (230 hp)
Transmissions: 5-speed man.
• 4-speed auto. OD
• 5-speed auto. OD
Dimension/Capacity
Height/length/width:
65.6/195.8/71.5 in.
Box length: 6.5–8/6.5 ft.

Headroom F/R: 40/38 in.
Legroom F/R: 41.9/32.1 in.
Wheelbase: 112–124/131 in.
Turning circle: 44 ft.
Passengers: 2/3
GVWR: 4,390–6,150/5,100–5,650 lb.
Payload: 1,250–2,600/1,450–2,000 lb.
Tow limit: 6,650 lb.
Ground clear.: 7.1 in.
Fuel tank: 57/68L/reg.
Weight: 3,500 lb.

MODEL HISTORY: The 2005 midsize Dakota is a much-improved, well-equipped pickup covered by a comprehensive powertrain warranty. Unfortunately, for a model launched in 1987, it's too little, too late. Owners still must contend with mediocre handling, a jittery, wandering ride, marginal braking, and subpar quality control.

2004 and earlier models are seriously underpowered when equipped with the standard 4- or 6-cylinder engine. With an optional, more powerful engine, the Dakota outclasses the compact competition for sheer towing power. As if they needed it, both optional motors, the V6 and V8, got a substantial horsepower increase in 1992.

There are plenty of used Dakotas around, but they aren't cheap, especially the 2001–2003 models that come with a 7-year powertrain warranty. If you buy outside of these years, plan on spending part of your savings on an extended warranty, preferably one sold by Chrysler. You'll need the extended protection because of the many engine, transmission, and electrical glitches and other mechanical and body failings that can inflate upkeep costs considerably.

1991—A V8 engine became available, 4-cylinder engines got 17 more horses, and the front end was restyled. **1992**—V6 and V8 engines gained 55 and 65 horses, respectively. **1993**—A depowered 4-cylinder engine, optional four-wheel ABS, stainless steel exhaust, and upgraded seat cushions. **1994**—A driver-side airbag and padded knee bolster, side door guard beams, and centre-mounted brakelights. **1995**—A shift interlock and a 4X2 Sport Club Cab debuts. **1996**—A "Magnum" 4-cylinder base engine and an upgraded automatic transmission (no real improvement). **1997**—A slight re-styling, dual airbags, a stiffer frame, and a tighter turning radius for slightly better handling (though ride remains choppy). **1998**—An optional 5.9L V8, de-powered airbags, and airbag off-switches. **2000**—Four full-sized doors (called the Quad Cab) and a new 4.7L V8; the 8-foot bed is gone. **2002**—Arrival of the SXT version, sporting 16-inch wheels and bucket seats. **2003**—Larger tires and an upgraded automatic transmission coupled with the 4.7L V8 and standard four-wheel disc brakes; the puny 4-cylinder engine was dropped. **2004**—Base V6 gets 35 extra horses, while the 4.7L V8 loses five horses. R/T model and its 5.9L V8 are gone.

COST ANALYSIS: Best alternatives: Considering its larger size and more powerful engines, the upgraded 2005 Dakota is the better buy at $23,000+. Save about $10,000 by purchasing a 2003 or 2004 model equipped with a small V8. Shopping in those same model years, you may want to look at a full-sized pickup like the Toyota Tundra or Tacoma, a compact Mazda B Series, or a Nissan Frontier. **Rebates:** $2,500 rebates and zero percent financing. **Delivery/PDI:** $880. **Warranty:** Bumper-to-bumper 3 years/60,000 km; powertrain 7 years/115,000 km; rust perforation 5 years/160,000 km. **Supplementary warranty:** Not needed if you can get the 7-year powertrain warranty. **Options:** Although the V6 is adequate for most light-duty chores, invest in the smaller V8 power plant for best performance and resale value. Four-wheel ABS is a must-have, given the poor braking performance with standard brakes. Remote keyless entry system is also a good idea. It turns on your dome light when pressed, cutting down search time in crowded parking lots. **Depreciation:** A bit slower than average. **Insurance cost:** Above average. **Annual maintenance cost:** Average; easily repaired by independent garages. **Parts supply/cost:** Good parts supply and reasonable cost; easy servicing. **Highway/city fuel economy:** *4X2 and 3.9L:* 10.4–14.8L/100 km; *4X4 and 3.9L:* 11.9–16.3L/100 km; *4X4 and 4.7L:* 11.4–16.5L/100 km; *4X4 and 5.2L:* 13.5–18.5L/100 km.

QUALITY/RELIABILITY: Very poor quality control. Transmission, axle, ball joint, and fuel system problems can take the truck out of service for considerable lengths of time. Fit and finish is below average. **Owner-reported problems:** Complaints target fuel and emissions control systems, transmission, chronic upper ball joint/control arm failures, brakes (premature wear and pulsation), clunks and rattles, and body defects. Other complaints include chronic stalling; excessive engine valve knocking and ticking; a noisy rear end; brake shudder; thunking, erratic-shifting transmission; squeaking ball joints; front wheel wells that have a large gap between where the inner fender ends and the frame starts, allowing water and snow to enter the engine compartment; window fogging; excessive interior noise and shake whenever rear window is opened; fuel tank thud when stopping; and left rear axle thumping noise. **Warranty performance:** Below average. "Goodwill" after-warranty assistance is spotty at best.

SAFETY SUMMARY: 1998–99 Dakotas have a towing capacity of only 907 kg (2,000 lb.) despite the fact that Chrysler's sales literature says they can tow over three times as much—2,903 kg (6,400 lb.). Chrysler Canada officials tell me the higher towing rating was a misprint and all owners who have complained were compensated. **Airbags:** Several reports of airbags failing to deploy and deploying when they shouldn't. **ABS:** Standard 2W; optional 4W. **Traction control:** Optional. **Head restraints F/R:** *1997:* ***; *1998:* ***/**; *1999:* ***; *2001–04:* ***/**. **Visibility F/R:** *****/***.

SAFETY COMPLAINTS: All years: Vehicle fires. • Airbag failures. • Sudden acceleration with cruise control engaged or due to sticking accelerator pedal. • Sudden failure and premature wearout of the upper ball joints. • Vehicle wanders all over the road. • Left in Park, vehicle rolls away on an incline. • Frequent transmission failures and noisy operation (grinds and clunks); it sticks in a lower gear. • ABS failures; pedal went to the floor without stopping vehicle. • Frequent replacement of front brake pads and rotors. **1998—** Windshield wiper falls off. • Instrument panel indicators not visible when headlights used during the day. • Driver-side seat belt locks when pulling across body to latch it; doesn't recoil properly when released. • The seat belt catch is too short, making it difficult to find, especially when the centre console is down. • Steering wheel locked up while driving. • Design of driver's door allows the door to hit windshield, resulting in a stress fracture. • Truck needs heavier shocks. • Wheel flaps pull away from the body of the vehicle. **1998—**Vehicle suddenly lost power and gas leaked out through disconnected fuel line quick connect fitting. • Fuel return line separated and resulting fumes were ignited by the catalytic converter. • An extra wheel stud found in brake system caused brakes to engage at 50 km/h, resulting in an accident and injury. • Seat belts failed to lock up and restrain occupants during a collision. • Front wheelwells have a large gap between the inner fender ends and the frame, allowing water and snow to enter the engine compartment. • High seatback posts to the left and right of windshield obstruct driver's field of vision. • Windshield optical distortions. • Side mirrors attract surface scratches. • Early motor mount rust-out. • Coolant system failure causes vehicle to overheat and lose radiator fluid. • Frequent engine oil leaks. • Chronic fuel pump and ignition system malfunctions. • Faulty powertrain control module (PCM). • Erratic cruise control operation. • When accelerating, transmission fails to fully engage and vehicle doesn't advance as expected. • Chronic drivetrain and rear-end noise, despite having the rear axle replaced three times. • Truck jumps around excessively when not hauling passengers or cargo. • Driver- and passenger-side doors broke while being shut. • Erratic fuel gauge readings.

1999—Reports of several engine fires of unknown origin. • Poor brake performance. • Front-brake lock-up on wet roads. **1999–2000**—Intermittent harsh shifting into Reverse:

A/T – Harsh Reverse Gear Engagement

NUMBER: 21-01-00   GROUP: Transmission   DATE: Feb 4, 2000

OVERVIEW:

This bulletin involves the replacement of the transmission valve body upper housing separator plate and a valve body check ball. In addition, for 2000 M.Y. vehicles equipped with a 46RE transmission this bulletin involves selectively erasing and reprogramming the JTEC Powertrain Control Module (PCM) with new software (calibration change 00Cal13/13A).

MODELS:

2000	(AB)	Ram Van
1999–2000	(AN)	Dakota
1999–2000	(BR/BE)	Ram Truck
2000	(DN)	Durango
1999–2000	(WJ)	Grand Cherokee

SYMPTOM/CONDITION:

The customer may experience a harsh engagement into gear when Reverse is selected. This condition may be intermittent, and may occur more frequently as the transmission fluid warms to normal operating temperatures.

2000—Vehicle caught fire (under hood) at stoplight, believed to be caused by faulty wire. • Another fire, this time started when transmission fluid was pumped out of filler tube onto hot exhaust pipe. • Airbags failed to deploy. • Broken axle caused vehicle to go out of control. • Rear brakes lock up intermittently. • Cruise control failed to disengage. • Goodyear Wrangler tire sidewall defect. • Chronic stalling. • Transmission fluid leaks onto engine. • Transmission jumped into Neutral while vehicle was underway. • Heater core fell off and slipped underneath brake pedal. • Exterior mirrors block visibility. • Seatback collapsed due to weld giving way. **2001**—Vehicle caught on fire while parked. • Several cases of sudden axle failure while vehicle was underway. • Transmission jumps out of gear while cruising. • Windows fog up due to inadequate heater and defroster. • No outside air flows in through the vents. • Poor braking. • Excessive brake pulsation. • Lug nut failure caused wheel to fly off vehicle. • Transmission can be shifted without applying brakes. • Brake release handle is easily broken. **2002**—Wheel bearing failures. • Automatic transmission jumped to Reverse when vehicle was put in Park with the engine running. • Shift lever indicator doesn't always show the correct gear. • Without any warning, transmission will shift from Overdrive to Second gear. • Sometimes driver must step on the brakes to get vehicle to shift. • Vehicle stalls upon acceleration. • Excessive steering-wheel play and steering randomly goes from heavy to light turning assist. • Instrument cluster light fuse blows repeatedly. **2003**—Gear shift lever can be inadvertently knocked out of gear. **2004**—Vehicle rolled over and driver suffocated from airbag or seat belt. • Front wheel fell off due to lack of an upper ball joint bolt. • Defective upper and lower ball joints replaced at owner's expense. • Steering lockup. • Hesitates when accelerating and pops out of gear.

Secret Warranties/Service Tips

1993–2002—Paint delamination, peeling, or fading (see Part Three pages 125–128). **1996**—Chrysler will install a free transmission cold-temperature cooler bypass kit on vehicles operating in temperatures of –20°C or colder. Failure to install this kit could damage the transmission. **1996–98**—Vehicle bucking during wide-open throttle operation may need an upgraded pressure sensor, says TSB #18-19-98. **1997–98**—A clunk or rattle felt in the steering wheel or column during slow turns, rough-road driving, and when braking may indicate the need to replace the intermediate shaft and retorque the bolts. **1997–2000**—A squeaking noise coming from the rear leaf springs can be silenced by replacing the spring tip liners and installing spring cinch clips and isolators. **1997–2003**—Upper and lower ball joints, control arm, and bushing failures. Sometimes, Chrysler offers a 50 percent replacement refund, which doesn't help much when applied to the full retail charge (see Durango "Secret Warranties" on page 185). **1998**—Cold-engine sag or hesitation may require an upgraded PCM (power control module). • TSB #18-34-97 tackles ways to correct an annoying spark knock when the 5.2L engine is warm and under moderate acceleration. **1998–99**—Poor AC performance may require an adjustment of the temperature control cable or replacement of the evaporator under warranty. **2000**—If the central timer module locks up, many of your power-assisted features and lights will malfunction and vehicle may not start. **2001**—Water leaks around the rear window. • Drivetrain noise or vibration. • Service 4X4 light comes on for no reason. • Vehicle may surge with cruise control engaged. • Steering-column popping noise. **2000–03**—Doors lock/unlock on their own. **2001–04**—Water leaks on passenger-side floor:

Passenger Side Floor Water leakage

Bulletin No.: 23-010-04   Date: April 29, 2004
This bulletin involves sealing the opening for the evaporator hose/drain tube with RTV sealer.
2001–04 Dakota
2000–03 Durango
2001–04 Caravan, Voyager, Town & Country.

2002—Automatic transmission filler tube rattle. **2002–03**—Reprogram the JTEC power control module if the truck won't shift out of Second gear when climbing a grade. **2003**—An erratic-shifting automatic transmission may require a re-calibrated powertrain control module (PCM) or transmission control module (TCM). • Customer satisfaction notification regarding the torque converter drainback valve. • Harsh shifts due to a sticking pressure sensor transducer. • Transmission shift/speed control improvements. • Transmission may overheat.

Dakota Profile

	1997	1998	1999	2000	2001	2002	2003	2004
Cost Price ($) (firm)								
4X2 (14%)	16,470	16,795	17,585	18,380	18,780	21,815	21,960	22,675
4X4 (18%)	21,140	21,490	22,295	22,375	27,915	25,670	30,250	—
Used Values ($)								
4X2 ▲	5,000	6,500	8,500	9,500	12,000	15,000	16,500	18,000
4X2 ▼	4,500	5,500	7,000	8,500	10,500	14,000	15,500	17,000
4X4 ▲	6,500	8,000	10,000	12,500	16,500	20,000	22,500	—
4X4 ▼	6,000	6,500	9,000	10,500	15,000	18,500	21,500	—
Reliability	❷	❷	❷	③	③	③	③	③
Crash Safety (F)	④	—	—	—	④	④	③	③
Ext. 4X2	④	④	—	—	—	③	③	—
Quad 4X2	—	—	—	—	—	—	④	—
Side (Ext. 4X2)	—	—	⑤	⑤	⑤	⑤	⑤	⑤
Quad 4X2					—	—	⑤	—
Offset	❶	❶	❶	❶	❶	❶	❶	❶
Rollover (Ext. 4X2)	—	—	—	—	④	④	④	—
Ext. 4X4					③	③	③	—
Quad 4X2	—	—	—	—	—	③	③	—

RAM ★★★★

RATING: *1500 series:* Above Average (2002–05); Average (1986–2001). *2500 and 3500 series:* Average (1986–05). **Strong points:** Average quality buttressed by a better-than-average warranty combined with assertive styling, a high-tech engine, full-time four-wheel drive, roomy cabs with good stowage utility, one of the longest and roomiest cargo boxes available, and a comfortable and well-designed interior with easily accessed and understood instruments and controls. The 1500-series models have better handling, improved steering, and fewer rattles. Other pluses: Powerful Hemi, V8, and V10 engines; reliable Cummins V6 diesel; good trailering capability; a smooth-shifting automatic transmission; and four-door versatility. **Weak points:** The 1500-series engines may be outclassed by Ford and GM power plants, but most carry a stronger warranty; Hemi V8 has had a few quality problems and the 2005's "cylinder deactivation" feature appears ominous; 2500 and 3500 models have been left in the Jurassic Age; 4X4 must be disengaged on dry pavement; outdated mechanical components, like an inconvenient transfer case and a solid front axle that makes for a jittery ride (2500/3500 only); poor V6 acceleration; rear entry/exit is problematic (Club Cab); back seat is rather tight, hard, and too upright; slow steering response; still bouncy over rough spots; controls aren't easy to calibrate; six-foot bed looks stubby; truck sits very high—shorter drivers and passengers will definitely have problems getting into this pickup; high hood hides obstacles from view; very poor fuel economy ties Ford pickups at about 21 km/L (11 mpg). As with Ford and GM trucks, Rams also have a disturbingly large number of safety- and performance-related defects reported to NHTSA. **New for 2005:** No major changes. **Likely failures:** Automatic transmission, suspension (ball joints), steering, fuel system, brakes, and fit and finish. Be wary of front differential damage caused by road debris striking the unprotected differential housing, as recounted by this Drumheller, Alberta owner of a 2003 Dodge Ram 3500:

> The design and strength of the front differential is inadequate when a rock or other objects can cause the gasket to leak out the oil which in turn results in a $7000 repair bill that Chrysler refuses to honour or take any form of responsibility as a possible defect. There should be some type of protection device around the housing for this one ton vehicle. They advertise it as "tuff"!!
>
> Since my vehicle was in the shop another truck came in with the identical problem. I wonder how many others are out there that Chrysler will continue to ignore?

Chrysler has a duty to protect vulnerable parts from forseeable road hazards. That's the logic behind bumpers.

2005 Technical Data

Powertrain (4X2/part-time 4X4)	Box length: 5.0/6.5/8 ft.
Engines: 3.7L V6 (215 hp)	Headroom F/R: 40.2/39.4 in.
• 4.7L V8 (240 hp)	Legroom F/R: 41/31.6 in.
• 5.7L V8 (345 hp)	Wheelbase: 138.7/154.7 in.
• 5.9LD 6-cyl. (215 hp)	Turning circle: 48 ft.
• 5.9L V8 (245 hp)	Passengers: 3/3
• 8.0L V10 (305 hp)	GVWR: 6,010–6,400 lb.
Transmissions: 5-speed man.	Payload: 1,400–1,850 lb.
• 4-speed auto. OD	Tow limit: 7,500 lb.
Dimension/Capacity (1500 4X2/	Ground clear.: 7.5–10.5 in.
4X4 Reg.)	Fuel tank: 98/132L/reg./diesel
Height/length/width:	Weight: 4,550 lb.
71.6/224/79.4 in.	

MODEL HISTORY: Not a spectacular performer, the Dodge Ram is a full-sized pickup that mirrors Ford and GM's truck lineups, with a bit more reliability and warranty protection thrown in. It's sold in 1500, 2500, and 3500 chassis designations (approximate load capacities: Half ton, three-quarter ton, one ton) with Regular Cab, Club Cab, and Chassis Cab configurations. Drivetrains include 4X2 and part-time 4X4 modes hooked to various engine offerings. Ram 3500 models have dual rear wheels.

Front-seat configurations allow for a centre console that can house a laptop computer, cellular phone, CDs, or cassettes. For nature lovers, a rear suspension Camper Package is an option with 2500 and 3500 series models.

The 2004–05 1500-series models come with a 3.7L V6 base engine and optional 4.7L and 5.7L V8s. The latter is called the Hemi, and is sold only with a 5-speed automatic transmission. The V6 and 4.7L V8 offer manual transmission or a 4- or 5-speed automatic, respectively. Automatics include a tow/haul mode for heavy loads.

Chrysler plays the nostalgia card with its 345-hp 5.7L Hemi high performance engine, last seen as an allegedly 425-hp powerhouse offered from 1965 to 1971. At the time it was offered as a $500–$1,100 option in Dodge Coronets and Chargers and Plymouth Belvederes and Satellites. Now the Hemi is an optional engine sold with the 1500 series and heavy-duty Ram pickups and the Dodge 300C/Magnum wagon. Drivers can expect to shave about three seconds off the 1500's 0–100km/h 10.5 seconds time, all the while praying the engine doesn't kill the tranny.

Here are some of the changes the Ram has undergone over the years. **1995**—Debut of the Club Cab equipped with a folding three-place rear bench seat. **1996**—An optional suspension package delivers extra towing and hauling capacity; increased power for the Cummins turbodiesel. **1997**—The 5.9L V8 got a 5-hp boost. **1998**—Launch of the Quad Cab full-sized four-door pickup and a passenger-side airbag with an On-Off switch. **1999**—Insignificant decorative touches. **2000**—Nothing significant. **2001**—Improved steering and an upgraded rear-suspension system. **2002**—Revamped handling and ride comfort. The 1500 models (2500/3500 versions were upgraded in 2003) got more aggressive styling, two new engines, roomier cabs, and optional side airbags. The two-door extended Club Cab was axed, Quad Cabs were given four front-hinged doors, and short-box models gained three inches of cabin length and lost three inches of bed length. The 4X4-equipped Rams got an independent front suspension. **2003**—2500 and 3500 series were revised and given the Hemi 345-hp 5.7L V8 and rack-and-pinion steering. The 1500 series got new wheels. **2004**—An expanded model lineup that includes a Hemi-powered Power Wagon off-roader and the SRT-10 Quad Cab, equipped with the Dodge Viper's 8.3L, 500-hp V10 engine.

These pickups aren't hard to find, though used prices for the first few years tend to be on the high side because young truck buyers are lured to anything with a cab, a bed, and an attitude. Buy extended coverage if Chrysler's base warranty has expired, particularly after the fourth year, when quality control problems multiply. Look for a Ram with running boards because the high step-up makes climbing aboard difficult and the lack of a third door complicates rear-seat access. Take a high-speed test-drive to see if you can handle the vehicle's wandering nature.

COST ANALYSIS: Best alternatives: With Chrysler holding the line on 2005 prices at $24,000 and $27,000 for the base 1500 and Quad Cab, you'd be better off with a 2005. Alternative pickups: A Toyota Tundra or a Nissan Frontier. **Rebates:** $3,000 rebates, plus zero percent financing. **Delivery/PDI:** $995. **Warranty:** Bumper-to-bumper 3 years/60,000 km; powertrain 7 years/ 115,000 km; rust perforation 5 years/160,000 km. **Supplementary warranty:** A good idea, see above. **Options:** Some options worth considering are power windows/locks, a transmission/oil cooler, and running boards. The 20- and 22-inch wheels degrade ride comfort. **Depreciation:** Slower than average. **Insurance cost:** Higher than average. **Annual maintenance cost:** Average. The powertrain warranty has kept repair costs down. **Parts supply/cost:** Good supply. Reasonable cost. No Hemi data yet. **Highway/city fuel economy:** *4X2 and 3.9L:* 11–15.9L/100 km; *4X4 and 5.2L:* 13.1–18.9L/100 km. New engines haven't been rated.

QUALITY/RELIABILITY: Below average quality and reliability. Powertrain, suspension, steering, brake, electrical, fuel-system components, and fit and finish are still not top quality. Hemi engines have had a problem with broken valve springs and rear main seal leaks. The Cummins diesel engine has performed exceptionally well. Some downtime due to automatic transmission malfunctions and breakdowns; not as severe as the Dakota or Ford F-Series, though. **Owner-reported problems:** Owners report chronic automatic transmission, electrical, ignition, engine cooling system, steering, suspension, fuel, brake, and body problems for all years. Cold or wet weather doesn't agree with these trucks, either—generating lots of reports of chronic hard starting and stalling, even when the engine is warm. Chrysler has done little to deal with this basic flaw, which has been a generic Chrysler problem for decades. The ignition system on 1993–96 models earns low reliability marks as well. There have been some reports of misaligned drivelines leading to excessive vibration and prematurely worn clutches. The body is squeak- and rattle-prone, water and air leaks are common, and rust tends to start fairly early.

Other owner-reported problems: Electrical fire at the power dispersement box under the hood; accelerator pedal jams while backing up; sudden transmission failure; poorly performing brakes must be adjusted at every oil change; premature (5,000 km) wearout of the rear-brake hubs and front-brake pads; complete ABS brake failure; weak stabilizer bar is easily bent when passing over potholes; lack of an anti-sway bar on the rear axle in the trailer towing package means excessive swaying causing steering instability; some trailer hitches are cracked; obstructive rear door latching mechanism prevents easy access to the rear seat; fragile right front ball joints; excessive vibration when approaching 100 km/h; very loose steering allows vehicle to wander all over the roadway; faulty steering gearbox; defective steering pump causes loss of steering control; truck changes lanes even though steering wheel isn't turned; constant pulling to the right on the highway; inadequate cooling due to AC freeze-up; odour coming from the AC ducts; oil filter adapter plate and speed sensor oil seepage; clunk or rattle felt in steering wheel after running over a rough surface; front disc brake noise on the 3500 series; clunking or rattling noise from the front suspension; ringing noise from the rear of the vehicle; excessive shimmy after hitting a bump or pothole; shudder when pulling away from a stop when near maximum GVWR; absence of a baffle in the fuel tank allows gas to slam forward and back in the tank, subjecting connections to stress and early failure; ignition fuse link blows intermittently, shutting down the vehicle; lapbelt rides too high on the abdomen and shoulder belts lie too close to neck and jaw. **Warranty performance:** Average. "Goodwill" payouts have no rhyme nor reason, but track in the 50 percent range with threat of small claims action to about 75 percent just prior to mediation/trial.

ROAD PERFORMANCE: Acceleration/torque: Owners report the Hemi has trouble getting up to speed, requiring a lot of throttle. Hill climbing is poor until the engine hits the higher rpms at nearly full throttle. Once the Hemi finds its sweet spot it does well, but towing at high rpms cuts considerably into fuel economy. The Cummins Turbo Diesel won't break any speed records, either, but it will haul just about anything when hooked to the 5-speed manual transmission. The 3.7L V6 is smooth and acceptable for light chores but the 4.7L V8 gives you the reserve power needed for heavier work. The 5.9L V8 is the engine of choice for hauling or towing anything weighing more than 1,800 kg (4,000 lb.). Shifting into 4X4 is done via a hard-to-reach floor lever; however, the 2002 and later 1500 offers an optional dashboard-mounted switch. Unlike GM's Silverado and Sierra, the 4X4 system can't be used on dry pavement. **Transmission:** The 4-speed automatic transmission shifts smoothly when it's working right. **Steering:** Vague and slow to respond. Excessive steering wander on Quad Cabs and extended cabs. **Routine handling:** The Ram's performance, ride, and handling are more trucklike than its Ford or GM rivals. The ride can be especially rough without a full load in back. **Emergency handling:** Although the 2002 1500 series rides well, other Rams are quite jittery on the highway (thanks to an antiquated solid front axle) and ponderous in their handling. They also have a lower ground clearance than their rivals. Rapid cornering isn't advisable due to excessive rear-end sway. **Braking:** Not impressive, in spite of rear-wheel ABS (100–0 km/h: 45m [147 ft.]). Some fading after repeated application.

SAFETY SUMMARY: A child safety seat can fit in the rear centre seat if an extended belt is used. Most early Dodge trucks won't have head restraints. **Airbags:** Many complaints of airbags failing to deploy or deploying when they shouldn't. **ABS:** Standard 2W; optional 4W; disc/drum. **Head restraints F/R:** *1997: *; 1999: **/*; 2001: *; 2002–04: ***/**.* **Visibility F/R:** ******.* **Maximum load capacity:** *1999 SLT 5.2L:* 574 kg (1,265 lb).

SAFETY COMPLAINTS: All years: Sudden acceleration. • Chronic stalling. • Airbags fails to deploy. • Airbag warning light frequently comes on. • Repeated ABS failures; pedal goes to floor without any braking effect. • Severe pull to the side when braking. • Warped rotors and worn out brake pads. • When parked, vehicle rolls down an incline. • Frequent transmission failures and fluid leaks. • Overdrive engages poorly in cold weather. • Vehicle wanders excessively at highway speeds; loose steering makes for imprecise corrections. • Steering wander is especially severe with diesel-equipped vehicles. • Vehicle sways and tilts when underway. **1997**—Many reports of fires with different causes, including an electrical short in the wiring that attaches to the brake lights; insulation on firewall cab and material close to exhaust pipe may ignite; the exhaust manifold heat melts the plastic tube that connects the clutch master cylinder to the clutch slave cylinder; overheated transmission fluid; and a cracked fuel rail that sprays fuel onto the firewall and engine. • Left rear dual wheel fell off vehicle due to bolt failure. • Other reports of wheel studs breaking off. • Left front wheel fell off due to connecting rod failure. • Sudden tire failure; tires ballooning in spots. • Vehicle pulls sharply to the side when the brakes are applied. • Sudden steering and brake failure. • Power-steering pump failures. • Broken throttle control rod causes engine to suddenly drop to idle. • Steering box failure. • Transmission slips into Neutral at highway speeds. • Transmission cooler quick connect failed, preventing engagement of 4X4. • Headlights flicker. • Dome light comes on when backing up, ruining night vision. • Lower splash guards needed for rear wheels to protect emissions canister from road debris and to protect rocker panels from severe damage. • Defective driver's door causes windshield to buckle up from the pressure exerted by the door. • Rear passenger fender discolours due to diesel exhaust fluid leak. • Hood flew up, cracking the windshield. • Driver-side rear-view mirror vibrates excessively. • Front windshield moulding melted. • Radio destroys cassette tapes. • Front seatbacks collapsed in a collision. • Seat belts are uncomfortably tight. • Fuel gauge reads empty with warning light on when the tank is 80 percent full. • Ice blocks windshield wiper blade whenever it snows. • At speeds of 70–90 km/h, windshield wipers fail to clean the windshield. • Location of cupholder allows liquid to spill into cab module, causing various component failures. **1998**—Vehicle suddenly accelerated when cruise control was engaged. • Severe pulling to one side when brakes are applied. • Mirror distorts images. • Seat belt solenoid short causes the passenger-side seat belt to lock up. • Michelin LTX side wall cracks. • Windshield wiper assembly failure caused the wiper arm assembly to pop off. • Horn is hard to activate. **1999**—Transmission suddenly jumps into Neutral (transmission shift sensor suspected). • Power-steering binding or lock-up. • Seat belt buckle won't latch. **2000**—The speed control fails to keep an even speed, and the automatic transmission is always "gear hunting." • Brakes don't stop the vehicle, require constant and expensive maintenance. • When braking, vehicle pulls violently to the side. • Power-steering and rear-wheel brake drum failures. • Michelin LTX tread separation. **2001**—Many reports of electrical shorts causing under-hood fires. • Fuse box caught fire because battery cable wasn't properly installed at the factory. • Evaporator canister, power-steering box and hose, and seat belt retractor failures. • Power-steering line blew out. • Brake-pad rivets come loose; and rear brake light fuses keep blowing. • Excessive crankcase oil vapours enter the passenger compartment. • Front suspension bottoms out on speed bumps. • Excessive vibration of side mirrors. • Rear window shattered. **2002**—Front end jumps from side to side when vehicle passes over uneven pavement or easily hydroplanes when passing over wet roads. • Bed may damage the cab. • Premature brake master cylinder failure. • Differential and rear axle bearing failed prematurely. • Automatic transmission stuck in Reverse. • Loose side-mounted rear-view mirrors. **2003**—Accelerator pedal fell off. • Stalling and hard starting. • Front suspension collapse. • Automatic transmission won't shift into Reverse. • Lowered tailgate falls onto the roadway when vehicle goes over a bump. **2003–04**—Ram 2500 and Ram 3500 pickups with automatic transmissions might roll backward when shifted into the Park position. NHTSA says 42 crashes and three injuries have been linked to the problem. **2004**—Fire ignited in the driver-side rear wheel well. • Brake lockup. • Sudden stalling while cruising. • Stalling Hemi engine (EGR valve on national backorder). • Excessive on-road vibration. • Erratic reading on odometer and speedometer after water gets into the wiring harness. • Wheel bearing failure. • Rear axle broke. • Coolant cap leaks. • Horn failure. • Headlight high beams aren't bright enough.

Secret Warranties/Service Tips

1993–2002—Paint delamination, peeling, or fading (see Part Three). **1994–98**—Left or right drifting when applying the brakes can be fixed by installing a wheel shim kit (#4856419). • TSB #18-29-95 gives an excellent summary of the causes and remedies for loss of power with the Cummins diesel engine and automatic transmission. • Excessive shimmying after hitting a pothole or passing over a bump can be corrected by replacing the steering damper and track bar. You may also have to add an auxiliary steering damper. • An oil canning noise coming from the box area can be silenced by installing isolators on two cargo box crossmember rails. **1994–99**—Engine knocking and high oil consumption may be caused by an intake manifold pan gasket oil leak. Stand fast for a refund of repair costs up to 7 years/160,000 km:

Engine – Spark Knock/Oil Consumption

NUMBER: 09-05-00   GROUP: Engine   DATE: Feb. 25, 2000
MODELS:

1994–99	(AB)	Ram Van
1994–99	(AN)	Dakota
1994–99	(BR/BE)	Ram Truck
1998–99	(DN)	Durango
1994–98	(ZJ)	Grand Cherokee
1996–98	(ZG)	Grand Cherokee

SUBJECT: Spark Knock and Engine Oil Consumption due to Intake Manifold Pan Gasket Oil Leak

OVERVIEW: This bulletin involves the replacement of the engine intake manifold plenum pan gasket.

Accelerated front and rear brake lining wear can be controlled by installing countermeasure linings developed to prevent early wearout. • A squeaking noise coming from the rear leaf springs can be silenced by replacing the spring tip liners and installing spring cinch clips and isolators. **1994–2000**—A rattle from the door area may be corrected by installing a revised window channel. **1994–2001**—If a higher-than-normal steering wheel movement is required to keep the vehicle from wandering (vehicle slow to respond to normal steering wheel input), then perform the Over-Centre Adjustment Repair Procedure. • Many 4X4 Rams with several years of hard use are developing steering wander due to worn track bars. To check a track bar, start the engine and observe the ends of the track bar while someone saws the wheel from side to side. Any movement at either end of the track bar indicates that the track bar is bad. If play is observed, replace the track bar. **1996–98**—Vehicle bucking during wide-open throttle operation may need an upgraded pressure sensor, according to TSB #18-19-98. **1997–2000**—A squeaking, creaking steering column likely needs a new lock housing and attaching screws. **1997–2002**—A power-steering hissing may only require replacing the power-steering hoses. **1998**—Cold-engine sag or hesitation may require an upgraded PCM (power control module). • TSB #18-34-97 tackles ways to correct an annoying spark knock when the 5.2L engine is warm and under moderate acceleration. • Troubleshooting tips for a sliding rear window that may be difficult to open, will not latch, or leaks water past the sliding rear window's lower run channel. • TSB #23-68-97 shows how to stop water from leaking through the side cowl panel. **1998–99**—A knocking or tapping noise coming from the engine compartment may be corrected by replacing the duty cycle purge valve bracket. **1999–2001**—Erratic engine operation:

Surge/Lack of Power in Third Gear/Erratic Shifts

NUMBER: 18-006-02 REV. C   DATE: June 3, 2002

OVERVIEW: This bulletin involves selectively erasing and reprogramming the JTEC Powertrain Control Module (PCM) with new software.

MODELS: 1999–2001 (BE/BR) Ram Trucks equipped with a 5.2L, 5.9L, or 8.0L engine.

SYMPTOM/CONDITION: Some vehicles may exhibit one or more of the following performance conditions:

1. Perceived lack of power in Third gear due to converter lock-up in Third gear. This reprogramming eliminates Third gear lock-up.

2. Surge after lock-up (40–45 mph) in Fourth gear. This reprogramming raises torque converter lock-up speed to 52 mph

3. Transmission does not upshift from Third gear after a 4–3 downshift. (Most often noticed when cruise control is engaged.)

POLICY: Reimbursable within the provisions of the warranty.

2000–02—Doors lock/unlock on their own. **2001**—Engine may not crank, due to a blown starter relay circuit fuse. • Engine cranks but won't start, or starts and stalls. • Low fuel output from the transfer pump may be the cause of hard starts or no-starts. • Vehicles used for extended heavy trailering may experience a loss of exhaust manifold bolt torque. • Troubleshooting tips for complaints of poor diesel engine performance. • Low engine power when transmission is in Overdrive. • Harsh transmission engagement when the torque converter clutch is applied. • Remedy for steering wander (1500 series). • Rear may sit too high to attach a fifth wheel. • Spark knock when accelerating. • Rear leaf spring clicking, squeaking noise. • Tie-rod adjusting sleeve slot may be the source of a high-pitched whistle. • Tapping or knocking during idle. **2001–04**—Water leaks on passenger-side floor (see Dakota "Service Tips"). **2002**—Hard starts and idle speed fluctuation in cold weather. • Inoperative tachometer. • Faulty oil pressure gauge. • Oil pan gasket leaks. • Water leak at grab handle. • Hood distortion and low spots. • Seat rocking movement when accelerating. **2002–04**—Water leaks at grab handle. **2003**—

Low start-up oil pressure with the Hemi engine requires the replacement of the oil pump pick up tube. • Brake vibration or shudder requires the replacement of many major brake components, says bulletin No.: 05-008-03, published November 28, 2003. • An erratic-shifting automatic transmission may require a re-calibrated powertrain control module (PCM) or transmission control module (TCM). • Instrument panel whistle. • Poor idle and coasting. • Lack of air from floor vents. • Buzzing, vibration from front of vehicle. **2003–04**—Loose, rattling bug deflector. **2004**—Poor sound quality from Infinity speakers.

Ram Profile

	1997	1998	1999	2000	2001	2002	2003	2004
Cost Price ($) (negotiable)								
D-150, 1500 (17%)	17,190	18,890	20,345	20,630	18,750	23,255	23,865	24,910
Quad Cab (18%)	—	26,375	27,250	27,595	27,280	27,280	26,900	—
SRT-10 (20%)	—	—	—	—	—	—	—	61,000
Used Values ($)								
D-150, 1500 ▲	6,500	8,000	10,500	12,000	14,000	15,000	18,000	21,000
D-150, 1500 ▼	5,500	7,000	9,500	11,000	12,500	13,500	17,000	19,500
Quad Cab ▲	—	12,000	13,500	15,500	17,000	19,500	22,000	—
Quad Cab ▼	—	9,500	12,000	14,000	16,000	18,000	21,000	—
SRT-10 ▲	—	—	—	—	—	—	—	54,000
SRT-10 ▼	—	—	—	—	—	—	—	51,000
Reliability	❷	❷	❷	❷	❷	③	③	③
Crash Safety (F)	⑤	—	—	—	⑤	④	④	⑤
Ext. cab	④	④	④	④	④	—	—	—
Quad cab	④	④	③	③	④	—	—	—
Side	—	—	⑤	⑤	—	—	—	③
Quad Cab	—	—	—	—	—	④	⑤	③
Offset	—	❶	❶	❶	❶	⑤	⑤	⑤
Rollover	—	❶	❶	❶	③	③	⑤	③

Ford

F-SERIES ★

RATING: *F-150:* Below Average (1990–2005); Ford's two redesigns have been tested and been found wanting. The F-Series trucks are versatile and brawny haulers, with much-improved handling incorporated into the 1996 model's redesign. On the other hand, quality control remains abysmally poor. Over the past decade, I've seen a dramatic increase in owner complaints relating to poor-quality powertrain components and serious safety-related defects that include sudden tie-rod separation, torsion bar failures, unintended acceleration, and the complete loss of braking. Service bulletins reinforce the fact that these trucks aren't well made. **Strong points:** Good choice of powerful V8 engines, easy and predictable handling, pleasant ride on bad roads, well-thought-out ergonomics, instruments, and controls, and fourth-door access. With a few exceptions (like tacky cloth seats), base models are nicely appointed, with lots of handy convenience features and a classy interior. Commanding view of the road, lots of cab space, and excellent interior ergonomics. Front bench holds three in relative comfort, though there's insufficient footroom for the front centre passenger. One of the quietest pickups available. **Weak points:** Needs to lose weight. Underpowered base V6 engine and 4.6L V8 doesn't have sufficient passing power; questionable engine, transmission, suspension/steering and brake performance and reliability; poor braking performance with four-wheel ABS; and an uncomfortable rear seat. Climate control system is a bit slow in warming up the cabin. There's no left-foot rest and the cramped and upright rear seats can't match GM for comfort. Cargo flexibility compromised by second row layout. An inordinate number of serious safety-related complaints have been collected by NHTSA with tie-rod end, front torsion bar failures, and steering vibration and drivetrain shudder heading the list. Warranty payouts have been unacceptably Scrooge-like in the past and fuel economy is astoundingly poor. **New for 2005:** No major changes.

2005 Technical Data

Powertrain (rear-drive or 4X4)
Engines: F-150: 4.2L V6 (202 hp)
• 4.6L V8 (231 hp)
• 5.4L V8 (235 hp)
F-250, F-350, etc.: 4.2L V6 (220 hp)
• 5.4L V8 (260 hp)
• 5.4L V8 (300 hp)
• 6.8L V10 (275)
• 6.0L V8 diesel (325)
• 7.3L V8 diesel (275 hp)
Transmissions: 5-speed man.
• 4-speed auto. OD

Dimension/Capacity (F-150)
Height/length/width:
72.8/220.8/78.4 in.
Box length: 6.5/8.0 ft.
Headroom F/R: 40.8/37.8 in.
Legroom F/R: 40.9/32.2 in.
Wheelbase: 138.5/157.1 in.
Passengers: 3/3
GVWR: 6,050–10,000 lb.
Payload: 1,950 lb.
Tow limit: 2,000–21,800 lb.
Ground clear.: 6.8 in.
Fuel tank: 131L/reg./diesel
Weight: 4,050 lb.

MODEL HISTORY: For almost a decade, Ford coasted on its past glories when it and GM were the only pickup game in town. Now, Chrysler, Nissan, and Toyota are all eating into its market share. Buyers are clamouring for more versatile and reliable trucks that mix hi-tech with dependability (or, in Chrysler's case, a better base warranty). Unfortunately, Ford's latest F-Series 2004 revamp has failed to catch on with buyers who are snapping up Dodge Ram, GM Silverado/Sierra, Nissan Titan, and Toyota Tundra pickups, forcing Ford to pay huge incentive bribes to buyers.

The most obvious changes on the 2004–05s are the F-Series' new angular styling, four-door configuration (a first for entry-level trucks); a bigger, quieter cab; a bed box that is 2-1/2 inches deeper; and an upgraded interior. Ride comfort is improved by a roomier interior and new rear suspension. SuperCab models gained half a foot in cab length, and larger rear doors and entry/exit handles. Other nice touches: A power-sliding rear window controlled by a button on the overhead console, power rear side windows, and an easier-to-lift tailgate that houses a torsion bar assist mechanism built into the tailgate.

Adding to the truck's performance are a stiffer frame, better shock absorber placement, rack-and-pinion steering, and a double wishbone design front suspension with coil-over shocks. Drivers will notice there's less "skipping" on washboard roads, less bounce, and great cornering, thanks to the 17-inch tires and larger leaf springs that reduce sway and enhance towing stability.

The Ford 4.2L V6 is rated better in fuel mileage than the 4.6L V8, but the V8 gets better mileage in the real world. The V6 also was known for oil pump problems and has been dropped from the reworked F-150. A new 300-hp 5.4L V8 engine, known for early-production glitches, was added. It features three valves per cylinder, variable-cam timing, and electronic throttle control that dealer mechanics are still trying to master.

The new F-150 allows you to ease down the steepest inclines in First gear without the need to ride the brakes, though overall braking has been improved as well. Fully vented four-wheel disc brakes with ABS and Electronic Brake Force Distibution (a system that varies braking according to perceived load) provides extremely smooth and predictable braking with little fade and no sudden jolts like we've felt with GM. Their complexity, however, could mean costly repairs later on.

Safety features have been augmented to include multi-stage front airbags, a sensor to determine if the front passenger seat is empty, five three-point seat belts with the front shoulder belts integrated into the seats, and a LATCH (lower anchors and tethers for children) system to facilitate the installation of child safety seats.

Pre-2004 models

The F-150 is Ford's base model, followed by the 250, 250 Heavy Duty, 350, and F-Super Duty. For 2001, the Super Duty F-650 Super CrewZer debuted as Ford's medium-duty pickup, aimed at the horse-trailering crowd. All versions are available with rear-wheel or 4X4 drive. A wide variety of wheelbase and box lengths is available.

There's a wide range of engines, making the F-Series a very versatile truck. The standard engine for the pre-2004 and Heritage F-150 is a 4.2L V6 power plant borrowed from the Windstar; two Triton V8s, based on a Lincoln engine; and a 7.3L diesel engine. A 5-speed manual transmission, a 6.8L V10, and a 4-speed electronically controlled automatic transmission are also likely to be found on these carried-over models.

For light-duty use, stick to the F-150 for the best combination of a tolerable ride, decent handling, and good load capacity. Various combinations of extended cabs and longer cargo boxes are available in all years, including the more heavy-duty F-250 and F-350 models. Keep in mind, however, that ride and handling suffer as size and weight increase.

Most of the engines have not changed radically for over 15 years. The basic

4.9L 6-cylinder engine, used through the 1996 model year, is a good, economical, light-duty power plant, understood by most dealer and independent mechanics. If you need more power, go directly to the small V8.

Transmission choices for these vehicles run the gamut from a primitive but sturdy 3-speed manual to the trouble-prone 4-speed automatic and 4- and 5-speed manuals. The 4X4 versions have been available since 1986.

Here's a short summary of model year changes over the past ten years. **1995**—Arrival of the 7.3L diesel engine. **1997**—The truck-buying public wasn't enthralled with the 1997 model's new design; buyers complain there's nothing really distinctive about the re-styling and quality deficiencies weren't seriously addressed. **1999**—A re-styled front end, upgraded front seats, and the arrival of a four-door SuperCab. **2001**—The F-150 Crew Cab debuted with four full-sized doors and a full rear passenger compartment; the 4.6L V8 gained 20 additional horses; the F-250 and F-350 got a horsepower upgrade for the 7.3L Power Stroke turbodiesel engine; the Trailer Tow package became standard on all models, as did four-wheel ABS; the Lightning got a slight increase in power and a shorter final drive ratio. **2002**—The midyear return of the Harley-Davidson Edition; SuperCrew models came with 20-inch wheels and special trim; the 260-hp 5.4L V8 was joined by a 340-hp supercharged variant. **2003**—Lightning models received a stiffer rear suspension to support a 635 kg (1,400 lb.) payload. **2004**—An entirely new model.

Hauling capacity, interior comfort, and handling vary greatly depending on the model chosen. Although a bit rough-riding, the half-ton suspension should serve well for most purposes. Early models had poor front-rear brake balance when carrying a light load, so when rear ABS was added in 1987, it was hailed as a much-needed improvement. The euphoria was short-lived, however; owners soon complained that the ABS locked up on wet roads and was failure prone. These same braking problems have continued to the 2004 models.

COST ANALYSIS: The 2005 F-150 XL sells for $27,500, which is only a few hundred more than last year's price. Since there's no real difference, choose a second-series 2004, if it's discounted sufficiently (about 20 percent). **Best alternatives:** Mazda, Nissan, and Toyota make pickups that are a lot more reliable and safer. Incidentally, the base Toyota pickups' used prices are very competitive after a few years on the market (see Tacoma section). **Rebates:** Look for a "take no prisoners" rebate war as GM fights to maintain its pickup gains. Chrysler and Ford will likely counter with $3,000 rebates and zero percent financing well into 2005. **Delivery/PDI:** $1,025. **Warranty:** Bumper-to-bumper 3 years/60,000 km; rust perforation 5 years/unlimited km. **Supplementary warranty:** An extended powertrain warranty figured into the base price is a must to counter Ford's poor quality control. **Options:** Get the small 4.6L 231-hp V8 engine or you'll be kicking yourself for getting stuck with the anemic V6. Other options you should consider: Four-wheel ABS (standard with most 2004 F-150s), remote keyless entry, and a heavy-duty battery. Short drivers may require the optional power seat with height adjustment, running boards, and extended pedals to get away from the airbag's explosive deployment. Parking-distance beeper is a waste of money. **Depreciation:**

Average. **Insurance cost:** Higher than average. **Parts supply/cost:** Parts are generally widely available from independent suppliers and of average cost, however, this may not be true for the 2004 redesigned versions. **Annual maintenance cost:** Higher than average; easily repaired by independent garages. **Highway/city fuel economy:** Very poor, real world fuel economy hovers around 21 L/100 km (11 mpg)—equal to the Dodge Ram. *4X2 and 4.2L:* 11.1–15.1L/100 km; *4X2 and 4.6L:* 11.3–16.2L/100 km; *4X2 and 5.4L:* 12.3–17.4L/100 km; *4X4 and 4.2L:* 12.2–15.9L/100 km; *4X4 and 4.6L:* 12.9–17.4L/100 km; *4X4 and 5.4L:* 13.6–18.6L/100 km.

QUALITY/RELIABILITY: Terrible. It's interesting how Chrysler, Ford, and GM trucks have similar patterns of powertrain, suspension, and brake failures. Could it be because they use the same suppliers and cost-cutters pirated from each other? Apparently, Ford's '96 and 2004 redesigns created more bugs than they fixed. In fact, the company's new flagship 6.0L diesel engines introduced in December 2003 were so badly flawed that Ford had to initiate a service program to fix them and buy back over 500 trucks. Their problems included a rough idle, loss of power, stalling, excessive exhaust smoke, leaky fuel injectors, high fuel consumption, and engine seizures. Ford says the engines are fine now, but there are many skeptics. Another serious defect afflicting 1996–2004 models that's likely to gain national attention soon is collapsing tie-rods/torsion bars in the steering/suspension system that throw the truck out of control when they fail. Ford has sent a letter to owners asking them to *please* have their vehicles inspected and repaired, at their own cost, of course (sigh, another example of Ford's crappy customer relations attitude). **Owner-reported problems:** Engine and automatic transmission breakdowns top the list. Owners report failure-prone engine gaskets (covered by a number of special warranty extensions—see "Secret Warranties/Service Tips"), timing belt tensioners, oil pumps, fuel and ignition systems, driveline (principally clutches); poor-quality front and rear brake components that include premature pad and caliper replacement and chronic rotor warping (also covered by a secret warranty—see Part Three); faulty powertrain control modules that cause sudden stalling at full throttle; excessive vibration felt throughout the vehicle; a lack of sufficient support in the driver's seat; and front suspension and steering problems. There are also body defects, including door cracks on 1997–2000 models covered in Ford SSM 12071 (*www.F150online.com/articles/cracks.html*) and confirmed by internal bulletins supplied by ALLDATA. Ford may replace the door or install a reinforced plate. Careful checking of frame rails and underbody panels is a must on older trucks. Dealers and owners alike report that late-model Ford trucks and sport-utilities are equipped with defective torsion bars, which usually fail while the vehicles are being driven, resulting in loss of vehicle control. Additionally, owner complaints target FX-15 air conditioner compressors; fuel and electrical systems; brakes; premature catalytic converter failure; and poor-quality fit and finish:

> My father purchased a 2003 model F-350 dually last fall for his new ranch truck. This spring when the frost came out of the roads (35 km of gravel) the dirt/mud stuck to the inner plastic fenders and both of

them were damaged.... There are a lot of these dually trucks in that area (Fort St. John, B.C.) and the body shop has said many that drive on the dirt roads have this problem.

Other complaints include excessive vibration and shaking at idle and at cruising speed; noisy steering and suspension; rear-end rattles; exhaust system leaks; loose manifold air intake hoses; transmission rear seal and bushing leaks, squealing, and humming; drive shaft clunks when accelerating or decelerating; excessive brake pedal pulsation when brakes are applied; and front shocks that leak oil. The 2001 models are particularly plagued by engine and rear-end failures. **Warranty performance:** Way below average. While reports of safety- and performance-related defects have soared, Ford's customer relations performance has soured.

SAFETY SUMMARY: 1997–2000 model year F-150, F-250 and Blackwood pickups are part of an Ontario class-action petition alleging faulty door latches (*www.willbarristers.com*). Earlier Ford pickups don't have head restraints. **Airbags:** A number of incidents where the airbags deployed without cause. **ABS:** Standard 2W; optional 4W. **Head restraints F/R:** *1997: *; 1999: **/*; 2001: ***/**; 2002–04: **/*; 2004: *****. 1999 and 2001 F-250: **; 2002–04 F-250: ***/*; 2002–04 F-350: ****. Lack of rear-seat head restraints on early production 2001s. **Visibility F/R:** *****. **Maximum load capacity:** *1999 F-150 XLT 5.4L: 585 kn (1,290 lb.).*

SAFETY COMPLAINTS: All years: Tie-rod and front torsion bar failures sending the truck out of control. • Sudden acceleration. • Sticking accelerator pedal. • Chronic stalling. • Airbag malfunctions. • Wheel lug nut failures. • Firestone and Goodrich tire tread separation. **1997**—Fire ignited in wiring harness. • Fire ignited underneath the truck between the cab and bed. • Fuel leak in engine compartment. • Fuel cut-off switch didn't work after collision. • Exhaust pipe location allows carbon monoxide to enter cabin. • Cruise control wouldn't disengage. • Throttle stuck wide open when piece of insulation lodged in the throttle linkage. • Driver-side and rear window exploded while driving. • Repeated ABS failures. • Brake pedal goes to floor while in idle. • Master cylinder failures. • Steering gearbox bolts pulled out. • Dangerously loose steering and excessive steering wheel vibrations. • Frequent tire blowouts. • Wheels split where they are joined, causing tire failure. • Stabilizer bar failure caused vehicle to collapse on its front tires. • Rear passenger-side wheel broke off the shaft. • Control arm rusted/cracked, causing left front wheel to break loose. • Aluminum wheels hold ice in winter, causing them to be unbalanced. • Wheel lugs break when anti-theft locking lug is torqued to specification (100 pound-feet). • Wheel lug bolts broke off while driving. • Many reports that vehicle rolled downhill with parking brake engaged. • Transmission sticks in Neutral. • Transmission seal leak. • Struts suddenly broke off axle, causing loss of tire and control. • Driver-side shoulder belt tightens progressively or won't stay locked in place. • Seat latch broke after car was rear-ended. • Bed seams not sealed, inviting premature corrosion damage. **1998**—Frequent failure of the engine idle pulley and serpentine belt, causing loss of control. • Passenger

was blinded by airbag deployment. • Gas rail leaks fuel onto the engine manifold. • ABS failures, resulting in complete loss of braking or extended stopping
distance. • Front-end stabilizer broke, causing loss of steering control. •
Steering shaft failure; front steering system fell from truck, causing loss of control and collision. • While vehicle was travelling at 100 km/h, both the
front-wheel bearing and drive shaft suddenly seized. • Frequent automatic
transmission failures, resulting in accidents. • Owner reports that the rod that
connects the axle to the transmission fell off. • Harsh, noisy transmission
shifting. • Excessive vibration makes the truck difficult to control at highway
speeds. • Rear end jumps about and is hard to control when driving over
bumpy surfaces. • On the extended cab, where the bench seats are located, the
rear windshield latch struck a child's head when going over a bumpy road. •
Spare tire cable broke, allowing the tire to fall from the vehicle. • Fumes enter
the interior when the defroster and heater are engaged. • Electrical shorts
caused by water leaking into the interior and engine compartment. • Doors
don't shut properly. • Frequent reports that the side windows suddenly explode
for unknown reasons. • Power-door lock failures. • Rear window seal leaks. •
Arm rest containing cupholder may suddenly flip up if the driver leans on its
rear portion. • Loose mounting bolt renders seat belt retractor inoperative. •
Rear seat belts aren't compatible with the safe installation of a child safety seat.
1999—Cruise control fails to disengage. • Brakes fail. • Engine gasket failures.
• Broken spare tire cable lets tire fall on highway. • Driver-side door cracks
just above window line (dealer replaced door). • Horn difficult to activate due
to small area that must be depressed. • Rear side window leaks. **2000**—Other
incidents of sudden, unintended acceleration in a variety of situations. •
Chronic stalling.

> I have a 2000 Ford F-150 pickup and the airbag restraint system ran-
> domly deactivates while driving. The problem corrects itself when the
> vehicle is restarted so it is difficult for the dealer to detect a problem
> although a code is flashed when this happens. The truck has been in
> for this problem 11 times and is currently at the Ford plant in Oakville
> for further investigation of the problem.

• Driver's face was burned when airbags deployed and gases caught on fire. •
Steering loss due to shearing of the sector shaft. • Loss of brakes caused by prematurely worn calipers and pads. • Truck parked with emergency brake set
rolled down incline. • Transmission torque converter may lock up without
warning. • Halogen lights look like high beams to other drivers. • Metal cable
broke, allowing spare tire to fall on the highway. • Left rear tire flew off truck.
• Radio heats up to point where tapes can melt. • Windows suddenly shatter
for no reason. **2001**—An incredible number of complaints have been registered by NHTSA. Owners cite most of the above defects, plus a host of new
safety-related failures. • A golf cart bumped the truck while it was parked and
it rolled about 15 feet. • Suspension is not strong enough for the rated towing
capacity. • On early production 2001s, rear seat doesn't have head restraints,

allowing passenger's head to hit the back window. • Frequent automatic transmission failures. • Driver's seat belt buckle won't fasten. • Sudden brake loss. • While parked on an incline, truck rolled away. **2001–02**—High seats positioned so that driver stares into the coloured top part of the windshield and inside rear-view mirror blocks forward visibility. **2002**—Fire ignited under the power-adjusted seat mechanism. • Automatic transmission slips in Reverse or downshifts; jerks when vehicle accelerates. • Headlights and dash lights fail intermittently. • Small wheel hubs cause vehicle to vibrate excessively. • Water leaks into the interior. • Speedometer often falls to zero. • Side window suddenly shattered while underway. **2003**—Faulty EGR valve causes throttle to stick wide open and brakes to fail. • Automatic transmission slippage and leakage. • Rear axle failure; wheel came off. • Left front wheel separated and truck ran into a wall. • Sudden tire tread separation. • Brake failure as pedal went to the floor. • Harley Truck Club (*www.nhtoc.com*) owners report that rubber strips on stainless steel gas pedals peel off, making the pedal too slippery. • Fuel tank leakage. • Driver's seat belt fails to lock up. **2004**—133 complaints have been logged by NHTSA; normally, one would find a couple of dozen. • Transmission slips. • Driving with rear window open makes the cabin vibrate violently. • Steering vibration (shimmy, "nibble") and rear end shudder at highway speeds:

> 2004 Ford F-150 has extremely high amount of vibration. Vibration is felt throughout the entire operating range in the cab of the vehicle from the floorboard to the roof. The vibration is so bad that it will literally put your feet to sleep after about fifteen minutes and your hands begin to go numb after about thirty minutes. The truck has been in the dealership on four occasions for repairs and nothing they have done has helped the problem in the least amount.

Painful, high-pitched noise comes from the dash area. • Tire chains cannot be used. • Tailgate fell off. • Wiper leaves a six-inch blind spot near the driver's side pillar.

Secret Warranties/Service Tips

1980–97—Bulletin #97-3-10 is an extensive guide to troubleshooting popping or creaking noises coming from the front frame or suspension brackets. **1993–2002**—Paint delamination, peeling, or fading (see Part Three). **1995–99**—Countermeasures to correct vibration, noise, and a harsh ride are all listed in TSB #99-11-1. **1997**—Ford will repair faulty engine gaskets free of charge up to 7 years/160,000 km under a special warranty program. **1997–98**—Stalling, engine miss, and surging may be caused by cold condensation from the AC dripping onto the heated exhaust gas oxygen (HEGO) sensor, causing thermocycling of the HEGO. This is a warranty repair covered by the emissions warranty. • Electrical accessories that short out may be contaminated by water leaks, says TSB #98-9-13. • Fuel may leak from the spring lock couplings when temperatures plunge. • A rear axle chatter when turning can be silenced by installing a new traction-lock clutch pack kit. • TSB #98-14-5 provides a correction for steering wheel clunk noise. • TSB #98-16-10 gives tips on fixing an inoperative seatback recliner. **1997–99**—If you have a hard time removing the key from the ignition, you may have a misaligned shift column shaft bushing. • A moaning noise coming from the front differential while in 4X2 mode may be fixed by replacing the front differential side and pinion gears with revised gears. • The source of an annoying whistle from the dash may be an air leak at an instrument panel grommet. • If the rear brake drum grabs when cold, install Ford's revised rear brake drum shoe kit. **1997–2000**—Ford will provide a free inner fender shield to protect the fender from rocks thrown up by the tires. • Free "goodwill" repairs for door cracks (TSB No.: 01-18-2; Date: 09/17/01). **1997–2002**—High idle speeds; throttle sticks in cold weather (Yikes!):

Engine – High Idle/Sticking Throttle

Article No. 01-21-5   Date: 10/29/01

IDLE – HIGH IDLE SPEEDS – THROTTLE STICKS AFTER STEADY STATE DRIVING IN EXTREME COLD AMBIENT TEMPERATURES – VEHICLES BUILT THROUGH 11/01/01 EQUIPPED WITH 5.4L ENGINE

ENGINE – 5.4L – PCV SYSTEM ICING – VEHICLES BUILT THROUGH 11/01/01

FORD:

1997–98   EXPEDITION, F-150, F-250 LD
2000–02   EXPEDITION, F-150

LINCOLN:

1998   NAVIGATOR

This article is being republished in its entirety to update the Model Year and vehicle applications and the Service Kit part number.

ISSUE: In rare instances, throttle sticking may occur on a few vehicles in very cold ambient temperatures after operating at steady speed or extended idle for a period of time. This may be due to ice build-up in the PCV gas on the throttle plate or throttle body.

1998—An automatic transmission ticking noise on initial start-up may be caused by the Overdrive clutch steel separator plates rubbing against the case internal spline. **1999**—Door locks that lock and unlock on their own need to have the GEM module serviced. **1999–2000**—Install a new clutch pack kit if the rear axle "chatters" when turning or cornering. **1999–2001**—Ford will repair or replace 5.4L engines with faulty head gaskets. The April 1, 2002, edition of *Automotive News* says the automaker spent about $5,300 (U.S.) to replace the engine and cylinder heads/head gasket. **2000**—Replace the intake manifold gasket and ask that "goodwill" cover the cost. **2001**—Automatic transmission clunk when shifting from Second to First gear. • Erratic 4X4 shifting; vehicle sticks in 4L gear. • High speed driveline vibration may damage drivetrain. • No-starts. • Tie-rod end squeaking. **2002**—Throttle may stick in cold weather. • Engine power loss in hot weather. • 4.6L engines may have a higher than normal idle speed. • Repaired aluminum engine heads may continue to leak coolant or oil. • Vacuum or air leaks in the intake manifold and engine. • Heater core leaks. • Faulty ignition switch lock cylinder. • Excessive front suspension noise when turning or shifting into Reverse. • A clunk may be heard when parking. **2003–04**—Remedies for 6.0L diesel engines that have fuel in oil, lose power, or run roughly (TSB #03-14-6):

Diesel Engine Driveability Concerns

Bulletin No.: 03-20-12   Date: 10/13/03

2003–04 EXCURSION, F SUPER DUTY

Some vehicles may exhibit various driveability conditions listed below:

^ Rough/Rolling Idle When The Engine Is Warm

^ Rough/Rolling Idle And White Smoke After Hot Restart

^ Lacks Power After Initial Start-Up

^ Cold Idle kicker Performance At Warm Ambient Temps

^ U0306 Codes After Reprogramming

^ P2263 Code Set During Extended Idle

^ False P0196 Codes

ACTION: Reprogram the PCM/TCM/FICM modules to the latest calibration level (B27.9) or later. This calibration should only be installed on customer vehicles that exhibit one of the conditions addressed above.

2004—Faulty handle cables could make it impossible to open the doors from the inside. • Steering wheel vibration at 97 km/h (60 mph) or higher may require replacing the steering gear.

F-Series

	1997	1998	1999	2000	2001	2002	2003	2004
Cost Price ($) (negotiable)								
XL (17%)	22,295	23,195	22,995	22,295	22,710	23,310	23,380	27,135
Used Values ($)								
XL ⋏	7,500	9,500	11,500	12,500	15,000	17,000	19,500	23,000
XL ⋎	6,000	8,500	10,000	11,000	13,500	15,500	18,000	22,000
Reliability	❷	❷	❷	❷	❷	❷	❷	③
Crash Safety (F)	④	⑤	④	④	⑤	—	—	⑤
Side	—	—	⑤	⑤	⑤	⑤	⑤	—
Ext. cab	—	—	—	—	④	④	④	—
Side	—	—	—	⑤	⑤	⑤	⑤	—
SuperCrew	—	—	—	—	—	⑤	⑤	—
Offset	❶	❶	❶	❶	❶	❶	❶	❶
Rollover	—	—	—	—	—	—	③	④
4X4	—	—	—	—	—	—	❷	—

Ford/Mazda

RANGER, B SERIES

RATING: Average (1984–2005). Mazda pickups are generally the least expensive of the "gang of three" Japanese pickups (Mazda, Nissan, and Toyota). Actually, from the 1994 model onward, your Mazda is really a Ford Ranger. Overall they're acceptable, but performance-wise they are only mediocre. Powertrain defects are worrisome. **Strong points:** Good engine performance (4.0L V6), well-designed interior, comfortable seating, classy interior trim, user-friendly control layout, four-door extended cab, good off-road handling, and good resale value. **Weak points:** Weak 4-cylinder engine (carried over into early 2001), barely adequate 3.0L V6; harsh ride, excessive braking distance, 4X4's extra height hinders easy entry/exit, rear doors are hinged at the back and won't open independently of the front doors, spare tire is difficult to remove, and many safety-related complaints reported to NHTSA. **New for 2005:** Nothing important.

2005 Technical Data

Powertrain (4X2/part-time 4X4)
Engines: 2.3L 4-cyl. (135 hp)
• 3.0L V6 (154 hp)
• 4.0L V6 (207 hp)
Transmissions: 5-speed man.
• 4-speed auto. OD
Dimension/Capacity (Reg. cab 4X2/4X4)
Height/length/width:
64.1/201.4/69.4 in.
Box length: 6/7 ft.

Headroom F/R: 39.3/39.1/39.6/36.5 in.
Legroom F/R: 42.4/36.2/42.5/35.1 in.
Wheelbase: 107.9/113.9/125.24 in.
Turning circle: 45 ft.
Passengers: 3/2
GVWR: 4,700/5,100 lb.
Payload: 1,250–1,650 lb.
Tow limit: 2,195–6,070 lb.
Ground clear.: 6.1/7.2 in.
Fuel tank: 64/79L/reg.
Weight: 4,150 lb.

MODEL HISTORY: Base Rangers come with a SuperCab option, there is 4X2 and part-time 4X4 versatility, and flare-side models are available with XL and XLT models. Mazdas follow the same program, shared among three badges, the B2500, B3000, and B4000, which are indicative of each model's engine size.

Properly equipped, these vehicles almost match the versatility of a full-sized pickup. Since the 4-cylinder engine is unsuitable for anything but the lightest chores, the larger V6 is the preferred engine choice. Its additional torque can better handle serious towing and off-roading, and fuel economy is practically the same as with the smaller V6.

An electric shift transfer case and shift-on-the-fly control are standard on 4X4 models. The upscale trim level should appeal to buyers who want to combine reliability with a more sedan-like interior.

Since 1994, the Ranger and its Mazda B Series twin have changed little. The 1995 models got a standard driver's airbag, a small horsepower boost, and four-wheel anti-lock brakes. The following year's models were the first in the industry to install an optional passenger-side airbag with a shut-off switch. The 1997 models were given an optional upgraded 5-speed automatic transmission.

Extensively redesigned for the '98 model year, these small pickups got more powerful, torquier engines; an upgraded standard 5-speed automatic; shift-on-the-fly 4X4; and 4X2s with standard power steering. Other '98 improvements included a stiffer frame, an upgraded front suspension, more precise power steering, three inches more of cab space, and a mild exterior re-styling with a lower hood line, new grille and headlights, a larger rear window, and 16-inch wheels.

1999—Ranger and B Series returned unchanged, except for the SuperCab's fourth door, while the following year's models got torsion bar suspension and a larger wheel/tire package for the 4X2. **2001**—Models got the Explorer's 207-hp, 4.0L SOHC V6; the flexible-fuel feature on the 3.0L V6 was dropped; and a new base 2.3L 4-cylinder replaced the 2.5L. ABS became a standard feature. **2002**—Models were joined by an XLT FX4 off-road 4X4 model, heavy-duty suspension, 31-inch tires, a heftier skid plate, and tow hooks. **2003**—The extension of Quadrasteer to other models and an improved electrical system and passenger-side airbag sensors. **2004**—Minor appearance changes.

COST ANALYSIS: $16,500, less a 10 percent discount for the base 2004 is the better buy. **Best alternatives:** Nissan Frontier and Toyota Tacoma are two other pickups worth considering. **Options:** The 4.0L V6, four-wheel ABS, running boards, transmission/oil cooler, remote keyless entry/anti-theft system, upgraded sound system, and power windows and door locks. Dealers are putting Firestone space-saver tires as spares; ask for regular-sized tires from a different manufacturer. Stay away from the weak 2.5L 4-cylinder engine. **Rebates:** $2,000 rebates and low financing rates on all model years. **Delivery/PDI:** $880; *Mazda:* $1,095. **Depreciation:** Much slower than average. **Insurance cost:** Average. **Annual maintenance cost:** Below average. **Parts supply/cost:** Excellent supply and relatively inexpensive from independent suppliers. **Warranty:** Bumper-to-bumper 3 years/60,000 km; rust perforation 5 years/unlimited km. **Supplementary warranty:** A good idea, judging by recent owner complaints. **Highway/city fuel economy:** *4X2 and 2.5L:* 8.8–11.7L/100 km; *4X2 and 3.0L:* 9.4–14L/100 km; *4X2 and 4.0L:* 9.7–13.9L/100 km; *4X4 and 3.0L:* 10.6–14.8L/100 km; *4X4 and 4.0L:* 10.9–14.7L/100 km. Owners report fuel economy is often way below these averages.

QUALITY/RELIABILITY: Assembly and component quality are below average. Reliability isn't impressive. Owners note serious engine problems (poor idle, surge, and stalling), erratic transmission performance and failure, brake, and fuel system issues, and breakdowns. **Warranty performance:** Below average with Ford; average with Mazda staffers. **Owner-reported problems:** Extremely poor gas mileage; 3.0L engines may have a spark knock (ping) under acceleration; the camshaft may have been incorrectly heat-treated; Flex-Fuel engines may experience a hard start or no-start; 4.0L engines may have excessive oil consumption, and surging, clogged, or plugged fuel injectors; transmission fluid leak from the transmission extension housing; oil leak from the rear seal of the transmission extension housing; no 4X4 Low range or be stuck in Low range; oil leak from the front axle pinion oil seal area; manual transmission clutch squawk noise on take-off; manual transmission–equipped 3.0L vehicles may maintain a too high engine idle when decelerating; automatic transmission fluid leaks at radiator; manual transmission buzzing, grinding noise during 2–3 upshift; steering vibration at idle or at blow speeds; wind noise from the windshield cowl, top-of-door glass seal, or the weatherstrip moulding area; poor AC performance; faulty dome and Door Ajar lights; front wipers operate when switch is Off; clutch squawking noise; chucking, squeaking noise from rear doors; rear-end sag; side mirrors flutter or shake at highway speeds; premature paint peeling and delamination.

SAFETY SUMMARY: NHTSA crash tests of a 1987 Ranger showed both the driver and the passenger would be well protected. The passenger-side airbag can be shut off to enable installation of a child safety seat. ABS is standard on rear wheels only, making for less-than-impressive braking with the 1997 version. **Airbags:** There have been reports of airbags failing to deploy or deploying when they shouldn't, resulting in severe injuries. **ABS:** Standard 2W; disc/drum. **Safety belt pretensioners:** Standard. **Head restraints F/R:** *Ranger: 1997–98: **/*; 1999: **; 2001–03: **/*; 2004: *****. B Series: 1997: **/*; 1999–2003: *; 2004: *****.* **Visibility F/R:** *****. **Maximum load capacity:** *1998 Ranger XLT 4.0L:* 549 kn (1,210 lb.).

SAFETY COMPLAINTS: All years: Ford Ranger and Mazda B Series truck passengers slam their heads into the back glass during sudden stops or in rear-end collisions. • Steering wheel lock-up. • Excessive shaking when cruising. • Malfunctioning airbags and burns caused by airbag deployment. • Defective tie-rod. • When parked on an incline with shifter lever in Park, vehicle jumps into Neutral and rolls away. • Transmission failures:

> I suffered a complete transmission failure and was forced to limp into a local Ford truck sales place. The failure occurred without any advance warning and left me limping along at 35–40 mph [55–65 km/h] on the I-90 thruway during rush hour, with heavy traffic travelling 65–70 mph [105–115 km/h]. I had totally lost Reverse gear and had substantial slippage occuring in forward gears.
>
> Ford tech consultants revealed that this is happening to many Ford Rangers, but no recall has been issued. Apparently, the torque on the transmission was increased without redesigning the transmission or seals to be able to withstand the higher torque.

• Drive shaft sheared off while driving at high speed. • Fuel leaks (tank and fuel lines). • Sudden acceleration, often when braking. • A faulty idle air control valve may be responsible for the vehicle not decelerating properly. • Stalling. • Complete loss of ABS. • Gas and brake pedals are too close together.

• Brakes don't work properly, with stuck brake calipers, overheating, and excessive pad and rotor wear. • Windshield wiper comes on by itself, or won't come on at all. • Tire tread separation. **Ranger: 1997**—When vehicle was rear-ended, front seat collapsed backwards, pinning rear-seated child against the back window. • A broken accelerator cable caused the Ranger to suddenly accelerate with no braking ability. • Several reports that the accelerator pedal broke away from the firewall. • Sudden steering loss; power steering is frequently lost in rainy weather. • While at the dealer for repairs, the transmission fell out. • Rear axle suddenly locked up, causing an accident due to loss of control. • Bent side axle housing. • While driving, one owner reported that the transmission suddenly shifted into Neutral as he was passing another vehicle. • The ABS warning light will come on intermittently for no apparent reason, even after the master cylinder has been replaced. • Poor suspension system causes vibration, bouncing, and an uncomfortable ride, resulting in loss of vehicle control. • Whenever truck passes over a pothole, it jumps to the side and practically goes out of control. • Rear seat belts failed to restrain children from injuries. • Bed liner plugs continually come out, resulting in the separation of the liner from the truck bed. • Inside door handles open the door even if the locks are engaged. • Hood supports failed, allowing hood to slam shut. • Sudden headlight failure. **1998**—Engine compartment fire. • Oil filter location makes it easy for the filter to touch the starter hot terminal, producing electrical sparks. • Strong odour emanates from the airbag (non-deployed), causing asthma attacks, hay fever symptoms, and light-headedness. • Two reports that the rear end suddenly locked up, completely severing the drive shaft and throwing the vehicle out of control. • Upper ball joint separation. • Incredible but true report that vehicle suddenly started on its own, forcing driver to run after the truck and jump in the cab to stop it. • Faulty fuel injection system causes vehicle to surge or hesitate. • Power-steering malfunction causes the power-steering fluid to crystallize, resulting in steering loss. • Defective, noisy upper and lower control arms. • AC compressor and condenser failure. • Driver-side upper door hinge bolt came off. • ABS continually locks up and smokes, which results in increased stopping distance. • Typically, when attempting to stop, the brake pedal stiffens but doesn't brake. • Excessive vehicle and steering wheel vibration when the brakes are applied. • Seat belt failed to lock up in a collision. • Jump seat only has lapbelts. • Passenger-seat recliner bar broke off. • Fuel gauge failures. • Premature wheel-bearing failures. • Driver-side window suddenly exploded. • Turning signal lever won't stay engaged. **1999**—Airbag-induced injuries. • Jerks to the side when braking or accelerating. • Chronic window fogging. **2000**—Left front wheel flew off vehicle. **B Series: 1997**—During highway driving, driver's knee bumped the ignition key and turned the key to the off position, resulting in no power, and the steering wheel locked with the key in it. **1998**—Severe shaking while underway. **1999**—Differential pinion gear self-destructed. • Emergency brake locked up, causing loss of control. **2000**—Power-steering fluid leaks onto engine. **2001**—Excessive wander on the highway, especially bad when passing over uneven terrain or after hitting potholes. • Inaccurate fuel tank level indicator and fuel gauge. • Fuel tank overflows when refuelling. • Faulty engine computer causes hard starts. • Brake line abraded by rubbing against leaf spring. • Excessive vibration called "harmonic imbalance" by dealer. • Passenger-side seat belt unbuckles at random. **2002**—A large number of serious safety-related incidents have been reported. • Sudden acceleration after vehicle jumps from Park into gear. • Premature clutch slave cylinder replacement. • Complete brake failure due to a defective idle control among other causes. • Rear shock absorbers quickly wear out. Front tire fell off due to defective carter pin. Interior and exterior lights go out intermittently. **2003**—Throttle sticks as pedal sinks to the floor. • Misaligned driver-side door allows wind and water entry. **2004**—Premature front tire wear. • Front seat pushed rearward and window popped out.

Secret Warranties/Service Tips

Keep in mind that Ford service bulletins will likely apply to Mazda. **Ranger: 1988–97**—Repeat heater core failures. **1989–99**—Poor radio reception, including whining and buzzing, may be caused by a faulty fuel pump. Install an RFI filter on the in-tank pump. **1993–99**—A buzzing or rattling noise coming from underneath the vehicle indicates the need to secure the heat shield. • A pinging or creaking driveline noise on 4X4-equipped vehicles may be silenced by replacing the transfer case rear output flange, says TSB #99-16-1. **1993–2002**—Paint delamination, peeling, or fading (see Part Three). • Loud AC clutch cycling. **1995–2000**—Temperature gauge fluctuation, or a knocking/ thumping noise coming from the engine compartment, may be fixed by installing a coolant by-pass kit. **1995–2002**—Automatic transmission slips or has a delayed engagement. **1997–2003**—Front-drive axle vent tube leaks. **1998**—TSB #98-8-13 troubleshoots clunking shifts and no or intermittent 4X4 engagement. • Erratic operation of the door chimes, speedometer, lamps, and windshield wipers may be due to a miscalibration of the generic electronic module or central timer module. • **1998–99**—An acceleration or deceleration thump or bump may be corrected by installing a revised drive shaft. • Hard starts and poor engine performance can both be traced to a chafed wire harness, says Ford TSB #00-5-4. **1999**—If the automatic transmission slips, is slow to shift, or won't shift, replace the EPC solenoid and bracket. • Water leaks through doors on four-door models. **1998–2000**—Excessive clutch noise on vehicles equipped with manual transmissions may require a new clutch disc and revised pressure plate assembly. **B Series/all years:** TSB #006/94 outlines all the possible causes and remedies for brake vibration or pulsation. **B Series: 1994–97**—A clutch that's hard to disengage may need a revised clutch slave cylinder with a new dust shield and upgraded lip seal. • Troubleshooting tips for driveline pinging and creaking. **1994–99**—Heat shield rattling can be prevented by installing four worm clamps. **1995–98**—A chattering noise heard when lowering the power windows can be silenced by installing a redesigned glass guide bracket assembly. **1995–2003**—Incorrectly-installed camshaft position (CMP) sensor synchronizer assemblies may cause loss of power, engine surge, hesitation, and rough acceleration. **1997–2003**—Front axle leaks:

Front Drive Axle Vent Tube Leaks

Bulletin No.: 03-5-8   Date: 03/17/03

1995–2001 EXPLORER
1997–2003 RANGER
2001–03 EXPLORER SPORT TRAC; EXPLORER SPORT
1997–2001 MOUNTAINEER

Article 02-4-2 is being republished in its entirety to update the model year applications.

ISSUE: Fluid may leak out of the front axle vent tube after being thrown toward the axle vent by the gears during vehicle operation.

ACTION: Replace the axle cover and install the Axle Cover kit (F6TZ-4033-BA).

1998–99—Hard starts and poor engine performance can both be traced to a chafed wire harness, a problem shared with Ford Ranger owners. **1998–2000**—Noisy manual transmission shifting is addressed in TSB #003/00. **1998–2003**—Wind noise around doors. • Seat track rattling. **1998–2004**—Driveline clunk remedy. **2000–03**—Persistent rotten-egg sulfur smell invades the cabin. **2001**—Unable to reach wide open throttle, lack of power. • 3.0L engine leaks oil at the oil filter mounting surface. • Vacuum or air leaks in the intake manifold. • 4.0L engine may lose power or have a low idle when first started. • Clutch may be hard to disengage. • Front axle squeal or whistle. • 4X4 SuperCab models may have a drive shaft thump and vibration when accelerating or stopping. • Inaccurate fuel gauge. • Front end may produce a squeal or whistle. • Delayed Reverse engagement. • Condensation leads to early fog lamp failure. • Heater core leaks. • Faulty speedometer. **2001–03**—Transmission whine on vehicles with the 4.0L engine:

1st/2nd Gear Whining Noise

Article No.: 02-22-2   Date: 11/11/02

2001–03 EXPLORER SPORT TRAC, EXPLORER SPORT, RANGER

ISSUE: Some vehicles may exhibit a gear whine type of noise in 1st and 2nd gear ONLY. This may be caused by the Reverse and Forward Planetary assemblies and/or the driveshaft.

2002—Check Engine light troubleshooting. • 4.0L engine may produce a spark knock or fluttering noise, or leak oil. • 2.3L engine may idle poorly and surge or hesitate when accelerating. • Automatic transmission fluid leaks. • Manual transmission–equipped vehicles may lose power when decelerating. • Damaged fuel return line. • Fluid leaks from the front axle vent tube. • Heater core leaks. • Air leaks or vacuum in the intake manifold or engine. • Faulty ignition switch lock cylinder. • Inaccurate temperature gauge. **2002–03**—Noisy manual transfer case shifter.

Ranger, B Series Profile

	1997	1998	1999	2000	2001	2002	2003	2004
Cost Price ($)								
Base/XL 4X2 (14%)	14,995	15,945	15,995	16,395	16,995	18,595	17,395	16,775
Base/XL 4X4 (16%)	20,795	20,245	20,295	21,395	24,675	23,715	24,495	—
Used Values ($)								
Base/XL 4X2 ⋀	4,500	6,500	8,500	9,500	11,000	13,000	14,500	16,000
Base/XL 4X2 ⋁	4,000	5,500	7,000	8,500	10,000	11,500	13,000	14,500
Base/XL 4X4 ⋀	6,500	8,000	9,500	11,500	13,500	16,000	19,000	—
Base/XL 4X4 ⋁	6,000	7,500	8,500	10,500	12,500	15,000	17,000	—
Reliability	③	③	③	③	③	③	③	③
Crash Safety (F)	④	④	④	④	—	④	④	④
Ext. cab	—	—	—	④	④	④	④	④
Side	—	—	⑤	⑤	⑤	⑤	⑤	⑤
Ext. cab	—	—	—	④	④	④	④	④
Offset	—	③	③	③	③	③	③	③
Rollover (4X2)	—	—	—	—	—	—	③	—
(4X4)	—	—	—	—	—	—	❷	—
Ext. cab (4X2)	—	—	—	—	—	—	③	—
Ext. cab	—	—	—	—	—	—	③	—
(4X4)	—	—	—	—	—	—	❷	—

General Motors

AVALANCHE ★★★

RATING: Average with an extended warranty (2002–05). **Strong points:** A Suburban clone; drives much like the similarly equipped Suburban and Silverado/Sierra; plenty of passenger and cargo room; up to 5,400 kilogram (11,900 lb.) towing limit; a nice choice of V8 powerhouse engines; a smooth powertrain (with some exceptions), and plenty of standard amenities. The 2004 model hydroboost brake feature enhances brake feel, but no word as to whether poor durability problem has been addressed. Four doors provide easy access for six occupants who are given plenty of head- and legroom. "Midgate" panel adds to the pickup's practicality. Angular styling similar to the Cadillac Escalade and Pontiac Aztek gives the Avalanche an aggressive stance. Other positives are a high ground clearance, and a slow rate of depreciation. **Weak points:** Excess weight cripples performance and fuel economy; excessive brake wear; suspension and steering vibrations; numb steering; and powertrain deficiencies similar to those afflicting the Suburban and Silverado. **New for 2005:** Nothing significant. **Likely failures:** Engine, transmission (clunky and glitch-prone), steering, seat belts, and airbags; and early brake-pad and rotor replacement. Owners mention that braking is dangerously poor on wet pavement, pad/rotor problems cause excessive vibration when braking, and components frequently overheat.

Service tips: Similar to the Suburban and Silverado. **2002–04**—Suspension clunk, slap. GM will replace the spring insert and insulator for free (see Silverado "Service Tips"). **2003–04**—Remedies for an inoperative front power window and steering wheel clunk.

MODEL HISTORY: Sharing 85 percent of its parts with the Suburban, the Avalanche is a full-sized, crew-cab pickup with a unique bed and cab design and performance features that make it one of the most versatile and powerful sport-utility/truck crossovers you can find. Yet, it looks like a gimmicky "what's that" kind of vehicle not seen since the El Camino sedan *cum* pickup, or the weirdly styled Aztek. Carrying a base 5.3L V8 engine mated to a rear-drive/4X4 4-speed automatic powertrain, the Avalanche comes, nevertheless, loaded with potential. For example, its Convert-a-Cab feature allows you to fold the rear passenger seat/midgate and extend the standard bed by about 34 inches, giving the bed an impressive 8'1" length. Or you can remove the rear window, fold the midgate, and get an open-air feel. The Avalanche won't win any fuel-economy or retained value prizes and its price and factory-related deficiencies will discourage all but the most daring (see Tahoe/Yukon "Service Tips"). Best advice, don't look for a Swiss Army knife SUV, determine your most basic requirements and buy a simpler, less costly and gimmicky pickup.

2005 Technical Data

Powertrain (4X2/4X4)
Engines: • 5.3L V8 (295 hp)
• 8.1L V8 (320 hp)
Transmission: 4-speed auto.
Dimension/Capacity
Height/length/width:
73.6/221.7/79.8 in.
Headroom F/R: 40.7/38.6 in.

Legroom F/R: 41.3/38.9 in.
Wheelbase: 130 in.
Turning circle: 43 ft.
Passengers: 3/3
Cargo volume: 53.9 cu. ft.
Payload: N/A
GVWR: 6,800–8,600 lb.
Tow limit: 8,200–12,000 lb.
Ground clearance: 8.6 in.
Fuel tank: 117-142L/reg.
Weight: 5,437 lb.

Avalanche

	2002	2003	2004
Cost Price ($) (negotiable)			
Avalanche (21%)	37,372	38,135	39,155
Used Values ($)			
Avalanche ⅄	26,000	30,000	34,000
Avalanche Ⓥ	24,000	27,000	32,000
Reliability	③	③	③
Crash Safety (F)	③	③	③
Rollover	❷	❷	—

C/K, SIERRA, SILVERADO

RATING: Below Average (1999–05); Average (1988–98). What a disappointment! GM invested billions in upgrades six years ago and came up with mediocre haulers. Duramax diesel has serious quality and performance issues, as well. **Strong points:** Well appointed, competent optional powertrain for towing and hauling, user-friendly controls for full-time, 4X4 system, effective brakes and responsive steering, well laid-out instruments and controls, seats are roomy and supportive, lots of leg clearance, a contoured cushion and a reclined seatback to further enhance comfort, doors open wide and feature useful pull-lever handles, a large cabin, a high ground clearance, good noise insulation, and a rattle-resistant body. Fairly good real-world fuel economy. **Weak points:** Base 4.3L V6 needs more grunt, transmission hunts for the right gear and produces an incessant whine, base suspension provides a too-compliant ride, there's insufficient room for the driver to reach between the door panel and seat to access the seat-adjusting mechanism, some engine noise intrudes into the cabin, serious reliability problems and an incredibly high number of performance- and safety-related complaints reported to NHTSA and confirmed through confidential bulletins and whistle-blowers. **New for 2005:** Nothing significant, giving the edge to the re-engineered Nissan Titan and Toyota Tacoma.

2005 Technical Data

Powertrain (rear-drive/4X4)
Engines: 4.3L V6 (200 hp)
• 4.8L V8 (255 hp)
• 5.3L V8 (270 hp)
• 6.0L V8 (300 hp)
• 6.0L V8 (325 hp)
• 6.6L V8 D. (215 hp)
• 8.1L V8 (340 hp)
Transmissions: 5-speed man.
• 4-speed auto. OD
Dimension/Capacity (1500)
Height/length/width:
70.8/246.7/78.5 in.
Box length: 6.5/8 ft.

Headroom F/R: 41/38.4 in.
Legroom F/R: 41.3/33.7 in.
Wheelbase: 133 in.
Turning circle: 45.3 ft.
Passengers: 3/3
GVWR: 1500: 6,200 lb./
  2500: 9,200 lb.
Payload: 1500: 747–1,965 lb./
  2500: 2,614–3,334 lb.
Tow limit: 3,700–15,900 lb.
Ground clear.: 6.9 in.
Fuel tank: 95–129L/reg., diesel
Weight: est. 4,300 lb.

MODEL HISTORY: Similar to Detroit's other pickups, these models come as 1500 half-ton, 2500 three-quarter-ton, and 3500 one-ton models. They come with a wide range of engine options, body styles, and bed sizes. The "C" designation refers to 4X2, and the "K" designation to 4X4. The 3500 series offers a four-door cab with a full rear seat. The variety of cab and cargo bed combinations, along with a choice of suspensions, makes these pickups adaptable to just about any use. Standard features include one of the biggest cabs among pickups, a fourth door, a three-piece modular truck frame, rack-and-pinion steering, and four-wheel disc brakes with larger pads and rotors.

An Auto Trac AWD drivetrain allows the driver to select an automatic mode that delivers full-time 4X4 (particularly useful if you live in a snowbelt area), while a 4-speed automatic features an innovative "tow/haul" mode that stretches out the upshifts to tap the engine's power at its maximum. There's also a potent family of four Vortec V8s in addition to a 6.6L turbodiesel (215 hp), 16-inch tires and wheels, and the highest minimum ground clearance among the Big Three pickups.

Chevy and GMC full-sized pickups are good domestic workhorses—when they're running. Of course, that's the problem—they're not dependable. On the one hand, these large pickups have a large, quiet cabin, and give relatively easy access to the interior. On the other hand, their size and heft make for lousy fuel economy, a mediocre ride, and subpar handling and braking.

Nevertheless, these are GM's most popular and highest-priced pickups. Although, reasonably priced on the used car market, new models will cost you the equivalent of a downpayment on a home.

Early full-sized GM trucks may look like bargains, but they have as many or more serious factory-related deficiencies as their smaller S-10 cousins. Consequently, be sure to get extended warranty coverage. Keep in mind that engine and automatic transmission failures are quite common and can, together, give you a $7,000 headache. Also, try to find a pickup with running boards already installed. You'll save a few hundred dollars and make entry and exit a lot easier. Check out towing claims carefully, as well. One owner reports that his truck was advertised as able to pull 3,856 kg (8,500 lb.), but the owner's manual says the towing limit is 3,402 kg (7,500 lb.).

From 1994 through 1998 GM's pickups were better built than its own compact versions and more reliable than the Ford and Chrysler competition. Earlier versions will have a 4-speed manual or 3-speed automatic transmission; later ones come with a 5-speed manual or a 4-speed automatic. Three-quarter-ton pickups offer more cargo capacity, but their harder suspension makes for an uncomfortable ride when lightly loaded and also affects handling.

1999–2004 models got many new features that make them more powerful, versatile, accomodating, and safer than previous models. However, these changes also made them less reliable than the pickups they replaced. Major powertrain, brake, suspension, electrical system, and body deficiencies have turned these "dream" machines into nightmares.

Redesigned Sierras and Silverados have been plagued with severe vibrations that GM has routinely ignored. Owners have affectionately nicknamed their trucks "Shakerados," and say that new frame braces added to the 2001s to stop the shakes haven't worked (*agmlemon.freeservers.com/index.html*).

Another generic failing is engine knocking or "piston slap," a term used to describe knocking engines. Owners claim the problem affects GM's 3.1, 3.4, 4.3, 4.6 (Northstar), 4.8, 5.3, 5.7(LS1), 6.0 or 8.1L engines, which were poorly designed and not given adequate quality control. We're not talking about a small amount of light tapping upon start-up that disappears completely upon engine warm-up: This is a loud, embarrassing, and damaging internal engine knock. There are currently six technical service bulletins that are relevant to piston slap: Engine Knock #01-06-01-022; Engine Knock

#01-06-01-028; Engine Knock #01-06-01-028A; Cold Engine Tick #01-06-01-005; Engine Oil Consumption #01-06-01-011; and Engine Oil Consumption #01-06-01-011A. For more details, check out *www.pistonslap.com/;* if the site has been shut down, simply "google" "GM piston slap." **2000**—The 2000 Sierra and Silverado came up with an optional fourth door on extended cab models and a small power boost for the Vortec 4800 and 5300 V8 engines. **2001**—Debut of three-quarter- and one-ton versions of the Silverado. They offered two engines: the 6.6L Isuzu-built Duramax V8 diesel and GM's homegrown 8.1L Vortec V8. A traction assist feature became available on rear-drive V8 automatics. The Sierra C3 luxury truck offered a number of new features, including a 325-hp 6.0L Vortec V8; full-time all-wheel drive (no two-speed transfer case for serious off-roading, though); upgraded four-wheel disc anti-lock brakes; an increased-capacity suspension system; and a luxuriously appointed interior. The Sierra HD truck lineup came with stronger frames; beefed-up suspensions, axles, brakes, and cooling systems; new sheet metal; bigger interiors; and three new V8s—a 6.6L Duramax turbodiesel and two gas engines, a hefty 8.1L and an improved 6.0L. One of the four transmissions, a new Allison 5-speed automatic, was designed especially for towing and hauling with GM's tow/haul mode and a new grade-braking feature. **2003**—Quadrasteer was expanded to other models, improved electrical system and passenger-side airbag sensor, a new centre console, and dual-zone temperature and steering wheel controls. **2004**—Standard cruise control, power door locks, and a CD player.

COST ANALYSIS: Best alternatives: Buy a discounted 2004, but remember, anything but a bare-bones version will be quite expensive. Your best alternatives are the Dodge Ram (mainly for the warranty and Hemi), Mazda B Series, Nissan Frontier V6 and Titan, and Toyota T100, Tacoma, or Tundra. **Rebates:** Expect $2,000–$3,000 rebates through 2005. **Delivery/PDI:** $1,000. **Warranty:** Bumper-to-bumper 3 years/60,000 km; rust perforation 6 years/160,000 km. **Supplementary warranty:** A good idea, judging by last year's high number of consumer complaints. **Options:** This is where GM really sticks it to you. Consider the remote keyless entry, upgraded sound system, heavy-duty battery, and transmission fluid and oil coolers. Be wary of the adjustable ride control option that adjusts the firmness of the shock absorbers to suit different loads; it doesn't make much difference. Test-drive before you buy. **Depreciation:** Slower than average. **Parts supply/cost:** Parts are widely available but are on the pricey side for post-'98 models, despite the availability of cheaper parts from independent suppliers. **Insurance cost:** Higher than average. **Annual maintenance cost:** Upkeep costs for these trucks are high, wiping out whatever savings are realized from buying an early version or frequenting independent garages. **Highway/city fuel economy:** *4.3L V6 and manual:* 9.5–14.1L/100 km; *4.3L V6 and auto.:* 10.6–14.6L/100 km; *4.8L V8 and auto.:* 10.5–14.6L/100 km.

QUALITY/RELIABILITY: Below average. Powertrain and brake repairs and troubleshooting excessive vibration complaints often sideline the vehicle for days at a time and repair suggestions don't make any sense:

> Then after the shimmy vibration continued, GM Tecnical Assistance to the dealership stated that all the 2004 Chevrolet Silverado 1500 Series have this vibration and it is classified as "beam shake". Their solution was to put 200 pounds of weight over the axle in the bed of the truck stating "It will ride like a Cadillac". The weight did not change the vibration and now they have a GM field engineer coming to look at the truck.

GM plant workers claim the porous frame on both vehicles cracks behind the cabin and near the tow hook. **Owner-reported problems:** Excessive engine knock (faulty engine-connecting rod bolts, confirmed by internal bulletins) and exhaust system noise; diesel engine ticking noise; Check Engine light often comes on and requires replacement of many emissions components before it goes out; rough idle; and excessive oil consumption. Many complaints of rear differential pinion seal oil leaks; transmission failures; shifts for no reason from 4X4 to 4X2 or 4X2 to 4X4 Low; delayed transmission shifting; failing to upshift; slipping in Overdrive; and shuddering in Drive or Reverse. Other problems: AC blower motor failure; excessive front-end vibrations felt throughout the chassis, steering, and floorboards at 100 km/h (dealers blame vibrations on Goodyear tires but problem persists after tires are replaced); defective lower control arm and steering bushings suspected as the cause of excessive vibrations; frequent and costly brake repairs involving rotor and pad replacement:

> I have a 99 GMC Sierra 1500 4WD (purchased new in Sept 2000) that went off the base warranty in October 2002. The vehicle currently has 37,000 km on clock.
>
> As I have found stopping distances to be increasing of late, I recently took the vehicle in for servicing. GM advised that it is "normal" for pads to be replaced every 15–20,000 km. I said I disagreed very strongly with this estimate, and that pads alone should last at least 25,000 km under any conditions. The GM rep also said brake rotors on these vehicles cannot be reconditioned (turning) as they are "too thin", and generally require replacement in the 50–60,000 km range. I asked if there were "known problems" with the brake system on these vehicles that contribute to these early failures. The representative said there were no known problems, just normal wear.
>
> After taking the vehicle to a third party for inspection, I was told that the pads are finished and that all four rotors must be replaced as they are rusted through. I inspected the vehicle myself in the shop and found that the third party was completely correct in this. The net cost for this work is expected to be in the $1600–$2000 range. I find the thought of a $2000 bill every three years for replacement brakes unacceptable.

Excessive brake noise and steering-column squeaks; inadequate front defroster; front-end popping noise; hubcaps often fly off vehicle; tires won't stay balanced; and poorly fitted trim and body panels. **Warranty performance:** Average. GM has a number of extended warranties in place to compensate owners for defects, but getting information on which "secret" warranties apply and obtaining compensation isn't easy.

SAFETY SUMMARY: Very few early versions were sold with front-seat head restraints, and the driver's head is very close to the rear window on regular cab versions. U.S. federal government researchers have opened an investigation into reports of erratic power-steering assist (1997–99). **Airbags:** Reports of airbags failing to deploy. **ABS:** Standard 4W; disc/drum. **Traction control:** Optional. **Head restraints F/R:** *C/K:* 1997: *; *Silverado 1500: 1999:* *; *2001–04:* **/*. **Visibility F/R:** *****. **Maximum load capacity:** 1999 LS Silverado 5.3L: 665 kn (1,465 lb.).

SAFETY COMPLAINTS: All years: Sudden, unintended acceleration. • Airbag failed to deploy. • Intermittent loss of power steering. • Brake failures (pedal goes to the metal with no braking effect) with ABS light lit constantly. • Brake pad failure and warped rotor. • Parking brake doesn't hold. • ABS doesn't engage; results in extended stopping distances and wheel lock-up. • Chronic stalling. • **1997**—Sudden acceleration from 50 to 130 km/h with the cruise control engaged. • Many complaints of sudden steering loss due to missing bolt that holds the steering shaft from the steering gearbox to the steering column. • Power steering locks up when the brakes are applied or when turning. • Power-steering assist feature (designed to engage at low speeds) operates erratically. • Failure of the steering-column wiring harness. • Rubber brake pedal pad comes off. • Fuel leakage caused by defective fuel pump gasket. • Engine surges; maintains a fast idle. • Premature failure of the front-wheel bearings. • Wheel rims rub against the brake calipers and suspension. • When making a sharp turn, front tire rubs against the frame and sway bar, destroying the tire. • Several complaints that wheels bend, causing repeated tire blowouts and excessive vibration. • While vehicle was parked on an incline, transmission slipped out of Park and vehicle rolled away. • Transmission Overdrive melted. • Several cases where the front brass bushing shattered and filings ran through the transmission. • Automatic transmission hesitates before shifting gears. • Chronic front suspension noise. • Continual rear suspension noise believed to be caused by insufficient padding of the rear spring leaves. • Rear-end clunk when coming to a stop. • Loose wiring to starter makes for hard starts. • Defective windshield wiper control. • Faulty seat belt retractors. **1998**—Steering column pulled out, causing loss of control. • Another owner reported loss of steering when the steering tie-rod end bolts failed, causing the rod to drop. • Fuel tank dropped to within a few inches from the ground, due to the failure of the bolt that attaches the tank to the frame. • ABS is ineffective when towing. • Middle seat lapbelt failed to restrain occupant in a collision. • Excessive drivetrain and suspension vibrations. • Automatic transmission seizes, leaks, and shifts harshly. • Vehicle surges and stalls when changing gears with the manual transmission. **1999**—Inability to shut off headlights without shutting down vehicle; delayed transmission shifting in cold weather; and broken spare tire cable that allows spare to fly off.

2000—A very common problem appears to be that the rear frame breaks, from the bottom up, from about two inches in front of the tow hook attachment. • Transmission jumped from Park into Reverse. • Fuel line leakage. • Several cases relating to a broken power-steering pump shaft. • Rear left emergency brake shoe and drum allows for salt and debris to get into drum and drum elbow. • Dash light failures and headlight switch burns out. • Many incidents of tire tread separation. • Excessive vibration felt throughout vehicle. **2001**—Left rear wheel fell off due to loose lug nuts. • Spongy brakes lead to extended stopping distance. • After driving in snow and parking vehicle, brakes wouldn't work. • Emergency brake gave way on flat ground. • When accelerating from a stop, vehicle momentarily goes into Neutral. • Sometimes, transmission suddenly shifts from Fifth to Third gear, or down to Second gear while cruising on the highway. • Defective transmission valve body results in transmission jumping out of gear. • Truck "drifts" all over the highway. • Driver's safety belt causes pain in the shoulder. • Upper ball joint and right sway bar ends may be missing nuts and cotter keys. • Fuel line leak allows fuel to spray out rear. **2002**—Fire ignited in the dash. • Throttle sticks. • Chronic engine surging when braking. • Automatic transmission suddenly downshifts when accelerating, as engine surges, then clunks into gear. • Steering wheel locks up while driving. • Passenger-side front end suddenly collapsed (replaced outer tie-rod end). • Steel wheel collects water that freezes and throws wheel out of balance. • Steering-column bolt came apart. • Interior rear-view mirror distortion. • Dimmer switch overheats. • Driver's seatback will suddenly fall backwards. • Head restraint blocks vision to right side of vehicle. **2003**—Fire ignited in engine compartment. • Cracked transmission transfer case. • Automatic transmission slips when shifting from First to Second gear. • 4X4 shifts erratically causing serious highway instability. • Seat belt and steering lock-ups. • Tailgate pops open. **2004**—Collapsed front axle assembly. • Sway bar mounting bracket broke, causing the frame and mounting bar to come off. • Brake failures when coasting downhill or when decelerating. • Brakes are too soft and set too close to the accelerator pedal. • Cruise control surges when going downhill. • Transmission suddenly jumped from Second gear to Reverse. • Steering lockup. • Tailgate came apart in owner's hands. • Doors won't unlock in cold weather. • Driver's door window shattered for no reason. • Hood coil spring failed, injuring owner. • Jack slipped off the vehicle. • Side mirrors constantly vibrate and are easily scratched when wiped off.

Secret Warranties/Service Tips

All models: 1996–98—Extremely cold temperatures may cause cracking of the inside of the differential seals. Replace with upgraded seals. **1996–99**—Engine bearing knocking on vehicles equipped with a 5.0L or 5.7L V8 may be silenced by using a special GM countermeasure kit to service the crankshaft and select-fit undersized connecting rod bearings. • No-starts, hard starts, and poor engine performance can all be traced to a faulty crankshaft position sensor. **1997–98**—Vehicles equipped with a 6.5L diesel engine with hard upshifts may need to reprogram the PCM/VCM. • An excessive ticking noise coming from the engine compartment may be silenced by replacing the EVAP

purge solenoid valve. **1998**—Engine stalling or surging and a slipping transmission may signal the need to repair the auxiliary oil cooler or replace the
transmission torque converter. • TSB #76-65-07 tackles correcting a 4.3L
engine fast idle or flare when manually shifting by performing a flash calibration under warranty. **1998–99**—If the 4X4 won't engage, you may need to
install a new transfer case actuator and shift detent plunger. • Before you spend
big bucks overhauling the transfer case, remember, a bump or clunk heard
upon acceleration may be silenced by simply changing the transfer-case fluid.
1999—If the front wheels slip while in 4X4, consider replacing the transfer-
case clutch plates and front-drive axle lubricant. • A steering column squeak
noise may be silenced by replacing the steering wheel SIR module coil
assembly. **1999–2000**—Wind noise coming from the side may be silenced by
replacing the quarter window assembly under warranty. **1999–2003**—An
exhaust moan or vibration can be corrected by installing an exhaust system
flex pipe kit. **1999–2004**—Chronic engine knock or piston slap. •
Prematurely worn and noisy brake rotors and pads may be replaced with
higher-quality aftermarket parts, for about half the price. • GM says in TSB
#00-05-23-005B that owners should invest in a GM mud flap kit
(#15765007) to make their rear brakes last longer. Again, save money by shopping independent retailers. • Inoperative power windows. • Remedy for
steering wheel clunk. • Suspension clunk, slap. GM will do this repair for free
as "goodwill" up to 3 years/60,000 km, and will offer a 50 percent refund
thereafter:

Suspension – Rear Leaf Spring Slap or Clunk Noise

Bulletin No.: 03-03-09-002A   Date: April 29, 2004

Rear Leaf Spring Slap or Clunk Noise (Replace Spring Insert and Insulator)
1999–2004 Chevrolet Silverado 1500/2500 Series Pickups
2000–04 Chevrolet Suburban 2500 Series
2002–04 Chevrolet Avalanche 2500 Series
2003–04 Chevrolet Express 2500/3500 Vans with 8500 GVWR (RPO C5F), 8600 GVWR (RPO C6P) or
9600 GVWR (RPO C6Y)
1999–2004 GMC Sierra 1500/2500 Series Pickups
2000–04 GMC Yukon XL 2500 Series
2003–04 GMC Savana 2500/3500 Vans with 8500 GVWR (RPO C5F), 8600 GVWR (RPO C6P) or 9600
GVWR (RPO C6Y)

Some customers may comment on a rear leaf spring slap or clunk noise. This noise is most
apparent when the vehicle is operated over irregular road surfaces.

2000–04—Troubleshooting delayed gear engagement. **2001**—Loose engine
connecting rod bolts may cause engine knock and complete engine failure. •
Loss of turbo boost accompanied by thick black smoke. • No-starts or hard
starts. • Excessive vibration and surging with the 6600 Duramax engine. •
Harsh shift remedies. • When in 4X4 and in Reverse gear, engine won't go
over 1000–1300 rpm. • Transmission slips when placed in 4X4. • 6-speed
manual transmission clutch fluid may be contaminated by water entering
through the reservoir cap. • Automatic transmission 2–4 band or 3–4 clutch
damage. • Inoperative wiper motor; fuse blows repeatedly. • Windows are slow

to defrost. • Steering-column lock shaft doesn't lock. **2001–02**—Troubleshooting tips to correct slow or no automatic transmission engagement, no-starts, or a blank PRNDL. • Secret warranty to pay for faulty fuel injectors (6.6L diesel):

Special Policy Adjustment

Bulletin No.: 04039 (Replace Injector)   Date: June 2004

2001–02 Silverado/Sierra (6.6L Duramax Diesel)

Condition: Some customers of 2001-02 model year Chevrolet Silverado and GMC Sierra vehicles, equipped with a 6.6L Duramax Diesel (RPO LB7 - VIN Code 1) engine, may experience vehicle service engine soon (SES) light illumination, low engine power, hard start, and/or fuel in crankcase, requiring injector replacement, as a result of high fuel return rates due to fuel injector body cracks or ball seat erosion.

SpecialPolicyAdjustment: This special policy covers the condition described above for a period of 7 years or 200,000 miles (320,000 km), whichever occurs first, from the date the vehicle was originally placed in service, regardless of ownership. The repairs will be made at no charge to the customer.

2001–03—The torque converter relief spring and lube regulator spring may need to be changed to correct automatic transmission delayed shifts or loss of power. GM service bulletins TSB #01-07-30-043 and 03-07-30-031 explain why the automatic transmission may slip or leak (see following). **2001–04**—6.6L Duramax diesel engine O-ring free replacement:

Diesel Engine Oil Leak

Bulletin No.: 02-06-01-023B   Date: January 26, 2004

Oil Leak At Oil Cooler To 6.6L Diesel Engine Block Mating Surface (Replace O-rings, Apply Sealant)

2001–04 Chevrolet Silverado 2500/3500
2001–04 GMC Sierra 2500/3500
2003–04 Chevrolet Kodiak C4500/5500
2003–04 GMC Topkick C4500/5500

Cause: Minor imperfections in the engine block machined surfaces at the oil cooler interface may allow oil seepage past the oil cooler O-rings.

2002—Check Engine light comes on as automatic transmission begins shifting erratically. • 1–2 shift shudder. • Diagnostic tips for a slipping automatic transmission. • Clunk noise from under the hood. • Clunk, bump, or squawk heard when accelerating or coming to a stop. • Shudder or vibration when accelerating from a stop. • Driveline growl or prop shaft ring noise. • Steering shaft clunk. • Noisy brakes. • Water leak at the roof centre clearance lamp. • Inability to control temperature setting. • Intermittent failing of the tail lights, backup lights, or trailer harness. **2003**—Harsh automatic transmission 1–2 shifting; slipping due to a faulty pressure control solenoid (Bulletin #03-07-30-020, May 2003) • Poor AC performance with 6.6L diesel engine. **2003–04**—Remedies for buzz noise or vibration felt in floor or throttle pedal. Inoperative front power window. **2004**—Cold engine rattling.

C/K, Sierra, Silverado

	1997	1998	1999	2000	2001	2002	2003	2004
Cost Price ($)								
C/K (17%)	19,750	20,995	21,735	—	—	—	—	—
Sierra, Silverado (18%)	19,750	20,955	21,895	22,100	22,060	22,410	23,240	24,070
Used Values ($)								
C/K ⋏	7,000	9,000	11,000	—	—	—	—	—
C/K ⋎	6,000	8,000	10,000	—	—	—	—	—
Sierra, Silverado ⋏	7,500	9,500	11,500	12,500	14,500	16,000	19,500	21,000
Sierra, Silverado ⋎	6,500	8,500	10,500	11,000	13,000	15,000	18,000	19,500
Reliability	③	③	❷	❷	❷	❷	❷	❷
Crash Safety (F)	⑤	—	—	—	—	—	—	④
Ext. cab	⑤	④	—	③	③	③	④	④
Offset	—	—	❷	❷	❷	❷	❷	❷
Rollover	—	—	—	—	—	—	④	④
Ext. cab	—	—	—	—	④	④	④	④
Ext. cab 4X4	—	—	—	—	③	③	③	④

General Motors/Isuzu

S-10, SONOMA, T-10/SPACE CAB, HOMBRE, CANYON, COLORADO   ★ ★ ★

RATING: *S-10, Sonoma, T-10:* Average (1999–2004); Below Average (1996–98); Not Recommended (1986–95). *Space Cab:* Below Average (1984–94); *Hombre:* Average (1997–2002). *Canyon, Colorado:* Average (2004–05).

These pickups are no match for the Japanese competition. While the quality control for GM's full-sized pickups has improved over the past five years, the S-10 has only recently shown small signs of improvement. There were no 1995 or 1996 Isuzu pickups sold in Canada; for the 1997 model year, the Space Cab was re-designated the Hombre. **Strong points:** A well-appointed pickup, good V6 acceleration, reliable and smooth-shifting automatic transmission, user-friendly controls and instruments, extended cab offers a spacious interior and storage space, airbag cut-off switch, easy loading and unloading, and one of the quietest interiors you'll find. **Weak points:** Wimpy 4-cylinder engine, harsh ride, poor handling, plastic door panels make for a tacky-looking cabin, difficult entry/exit on 4X4 version, awkward rear access almost makes the optional third door a necessity, limited rear-seat room, jump seats in the extended cab are tiny and uncomfortable, and an extraordinary number of safety-related defects have been reported to NHTSA. *Colorado:* No outside key door lock. **New for 2005:** Nothing significant. **Likely failures:** Automatic transmission, fuel system, upper control arm bushings wire harness melting, and worn brake rotors and pads. *Colorado:* General tire side wall blowout, water leaks, and a bad odour from the AC.

2003 Technical Data

Powertrain (4X2/part-time 4X4)
Engines: 2.2L 4-cyl. (120 hp)
• 4.3L V6 (175–190 hp)
Transmissions: 5-speed man.
• 4-speed auto.
Dimension/Capacity (Reg. cab/Ext. cab)
Height/length/width:
63.3/189/67.9 in.
Box length: 6/7.5 ft.
Headroom F/R: 39.5/39.5 in.
Legroom F/R: 42.4/42.4 in.

Wheelbase: 108.3/117.9–122.9 in.
Turning circle: 51 ft.
Passengers: 3/2
Cargo Volume: 48.1 cu. ft.
GVWR: 4,200–5,150 lb.
Payload: 1,150–1,633 lb.
Tow limit: 2,100–5,200 lb.
Ground clear.: 6.8–10.3 in.
Fuel tank: 76L/reg.
Weight: 3,350 lb.

2005 Canyon, Colorado

Powertrain (4X2/part-time 4X4)
Engines: 2.8L 4-cyl. (175 hp)
• 3.5L 5-cyl. (220 hp)
Transmissions: 5-speed man.
• 4-speed auto.
Dimension/Capacity
 (Reg. cab/Ext. cab)
Height/length/width:
64.8/192.4/67.6 in.
Box length: 6/7.5 ft.
Headroom F/R: 40/37.9 in.

Legroom F/R: 44/23.1 in.
Wheelbase: 111.3 in.
Turning circle: 40.7 ft.
Passengers: 3
Cargo Volume: 43.9 cu. ft.
GVWR: 4,700–5,300 lb.
Payload: 1,503–1,613 lb.
Tow limit: 4,000 lb.
Ground clear.: 8.5 in.
Fuel tank: NA/reg.
Weight: 3,452 lb.

MODEL HISTORY: These mostly identical pickups (some differences in trim and equipment) are compact, light-duty vehicles that are available in regular and extended cab versions. For easier entry/exit, a driver-side third door is available on the extended-cab pickups.

There are lots of suspension packages to choose from, ranging from a "Smooth Ride" package for paved roads and light trailering to "Wide Stance Sport Performance" for off-roading and trailering. The trucks are available in 4X2 and part-time 4X4 drive. A 2.2L 4-cylinder or 4.3L V6 power plant is hooked to a 5-speed manual or 4-speed automatic transmission.

The 4X4 is engaged with InstaTrac shift-on-the-fly. There is low range for off-roading. The Highrider off-road package rides on 31-inch tires, an off-road suspension, and a reinforced frame.

These attractively styled S-series pickups do have some good points, like a powerful V6 and user-friendly controls. But these advantages have to be weighed against some rather serious shortcomings: a wimpy 4-cylinder engine (also a Canyon and Colorado problem), a clunky and quirky automatic transmission, difficult entry/exit, a harsh ride, and excessive gas consumption. S-10s don't offer any space or load capacity advantages over their Japanese counterparts.

1996—Performance was enhanced on the through the addition of improved V6 engines, a smoother 4-speed manual transmission, a sportier suspension, four-wheel ABS, and a third-door access panel on the driver's side of extended cabs. **1997**—GM strengthened the frame on the 4X2s and added a smoother-shifting automatic throughout the lineup. **1998**—De-powered airbags, four-wheel disc brakes, and a more refined transfer case on vehicles equipped with an automatic transmission. **1999**—Extreme sport package replaced the SS, more automatic transmission enhancements were carried out to improve sealing and durability, and a new Auto Trac electronic push-button transfer case was added. Again, the following year, GM felt compelled to upgrade the engine (same horsepower, though), manual transmission, ABS, and exhaust system. **2000**—Trucks carrying the ZR2 package were given a new axle ratio for better acceleration.

2001—A new four-door crew cab 4X4 version was offered, with enough room for five (small) passengers, plus an InstaTrac 4X4 system and SLS trim. Powertrain upgrades included an advanced control module for the V6 and Flex-Fuel capability for the 4-cylinder. There were also new aluminum wheels with the sport suspension, and programmable power door locks. **2002**—Standard air conditioning and a long cargo bed option (initially dropped, then reinstated). **2003**—A new fuel injection system and a minor face-lift. **2004**—No significant changes, except for the Colorado and Canyon's arrival in early 2004. S-10 continues only as a $33,000 4X4 four-door Crew Cab for 2004. This is the S-10's last model year.

Space Cab, Hombre

This Isuzu-built pickup, once sold through GM's short-lived Passport division, is acceptable, basic transportation in small-truck guise. Its main drawbacks are an underperforming engine, spongy brakes, and spotty reliability. Sales were fairly brisk at first, but declining demand led to a reduction in the models available during the last few years.

The standard engines are weak 2.2L and 2.3L 4-cylinders; if you intend to do hauling or light towing, look for a version equipped with the optional 2.6L 4-banger mated to a 5-speed manual or 4-speed automatic transmission. For off-roading, the 4X4 is the best choice, with its GM-built V6 coupled to a 5-speed manual gearbox. Unfortunately, it sells for too high a premium.

The 1997–2000 Hombre is essentially a Chevrolet S pickup with Isuzu sheet metal; therefore, quality control is only marginally better than what you'd find with GM's homegrown counterpart. Initially, the only engine choice was GM's anemic 4-banger. **1997**—Included an optional extended cab housing and a better-performing 4.3L V6. **1998**—Was given 4X4, dual airbags, and a passenger-side airbag cut-off switch. The next two model years saw few changes, as these vehicles remained near-mirror images of GM's S-10, lacking some configurations such as V6-equipped regular cabs and manual transmission-equipped 4X2 V6 extended cabs.

Canyon, Colorado

Replacing the S-10, these $19,000 small, light-duty pickups sacrifice hauling capacity for good fuel economy and a softer, quieter ride. They are slightly larger than the S-10 and will come with 4X2 or 4X4 drive and in regular-cab, extended-cab, and crew-cab configurations. Three suspension packages will be available: standard, sport, and off-road.

The new 3.5L inline 5-cylinder is derived from GM's 4.2L inline-six, first used in the 2002 Chevrolet TrailBlazer. Dual balance shafts within each engine help eliminate vibrations, while variable valve timing improves idle smoothness, reduces emissions, and increases gas mileage. Other features include a shift-on-the-fly 4X4 system, an optional locking differential, and traction control. On the minus side, no V6 is available, towing capacity is limited, and the 5-cylinder engine is unproven.

Both mid-sized pickups include federally mandated child-seat anchors, four-door child locks, front-seat airbag Off switches for regular cab models, and the same three-point safety belts found in automobiles.

Main competitors: Ford Ranger, Dodge Dakota, Toyota Tacoma, Nissan Frontier, Mazda B Series Crew Cab, Dodge Dakota Quad Cab, Nissan Frontier Crew Cab, Toyota Tacoma Crew Cab, and Ford Explorer Sport Trac. Of this group, the Mazda, Nissan, and Toyota pickups are your best bets.

COST ANALYSIS: Theoretically, $17,000 will put you into an unadorned 2005 Canyon or Colorado, if you're lucky enough to find one. Dealers are feature-loading these pickups with several thousand dollars worth of non-essential options. **Best alternatives:** S-10 sales have been terrible, so expect lots of discounting on the 2004 models as they face additional heat from the Canyon and Colorado. Don't buy the new Colorado or Canyon during their first year on the market. Remember, there is a lot of overlapping of features between GMC, Chevrolet, and Isuzu pickups. You may be able to find a better equipped GM or Isuzu version of the Sonoma carrying a different nameplate. Best alternatives: Mazda B Series, Nissan Frontier, or Toyota Tacoma. **Rebates:** $1,500 rebates, plus zero percent financing on the 2004 and 2005 models. **Delivery/PDI:** $850. **Warranty:** Bumper-to-bumper 3 years/60,000 km; rust perforation 6 years/160,000 km. **Supplementary warranty:** An extended powertrain warranty would be a good idea. **Options:** The V6 is a prerequisite if you plan to use an automatic transmission. Ensure that suspension package, payload, and towing capacities meet your requirements. **Depreciation:** Average. **Insurance cost:** Average. **Annual maintenance cost:** Higher than that of most pickups in this class. **Parts supply/cost:** Good supply and reasonably priced parts. **Highway/city fuel economy:** *4X2 and 2.2L:* 8.5–12.4L/100 km; *4X2 and 4.3L:* 10.1–14.2L/ 100 km; *4X4 and 4.3L:* 10.6–14.7L/100 km.

QUALITY/RELIABILITY: Average. Fit and finish isn't as good as most other pickups; excessive wind noise, especially with the Colorado, the thickness of the paint coat varies considerably and will chip easily (midnight blue). **Owner-reported problems:** Engine and automatic transmission malfunctions and excessive knocking noise, electrical shorts, power window failures, inaccurate fuel gauges, plastic expensive and frequent oxygen sensor replacements and brake repairs, and poor body assembly. *Colorado:* Fuel lines are easily cracked and driver-side door water leaks; lumbar support may be too high for some people. **Warranty performance:** Average.

SAFETY SUMMARY: The lack of head restraints on early models is a safety hazard. U.S. federal government researchers have opened investigations into reports of ABS failures (1991–94); the spare tire falling off the vehicle (1991–96); and post-crash fuel leakage (1994–99). There are over a thousand reports of safety-related failures registered by NHTSA for the 1995 model year alone. The most frequent failures are sudden, unintended acceleration; head restraints that can't be adjusted and are too low to be effective; airbags that fail to deploy; blown engine head gaskets; ABS that doesn't brake but does break; intermittent windshield wiper failures (they also often stop in the middle of the windshield); tires that rub the front wheelwell when turning; and spare tires that fall off on the highway. **Airbags:** The airbag cut-off switch permits the use of a child safety seat up front. **ABS:** Standard 4W; disc/drum. **Safety belt pretensioners:** No. **Head restraints F/R:** *S10: 1997:* *; *1998:* ****; *1999:* **** *2001–03:* ****/*. **Visibility F/R:** *****/***. **Maximum load capacity:** *2001 S-10 LS V6:* 454 kg (1,000 lb.).

SAFETY COMPLAINTS: All years: No airbag deployment. • Chronic stalling. • Transmission and differential failures. • ABS failures. • Premature front pad wear and rotor warping. • Plastic gas tank is easily punctured. • Driver's seat slides back and forth while driving. **S-10, Sonoma, T-10: 1998**— Engine compartment fire ignited while vehicle was parked for about an hour. • Another fire erupted in the dash area while vehicle was being driven. • Defective door latch allowed the driver-side door to swing open while vehicle was underway. • Others report that the doors don't close properly, allowing water to enter the interior and hit the third door. • Easily broken door handles. • Right front seat belt failure. • Spare tire rod broke, throwing tire onto the highway. • Excessive steering wheel vibration. • Vehicle pulls to the side and wanders over the highway. • Engine head gasket failures. • Faulty fuel injection system. • Both rear wheels suddenly locked up at 100 km/h. • Burst transmission fluid line. • Low-mounted gas pedal forces short drivers to sit dangerously close to the airbag housing. • Third brake light shorts out. • Water leaks behind the jump seat. **1999**—Transmission lock-up, poor braking perfor-mance, and headlight failures. **1999–2000**—461 complaints recorded by NHTSA. • AC froze, causing the serpentine belt to catch fire. • Oil lines and oil pan gaskets frequently fail. • Wiring harness caught fire while vehicle was parked. • Stuck gas pedal. • Transfer case gets stuck in 4X4 High and Low. • Vehicle jumps out of First gear when accelerating. • Reverse band slips and spreads fibres throughout transmission and converter. • Drive shaft broke while vehicle underway. • Rear-end pinion seal failed. • No-starts and hard starts. • Cruise control doesn't shut off when brakes are applied. • Battery leaked acid onto brake line, resulting in complete loss of braking. • Brake lock-up caused vehicle to go out of control. • Broken driver and passenger seat recliners. • AC wires burned out clutch fan. • Bad relay causes sudden dash light and headlight failure. • Wipers don't operate properly. • Horn goes off by itself. • Exhaust fumes leak through ventilation system. • Right and left side wheels fell off due to a missing cotter pin. • Spare tire cable broke, allowing tire to fly off. • Goodyear Wrangler tire tread separation. • Loose ball joints cause excessive tire wear. • Doors have fallen off due to hinge weld failure. • Third door handle breaks easily. • Rearview side mirror falls off. • Side window shattered as door was closed. • Loose front seats and headlight failures. • Payload label may be incorrect. **2001**— Over 150 complaints recorded by NHTSA. • ABS engages when vehicle passes over a bump. • Engine surging. • During a collision, airbags deployed and ignited a fire. • Vehicle rolled down driveway even though engine was shut off and parking brake was applied. • Undercarriage fires. • Tire tread separation. • Steering stiffens. • Loose passenger seat. • Wipers stop in middle of windshield. **2002**—Stuck gas pedal (not carpet related). • Axle suddenly snapped. • Harshshifting automatic transmission. • Door water and air leaks. **2003**—Long hesitation when accelerating and then suddenly drops into first gear. • Airbags didn't deploy. • Quirky steering; suddenly pulls to one side. • Goodyear sidewall defect; and Uniroyal tires wobble. • Faulty fuel gauge. • Fuel tank always overflows when refuelling. • Excessive on-road vibration. • Tailgate fell off. • Driveshaft fell out. • Primary hood latch releases while driving. • Headlights dim without warning. **Hombre: 1997**—Tall drivers not protected by head restraints. • Cracked rear axle caused transmission lock-up. • Electrical shorts cause lights to go out. • Poor brake performance. • Engine ingested water in sufficient quantity to cause hydraulic lock-up of the engine pistons. **1998**— Brake failure. • Sudden breakage of the front axle. **2000**—Sudden steering rod failure while underway. **2003**—Manual transmission pops out of gear. **Canyon and Colorado: 2004**—Engine surging. • Brake pedal went to floor without effect. • Tailgate fell down while driving. • Transmission failures. • Excessive on-road vibration.

Secret Warranties/Service Tips

S-10, Sonoma, T-10: 1993–99—Cure AC odours by installing GM's cooling coil coating kit. **1993–2002**—Paint delamination, peeling, or fading (see Part Three). **1995–2001**—Hood hinge rattling. **1995–2002**—A rough idle or Check Engine light warning may only signal the need to clean the fuel injection system **1996–97**—Excessive engine noise can be silenced by replacing the valve stem oil seal. • A chronic engine miss may be caused by a faulty oxygen sensor. **1996–98**—Pickups that idle roughly after sitting overnight may only need a fuel injector cleaner, says TSB #87-65-07A. • If the engine overheats, the heater won't work, and you find rust in the coolant, try GM's suggested engine flush before paying for more expensive work. **1997–2001**— Transmission stuck in Third gear, MIL lamp comes on, and instrument cluster is inoperative. **1998**—If the blower fan runs continuously with the ignition off, consider replacing the AC control assembly. **1998–99**—Incorrect fuel gauge readings can be corrected by reprogramming the VCM module. **1998–2002**—AWD malfunctions (see following).

Drivetrain – Noise/Vibration/Leaks/Slipping in 4X4

Bulletin No.: 02-04-21-005A   Date: February 2003

Subject: Slips in 4X4, noise, vibration, leaks, hot odour (diagnose and repair front differential and/or transfer case)
1999–2000 Cadillac Escalade
1998–2002 Chevrolet S-10, Silverado, Blazer, Suburban, Tahoe
2002 Chevrolet Avalanche
1998–2002 GMC Sierra, Sonoma, Jimmy, Suburban, Yukon, Yukon XL
with Autotrak transfer case (RPO NP8) (selector pad on instrument panel must have auto 4X4, 4HI, 4L0, and 2HI selections)

Cause: The front axle may have excessive preload in the pinion or carrier bearings or may be locked up, not allowing the pinion to rotate freely.

2000–03—Hard starts, poor idle, and misfires. **2001**—Incorrectly oriented engine oil cooler hose. • Harsh shifts. • Automatic transmission 2–4 band or 3–4 clutch damage. • Security lamp flashes • Engine stalls, or won't start. • Rear suspension popping noise when going over a bump or when turning. • Lights flicker while driving at night. **Space Cab, Hombre: all years:** Replace the distributor seal to stop engine oil from leaking into the distributor. • Knocking from the steering column when the wheel is turned from side to side can be fixed with a steering shaft repair kit (#8-97077-575-0) and rubber boot (#8-97079-655-0). • TSB #SB96-11-L002 suggests the front fender inner liners be replaced to prevent ice buildup around the lower door-to-fender area, which can damage the door and fender. **Canyon and Colorado: 2004**—Automatic transmission slipping. • Hot exhaust popping or snapping. • GM says it's normal to hear a shift clunk (sigh).

S-10, Sonoma, T-10/Space Cab, Hombre Profile

	1997	1998	1999	2000	2001	2002	2003	2004
Cost Price ($) (negotiable)								
S-10, S-14 (15%)	15,300	16,190	16,410	16,495	18,217	17,060	17,870	—
T-10 4X4 (15%)	20,015	21,150	21,370	21,170	26,097	—	—	—
Sonoma (15%)	15,300	16,190	16,410	16,495	17,025	17,060	17,870	—
Sonoma 4X4 (15%)	15,300	16,198	16,410	16,495	17,025	19,128	17,860	
Hombre (12%)	14,614	14,825	13,995	14,095	14,095	—	—	—
Hombre 4X4 (16%)	—	—	22,961	26,995	27,595	—	—	—
Canyon/Colorado (16%)	—	—	—	—	—	—	—	16,995
Used Values ($)								
S-10, S-14 ∧	4,500	5,500	6,500	8,500	10,000	11,500	13,000	—
S-10, S-14 ∨	3,500	4,500	5,500	7,000	8,500	10,000	11,500	—
T-10 4X4 ∧	5,500	6,500	8,000	10,000	11,500	—	—	—
T-10 4X4 ∨	4,500	5,500	6,500	8,500	10,500	—	—	—
Sonoma ∧	4,000	5,000	6,500	8,500	9,500	10,500	13,000	—
Sonoma ∨	3,500	4,000	5,000	7,000	8,500	9,500	11,500	—
Sonoma 4X4 ∧	5,000	5,000	6,500	8,500	9,500	10,500	13,000	—
Sonoma 4X4 ∨	4,000	4,000	5,000	7,000	8,500	9,500	11,500	
Hombre ∧	3500	4,000	5,000	6,000	6,500	—	—	—
Hombre ∨	3000	3,000	4,000	5,000	6,000	—	—	—

Hombre 4X4 ∧	—	—	6,500	7,500	8,500	—	—	—
Hombre 4X4 ∨	—	—	5,000	7,000	7,500	—	—	—
Canyon/Colorado ∧	—	—	—	—	—	—	—	14,000
Canyon/Colorado ∨	—	—	—	—	—	—	—	12,500

Reliability

S-10, Sonoma, T-10	❶	❷	③	③	③	③	③	—
Space Cab, Hombre	③	③	④	④	④	④	④	—
Canyon/Colorado	—	—	—	—	—	—	—	③

Crash Safety (F)

S-10 4X2	③	—	—	③	③	③	③	—
Ext.	③	④	❷	❷	❷	❷	❷	—
S-10 4X4	—	—	—	—	❷	—	—	—
Sonoma	③	④	❷	③	③	—	—	—
Sonoma Ext.	—	—	—	❷	❷	—	—	—
Hombre	—	—	—	③	—	—	—	—
Canyon/Colorado	—	—	—	—	—	—	—	④
Side								
S-10 4X2	—	—	—	④	④	④	④	—
Ext.	—	—	③	③	③	③	③	—
S-10 4X4	—	—	—	—	③	—	—	—
Sonoma	—	—	—	④	—	—	—	—
Sonoma Ext.	—	—	—	③	—	—	—	—
Space Cab, Hombre	—	—	—	④	—	—	—	—
Canyon/Colorado	—	—	—	—	—	—	—	④
Offset	—	❷	❷	❷	❷	❷	❷	—
Rollover	—	—	—	—	③	③	③	—

Nissan

FRONTIER, PICKUP

RATING: Recommended (2005). Nissan has hit a home run with its 2005 Frontier. Year after year, this Nissan pickup performs well without any serious complications and this "Baby Titan" is destined to continue the tradition. It's as good as the Mazda and Toyota competition and better than Chrysler's over-hyped semi-Hemi, Ford's quality-challenged Rangers, and GM's puny, Isuzu-bred Canyon/Colorado "munchkins" and Silverado/Sierra "Hulk." Above Average (1985–2004). Let's face it, the pre-2005 models are mediocre performers, nevertheless, they are reliable, relatively inexpensive, competent for light chores, easy to maintain, and fun to drive. **Strong points:** *2004:* Excellent V6 performance, nice handling, very comfortable ride up front, a high resale value, and an airbag cut-off switch. Crew Cabs have convenient front-opening rear doors that open independently of the front doors. Easier rear access with the four doors than you'll find with Ford or Mazda. **Weak points:** The new 4.0L will run on regular fuel (wink, wink, nudge, nudge), but 91-octane is recommended. Test-drive your choice for engine performance;

Nissan has been notorious for overrating their engines. *2004:* Poor acceleration (4-cylinder); choppy ride over uneven terrain ("rear-end hop") is accentuated with an empty load; lots of body lean when cornering; slow, vague steering offers little feedback; mediocre braking; drive shaft carrier bearing failures on earlier models; automatic transmission shifter obstructs view of the climate controls and blocks access to the wiper switch; difficult rear entry/exit (King Cab); low seats make the height-adjustment feature essential for many drivers and the King Cab's rear jump seat is laughably small; limited rear legroom on the hard rear bench seat; small cargo bed on the Crew Cab; few standard features, the cabin looks like "plastic central," and many gauges are too recessed to be easily read. Lots of engine, wind, and tire noise. Mediocre fuel economy on 2001–2004 models. Triple-whammy safety complaints: sudden acceleration, brake failures, and Firestone tire defects. **New for 2005:** Almost everything. Frontier morphs into a burly-looking, small-scale version of the Titan pickup with larger dimensions, additional power, and important safety and convenience enhancements. **Likely failures:** Automatic trans-mission, drive shaft, oxygen sensor, and brakes.

2004 Technical Data

Powertrain (rear-drive/ part-time 4X4)
Engines: 2.4L 4-cyl. (143 hp)
• 3.3L V6 (180 hp)
• 3.3L super V6 (210 hp)
Transmissions: 5-speed man.
• 4-speed auto. OD
Dimension/Capacity
Height/length/width:
65.9/196.1/71.9 in.
Box length: 4.6 ft./6.2 ft.

Headroom F/R: 39.6/36.5 in.
Legroom F/R: 42.5/35.1 in.
Wheelbase: 104.3/116.1 in.
Turning circle: 33.6 ft.
Passengers: 3/2+2
GVWR: 4,701–5,202 lb.
Payload: 1,061–4,141 lb.
Tow limit: 3,500–5,000 lb.
Ground clear.: 7.1–7.9 in.
Fuel tank: 60L/reg.
Weight: 3,205 lb.

MODEL HISTORY: Forget the 2004 specs above, the 2005 Frontier is a significantly improved pickup that's larger, more powerful, easier to handle, and safer than ever before. Wheelbase, is a whopping 9.8 inches longer, width goes up 1.6 inches, height increases by 3.0–3.5 inches, and overall length is stretched by 9.8 inches. Somebody mention power? The entry-level King Cabs get a new 2.5L 4-cylinder engine, while most other models will use a new 250-hp 4.0L V6. A 6-speed manual replaces last-year's 5-speed and a 5-speed automatic replaces the 4-speed automatic. There's also a new dual-range 4WD setup with shift-on-the-fly electronic control, rack-and-pinion steering, and a slew of handling improvements. Occupant crash protection is improved through the use of new front side airbags and optional curtain side airbags triggered by rollover sensors.

Frontier pickups have always been reliable and versatile haulers. Most models used a lethargic 143-hp 2.4L 4-cylinder, supplemented by a better-performing, 180-hp, 3.3L V6, and a barely-worth-the trouble, premium-fueled and temperamental, supercharged 210-hp V6 variant.

The King Cab V6 addition gave these pickups the power boost they lacked in the past. ABS is standard on the rear wheels and optional on all four wheels. It's standard, however, on all recent 4X4s, Crew Cabs, and on the Desert Runner.

Introduced in 1985, these pickups are more comfortable, perform better, and aren't as rust-prone as their Datsun predecessors. The different 4-cylinder engines offered through the years have all provided adequate power and reasonable reliability. Engine choices through the '90s include the 2.4L 4-cylinder or the more powerful 3.0L V6 borrowed from Nissan's 240SX. Although the powerful 6-cylinder is more fuel thirsty, it's the engine of choice for maximum hauling and off-roading versatility.

You won't have to look far to find a reasonably priced used Nissan pickup. These small pickups, like Mazda's trucks, didn't cost much when they were new and their used prices have drifted downward accordingly. On newer models, though, you'll find prices have firmed up considerably due to the general popularity of two- and three-year-old crew cab pickups and down-sized sport-utilities. Depending on the year, you'll find a standard 4- or 5-speed manual or an optional 3- or 4-speed automatic. Later 4-speed automatics have a fuel-saving lock-up torque converter, but a manual transmission will get the most power and economy out of these motors. The 4X4 option is available with either manual or automatic hubs. The manual version is a pain because you have to stop and turn the hubs. The automatic form isn't much better because it can't be engaged above 50 km/h, and to disengage it you have to stop and back up a metre or two. These pickups handle impressively well and have firm but reasonably comfortable rides, although some owners say the bucket seats only fit bucket bottoms. The king cab is a must for tall drivers or those who require extra interior storage space. Don't look for a fourth door—Nissan didn't offer one until the 2000 model year.

1995—Rear wheel ABS added. **1998**—A larger, roomier model debuted with more refined interior ergonomics. **1999**—King Cabs got more powerful V6 engines and a host of other standard and optional features. **2000**—A crew cab model was given a full-sized forward-hinged fourth door and a short bed. **2001**—A supercharged, 210-hp V6 on SE king and crew cabs along with a slight restyling and standard 17-inch wheels. Other additions: a new instrument cluster, interior upgrades, and a security system. **2002**—The regular cab model was dropped, crew cabs were offered with a long bed, and all pickups got a re-styled interior. **2003**—6-cylinder engines for the four-wheel-drives, crew cabs got ten more horses, and more options like a tire-pressure monitor and antiskid/traction control.

COST ANALYSIS: $23,498 is the price for the base 2004 Frontier King Cab XE; and it will be heavily discounted as buyers turn to the better performing, more feature-laden 2005. Take the hint: Save your pennies for a much-improved second-series 2005 version and pay the predicted 4-percent increase. I know, they'll try to charge you 10 percent more, but stand fast and most dealers will accept splitting the difference (all the while, hoping to skin you alive with an inflated preparation and freight fee). Be ready! **Best alternatives:** Some other pickups you might want to consider: Mazda B Series and Toyota Tacoma.

Rebates: $1,500+ rebates, plus zero percent financing. **Delivery/PDI:** $950. **Warranty:** Bumper-to-bumper 3 years/60,000 km; powertrain 5 years/100,000 km; rust perforation 5 years/unlimited km. **Supplementary warranty:** An extended warranty isn't needed. **Options:** The supercharged V6 is an extreme solution to the small engine's deficiencies. The other V6 is the best compromise. Other options to consider: a limited-slip differential, four-wheel ABS, and running boards. Don't go for the Off-Road Package unless you crave a bouncier ride. **Depreciation:** Slower than average. **Insurance cost:** Average. **Parts supply/cost:** These trucks have been around for decades with few design changes, so parts are widely available and relatively inexpensive. **Annual maintenance cost:** Below-average maintenance costs; the simple design makes for easy servicing by any independent garage. **Highway/city fuel economy:** *2.4L and auto.:* 9.1–12L/100 km; *3.3L V6 and 4X4:* 11.5–15.3L/100 km.

QUALITY/RELIABILITY: Assembly and component quality are above average. Fortunately, Nissan products are generally so well made that they don't need lots of warranty work. But when they do, owners report that the company's customer relations staff in Canada aren't all that sensitive to their needs. For example, in several instances, Nissan Canada and its Infiniti spin-off have refused to recognize goodwill programs detailed in the company's U.S. service bulletins. Their reasoning: Nissan Canada isn't obligated to give the same treatment to Canadian owners. Yikes! **Owner-reported problems:** Engine exhaust intake manifold failures have been common during the past five years; drive shaft and ball joint defects cause excessive vibration; minor trim and accessory defects; premature front-brake wear; and electrical short circuits.

ROAD PERFORMANCE: Acceleration/torque: The fuel-sipping 4-cylinder engine is adequate for light-duty use. However, add an automatic transmission and you'll wish you had the V6. The supercharged V6 is an impressive performer that's less noisy than the 4-banger. **Transmission:** Easy-shifting manual transmission, and the electronically controlled automatic transaxle is both smooth and predictable. **Steering:** Acceptable, but not very responsive or precise; 2005 model corrects this problem. **Routine handling:** Average for a truck; improved with the upgraded suspension, added in 1998 and steering/suspension improvements found on the 2005s. Firmer ride with long wheelbase and supercharged models. **Emergency handling:** Better than average, in spite of the pickup's heft and size. **Braking:** Mediocre (100–0 km/h: 44 m[143 ft.]).

SAFETY SUMMARY: Crash-tested 1989 and 1991 versions passed with flying colours—neither the driver nor the passenger would be seriously injured. **Airbags:** There have been reports of airbags failing to deploy or deploying when they shouldn't, resulting in severe injuries. **ABS:** Standard 2W, 4W. **Safety belt pretensioners:** Standard. **Traction control:** Optional. **Head restraints F/R:** *1997:* *; *1998:* ***/**; *1999:* ***; *2001:* ***; *2002–04:* **. **Visibility F/R:** *****.

SAFETY COMPLAINTS: 1997—Brakes lock up in emergency braking situations. • Leaking rear axle seals. • Excessive shaking when vehicle is driven at 80 km/h. **1998**—Accelerator sticks when shifting gears. **1999**—Rattles inside steering column. • Exhaust leak under driver's seat. • Drive shaft failure. • Driveline vibration upon acceleration. • Tires lose traction on wet roads. **1999–2000**—Brake pedal goes to floor without braking. • Stalling at full throttle. **2000**—Under-hood fire. • Sudden acceleration. • Severe vibration during acceleration or while pulling a load. • Front-end bushing bolt sheared. • Loss of brakes. • Brake master cylinder failure. • Faulty drive shaft carrier bearing; Nissan's "fix" is inadequate. • When parked on an incline, emergency brake failed and truck rolled into garage door. • Too-soft suspension causes serious swaying. **2001**—Airbags failed to deploy. • Front passenger seat belt can't be pulled out for usage (on national back order). • High idle at low speeds with clutch depressed. • Fuel overflows from filler neck when refuelling. • Brakes lack sufficient hydraulic pressure to stop vehicle. • Blocked cowl vent restricts fresh air flow. **2002**—No airbag deployment. • Automatic transmission jumped out of Park into Reverse. • Leaking fuel tank. • Brake failure. • ABS light comes on for no reason. • Sudden loss of power due to defective oxygen sensor, or kicking in of Nissan speed limiter. • Controller fuse blows repeatedly, shutting vehicle down. • Gas and brake pedal set too close together. • Tail light fills with water. • Defective sidewalls on General Grabber tires. **2003**—Sudden, unintended acceleration when brakes are applied. • Engine has to be shut down to turn off AC if defroster is engaged. **2004**—Slipped out of Park and rolled downhill. • Excessive vibration due to corroded upper and lower ball joints.

Secret Warranties/Service Tips

1996–2002—Troubleshooting tips for noisy, hard transfer-case shifting. **1998–99**—An easy fuel gauge fix is outlined in TSB #NTB99-064. **1999–2000**—A pop or clunking noise is addressed in TSB #NTB00-075. **1999–2001**—Repair tips for a cracked exhaust manifold set the stage for after-warranty assistance since this bulletin shows it's a recognized defect:

Exhaust Manifold (R/H) – Ticking/Exhaust Noise

Bulletin: NTB01-038   Date: May 22, 2001

1999–2001 Frontier (D22)
2000–01 Xterra (WD22)

If a cracked right-hand exhaust manifold is discovered during unrelated service when the exhaust heat shield is removed, a replacement right-hand exhaust manifold is available to correct the incident. If one of these symptoms should occur, use the service procedure provided in this bulletin to diagnose the condition, replacing the right-hand exhaust manifold and related parts as described.

1999–2004—A faulty radiator cap may be the cause of coolant loss or engine overheating. **2000**—Idle fluctuation when coasting to a stop with the clutch depressed. • Remedy for excessive body vibration at 100 km/h. • Water may enter the distributor assembly. • Rough idle or excessive engine vibration at idle. • Clunk or rattle heard when turning the steering wheel. • Front bumper rattling. • Troubleshooting squeaks and rattles. **2000–03**—ABS trouble light stays lit. **2001**—Cloudy, hazy appearance of plastic headlamp. Warm air from fresh air vents. • Speedometer may not work. **1999–2002**—Loss of super-charged engine power. • Surging, no automatic transmission upshift. • Steering pull during braking. • MIL light may malfunction. • Silencing bearing noise from the transfer-case area. • Knocking noise above idle. **2003**—Remedy for AC that won't turn off. **2003–04**—Cold engine startup rattle.

Frontier, Pickup Profile

	1997	1998	1999	2000	2001	2002	2003	2004
Cost Price ($) (negotiable)								
4X2 (15%)	13,798	14,498	14,498	14,498	20,998	22,890	23,498	23,450
4X4 (16%)	20,498	20,999	21,498	21,498	26,498	27,553	27,398	27,400
Used Values ($)								
4X2 ⋀	5,000	6,000	7,500	9,500	12,500	14,500	16,500	19,500
4X2 ⋁	4,000	5,000	6,000	7,500	11,500	13,500	15,500	18,000
4X4 ⋀	7,500	8,000	9,500	11,000	15,500	18,500	20,500	23,000
4X4 ⋁	6,500	7,000	8,500	10,000	14,500	17,000	19,500	21,500
Reliability	④	④	④	④	⑤	⑤	⑤	⑤
Crash Safety (F)	❷	❷	③	③	—	④	④	④
Side	—	—	—	④	④	⑤	⑤	⑤
Offset	—	❷	❷	❷	❷	❷	❷	❷
Rollover	—	—	—	—	③	③	③	—

TITAN ★★★★

RATING: Above Average (2004–05). **Strong points:** Powerful V8 engine has slightly more torque than the Chrysler Hemi does, and notably more than the Ford, Chevrolet, or GMC V8s in standard-duty trucks; good off-road perfor-mance and braking; a roomy interior; the King Cab's rear doors swing back almost flat against the side of the cargo box; high-utility bed option is a hauler's dream; a security system with an immobilizer is standard; high-quality, factory-applied, spray-on bed liner; optional adjustable pedals; superior build quality; predicted high resale value and reliability; 5-speed automatic boosts fuel economy. **Weak points:** The only engine available is a fuel-thirsty 5.6L gasoline V8; a jumpy throttle causes jerky acceleration; one wheelbase must fit all; if you want more passenger space with the Crew Cab you give up a foot of bed length; no standard regular cab or heavy-duty versions; part-time 4X4 must be shifted out of 4X4 on dry or hard surfaces; Chevy and GMC have a full-time system; excessive on-road vibration and a hopping ride; nonstop exhaust roar; serious premature brake wear and airbag sensor defects; a plastic-laden interior; no crashworthiness tests, yet; and freight and PDI fee price gouging. **New for 2005:** Nothing much. **Likely failures:** Brake master cylinder rotors, calipers, and pads, power windows, AC, accessories, FM radio, and fit and finish (front and rear doors and door locks).

2005 Technical Data

Powertrain (4X2/part-time 4X4)
Engine: 5.6L V8 (305 hp)
Transmission: 5-speed auto.
Dimension/Capacity
Height/length/width:
74.4/224.2/78.8 in.
Box length: 6.7 ft.
Headroom F/R: 40.9/38.9 in.
Legroom F/R: 41.8/33.6 in.

Wheelbase: 139.8 in.
Turning circle: 41 ft.
Passengers: 3/2
GVWR: 16,200 lb.
Payload: 1,875 lb.
Tow limit: 9,400 lb.
Ground clear.: 9.7/11.5 in.
Fuel tank: 76L/reg.
Weight: 4,700 lb.

MODEL HISTORY: Introduced as a 2004 model, this is the full-sized pickup Toyota should have built. Titan's bold, rugged styling harkens back to the macho "in-your-face-styling" of the Dodge Ram in its incarnation as the star of the movie *Twister* starring. An important difference is that the Titan delivers high-tech refinements along with proven reliability, two elements missing from the Chrysler, GM, and Ford lineups. This large pickup has lots of engine torque, headroom, rear-seat legroom, and 4X4 ground clearance. The Titan's also particularly innovative in offering a factory-sprayed bedliner, a lighted tailgate, a cargo access area in the rear quarter panel and king cab rear doors that swing open 168 degrees. It's also the first truck in its class with an optional locking rear differential.

Standard features include a 5-speed automatic transmission, air conditioning, power rack-and-pinion steering, lockable tailgate, fold-flat front seats and four-wheel disc brakes with ABS.

COST ANALYSIS: Best alternatives: There's no reason to buy a 2005 model; go for a 2004 model built after June 2004 to keep first-year glitches to a minimum. Base price for a 4X2 is estimated to be $27,000; $30,000 for the 4X4 version. Bargain down Nissan's excessive freight and PDI fee. Ford F-150, Chevrolet Silverado, and Dodge Ram come up way short for reliability. Toyota's Tundra is smaller and a bit more problem prone (see Tundra's Safety Complaints). **Rebates:** Not likely, though some financing incentives may kick in early next year.

QUALITY/RELIABILITY: Good, though, there are some major deficiencies. It's worrisome that Dana makes both axles, both differential gears, and the all-aluminum propeller shaft. The quality of this company's powertrains on Chrysler Jeeps hasn't been impressive. Owners report brake rotors warping within a few months; terrible radio reception, which fades out of stereo and FM mode, and the $1,800 premium Fosgate radio uses cheap Clarion components; power window malfunctions; rear axle leakage; dash rattles; steering wheel clicks; and easily chipped paint.

SAFETY COMPLAINTS: 2004—Vehicle jumped out of Park into Reverse while parked (also a Frontier problem). • Complete steering loss. • Airbag disabled even though a 170-pound passenger is seated. • Headlight switch easily bumped On or Off—not enough resistance to rotation. • Rotors are too small for the Titan, warp easily.

> The vehicle is now in the shop with 12,113 miles [19,494 km], having the rotor replaced again. I believe that there is a defective part manufactured for this vehicle. My driving habits are not such that they would cause this much excessive brake rotor warping. These brakes are not cheap to replace, I think it is unrealistic to advertise a vehicle can tow 9,400 lbs [4264 kg] and cannot even stop with its own body weight, less any towing. The brake system in my opinion is undersized or there is a manufacture spec that is not being met. God forbid I actually used this vehicle to tow, as advertised.

Secret Warranties/Service Tips

2004—Warranty payout guidelines and troubleshooting tips for brake shudder and vibration are detailed in TSB #: BR00-004a and NTB00-033a, dated June 11, 2003. • Slow tire leak. • Inoperative DVD. • Coolant leaks and engine overheating blamed on faulty radiator cap.

Subaru

BAJA

RATING: Not Recommended (2003–05). A Legacy spin-off going into its third year, Baja is touted as a crossover that's part wagon and part pickup, and winds up offering little that is useful or fun. **Strong points:** Poor sales mean deep-discount prices; uniquely styled like a mini-Avalanche; uses a shortened Legacy platform. **Weak points:** Way overpriced; uncomfortable upright rear seating; bed is too short to carry a bike without extending the tailgate into part of the bed; no 5-speed automatic transmission; absence of a folding midgate means the flip-and-fold versatility isn't as practical as Subaru pretends; essentially a resurrected Subaru Brat (1977–87). Head restraints ranked "marginal" by IIHS. **New for 2005:** Nothing significant. **Likely failures:** Front brakes and fit and finish.

MODEL HISTORY: The Baja costs $35,595 and is basically a Legacy Outback with its rear roof chopped off and six inches added to the rear floor to make a mini pickup bed. Like the Chevy Avalanche, the Baja has a "switchback" door similar to the trunk pass-through door in a sedan, creating a 7.5-foot cargo bed. The car/truck comes with standard four-wheel disc ABS, AC, sunroof, anti-theft device, front passenger side-airbag, a 5-speed manual or 4-speed automatic transmission, and upgraded child restraint anchors.

Baja projects a rugged, utilitarian look with its large fender flares, 16-inch alloy wheels, and sport bars, but its 165-hp flat 4-cylinder engine fails to deliver the driving performance its styling promises. Nevertheless, if you're not in a hurry to go anywhere and value fuel economy over driving thrills, the all-wheel drive Baja will do nicely.

Toyota

TACOMA

RATING: Recommended (2005); Above Average (1987–2004). This is a low-tech, relatively reliable, unadorned pickup. The 2005 improvements make Tacoma a big pickup player. **Strong points:** Incredibly powerful 4- and 6-cylinder engines give smooth performance without guzzling fuel; ride and handling improved with firmer, shorter springs, gas shocks, a limited-slip differential, and larger tires; towing capability increased by 680 kilograms (1,500 lb.); upgraded interior and a new composite cargo bed with extra storage compartments and adjustable tie-down anchors; additional interior room makes back seats acceptable for adult passengers. *2004*: Competent V6 engine performance; rugged, impressive off-road capability; good braking; roomy interior; good build quality; high resale value; above average reliability; slow depreciation, and good fuel economy somewhat offset the stiff purchase price. **Weak points:** Handling is still a bit trucklike; 6-speed manual transmission is a bit clunky; rear drum brakes (Toyota says they perform better in wet conditions). *2004:* mediocre ride and wet-weather handling; bereft of many standard features offered by competitors; front seat is set too low and far back; cushions are too small in the rear seat, where legroom is limited; climate controls are obstructed by the cupholders; smaller bed than many competitors; StepSide bed is quite narrow; difficult entry/exit requires a higher step-up than with other 4X4 pickups; less towing capability than domestic competitors; and may not achieve stated towing capacity; be very wary. Lots of engine and road noise. Freight and PDI fee price gouging ($1,245). **New for 2005:** Almost everything. This is a longer, more powerful truck. **Likely failures:** Automatic transmission, brakes, and accessories.

2005 Technical Data

Powertrain (4X4 or 4X2/part-time 4X4)
Engines: 2.7L 4-cyl. (164 hp)
• 3.4L V6 (245 hp)
• 4.7L V8 (245 hp)
Transmissions: 6-speed man.
• 5-speed auto.
Dimension/Capacity
Height/length/width:
65.7/190.4/72.2 in.
Box length: 74.5 in.

Headroom F/R: 38.4/35.5 in.
Legroom F/R: 42.8/27.2 in.
Wheelbase: 109.4 in.
Turning circle: N/A
Passengers: 3/2
GVWR: 4,244–5,104 lb.
Payload: 791–1,200 lb.
Tow limit: (4X4) 6,500 lb.
Ground clear.: (4X4): 6.5 in.
Fuel tank: 57L/reg.
Weight: 3,140 lb.

MODEL HISTORY: Redesigned for the first time in ten years, the 2005 Tacoma targets the Dodge Dakota crowd with a powerful V6 and a 6-speed manual/5-speed automatic transmission, to counter Dodge's less sophisticated powertrain setup. Set on the same platform as the 4Runner and Lexus GX 470, Tacoma is about a half-foot longer, four inches wider, and two inches taller, than last year's version. Interior dimensions are larger and a long-bed version of the Crew Cab and the high-performance Access Cab X-Runner street truck, have been added.

The entry-level 4X2 Regular Cab has more standard features this year, such as anti-lock brakes, a CD stereo, multiple power points, and a coolant temperature gauge. Interior amenities are also classier this year, with quality materials and a more stylish design.

This compact pickup is available as a Regular Cab, Xtracab, or Double Cab (a four-door crew cab) in 4X2 or 4X4. There's no denying the added convenience of four doors, but the Double Cab also provides a 60/40 folding rear bench seat for more versatility. The new 245-hp V6 is best in class: it beats the Dodge 3.7L 215-hp V6, Ford's 4.2L 202-hp V6, and the GM 4.3L 200-hp V6. Available engines on 2004 and earlier models are a 2.4L and 2.7L 4-cylinder and a 3.4L V6. A dealer-installed supercharger package will give the V6 50 additional horses (295-hp). The shift-on-the-fly 4X4 system is optional on 4X4 trucks and standard on the 4X4 SR5 V6.

Toyota has been building good cars for quite a while, but its pickups have always missed the quality and performance mark by a little bit because they were either undersized, underpowered, or both. Mechanical reliability is better than that of American pickups, but that's not saying much. Tacomas don't offer a lot of razzle-dazzle, or car-like handling, but they aren't dangerous to life, limb, or your pocket-book.

Over the years, these small pickups have changed little: **1990**—SR5 V6s got standard rear-wheel ABS. **1991**—A wider distribution of shift-on-the-fly 4X4 and ABS and no more manual transmission. **1993**—Introduction of the full-sized T100, a one-ton model, carrying a 150-hp V6 capable of handling 1168 kg (2,575 lb.). **1994**—Dropped the long-bed option and added side-door beams. **1998**—Fresh styling and a passenger-side airbag and cut-off switch. **1999**—Seat belt pretensioners and force limiters. **2000**—4X4 improved gearing. **2001**—Debut of the Double Cab and a new StepSide version, revised front styling and new alloy wheels, a differential locking system, 31-inch tires on alloy wheels, and a tachometer. **2003**—Standard ABS and upgraded child restraint anchors.

Reliability was compromised during the past several decades by lapses in quality control leading to expensive V6 engine head gasket failures through 1996. Engine, automatic transmission, and brake problems have carried over to the latest models. Fortunately, they have been covered by after-warranty assistance programs that have compensated owners long after the original warranty has passed.

COST ANALYSIS: If you absolutely *must* get a new Tacoma, understand that it will cost you at least $1,500 more than last year's $23,750 base price. If you want the AWD version, it'll cost you about $3,000 tacked onto last year's $28,500. Of course, you should cut down Toyota's huge freight and PDI fee by about half. Pssst! The 2000 or earlier versions are your best buys from a price/quality perspective. In 2002–04 models 2,250 kilogram (5,000 lb) towing capability may not be possible. Watch out! **Best alternatives:** The Mazda B Series or Nissan Frontier are credible alternatives. Watch out: As with Mazda's B Series, you'll pay way over the base price for a loaded version. It's interesting that the new 4X4 versions that sell for about $10,000 more than the 4X2 version depreciate almost to the 4X2 level after five years on the market. **Rebates:** Look for $1,000–$2,000 rebates and zero percent financing. **Delivery/PDI:** $1,245. **Warranty:** Bumper-to-bumper 3 years/60,000 km; powertrain 5 years/ 100,000 km; rust perforation 5 years/unlimited km. **Supplementary warranty:** An extended warranty isn't necessary. **Options:** ABS and running boards. Ditch the Firestones. **Depreciation:** Slower than average. **Insurance cost:** Average. **Parts supply/cost:** Parts are easily found at dealerships and independent suppliers. Parts costs are very reasonable. **Annual maintenance cost:** Far below average when compared with the American competition and most other Japanese automakers. Good dealer network and service. **Highway/city fuel economy:** *4X2, 2.4L, and automatic:* 8.8–11.1L/100 km; *4X4 and 2.7L:* 10.4–13.1L/100 km; *4X4 and 3.4L:* 10.9–13.6L/100 km.

QUALITY/RELIABILITY 2004: Better than average. Not as good as it once was and the 2005's changes will likely bring their own set of problems. Nevertheless, there's seldom a need to take these pickups out of service for repairs. **Owner-reported problems:** Powertrain and brake failures, electrical shorts, and subpar fit and finish. Some reports that the driver's seat lumbar support is painful on long drives. **Warranty performance:** Better than average. Toyota technical service bulletins usually advise dealers to carry out factory defect repairs only if the customer complains.

SAFETY SUMMARY: Xtracab's right rear seat will accommodate a child safety seat. Owners report that the truck's suspension can barely handle a 227 kg (500 lb.) payload, despite Toyota's assertion that it has a 544 kg (1,200 lb.) rating. **Airbags:** Front. There have been reports of airbags failing to deploy. **ABS:** Optional 2W and 4W. **Safety belt pretensioners:** Standard. **Head restraints F/R:** *1997: ***/**; 1998: ***/**; 1999: *; 2001–04: *; 1999 Extended Cab: **.* **Visibility F/R:** *****. **Maximum load capacity:** 1,470 lb.

SAFETY COMPLAINTS: All years: Airbag malfunctions. Sudden acceleration. • Brake failures, overheating, extended stopping distance, and prematurely worn calipers and rotors. • Vehicle wanders all over the road after hitting a bump. • Firestone, Goodyear, and Dunlop tread separation. • Loose or poorly-fitted trip panels. **1997**—Faulty seat belt retractors. • Unstable suspension can lead to loss of control. • Rear leaf springs don't meet Toyota's load specs. • Headlight failure. **1999**—Stuck accelerator. • When airbag deployed, it melted a hole in the dash. • ABS brakes locked up. • Truck accelerates when heater motor comes on. • Shift lever jumped out of First into Second gear. • Transfer-case seizure. • Left front axle assembly failure due to front ball-joint nut defect. • Rear differential failed. • Check Engine and airbag warning lights stay on constantly. • Rear leaf spring and overload spring break easily when passing over rough terrain. **1999–2000**—Under-hood fires. • Excessive vibration when underway. • Turn signals don't work. **2000**—Parking brake failed. • Side mirror is hard to focus. • Nothing in place to prevent rear-seat passengers' heads from striking the rear window in a collision. **2001**—Incorrectly installed ABS sensor led to brake failure. • Vehicle is prone to hydroplane over wet roads at relatively slow speed. • Intermittently, alarm system fails to unlock vehicle. • Loose front-drive shaft bolts. • Rear wheel fell off. **2001–04**—Dash pad rattle repair tips. **2002**—Brake and gas pedal mounted too closely together. • Brake master cylinder leaks. • Automatic transmission shudders, clunks, surges, shifts erratically, and jumps from gear to gear • Transmission line blew out. • Defective front and rear shock absorbers. • Water enters the cabin through the driver-side support handle. • Defective wheel rims and tires. • Poorly designed jack handle makes for risky tire-changing. **2003**—Sudden rollover. • Truck sways and pitches excessively. • Water leaks onto the driver-side floor and through the passenger door. • Doors don't close fully and lock. **2004**—Excessive exterior mirrors fogging. • Goodyear Wrangler sidewall blowout. • Parking brake hits driver's knee.

Secret Warranties/Service Tips

All years: If there is a delay when shifting from Park or Neutral to Reverse, Toyota will install an upgraded B3 return spring, B3 Brake piston o-rings, and a low-coast modulator spring to correct the problem. Toyota doesn't say if the repair will be covered by its base warranty or "goodwill"; however, a good rule of thumb is that any transmission malfunction, like a delay, in this case, would be the automaker's responsibility for at least the first 7 years/160,000 km. • To minimize noise when shifting 4X4 automatic transmissions, Toyota will change various transmission components under the base warranty. A Toyota insider tells me that the work will also be done for free up to 5 years/ 80,000 km under a "goodwill" special policy. • Consult TSB #AC002-97, issued May 9, 1997, to eliminate musty odours emanating from the AC. Usually, the problem is caused by a blocked evaporator housing drain pipe. • Exhaust "rotten-egg" smell countermeasures. • TSB #BR95-003 says Toyota has a new brake pad kit that reduces brake noise and increases brake durability. • Consult TSB #BR94-002 and #BR95-001, where the company outlines all the possible ways brake pulsation/vibration can be further reduced. Incidentally, this problem has affected almost all of Toyota's cars and trucks over the past decade. • Toyota has also developed a new grease to prevent brake pad clicking. **1995–2000**—That undercarriage noise you hear may be caused by a loose exhaust manifold heat shield. **1997–98**—Transmission chatter can be silenced by adding a check ball to the transmission valve body. **1999**—Install an upgraded clutch pedal kit to silence pedal squeaking. **2000**—Tips on plugging body water leaks. • Fix to prevent paint chipping on the rear quarter panels. • Shoulder belt dirt buildup. • Squeak and rattle noises from the idler pulley. **2001**—Faulty power door locks. **2001–02**—Tube step knocking, squeaking, and rattling fix. • Dash pad rattles. • Loose fender flare pad. • Tearing of the seat material on Double Cabs. **2002**—Vehicle pulls to one side. • Off-centre steering wheel. • MIL light stays lit. **2001–03**—Special Campaign relative to the fuel inlet protector.

Tacoma Profile

	1998	1999	2000	2001	2002	2003	2004	2005
Cost Price ($) (negotiable)								
Base (15%)	15,548	16,395	17,605	21,630	22,000	22,370	22,570	22,125
4X4 (17%)	24,868	25,705	26,150	27,045	27,500	28,065	29,400	29,240
Used Values ($)								
Base ⋀	6,500	8,500	8,500	13,500	15,500	17,500	20,000	—
Base ⋁	5,500	7,500	7,500	12,000	14,000	16,000	18,000	—
4X4 ⋀	8,500	10,500	10,500	16,000	18,000	20,000	22,000	—
4X4 ⋁	7,500	9,500	9,500	14,500	16,500	18,500	20,500	—
Reliability	④	④	④	④	④	④	⑤	—
Crash Safety (F)								
4X2	—	—	—	—	—	④	—	—
Ext. Cab.	④	④	—	③	③	③	③	—
Double	—	—	—	—	—	—	④	—
Side								
4X2	—	—	—	—	—	⑤	—	—
Ext. Cab	—	❶	❶	③	③	③	③	—
Double	—	—	—	—	—	—	⑤	—
Offset	③	③	③	③	③	③	③	—
Rollover	—	—	—	❷	❷	❷	④	—

TUNDRA ★★★

RATING: Average (2004–05); Below Average (2001–03). Rating has been downgraded this year due to better performing models, higher levels of quality control, and cheaper prices available from the competition. A high number of brake and transmission failure complaints is also a factor. **Strong points:** Twin-cam V8 acceleration; low-range gearing for off-roading; smooth, quiet ride; a roomier Double Cab (2004); passenger-side airbag can be switched off with a key; well appointed; easy front access; good fit and finish; standard transmission and engine oil coolers; slow depreciation; better-than-average predicted reliability. **Weak points:** $1,245 freight and PDI fee (price gouging: oh, what a feeling!); less engine torque than the competition; difficult rear exit/entry; 4X4 can't be used on dry pavement (unlike the GM Silverado and Sierra); excessive body sway and tends to be a bit bouncy; poorly performing rear brake drums; rear-hinged back doors on the Access Cab don't open independently of the front doors; no four-door Crew Cab model available, and V8 requires premium fuel. The 2003 and earlier models aren't as roomy in the rear half of the extended cab as other extended full-sized trucks—you feel like you're entering a Dodge Dakota or Ford Ranger; paint not up to Toyota standards; weak door indents; dash LCDs are unreadable with sunglasses; bland styling; incredibly high rate of safety-related defects involving brake, airbag, and seat belt failures. **New for 2005:** Nothing significant.

2005 Technical Data

Powertrain (4X2/4X4)
Engines: 3.4L V6 (190 hp)
• 4.7L V8 (240 hp)
Transmissions: 5-speed man.
• 4-speed auto.
Dimension/Capacity
Height/length/width:
70.5/217.5/75.2 in.
Box length: 76.5/98.2 in.
Headroom F/R: 40.3/37 in.

Legroom F/R: 41.5/29.6 in.
Wheelbase: 128.3 in.
Turning circle: 44.9 ft.
Passengers: 3/3
GVWR: 3,795–5,700 lb.
Payload: 1,500–1,800 lb.
Tow limit: 5,100–7,500 lb.
Ground clear. (4X4): 11.4 in.
Fuel tank: 100L/reg.
Weight: 3,861 lb.

MODEL HISTORY: Larger, stronger, safer, and roomier than its T100 predecessor, the 2001 Tundra was Toyota's first serious foray into the lucrative, though crowded, full-sized pickup market. Unfortunately, Toyota's truck wasn't quite full-sized and sales suffered. **2002 Limited**—A standard in-dash CD changer, antilock braking, and keyless remote entry. 2003—A new V8-equipped Access CAB StepSide model, ABS, grille, bumper, power-sliding rear window (Limited), 17-inch wheels (optional on the SR5), new centre console, and vinyl flooring. **2004**—A more powerful, brawnier Double Cab that gains a foot in wheelbase and length, and three inches in width.

Toyota stretched its Dana-built frame, making the 2004-model Tundra a full-size pickup, competitive with Detroit's Big Three. Buyers were offered an entry-level two-door cab and 8-foot cargo bed, or in Extended Access Cab with a 6.5-foot bed and three-place 60/40 rear bench seat.

The 2004 models come in large and larger sizes, starting at $23,700 for a base 4X2 version and $29,500 for a 4X4. The four-door Access Cab is available for about $36,000. Hauling is also made more convenient through the inclusion of a base 8-foot bed or a 6.5-foot bed found with the four-door version. Two engines are offered: a 190-hp 3.4L V6 or a 240-hp 4.7L V8.

COST ANALYSIS: Best alternatives: The 2004s are the better choice, if you need the extra cabin space and four-door convenience. You'll pay less for last year's Mazda B Series or Nissan Frontier, but performance won't be comparable. Choose optional equipment judiciously—you could pay almost $40,000 for a loaded version. **Rebates:** Look for $2,000 rebates and low financing on the 2004s. **Delivery/PDI:** $1,245. **Options:** Recommended: running boards and the All Weather Guard package that includes a heavy-duty starter and heater. **Depreciation:** Much slower than average. **Insurance cost:** Higher than average. **Parts supply/cost:** Most parts are widely available and of average cost. Some drivers wait as long as two months for powertrain components. **Annual maintenance cost:** Maintenance and repair costs have been much less than average. **Warranty:** Bumper-to-bumper 3 years/60,000 km; powertrain 5 years/ 100,000 km; rust perforation 5 years/unlimited km. **Supplementary warranty:** An extended warranty is a waste of money. **Highway/city fuel economy:** *4X2, 3.4L, and man.:* 11.1–14.3L/100 km; *4X2, 3.4L, and auto.:* 10.9–14.1L/100 km; *4X4, 3.4L, and man.:* 12.1–15.4L/100 km; *4X4, 3.4L, and auto.:* 12.3–14.4L/100 km; *4X2, 4.7L, and auto.:* 11.9–15.6L/100 km; *4X4, 4.7L, and auto.:* 12.6–15.4L/100 km.

QUALITY/RELIABILITY: The large number of brake defects and failures impinges upon Toyota's reputation for reliability and puts its customers' lives and wallets in jeopardy. **Owner-reported problems:** Excessive front-brake vibration or pulsation makes vehicle almost uncontrollable and causes the Tundra to shake violently when brakes are applied; brake drums and rotors warp within 7,000 km; steel wheels rust prematurely; chronic rear axle noise; ABS brakes make a loud banging sound upon engagement; V8 engine knocking when started in cold weather; excessive drivetrain vibration at 100 km/h; automatic transmission binding; 4X4 system grinds and pops out of gear; paint is easily chipped; oil dipstick is incorrectly calibrated or too short, leading to incorrect readings; exhaust smells like rotten eggs. **Warranty performance:** Generally very good, but Toyota must stop blaming its customers for front- and rear-brake defects.

SAFETY SUMMARY: Airbags: Front only; there have been reports of airbags failing to deploy. **ABS:** 2W optional; disc/drum. **Safety belt pretensioners:** Standard; seat belt failures are also common. **Head restraints:** *2001–02:* ****; *2003-04:* ****/***. **Visibility F/R:** *****. **Maximum load capacity:** *2000 SR5 4.7L:* 608 kg (1,340 lb.).

SAFETY COMPLAINTS: All years: Airbags failed to deploy. • Seat belt/retractor failures. • Vehicle rolled away after it was put in Park and the emergency brake was applied. • An incredibly high number of brake complaints relative to brake failures, rotor and drum warping, and excessive vibration/shudder. • Brakes overheat and fade after successive application; extended braking distance. • Ball joint failure caused wheel to separate. • Loose poorly fitted trim panels. **2001**—Sudden, unintended acceleration caused by faulty oxygen sensors, which are frequently back-ordered. • Exhaust manifold cracking. • With a full fuel tank and when riding uphill, gas fumes enter the cabin. • Gear selector fails to engage the proper gear. • When applying lube to the drive shaft bearings the grease just squirts around the fitting, not in. • Broken weld in tow hitch caused accident. **2002**—Cab separated from chassis. • Automatic transmission goes into the wrong gear or slams into gear. • Sudden brake lock-up. • Lug nuts are easily broken when tightened. • Bent wheel rims. • Bridgestone tread cracking. • Tires hydroplane easily. **2003**— Sudden tie-rod failure caused Tundra to flip. • Transfer case malfunction leads to reduced power and excessive vibration. • Vehicle stalls out. **2004**—Sudden, unintended acceleration. • Defroster brings in carbon monoxide. • Goodrich Rugged Trail tire cracks. • Rear window popped out and sunroof exploded.

Secret Warranties/Service Tips

2000–02—Hard/no-starts:

Engine No Start Condition

Bulletin No.: EG016-02   Date: August 30, 2002

2000–02 Tundra (2UZ-FE)
2001–02 sequoia

This may be caused by an inoperative fuel pump and/or blown EFI fuse. The Fuel Pump Assembly and Pick-up Sock have been improved to correct this condition.

Damaged front seat cover. **2000–04**—If the AC doesn't sufficiently cool the cabin, TSB #AC004-04 says the water control valve is the likely culprit. **2001**—New parking struts developed to reduce rear brake vibration. • Inaccurate temperature gauge. • Inadequate application of seam sealer in driver's footwell area. • Loose antenna mast. • Improved durability of the quarter-window lock. **2001–03**—Oil pressure gauge reads abnormally low. • Front-brake repair tips. • Troubleshooting brake vibration. • "Rotten-egg" exhaust smell (a replacement catalytic converter has been devised). **2002**— Vehicle pulls to one side. • Off-centre steering wheel.

Tundra Profile

	2001	2002	2003	2004
Cost Price ($) (negotiable)				
Base (16%)	23,110	23,520	23,520	24,565
4X4 V8 (17%)	28,600	29,270	29,270	30,320
Used Values ($)				
Base ∧	15,500	17,000	20,000	21,000
Base ∨	14,000	16,000	18,500	20,500
4X4 V8 ∧	19,000	21,500	23,500	26,000
4X4 V8 ∨	18,000	19,500	22,500	24,000
Reliability	④	④	④	⑤
Crash Safety (F)	③	④	④	④
Side	—	⑤	⑤	⑤
Offset	⑤	⑤	⑤	⑤
Rollover	③	③	③	—

Internet Sleuthing

You can find lots of information about SUVs, trucks, and vans on the Internet. But, you do have to be sure that what you find is truthful and unbiased.

Automobile companies have helpful—though self-serving—websites, most of which feature detailed sections on history, research and development, and all sorts of information of interest to auto enthusiasts. Some automakers, such as Toyota, will even give you an online appraisal of your trade-in. Manufacturers can easily be accessed through Google's search engine under the automaker's name followed by *.com* or *.ca*. For extra fun and a more balanced presentation, put in the vehicle model or manufacturer's name, followed by "lemon."

Auto Safety, Costs, Servicing, and Reviews

Alberta Vehicle Cost Calculator
(*www1.agric.gov.ab.ca/app24/costcalculators/vehicle/getvechimpls.jsp*)
Estimate and compare the ownership and operating costs of vehicles with variations in purchase price, options, fuel type, interest rates, or length of ownership.

ALLDATA Service Bulletins (*www.alldata.com/consumer/TSB/yr.html*)
Free summaries of automotive recalls and technical service bulletins. Detailed summaries will cost only $25 U.S. for hundreds of bulletins applicable to your vehicle, dating back almost 30 years.

American Automobile Association (*www.aaa.com*)
The AARP (American Association of Retired Persons) on wheels.

The Auto Channel (*www.theautochannel.com*)
A multimedia resource with excellent information needed choose a new or used vehicle. Links to articles on an astounding variety of auto-related topics. Updated daily.

Autopedia (*www.autopedia.com/index.html*)
An online automotive encyclopedia that's easy to use.

BBC TV's *Top Gear* Car Reviews (*www.topgear.com*)
Hated by European automakers, *Top Gear* gives raw, independent reviews of the
best and worst European-sold vehicles, auto products, and industry practices.

Canadian Automobile Association (*www.caa.ca*)
A bilingual AARP on wheels. Has a nice checklist for "Keeping Track of Your
Own Vehicle Costs" in their "Driving Costs" pamphlet at *www.caa.ca/e/*
automotive/pdf/driving-costs-03.pdf.

Canadian Driver (*www.canadiandriver.com*)
An exceptionally well-structured and current Canadian website for new- and
used-vehicle reviews, MSRPs, and consumer reports. Other auto magazines
websites:

- *Automotive News* (*www.autonews.com*)—Engine "sludge," GM "piston
  slap," etc.
- *Car and Driver* (*www.caranddriver.com/default.asp*)—Good recent hybrid
  report.
- *Motor Trend* (*www.motortrend.com*)
- *Road & Track* (*www.roadandtrack.com*)

Carfax (*www.carfax.com*)
Use Carfax (tel.: 1-888-422-7329) to see if an American- or Canadian-sold
vehicle has been "scrapped," had flood damage, is stolen, or had its mileage
turned back. There's a fee of $14.95 U.S. ($23.39 Cdn.) if the order is placed
via the Internet. Be careful. The free report may tell you of several "hot" leads
and when you pay to get the specifics, they may only be the number of times
the vehicle has taken an emissions test.

Cartrackers (*www.cartrackers.com*)
Used vehicles, consumer advice, and environmental issues are all well-covered
in this site that features a terrific auto image gallery and an excellent automotive glossary.

CBC TV *Marketplace* (*www.cbc.ca/consumers/market/files/cars/index.html*)
An impressive array of auto consumer info based on investigative reports and
other sources. Well-researched, useful Canadian information.

The Center for Auto Safety (*www.autosafety.org*)
A Ralph Nader–founded agency that provides free online info on safety- and
performance-related defects on each vehicle model. Free vehicle reports based
on owner complaints and service bulletins are sometimes dated. Still, a good
place for safety- and performance-related defect listings.

***Consumer Reports* and Consumers Union** (*www.consumerreports.org*)
It costs $4.95 a month to subscribe online, but *CR*'s database is chock full of
comparison tests and in-depth stories on products and services, including a

"Cars for Teens" special feature. Download info like crazy during first month of your subscription, and then wait awhile, until the need arises to renew your subscription.

Crashtest.com (*www.crashtest.com/netindex.htm*)
A website where crash tests from around the world can be analyzed and compared.

DaimlerChrysler Problems Web Page
(*www.wam.umd.edu/~gluckman/Chrysler*)
This is a great site for technical info and tips on getting action from DaimlerChrysler.

Edmunds.com and Kelley Blue Book (*www.edmunds.com, www.kbb.com*)
In-depth reviews and owner critiques of almost every vehicle sold in North America, plus an informative readers' forum. Ignore the zip code request.

Ford Insider Info (*www.blueovalnews.com*)
This website is the place to go for all the latest insider info on Ford's quality problems and future models.

Lemon-Aid (*www.lemonaidcars.com*)
The official website of the *Lemon-Aid* annual consumer car guides. It always needs updating, and, like universal health care and Buckley's Mixture, is for Canadians only.

Metric Conversion Online (*www.sciencemadesimple.net/conversions.html*)
A great place to instantly convert gallons to litres, miles to kilometres, etc.

National Highway Traffic Safety Administration
(*www.nhtsa.dot.gov/cars/problems*)
This American site has a comprehensive, free database covering owner complaints, recall campaigns, crashworthiness and rollover ratings, defect investigations, service bulletin summaries, and safety research papers.

The SUV Info Link (*www.suv.org*)
This Friends of the Earth website shows why SUV ownership is bad for the environment.

Finally, here are a number of other websites that may be helpful:

- *www.automotiveforums.com*
- *www.consumeraffairs.com/index.html*
- *www.consumeraffairs.com/automotive/ford_transmissions.htm*
- *www.epa.gov/otaq/consumer/warr95fs.txt*
- *everythingfordrivers.com/carforums.html*
- *www.freelanderliving.com/default.asp*

- *us.lexusownersclub.com*
- *www.troublebenz.com/my_opinion/actions/links.htm*
- *www.myvwlemon.com*
- *www.thesamba.com/vw/forums*
- *www.suv.com/indextoc.html*
- *www.vehicle-injuries.com/suv-safety-news.htm*
- *www.worktruck.com*

"Beater" Bargains and Luxury "Lemons"

There are lots of cheap SUVs, trucks, and vans out there that are good buys. The problem is knowing which models to choose and how to avoid getting cheated.

First, consider the following 10 rules:

1. Looks don't matter. GM's Astro and Safari minivans are boxy and bland, but they're fairly reliable, cheap, and easy to find.
2. Used is always a better buy than new. There's less depreciation and no bogus administrative or freight charges.
3. American front-drives are usually poor buys. They are less reliable than rear-drives and cost more to repair.
4. Be wary of "orphans" like the Ford Windstar, Jeep Cherokee, and Toyota Previa. Parts will be hard to find and no one will want to service them.
5. Stay away from European luxury "lemon" SUVs like the Mercedes M-Class and BMW X3 and X5. They are way overrated and overpriced. Parts and servicing can be a problem, and quality control is declining. Heck, recent polls show that Europeans don't trust their own automakers, and tend to prefer Japanese makes. *Mais, oui!!*
6. Don't worry about paying too much for a Japanese model, you'll get the excess back when you sell.
7. Look for 5-year-old Japanese models, or a 3-year-old Hyundai Santa Fe. Stay away from Mitsubishi until they become financially viable, or their key executives get out of jail.
8. Buy small, entry-level Japanese pickups from Mazda, Nissan, and Toyota.
9. Shop for rear-drive, full-sized vans, instead of American minivans; high gas prices have sent their resale value somewhere south of Patagonia. A few thousand dollars more off the selling price will buy lots of fuel.
10. Don't buy for fuel economy alone: A 4-cylinder minivan or SUV *is* cheap to run, but highway merging will scare the heck out of you. Plus, don't believe the hybrid- and diesel-savings hype; your hybrid fuel economy may be 40 percent *less* than what is advertised and diesels have become almost as tempermental and failure-prone as gasoline-fed engines (hear that, Ford Powerstroke and GM Duramax?).

Pre-loved and broken-in

It's getting pretty hard to find a vehicle 10 years old or more that's safe and reliable. Personally, I'd be reluctant to buy any decade-old vehicle anywhere east of Manitoba, or one that has been brought in from another province. Apart from salt being a real body killer, it's just too easy to fall prey to scam artists who cover up major mechanical or body problems resulting from accidents or environmental damage.

Nevertheless, if you know the seller, and an independent mechanic gives you the green light, you might seriously consider a 10-year-old, beat-up-looking pickup or van. Look for one of those listed below, or if you have a bit more money to spend and want to take less of a risk, look up the 1997 and later Recommended or Above Average models found in Part Four.

Best Choices

The following new and used choices will help you hunker down and get reliable, safe, fuel-efficient, and inexpensive wheels that will tide you over until you can get that more expensive "dream machine" you've always wanted.

Warning: No matter what you buy, or how much you spend later on, you're likely to think of your first "beater" as one of the best cars you ever owned. Furthermore, you'll quickly learn to drive with the windows and sunroof closed, to avoid the painful, deafening "booming" noise so common to most SUVs, trucks, and vans.

Pickups

As a general rule, old trucks aren't very collectible, unless they were utilized for a specific purpose, like fire trucks, army vehicles, or commercial vehicles (milk trucks, etc.). For most small trucks made by the Detroit Big Three that are 10 years old, you can expect to pay $1,500–$2,500. Asian imports may cost about twice as much, due to their reputation for being better made and more reliable. If you're looking for a larger pickup, the price may vary from $3,000 to $5,000, with no real Asian competition in sight.

Old trucks are bought for function, not appearance. Full-sized Chrysler, Ford, and GM pickups from the first half of the '70s are all practically equal in performance and reliability (although Ford vehicles were extremely rust-prone). After 1976, stringent emissions regulations mandated the use of failure-prone fuel injectors, computer modules, and catalytic converters. As leaded fuel was phased out, vehicles became much more complicated to troubleshoot, more expensive to repair, and less reliable.

Post-'76 GM trucks are afflicted by poor-quality computer modules that make for hard starts and poor engine performance, early catalytic converter failures, unreliable diesel engines, and poorly engineered braking systems where the rear brakes are vulnerable to premature backing plate corrosion. GM's use of the "side-saddle" gas tank design also led to additional risk of fire in a collision.

From late 1998 to the present, GM's truck quality has improved ever so slightly. Yet, engines, brakes, transmissions, and fit and finish continue to be major trouble spots.

From the late '70s until today, Ford's trucks are noted as gas hogs; their fuel and ignition systems often fail, causing fires and full-throttle stalling; and fuel pumps, AC, and electrical systems can be chronically dysfunctional. Automatic transmissions have become "bump and jump" affairs, and collapsed coil springs and steering/suspension tie-rod failures bring new meaning to "off-roading."

But Chrysler's trucks are no better, except for their fairly reliable Cummins diesel powerplants. And even these engines can get nasty. Chrysler's trucks have always been plagued by persistent brake, computer module, suspension, and automatic transmission failures. They have a tendency to wander all over the road and are often hard to troubleshoot.

Recommendation: Stick with the smallest Japanese-made truck you can find that will do the job. This means choosing a small pickup like the **Mazda B-series**; **Nissan King Cab**; or **Toyota Pickup**, **Tacoma**, and **T100**. Even though these vehicles are recommended, they should be inspected for brake, steering, and engine head gasket problems. Also check for undercarriage corrosion, particularly with older Toyotas and Mazdas.

Avoid: Steer clear of Japanese pickups sold under an American label, like the Mitsubishi-built 1981–93 **Chrysler Ram 50** ($500–$700), plagued by poor NHTSA crash scores, weak engine piston rings, prematurely worn timing chains, failure-prone automatic transmissions, and a rust-prone body. The 1980–82 **Ford Courier** (a Mazda import worth barely $500) is another truck to avoid. Its main traps for the unwary are poor crashworthiness; excessive corrosion afflicting suspension, steering, and brake components; and failure-prone engine head gaskets, automatic transmission, front brakes, and electrical systems. And don't get caught with a 1980–82 **VW Rabbit Pickup** ($300–$500), due to its poor parts availability; lack of service support; unreliable electrical, fuel, and cooling systems; troublesome brakes; front suspension components; and diesel engine head gaskets. Also, be wary of the failure-prone 1982–84 **Dodge Rampage pickup**, which should cost no more than $300–$500.

Sport-utilities

Anyone buying a decade-old or older sport-utility is asking for trouble. The danger of rollover is quite high (particularly with Ford, Isuzu, and Suzuki versions), overall quality control is very poor, and performance is mediocre. Furthermore, don't assume that European luxury SUVs are more reliable. To the contrary, **Land Rover** and **Mercedes-Benz** SUVs have garnered a reputation for poor-quality vehicles with head-spinning depreciation.

Land Rover, for example sells the **Range Rover**, **Discovery**, and **Freelander** in Canada. The cheapest of the three is the $35,000 Freelander, launched in 2002, now worth about $17,000. Range Rover and Discovery versions lose their value in the blink of an eye: A 1996 $42,000 Discovery is now worth about $8,000, and the same-year Range Rover, originally priced at $80,000, now sells for $11,000. This rapid depreciation would be a good thing if these cars were reliable—but they're not.

More softly styled than its larger, squared-off Discovery brother, the Freelander is an underpowered, small, cramped truck with luxury SUV pretensions. Don't look for the seat height adjustment control—there isn't any (posing a serious problem for tall drivers). Headroom is at a premium for tall drivers, and storage space behind the back seats is clearly inadequate. Ground clearance is also quite low when compared with the competition. When pushed, the 174-hp V6 engine whines and struggles to hold its own. A stick-shift isn't available, so there's no way to improve the mediocre 15L/100 km average fuel economy.

The 1998–2001 **Mercedes-Benz ML320**, **350**, and **430** models are a far cry from cheap wheels even though they too depreciate about 50 percent after five years (a $39,000 1996 ML320 is now worth about $16,000). The main drawbacks of these luxury SUVs are poor quality control; unreliable, limited servicing; and so-so parts availability. Owners report automatic transmission failures, frequent engine oil leaks and engine oil sludge, and electrical system shorts. Other problem areas include brake pads, rotors, master cylinder, fuel pump, oxygen sensor, mass airflow sensor, and fit and finish.

After settling out of court $38 million worth of engine sludge complaints on its own luxury models, Mercedes is now faced with hundreds of complaints that Chrysler's 2.7L engines have the same costly defect.

Recommendations: The **Jeeps** are the best of a bad lot, particularly the **Wrangler** versions. Their rollover tendency isn't as great as other small sport-utilities; parts are more easily obtainable; and servicing, if not given with a smile, at least isn't accompanied by a snarl or head scratching. Nevertheless, the early **CJs** and **Wagoneers** have been known for their rattle-prone bodies, air and water leaks, electrical glitches, and high-cost brake maintenance. Expect to spend $2,500 tops for the entry-level CJ and a thousand more for a Wagoneer.

Selling for as little as $5,000 for a 1996 Rodeo S, Isuzu's 1993–2004 **Ascender**, **Axiom**, **Rodeo**, **Rodeo Sport**, and **Trooper** are ideal SUVs for light city commuting. Although they look tacky and feel outdated, these Isuzus are competent performers with a powerful V6; shift-on-the-fly capability; versatile transmission; nice, predictable rear-drive handling; a spacious interior; and very few complaints of safety-related defects. Less attractive characteristics: a wimpy 4-cylinder engine; part-time 4X4 that can't be used on dry pavement; a harsh ride over bumpy terrain; excessive body lean when cornering; obstructed rear visibility, narrow rear doors; excessive road and engine noise; and poor fuel economy. Some of the safety-related failures tabulated by

NHTSA include brake loss, sudden unintended acceleration, and automatic transmission failures.

Of course, if you don't mind paying a little more, there's nothing wrong with a 1987–89 **Toyota Land Cruiser**, selling for about $5,000. Just be sure to pull the wheels off to examine the brakes, check for undercarriage corrosion, and make sure the engine head gasket is okay.

Avoid: Ever heard of American Motors? Well, back in 1981 they came out with the first 4X4 passenger car/sport-utility, called the **Eagle** (others called it the Turkey), which was basically a Concord 4X4. It now sells for about $800. Be wary of its failure-prone drivetrain, ignition system, and clutch master; slave cylinder leaks; low rust resistance; and marginal crash protection. But at least it didn't roll over, something that can't be said for Ford's Bronco II.

Don't buy Ford's 1981–90 **Bronco II**, even though its $500–$2,000 price may seem like a bargain. It's one of the most unreliable, rollover-prone, rust-attracting 4X4s ever built. You can cut repair costs by using independent garages, but parts can be quite expensive (especially TFI ignition components and computer modules). Between 1985 and 1989, the Bronco II was the undisputed leader in rollover deaths in the U.S. According to internal memoranda, Ford released the Bronco II in 1981 with full knowledge of the stability dangers inherent in the design. Critics contend that the present-day Explorer's rollover problems can be traced back to its Bronco heritage.

This sport-utility suffers from worse-than-average reliability. The 4-speed automatic transmission has been the worst contributor to owners' woes. The complicated electronic fuel-injection system is a headache to diagnose and has a bad repair history. Brakes and 4X4 components are also often included on the list of potential problems. Overall, body assembly and paint quality are mediocre.

Now discontinued, the **Lada Niva** is a cheap Russian import ($500–$2,000 for 1990–97 models) that uses poor-quality body and mechanical components on a 20-year-old 4X4 design. The vehicles are noisy and trucklike on the road, the dealer network is non-existent, and parts are hard to find. Defective fuel and ignition systems (particularly the ignition control module) and a poorly designed electrical system are the most common problems. Frequent carburetor replacements, at $325 plus tax (if you can find a replacement carburetor at all), are rendered necessary due to the butterfly shaft warping or corroding—the result of an inherently defective design. Front brakes need to be replaced often; and transmissions, engine head gaskets, and differentials aren't durable either. Ladas were never crash-tested nor airbag equipped.

The 1987–94 **Suzuki Samurai** is another orphan you shouldn't buy, despite its low cost ($500–$1,000). Although parts costs are average, owners have complained that the parts themselves are almost impossible to find. Crash tests of the 1986 model concluded that the driver and passenger would have sustained severe leg trauma. Unsteady road manners, coupled with a high centre of gravity, make the Samurai susceptible to sudden rollovers if the vehicle is not driven carefully, especially on rough terrain. This is particularly true of the 1987–88 models, where NHTSA records show the largest grouping of owner complaints and accident injury reports.

Minivans and wagons

Assuming you can't afford the big bucks for a Honda Odyssey or Toyota Sienna, you have a number of cheaper, old minivans to choose from: **Chrysler's Colt/Summit/Vista wagons**; **Ford's Aerostar**; **GM's Astro** and **Safari**; and **Nissan's Axxess**.

Recommendations: Chrysler's Colt, **Summit**, and **Vista**. Priced from about $700 for an '88 version to about $1,500 for a '95, these are three of the best small cars and wagons that Chrysler doesn't make (they're all Mitsubishi imports). The only exceptions are the 1985–88 models, which were quite troublesome.

The Vista and the Summit wagon are small minivans with five- to seven-passenger seating. They have excellent crash ratings and are more reasonably priced, practical, and fuel efficient than many other small wagons. The five-passenger Colt wagon, like the Summit and Nissan Axxess, offers the extra versatility of a third seat in the back and a tall body. As such, it makes a great car for a small family with space to haul loads to the cottage. The wagon series is available in 4X4 (not recommended) and uses practically the same mechanical components as the other Colt models. The Summit wagon is essentially a wagon version of the Colt 200 and sells for a bit more.

On post-1990 Colts and Summits, the 2.4L head gasket may fail prematurely. Shocks aren't very durable, braking isn't impressive, and the front brakes have a short lifespan. Emission components, such as the oxygen sensor, often fail after two years of use. A few owners have reported automatic transmission failures. Be especially wary of the troublesome 4X4 powertrain on 1989–91 wagons and the 16-valve turbo, dropped in 1990. Owners of the 1993 wagon complain of poor heating and defrosting. Surface rust is common, as are rust perforations on door bottoms, the front edge of the hood, and the rear hatch.

The 1995–97 **Ford Aerostar** isn't a bad choice, though 1986–94 models are risky buys. A 1992 XL would cost about $2,500, while a fully equipped 1997 version (1997 was the Aerostar's last year) should cost between $4,000 and $5,000. These primitive rear-drives are brawnier and more reliable than Chrysler's or Ford's front-drive minivans (exception made for the failure-prone 4X4 system), and they've posted impressive crashworthiness scores since 1992. Just make sure Ford pays for cracked coil springs up to 10 years of use.

The 1986–94 models are at the bottom of the evolutionary scale as far as quality control is concerned. However, the last three model years showed lots of improvement. Repair costs are reasonable (except for high automatic transmission, AC, and computer module costs), and many of the Aerostar's myriad mechanical and body defects can be fixed quite easily by independent garages. The Aerostar's modern, swoopy shape belies its limited performance capabilities: The 3.0L and 4.0L engines are unreliable through the 1991 model year, and the 3.0L is a sluggish performer. Older 2.3L and 2.8L engines can barely pull their own weight. The failure-prone 4-speed automatic transmission often has a hard time deciding which gear to choose, and the power steering transmits almost no road feel to the driver. The ride is bouncy, handling is sloppy, and braking performance is poor. Reliability problems on all models make early Aerostars risky buys, especially if the previous owner has been less than fastidious in maintenance and repairs.

Valve cover and rear main oil seal leaks are frequent, and leaks from the front axle vent tube often require the replacement of the front axle assembly. Even oil pans, which you wouldn't normally associate with leaks, tend to leak as a result of premature corrosion (a big-buck repair). Fuel injectors are either faulty or plugged. A grinding/growling coming from the rear signals that the in-tank electric fuel pump is defective. Other problems include expensive electronic and electrical system glitches; power-steering, suspension, and brake defects; and premature and chronic air conditioner condenser and compressor breakdowns.

Nissan's 1991–95 **Axxess** minivan is a good choice. It's fairly reliable, easily serviced, and has posted respectable crash-safety ratings. You get carlike handling and ride comfort and as much space as the higher-priced Honda Odyssey. As with most minivans equipped with a full load and a small engine, acceleration isn't confidence inspiring on the highway. However, the Axxess is ideal for city-to-suburb commuting. What further sets the Axxess apart is its reasonable price and better-than-average reliability. Prices have remained stable, ranging from $2,500 to $3,500 for the top-of-the-line SE. You may have trouble finding one; word has gotten out that they are "beater" bargains.

Avoid: Stay away from bargain-priced minivans that require frequent and costly repairs. Chief among these are $2,000–$3,500 **Chrysler minivans** (1991–96) and $2,500–$4,000 **Mercury Villager/Nissan Quest** models (1993–96). Chrysler minivans had engine, drivetrain, suspension, electrical and fuel system, AC, brake, and body deficiencies galore. Early Villagers and Quests had chronic engine exhaust manifold stud failures that could cost thousands of dollars to replace. **VW Campers** are a good idea poorly executed. These minivans are nicely laid-out, but they aren't reliable and servicing is practically non-existent. Plus, they are relatively costly: $3,500–$4,500 for a 1985–89 model.

The VW Camper allows you to wait for the tow truck—in comfort.

Lemon-Proofing before You Buy

Now that you've chosen a vehicle that's priced right and seems to meet your needs, take some time to assess its interior, exterior, and highway performance with the checklist below. If you're buying from a dealer, ask to take the vehicle home overnight in order to drive it over the same roads you use in your daily activities. This will give you important insight into how well the engine handles all of the convenience features, how comfortable the seats are during extended driving, and whether front and rear visibility is satisfactory without your having to double up like a pretzel to avoid dash glare (a Volvo problem, particularly). Of course, if you're buying privately, it's doubtful you will get the vehicle for an overnight test—you may have to rent a similar one from a dealer or rental agency.

Safety Check

1. Is outward visibility good in all directions?
2. Are there large blind spots impeding vision (such as side pillars)?
3. Are the mirrors large enough for good side and rear views?
4. Does the rear-view mirror have a glare-reducing setting?
5. Is there a rear window washer and wiper?
6. Are all instrument displays clearly visible (not washed out in sunlight), is there daytime or night driving dash glare upon the windshield, and are the controls easily reached?
7. Are the handbrake and hood release easy to reach and use?
8. Does the front seat have sufficient rearward travel to put you a safe distance from the airbag's deployment (about a foot) and still allow you to reach the brake and accelerator pedals? Are the brake and accelerator pedals spaced far enough apart?
9. Are the head restraints adjustable or non-adjustable? (The latter is better if you often forget to set them.)
10. Are the head restraints designed to permit rear visibility? (Some are annoyingly obtrusive.)
11. Are there rear three-point shoulder belts similar to those on the front seats? Two-point belts aren't as good.
12. Is the seat belt latch plate easy to find and reach?
13. Does the seat belt fit comfortably across your chest?
14. Do you feel too much pressure against you from the shoulder belt?
15. Does the seat belt release easily, retract smoothly, and use pretensioners for maximum effectiveness?
16. Are there user-friendly child seat anchorage locations?
17. Are there automatic door locks controlled by the driver or childproof rear door locks? Does the automatic side sliding door latch securely and immediately stop when encountering an object as it opens or closes?
18. Do the rear windows roll only halfway down? When they are down, are your ears assailed by the wind "boom," or does the vehicle vibrate excessively?
19. Are the airbags de-powered?
20. Are there side airbags that protect the head and torso (not recommended for kids)?

Exterior Check

Rust

A serious problem with the roofs of GM vans for more than two decades, rust is a four-letter word that means trouble. Don't buy any used vehicle with extensive corrosion around the roof-rails, rear hatch, wheelwells, door bottoms, or rocker panels. Body work in these areas is usually only a temporary solution.

Cosmetic rusting (rear hatch, exhaust system, front hood) is acceptable and can even help push the price way down, as long as the chassis and other major structural members aren't affected. Bumps, bubbles, or ripples under the paint may be due to repairs resulting from an accident or premature corrosion. Don't dismiss this as a mere cosmetic problem; the entire vehicle will have to be stripped down, re-primed, and repainted. GM has a secret warranty covering these hood repairs that can be extrapolated to other models and different body panels (look in the van ratings).

Knock gently on the front fenders, door bottoms, rear wheelwells, and rear doors—places where rust usually occurs first. Even if these areas have been repaired with plastic, lead, metal plates, or fibreglass, once rusting starts, it's difficult to stop. Use a small magnet to check which body panels have been repaired with non-metallic body fillers.

Use a flashlight to check for exhaust system and suspension component rust-out. Make sure the catalytic converter is present. In the past, many drivers removed this pollution control device in the mistaken belief that it would improve fuel economy. Police can fine you for not having the converter and force you to buy one ($400+) before certifying your vehicle.

Tires

Be wary of tire makes that have a poor durability record. Stay away from Firestone/Bridgestone makes. Don't be concerned if the tires are worn, since retreads are inexpensive and easy to find. Look at tire wear for clues that the vehicle is out of alignment, needs suspension repairs, or has serious chassis problems. An alignment and new shocks and springs are part of routine maintenance and are relatively inexpensive in the aftermarket. However, if it's a 4X4 or the MacPherson struts have to be replaced, you're looking at a $1,000 repair bill.

Accident damage

Accident repairs require a further inspection by an independent body shop in order to determine if the frame is aligned and the vehicle is tracking correctly. Frameless minivans need extensive and expensive work to straighten them out, and proper frame and body repairs can often cost more than the vehicle is worth. In British Columbia, all accidents involving more than $2,000 in repairs must be reported to subsequent buyers.

Here are some tips on what you can do to avoid buying a damaged vehicle. First, ask the following questions about the vehicle's accident history:

- Has it ever been in an accident?
- If so, what was the damage and who fixed it?
- Is the auto body shop that repaired the vehicle registered with the provincial government? Is there any warranty outstanding? Can you have a copy of the work order?
- Has the vehicle's certificate of title been labelled "salvage"? ("Salvage" means that an expert has determined that the cost to properly repair the vehicle is more than its value. This usually happens after the vehicle has been in a serious accident.)

If the vehicle has been in an accident, you should either walk away from the sale or have it checked by a qualified auto body expert. Remember, not all salvage vehicles are bad—properly repaired ones can be a safe and sound investment if the price is low enough.

What to look for

1. If the vehicle has been repainted recently, check the quality of the job by inspecting the engine and trunk compartments and the inside door panels. Do it on a clear day so that you'll find any waves in the paint.
2. Check the paint—do all of the vehicle's panels match?
3. Inspect the paint for tiny bubbles. They may identify a poor priming job or premature rust.
4. Is there paint overspray or primer in the door jambs, wheelwells, or engine compartment? These are signs that the vehicle has had body repairs.
5. Check the gaps between body panels—are they equal? Unequal gaps may indicate improper panel alignment or a bent frame.
6. Do the doors, hood, and rear hatch open and shut properly?
7. Have the bumpers been damaged or recently repaired? Check the bumper support struts for corrosion damage.
8. Test the shock absorbers by pushing hard on a corner of the vehicle. If it bounces around like a ship at sea, the shocks need replacing.
9. Look for signs of premature rust or displacement from a collision on the muffler and exhaust pipe.
10. Make sure there's a readily accessible spare tire, a jack, and tools for changing a flat. Also look for premature rusting in the side wheelwells and for water in the rear hatch channel.
11. Look at how the vehicle sits. If one side or end is higher than the other, it could mean that the suspension is defective.
12. Ask the seller to turn on the headlights (low and high beams), turn signals, parking lights, and emergency blinking lights, and to blow the horn. From the rear, check that the brake lights, backup lights, turn indicators, tail lights, and licence plate light all work.

Interior Check

The number of kilometres on the odometer isn't as important as how well the vehicle was driven and maintained. Still, high-mileage vehicles depreciate rapidly because most people consider them to be risky buys. Calculate 20,000 kilometres per year as average and take off about $200 for each additional 10,000 kilometres above this average. Be suspicious of the odometer reading. Confirm it by checking the vehicle's maintenance records.

The interior will often give you an idea of how the vehicle was used and maintained. For example, sagging rear seats and a front passenger seat in pristine condition indicate that your minivan may have been used as a minibus. Delivery vans will have the paint on the driver's door sill rubbed down to the metal, while the passenger door sill will look like new.

What to look for

1. Watch for excessive wear of the seats, dash, accelerator, brake pedal, armrests, and roof lining.
2. Check the dash and roof lining for radio or cellular phone mounting holes (police, taxi, delivery van). Is the radio tuned to local stations?
3. Turn the steering wheel: listen for unusual noises and watch for excessive play (more than an inch).
4. Test the emergency brake with the vehicle parked on a hill.
5. Inspect the seat belts. Is the webbing in good condition? Do the belts retract easily?
6. Make sure that door latches and locks are in good working order. If rear doors have no handles or locks, or if they've just been installed, your minivan may have been used to transport prisoners.
7. Can the seats be moved into all the positions intended by the manufacturer? Look under them to make sure that the runners are functioning as they should.
8. Can head supports be adjusted easily?
9. Peel back the rugs and check the metal floor for signs of rust or dampness.

Road Test

1. Start the vehicle and listen for unusual noises. Shift automatics into Park and manuals into Neutral with the handbrake engaged. Open the hood to check for fluid leaks. This test should be done with the engine running and be repeated 10 minutes after the engine has been shut down following the completion of the test-drive.
2. With the motor running, check out all dashboard controls: windshield wipers, heater and defroster, and radio.
3. If the engine stalls or races at idle, a simple adjustment may fix the trouble. Loud clanks or low oil pressure could mean potentially expensive repairs.
4. Check all ventilation systems. Do the rear side windows roll down? Are there excessive air leaks around the door handles?
5. While in Neutral, push down on the accelerator abruptly. Black exhaust smoke may require only a minor engine adjustment; blue smoke may signal major engine repairs.
6. Shift an automatic into Drive with the motor still idling. The vehicle should creep forward slowly without stalling or speeding. Listen for unusual noises when the transmission is engaged. Manual transmissions

should engage as soon as the clutch is released. Slipping or stalling could require a new clutch. While driving, make absolutely sure that a four-wheel drive can be engaged without unusual noises or hesitation.

7. Shift an automatic transmission into Drive. While the motor is idling, apply the emergency brake. If the motor isn't racing and the brake is in good condition, the vehicle should stop.

8. Accelerate to 50 km/h while slowly moving through all gears. Listen for transmission noises. Step lightly on the brakes; the response should be immediate and equal for all wheels.

9. In a deserted parking lot, test the vehicle's steering and suspension by driving in figure eights at low speeds.

10. Make sure the road is clear of traffic and pedestrians. Drive at 30 km/h and take both hands off the steering wheel to see whether the vehicle veers from one side to the other. If it does, the alignment or suspension could be defective, or the vehicle could have been in an accident.

11. Test the suspension by driving over some rough terrain.

12. Stop at the foot of a small hill and see if the vehicle can climb it without difficulty.

13. On an expressway, it should take no longer than 20 seconds for most cars and minivans to accelerate from a standing start to 100 km/h.

14. Drive through a tunnel with the windows open. Try to detect any unusual motor, exhaust, or suspension sounds.

15. After the test-drive, verify the performance of the automatic transmission by shifting from Drive to Neutral to Reverse. Listen for clunking sounds during transmission engagement.

Many of these tests will undoubtedly turn up some defects, which may be major or minor (even new vehicles have an average of a half-dozen major and minor defects). Ask an independent mechanic for an estimate and try to convince the seller to pay part of the repair bill if you buy the vehicle. Keep in mind that many 3- to 5-year-old vehicles with 60,000–100,000 km run the risk of an engine timing belt or timing chain failure that can cause several thousand dollars worth of repairs. If the timing belt or chain hasn't been replaced, plan to do it and deduct about $300 from the purchase price for the repair.

It's important to eliminate as many duds as possible through your own cursory check, since you'll later invest two hours and about $100 for a thorough mechanical inspection of your choice. Garages approved by the Automobile Protection Association or members of the Canadian Automobile Association usually do a good job. CAA inspections run from $100 to $150 for non-members. Oil company affiliated diagnostic clinics are recommended only if they don't do repairs. Remember, if you get a bum steer from an independent testing agency, you can get the inspection fee refunded and hold the garage responsible for your subsequent repairs and consequential damages, like towing, missed work, or a ruined vacation. See Part Three for details.